Fifth Edition

Creating Writers

Through 6-Trait Writing Assessment and Instruction

Vicki Spandel

Writer in Residence, Great Source Education Group

With a Foreword by Cindy Marten

PEARSON

Boston   New York   San Francisco
Mexico City   Montreal   Toronto   London   Madrid   Munich   Paris
Hong Kong   Singapore   Tokyo   Cape Town   Sydney

This book is lovingly dedicated to Don Graves,
who taught us—and continues teaching us—
to trust the voice within.

Executive Editor: Aurora Martínez Ramos
Editorial Assistant: Kara Kikel
Director of Professional Development: Alison Maloney
Marketing Manager: Danae April
Production Editor: Janet Domingo
Editorial-Production Service: Kathy Smith
Design and Electronic Composition: Schneck-DePippo Graphics
Composition and Prepress Buyer: Linda Cox
Manufacturing Buyer: Linda Morris
Cover Administrator: Kristina Mose-Libon

For related titles and support materials, visit our online catalog at www.pearsonhighered.com.

Between the time website information is gathered and then published, it is not unusual for some sites
to have closed. Also, the transcription of URLs can result in typographical errors. The publisher would
appreciate notification where these errors occur so that they may be corrected in subsequent editions.

Library of Congress Cataloging-in-Publication Data
Spandel, Vicki.
    Creating writers : through 6-trait writing assessment and instruction /
    Vicki Spandel ; with a foreword by Cindy Marten.-- 5th ed.
        p. cm.
    Includes bibliographical references and index.
    ISBN 0-205-61910-X
    1. English language—Rhetoric—Study and teaching. 2. English language—Composition and
    exercises—Study and teaching. 3. Report writing--Study and teaching. 4. English language—
    Ability testing. 5. College prose—Evaluation. 6. School prose—Evaluation. I. Title.
    PE1404.S69 2008
    808'.042071—dc22   2008008664

Printed in the United States of America
10 9 8 7 6 5 4 3 2   EB   12 11 10

**Allyn & Bacon
is an imprint of**

www.pearsonhighered.com

ISBN 13: 978-0-205-61910-8
ISBN 10:   0-205-61910-X

Contents

5 Adding Flavor: Voice, Word Choice, and Sentence Fluency   85

6 Framing the Picture: Conventions and Presentation   113

7 Using Traits to Support Writing Process   137

8 Unlocking the Door to Revision   153

9 Troubleshooting: Dealing with Common Writing Problems   209

10 Listening to Teachers' Voices   249

11 Going Informational   269

12 Exploring the World of Beginning Writers   307

13 Communicating with Students 349

14 Expanding the Vision 373

Appendices 382

Foreword

"It is only with the heart that one can see rightly; what is essential is invisible to the eye."
—Antoine de Saint-Exupéry, *The Little Prince, 1943*

My wish is for all children to have a writing teacher who knows how to listen deeply. In the Chinese language the word "to listen" is depicted with a character that embodies the elements necessary for authentic listening: ears, eyes, attitude, undivided attention and my favorite . . . heart. Indeed, listening to a piece of writing involves not just what you can see with your eyes or hear with your ears. The power of the traits is and always has been their ability to help us see with our hearts and make the invisible visible. A piece of writing that falls before our eyes should always be "seen" as a sacred offering and our job is to receive it completely for the gift that it is. That is not as easy as it sounds. Sometimes the "writing gift" we get excites us no more than socks on Christmas morning. Yet once we teach ourselves to truly listen, we may hear more voice than we originally knew was there. This is where Vicki's work, especially in this fifth edition, comes in.

You may wonder—*why a fifth edition?* Think of a pair of glasses you've had for a long while. You'd like to see clearly again—to sharpen the focus. In this edition, Vicki sharpens our focus. This fifth edition is worth every hard-earned penny you make. That's not surprising though, since it's coming from the queen of revision. If anyone knows how to revise with passion, voice, purpose, and power, it is Vicki Spandel. She understands that the heart and soul of revision lies in a continually deepening understanding. Vicki shares her ongoing learning about writing and teaching in this brilliant fifth edition. The clarity and depth of this revision gives us the most supportive and accessible version to date of a book that has changed the face of writing education in America. It is also the most intimate version. You will feel as if you are sitting at Starbucks with Vicki having a one-on-one conversation about the magic of teaching a child to write.

Specific features make this new edition especially worthwhile. They include new lessons—and revision ideas connected directly to writing samples. Those samples alone make this book a precious resource.

This edition also includes many new book recommendations. Vicki always seems to have the perfect mentor text at her fingertips. I love listening to her read because she makes you fall in love with the literature. When Vicki recommends a book I feel I *have* to buy it so I can share it with my students. But I used to wonder, "How in the world does she FIND these perfect passages? She must read constantly!" In this fifth edition she shares with us not only the books *she* uses to teach, but ways of finding our own jewels. That is a priceless gift. It makes us more independent as teachers who are always on the lookout for powerful mentor texts.

The fourth edition of *Creating Writers* came to us at a time when measurement and accountability started playing the starring role in education across the nation. Mandates to evaluate and measure our students flooded the schools and the stakes were very high. With this fifth edition, the stakes remain high, and the need for an assessment vision to guide us is stronger than ever.

The best assessments give us valid results without asking us to sacrifice our humanity. Nobody has really figured out how to measure voice using a scantron! We also don't know how to measure love, peace, kindness, perseverance, tolerance, hope, optimism, resourcefulness, commitment, loyalty, respect, compassion, or dignity. But these incalculable qualities are the reason behind most writing. We don't write *just* to meet a standard, after all. We write to touch a human heart. This book shows us how to help students do both.

For years as a writing workshop teacher I looked at writing with novice eyes. I knew how to edit a piece of student writing. But when it came to revising, I was as lost as my students. I think I could tell when a piece of writing wasn't good, but I couldn't explain why, nor could I teach students how to improve the piece. After reading Vicki's first edition of *Creating Writers,* I realized that for too long I had been looking only at surface structures like grammar, spelling, and punctuation. What I found in the traits was a way to see the hidden structures of writing. I've learned to teach children to find their voice and value their ideas; I've learned to *teach* revision instead of assigning it. Teachers who understand that writing is more than surface structures hold the power to change the world. That's because children lucky enough to have this kind of teacher learn how to communicate with clarity and conviction. Their voices will be heard.

There are no short-cuts in creating writers. I know that the six-trait model has sometimes been misused and distorted. I've seen it separated from the writing process. I've seen it used as a gimmick or a trick or held up as a district writing curriculum. This book helps us once again see the traits as a shared vision for good writing. The heart of writing workshop begins to beat when we learn to listen to our students and

find the voice in their writing. It's the trait that matters most, yet it can be the most difficult trait to grasp. Vicki's book will help you understand what voice is about—and with that understanding, you will feel your passion for teaching writing grow.

Vicki gives us a language for navigating the deep structures of writing where idea development, voice, sentence fluency, and word choice reside. Thanks to her endless work, supportive words, and rich examples, we are able to teach and assess in ways that create strong writers. This book is dedicated to my personal mentor, Don Graves, who taught us to trust the voice within. Take those words to heart and trust the voice within YOU, dear teacher. Your voice matters deeply. Use it with your children and together we *will* change the world!

Cindy Marten
Vice-Principal, Central Elementary School
San Diego City Schools
Author of *Word Crafting: Teaching Spelling Grades K–6*

Preface

When the previous—fourth—edition of this book first came out, I could not wait to sign copies for people who purchased it at conferences and workshops. (And *thank you*, by the way.) One woman was a bit hesitant. In her hands she held her much "loved" third edition, which she was reluctant to let go of for it held all her notes and bookmarks. It was smudged and wrinkled with a nicely broken-in cover, a veritable reader's garden sprouting colored tabs out the top and sides. I loved it—and I understood completely. I read with a pen in my hand and mark *everything*—which is why this text is filled with the voices of all those people who "talk writing" in my head all the time.

Maybe you have a second, third, or fourth edition of this book, and so you're thinking, "Do I really *need* a fifth edition? Is *this* the time to break down and buy this book—again?" Yes—and yes. First, think what a wonderful contribution you'll make to my retirement. I am joking—a little. The real reason is this. Anyone who teaches knows it takes time to "get it." To figure out how to say what it is you really want to say, to make the world of whatever you're teaching accessible. To let people inside. This is the book that let's you inside the world of the six traits. The book that will make you say, "I can teach this. I can *do* it—and I know it will make a difference." And guess what—it *will*.

I don't know if there is any way to explain how much I love what I do. My work allows me to interact with teachers, the most giving people on the planet. Teachers give up what is most precious—their personal energy, stamina, and time—just so that someone might see the world a little differently or walk an easier path. How selfless can you get? When I do a workshop for teachers, I look out onto a sea of faces and "read" to the best of my ability who they are, what they are thinking and feeling, and what is making sense to them (or isn't). The questions these teachers—perhaps you—have asked over the past several years have inspired this revision. It is different from its predecessors in many ways, but it took awhile to get here.

A few years ago, a young boy whose teacher was coming to one of my workshops, asked, "My God, how old *is* she? You told us the traits had been around as long as writing itself!!" I relish this story—and it makes me think of the very first edition of this book—which was not inscribed on cave walls (sorry) but only goes back to 1990, and was co-authored by my beloved friend, Rick Stiggins (president of Portland's Assessment Training Institute, now part of ETS). That early (rather skinny) edition focused heavily on quality writing assessment, but through the years, the book has evolved into something quite different: a look at how to use assessment wisely and well to help students revise with power. At most of my workshops, two-thirds to three-fourths of the educators with whom I work have been to a previous workshop or have taught these traits to their students. Because there are so many people out there now doing six-trait workshops, though, and because too many of them (annoyingly) present the traits as a quick-fix, silver bullet approach to writing, not everyone understands how the traits work or why. A book I wrote in 2005, called *The 9 Rights of Every Writer* (Heinemann) was my passionate protest against the shortcut, formula-of-the-week approach to writing that is too often seen as a lifeline instead of the anchor that it truly is. I want to wring my hands and tear my hair out when I see how many people view the traits as yet another in a long line of formulas. But hair tearing is not helpful—and so I wrote this fifth edition instead.

As you sit in your comfy chair sipping herbal tea and merrily reading along, I want you to imagine I am having a conversation with you—because I am. As I revised each chapter, I pictured you—the teacher—looking at a face in a conference and asking yourself, "How can I help this writer?" Or kneeling by a desk looking at a student's writing and saying, "What question will unlock this for her—or at least get her to pick up her pencil?" Helping you answer these questions—in a variety of ways—drove my revision.

This edition has **new lessons**—and **lesson ideas connected to most of the student sample papers, as** well. This is a brand new feature. It's one I would have loved as a teacher, and I hope you like it, too. I have also tried to make clear not just what books *I* use to teach, but rather—and this is more helpful—**how to choose the books that will work *for you*.**

Some **new teachers' voices** appear in Chapter 10, *Listening to Teachers' Voices*, and what they add to our understanding of how to teach writing well will inspire you. Throughout that chapter, I also identified the **"Key Strategies"** that make every single one of these teachers' classrooms a remarkable, unique place in which to learn.

The **writing guides are newly revised**, again with suggestions and guidance from teachers throughout the country. They are even more explicit, and I think make the range of performance across traits more clear. As always, they remain open to interpretation and further revision by you and your students. The **six-point scale for students is now re-formatted** to underscore the "leaping the river" metaphor that helps make it easy to teach, with scores of 1, 2 and 3 reflecting need for revision, and scores of 4, 5, or 6 indicating predominant strengths. The **five-point scale** is used far less these days, but if you prefer it, it is still here, also **in a brand new format.** I have revised it as a **three-level scale** which—for the first time—can be adapted as a five- or six-point rubric. This flexibility means you can have your cake and eat it, too: the verbal richness of the five-point, with the expansiveness of the six.

Reviewers and teachers alike requested **more emphasis on informational writing**—and so you'll notice that shift, both in student samples and in lessons.

Many new papers make their debut in this edition—but because they do, others had to go. This was a *difficult* choice, but unavoidable. I cannot go on making this book longer and longer, you see—unfortunately. It isn't just that people can no longer carry it. It's also that my editor—the brilliant and inspirational Aurora Martínez Ramos—told me I had to stick (more or less) with the same length. Have you any idea how difficult this makes revision? Well, trust me—it was a challenge. Every time I added something (and there are *a LOT* of something's), something else had to hit the cutting room floor. If one of your favorite papers met this fate, I am sorry. I loved them, too. I carry many of them with me. Just know that many new favorites await you. The students who contributed to this edition had much to say—and said it with flair. I think you'll enjoy making new friends.

Chapter 12, *Exploring the World of Beginning Writers*, now includes brand **new primary continuums** developed for this edition's complementary text, *Creating Young Writers*—now in its second edition. That second edition, along with Chapter 12 from this text, offers many teaching ideas useful for working with challenged writers of *any* age, and I hope you will look at them through this lens as well.

The book is set up to be used in a class or study group, and I hope you will use it just that way so that you can talk about the content of each chapter and how it applies to your classroom. **Study Group questions and activities** appear at the end of each chapter. You don't have to do them all—but look through them—and do *some*.

Teachers also wanted more lessons—an extension of what appears in this book. To create these, I took each trait apart, asking, "What do writers actually *do* when they revise under the umbrella of this trait?" And the result is **a new collection called *Creating Revisers and Editors***, a series of individual, writing small/revising small lessons that extend everything in this book. These complementary editions are also published by Pearson Education, and will be issued grade by grade, beginning with grades 3 and 4, but eventually extending from grades 2 through 8. If teaching highly focused revision and editing skills appeals to you, please watch for them. If you are currently using the *Write Traits Classroom Kits* (written by my co-author Jeff Hicks and me, and published by Great Source Education), please know that the new *Creating Revisers and Editors* fully complements lessons in those kits—and is *not* a repetition of what you will find there.

If you are new to trait-based teaching, I want to say two things to you. First, the six traits support and enrich writing process at every step. They not only make revision manageable, but they make it make sense, period. If you want your students to taste writing success—success you can see and measure—this is your book. Trying to teach revision without the traits—or at least *your own personal version* of writer's language—is like trying to teach math without any names for the numbers or for the math processes through which you will manipulate them.

Second, because the traits are *not a curriculum* in any sense or form, they will not take over your classroom like unchecked ivy (as many writing *programs* do these days) or replace *anything you are doing now*. Rather, they will fit in with, adapt to, accommodate, and expand your current practice, helping students gain more than ever from process, writing workshop, response groups, conferences, and all verbal feedback.

Like a good rail fence, the traits provide enough structure to lean on—but the structure is open and supportive, not restrictive. You can look through and beyond it, and one day you find yourself sitting on it and looking off into the horizon and realize that even though it was holding you up the whole while, you barely knew it was there.

Acknowledgments

Countless people have contributed to the development of this book—to mention everyone, I would need another book, but know you are loved and appreciated even if your name is not on these pages. First and foremost, I want to acknowledge how much all teachers, including myself, owe to the tens of thousands of student writers who have taught us all so much. The original six-trait model was built upon their voices, and without them, neither this book nor the six traits themselves would exist.

Special thanks to the many student writers whose work appears in this edition—and to those for whom we could not make room, much as we wanted to. Your contributions were greatly valued. We have sought permission for each paper and copyrighted selection in this book. If for any reason you feel your work has been published without permission, we will happily correct that oversight.

Thank you to all of the teachers who invited me into their classrooms to share lesson ideas and work with their students, and who shared instructional strategies or lessons with me.

My deepest thanks to *all* those people who have been my personal teachers through the years: in particular, to Cindy Marten, who knows that genius is hollow without compassion, and whose spirit *("Work hard, Be kind, Dream big")* will guide—I believe—our nation's very destiny in literacy; to Don Graves, the gentle man to whom this book is dedicated, who taught so many of us the importance of voice and who shaped, in a very direct way, a view of assessment that dared to look beyond conventions to the soul of writing; to my cherished friend and mentor Donna Flood, who has supported this project in a thousand ways through her own teaching and writing,

whose intelligence guides me like a light in the dark, and who continues to share her vast knowledge, wisdom, sensitivity, and gentle humor with all students and teachers lucky enough to know her; to the inimitable Barry Lane, the finest teacher of revision skills I've yet to encounter, and unquestionably the wittiest, who always seems to make me laugh just when I need it most, who gets workshop participants to perform interpretive poetry in ways they never imagined themselves doing in public, and who is gifted enough to write *music about revision*; to Monica Mann, Gail Lee, Sean Doi, and Sandra Haynes, who opened so many, many doors for me, and to all my friends (students and teachers alike) in Hawaii whose aloha spirit (like the music of Israel Kamakawiwo'ole himself) keeps me going and fills my heart; to the incredible Leila Naka, who embodies the best of what education should be, who can say more with her wise, smiling eyes than most people could say in six books, who has helped countless teachers see the traits as a vision and not a program, and whose generosity of spirit touches everyone she meets; to Richard (aka Rick) Stiggins, the guru of classroom assessment (and fly fishing), who has always encouraged *me* to "work hard" and "dream big," and whose vision of quality assessment guides every facet of my educational life (and would even influence my fishing if I could ever make time for it); to the comical, inspirational Rosey Comfort, who never found a formula she couldn't outwit and who, as a force to be reckoned with, coaxes the kind of writing from her students that rocks the world; to the remarkable Judy Mazur, whose humbleness belies the fact that *no one anywhere* does writing workshops or conferences or sharing time more brilliantly or with more grace and vitality—and who is deeply loved by the students for whom she opens doors every single day of her life (Thank you, Judy, for just letting me be there); to Barbara Andrews, whose inventive and tireless spirit brings the traits to life every day for her brilliant middle school writers, and who never runs out of new ways to teach; to the extraordinary Sally Shorr, whose understanding of writing process is unsurpassed, and who has so often been for me the person Mem Fox calls "the watcher," the heart to whom you write, whose voice inspires your own; to the phenomenally talented Lois Burdett, who let me watch as she coached her second graders through *Macbeth*, and who taught me to "take the lid off" because there are no limits to what children of any age can do; to Tommy Thomason and Sneed B. Collard, my writer-teacher friends, who do not just *talk* writing, but also *do* it; to the incredible trainers of the Write Traits team (matchless, best in the world), most especially my long-time friends Darle Fearl, Jeff Hicks and Fred Wolff, who have unerringly guided me to the BEST books all these years, and who have taught me more through casual conversation than I learned from most courses; and to all my friends at Great Source Education, particularly three very special people who helped build a bridge between two publishers: Susan Rogalski, Sue Paro, and Karin Huang—my thanks to you for your encouragement and understanding.

My continued appreciation to those who started the ball rolling so long ago. In particular, thanks to my dear friend Carol Meyer, former assessment and evaluation specialist for Beaverton (Oregon) School District #48, and to those 17 teachers who made up the Analytical Writing Assessment Model Committee. Thank you all for hanging in there through mountains of student essays and countless early drafts. Thank you for making history and letting me be there.

No book comes together without extensive behind-the-scenes effort. I wish to thank my editor, Aurora Martínez Ramos, who has encouraged me to make this book the extension of myself I always wanted it to be. I am also deeply indebted to Barbara Andrews, Rosey Comfort, Judy Mazur and her parent helper Teresa Weaver, and all the participating student writers for their time and skill in providing (from their own classrooms) the photos for this book that illustrate six-trait writing workshop in action. My sincere thanks also to the reviewers of this edition: Patricia L. Ball, Milwaukee Public Schools; Tamara Doehring, Melbourne High School; Dena Harrison, Mendive Middle School; Erin Helme, Upland Terrace Elementary; Donna C. Horton, Hillcrest Middle School; Laura Lundy, Medford Area Public School District; and Dan Ryno, Jury Elementary School.

Thanks of course to my family, whom I hardly ever see because that is the way of things for writers. Thank you to my husband and best friend, Jerry—for cooking (*really* good food), making (*really* good Kona) coffee, listening, encouraging me, remaining calm through all computer crises, and putting up with a houseful of manuscript bits and pieces. Thanks to my remarkable, loving, and disarmingly humorous children, Nikki and Michael, my wonderful son-in-law Chris (all writers, though they don't make a living at it)—and my grandson and future writer Jack (now 3), who has already figured out that once they let you at the keyboard, all things are possible. And thanks to Ann Marland, an adopted member of our family, who is Auntie Ann to my children. You have to love a friend who sticks with you no matter where you relocate.

Somewhere in Montana lives the woman who in many ways is more responsible for this book than anyone else. Her name is Margery Stricker Durham, and she taught me to write. I took seven classes from her (both graduate and undergraduate) and she never covered the same ground twice. On the first day of class, she walked into the room (all 90 pounds of her), pulled off her wild raccoon hat to revel equally wild hair underneath, and wrote her name on the board: S-T-R-I-C-K-E-R. "My name is Stricker," she said. "If you're late, don't bother coming. If you don't do the work, don't waste my time." I loved her immediately. I was only late once (and came anyway)—and I did the work. And I found what I had been looking for all my life without knowing it—a teacher who waited for my writing, read every word, and wrote back. She taught us that literature was a reflection of life. She taught us that history wasn't just something from long ago, but was unfolding all around us. She taught us to see books, paintings, architecture, music and other expressions of the human spirit as an interconnected record of intelligent thought. She taught us to think. It is the finest, most unselfish gift we give one another—and is the reason teachers are so loved. Dear Margery, I think of you each day of my life—and always will.

Creating a Vision

The best change occurs slowly and comes from teachers themselves. It takes longer but it lasts.

—**Donald H. Graves**
Testing Is Not Teaching, 2002, p. 52

Good assessment always begins with a vision of success.

—**Rick Stiggins**
President, Assessment Training Institute

I wish we could change the world by creating powerful writers for forever instead of just indifferent writers for school.

—**Mem Fox**
Radical Reflections, 1993, p. 22

Six-trait writing is not a curriculum. It is not a program. It is a vision—a way of thinking and talking about writing that helps teachers, and even more important, helps students answer the question all writers must ask: *What makes writing work?* Answering this question enables students to revise with purpose and, in addition, makes the teaching of writing easier.

Easier is good. No teacher anywhere these days is saying, "I don't know what it is with this skimpy curriculum. I simply *cannot* fill the days." While trait-based assessment and instruction cannot make classes smaller or make testing go away, it can ease writing teachers' stress by showing them how to help students

- Take charge of their own writing process.
- Understand the difference between strong and weak writing—and use that knowledge to write stronger drafts.
- Revise and edit their own writing because they can "read" it and because they know what to do to make it better.

All this sounds a little like magic, but really, it's logic. The key has been right before us the whole time; we had only to unlock the door. The key is language—*writers'* language that opens the door to revision.

 # Who Invented the Six Traits?

No one. Though the number of persons who take credit for having "invented" or "developed" the six traits seems to grow geometrically each year, the truth is that the traits themselves are not *anyone's* invention. Like stars or far-off planets awaiting discovery, the traits have been around as long as writing itself and are an inherent part of what makes writing work. What *is* new (within the last few decades) is a written description of what the traits *look like* at different levels of performance. In other words, a *rubric,* or *writing guide,* if you prefer that term.

The original six-trait rubric for assessing and teaching writing came *from teachers.* It was developed in 1984 by the Analytical Writing Assessment Committee, a group of seventeen teachers from the Beaverton, Oregon, school district with whom I was privileged to work. Since its inception, the six-trait model has been revised numerous times and currently exists in both five- and six-point versions. The six traits include

Ideas—The heart of it all, the writer's main message and the details, evidence, or anecdotes that support or expand that message.

Organization—The internal structure (skeleton, if you will) of a piece that gives support and direction to the ideas.

Voice—The writer's fingerprints preserved on the page, that special something that keeps readers reading.

Word choice—A knack for selecting the *just right* word or phrase that makes everything come clear for the reader.

Sentence fluency—Rhythm and flow, the music and poetry of language—how it all plays to the ear.

Conventions—Skill in using an editor's tools (punctuation, spelling, grammar, capitalization, and layout) to enhance readability and meaning.

Paul Diederich: The Inspiration

Beaverton's innovative research design was based largely on work done by Paul Diederich (as documented in *Measuring Growth in English*, 1974) in the 1960s. Diederich had been curious to know whether people could agree on what makes writing work and whether they could come up with language to describe what they found. His research method was ingenious in its simplicity. He assembled a group of fifty or so writers, editors, attorneys, business executives, and English, natural science, and social science teachers and asked them to read numerous student essays and rank them into three groups: effective, developing (about halfway home), and problematic. Then—this is the interesting part—they were asked to record their reasons for ranking the papers as they had. In the process, they discovered something rather striking: In most cases they were influenced by nearly identical qualities (traits) in the writing. Here (listed here in order of apparent influence) are the traits Diederich's team identified:

- Ideas
- Mechanics (usage, sentence structure, punctuation, and spelling)
- Organization and analysis
- Wording and phrasing
- Flavor (voice, tone, and style)

Confirmation from Purves and Murray

Over the years, Diederich's method has been replicated by other researchers, including Alan Purves (1992). In his work on international writing assessment, Purves and his team of raters identified these *significant* traits:

- Content (what we call ideas)
- Organization
- Style and tone (what we call voice, word choice, and sentence fluency)
- Surface features (essentially conventions, but also including neatness)
- Personal response of the reader (essentially, response to the quality we call voice)

In 1982, Donald Murray (pp. 66–67) identified these six traits—also closely aligned with those in this book:

- Meaning
- Authority
- Voice
- Development
- Design
- Clarity

Meaning and clarity equate with the trait of ideas, design with organization, voice and authority with voice.

Beaverton: The First Six-Trait Rubric

Inspired by Diederich's research design, the seventeen-member Analytical Assessment Model Committee set about replicating it. Carol Meyer (then director of evaluation and assessment for the district) and I were privileged to direct and work with this team. We spent weeks reading student papers at every grade level from 3 through 12, sorting them into high, middle, and beginning levels and documenting our reasons for ranking them as we did. Eventually, we arranged our documentation along a continuum of writing performance, and the result was a draft of what would eventually become the six-trait assessment model (see Figure 1.1 for an in-process draft of the original rubric).

Shortly thereafter, Portland Public Schools conducted a similar study—in which I also participated. Minus any collaboration with Beaverton, Portland came up with virtually identical traits, their list also closely matching that of Diederich. Since Portland had no knowledge of Beaverton's work or Diederich's, this similarity demonstrated to us all that teachers *do* in fact share common values about what is important in writing.

The six-trait model is now used in virtually every state by one or more districts—and in many states, the model is very closely aligned to state standards. (See Appendix 9 for sample correlations between the six traits and selected state standards of writing.)

The model also has spread throughout the world so that many teachers from South America to Africa and the Far East are now using some version of six-trait writing. Its wide use is largely due to two things: First, it simply reflects the heart and soul of what good writing is about, with definitions expressed in clear, easy-to-understand language from which teachers can teach. Second, it has a kind of déjà vu feel to it, echoing good teaching practice that process-based writing teachers have been using for years. It gives teachers language for saying the things they always wanted to say, but for which they did not have the words. In this sense, the six traits are writing teachers' gift to themselves.

FIGURE **1.1** In-Process Draft of the Original Six-Trait Rubric

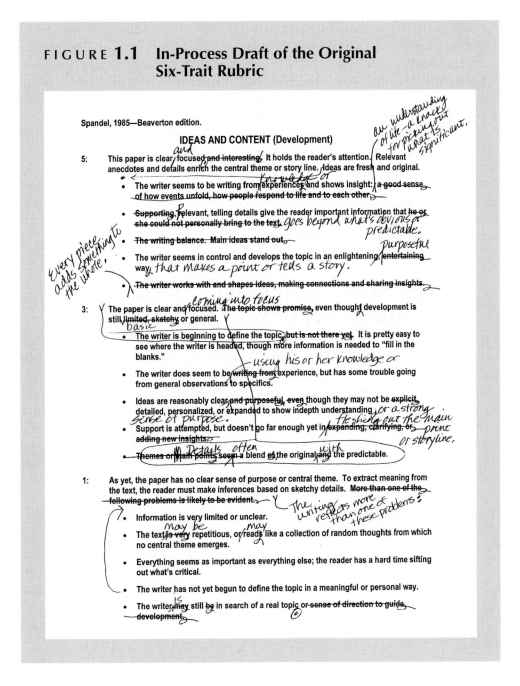

Assessing to Learn: The Bridge to Revision

Isn't assessment an odd place from which to begin writing instruction? Actually, no. It's the very best place, once we understand what assessment is.

When we think *assessment*, we usually think *grading* or *testing*. This is a very limited view. Assessment is looking within. It is the door to understanding.

As Lucy Calkins so eloquently points out in her revised edition of *The Art of Teaching Writing* (1994), we assess to *learn*: "If . . . children can't talk easily about texts, they will have a hard time being critical readers of their own or anyone else's writing" (p. 326). They will also have a difficult time revising. You cannot repair a car until you know what is not working. You cannot revise writing unless you can hear problems within the text.

Looking deep within is essential not only to students' understanding of their own writing but also to the very act of writing itself. "We teach [students] how to read books," Donald Graves (1994, p. xvi) points out, "but not how to read their own writing. Unless we show children how to read their own writing, their work will not improve." But if we *do* show them, their skills will soar. The very core of this book rests on one foundational belief: *What you can assess, you can revise.*

Ten Reasons to Make Six-Trait Writing Part of Your Instruction

Look again at the list of traits and ask yourself, "Could I seriously teach writing without emphasizing the importance of good ideas and organization? Without worrying about the words my students use or how they construct sentences or whether their text is conventionally correct? Without stressing the importance of audience?" Of course not. If you are currently teaching writing using a process-based approach, you are already teaching the traits—in some form. This book will help you streamline and organize the best of what you already do—and give you a language for talking to students about writing.

Here are ten important reasons to include six-trait writing in your instructional vision of success:

1. The model defines clearly what it means to write well.

2. Using a rubric you believe in keeps your assessment consistent and honest.

3. The six traits make writing and revising *manageable*.

4. The traits support and strengthen writing process.

5. Trait-based instruction makes revision and editing purposeful.

6. Making students partners in writing assessment empowers them.

7. Learning to assess with confidence increases student motivation while promoting thinking skills.

8. Six-trait instruction connects reading and writing by encouraging students to read like writers—and write like readers.

9. Six-trait writing is *real*.

10. Working with well-written writing guides can save you assessment time.

Let me expand, very briefly, on each of these.

1. Defining "Good" Writing

Do you recall as a student wondering what on earth it was the teacher wanted? My third grade teacher liked l-o-n-g pieces of writing, regardless of what we actually wrote, so we filled pages, whether we had something to say or not. My fourth grade teacher did not care a whit about length; penmanship was the target to hit. Mine was good, so I sailed through that year effortlessly (and mindlessly), while my friend Gary spent hours inscribing, "I will write neatly" (a promise he never fulfilled). In fifth grade, the teacher wouldn't allow anyone but herself to touch her desk; she valued neatness and organization above all things. I had the straightest margins in town, so it was a whiz-bang year. Then, in sixth grade, the roof caved in; that was the year we had to *think*. None of us had seen this lightning bolt coming, so we were unprepared. We floundered. And that, of course, was only the beginning. Each successive year brought its own challenges and revelations about what teachers "really wanted": research, citations, expanded ideas, condensed ideas, three paragraphs, five paragraphs, ten pages with documentation, details, quotations, objectivity, analysis. More. Less. Everything. How much more successful we would all have been had our teachers shared a common vision instead of giving us an endless succession of mysteries to solve.

2. Keeping Assessment Consistent and Honest

Have you ever come to the bottom of a thick stack of papers you are reviewing/grading, and thought to yourself, "I really *should* start over—I would assess those early papers *sooooo* differently now"? If you have had this experience, or if you have wondered whether you assess differently class to class, day to day, or in some way that conflicts totally with what a colleague is doing, then you know the value of consistency and how hard it is to achieve. Rubrics give us a reference point, a safe harbor to which we (and our students) can return. And if our thinking or what we value changes over time, we can revise our rubrics to reflect that new thinking.

3. Making Writing Manageable

One of my favorite writing stories comes from author/teacher Anne Lamott, who tells of her older brother, just ten at the time of the story, who was struggling to complete a research report on birds that he had had three months to write. The boy was close to tears, surrounded by papers and books, overcome by the daunting task ahead. Anne's father put a reassuring arm around her brother and said, "Bird by bird, buddy. Just take it bird by bird" (Lamott, 1995, p. 19). In this anecdote, Lamott perfectly captures how overwhelming writing can feel (to say nothing of the *teaching* of writing). Because the six traits define writing, they allow us to take it "bird by bird." So one day perhaps you teach a lesson on leads, and on another day you show students how to come up with a good title or use transitional phrases effectively. Step by step, you create writers who are confident in what they do.

4. Strengthening Writing Process

Do you believe in process or use a writers' workshop approach in your classroom? Do you give your students time to write, revise, and edit? Model writing for them? Read to them? Confer with them and encourage response groups? Good. You will not need to give up *any* of these tried and true instructional strategies, nor should you. Each and every one will be strengthened by your use of writers' vocabulary—six-trait language. Trait-based instruction *enhances* a process-based approach to writing instruction; *it does not replace it.*

Students who know the language of the traits respond easily—and helpfully—to peers in a response group: *I could really hear your voice, Your lead made me expect something different, The word choice was very strong—I could picture the band playing.* Trait-savvy students come to conferences with a question in mind: *I need help with my conclusion, This dialogue isn't sounding right.* A shared vocabulary turns us all into writing coaches and enriches our understanding of how writing works.

5. Making Revision and Editing Purposeful

Look carefully at Figure 1.2. What do you see? Perhaps you see a tall, elegant vase. But if you look at the picture another way, you'll see two women looking at each other. A good writing rubric should be just like that. Look at it one way, and it's a tool for assessment. Look at it another, and it becomes a guide to revision—adding detail, focusing on one main message, rewriting a lead or conclusion, or adjusting voice or wording to meet the needs of an audience: These *are* the things writers do when they revise. Scoring guides reveal revision possibilities.

6. Empowering Students

When we make students partners in the assessment process, they become much less dependent on us to give them a specific blueprint for revision: *"You need to cut this first paragraph. . . . I'd add more detail here. . . . You might think about changing the structure of this sentence."* Writing is mostly problem solving, after all. You cannot get better at it if someone else is always solving all the problems for you. In classes where the traits are taught as part of a process-based approach, students use rubrics to guide the way they view their own and others' writing, talk about writing, and use literature as models of what to do or not do. They take charge of their own writing process instead of looking to us for all their revision cues.

7. Promoting Student Motivation— and Encouraging Thinking Skills

Research by Paulette Wasserstein (1995) shows that students learn best when they are challenged, actively engaged, and asked to be self-reflective: "Hard work does not turn students away, but busywork destroys them" (p. 43). With six-trait assessment, students become part of a writing community in

FIGURE **1.2**
Two-Way Picture

Writing begins with listening. Don't we all, as writers, want to be listened to?

—Arlene Moore
K–1 teacher,
Mt. Vernon, Washington

which their opinions about the quality of writing are frequently, actively sought. Having your opinion valued makes you feel that your presence in the classroom has purpose.

Many students simply do not like to write, are afraid to write, or feel that they have nothing important to say. For these—and for *all* students—Richard Strong and his colleagues (Strong, Silver, and Robinson, 1995, p. 10) suggest that three factors are essential to motivation:

- We must clearly articulate the criteria for success and provide clear, immediate and constructive feedback.
- We must show students that the skills they need to be successful are within their grasp by clearly and systematically modeling those skills.
- We must help students see success as a valuable aspect of their personalities.

We do all three with six-trait assessment. Rubrics define success in student-friendly language. The immediate feedback is there if students are taught to understand the criteria within the rubric and use those criteria to assess their own work. Modeling (second bullet) is key. You are modeling writing success every time you write or read with students, share your own writing, or share and discuss writing samples that show what to do—or not do. Finally, in order for success to become part of you (third bullet), you must experience it. Many of our students have *never* experienced the joy of that moment when you hear your own voice or see how much your writing has touched someone. All the assessment and monitoring in the world will not do as much for those students as one genuinely appreciative voice saying, "I *loved* that. Please write more." Among the true advantages of the six-trait model is that it offers *every* student multiple opportunities for success.

Consider fourth grader Rocky. In his first few years of school, he rarely wrote more than a line or two. Negative comments and multiple corrections taught Rocky an important lesson: Keep it short. Get in and get out; that way, they can't hurt you too much.

When he had an opportunity to serve as an assistant to Harry, the school custodian, it was an enormous boost to Rocky's spirit. In addition, Rocky encountered a teacher who could see beyond his conventional problems and who encouraged him to express his voice on paper. Not surprisingly, he chose the topic most important to him at the time: his friend Harry (see Figure 1.3).

> Many of my teacher education students, after twelve years at school, come to me helpless and fearful as writers, detesting it in the main, believing that they can't write because they have nothing to say because they haven't cared about saying anything because it hasn't mattered because there's been no real investment for so long.
> —Mem Fox
> *Radical Reflections,*
> 1993, p. 21

> Teachers should focus on students' strengths rather than on deficiencies.
> —Kathleen Strickland and James Strickland
> *Reflections on Assessment,*
> 1998, p. 25

FIGURE 1.3   Rocky's Paper on Harry

Harry is the one that made me stop fighting help me focos and do my work.

Ever sense I've been friends with Harry I've got all A & B on my reportcards. He's brought me to his camp, brought me fishing, let me sleep over his house I think hes the best friend a kid could have.

He brought me to eat at a resteront in Wiscasset. He bouht me an carereokey isn't that so nice. Harry and I play the gutar together my gutar is alatrek his I have know idea. Harry plays like the greatest singer there is. I help Harry at lunch time he let's me help him dump trays.

The day Harry and I stop being friends is the day I die, and that's along time from now.

from Rocky
Grade 4

> Every student ought to have the equivalent of a baseball card—many different kinds of abilities measured and a brief narrative report—if we are seriously interested in accurately documenting and improving complex performance.
>
> —Grant Wiggins
> "Creating Tests Worth Taking,"
> 1993, p. 33

Rocky's paper contains a number of conventional errors. His teacher, however, chose to focus on other features: "Your ideas are so clear in this piece. I can tell from your paper what a special friend Harry is. And your voice in this last paragraph really shines."

That night Rocky went home and told his mother, "I can write."

8. Connecting Reading and Writing

In her brilliantly insightful book, *What You Know by Heart* (2002), Katie Wood Ray points out that "every single text we encounter represents a whole chunk of curriculum, a whole set of things to know about writing" (p. 92). When we teach our students to read not just for meaning but also to discover clues about the writer's craft, we make every reading venture a lesson in how to write. The same things that help Gary Paulsen or Sandra Cisneros put voice into their writing work for student writers too. Professional writers do not inhabit a different universe or use secret skills unavailable to our students. They too must consider which details to include or omit, how to begin and end, and how to make sentences sing. Their text has much to teach—if we read like writers.

> Feedback has been shown to improve learning when it gives each pupil specific guidance on strengths and weaknesses, preferably without any overall marks.
>
> —Paul Black and
> Dylan Wiliam
> "Inside the Black Box: Raising Standards through Classroom Assessment," 1998, p. 140

9. Writing for Real Purposes

This book isn't *just* about success in grade school or high school or college—or improving scores on state tests. It is about students becoming strong and confident writers in any context for any purpose.

The College Board's National Commission on Writing issued a report in 2003 (*The Neglected "R": The Need for a Writing Revolution*) that cites several critical writing skills students need to work successfully in a twenty-first-century environment. Among them are "first-rate organization" (p. 16), ability to generate "convincing and elaborate" text, the use of "rich, evocative and compelling language" (p. 17), knowledge of "mechanics of grammar and punctuation" and a "'voice' and . . . feel for the audience" (p. 20). Do these traits sound familiar? We should not be surprised. The six traits are, after all, the very foundation of good writing—not a tack-on to good writing but the essence of writing itself.

> Writing well is not just an option for young people—it is a necessity.
>
> —Steve Graham
> and Dolores Perin
> *Writing Next,* 2007, p. 3

This same report points out that many Americans "would not be able to hold their positions if they were not excellent writers" (p. 10). But this is only the beginning. "At its best," the report continues, "writing has helped transform the world. Revolutions have been started by it. Oppression has been toppled by it. And it has enlightened the human condition. American life has been richer because people like Rachel Carson, Cesar Chavez, Thomas Jefferson, and Martin Luther King, Jr., have given voice to the aspirations of the nation and its people. And it has become fuller because writers like James Baldwin, William Faulkner, Toni Morrison, and Edith Wharton have explored the range of human misery and joy" (p. 10).

Our student writers will soon add their voices to the mix. What sorts of things will they write about in the twenty-first century? With each year, we view our solar system and indeed our whole universe differently. New moons and planets appear, while others, like Pluto, retire. Everyone has a Web site. Through DNA research we track the genetic history of the human adventure, capture criminals, and clone sheep. We discover life forms we didn't know existed, predict the demise of polar ice caps and the rise of oceans, and design self-parking cars and fire-fighting robots.

What will make us care about these things? What will help us to understand, recall, or connect them to our own lives? Writing. In their capacity as writers, our students will document these discoveries and thousands of others through film and television scripts, essays, textbooks, travel brochures, voter pamphlets, greeting cards, cartoons, letters and journals, poems, legal briefs, medical reports, advertisements, picture books, novels, editorials, song lyrics, and countless other forms. Someone will probably write a play satirizing overdependence on e-mail or script a new "Planet Earth" documentary. We will all, through most of our working lives, be writing to inform; to record; to define and explain concepts; to condense, summarize, and interpret data; to teach; to persuade, prompt, amuse, or inspire; and generally, to make sense of the world. And because, as Mem Fox (1993, p. 38) tells us, "No one writes for no one to read," knowing how to touch a reader's soul can only help us to do it better.

> Survey results [of 120 major U.S. corporations] indicate that writing is a ticket to professional opportunity. . . . "In most cases, writing ability could be your ticket in . . . or it could be your ticket out," said one respondent.
> —The National Commission on Writing
> September 2004, p. 3

> I will create a class culture of questioning. . . . If I have 120 students, I will have 120 teacher's aides. I will train students to assess and reflect on their own work daily and take charge of their learning.
> —Barry Lane
> *Reviser's Toolbox,*
> 1999, p. 194

10. Saving Assessment Time

Wait just a minute, now. Rubrics as *time savers*? Surely, you're saying to yourself (feeling somewhat protective of those few precious moments not already eaten up by lesson planning and preparing for the state test), a teacher cannot *save* time by assessing students' writing performance on *six traits*. You'd have to read a paper six times to make that work, wouldn't you? No, actually. One thorough, attentive reading will do. Internalizing the traits and *teaching them to students* is the secret, though.

Paul Diederich (1974) effectively demonstrated the practical value of good criteria in a study showing that teachers who marked student essays line by line spent, on average, a remarkable *eight minutes per essay*. This means that a teacher with 130 students (a much smaller class load than many have these days) could spend nearly eighteen hours per assignment *just responding to students' work*. (As a teacher, you might wish to have this figure handy the next time someone asks, "Why don't teachers assign more writing?") But here's the interesting part: When teachers abandoned their old ways of grading, stopped functioning as editors for their students, used consistent criteria that were *familiar to student writers*, and kept their comments to a minimum (brief marginal notes on what

the student had done well plus one short suggestion), that time dropped to just two minutes per paper—*one-fourth the time they had been spending.*

Rubrics act as a kind of shorthand between you and the student. You don't need to say everything; the rubric says some things for you. Then you can add a personal comment that gives your students what they hunger for most: your own words about how the writing touched you.

Building a Personal Vision

Any vision of success in writing must reflect classroom culture and embrace both product and process. You must build this vision for yourself. Let me suggest, though, some elements that I believe are critical, and as you go through the book, continue to reflect on the role traits might play in shaping *your* personal vision.

In my vision, *successful writing* would meet the criteria spelled out in the six-trait rubrics within this book. But focus on *product* tells only one part of the story. The vision must also incorporate a successful *classroom culture,* one that would

- Encourage exploration and risk.
- Help students find and develop their own voices.
- Respect choice.
- Provide a rich array of resources—human, technological, and academic.
- View "failure" as an opportunity for learning.

And finally, that vision must embrace the teaching of writing as a *process,* encouraging students to

- Write frequently.
- Choose topics of personal importance.
- Write in many genres and for diverse audiences.
- Understand the value of research in *all* writing—including narrative.
- Use lessons learned from mentor texts to enrich their own writing.
- Develop personal strategies for prewriting, drafting, revising, and editing.
- Assess their own work as a first step in revising and editing well.
- Keep personal portfolios to trace their journey as writers.
- Publish on their own initiative.
- Recognize that a reader's enthusiasm can mean as much as—even more than—publishing itself.
- Read like writers—and write like readers.

- Feel they are part of a writing community.

- Love writing.

In the chapters that follow, we will explore ways of making this vision a reality.

Chapter 1   In a Nutshell

- Six-trait writing is not a curriculum but a vision—a way of thinking about writing.

- Students who can "read" their own writing stand a better chance of revising effectively: *What you can assess, you can revise.*

- The six traits are not an invention but an inherent part of what makes writing work.

- The original six-trait rubric was developed *by* teachers *for* teachers.

- The six-trait rubric (or any good rubric) is not just a tool for assessment but a guide to thoughtful, effective revision.

- Assessment provides an important link to instruction because it takes us inside a process or concept, such as writing.

- We assess to understand, and once we understand, we can write and revise with purpose.

- To be effective teachers of writing, we must first teach ourselves what good writing is, and then we are better equipped to teach our students.

- There are (at least) ten reasons to make six-trait writing part of your personal vision for writing success: It provides—a language for talking about writing, consistency in assessment, a way of making revision and editing manageable, support for writing process, a guide to purposeful revision and editing, empowerment for students, increased motivation and thinking skills, a way of linking reading and writing, a foundation for real-world writing, and a way of saving assessment time.

- A personal vision of success in writing helps students to understand expectations—and thus increases their chances of success.

- Such a vision must incorporate attention to both process and product, as well as classroom culture.

Study Group   Interactive Questions and Activities

1.   **Discussion.** Within your study group, brainstorm ways in which your own teachers K through college created (or failed to create) a clear vision of success. Talk about ways in which this vision changed year to year, and the ways in which these shifting visions influenced your teaching.

2. **Activity and Discussion.** List the explicit writing skills you think today's students will need to enter the workforce. Then, visit any large local employer and interview someone from the administrative staff on this topic. Do you need to revise your list in any way?

3. **Activity.** Document your vision of success. You might do this as a list, essay, or poem. Focus on both product—the actual writing—and process. Expand your vision through quotations, anecdotes, or samples of student work, and make it part of a portfolio.

4. **Activity and Discussion.** With students or colleagues, compile a group list of *all the writing* you do over the course of a month. As a group, for how many purposes did you write? For how many different audiences? What forms did your writing take? Compare what you discover to the forms and purposes for writing students

experience within your classroom. To what extent is your writing curriculum preparing students for twenty-first-century writing? To what extent can students take the writing skills they are learning now on to college or into the world of work—or both?

5. **Discussion.** How would your *students* (if you are now teaching) rate your individual vision of success? How would you rate it?

_____ Very clear. Students know precisely what is expected.

_____ Somewhat clear. I find myself clarifying what I expect quite often.

_____ Unclear. I know good performance when I see it—but I have a hard time defining it ahead of time.

6. **Activity and Discussion.** On a six-point scale, how much would you say you are using the traits right now in your writing instruction? Rate yourself, compare with colleagues, then return to this question and rate yourself again once you have finished the first nine chapters of this book:

1	2	3	4	5	6

Not at all   *Every day*

Reflections on Writing

I write because I am a visual learner. Seeing something in text makes me learn it. I also write because I like to read. I can go back to something I wrote months or even years ago and have a great time reading what I wrote myself!

—**Sammy Geiger**, student writer

When first entering this galaxy of writing, you fear doing something wrong, of messing up, of being a bad writer. It takes a while to let that go, to just rocket off and take what comes.

—**Elisabeth Kramer**, student writer

Creating Assessment to Match the Vision

Good teaching is inseparable from good assessing.

—Grant Wiggins
"Creating Tests Worth Taking," 1992, p. 28

Our politicians believe that all tests are automatically good. They'd better take a second look at assessment approaches.

—Donald H. Graves
Testing Is Not Teaching, 2002, p. 3

The key assessment question comes down to this . . . Do I know the difference between successful and unsuccessful performance and can I convey that difference in meaningful terms to my students?

—R. J. Stiggins
Student-Involved Classroom Assessment, 2001, p. 196

Good assessment does not just happen. It takes planning. Tests are not inherently good, nor is assessment inherently beneficial or even helpful. When we judge the quality of our writing assessment, there are eight keys to success that we should be measuring our assessments against all the time. After considering these, we'll look at the lessons large-scale and classroom assessment have to offer us—and each other.

Keys to Quality Assessment

Key 1—Make the Target Visible

Good assessment is never about entrapment of students (or teachers, for that matter). It's about giving students an opportunity to show what they can do. As my friend and colleague Rick Stiggins is fond of saying, "Students can hit any educational target that holds still for them." When we define our expectations (as in a rubric), we dramatically increase the chances that students will perform better just by virtue of the fact that we have made clear what it is we want; we have held the target still.

Key 2—Construct Rubrics with Thought and Care

In constructing good rubrics, the language we use is critical. For example, beginning-level criteria point out problems with writing but do not point fingers at the writer: e.g., "Details are poor." Wording matters deeply because the language we use teaches students to think about themselves and about their work. Grant Wiggins (1992) reminds us that to the extent possible, "scoring criteria should rely on descriptive language, not on evaluative and/or comparative language such as 'excellent' or 'fair'" (p. 30). Such words are impossible to define rater to rater and promote inconsistencies in scoring. Furthermore, descriptors such as *excellent* or *poor* indicate a fundamental misunderstanding of how writing works. It does not start out being *poor* and suddenly become *good*. It begins with a small idea, like the planting of a seed, and grows as the writer's understanding grows, reflecting that expanded thinking. A score of 1 does not say, "You failed," but rather, "You put something on paper. You made a beginning. Now let's see how to make it stronger."

Wiggins also encourages us to focus on "the most salient characteristics" of performance at each level—those things, in other words, that would truly cause us to score a performance higher or lower. He also suggests linking criteria to "wider-world" expectations. In other words, we need to ask, Does what we are teaching and emphasizing lead to successful performance in a broader educational sense—out there in the competitive real world?

Once we are convinced that the criteria we have come up with are significant and that they are worded in a clear and constructive fashion, we arrange them along a continuum like that in Figure 2.1. This helps us and our students to understand what ideas look like as they grow.

A good rubric is also enhanced by examples that show the trait in action. This excerpt from Roald Dahl's classic *Matilda* is an excellent illustration of *detail*:

When she marched—Miss Trunchbull never walked, she always marched like a storm-trooper with long strides and arms aswinging—when she marched along a corridor you could actually hear her snorting as she went, and if a group of children happened to be in her path, she ploughed right on through them like a tank, with small people bouncing off her to left and right [1988, p. 67].

> We must speak to our students with an honesty tempered by compassion: Our words will literally define the ways they perceive themselves as writers.
>
> —Ralph Fletcher

■ Beware of "Armchair Criteria"

Too many rubrics consist of "armchair criteria" hastily scribbled down without validation through actual examples. This method of criteria development is dangerous because what is in our imaginations may or may not reflect real-life performance. If we want to know what's important in public speaking, for instance, we should listen to speakers and watch their behavior. To assess writing well, we must look at examples of text and assess our own responses—and we must expect a few surprises.

We may start out believing that correctness is what we'd most like to see in a strong piece of writing; then we look carefully at the examples that move us most. When I curl up to read Annie Proulx's *Close Range* (1999), I cannot really say I do not care about the punctuation and spelling. Of course I do. Still, I don't put the book down and say to myself, "Wow. Now *that* was an exciting use of commas." But you can believe I am closely tuned in when Proulx writes, "In the long unfurling of his life, from tight-wound kid hustler in a wool suit riding the train out of Cheyenne to geriatric limper in this spooled-out year, Mero had kicked down thoughts of the place where he began, a so-called ranch on strange ground at the south hinge of the Big Horns" (p. 19). I read this compelling line over and over, thinking what a fine choice *unfurling* is and how well the contrast of *tight-wound kid* and *geriatric limper* works or how often I feel that I am living in a *spooled-out year* myself. My response tells me that a good rubric should include features such as word choice and voice. Only writing that teaches and touches us can show us which traits count and how they look in action.

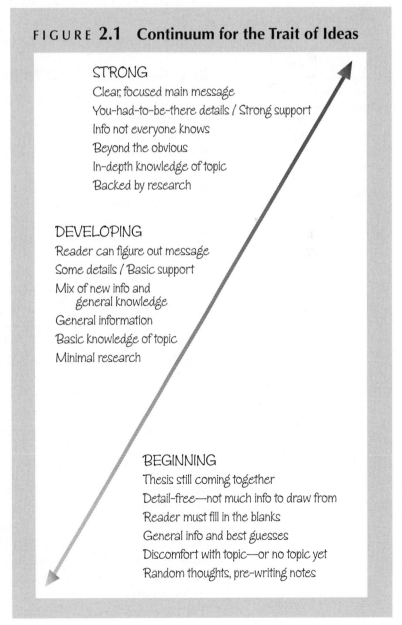

FIGURE **2.1** **Continuum for the Trait of Ideas**

STRONG
Clear, focused main message
You-had-to-be-there details / Strong support
Info not everyone knows
Beyond the obvious
In-depth knowledge of topic
Backed by research

DEVELOPING
Reader can figure out message
Some details / Basic support
Mix of new info and general knowledge
General information
Basic knowledge of topic
Minimal research

BEGINNING
Thesis still coming together
Detail-free—not much info to draw from
Reader must fill in the blanks
General info and best guesses
Discomfort with topic—or no topic yet
Random thoughts, pre-writing notes

Here are a few guidelines to help you recognize good criteria when you see them. They

- *Are clearly written*—easy to understand, explicit, and complemented by samples of strong and weak performance.
- *Focus on significant aspects* of performance (organization), not on trivia (size of margins).
- *Create clear distinctions* among performance levels so that raters have little difficulty agreeing on scores.
- *Thoroughly cover what is important* to quality performance; they do not pass over vital qualities (such as voice) just because they're difficult to define.
- *Use positive language,* even to describe beginning performance levels, thereby teaching students to think about themselves and their work in positive terms.
- *Are easy to teach from* because they are written in student-friendly language.
- *Are generalizable across tasks* so that it is not necessary to invent brand-new criteria for every new assignment.
- *Are forever changing* as we refine our thinking.

Key 3—Assess What Matters, Not What's Easy to Measure

Barry Lane (author of *After THE END* and *The Reviser's Toolbox*) tells the story of a high school teacher who commented on one piece of his writing, "It's nice to read typewritten work." Yes, it is. But it's even more rewarding to read work that reflects thinking. The obvious and easy thing to assess is not always what we value most. It is critical to distinguish between the two because what we assess is what we'll get.

In *Reflections on Assessment*, Kathleen and James Strickland caution that "many rubrics we use are invalid because we don't score what's important in the real-world application of the content being assessed. Instead we design rubrics to assess what's easiest to describe rather than what really matters" (1998, p. 81).

As teachers of writing, we usually mean well. We start out on a noble mission in pursuit of content, voice, fluency, or organization (and even go so far as to tell students that this is what we will be looking for), but we get bushwhacked by a pet peeve and wind up basing the grade on neatness, choice of topic, use of a pen rather than a pencil, or how closely the writer follows the assignment. One teacher actually gave an F to a third grade student who had written a clever, original fairy tale—in purple ink; the teacher did not consider this color appropriate for a serious writing assignment. We might counter that giving a low grade for such a superficial reason is not appropriate in serious assessment.

Key 4—Match the Assessment Approach to the Task

Most large-scale writing assessment today involves *direct assessment,* a form of performance assessment that requires students to actually write. *Indirect assessment* is, as its name implies, a somewhat more roundabout way of getting at *writing-related skills,* through fill-in or multiple-choice questions, such as that shown in Figure 2.2.

Though indirect assessment of writing is rare these days, its inherent emphasis on conventions continues to influence many *direct* tests of writing. It is far easier to write multiple-choice test items about grammar and punctuation than about concepts such as voice and organization. Thus indirect assessments of writing have traditionally tended to favor conventions, and this favoritism still affects the way some rubrics are constructed and the way many writing samples are scored. Too frequently, raters do not look beyond the conventions, and they may miss a lot. Writers who are passionate and clear thinking *sometimes* spell and punctuate well, too—but not always. Similarly, strong conventions have saved many a banal, content-free paper from the relatively low scores it would have earned in other traits had raters been focusing on the message more than on correctness and appearance.

FIGURE **2.2** **Sample Multiple-Choice Question**

Which of the following is not a complete sentence?

1. As of February 1, his projection seemed accurate.

2. How accurate could that February 1 projection be?

3. Accurate: That was the word for the February 1 projection.

4. An accurate projection, no doubt, as of February 1.*

5. All of the above are complete sentences.

■ Forms of Direct Assessment

Assessors have searched for years for some formulaic method of assessing writing that would eliminate pain, time, and expense. Some methods have included such things as counting numbers of words per sentence (think how high legal contracts would score on this one) or favoring complex sentence structure over simple. Unfortunately for those who favor the quick approach, no one as yet has been able to pinpoint any definitive relationship between writing quality and something so superficial as words per sentence or numbers of interlinked independent clauses (Huot, 1990). All widely accepted methods of direct writing assessment demand careful reading and attention to qualities that reflect thinking, e.g., idea development and organization of information.

Of the three most used scoring methods for direct assessment, *analytical scoring* (of which the six-trait model is one example) has become the most popular because, most assessors agree, it provides the richest information for the time invested. To best appreciate the advantages of this approach, it is worth looking at it in comparison with two other scoring methods: *holistic* and *primary trait*.

■ Holistic Scoring

Holistic scoring is based on the premise that the whole is more than the sum of its parts and that the most valid assessment of writing will consider how all components—ideas, mechanics, voice, and so forth—work in harmony to achieve an overall effect. Most often a holistic approach is based on explicit criteria, in which case it is termed *focused holistic scoring*. See Figure 2.3 for an example of a focused holistic scoring scale. When raters assign scores by matching students' papers to exemplars (also known as *anchor papers*), samples that typify performance at various score points, the process is called *general impression scoring*.

Because each paper receives only one score, holistic assessment has limited effectiveness in diagnosing writing skills or problems, and therefore is of

FIGURE 2.3 Focused Holistic Scale

Holistic Six-Trait Scale*

Strengths Outweigh Problems at the 4 to 6 Level

6

- Clear, focused main idea enriched with telling, unusual details
- Inviting lead, satisfying conclusion, reader never feels lost
- Irresistible voice that asks to be shared
- Vivid, memorable, precise words—no wasted words
- Clear, fluent sentences that make expressive reading easy
- Only minimal touch-ups needed prior to publication

5

- Clear, focused main idea with striking details
- Strong lead and conclusion, structure that guides the reader
- Individual, confident voice speaks to readers
- Accurate, well-chosen words that make meaning clear
- Clear, fluent sentences that make expressive reading possible
- Very light editing needed prior to publication

4

- Clear main idea, supported by details (description, examples, etc.)
- Functional lead and conclusion, reader can follow story/discussion
- Moments of strong voice speak to readers
- Functional, clear language carries general message
- Clear sentences that can be read without difficulty
- A good once-over needed prior to publication

Problems Outweigh Strengths at the 1 to 3 Level

3

- Main idea can be inferred—a broad, unexpanded overview
- Some details/elements could be relocated—lead and conclusion are present, structure may be formulaic
- Voice comes and goes—or not always a good fit with audience
- Marked by tired, overused words, phrases—OR overwritten
- Limited variety in sentence length, structure
- Thorough editing needed prior to publication

2

- Reader must guess at main idea—few details or just a list
- Hard to follow, lead and/or conclusion missing
- Distant voice—writing to get it done
- Filled with tired, overused language—OR overwritten, wordy
- Problems with repetitive, awkward, or run-on sentences
- Line-by-line editing needed prior to publication

1

- Main idea yet—random collection of thoughts
- Reader consistently goes back—no apparent link thought to thought
- Hard to "hear" the writer in the text
- Word choice confusing, general, repetitive, vague, or incorrect
- Hard to tell where sentences begin or end—many problems
- Word-by-word editing needed prior to publication

*Please note that a perfect match is not necessary. Choose the set of descriptors that best fits a given writing sample.

less value in the classroom than an analytical approach. As you can see from looking at Figure 2.3, a holistic scale implies, by the way it is constructed, that strengths or problems move up or down the scale together. Sometimes that is true. But many writers show great strength in one area—particularly ideas or voice—while such traits as sentence fluency or conventions are less developed. The holistic scale makes no allowances for such differences. Thus raters are left to make the best match they can, and a score of, say, 3 may indicate weakness in ideas *or* organization *or* conventions—and there is no way to know for sure without further analysis. All the same, because of its appealing simplicity, holistic scoring is well suited to offering a broad, general impression of group (versus individual) performance.

■ Primary-Trait Scoring

Primary-trait scoring is based on the premise that all writing is done for an audience and that successful writing will have the desired effect on the audience, mainly due to the impact of the primary, or most important, trait within the piece.

Let's say a writer is putting together a set of directions on assembling a bicycle that will be included with the bicycle components shipped to customers. Of course, it is important to write clearly, to use terms correctly, and to have sound mechanics, but perhaps the most critical trait of all is to organize the steps correctly.

Primary-trait assessment has never really caught on in large-scale state or district writing assessments because many educators feel that it is too limited in scope to provide all the feedback they want about their students' writing. On the other hand, it can be useful at the classroom level for teachers who wish to focus on a particular skill. For instance, if a teacher is helping students learn to write good business letters, a primary-trait approach can encourage them to pay particular attention to the right business tone or appropriate format.

■ Analytical Assessment

Because of its strong, natural link to revision, analytical assessment has become far and away the most preferred form of direct writing assessment at classroom, district, and state levels. Analytical scoring acknowledges the underlying premise that the whole is more than the sum of its parts, but it adds that if we are to teach students to write, we must take writing apart—temporarily—in order to focus on one skill at a time (remember—"bird by bird").

In order for analytical scoring to work well, all traits must be significant; e.g., use of voice appropriate to purpose and audience would seem important to most readers; placement of a title in the center of a page, less so. A good scale has *horizontal integrity*. That is, traits are distinct enough from one another that we do not wind up scoring the same thing twice. For example, we would just be duplicating efforts (and assessing unfairly) if we scored *ideas, content,* and *meaning* as separate traits because all cover basically the same thing.

A good scale also has *vertical integrity*. In other words, the "distance" from a 1 to 2 is the same as from a 2 to a 3 and so on. Definitions must reflect this difference. Vertical integrity also demands that any factor (leads or transitions) considered at one level must be considered at *all* levels. (See Figure 2.4 for an illustration.)

Key 5—Consider Multiple Samples

Hoping one writing sample will "tell all" is risky. Reviewing multiple samples collected over time (and across forms of writing) gives us a more accurate picture of student proficiency and helps to minimize bias. Such an approach is particularly important in high-stakes decisions such as graduation, entrance into college, and so on.

The value of this multisample approach is confirmed by Alan Purves' (1992) ten-year study of primary and secondary writing within fourteen international school systems, including those in the United States, England, Finland, Wales, Italy, Chile, Nigeria, New Zealand, and others. Among this study's many intriguing findings is this conclusion: "To make any assessment of students' [overall] writing ability, one at least needs multiple samples across the domain" (p. 112). Most of us would agree without thinking twice, but the "one sample tells all" approach is used widely at district and state levels, where funding is scarce and time short. This is unfortunate because significant decisions affecting both teachers and students are often based on this scant, limited information.

The issue is this: Writing involves a continual cycle of defining a topic, gathering information, planning and designing, drafting, reviewing and revising, and editing. In short, it's exquisitely complex. The more complex the target, the more samples we need to ensure that any measurement is accurate (Arter and Chappuis, 2006, p. 101). Calculating a student's ability to run the 50-yard dash in under 30 seconds is one thing—gauging that student's ability to *write* is quite another. But often we behave as though these two achievements were comparable.

At the classroom level, we know instinctively that we need as much information as possible, yet

> Since single assessments are unlikely to be able to show the range of a student's abilities—and cannot conceivably measure growth—a writing assessment, ideally, should rest on several pieces of writing, written for different audiences and on different occasions. Writing assessment is a genuine challenge.
>
> —The National Commission on Writing
> *The Neglected "R,"* 2003, p. 21

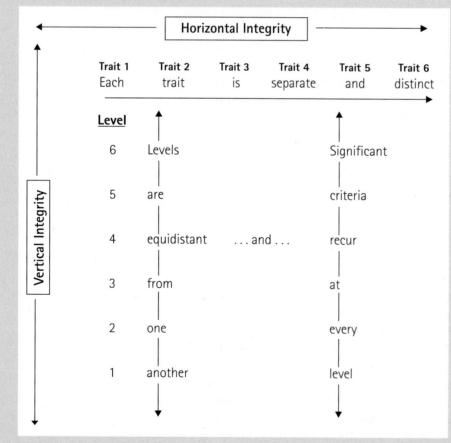

FIGURE **2.4** **Horizontal and Vertical Integrity**

Horizontal Integrity

Trait 1	Trait 2	Trait 3	Trait 4	Trait 5	Trait 6
Each	trait	is	separate	and	distinct

Vertical Integrity

Level

6	Levels		Significant
5	are		criteria
4	equidistant	. . . and . . .	recur
3	from		at
2	one		every
1	another		level

the reality of huge class loads makes us ask, "What's reasonable?" Because each classroom is different, we may never come up with a magic formula to tell us precisely how many samples we need for grading purposes. Yet there are guidelines to help us. First, the number of samples we can grade should not restrict how much students write. Not every piece of writing needs to be assessed. Students may keep files of drafts from which they select only a few to revise and hand in for formal assessment. Such assessment may occur only about once every week or two. This plan will easily result in four to six samples per grading period, a good minimum body of work on which to base defensible conclusions about student performance. Teachers who are able to do more (especially if students are writing in more than one genre), of course, will receive a proportionately more thorough picture of students' writing skills. Smaller assignments mean less to assess, and so minimizing assignment length in favor of more opportunities to write seems a good strategy if we wish students to receive as much feedback as possible. (See Chapter 13 for a more thorough discussion of grading.)

Let's not forget too that students who are skilled self-assessors are assessing and reflecting on their own work all the time. They self-assess as they plan, read their work, and revise until it becomes as natural as breathing. This self-assessment, in which the student goes inside the writing and thinks her way out, is the most important assessment by far, for it is the student (with guidance from the teacher) who has the power to change her writing and the way in which she writes. No matter how much data we scramble to collect, until the student knows what to do, assessment from without has no impact.

Key 6—Minimize Bias

Bias involves basing a writing assessment score or grade on some factor unrelated to actual writing performance, e.g., length of the document, handwriting (for pieces that are not word processed), previous performance, choice of topic, and so on. In large-scale writing assessment, raters may fail to use criteria, misinterpret those criteria, place too much emphasis on one factor while disregarding others, or ignore criteria altogether in favor of some personal basis for making a judgment; e.g., "This student wrote a science fiction piece, and I just don't like science fiction." Not surprisingly, many of these same factors influence teacher grading at the classroom level. (See Chapter 3 for a list of common pet peeves and other causes of bias among raters or classroom teachers.)

■ Isn't Bias Just Another Word for Subjectivity?

In a word, no. *Subjectivity* refers to the application—not the misapplication—of human judgment. Whether a test is *subjective* or *objective* has nothing to do with fairness or bias; it has to do with when human judgment is applied.

In direct writing assessment, judgments are made *during scoring;* such assessment is therefore known as *subjective.* In multiple-choice tests, human judgment is applied *during test construction* but not during scoring. In designing a multiple-choice test, someone must determine which content to include, which questions are significant enough to bother asking in the first place, how those questions will be worded, and which possible answers are plausible enough to look correct yet not so plausible as to *be* correct. These

> We often need to gather several samples to get a stable view of student achievement because the behaviors we are assessing are complex.
> —Richard J. Stiggins, Judith A. Arter, Jan Chappuis, and Stephen Chappuis
> *Classroom Assessment for Student Learning,* 2006, p. 198

> Careful research shows us what common sense tells us is obvious: no matter how trustworthily we may evaluate any sample of a student's writing, we lose all that trustworthiness if we go on to infer from just that one sample the student's actual skill in writing.
> —Peter Elbow
> *Embracing Contraries,* 1986, p. 37

> Current approaches to evaluation have it backwards. At the moment, the most important evaluator is some person out of town who knows nothing of the teaching situation. In fact, the student, who is closest to the work . . . ought to be and is the most important evaluator.
> —Donald H. Graves
> *Testing Is Not Teaching,* 2002, p. 28

Even though people often think of selected response tests as objective measures of learning, selecting the content for the test is itself a subjective exercise. . . . It is a matter of professional judgment, just as is determining how to teach the material in the first place.

—Richard J. Stiggins,
Judith A. Arter, Jan Chappuis,
and Stephen Chappuis

*Classroom Assessment for
Student Learning,* 2006, p. 133

are all subjective judgments. Because multiple-choice (or fill-in or true-false) tests frequently are scored by machine, however, no human judgment is applied *during scoring.*

This common misperception about objectivity is important because it causes some assessors as well as the general public to place undue faith in "scientific" testing approaches, such as multiple-choice tests, when in truth, such methods are incredibly ill-suited to the measure of writing proficiency. By extension, some people may also place undue faith in grammar and usage drills, sentence diagramming, memorization of formulas, vocabulary lists, spelling tests, and other shortcuts to the *teaching* of writing. Research cited in the National Commission on Writing's report, *The Neglected "R"* (2003), notes that "writing extends far beyond mastering grammar and punctuation. The ability to diagram a sentence does not make a good writer. There are many students capable of identifying every part of speech who are barely able to produce a piece of prose" (p. 13). Writing as thinking demands creative instruction and assessment by thoughtful readers, not machines.

■ A Little Subjectivity = Brain at Work

We must also be cautious about taking the position that subjectivity is somehow inherently wrong or that it invalidates the assessment process. There's nothing wrong with subjectivity if it's applied with consistency and intelligence. After all, lots of things in this world—films, books, restaurants, and performers in the Olympics—are rated subjectively; but we trust those ratings when they are given based upon relevant, consistent criteria and by persons with the training, insight, and experience to make ratings meaningful.

Key 7—Ensure That Assessments Are Both Reliable and Valid

Consistency, sometimes called *reliability,* depends on the specificity of the scoring criteria and the quality of rater training. When the criteria are highly refined and very explicit, and when the raters are very thoroughly trained and feel confident in applying those criteria (so confident that they could score a paper without even looking at the criteria, but they look anyway), the likelihood of their scoring consistently increases dramatically. This is important not only in large-scale assessment but also in the classroom.

A good assessment of writing is also said to have *validity,* the closest possible connection with the knowledge or skills we wish to assess. To determine whether a writing assessment has validity, we should ask questions like these:

1. Would a student who performed well on this assessment also do well in other writing contexts—in a college course, for example, or in a job demanding strong writing skills?

2. Would a student who did well on this assessment perform well on other well-constructed writing assessments—whether at the state, district, or classroom level?

3. Would a student participating in this assessment have a chance to demonstrate the kinds of skills most essential to writing competence?

4. Would a teacher or professional writer or editor looking at this assessment say, "Yes! That's *exactly* what we should be testing"?

Direct writing assessment has a potentially high degree of validity because, after all, students really are writing. The problem is, good writing assessment takes effort and time—enormous quantities of each. And while we always seem to find time to assess, we often find ourselves in a rush when it comes to doing it well. We are so concerned with speed and convenience that what we wind up measuring (often) is hasty drafting, not reflective thinking.

Key 8—Know What Questions We're Asking

We might begin by asking whether we need assessment results to assign grades, decide who will graduate, determine which candidates will be accepted into an institution or program, decide whom to hire, show how well an educational program or strategy is working, measure students' content knowledge (in math or science, let's say), inform writing instruction, or for some other purpose.

When we know precisely what questions we're asking, we can design an assessment that will actually give us the answers. Let's say one question is, "Will a process-based instructional approach help students write well?" In fact, we ask this very question all the time. Logic suggests that if we really wanted the answer, we would invite students to plan, draft, revise, and edit— even to choose their own topics or conduct research informing them about those topics. And that is how we generally assess writing at the classroom level.

District and state assessments, by contrast, are usually set up to answer the question, "Under timed conditions, can students create a clear and coherent *first draft* based on an assigned topic?" It is perfectly fine to ask this question. What is *not* fine is to set up an assessment that asks one question, and then to use and report results as if we had asked—and answered—another. Only when we are both precise and honest about *why* we are assessing can we hope to figure out *how* we should be assessing.

> Research is crystal clear: Schools that do well insist that their students write every day and that teachers provide regular and timely feedback with the support of parents.
>
> —National Commission on Writing
> *The Neglected "R,"* 2003, p. 28

Large-Scale and Classroom Assessment: Lessons from Two Perspectives

We often expect assessment, especially large-scale assessment, to magically improve performance, when the reality is that only instruction can do that. If assessment alone were the key, we would need only to weigh ourselves daily to lose weight. Would that it were so. If you think this sounds silly, ask yourself what it is we do when our student writers do not perform as we feel they should. We assess more often, make our standards more rigorous, and heighten our expectations. Well, then, perhaps if we weighed ourselves *hourly* . . .

Assessment serves us best when we use it to support, not direct, instruction. We must use results responsibly, as indicators. A writing assessment is one indicator of writing proficiency. We don't, if we are wise, rely on one indicator to tell us *everything*. Nevertheless, large-scale assessment has much to teach us about classroom assessment and instruction—and vice versa.

Lessons Learned from Large-Scale Assessment

Lesson 1: Prompts Count!

Several years ago I came across a newspaper article entitled, "Most Students Stumble on Writing Exam" (*The Oregonian,* September 29, 1999). The article began by stating that "only one in four U.S. students is able to write reports, narratives and persuasive pieces at a proficient level, according to the U.S. Department of Education." This "proficient level" is not defined in the article, but we are told that the results are based on two writing samples, with 25 minutes of writing time allowed for each. We are also given one of the prompts:

> Imagine this situation! A noise outside awakens you one night. You look out the window and see a spaceship. The door of the spaceship opens, and out walks a space creature. What does the space creature look like? What do you do? Write a story about what happens next [National Assessment of Educational Progress].

Do you see anything wrong with this picture—this so-called test of writing proficiency? The 25-minute time limit says clearly to students: "Writing is a quick activity that requires little thinking or reflection. If you cannot do it quickly, you are not proficient. Revision is not important; if it were, we would have provided time for it."

This prompt, I suggest, would make almost any thinking person "stumble." Written for eighth graders, it does not take into account what might interest or intrigue them, nor is it written at their level. Notice the short, simple sentences; it's almost a parody of a basal reader: *Open, spaceship, open. Walk, space creature, walk.* Further, it begins with a highly unlikely premise: a spaceship landing outside someone's window. Come on.

The 2002 prompts showed no improvement: "You wake up one morning, and there are clouds on your breakfast plate." Maybe it's a foggy day. If I cannot write to this prompt, there's a so-called alternative: "You look out the window and see stars littering the streets." Last time we looked, weren't stars rather large—and *hot?* In any case, students are further instructed to write a story called "The Very Unusual Day." They are given 25 minutes. "Faced with that task," the article (*USA Today,* July 11–13, 2003) continues, "fewer than one in five fourth-graders could write a respectable story." Really? So—given a wholly implausible premise completely outside the range of human experience, nine-year-olds could not concoct fanciful, coherent stories sufficiently riveting to engage an adult audience? Imagine that. This article ("Most Students Unable to Write Respectably") concludes with some thoughtful remarks by Gerald Bracey of George Mason University, Fairfax, VA. Bracey is said to be critical of the way writing tests are scored: ". . . by $7-an-hour temps who spend, at most, 30 seconds on an essay." If that 30-second estimate is correct, these "raters" are scoring roughly 120 essays an hour. At $7 an hour, that's about 6 cents per essay to discover what any teacher of writing could have told them: 25 minutes is an insufficient amount of time to rescue prompts that force students into a mental clash with common sense.

I've often wondered who in our national, state, or local government keeps an eye on the type of learner we are trying to develop in our public schools. Until we can begin to agree on what basics make up this ideal learner, it will be difficult to consider the best assessment approaches to tell us if our schools are succeeding.

—Donald H. Graves
Testing Is Not Teaching,
2002, p. 23

Because the identity of prompt writers is hard to discover (I think there is a Prompt Writers Protection Program), they often live to write another day. In all fairness to prompt writers everywhere (I have been one myself and have written my share of losers), let me say at the outset that writing good prompts is very hard. On a scale of 1 to 10, measuring difficulty and tendency to promote frustration, prompt writing is roughly an 8. This is one of many reasons we should (1) provide students with choices across topic and mode and (2) whenever possible allow students to write on self-selected topics. In addition, though, we should scrutinize prompts (in the classroom and out) to be sure that they open doors for students instead of locking them.

All prompts miss the point, which is this: An important part of what we should be assessing in writing is the student writer's ability to define a personal topic or come up with a research question worth pursuing. Any time we assign writing, we do part of the thinking for the writer. And in the end, the only person to whom I can effectively assign writing is myself.

Given that caveat, some assigned prompts are far superior to others. They are open-ended, allowing writers freedom to draw upon their personal knowledge and experience in creative ways, and to take a core idea in numerous directions—including directions the prompt writer could not foresee. See Figure 2.5 for a list of my favorites. These prompts are what I would term *functional*. They are not great. All the great prompts belong to the student writers who thought them up. Further, I don't claim any of them will cause students to cry out, "Quick! A pen!" Yet I believe each has potential to elicit strong writing. Notice the **boldfaced print** that offers students a clue about the kind of writing asked for. (One legitimate reason for imposing a prompt is to guide the writer into a particular genre—expository, persuasive, narrative.)

My friend and colleague Barry Lane (1993, p. 56) often favors a single-word or phrase approach to prompts. See Figure 2.6 for a brief list of his favorites.

Picture prompts nearly always work well because they assign no parameters. Students are free to use their imaginations to construct any content they wish, for any purpose they deem fit. If you have ever asked your students to write in response to *The Mysteries of Harris Burdick* (1996, Boston: Houghton Mifflin), for example, you know how powerful and provocative a picture can be. Picture prompts stimulate thought and invite voice. Most prompts are overwritten. Barry Lane gets around this problem with single-word or phrase prompts, and that is one good solution. The picture prompt goes even further.

Writing good prompts is a challenge. See Figure 2.7 for a few rules of the road to keep in mind.

Lesson 2: "Off Topic" Is Often "Off Base"

Many papers in district or state assessments (way too many) judged as "off topic" are in reality highly individual, even ingenious responses to a vague or uninspiring topic. Prompts are not holy writ. They are invitations to write, nothing more. Often students who wander "off topic" are penalized for thinking in an original manner, the very thing our instruction seeks (or should seek) to promote. In reality, these writers are finding their way *into* their own personal topics, "prompted" by a word, an association, or a

> "Why don't students put more voice into their writing?" we ask. Why don't caged animals run more?
>
> —Vicki Spandel
> *The 9 Rights of Every Writer,*
> 2005, p. 31.

> Current approaches to assessing writing usually provide a single prompt. . . . A far more demanding yet fairer approach, for both students and teachers, is to have students write on a topic that interests them and on which they have already prepared their ideas by reading and turning possibilities over in their minds.
>
> —Donald H. Graves
> *Testing Is Not Teaching,*
> 2002, p. 46

FIGURE **2.5   A Few Good Prompts**

1. Think of something you own that means a lot to you that was NOT purchased in a store. **Explain** why it is important to you—**OR, write a story** connected to this object.

2. Can very young and very old people be friends? Use your experience and judgment to **write a convincing paper** that answers this question for your reader.

3. Some people think pets are essential to happiness. Others think they are mostly a nuisance. Which side are you on? **Write an essay** that would **convince readers** to agree with you.

4. Think of a place so important to you that you would like to return to it many times. **Describe it** so clearly a reader can see, hear, and feel what it is like to be there.

5. Imagine it is ten years in the future. **Write any report** you think might appear on the front page of a major newspaper.

6. Think of a story (funny, sad, frightening, or embarrassing) that you might still enjoy telling to friends when you are older. **Write your story** as if it will be published in a magazine.

7. Think of a teacher (friend, family member) you will never forget. **Tell one story** that comes to mind when you think of what makes this person unforgettable.

8. Some people feel that video games and other electronic media have decreased our ability to concentrate and learn. Do you agree—or not? **Write a convincing paper** based on your experiences and observations.

9. Imagine you are a historian living 100 years in the future. You are **writing a description** of planet Earth in the year 20___. Think carefully about what you will say because your writing will be published in a science **textbook.**

10. What is it like to be in your place in your family—youngest child, oldest, middle, only, twin, or whatever? **Write a persuasive essay** that defends your position as best, worst, or just OK.

11. What might be the title and subject of the best-selling fiction or nonfiction book twenty years from now? **Write copy** that could be used on a **book jacket** to **help sell** the book.

12. The year is 2050. You have been asked to **write an updated version of the story** "Goldilocks and the Three Bears" [or substitute any story or fable]. Make sure your story contains details that make it authentic for the time. Think of how the characters speak, dress, and act.

13. What if you could spend one day with any person, real or fictional, from the past or present? Who would you choose and why? **Write an account of your time together** as if it has already happened.

14. The year is 2075. **Write an editorial protesting** the threatened extinction of an animal no one—not even scientists—ever thought would be endangered. **Convince** readers to take steps.

recollection. It's ironic to impose our topics on students and then complain when the responses lack individuality, imagination, or voice. It's like saying that someone else fails to wear your clothing with flair.

Lesson 3: We Must Be Very, Very Good Assessors

Most writing teachers are fair spellers and can recognize a comma splice at 10 paces, and so the old world of assessment, with its emphasis on conventions, felt safe. Now the National Commission on Writing (2003, p. 16) tells us that we need students who can create "precise, engaging, coherent prose." Our state standards and our rubrics typically echo such lofty goals, and this is a good thing. But keep in mind that when we raise the bar for our students,

FIGURE **2.6** **Barry's Prompts**

1. Lost
2. Running away
3. Big fat nuisance
4. No longer a child
5. Funny now—not then
6. Unbelievable
7. The other side
8. The one thing
9. The key
10. I just couldn't
11. Better than I thought
12. Who knew?
13. On sale
14. Just think…
15. A courageous moment
16. Lines
17. I remember…
18. Garbage
19. Let's face it
20. It bugs me
21. Footprints
22. Home

we raise it for ourselves as assessors, too. We must know the precise from the imprecise, the engaging from the voiceless, the coherent from the disorganized. Do we? We must not ask of our students what we are not prepared to assess with consistency and perception. A well-planned assessment is a contract. It pledges, "If you present clear and expansive ideas, I will understand; if you organize information effectively, I will follow; if you write with voice, I will hear you."

Lesson 4: On-Demand Writing Is a Genre onto Itself

Faced with an on-demand writing task, students must know how to *use* their time. We must teach them to scan the landscape so that they have some idea of how long a writing task will take. We must teach multiple forms of prewriting so that if they do not have an opportunity to talk or read, they can use webbing or listing. We must also teach them to read and respond to

Excluding those times when a writer is asked to or must address a specific question *(Explain your goals as a graduate student in psychology)*, writers do not wander off topic, but rather onto their real topics.

—Vicki Spandel
The 9 Rights of Every Writer,
2005, p. 35.

FIGURE 2.7 Rules of the Road for Writing Prompts

1. Consider the grade level and experience of the student writers. The topic should be reasonably familiar because they won't have time or opportunity for research. It should also be *interesting*—unless you want voiceless responses.

2. Do not give students any prompt you would not wish to write on yourself. The revenge factor is built in—you'll have to read the results.

3. Ask a question to which you don't already know the answer—and one that each respondent will likely answer differently: *What things were easier—or harder—for your parents when they were your age?*

4. Avoid issues that are likely to trigger emotional response: *Explain why you think the United States is or is not ready for a woman president.*

5. Avoid prompts that can be answered with a simple *yes* or *no*: *Should the driving age in your state be lowered to fourteen?*

6. Avoid "helpful hints" that make it hard for the writer to use *any* imagination: *Write about a time you will always remember. It could be a happy or sad time; a funny, embarrassing, or exciting experience; a memory from long ago or something recent. Include sights, sounds, smells, and feelings to put your reader right at the scene.* (Oops—time's up and we've only read the prompt.)

7. Does it matter if students write a narrative, expository, or persuasive piece? If it does, be very careful to word the prompt in a way that cues them in:

   For narrative: Tell the story,
   Tell about a time when,
   Give an account,
   Tell the story of

   For expository: Explain, Give directions for,
   Analyze, Tell how,
   Help the reader understand,
   Teach someone

   For persuasive: Persuade, Convince,
   Make an argument for, Share your
   position/opinion/view

   For descriptive: Describe, Help your reader picture,
   Make a movie in the reader's mind,
   Put the reader at the scene

8. Whenever possible, allow students to select *their own topics*. Their ability to do so can be part of what you assess.

9. At a minimum, *give students choices*. Just having a choice often helps students feel more positive about the whole assessment process.

prompts quickly. See Figure 2.8 for twelve writing tips that can be helpful in a formal, large-scale testing situation.

It can ease student stress enormously to have an in-class "prompt day," during which you and your students play the guessing game "What does the prompt writer want?" You can access hundreds of prompts online by typing in "student prompts" or, for older students, check out the book *411 SAT Writing Questions/Essay Prompts*, published by Learning Express. I'm not suggesting writing to these prompts, which eats up an inordinate amount of valuable instructional time. Rather, just talk about them. *What is the heart of the question being asked? What kinds of support might readers be looking for? What can I do if this seems outside my range of experience?* And—this is critical— *What kind of response (narrative, informative, persuasive) is called for?*

FIGURE **2.8** **Twelve Tips fpr Succeeding on Writing Tests**

1. **Read the prompt carefully.** Figure out the main focus (what the prompt writers want you to talk about) and the best form (story, expository essay, persuasive argument, description) to use.

2. Take a minute to settle on the **main thing you want to say**. Express it in one sentence and say it to yourself—on scratch paper or aloud.

3. **Make a general plan** to follow in a flexible way—not the very things you will say, but the kinds of things you will say. For example, if you're writing a persuasive essay, your plan might look like this: (1) A lead that lays out the issue in an interesting way, (2) What I believe, (3) Reasons I believe as I do, (4) How the other side sees things—and why, (5) Flaws in the opposition's arguments, (6) The serious consequences of not coming to the "right" conclusion.

4. In a persuasive or expository piece, **state your main idea outright**—and right up front. Don't make a tired reader guess. Make sure everything in your piece relates to that main point or argument. Don't wander from the path even if you have something interesting to say. Save that kind of writing for when you get published.

5. Spend time on a **strong lead and conclusion**. Use the lead to wake your reader up—and set up what follows.

6. In your conclusion, don't summarize or review old ground. **Cite something significant** (perhaps unexpected) **you gained** from your experience or observations.

7. **Don't try to tell everything.** Choose two or three key events in a story (including a *turning point*), and three or four key points in an essay or argument. Choose what is most interesting—and what the reader is *least likely to know already*.

8. If your writing includes characters, **have them speak** and make what they say important. If it doesn't, quote someone—even if it's someone you know.

9. If your writing includes a setting, focus on **sensory details**—sounds, smells—that not everyone might notice.

10. Think of adjectives and adverbs as salt and pepper. Use them sparingly. Let precise **nouns and active verbs carry the weight** of meaning.

11. **Tell the truth.** When it comes to putting voice in writing, there is no substitute for saying just what you mean.

12. Think carefully about your title and **write it last**. It will look as if your piece flowed right out of the title—when just the opposite is true.

Another helpful strategy to teach students is 2-minute planning. Once you know what's being asked, how do you shape your answer? In on-demand writing, I have usually posed three or four key questions I would answer. I use this approach because it takes me only 60 seconds. Some students might feel more comfortable with a general kind of outline (like that described in Figure 2.8), while for others, a quick bulleted list of things to touch on will do the trick.

We always say to students, "Think about your audience," but do we tell them who it is? In on-demand writing, it will *not* be a patient teacher who will come to the end of a piece he or she has already spent 10 minutes on and say, "I'd better read that again—maybe I missed the point." Picture a tired reader, pressured from having to read too many essays too quickly, distracted by the hundreds of other readers around her, weary from a thousand overly structured responses to a prompt that she doesn't like one bit better than the students did, having 2 minutes (tops) to spend, and longing for a paper that (1) states the main idea clearly and boldly, right up front, and (2) treats

> "We would rather see one or two examples that are well-developed than three examples that are just like stones skipping across a pond."
>
> —**Bernard A. Phelan**
> High School Teacher and Advisor to the College Board, in David Glenn, *The Chronicle of Higher Education*, 2007, p. 2

the reader to a moment of voice that allows a precious mental break. Once you've got that image vividly imprinted in your mind, you're in a much better position to write.

Lesson 5: Rubrics Can Be Dangerous

When they are skillfully designed and properly used, rubrics can be among the most valuable educational tools we have. They make previously mysterious expectations clear, and this is not just a matter of good instruction. It's a matter of ethics.

Rubrics can be misused, however, particularly when written in a way that quantifies writing performance. We must be careful not to ask for three supporting details, five sentences, ten-word sentences, no more than three errors, and so on. Writing is not a numbers game—and any criteria expressed in a reductive manner defeat the *main* purpose for which rubrics are designed: to give students (and all of us) insight into what makes writing work. Language like "Takes reader on a journey of understanding," "Reveals the human spirit," or " Makes reader want to say 'Listen to this'" (see Figure 3.6, page 44) allows for open interpretation of text, and encourages readers (and students) to think beyond the rubric itself and create their own personal, ever-expanding definitions of fine writing.

Lesson 6: Writing Matters

The single finest thing large-scale assessment does is to remind us just how important writing is. Even when the assessment itself is flawed, it reminds us that writing is thinking on paper, that it is important to do and important to teach, and that students who can write can do almost anything.

Lessons Learned from Classroom Assessment

Lesson 1: Writing Takes Time—and Resources

In a classroom where writing workshop is a way of life, students have both time and opportunity on their side. They are not mentally bludgeoned by topics that inhibit thinking and creativity, nor are they held to deadlines not even a professional writer could hope to meet. They can often choose their own topics, and take time to plan their writing, sometimes collaborating with other student writers to expand their thinking. They have access to the kinds of resources, including dictionaries, handbooks, and spell-checker, that professional writers would turn to without a thought. In the real world, writers do not work alone. Only in an academic context are such foundational, sensible behaviors as consulting a colleague or checking a reference book looked on as "cheating." Large-scale assessment would do well to look more closely at the way writers actually work.

In years past, the state of Kentucky has taken a refreshingly different approach to large-scale writing assessment (Hillocks, 2002, pp. 163ff.), coming much closer to what happens in many classrooms. As part of their state tests, Kentucky students have been asked to respond to an on-demand prompt, but also compile a portfolio spanning a significant block of time—thereby showing change and growth. George Hillocks Jr. calls this approach "an opportunity for students to show their best work developed over a series of drafts, replete with feedback, revision, editing, and time to think carefully." He adds that this is "writing as real writers do it" (p. 163).

Lesson 2: Writing Process Must Be Learned

Writing process is magical—*if* students make use of it. They cannot do so automatically, and simply providing time to write (or revise and edit) is not sufficient. We must show them what prewriting, drafting, revision, sharing, and editing are all about—not by talking about them but by being writers ourselves. They must see us do it. They must also see our own "before" and "after" samples so that they know what is possible in revision, and our rubrics must reflect the kinds of changes they *see* before to after.

Lesson 3: Choosing a Topic Is Not Just a Privilege— It's an Art

Many student writers do not know how to choose their own topics because someone else has frequently done this part for them. We must model for them what it means to sift through your life as an archaeologist sifts through sand and pick what should be recorded on paper. It's not that simple. Try it. Grab a piece of scratch paper right now and jot down five possible topics you could write on. And if you can do this, do it at your very next opportunity *while your students are watching.*

> Teachers should write so they understand the process of writing from within.
>
> —Donald M. Murray
> *A Writer Teaches Writing,*
> 2004, p. 74

Lesson 4: We Need to Model Revision, Too

Did you see any of your teachers write? I did not. So naturally, I did not see them revise either. If you did, you were lucky.

Many students breeze through prewriting and drafting; then they hit a brick wall. In the absence of any models or guidelines, they often settle for neatening up the piece, making it longer, or using a spell-checker. Time is not the whole answer either. Time to revise is of minimal help to the student who does not know how to narrow and define a topic, craft a good lead, play with phrasing, "hear" the conclusion, or fine-tune voice.

The good news is that teaching revision based on sound writing criteria is so much easier that teachers doing it for the first time can hardly believe the difference. When students have a repertoire of revision strategies (spelled

> When [a student] writes, she is on the inside looking out; later, as she rereads her work, she is on the outside again, wondering whether the page properly reflects her feelings and her ideas.
>
> —Donald H. Graves
> *Testing Is Not Teaching,*
> 2002, p. 59

> We need to avoid assessment environments steeped in mystery and illusion, intimidation and vulnerability, stress and anxiety. . . . Maximum anxiety does not lead to maximum learning.
> —Richard J. Stiggins
> *Student-Involved Classroom Assessment*, 2001, p. 3

out right on the rubric), and when they can rehearse revision on the work of others, they are only one tiny step from assessing—*and then revising*—their own work.

Lesson 5: The "Hurry Up and Write" Approach = More Stress, Less Quality

Most people drive 10 miles (or more) over the speed limit and grow impatient with those who observe it. We love *fast* food, *instant* messaging, *speed* dialing, and *rapid* transit. Our reverence for speed has an unfortunate impact on assessment. It creates stress, for one thing. Writing is not by nature a speedy activity but a reflective one. Until we recognize this, our large-scale measurements cannot dip beneath the superficial. In addition, stress potentially reduces quality. Some students freeze under pressure and write nothing. Others resort to formulaic writing because it's quick and easy to produce— and also voiceless and tedious to read. In the end, because formulaic writing requires no synthesis of ideas or creative organization, it results in a *lowering* of standards for quality writing—just the opposite of what we wanted.

> Currently, we are testing what we value, quick thinking. But what about long thinking? . . . Can we identify and encourage the children who can formulate a question, find the information, design an evaluation, and know whether they have answered their original question?
> —Donald H. Graves
> *Testing Is Not Teaching*, 2002, p. 34

Lesson 6: Good Writing Demands Revision

Instead of throwing topics at students like darts, we need to ask them what information they'd like to share and in what form they'd like to share it (e.g., report, children's book, interview for a journal). Instead of assessing rough drafts students have dashed off in minutes, let's gather and hold them for a time, discuss and model revision, and then return the drafts to students for refining and polishing. Let's give students realistic time frames. State legislatures may set limits on the number of hours that can be devoted to testing, thereby slicing time for revision and editing (Hillocks, 2002, p. 114). How contrary to real-world writing can you get? How many students would be hugging Harry Potter books if J. K. Rowling's editor gave her one week per edition or demanded to print the first draft? We already know how many things students cannot do when confronted with assessment hurdles. Aren't we just the least bit curious to know what they can do if we set it up right?

> Teachers are buried in an avalanche of expectations: standards, testing, and expanded curricula. The expectations come from every level of government and administration as well as from parents and the community. They are rarely part of a long-term plan carefully developed in conjunction with the teachers.
> —Donald H. Graves
> *Testing Is Not Teaching*, 2002, p. 50

Lesson 7: Teachers Themselves Should Lead Us

Remember, the six traits did not come from any educational agency, research organization, publishing house, or testing firm. They came from teachers. They came from *you*. When classroom teachers guide how writing assessments are administered and scored, students will not lie awake the night prior to a writing assessment, cry when they stare at a sheet of blank paper, or glaze over in bewilderment when they cannot figure out what a poorly worded prompt is asking of them. Instead, they will walk into any assessment situation, any time, any place, with the confidence that comes only from knowing that you write well enough to meet head-on any assessment they can throw at you.

Chapter 2   In a Nutshell

- Good assessment does not just happen; it requires thoughtful planning.

- Important keys to quality writing assessment include these:
  - Making the target visible
  - Constructing rubrics with care
  - Assessing what is important
  - Matching the assessment approach to the task
  - Reviewing multiple samples before drawing conclusions
  - Minimizing bias
  - Ensuring reliability and validity
  - Inviting parents to help support our instruction

- Assessment measures student proficiency; it does not change performance in and of itself. Only instruction can do that.

- Both classroom and large-scale writing assessment have important lessons to teach about how assessment works best.

- From large-scale assessment we learn that prompts count; the concept of "off topic" is often misapplied to writing that reflects a process of discovery; we must be very good assessors if we ask students to meet complex standards; on-demand writing is a genre onto itself; rubrics can be dangerous if misused; and writing matters.

- From classroom assessment we learn that writing takes time; writing process must be learned; choosing a topic is not just a privilege—it's an art; if students are to engage in true revision, we must show them how; the "hurry up and write" approach yields more stress and less quality; revision is essential to good writing; and teachers themselves should lead us in this endeavor.

Study Group   Interactive Questions and Activities

1. **Discussion.** In his eloquent book *Testing Is Not Teaching* (2002), Donald Graves presents an alternative writing assessment plan (p. 46) in which students would have from May to September to explore personally important topics, concurrently developing a list of six or seven on which they felt qualified to write. In May, the teacher would select two items from this list, and the student would write to those items, using a genre specified by the teacher. Compare this approach to the on-demand assessment favored by most districts or states that assess writing. What advantages does Graves's approach offer? How would our view of assessment need to change in order to support Graves's plan?

2. **Activity and Discussion.** Review the eight keys to successful assessment that appear in this chapter. How many apply to your classroom, school, or district? What (very specific) changes would you make if you could? On a scale of 1 to 10, how would you rate the quality of writ-

ing assessment in your classroom, school, or district?

3. **Activity.** With your group, write several prompts that could be used in a district writing assessment. Analyze your list. Which ones seem strongest? Why? Try writing to one or more and analyze your results in terms of whether (1) the prompt is both clear and interesting to *you, the writer;* (2) the audience is clearly defined; (3) the prompt encourages diverse responses; and (4) it is easy to tell what kind of writing—expository, narrative, descriptive, persuasive—the prompt is calling for.

4. **Activity.** Ask each person in your group to look up a different prompt online (just type in "student writing prompts" for numerous lists, including picture prompts). Respond to the prompts, allowing yourselves a limited amount of time. What conclusions can you draw from this experience?

5. **Activity and Discussion.** Choose any rubric *not included in this book*. (It need not relate to writing.) With a partner or group, analyze the effectiveness of this rubric on a scale of 1 to 12, based on each of the following criteria:

_____ Clarity (2 points possible)

_____ Positive language (2 points)

_____ Horizontal integrity (2 points)

_____ Vertical integrity (2 points)

_____ User friendliness (2 points)

_____ Absence of quantifiable criteria, such as *number of supporting details* (2 points)

6. **Activity and Discussion.** Does your state assess writing? Using the keys to success, create a short evaluation of your state's assessment methods. How closely does it align with your vision of good writing and writing instruction? Share your evaluation by writing to a state legislator or someone who helps design or direct the assessment.

7. **Activity and Discussion.** If your district assesses writing now, do you know—precisely—for what purpose(s) the results are used? Does the design fit the purpose well? If not, how could you revise it so the information gathered would better answer assessors' questions?

Reflections on Writing

Most of all, I write to soar. To soar through the clouds of imagination, dreams and possibilities. To soar on the words of hope. I am an eagle, catching the air and rising up to greatness.

—**Maegan Rowley,** student writer

Everything I see and hear I am thinking of how I can use it in a story, painting a parallel world where florid strokes of life and death sashay across the canvas. This would surprise most people who know me, because on the outside I am quiet, calm, collected, rational, and all those other good words that mean you are grounded here in this reality called life. But I am never fully here.

—**Simona Patange,** student writer

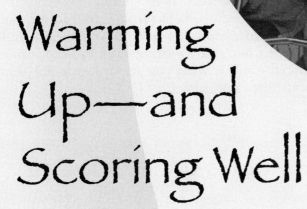

Warming Up—and Scoring Well

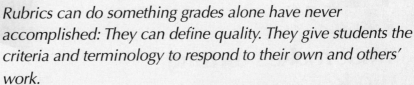

Rubrics can do something grades alone have never accomplished: They can define quality. They give students the criteria and terminology to respond to their own and others' work.

—Kathleen Strickland and James Strickland
Reflections on Assessment, 1998, p. 77

As a group, these studies indicate rather clearly that engaging young writers actively in the use of criteria, applied to their own or others' writing, results not only in more effective revisions but in superior first drafts. . . . Most of them show significant gains for experimental groups, suggesting that the criteria learned act not only as guides for revision but as guides for generating new material.

—George Hillocks Jr.
Research on Written Composition: New Directions for Teaching, 1986, p. 160

Whether you are introducing the traits to students, colleagues, or parents, it helps to begin with this foundational question: *What makes writing work?* A few years ago, I asked this question of fifth graders who had no previous experience with trait-based instruction. In Figure 3.1 you will see the responses I received. Notice the overwhelming emphasis on conventions—on *getting it right*. Where does this come from? Perhaps a misperception that these are the things most teachers value (some do, it's true, but not all). Or perhaps these students had been praised (by teachers *and* parents) for correct spelling, strong punctuation—even neatness. Such things are important but are not the qualities that engage readers. Have you ever in your life said to someone, "You *must* read this book. *Killer* margins"?

We need to help students think like readers by sharing text that moves them. This is what I did, reading to the fifth graders from Gary Paulsen, Louis Sachar, Mem Fox, Sandra Cisneros, and other writers with great margins (just kidding). Their concept of what makes writing work evolved within a very short time, and the initial result is what you see in Figure 3.2—comments from the same students three weeks later.

FIGURE **3.1** What Makes Writing Work

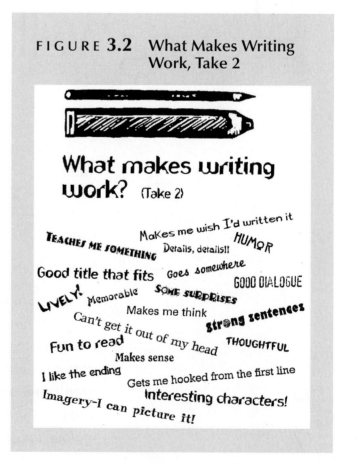

FIGURE **3.2** What Makes Writing Work, Take 2

Building a Community of Writers

Students need to see that they are part of a larger community of readers and writers, that what speaks to them from the page is also what speaks to teachers, and further, that what defines quality in professional writing also defines quality in student writing. There are no classes of writing. There is just writing.

Once students were happy with their list of things that make writing work, I asked if they would like to compare their thoughts with a list of things *teachers* valued. They were very eager. When I passed out six-trait rubrics written in student-friendly language (see Chapter 8 for copies), their response was, "These are the same things we said." Absolutely. Our sense of community had begun.

Responding to Writing

You cannot simply have someone talk to you about writing features such as *ideas* or *voice*. You need physical samples to fix in your mind what these concepts are about, and it helps to begin with a contrast. I like to use "The Redwoods" (a paper written by one of my own students) and "Mouse Alert," written by a middle school student I coached.

You could use these same papers (Figures 3.3 and 3.4) when introducing the six traits to students or to adults (colleagues, parents). Begin by copying the papers onto overhead transparencies and then (1) *reading each aloud,* (2) asking respondents to discuss each paper with a partner, and finally, (3) discussing the paper with the whole group.

Reading aloud is important. We are very visual in our response to writing, and hearing a piece causes us to assess with our ears— not just our eyes. When you read, project as much voice as the piece will allow, helping readers to interpret the writer's intended message. Don't worry that you will put in voice that isn't there. Trust me: In the end, even the finest of actors can only make a script so good.

What are *your* personal reactions to "The Redwoods" (Figure 3.3)? If you are like most readers/ listeners (including that group of fifth graders), your responses probably match some of these:

- Boring—it put me right to sleep.
- Safe.

FIGURE 3.3 The Redwoods

Last year, we went on a vacation and we had a wonderful time. The weather was sunny and warm and there was lots to do, so we were never bored.

My parents visited friends and took pictures for their friends back home. My brother and I swam and also hiked in the woods. When we got tired of that, we just ate and had a wonderful time.

It was exciting and fun to be together as a family and to do things together. I love my family, and this is a time that I will remember for a long time. I hope we will go back again next year for more fun and an even better time than we had this year.

- The person was writing just to get it done.
- Conventions are pretty good—but otherwise. . . .
- It doesn't *say* anything.
- The organization isn't too bad.
- *What* Redwoods? The title doesn't go with the paper.
- It's not *that* bad for third or fourth grade—I assume that's what it is, right?

I often do *not* share the grade level of this writer until after people have had a chance to respond to the paper because it is fun to guess. Actually, the writer is an eleventh grader. Knowing the grade level leads to some intriguing discussions about assumptions we often make as we read (including the sex and age of the writer) and why we make them. (This is a female writer, by the way.) Once they know the grade level, teachers often say, "Well, for *eleventh* grade I expected more, you know? If you'd told me it was third grade, I would have felt different." But would they really? Would *you?* I agree that the conventions would be excellent if this were a third grade paper. But would it *say* more? Or could we say, "Well, for grade 3, this is a powerhouse in voice." Hardly. When the voice is missing, it is just missing.

> I have taught college students and first graders in the same day. I can see the same qualities emerging in their work. I see detail. I see voice. I see various forms of organization.
>
> —Barry Lane
> "Quality in Writing," 1996, p. 4

Still, as one teacher pointed out, "Look, she's in eleventh grade, and she wants to go vacationing with her family. I'd like to give her a couple points for that." Me, too. There's a likable tone to this piece that makes me want to say, "Come out of hiding. I know you have more to share." One lesson of "The Redwoods" is that sometimes there is a story buried beneath the story that we get.

You might be thinking too that the assignment was some offshoot of the cliché "My Summer Vacation"—but you would be mistaken. The assignment was to create a scenario in which the five senses play an important part. "The Redwoods" was a stellar choice, but the writer did not exploit the opportunity.

Now for the contrast. I chose the paper "Mouse Alert" (Figure 3.4) as a companion to "The Redwoods" because this writer also chose to write about family vacation, making the two papers easy to compare.

Does this sound more like the real-life vacations you recall? In place of the "wonderful time" of "The Redwoods," we learn immediately that "Nothing went the way it was supposed to." We are immediately intrigued. It is comforting to know that someone else deals with bickering siblings, poked-out windows, and mice in the walls. This writer has learned an important secret: Vacations on which all goes wrong may be miserable to live through, but they are often the stuff of good writing. Teachers' comments on "Mouse Alert" typically include these:

- I can just *see* it. I feel like I'm *in* that car. (Actually, I was once.)
- I love the line "Her eyes were as big as her fists."
- He's having a good time. (Most readers assume that the writer is male.)
- I know these people.

FIGURE 3.4   MouseAlert

As soon as school was out, we left on vacation. Nothing went the way it was supposed to. Dad backed into a tree on the way out of the drive-way, pushing the bike rack through the rear window and nearly scaring my sister to death. She was cranky the rest of the trip. We had to take our other car, which is smaller and you can't hook the bike rack up to it. Now my sister and me were crowded together so much she kept complaining about me breathing on her and taking up all her air and foot room. Plus now Dad knew a big bill would be waiting for him when we got home. It put everyone in a lovely trip starting mood.

We were supposed to go to Yellowstone Park. Well, actually, we did but just barely. I think we hold the world's record for shortest time spent in the park. This was all due to my mother's new attitude toward animals. The night before yellowstone we stayed in a cabin on the edge of the park. It had a lot of mice, but most of them had the good sense to stay hidden in the walls. One poor furry guy had a death wish and showed himself. The whole family went into action. My father got a broom, which looked like an oversized weapon for a mouse. My mother hugged her pink flanel nightgown around her knees, jumped up on a wood chair and started shrieking "Kill him! Kill him!" Her eyes were as big as her fists. I had never seen her quite so blood thirsty. My sister spent the whole time dancing on the bed crying her eyes out and yelling, "Don't kill it Dad! Don't kill it!" It was up to Dad and me to trap it. We got it in a pickle jar and took it down to the lake and let it go. It seemed really happy to get away from us. I thought I knew how it felt.

The next day we raced through Yellowstone and then headed home. My Mother said she had enough of animals. For weeks afterwards, this was the big story she told everyone who asked about our vacation. You'd have thought the whole point of our trip was to go on a mouse hunt. Dad said all the money we saved by not staying at Yellowstone could go to pay for the broken car window, so for him the trip worked out perfect. As for me, I'm still planning to get back to Yellowstone one day. I want to see something bigger than a mouse.

- I can see the pickle jar, and I even smell the pickles.
- This writer is a storyteller.
- Great images—love Dad backing into the tree and Mom in the nightgown.
- Who *is* this kid? Can I get him next year?
- It comes full circle—great organization.
- You get every point of view—even the mouse's!

Students love this paper, too. Details and voice shine. True, there are minor problems with conventions, many more than in "The Redwoods," but the text is also more complex. Moreover, we tend to be forgiving of conventional errors when we are having a good time. If the writer of "The Redwoods" made this many errors, we might not be so forgiving. (Oh, and P.S.—this writer is also female.)

 # What Teachers Value in Writing

We have seen how teachers responded to "The Redwoods" and to "Mouse Alert." Take additional teacher comments, based on responses to *many* pieces of writing, group them together by trait, and Figure 3.5 is the result: What teachers value in writing.

Most likely you recognize many things that *you* value on this list. Understand, though: A list, however complete, is not yet a rubric. Why not? Because it does not yet define performance at multiple levels. Put these same qualities along a performance continuum beginning level (1) to strong or proficient (5 or 6), and you have a rubric.

The writing guide in this chapter (see Figure 3.6) covers virtually *any* type of prose writing: narrative, expository/informational, persuasive, descriptive, and so on. Unless you are deeply committed to the four- or five-point scale, I strongly recommend use of the six-point. It has room to show growth and is *very easy* to teach to students conceptually.

Scores of 1, 2, or 3 represent significant need for revision on a particular trait. When you "leap the river" into the land of proficiency (scores of 4, 5, or 6), strengths outweigh problems and less revision is needed. Have a look at the six-point scale in this chapter. Then we'll explore differences among the four-, five-, and six-point scales a bit further.

For other writing guides . . .

What about a student-friendly version of this writing guide?
See Figure 8.1 (page 159) for the student-friendly version of the scale in this chapter.

What if I prefer a five-point scale?
In the Appendix you will find three-level scales for both teachers (Appendix 1) and students (Appendix 2). I have modified them so that they can be used as five- or six-point scales—your choice. These scales have the advantage of richer language because performance is defined only at three levels: beginning (1 or 1-2 split), developing (3 or 3-4 split), and strong (5 or 5-6 split).

What if my students are doing research-based writing? Can I adapt the scale for that purpose?
Already done. See Figures 11.1 and 11.2 (pages 271, 274), for teacher and student versions of an informational scale.

Where will I find a Spanish translation?
See Appendix 3 for a Student Writing Guide in Spanish. See Appendix 4 for a Student Checklist in Spanish.

FIGURE **3.5**   **What Teachers Value in Writing**

Ideas

Clear—makes sense
Topic narrowed to manageable size
Focuses on key message(s)
Teaches me something
Holds my attention
Fresh, original perspective
Important, telling details that go beyond common
    knowledge
Minimal "filler" (unneeded information)
Shows insight
Authenticity

Organization

Inviting lead that draws me in
Starts somewhere, goes somewhere
Provides connections—detail to detail,
    paragraph to paragraph
Well paced, spending time where it matters
Like a good road map—easy to follow
Satisfying conclusion—sense of resolution
Doesn't end with "Then I woke up and it was a
    dream"
Doesn't end with truisms or clichés or literal
    summaries

Voice

Sounds like this writer—no other
Writer is "at home" in the writing
Writer seems engaged with topic
Brings topic to life
Shows concern for me—the reader
Individual, distinctive—unlike others
Makes me respond—cry, laugh, smile,
    get chills
Confident—writer knows his/her stuff
Lively, energetic, spontaneous

Word Choice

"Just right" words
Memorable words—worth highlighting, quoting
Creates word pictures, movies in the mind
Accurate, precise
Enlightening—helps me "get it"
Strong verbs
No modifier "overload"
Simple language used well
Repeats only as necessary—or for effect
Uses language to teach—not to impress
Defines difficult terms

Sentence Fluency

Easy to read aloud
Rhythm, cadence, flow
Easy to read with voice
Carefully crafted sentences
Variety in length, structure
Concise, direct sentences in informational
    writing
Fragments used only for effect
Authentic dialogue
Consistency in tense (present, past, future)

Conventions and Layout

Clean, edited
Free of distracting errors
No "mental editing" needed
Conventions guide reader through text
Conventions support meaning/voice
Design draws reader's eye to key points
Avoids distracting visuals—hard to read fonts
Uses graphics, as needed, to enhance text
Makes good use of white space

FIGURE **3.6** **Teacher Six-Point Writing Guide**

Ideas

6
- ☐ Clear, focused, compelling—holds reader's attention
- ☐ Striking insight, impressive knowledge of topic
- ☐ Takes reader on a journey of understanding
- ☐ Significant, intriguing info prompts reader's own thinking

5
- ☐ Clear and focused
- ☐ Reflects thorough knowledge of topic
- ☐ Authentic, convincing info from experience/research
- ☐ Clear main idea well supported by details

4
- ☐ Clear and focused more often than not
- ☐ Writer knows topic well enough to write in broad terms
- ☐ Some new info, some common knowledge
- ☐ Main idea can be easily inferred, quality details outweigh generalities

3
- ☐ Clear, focused moments overshadowed by undeveloped text
- ☐ Writer needs greater knowledge of topic—gaps apparent
- ☐ Marked by common knowledge and best guesses
- ☐ Generalities or lists of undeveloped points

2
- ☐ Writer lacks clear vision—still defining topic, key question
- ☐ Writer struggles with insufficient knowledge—writing is strained
- ☐ Broad unsupported observations, invented details
- ☐ Filler—writing to fill space

1
- ☐ No main idea, purpose, theme, or story as yet
- ☐ Writer seems uncomfortable with topic?or changes subject
- ☐ Hastily assembled notes, random thoughts
- ☐ Writer needs to define topic—then gather information

Organization

6
- ☐ Thoughtful structure guides reader effortlessly through text
- ☐ Provocative opening—enlightening conclusion
- ☐ Transitions suggest connections reader might not think of
- ☐ Design enhances reader's understanding—pacing is just right
- ☐ Unexpected turns, surprises lend creative twists

5
- ☐ Purposeful structure helps reader follow writer's thinking
- ☐ Strong lead—conclusion that provides closure
- ☐ Thoughtful transitions clearly connect ideas
- ☐ Design helps reader process ideas—pacing makes main ideas stand out

4
- ☐ Organization makes it fairly easy to follow story/discussion
- ☐ Functional lead and conclusion
- ☐ Helpful transitions often suggest connections
- ☐ Overall design works—writer *sometimes* dwells on trivia or skims over complex topics

3
- ☐ Reader can follow story/discussion if he/she is attentive
- ☐ Lead formulaic or misleading, conclusion formulaic or abrupt
- ☐ Transitions *sometimes* missing or mechanical
- ☐ Structure may be formulaic or confusing—pacing rushed or sluggish

2
- ☐ Hard to follow, even with effort
- ☐ Lead or conclusion missing, formulaic, or misleading
- ☐ Transitions unclear, missing, or not helpful in linking ideas
- ☐ Significant re-organization needed—pacing feels random

1
- ☐ Reader feels lost
- ☐ Starts right in (no lead)—just stops (no conclusion)
- ☐ Transitions missing—perhaps points *aren't* connected
- ☐ Disjointed collection of details/thoughts with no structure, design

FIGURE 3.6 Teacher Six-Point Writing Guide, *continued*

Voice	Word Choice
6	**6**
☐ As individual as fingerprints	☐ Everyday language used in original ways
☐ Begs to be read aloud—reader can't wait to share it	☐ You want to read it more than once—to savor it
☐ Uses voice as tool to enhance meaning	☐ Every word carries its own weight
☐ Passionate, vibrant, electric, compelling	☐ Powerful, stunning verbs, unique phrasing
☐ Reveals the human spirit	☐ Words capture what is hard to express
5	**5**
☐ Original—definitely distinctive	☐ Natural language used well
☐ A good "read aloud" candidate	☐ Engaging—makes you want to keep reading
☐ Voice appealing and well-suited to topic/audience	☐ Well-chosen words enhance meaning—concise
☐ Spontaneous, lively, expressive, enthusiastic	☐ Strong verbs, striking phrasing
	☐ Words appeal to senses, create clear images
4	**4**
☐ Sparks of individuality	☐ Functional, clear language used correctly
☐ Reader might share a line or two	☐ Easy to understand, some eye- and ear-catching phrases
☐ Voice fades at times—acceptable for topic/audience	☐ Vague words (*fun, nice*) or wordiness—meaning still clear, though
☐ Pleasant, sincere, emerging, earnest	☐ Some strong verbs
	☐ Strong moments outweigh clichés, tired words, overwritten text
3	**3**
☐ Voice emerges sporadically—then retreats	☐ Language clear on general level—"first thoughts"
☐ A "share-aloud" moment	☐ Broad brushstrokes with an occasional stronger moment
☐ Voice seems mechanical, not always directed to audience	☐ Vague words or wordiness water down the message
☐ Quiet, subdued, restrained, inconsistent	☐ Overused modifiers/weak verbs outnumber strong moments
	☐ Reader may encounter clichés, or overwritten text (writing to impress)
2	**2**
☐ Writer seems to be in hiding	☐ Tired words, the *wrong word*, or thesaurus overload
☐ A *hint* of voice—text not ready for sharing	☐ Have to search hard for moments that work well
☐ Just a whisper—OR, the wrong voice for audience, purpose	☐ Word choice and wordiness *cloud* the message
☐ Remote, encyclopedic—OR inappropriately informal	☐ Adjective avalanche—where are the *verbs?*
	☐ Reader must work hard to get the picture
1	**1**
☐ No sense of person behind words—is anyone *home?*	☐ Words chosen to fill the page
☐ Reader feels no invitation to share text aloud	☐ Apparent struggle to get words on paper
☐ No apparent engagement with topic, concern for audience	☐ Language does not speak to reader
☐ Voice . . . just . . . missing	

FIGURE 3.6 **Teacher Six-Point Writing Guide,** *continued*

Sentence Fluency

6
- ☐ Easy to read with inflection that brings out voice
- ☐ Lyrical—dances along like a script, poem, or song
- ☐ Stunning variety in style, length
- ☐ Fragments effective, dialogue authentic/dramatic/performable
- ☐ Makes reader want to say, "Listen to this"

5
- ☐ Can be read with expression
- ☐ Easygoing rhythm, flow, cadence
- ☐ Significant variety in style, length
- ☐ Fragments add emphasis, dialogue authentic

4
- ☐ Natural phrasing—easy to read
- ☐ Rhythmic flow dominates—a few awkward moments
- ☐ Some variety in style, length
- ☐ Fragments not a problem, dialogue natural

3
- ☐ Mechanical but readable
- ☐ Gangly, tangly, never-ending or chop-chop-choppy text common
- ☐ Repetitive beginnings, little variety in length
- ☐ Fragments (if used) do not work, dialogue (if used) a little stiff

2
- ☐ You can read it if you're patient—*and* you rehearse
- ☐ Many run-ons, choppy sentences, non-sentences, or other problems
- ☐ Minimal variety in style, length
- ☐ Fragments (if used) are oversights, dialogue hard to perform

1
- ☐ Hard to read, even with effort
- ☐ Missing words, awkward moments, irregular structure
- ☐ Hard to judge variety—hard to tell where sentences begin
- ☐ Fragments (if used) impair readability, dialogue hard to read

Conventions

6
- ☐ Thoroughly edited—only the pickiest editors will spot errors
- ☐ Conventions *enhance* meaning, voice
- ☐ Complexity of text showcases wide range of conventions
- ☐ Enticing layout *(optional)*
- ☐ Virtually ready to publish

5
- ☐ Edited well—minor errors that are easily overlooked
- ☐ Conventions support meaning, voice
- ☐ Sufficient complexity reflects skill in numerous conventions
- ☐ Pleasing layout *(optional)*
- ☐ Ready to publish with light touch-ups

4
- ☐ Noticeable errors—reader breezes right through, however
- ☐ Errors do not interfere with meaning
- ☐ Shows control over basics (e.g., caps, end punctuation)
- ☐ Acceptable layout *(optional)*
- ☐ Good once-over needed prior to publication

3
- ☐ Erratic editing—noticeable, distracting errors
- ☐ Errors may slow reader or affect message in spots
- ☐ Problems even with basic conventions
- ☐ More attention to layout needed *(optional)*
- ☐ Thorough, careful editing needed prior to publication

2
- ☐ Minimal editing—frequent, distracting errors
- ☐ Errors get in the way of message, require frequent rereading
- ☐ Numerous errors even on basics
- ☐ Limited attention to layout *(optional)*
- ☐ Line-by-line editing needed prior to publication

1
- ☐ Not edited yet—serious, frequent errors
- ☐ Reading/processing text takes attentive effort
- ☐ Errors on basics obscure meaning, put up road blocks
- ☐ No apparent attention to layout *(optional)*
- ☐ Word-by-word editing needed prior to publication

War of the Rubrics

Across the country, states and teachers are using five- *and* six-point scales (even four-point in some cases). You may be wondering what difference this makes, and curiously enough, it does not make as much as you might think. The reason for this is that virtually all scales are *conceptually* three-level scales. Each reflects a range of proficiency from beginning (lowest scores) through developing (middle scores) to strong (highest scores).

No matter how many numerical points we may put along our performance continuum, it does not change this basic concept. If we want a six-point scale, for example, we simply define the beginning-level scores as 1s and 2s, developing scores as 3s and 4s, and strong performance scores as 5s and 6s. We could even put 100 points along our continuum if we seriously believed we could distinguish between, say, a 72 and a 73.

Of course, it is ridiculous to suggest anything even approaching such precision. If you cannot tell a 7 from an 8 (and cannot find a sample 7 or a sample 8 to show what you mean), your points are no longer meaningful. George Hillocks (2002, p. 6) suggests that with a scale of six or seven points we have hit the limits of what we can conceptually grasp.

> Many years ago, psychologists found that there is a limit to what we can hold in short-term memory and the number of criteria we can use in making absolute judgments. George A. Miller (1956) called it "the magic number 7, plus or minus 2."
> —George Hillocks Jr.
> *The Testing Trap: How State Writing Assessments Control Learning,* 2002, p. 6

■ Four-Point Scale

The four-point scale is concise and provides definitions of performance at all four levels: 4 is proficient, 3 is midlevel tending up, 2 midlevel tending down, and 1 signifies beginning performance. Although its simplicity makes it popular for large-scale assessment, I am not a fan of the four-point scale for classroom purposes. Having a limited number of descriptors can oversimplify qualitative differences in performance, and further, such a compressed scale does not allow much room for growth. The smaller the scale, clearly, the more a student writer must improve to move up even one point. Also, in my experience, many readers are reluctant to assign scores at the top of a scale ("No room left to improve") or the bottom ("No one is *that* low, surely"). As a result, most papers scored on a four-point scale receive scores of 2 or 3, turning the scale effectively into a two-point rubric—*almost made it* (3) versus *problematic but redeemable* (2). In any assessment, it is critical to use *the full scale*—or to revise it if you feel uncomfortable with that.

■ Five-Point Scale

Because performance on the five-point scale is defined in writing at only three of the five levels, the language at those levels is rich and detailed, making it extremely easy to understand what we mean by beginning, developing, and proficient within each trait. Review the five-point rubric (see the 3-level rubric in the Appendix), and you will see at once that this is so. This detail within the descriptors makes the five-point easy to internalize for both teachers and students. This is the scale's big advantage.

Critics have two problems with the five-point scale. First, performance is not defined for the scores of 4 and 2. Personally, I do not find this troubling. The 4 and 2 are compromise scores—which will exist no matter *how* many points we put on the scale. There is always someone who wants to assign a score of 4.5.

The second criticism is that the five-point scale has a built-in midpoint "dumping ground" (score of 3)—the score we assign a performance when we are tired or have difficulty balancing out the strengths and problems in our minds. This does happen, but the problem is not as extensive as some critics would suggest. Many pieces truly *are* a balance of strengths and problems. A score of 3 is not always a cop-out; it's often real. The notion that expanding the scoring scale will reduce the number of 3s is the height of irony. The problem lies with the *writing*—not with the scale.

The three-level scales (teacher and student versions) that appear in the Appendix can be used as five-point scales (or six-point, if you prefer). I have modified them slightly from the original five-point versions so that it is now easier to break out the strengths and problems at the midlevel, and so that the upper level is strong enough to allow for scores of 6. The scale is simple to use either way. The beginning level is a 1 or 2, depending on the number and severity of the problems identified. The midlevel is a 3 or 4, depending on the relative balance of strengths and problems. And the upper level is a 5 or 6, depending on whether *many things* are true of a piece (5) or virtually *everything* is true (6).

■ Six-Point Scale

The six-point scale (see Figure 3.6) was developed to serve two purposes. First, it breaks out the midpoint score to a 3-4 split. A score of 3 is a midlevel score leaning down. A score of 4 is a midlevel score leaning up. I call the six-point scale the the River" model because as you cross from 3 to 4, it's like leaping into the "land of proficiency." Remember jumping a creek as a child? Maybe you just made it, pulling yourself up by a tree branch—that's a 4, a "just made it." Or maybe your feet found no purchase, and you slipped down the muddy bank and into the water—that's a 3, "not quite." The student version of the scale (see Figure 8.1, page 159) is formatted to illustrate this "leap," with scores of 4, 5, and 6 on one side, and scores of 1, 2, and 3 on the other.

Second, this scale provides a "place" (score of 6) to put those performances that not only meet but in many respects exceed usual expectations for grade level, performances that are striking, memorable, and worthy of sharing for instructional purposes.

The six-point scale offers two other distinct advantages: (1) it defines performance at all six levels, which many teacher/raters like (even if the descriptors are a bit more compressed), and (2) it is expansive enough to capture even relatively modest growth in writing skills. It is far easier to go from a 3 to a 4 on the six-point scale than on the four-point, and for purposes of tracking growth at the classroom level, this offers a distinct advantage.

Throughout most of this book I will share suggested scores based on both scales, but precise scores are much less important than your overall sense of whether a paper is at a beginning (1–2), developing (3–4), or strong (5–6) level and *why*. When you teach the traits to students, use this very same approach, scoring a paper and discussing its strengths and weaknesses. Use weaker papers as models for practice revision. As you work with students, keep your eye always on what is most important: (1) conversation about writing, (2) a growing sense of shared values that creates a community of writers, and (3) your students' growing repertoire of lessons learned based on the papers you read and share. If you like, you can simply ask students, "Does it leap the river—or not?"

Getting Ready to Score Papers

Our earlier assessment of "The Redwoods" and "Mouse Alert" focused on general personal responses. This time we'll put scores on the papers using the five- or six-point rubrics (your choice—I will give you scores on both).

Print out both papers and the rubrics so that you can see them easily and write on them. Then score both "The Redwoods" and "Mouse Alert" on *all six traits*. Don't worry about getting the "right answer." Ask yourself whether each paper is *strong* or *in need of revision* on a particular trait, *then* zero in on the specific score that seems most appropriate. This practice teaches *you* the traits so that later, you will know just what you are teaching students when you focus on, say, *ideas*. If possible, work with a partner so that you can discuss each paper throughout your practice. This is what you want students to do also.

If you are working with a group, you can record your scores on the scoring grid master in Figure 3.7. Simply write, in the appropriate box, the number of people who give a paper each possible score, e.g., how many 6s in ideas, how many 5s, how many 4s, and so on.

If your personal scores differ markedly and repeatedly from those of others in your group and from those suggested in this book, it is quite possible you are either (1) not sufficiently familiar with the scoring guide to use it consistently or (2) influenced by elements other than the traits of writing (such as topic choice). I'll touch on causes of rater bias in a minute. For now, let's consider recommended scores for these two introductory papers. Suggested scores on the five-point rubric appear first, followed by bold-face for the six-point rubric.

FIGURE **3.7**　**Scoring Grid Master***

	I	O	V	WC	SF	C
6						
5						
4						
3						
2						
1						

* Can be used with six-point or five-point analytical scale.

Suggested Scores and Comments

"The Redwoods" (Grade 11, Narrative)

Ideas: 2, 3 (a 2 on the five-point scale and 3 on the six-point scale)
Organization: 3, 4
Voice: 1, 2
Word choice: 2, 3
Sentence fluency: 3, 4
Conventions: 4, 4

■ Lessons Learned from This Paper

• Conventions alone will not carry the day.

• Don't be afraid to let the "buried" story out!

- Voice dies without details.
- Tell the truth.

■ Comments

This paper is classic in its total restraint. It's safe and impersonal. The writer is barely here. It communicates, but only on the most general level. There's a moment—just a *moment*—of voice: "I love my family, and this is a time I will remember for a long time." It's as if the writer wants to move in for a chat but can't quite bring herself to do it. The language is masterfully vague, and there is a significant lack of involvement in the topic. What about this "wonderful time"? *How* was it wonderful? What is the brother really like? Comical? Pesky? Rude? What happened on this trip to delight, surprise, annoy, or captivate this writer? Imagine making a film of this paper: *Redwoods, the Movie. Could* you? Not without fleshing out ideas and characters. Conventions are clean but extremely simple for eleventh grade (hence the slightly lower scores on that trait). *Note:* I have searched for years for a replacement for "The Redwoods," but papers so smoothly written yet impressively content-free are hard to come by.

"Mouse Alert" (Grade 7, Narrative)

> *Ideas:* 5, 6
> *Organization:* 5, 6
> *Voice:* 5, 6
> *Word choice:* 4, 4
> *Sentence fluency:* 5, 5
> *Conventions:* 3, 4

■ Lessons Learned from This Paper

- Writing "small" (focusing on the mouse incident) works better than telling everything (Imagine "My Trip to Yellowstone").
- Readers do not expect (or want) your family to be perfect; real people are more interesting.
- Sensory details put the reader at the scene.

■ Comments

This story is deliciously crammed with tiny acts of everyday heroism. Nothing much goes right, but everything from Dad backing into the tree to the mouse hunt, the big release, and the race through Yellowstone is extraordinarily visual (you *could* make a movie of this, with Chevy Chase or Steve Martin as Dad) and a tribute to the pitfalls of planning. These people are extremely human—unlike the people in "The Redwoods." They argue. They worry over money, mice, and who gets enough air in the car. We can picture Mom in her nightgown and smell the aroma of the pickle jar. Readers are often sorry this piece is so short, and that is about the best compliment you can give a writer. Conventions need work, yes, but we tend to forgive these problems because we're enjoying the ride, and this writer will find a professional editor one day.

The Write Connection

"The Redwoods"

Rewrite the lead for "The Redwoods," giving it the same voice as that in "Mouse Alert."

Rewrite the paper from another point of view—or more than one. How does Mom see the trip? Dad? The brother? The family pet?

The Write Connection

"Mouse Alert"

Imagine that "Mouse Alert" is going to be published in a school anthology of student writing. Edit it for this purpose, finding and correcting as many errors as possible.

Making Your Scoring Consistent

Before extending our scoring practice trait by trait (in Chapters 4, 5, and 6), let me offer some tips to make your assessment even more consistent and efficient.

1. Remember—There Is No "Right" Score

All the student papers in this book have been scored by experienced teachers/raters. Their suggested scores *should not be considered the "correct" scores*. There is no such thing. They are *suggestions* and cannot be more. The goal is to come up with a *defensible* score, one based on thorough reading of the paper and analysis of the rubric—never on personal bias or casual observation.

If you disagree by one point on a given score, you can still consider that agreement. On a continuum, remember, a high 3, let's say, and a low 4 would actually be quite close (see Figure 3.8).

2. Refer to the Scoring Guide Often

Once you have chosen a scoring guide (five- or six-point), read it through thoroughly, like a recipe that you don't know well yet; don't skim. Print out a copy so that you can write on it and highlight phrases that speak to you. Make it your own. Don't try to memorize it, though. You'll be surprised how quickly it will feel as comfortable and familiar to you as your name and address. (*Tip:* Score one paper a day for 20 days, recording scores for all six traits each time, and you'll find that at the end of that time, you are both fast and consistent.)

3. Ask, "Does It Leap the River?"

Scoring with a rubric is a balancing act: strengths versus problems. Where does the paper fall? If you are using a six-point scale, ask this question first: Does the paper "leap the river" into the land of proficiency (score of 4, 5,

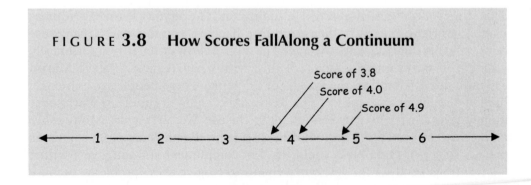

FIGURE **3.8** **How Scores FallAlong a Continuum**

or 6)? Then you'll have a good notion of just where to place a paper along the continuum.

4. Remember That a Score of 1 Indicates Beginning Performance, Not Failure

When you give a score of 1, you are saying to the student, in effect, "You have made a beginning. You put something on paper, and you get a point for that. Now we'll build from there."

5. Remember That a Score of 5 or 6 Represents Strength and Proficiency, Not Perfection

If you believe that a performance is strong, let your score show that. Papers that receive 5s and 6s are not all alike. Some are hilarious, and some are profoundly moving or well researched. If you feel that a paper has strength, go for the gusto; don't wait for that mythical "better" paper that still waits round the bend. You can give another 5 or 6 tomorrow.

6. Take Your Time

Beginning raters worry about time, and so often rush through the paper and spend time going through the rubric, agonizing over whether to give a 2 or 3. Don't do this. Spend your time *reading the paper*. Get inside the writer's thinking. Pay attention to details. Notice how it begins and ends. When you turn to the rubric, the "right" score will jump out at you.

7. Consider Grade Level, But Don't Make It the Factor

Grade level does not count as much as performance per se—but it still counts. After all, expectations for a second grader should be different from those for a twelfth grader. That's why we are surprised to learn that the author of "The Redwoods" is a high school student. Nevertheless, we can—and should—have high expectations at *all grade levels*. We should not expect, for example, that students in second or third grade will have only minimal voice. It does not work that way. What changes, with experience and sophistication, is a writer's control over a trait. So an eleventh grader might have more consistent voice throughout a piece of writing, but a third or even a first grader could have moments of voice that would rival that of any writer. Similarly, it is quite appropriate to say, "That is stunning word choice for a primary student." This is just the sort of thing we *should* be noticing. We must also remember that high school students have not reached the pinnacle of writing performance; we learn to write throughout our lives.

8. Watch Out for Rater Bias

Many little things can get in the way of scoring fairly or appropriately. Here are a few pitfalls to watch out for, whether in large-scale assessment or in the classroom.

> In addition to avoiding unclear language, rubrics should not use negative language.
> —Kathleen Strickland and James Strickland
> *Reflections on Assessment,* 1998, p. 85

> The most fundamental criteria don't change very much [across modes]. For example, vivid and explicit detail is as important in a short story as it might be in a business letter or research paper.
> —Barry Lane
> "Quality in Writing," 1996, p. 4

■ The Positive-Negative Trend

This trend reflects a tendency to be too hard (or too easy) on everyone as a matter of principle. We've all known the teacher who cannot bear to give anything but an A—or the one who is holding As in reserve for that special student he or she hopes to meet one day.

■ The Trait Error

Research cited by Brian Huot (1990) shows that readers do not always know what trait they are responding to as they read; they may *think* they are scoring organization, for example, when in fact it is the voice of the piece or the conventions to which they are reacting.

■ Appearance

We may find ourselves irritated by messy or tiny handwriting, especially when we're tired. But poor handwriting, while often annoying, is not the same thing as weak voice, unsupported ideas, or faulty conventions and should not influence trait-based scores.

■ Length

Is longer better? We might like to think so. In fact, though, many students who write well for one or two pages have enormous difficulty sustaining the flow. They just run out of juice. Furthermore, ability to condense is often a virtue; it may give voice just the boot it needs.

■ Personal Preferences

So you love football? Hate cats? Vice versa? These little quirks and preferences can and do get in the way of fair scoring.

■ Preconceptions

Researcher and writer Paul Diederich (1974) discovered that raters actually scored the very same essays higher when told they had been written by honors English students. If I told you "The Redwoods" was written by Hemingway, would you see it differently?

■ Skimming

Some readers think that they can tell after the first few lines whether a paper will be strong or not. Rarely is this true. A strong lead may disintegrate into generalities; a slow start may explode into a burst of inspiration on page two.

■ Self-Scoring

Are you a perceptive reader? If so, be careful that you score the work of the writer and not your own talent in deciphering the hidden message.

> In the past 30 years, researchers and theorists have come to know that teaching writing entails teaching thinking.
> —George Hillocks Jr.
> *The Testing Trap: How State Writing Assessments Control Learning,* 2002, p. 6

■ Vulgar Language

How do you respond to vulgar language in student writing? To profanity? To extreme violence? Some people have a very ho-hum attitude; others are readily offended.

My position usually has been this: If the language works in context and is not used simply to distract or shock the reader, I assess the work as I would any piece of literature. Profanity is part of the landscape in a narrative on war; it may seem jolting, cumbersome, or self-conscious in a persuasive essay on school locker searches. The question (for me) is not really about violence or profanity per se but about whether the writing works and whether the language is appropriate for the context and intended audience.

> The plot may be filled with blood and guts, but it's fine writing that keeps the audience rapt: it's exquisitely constructed sentences; it's carefully honed cadences; it's the marvelous satisfaction of the sensual rhythm of perfect prose.
>
> —Mem Fox
> *Radical Reflections,*
> 1993, p. 54

9. Be Aware of Pet Peeves

Everyone has a pet peeve. Some of us have many. The trick is to know what they are so that they will not trap you into assessing unfairly by *over*reacting. See Figure 3.9 for a list—and as you read through them, ask whether you notice any of your own pet peeves.

Keep a list of your own pet peeves. Share it openly with your students. It can teach us all a little about the way we respond to writing.

10. Remember That No Rubric Tells All

Writing guides (a term I prefer to *rubrics* because it does not sound so authoritative) are by nature simple documents, intended to capture the essence of performance we are *likely to see* at various levels. They cannot capture *everything* because the variety in writing samples is infinite.

In *The 9 Rights of Every Writer* (2005), I tell the story of a student paper titled "Ginweed" that I have carried with me since 1987. That's a long while to care about a piece of writing. Each time I read the story of a young boy and his 4-H calf, I am moved all over again. I laugh, I get tears in my eyes, and the unexpected ending still gives me chills. The county fair judge in the piece still reminds me of actor Melvin Douglas in the classic film *Hud*—especially when he remarks, "When you got a Jersey like this, it almost makes me want to change breeds" (pp. 93–95). But of course, I could not very well incorporate such personal responses into a writing guide:

- Causes the reader to tear up
- Compels the reader to treasure it for twenty years or more
- Reminds the reader of famous people

Personal responses cannot be and *should not* be transformed into expectations. This is why our comments matter so much. The writing guide is the right place to make important expectations known, but a score, no matter how accurate, can never take the place of words from our heart. We need both.

FIGURE **3.9** **Pet Peeves**

- *Big, loopy writing*
- **Teeny-tiny writing**
- No margins!
- Commas or periods outside the quotation marks
- Shifting tenses with no reason
- Writing in ALL CAPITAL LETTERS
- Mixing *it's* and *its*
- Mixing *are* and *our*—Do they even sound alike?
- Mixing *their*, *there*, and *they're*—when we just finished a unit on it
- *Goes* for *said*, as in *So he goes, "Let's dance," and I go, "Yeah, cool."*
- Endless connectives: *and, but then, because, and so, so then, so*
- The words and phrases *yuck, awesome, dude, radical, rad, in the zone, humongous, pushing the envelope, I mean, like, As if, cool* (I use *cool,* but hate it in print)
- Missing words—Didn't the writer notice?
- Sudden endings
- Writing just to fill the page—nothing goes with anything else
- Empty words used to snow the reader: *His unobstructed prejudice presupposed the obliteration of his potential. Just say, His prejudice held him back.*
- *The End* (as if I would look for more)
- The phrase *You know what I mean?* (I can't tell if it's more annoying when I do or when I don't)
- *Alot* (If you can have *alot,* what's wrong with *alittle?*)
- No punctuation at all—like driving without traffic signs
- No title—Take a minute and think of one
- A title that doesn't seem to go at all with the paper
- A lead that repeats the prompt or assignment—If I can't tell what the topic is, there's a problem with the writing
- Exclamation points after every breathless line!!!!!!!!!!!!!!!!!!!!!!!!!!
- *Between you and I* (versus *me*)
- *Me and my friend . . .* (as a sentence subject)
- *Her and me . . .* (as a sentence subject)
- Cliché adjectives: *crashing waves, blue skies, fluffy clouds*
- Tired words: *nice, good, great, wonderful, special, exciting . . .*
- No paragraphs!
- Paragraphs for every single sentence
- Cliché leads: *In this paper . . . Hi, my name is . . .*
- The ending *That's all for now . . .*
- Fifteen *different* **fonts** on **one** page

Chapter 3 In a Nutshell

- The question "What makes writing work?" underlies the search for the six traits and is a good place to begin teaching them.

- Contrast (as seen in "The Redwoods" and "Mouse Alert") is important in teaching writing and provokes discussion of those qualities that define strong writing.

- Ask your students what makes writing work, and they are likely to come up with the same qualities as teachers; then they "own" the traits, too.

- While four-, five-, and six-point scales all offer certain advantages, this book encourages use of a five- or six-point scale in the classroom, where it is important to show growth.

- Many factors, including the length of a paper or the topic, can trigger bias. Knowing what causes bias minimizes its effects.

- Teaching yourself the traits *first* paves the way for you to teach them to students through scoring, discussion, and focused lessons.

Study Group Interactive Questions and Activities

1. **Activity and Discussion.** Ask your group the question posed in this chapter: What makes writing work? Record your answers. How do your answers compare with the list of things teachers value in writing (Figure 3.5)?

2. **Activity and Discussion.** In *Embracing Contraries*, Peter Elbow (1986) describes research conducted by Alan Purves (1992) in which it is shown that readers make more accurate and reliable judgments about the features of student writing if they are also asked to give a quick account of their "subjective responses or feelings" (p. 230). Elbow hypothesizes that giving voice to a personal response allows a rater to be more objective in scoring. Do you agree? Try it. As a group, score any piece of writing, first voicing your subjective response, and then putting a score on the paper. Does it help to be "subjective first"?

3. **Activity and Discussion.** Make a group list of your pet peeves. Compare it with the list in Figure 3.9. Is yours longer? What did you include that is not in the figure?

4. **Activity and Discussion.** Expand your scoring skills by looking at writing *not generated by*

students. Consider a film review, advertisement, excerpt from a textbook, brochure, letter to the editor, lease agreement or other contract, driver's manual, or any writing that is part of your life. Consider how you might write a lesson based on this kind of scoring.

5. **Activity and Discussion.** Be daring. Ask each person in your group to submit a piece of original writing to be scored by the group—anonymously. Word-process them and leave names off. Give copies to each member of the group and tally scores—or simply identify the strongest trait and the one that most needs revision. Can your response to having your own work assessed in this way influence the way you respond to students? How?

6. **Activity and Discussion.** With your group, score any writing sample using both five- and six-point scales. Talk about which you prefer and why.

7. **Discussion.** Rubrics and scoring guides are never perfect. They always need revision and adaptation. What, in your mind, are the characteristics of a good scoring guide, and why is it so hard to capture on paper what's in our hearts and minds?

Reflections on Writing

I write because I like hearing the river of words flow like the ocean, so smooth and graceful. I like to read it over and over until the words ask me to stop.

—Ryan Sterner, student writer

Writing is everything because it can be about everything. You can write about anyone, any place, any thing. There are no limitations. Even grammar and correct spelling aren't barriers. How many times did Mark Twain spell something "wrong" when writing dialogue for Huckleberry? Here, with pen and paper, there is the possibility of freedom.

—Elisabeth Kramer, student writer

CHAPTER 4

Building a Foundation
Ideas and Organization

This cannot be stated bluntly enough: The writer must have something to say.

—Ralph Fletcher
What a Writer Needs, 1993, p. 151

An effective piece of writing says one dominant thing. As Kurt Vonnegut, Jr., says, "Don't put anything in a story that does not advance the action." The same thing can be said for argument, memo, technical writing or poetry. Every element in the text supports and advances the main point. Planning starts with the search for that dominant meaning.

—Donald M. Murray
A Writer Teaches Writing, 2004, p. 18

The need to write, the itch to write, begins with a story to tell, a point to make, an argument to put forth, a descriptive picture to paint—*ideas* that shift and change and grow with the act of writing. That act, the writing process, is driven and shaped by questions: "Where do I begin? What do I say first—and next, and after that? How do I bring it all to resolution?" These are the questions of *organization*. Of course, organization is flexible and grows to accommodate the ideas. As Donald Murray (2004, p. 18) says, "The writer does not arrive at the final destination before taking the trip," so while it helps to imagine what that destination might be, unanticipated side excursions often enrich the journey.

This chapter has two purposes:

1. To give you a chance to teach the traits of ideas and organization *to yourself first* by assessing, discussing, and reflecting on student work.

2. To discover papers that you can share with your students as you teach them these same traits.

Papers included in this chapter are scored for all six traits. This lets you keep the bigger picture in your mind as we go, even though I will introduce one trait at a time—just as you will do with your students.

Everything you do in this chapter you can do with students, and presenting papers to score and discuss is a good first step in teaching the traits. The discussion this generates will amaze and delight you. And as you talk, your students will be teaching themselves and one another countless lessons about what to do—or *not* do—as writers.

In this edition, I open the discussion of each trait with a "trait shortie"—a summary of the trait that you can share with your students. The shorties highlight the features of each trait that will later provide *the focus for your instruction*. This edition also includes a feature I have called the "Write Connection," which is a revision or editing activity inspired by each of the papers included in the book.

Ideas: The Heart of It All

Getting a Mindset

Ideas are the heart of the writer's message—which may take any of several forms—story, argument, informational summary, and so on. All other traits take their cue from this foundational trait and work in harmony to ensure that the message from writer to reader is clear and intriguing.

FIGURE **4.1**   Trait "Shortie" for Ideas
Use this summary to introduce the trait to students.

Ideas & Development
The Message

- Clear main message, point, thesis, storyline

- Narrow, manageable topic

- Rich, intriguing details expand the message

- Insight

- Knowledge from experience, research

- Compelling, holds reader's attention

© 2009. Allyn and Bacon, an imprint of Pearson Education, Inc.
Developed by Vicki Spandel for *Creating Writers*, Fifth Edition.

 # Practice Papers

What To Do

- Be sure that you have a printed copy of the scoring guide in front of you.
- Have a copy of the scoring grid (Figure 3.7, page 50) if you are working with a group.
- Make copies of papers so you can write on them.
- Make overheads of the papers if you wish to share them aloud.
- Read each paper aloud prior to scoring.
- Score papers using a five- or six-point rubric.
- Discuss your scores and the reasons for them with a partner or group.
- Check your scores against the suggested scores provided in this book.
- Consider the "Lessons Learned" for each paper.
- Share the Write Connection with students.

The Inside Track on Ideas

A good writer never tells everything but seeks those details that put us right at the scene. The writing becomes real, and we are absorbed into it effortlessly.

Consider this passage from Walter Dean Myers's book *Slam* (1996), in which the main character describes the sounds of the city:

> When it's late night you hear the sound of car doors and people talking and boom boxes spilling out the latest tunes. When it rains the tires hiss on the street and when there's a real rain with the wind blowing sometimes you can hear it against the tin sign over Billy's bicycle shop. If there's a fight you hear the voices rising and catching each other up. The sound of broken glass can cut through other noises, even if it's just a bottle of wine somebody dropped. And behind all the other sounds there's always the sirens, bringing their bad news from far off and making you hold your breath until they pass so you know it ain't any of your people who's getting arrested or being taken to the hospital. *[p. 2]*

It isn't the amount of detail that counts, but how vivid it is. As Grant Wiggins (1992) reminds us, "too many essay scoring systems reward students for including merely more arguments or examples; quantity is not quality, and we teach a bad lesson by such scoring practices" (p. 30).

Paper 1   **Making Decisions** (Expository, Grade 8)

When making a decision, take your time and not rush into a hasty conclusion. Clarify the decision you are making. Be sure you understand all aspects of your decision, without confusion. Reason out the consequences your decision will effect. Question whether the concluding effects will be positive or negative.

Before proceeding ahead with any decision making process, devise other alternatives, if any, noticing who and what may be effected. Be sure to ask others for their opinion on the subject. Keep in mind, however, that their opinion may not be correct or even helpful. Quality decision making depends on facts, not opinions. Eventually, your decision will have an impact on other things. These impacts cannot always be foreseen. Take your time in determining which impacts are most effected, and be careful in the end.

The Write Connection

"Making Decisions"

Revise "Making Decisions" by including a specific example of one hard-to-make decision and exploring the consequences. As an added bonus, try simplifying and "humanizing" the language so it sounds as if it's written by a real person, not a computer.

■ **Suggested Scores for Focus Trait: Ideas**

Ideas: 1-2, **2** (a 1-2 split on the five-point scale, **2** on the six-point scale)

■ **Lessons Learned from Paper 1**

- Generalities weaken ideas.
- Specific examples (in this case, a decision with good or bad results) are a must.

■ **Comments**

This paper *seems* to say something. The problem is, it's a compilation of generalizations and platitudes.

No people populate this paper. It is sterile. The strengths of the piece (compare the text of any inflated political speech) are fluency and conventions. While it says virtually nothing, it flows smoothly enough to come across as authoritative. The language is sophisticated but imprecise: "Take your time in determining which impacts are most effected." This probably means "Take time to figure out how your decision will affect your life." That revision is clear—but still general. Think how different this paper would be if the writer had chosen one difficult decision (say, leaving home or giving up drugs) and given us possible outcomes; then the writer might have gotten more involved, and so might we.

■ Suggested Scores for Other Traits

Organization: **1, 2**
Voice: **2, 2**
Word choice: **2, 2**
Sentence fluency: **4, 4**
Conventions: **4, 4**

> [Gary] Klein studied nurses, intensive care units, firefighters, and other people who make decisions under pressure, and one of his conclusions is that when experts make decisions, they don't logically and systematically compare all available options. That is the way people are taught to make decisions, but in real life it is much too slow.
>
> —Malcolm Gladwell
> *Blink,* 2005, p. 107

Paper 2 **Harder Than You Think** (Personal Essay, Grade 10)

I walk up the hill with my friends, turn into our cul-de-sac, go to the front door, put the key in the lock, turn, and step in. The house breathes a kind of spooky hello as I set my books down and go to the kitchen where the inevitable note is waiting: "Have a snack. Be home soon. I love you." As I'm munching cookies, I think how I'd like to go out and shoot a few hoops if I had someone to do it with. You can play Nintendo by yourself, but it isn't the same. So I forget that for now. I should be doing my Spanish homework anyway. Too bad I don't have an older brother or sister to help conjugate all those dumb verbs. I could call a friend, sure, but if I had a brother or sister, I'd have a built-in friend.

While I'm feeling so sorry for myself, I hear my friends Kelly and Kyle across the street. She's screaming bloody murder because he is throwing leaves in her hair and threatening to put a beetle in her backpack. She has just stepped on his new Nikes. I do not have these squabbles. I guess the big advantage, if you call it that, to being an only child is my room is my own. Nobody "borrows" my CDs or my books or clothes. I also get a bigger allowance than I probably would if I had siblings. My parents take me everywhere, from the mall to the East Coast. Maybe they wouldn't if they had other kids. (On the other hand, it would be more fun going if I had someone my own age.)

All these great advantages are overshadowed by one big disadvantage, though, and it's the main reason I would change things if I could. When you are an only child, your parents depend on you to be the big success all the time. You are their big hope, so you cannot fail. You have to be good at sports, popular, and have good grades. You need a career goal. You have to have neat hair and clothes that look pressed. You have to have good grammar, clean socks, good breath, and table manners. If you've ever felt jealous of somebody who is an only child, don't. It's a lot of pressure. I often wish for a little screw-up brother my parents could worry about for a while.

So—while having a neat room with nothing disturbed is great, I'd take a brother or sister in a minute if I could. The big irony is, if I had that mythical brother or sister, I would probably be wishing myself an only child again the first time my baseball shirt didn't come back or my stereo got broken. Life is like that. What you don't have always seems to be the thing you want.

The Write Connection

"Harder Than You Think"

Revise *just the lead* for "Harder Than You Think" by condensing it. Ask yourself, "Where does the paper really take off?" Then, compress everything before that. What is the effect of this revision on the paper as a whole?

■ **Suggested Scores for Focus Trait: Ideas**

Ideas: 5, 5 (a 5 on the five-point scale, 5 on the six-point scale)

■ **Lessons Learned from Paper 2**

• Beginning with an anecdote or image sets the scene.

• Multiple examples make an argument convincing.

■ **Comments**

I like this paper. It's authentic. The writer uses two contrasting examples—the neighbor children squabbling and his own home life—to make some key points about how peaceful yet rather lonely it can be to go through life as an only child. The examples are realistic, and the writer seems to have thought through what he has to say. The opening paints a clear picture of life as an only child; some readers feel that it could be condensed. The ending is even stronger, and it makes an important point, too—without being redundant. The voice, a definite presence in paragraphs 1 and 2, springs to life in paragraph 3, bolstered by precise, original ideas. This is a fluent, well-edited, readable piece.

■ **Suggested Scores for Other Traits**

Organization: 5, 5

Voice: 5, 5

Word choice: 4, 5

Sentence fluency: 4, 5

Conventions: 5, 6

 # Organization: Showcasing It

Getting a Mindset

Imagine that you are designing a display window for a department store. What you put into the window represents your *ideas*. How you arrange it is your *organization*. Organization is an evolutionary trait. It wraps itself around the ideas as they grow and change, just as your skin wraps around you. Take something out of your window display, and you cannot just leave a hole there. You rearrange so that no one notices. Got a new item to display? You make space. Good organization is similarly quiet and unobtrusive. Without drawing attention to itself, it makes ideas shine.

FIGURE 4.2 Trait "Shortie" for Organization
Use this summary to introduce the trait to students.

Organization
Design & Flow of Ideas

- Enticing lead pulls readers in

- Clear design guides readers, enhances understanding

- Strong transitions tie ideas together

- Good pacing—time spent where it counts

- Ending wraps up discussion

© 2009. Allyn and Bacon, an imprint of Pearson Education, Inc.
Developed by Vicki Spandel for *Creating Writers*, Fifth Edition.

Practice Papers

What To Do

Follow the same directions given for *ideas*—this time making sure that you have the scoring guide for *organization* in front of you.

The Inside Track on Organization

Good writing is writing by design. We don't want to be hit over the head ("*My first point. . . . Next I'll explain. . . . Now, for the third step. . . . Having considered all three reasons. . . .*"), but we want the comfort of knowing that the writer knows where he or she is headed. Look for a powerful lead that truly sets up the piece and tells you that this writer has a sense of direction. Look for an insightful conclusion that shows that the writer made some discoveries and is hoping that you did, too. In addition, good writing should follow a pattern—however flexible. Like a roadmap, that organizational pattern gives the reader a clear main path that makes the writing (even with surprise twists) easy to follow. Notice how author Jeffrey Eugenides (2003) guides the reader's eye in this description of the new family car from his Pulitzer Prize–winning novel *Middlesex:*

> Not a spaceship then, but close: a 1967 Cadillac Fleetwood, as intergalactic a car as Detroit ever produced. (The moon shot was only a year away.) It was as black as space itself and shaped like a rocket lying on its side. The long front end came to a point, like a nose cone, and from there the craft stretched back along the driveway in a long, beautiful, ominously perfect shape. There was a silver, multi-chambered grille, as though to filter stardust. Chrome piping, like the housing for circuitry, led from conical yellow turn signals along the rounded sides of the car, all the way to the rear, where the vehicle flared propulsively into jet fins and rocket boosters [p. 253].

Paper 3 | **Some Cartoons Are Violent!** (Persuasive, Grade 3)

Some cartoons are violent. And sometimes ther not! Some ar just funny like Tinny Tunes but some aren't. Take loony Tunes wich is violent but ther not all violent. They could be both. I wach cartoons alot and some are violent. Thers boms that get thrown down in som cartoons. and blows them up. But me I like cartoons some of the time. never will I stop waching but well more are violent than the loony toons. but if I were to mak a cartoon myself I would have well mabe just 1 mane violent thing and then just keep the rest funny OK?

■ Suggested Scores for Focus Trait: Organization

Organization: **1-2, 2** (a 1-2 split on the five-point scale, **2** on the six-point scale)

■ Lessons Learned from Paper 3

- Choose a side before trying to persuade others.
- Organization is very difficult when the main idea is unclear.

■ Comments

The questions of how much violence is too much and whether violence has redeeming social or artistic value continue to plague television and film executives, so we should not be too surprised that this question proved challenging to a third grader. Nevertheless, this young writer takes an exuberant stab at the prompt she is dealt. She sticks with the main theme—violence—but has a very hard time choosing sides. Her thinking goes something like this: A little violence in cartoons is entertaining; too much could be a bad thing (for reasons not fully explored)—but won't hurt me because I know it's phony! What this piece lacks in persuasive logic and organization (it's almost humorously random), it makes up for in voice. The writer is clearly speaking to an audience. By the end of the essay she is negotiating for position: How about just one violent episode per cartoon and keep the rest funny—what do you say? Had she begun here (the point to which her thinking led her), both ideas and organization would have been stronger.

The Write Connection

"Some Cartoons Are Violent!"

Revise "Some Cartoons Are Violent!" by first having a discussion about whether cartoons really *are* too violent. Try to imagine the arguments each side would pose, and list them. Which side is stronger? Watch a few cartoons. Take notes so you can sound like an authority. How do *you* feel as a viewer? Whichever side you take, offer two to three examples to support your side of the argument. How do the cartoons affect you? How might they affect someone younger?

■ Suggested Scores for Other Traits

Ideas: 2, **2**

Voice: 4, **4-5**

Word choice: 3, **3**

Sentence fluency: 3-4, **4**

Conventions: 2, **2**

Paper 4 **The Baseball** (Narrative, Grade 5)

I remember the day I got it well. It was an everyday type day until the doorbell rang. I got up to awnser it. But my sister beat me to it, as usual. It was dad's friend Tom. He got back from a New York yankes baseball fantasy camp a couple weeks ago. I said hi to him and he asked me if I knew who Micky Mantel was. I said of corse I do. At that point I was a little confused. Thenhe haded me a baseball. It wasn't the kind of baseball we use in little luege. It was nicer than that. Made of real leather. It even smelled like leather. Like the smell of a new leather jacket. And the seems were hand stitched too. I turned it around in my hand then I saw it. I saw a Micky Mantel aughtograph. I couldn't believe it. I had an aughtograph in ink of one of the greatest baseball players of all time. Wow. I teushered it ever since that everyday type day that changed at the ring of a doorbell.

■ Suggested Scores for Focus Trait: Organization

Organization: 5, **6** (a 5 on the five-point scale, **6** on the six-point scale)

■ Lessons Learned from Paper 4

- The lead and conclusion really do frame the writing.
- Only bring it up (e.g., Mickey Mantle) if it matters.

■ Comments

Small moments make the best stories, as this writer shows us so well in his tale of the "everyday type day that changed at the ring of a doorbell." Notice how the story comes full circle, beginning with the doorbell and returning to it at the end, when it's even more powerful because now we know its importance. Throughout, ideas drive the organization, which is why the piece works so well. You have to respect a writer who, even as a fifth grader, is so careful with his details. There is a reason behind everything. Consider the question about Mickey Mantle. It's not a throw-away detail; it matters. The writer does not understand why the question is important at first, and neither do we, but all becomes clear by the end of the story. Notice the moment of revelation: *"I turned it around in my hand then I saw it. I saw a Micky Mantel aughtograph."* Good organization thrives on high points.

> "If in the first chapter you say that a gun hung on the wall," Chekhov said, "in the second or third chapter it must without fail be discharged."
>
> —Playwright Anton Chekhov, quoted in Ralph Fletcher
> *What a Writer Needs,*
> 1993, p. 51

The Write Connection

"The Baseball"

Edit "The Baseball" by correcting all conventional errors, but not changing wording or sentence structure. Were there more errors than you thought when you first read it? Why don't we notice them more?

■ **Suggested Scores for Other Traits**

Ideas: 5, **6**

Voice: 5, **6**

Word choice: 4, **4**

Sentence fluency: 4, **4**

Conventions: 2, **2**

Looking at Additional Papers

In the remainder of this chapter we will consider additional papers, this time focusing scoring practice on two traits, *ideas* and *organization*. (Scores for all traits are given, but the practice will focus on these two.) This will enable you to see how the two traits work together (and begin to think about how they interact with other writing traits as well). Follow the same format and procedures; but this time give each paper two scores. Check your responses against the recommended scores.

Paper 5   **Unscripted Television: Enjoy It While You Can**
(Persuasive, Middle School)

After several decades of sitcoms, news shows, detective and adventure shows, most Americans feel they can predict the outcome of just about anything on television after five minutes. You can't always predict who gets voted off "Survivor" or who the American Idol will be, though. Sometimes it's refreshing not to know the ending. Reality TV should really be called "unscripted" TV since this is the factor that makes it different and (for now, anyway) appealing. Will it have a lasting impact? That's doubtful. Does anything on television?

For now, the only thing we can say for sure is that unscripted television reflects our culture. Reality TV tends to show a lot of gossip and intrigue. We see people scheming to outdo or outwit one another for money. This isn't very attractive, but it's a little naïve to say reality TV is a bad influence when in fact, it only shows who we really are. Reality shows often feature hosts who push people into dangerous or humiliating situations (which frankly, most of them seem to enjoy—or else they enjoy whining about it). And sometimes people on the shows are very rude, too. Will this teach Americans to be rude? Get real. We're already rude. Have you driven on a freeway lately?

Unscripted TV is mostly about entertainment—not character building or enlightenment. People watching "Survivor" don't necessarily think they are like the person on the show—or

(continued)

that they should be like that person. Rather, they wonder what they would do in the same situation: Would I be that low? Would I betray my friend? Would I dare do that stunt? This is no different from watching "Jeopardy" and asking yourself the questions contestants try to answer. (By the way, people on "Jeopardy" are trying to bump each other off just like contestants on "Survivor"—they just use their knowledge instead of winning challenges or telling lies, but they're equally money hungry.)

    Reality shows (unscripted shows) are entertaining because they let us ask ourselves what we would do in similar situations. When it comes to entertainment, however, Americans are very unpredictable. Nothing lasts forever, even "Seinfeld." So when it comes to reality TV, there might be one "survivor," and the rest will disappear. Being the last survivor does not necessarily make you the best, however. Look at the cockroach.

■ Suggested Scores for Focus Traits: Ideas and Organization

Ideas: 5, 6

Organization: 4, 5

■ Lessons Learned from Paper 5

- It is possible to have more than one key point—if you can keep all the balls in the air.

- Connecting with the reader (*Have you driven on a freeway lately?*) is a useful strategy to increase voice.

■ Comments

The main point of this paper is that reality television is unlikely to have any lasting impact on American culture. As part of this discussion, however, the writer makes some other intriguing points as well: Reality television is actually unscripted television; it's appealing because we do not know what will happen next; it's a reflection of our culture; and it isn't bad for us because we're already rude and wretched. I had no problem following this discussion, although some readers feel that it jumps from point to point. I simply felt that the writer had a lot of related points to make (it's a complex paper), but you may agree with the slightly lower organization scores. Virtually everyone likes the ending, and by the last paragraph, voice is in full swing.

■ Suggested Scores for Other Traits

Voice: 5, 6

Word choice: 4, 5

Sentence fluency: 5, 6

Conventions: 5, 6

The Write Connection

"Unscripted Television: Enjoy It While You Can"

Use research of different kinds to expand the power of this essay. For example, how many Americans actually watch reality shows? What sorts of ratings do they get? Consider looking up this information on the Web and including it in the essay. Conduct an informal "person on the street" survey and include one or two relevant, interesting quotations to lend the piece authenticity. Finally, watch one or two reality episodes yourself, taking notes, and use an actual example (cited correctly, of course) to show the "gossip and intrigue" or "people scheming to outdo or outwit one another." *Or*—you may find that by viewing a show for yourself you discover another side of reality TV this writer has not considered yet!

Paper 6 **Einstein** (Expository, Grade 5)

Who lived about 100 years ago? Who made great mathematical theories and ecuations? Albert Einstein, one of the greatest scientists who ever lived! Of course, all scientists are great, but Albert was special. He could look at the smallest thing, study it for hours, and see things others would just miss! He had an eye for detail, and he was never bored. Ever. Even when he was all alone!

What kind of family do you think a genius would have? Not much different from yours or mine, actually. Alberts' parents didn't even know for a long time that he had a great mind. They worried about him because he was alone so much. He liked staring at the stars for hours on end instead of playing with other kids. They didn't think this was normal. They worried that he didn't like to play war games. Instead he would just sit with his blocks and work them into different shapes for hours! What kind of kid was this? finally, when Albert's father realized he was a genius, he felt very proud.

You would think a genius like Albert Einstein would love school. Wrong! he hated it! the only classes he liked were math and physics. Albert was so good at math he had to go to a special school to take classes. His math and physics teachers inspired him to become a great scientist.

Albert invented many math theories, but he is most famous for the theory of relativity, which people find fascinating even though they do not understand it. Albert also invented two bombs: the hydragen bomb and the adom bomb.

Einstein made a difference in the world because of his great math theories and his many ecuations. Even though Einstein is dead now, teachers are still teaching his theories. Who knows? People could still be teaching them right on years after you and I are dead, too.

The Write Connection

"Einstein"

What questions do *you* have about Einstein? Pose six. Put them in the order in which you'd like them answered. Then try answering them by looking up Einstein on the Web or checking Walter Isaacson's remarkable biography: *Einstein: His Life and Universe* (2007, Simon and Schuster). Use what you find to expand this essay, keeping what you find helpful from the original. Include the best quotation you can find from the Isaacson book. When you finish, try coming up with a more original title.

■ **Suggested Scores for Focus Traits: Ideas and Organization**

Ideas: 3-4, 4

Organization: 4, 4

■ **Lessons Learned from Paper 6**

- Small details (Albert staring at the stars) add interest.
- Gather enough information before writing.

■ **Comments**

Although this piece is not a powerhouse, it has a kind of quirky appeal. The picture of Einstein as a child offers a fresh, interesting spin on a popular biography. Who knows? Maybe Albert's parents *did* fret over his less than social side. Of course, there must be more to the story, and that is the problem here: What's done is fairly good, but details are sketchy. The lead and conclusion work reasonably well; this writer needs only a good punch line— a significant moment, turning point, or spectacular surprise—to bring the organizational structure of the piece together. One other problem plagues the piece (as it does many assigned topics); namely, the writer seems to find

Einstein mildly interesting but not quite fascinating. One moment of true joyful discovery could have boosted this piece from pleasantly engaging to riveting. All the same, voice ("What kind of kid was this?") is the strength. Given the right topic, this curious writer will fly.

■ **Suggested Scores for Other Traits**

Voice: 4-5, **5**

Word choice: 3-4, **4**

Sentence fluency: 3-4, **4**

Conventions: 3, **3**

| Paper 7 | **Writing Today** (Persuasive Essay, Grade 9) |

"Good afternoon students. Today, we are writing a creative story. It can be about *anything you want.* Take your time and use your imaginations!"

Ha. Maybe in the "old school" days. Now, fast-forward to the present. This past year, as a freshman, I walked into class and heard, "Good afternoon students. Today, you have fifteen minutes to write a proficient, five-paragraph essay discussing the themes in the poem we analyzed yesterday. This is a practice for the *actual* Proficiency Assessment Test; if you do not pass the test next week, you will take it again this spring; if you fail it again, you will take in fall of your sophomore year; if you fail once more you will take it spring of your sophomore year. After that you have two more chances as a junior to make the grade, and if you should fail for a sixth time you will not receive your diploma." *No pressure, no pressure . . .*

These tests don't just happen in English class. I recently finished three Body of Evidence assessments in science, and one BOE in world history. All are mandated.

Personally, I feel that I am growing less interested in creative writing—or *any* writing. When I was asked to write a poem for an assignment, I found myself arguing the prompt I was to write.

Last year, as an eighth grader, I was home-schooled. I completed a 20 page children's book about a trip to the moon, and started another. I wrote a collection of horse poems, and photographed my horses to accompany them. Right now, I have no ambition to sit at the computer and finish my new story. I hesitate to pull up that children's story for fear I can't start again at the same level of creativity.

A family friend who is a first grade teacher used to constantly have hands-on projects in all subjects. Now, each morning she sits her seven-year-old kids down and reads them words from a prescribed text. This program was implemented by the district, and recommended by the state to teach children how to read. How much do you suppose these children love reading and writing? The first grade teacher doesn't have time this year to do the penguin project. First graders in her class used to make life-size paper penguins and write stories about them. It was great for them to see the actual size of the Emperor Penguin (who is usually taller than the kids who make him), and to use their imaginations to decorate him and write stories about him. If there is no time for play, fun,

(continued)

or excitement, how will these children grow to love school? How will they grow up to be individuals without time to develop the personal skills needed to succeed in a social context? According to the government and state, no child will be successful without passing the tests in schools today, which may not be in sync with the curriculum. Now I realize that all those times I sat through hours of testing I could've been learning how to break a horse, draw a picture, or braid leather. Maybe schools today should specialize in techniques that prepare students for the real world.

Maybe one day I will walk into a class and hear the teacher say, "Good afternoon, students. Take out paper and pencil, and with your words, paint me a picture of where you will be in the future."

I know that in that future, I will be sitting on a horse in the middle of a mountain range. I will pull a piece of paper and pen from my saddle bag and start to write. The unconventional tests, the B's, C's, and even A's I earned in school will not matter to me. I will feel confident that I can succeed in life no matter how I do on tests and assessments that have nothing to do with my intelligence or my work ethic.

The Write Connection

"Writing Today"

The author makes the comment that schools should spend more time preparing students for the "real world." Advocates of today's testing programs might argue that they are doing just that. They might feel reading and math are more relevant to success than the author's examples of breaking a horse or drawing a picture. What do *you* think? Use the last sentence of paragraph 6 as the basis for a new paper, and take either side. You may wish to cite several items from a current test (Look up ETS* online for samples), include quotations from one or two educators, and also interview someone from the world of business who can offer an employer's perspective.

*Educational Testing Service

■ Suggested Scores for Focus Traits: Ideas and Organization

Ideas: 5, 6

Organization: 5, 6

■ Lessons Learned from Paper 7

- A direct quotation is a good way to open.
- A specific example (first grade teacher with the penguin project) drives a point home better than a generalization.
- A strong image (the writer on her horse) makes a good ending.

■ Comments

This piece is clear and easy to follow. The writer makes her thesis known—too much testing is destroying many students' interest in writing—without ever stating it directly. It takes a strong writer to do this. Voice in this piece comes from the writer's confidence and conviction. She is persuasive without fretting over whether the reader will agree on all points. She doesn't hesitate or qualify her comments; I like that. The word choice is strong, but natural. Sentences flow well, and conventions are excellent.

■ Suggested Scores for Other Traits

Voice: 5, 6

Word choice: 5, 6

Sentence fluency: 5, 6

Conventions: 5, 6

Paper 8   ## A Great Book (Literary Analysis, Grade 8)

There are many themes in To Kill a Mockingbird. Three of the themes that stand out are fairness, justice and courage. These themes are widely spread throughout the book. Harper Lee helps explain these themes through her characters and the way she writes about them.

Fairness is one of the many interesting themes in this great book. The main character Atticus shows the importance of fairness by the way he tries to treat others. Other characters demonstrate fairness as well.

Respect is another important theme of the book, though not as frequent as some of the other themes. Atticus shows respect for his community and for Tom Robinson, and they respect him as well. This is one of the main themes throughout the book.

Courage is a very important theme in this book. Jem shows courage in several parts of the book. Atticus shows courage by defending Tom in the trial.

These three themes of courage, fairness and justice are important parts of this book just as they are important to our society.

■ Suggested Scores for Focus Traits: Ideas and Organization

Ideas: 2, **2**
Organization: 3, **3**

■ Lessons Learned from Paper 8

- Organization can be too predictable.
- Organization without content is hollow.
- Literary analysis demands quotations and/or characters "in action."

■ Comments

Here's a cheery but lightweight analysis of Harper Lee's novel, *To Kill a Mockingbird.* The paper is fluent, pleasant, and noncontroversial. It says virtually nothing except that, apparently, there are some "themes in this great book." This is a handy approach because this report can now be used for other books, too—*Moby-Dick, The Great Gatsby,* or really, any book having themes.

Oddly enough, the organization is stronger than the content only because the writer presents points in an orderly fashion, skipping right along, never pondering, reflecting, or enlightening us for a moment. Where are the specifics, the examples, the quotations? We want to picture Atticus thundering away in the courtroom or see Scout reaching out to Boo Radley. The organization is not driven by the content, however; the opposite is true, and this is why the piece lacks punch. It's a fill-in-the-blank paper. The voice is not daring, revealing, or personal. It's distant, almost a dust-jacket voice, except that we're tempted to ask (don't say you didn't think of it), "Did you actually *read* the book?" Did you notice that the "great themes" started out as fairness, justice, and courage but shifted to fairness, *respect,* and courage?

The Write Connection

"A Great Book"

If you happen to be reading *To Kill a Mockingbird* in your classroom, try exploring one or more of the four themes this writer mentions: *fairness, justice, respect,* and *courage.* First, state the theme as a sentence, not a word: *Courage sometimes means doing the unpopular thing.* Then, look for (1) an image or scene, (2) a character's response to a situation, and (3) a quotation that help show how that theme plays out in the book. Armed with these specifics, write one paragraph exploring one theme.

■ **Suggested Scores for Other Traits**

Voice: 2, 2
Word choice: 2-3, 3
Sentence fluency: 3-4, 4
Conventions: 4, 4

Paper 9 **Writing Is Important** (Expository, Grade 11)

Writeing is important. It allows you to express your thoughts but also your feelings. through writeing you provide entertenement and information which is useful to others. Writeing is both useful and enjoyable. it helps you explore ideas and issues you might not think of otherwise. If you are going to write, you will need plenty of information.

Writeing well means knowing what you are talking about. This takes research and information. If you do not know enough about your topic, your reader will not be convinced. It also means putting feelings into your paper. no one wants to read something where the writer sounds bored and like they wish they were doing something else. it can take courage to say what you really think and feel but it is worth it. You will get your audiences attention.

third, keep your writeing simple if you want it to be affective. Trying to impress people with big long super complicated sentenes and five dollar words does not work. They might just decide reading your writing is not worth the time and trouble it takes. So keep it simple if you want to have an audience.

the most important advice of all is to write about what you know about the best. If you are a good auto mechanic for instence maybe you should write about cars or if you have a summer job at the veterianians office, you could write stories about the animals you treat. If you try to write what you do not know it will be obvous to your audience and they will not believe in you. Use what you know and use your experences from everyday life

writeing is important in all occupations. Today, it is more true than ever before. If you do not believe it just ask around. Everyone from doctors and dentists to garage mechanics and salesmen have to write as part of their job. But the most important reason is because writeing is a way of sharing the ideas that belong to you. If you work on your writeing skills, It just might help you in ways you have not even throught of.

■ **Suggested Scores for Focus Traits: Ideas and Organization**

Ideas: 4, 4
Organization: 2, 3

■ **Lessons Learned from Paper 9**

• Writing about two things at once makes a piece hard to follow.
• A good ending sometimes makes the best beginning.
• If you shift focus, toss the reader a transition.

■ **Comments**

Despite some banal truisms, this writer makes some insightful points, but they need to be ordered, expanded, and set up better. The writer is trying to tell us two things, really: Everyone writes, making it an important skill (see the final paragraph), and several things (knowing your topic, keeping it simple, having the courage to say what you think) are key in writing well. These ideas could easily be connected with thoughtful transitions, but that hasn't happened as yet. The lead is stiff (the writer is still warming up); the conclusion is far stronger and could be bumped right up front. It sets the stage for why writing well is important in the first place. The voice comes and goes, and word choice is fairly routine. Many sentences are short and choppy, which breaks the flow and creates the impression that the thinking is simplistic, too—which it is not. Careful reading could correct many small problems with conventions.

■ Suggested Scores for Other Traits

Voice: 3-4, **4**

Word choice: 3, **4**

Sentence fluency: 3-4, **4**

Conventions: 2-3, **3**

The Write Connection

"Writing Is Important"

Try starting this piece from the final paragraph. See where it takes you—and do not feel compelled to use what's in the rest of the paper. Do, however, interview a doctor, dentist, mechanic, salesperson—or someone from any occupation—for ammunition to prove that writing *is* important in all occupations. See what you find out.

By the way, what *are* the keys to writing well? Try a second paragraph on this topic—taking a cue or two from this writer, but coming up with your own ideas.

Paper 10   Under the Knife (Expository, Grade 12)

Nip, tuck, trim, suck, lift, stitch, and peel. These words describe what we know as cosmetic surgery. Cosmetic or plastic surgery has over the years been tainted with the idea that it is purely vanity surgery for those of the rich and famous. But today it has evolved into much more.

Throughout the country people, in particularly women have been obsessed with the way they look. Women want to be more professional, young, and lively in order to compete with men in the work place, often times going to the extreme to get what they want.

Then there is the fashion media on TV, in books, magazines, stores and on the internet. Images of fake plastic smiles and Barbie figures are paraded in front of us, telling us in an unspoken language, this is what we should look like. This will make you happy. But is this really true? I tend to disagree.

No matter the motive the fact still remains that plastic surgery is an increasing trend in today's society that needs to be closely monitored. I don't know of one person that is completely satisfied with the way they look. Does your bust size really determine your amount of happiness and quality of life? No, it should not but does that mean cosmetic surgery is wrong? No.

Everyone is responsible to take care of their own body. So you exercise and diet correctly and everything should be under control. Some people may still not be satisfied and that's okay, as long as your health comes first. With any surgery you must look at the risks involved and weigh your choices wisely. Breast implants for example are dangerous and could cause severe problems such as poisoning or even death. This is not a wise decision. Obesity is dangerous to your health, therefore liposuction or stapling your stomach might be your best option when exercise and dieting fail.

(continued)

I believe that improving the way we look is always a good thing. But as with everything moderation is the key. Cosmetic Surgery is not a cure all. You have to like who you are on the inside first, than look at the outside and see what you can improve. If you're not happy with yourself when you go under the knife, chances are you won't be happy with your self when you come to. Looking good on the outside may improve your self esteem but not your self worth.

So what makes you a happy person, how do you improve your quality of life? By a use of many different means. Be healthy; surround yourself with things that make you happy. Don't look to the knife to make you happy, rather look at it as a means of self improvement. Everyone is an individual work of art; make it reflect the you inside.

■ **Suggested Scores for Focus Traits: Ideas and Organization**

Ideas: 4, **4**

Organization: 4, **4**

■ **Lessons Learned from Paper 10**

- Trying to round up too many ideas—even if they're related—makes organization challenging.
- A clearly expressed thesis can help to keep your reader on track.

■ **Comments**

This piece is about a draft away from achieving its potential. It has a strong title, lead, and conclusion. The voice is evolving and shows much promise. The problem is, it's hard to get a grip on what the writer thinks: Cosmetic surgery has a reputation as pure vanity surgery, women are obsessed with looks and so may take risks, the media are not helping, and surgery won't make you happy—yet "improving the way we look is always a good thing," and we should look at cosmetic surgery "as a means of self-improvement." We wind up feeling a bit confused. The writer *does* tell us that moderation is the key; perhaps this is a place to begin. She may be saying that surgery isn't a good recourse except when the need is extreme. I like the ending—"Everyone is an individual work of art." But if that's so, why do we need surgery? A better-defined thesis, clearly expressed, will give this "almost there" piece the strong sense of direction it needs—organization, voice, word choice, and fluency will all come along for the ride.

■ **Suggested Scores for Other Traits**

Voice: 4, **4**

Word choice: 3, **4**

Sentence fluency: 3, **4**

Conventions: 4, **5**

The Write Connection

"Under the Knife"

Turn this confusing discussion into a powerful persuasive essay. First, take a stand. Is cosmetic surgery a good thing for improving self-esteem or merely a superficial "fix" for people who think appearance matters more than who we are inside? Find examples (consider people who have had or performed cosmetic surgery) to back your position. You can use this writer's piece as a framework for your essay, but feel free to nip, tuck, and trim.

Paper 11   Be Happy With What You Have (Literary Analysis, Grade 3)

In the intelligent story *The Knee High Man* by Julius Lester, Lester tries to tell us that you should be happy with what you have. It is about a man that is only knee high. He soon wants to become the size of everyone else. He goes to friend after friend to ask how he can become tall, but they all just tell him nonsense. He finally goes to the owl, who is very wise, and the owl tells him that the size he is now is just fine.

Julius Lester wants us to know that we should be happy with what we have. One example is when the owl tells the knee high man that he could "climb a tree if you want to see far." The point is that he does not need to be big at all. If he ever got big, he might not even like it. If you want something you don't have, think to yourself first, "Do I really need it?"

I definitely agree with the author's message. This story reminds me of the saying, "The grass isn't always greener on the other side," and "Is the glass half full or half empty?" This story teaches readers the important lesson of thinking about whether you really need something. Maybe what you already have is just fine. If you have not learned that lesson yet, you are never too old to learn.

■ Suggested Scores for Focus Traits: Ideas and Organization

Ideas: 4, 5
Organization: 4, 5

■ Lessons Learned from Paper 11

- Good literary analysis does not require repeating the plot.
- In a strong literary analysis, the writer explains the author's point(s).
- Including at least one carefully selected quotation spices up the piece!

■ Comments

This writer tells us enough about the book *The Knee High Man* that even if we have not read it, we get the idea. She does not tediously repeat the plot. How wonderful. She gets to the main theme quickly: *We should be happy with what we have.* The piece loses a bit of momentum in the third paragraph, largely because the writer does not tell us just *how* the theme of Lester's book relates to the old sayings she quotes—and the final lines are a bit redundant. At the same time, this is a fine effort from a third grader, much stronger than "A Great Book," which is from a far older writer. The voice is strong, especially in the first paragraph: "they all just tell him nonsense." The word choice is beyond functional, though repetitious in the conclusion. Sentences are somewhat varied (*He, This story,* and *If* are repeated quite a lot) and smoothly crafted—and conventions are superb.

■ Suggested Scores for Other Traits

Voice: 4, 5
Word choice: 4, 5
Sentence fluency: 4, 5
Conventions: 5, 6

The Write Connection

"Be Happy With What You Have"

Highlight the first four words of each sentence. Then see if you can revise this piece so that each sentence begins differently.

As a second step, read *The Knee High Man* by Julius Lester. Then try revising the conclusion by either using a quotation from the story or making the connection to the old sayings this author quotes.

Paper 12   **How to Be a Good Driver** (Expository, Grade 12)

Being a good driver is not a big fat secret. I have been driving for just over two years and I know what it takes: caution, the alertness of a cat on the hunt, and knowledge of your car. It takes a little luck, too—but that part will always be beyond your control.

If you want a clean driving record like mine—no tickets, no pull-overs—you must be cautious. That's number one. I don't tailgate, and I don't barrel into intersections without looking. I don't back up till I'm sure there's no one behind me, either. Also—fussy people will appreciate this one—I don't park so close to the car next to me you need a can opener to separate us. I know banging a car door into the next guy isn't like a head-on collision—but it still causes damage, both to your car and to your mental health. Courtesy and common sense are important components of caution, you see.

Right up there with caution is a sense of alertness. I don't mean gripping the wheel with everything you've got (like I see some drivers do) and staring straight ahead like your neck won't move. Alertness means being aware of all the other vehicles around you at all times, and that includes those way, way out there in the distance (as well as those behind and to the sides). There could be an accident or stalled vehicle a half mile out, so anticipate. Assume the guy next to you will cut you off, pull right in front of you barely missing your front fender, and then slow down—for reasons known only to him and his therapist. This kind of irritating maneuver is all too common. That guy behind you? The one following too close? He doesn't know you're going to need to stop for some kid or dog that's about to run into the road. If you didn't know he was even there, that means you're not looking in your rear-view mirror enough. You should also assume that people approaching a yellow light at an intersection will storm on through. Heck—at least one guy is going to sneak through on the red. Be ready. That's what it means to be alert. It could save your life.

Finally, you need to know something about how your car works. Could you change a tire if you had to? If not, stay out of remote areas and at least have a cell phone. (Or drive with a buddy who can change tires!) Watch that gas gauge; boy, nothing ruins a good time like hiking down the road for gas. Also, don't allow people to make a lot of noise in the car. Make them wear seat belts. Keep the radio to a level where you might hear a police or fire siren a block away. Occasionally, turn the radio off so you can see if your car is making unusual noises, like the sound of a muffler scraping on pavement.

See how much of this is common sense? Yet, how much of it is included in the typical driver's test? That's right! Almost none! Know what that means? See those people out there on the highway? That's right! They're not ready to drive—but they're driving anyway! So, be defensive. Be alert, cautious, and knowledgeable, and with some luck thrown in, you'll have a chance.

■ **Suggested Scores for Focus Traits**

Ideas: 4, 5

Organization: 5, 6

■ **Lessons Learned from Paper 12**

- The five-paragraph organizational structure *can* work—IF you really do have three legitimate points to make and IF you handle transitions creatively and smoothly.

- Similarly, a summary ending can work IF you take a fresh perspective and avoid word-for-word restatement.
- Humor and understatement are as effective in expository writing as in narrative.

■ Comments

This paper is fun to read and easy to follow. The already convincing arguments could be strengthened by statistical support: e.g., the number of traffic accidents triggered by tailgating. Still, the writer is direct, confident, and not afraid to weave in humor, though he does not rely on it; he has specific points to make and delivers them clearly and forcefully. What could have dissolved into formula works this time because the writer really has three clear points to make: the need for caution, alertness, and knowledge of one's car. In this case, the structure enhances the message instead of fighting it, and that's what good organization should do. Some readers believe the language is too casual (*some kid, one guy*), though it can be argued that this conversational tone adds to the voice. Expressions like *irritating maneuver* and *storm on through* push me to a 6 in word choice.

■ Suggested Scores for Other Traits

Voice: 5, 6
Word choice: 4, 5
Sentence fluency: 5, 6
Conventions: 5, 6

The Write Connection

"How to Be a Good Driver"

Many readers object to the overall informal, sometimes conversational tone in this piece. Do you agree? With a partner, review the paper *first* to check for strong moments: Highlight any you find. You do not want to lose these! Then, check to see where you might revise the word choice to make it *slightly* more formal. (Imagine it will be published in a literary journal that does not favor informalities.) When you have made all the changes you believe are needed, read the result aloud. Is the word choice stronger? Were you able to retain the voice?

Paper 13   The Funeral of My OREO (Narrative, Grade 4)

I look at my pray, drooling, like a tiger looking at an antelope in the wet forests of India. I pounce. "Natalie," my weird brother announces his presence "be nice." I look regretfully at the hurt OREO. I had snuck a poor OREO from the vet hospital while my dog had an appointment.

I am about to tell you of the steps with which I dissect my OREO. I let it suffer slowly. I do this by, so very carefully, lifting off the top cookie so the frosting is saved.

Then, I nibble on the chocolate cookie. I do this like a mouse until it's gone. I then clean the chocolate off my face.

After that, I start to eat the rest of the cookie. I start by taking tiny bites. After I chew about a millimeter away, I eat the cookie in bigger bites.

Finally, I finish. But there's only one problem . . . I now have a whole lot of chocolate crumbs spread all over the table! The tiger in me sweeps the remains of its prey out of the den with a broom and curls up on the couch until the time comes to devour yet another OREO!

The Write Connection

"The Funeral of My OREO"

It's funny how one small hiccup can disrupt the organizational flow. Is the writer in this piece a tiger or a mouse? Make a decision and revise the piece to keep the metaphor consistent. Also, right now the last line in paragraph 1 is almost a throw-away interruption. But what if the piece started here? What if the writer used the tiger metaphor to dramatize the initial "capture" of the OREO? Try it.

Bring a little sentence fluency into play and revise so that *no sentences* begin with *I*.

■ **Suggested Scores for Focus Traits: Ideas and Organization**

Ideas: 4, 5

Organization: 5, 6

■ **Lessons Learned from Paper 13**

- One metaphor at a time.
- Let paragraphs reflect your organization.

■ **Comments**

Adopting the persona of the tiger hunting its prey is very effective—as is the interchange with the "weird" brother that snaps the writer (temporarily) back to reality. Unfortunately, the writer forgets herself briefly and turns into a mouse in paragraphs 3 and 4 (this is what lowered the ideas scores). She's back to her tiger self in the final paragraph, and a good thing too, or we'd miss the predatory sweeping of the crumbs. The tiger metaphor gives this piece plenty of voice, and the notion of a cookie as prey is irresistible. Word choice is very strong: *drooling, announces his presence, look regretfully, let it suffer, dissect, nibble, sweeps, devour.* Too many sentences begin with *I*, but this is a relatively simple thing to remedy. Conventions are strong.

■ **Suggested Scores for Other Traits**

Voice: 5, 6

Word choice: 5, 6

Sentence fluency: 3, 4

Conventions: 5, 6

Paper 14   **Computing Batting Averages** (Expository, Grade 6)

Math is all around us in almost everything we do. Math is involved in banking, shopping, the weather, the national economy and just about every thing we do. It is hard to think of even one thing that doesn't use math in one way or another.

You wouldn't think math would be such a big part of sports but it is. Take baseball for example. In baseball people use math for many things. One example is figuring out batting averages. This is important because when players see how well they are doing, they have a way to improve. How would players improve if they didn't know how well they are doing.

A batting average is really like a percentage. To find out your batting average, all you need are two numbers: how many times you are up and how many times you hit safely (meaning that you get at least to first base on a hit). Then

(continued)

you need to divide the number of times you hit safely by the total number of times you are up to bat.

Here is an example of a batting average. Lets say you are up 50 times and hit safely 25 of those times. Your batting average would look like this: 25/50. You would have a batting average of .500, which is pretty good. Suppose you hit safely every time you were up. Your batting average would then be 50/50, or 1.000—which is pronounced "one thousand". This were we get the famous saying "batting a thousand." Of course, nobody could ever bat this well in real life.

With the use of batting averages it is easy to set goals for yourself and see how well you are doing. A good batting average for a pro ball player is somewhere between .300 and .400. The all time record is held by Ted Williams, who batted .410.

My best batting average was in the summer of 1998, when I averaged .370. Maybe it was me, or maybe it was the pitching!

Think about your own life for a minute and you'll be surprised what a big role math plays.

■ Suggested Scores for Focus Traits: Ideas and Organization

Ideas: 4, **4**

Organization: 3, **4**

■ Lessons Learned from Paper 14

• Sometimes your paper starts with the second paragraph.

• You may not need that last line.

■ Comments

This paper is flanked by generalities that hurt the forcefulness of the whole piece. You don't always have to link your little point to a larger worldview. Let it go. Readers will make their own connections. The explanation of how to compute batting averages is clear and easy to follow. The voice is pleasant and reasonably engaging, although the piece is not quite a read-aloud yet. Or is it? Cut the beginning and ending, and what's left has more voice. Excellent conventions. And I'm told that the true average for Ted Williams is .406. Details, details.

■ Suggested Scores for Other Traits

Voice: 3, **4**

Word choice: 4, **4**

Sentence fluency: 4, **4**

Conventions: 5, **6**

The Write Connection

"Computing Batting Averages"

How important are the opening and closing paragraphs in this piece? Would the lead and conclusion actually be stronger if the writer began and ended with baseball? Try revising to begin and end differently, eliminating all generalities about math in our everyday lives. Is the paper stronger?

Paper 15 **Cats or Dogs** (Persuasive, Grade 6)

Cats or dogs, that is the question. My opinion is I like both. Cats are one of the most groomed animals in the world. Dogs are one of the most loyal. There are just some problems about both.

I really like cats because they are so clean. They always like to clean there selve's a lot. Most cats are very well mannered and they love people. They are also very fast. I have a cat, kind of. They really like string.

I also like dogs. They can run real fast to. I really like dogs because they can jump real high and catch a Frisbee. They can also do a lot of tricks like swimming.

There are some problems with both. I wish I could have both but it can't happen. Dogs just like to chase cats. Cats cough up fur balls. Dogs bark and eat lots of weird stuff. Now you see the reasons I like both. I really like cats. Dogs I really like to but there are some problems. I just can't decide.

■ **Suggested Scores for Focus Traits: Ideas and Organization**

Ideas: 3, **4**
Organization: 2, **2**

■ **Lessons Learned from Paper 15**

- Comparison papers need to be set up carefully.
- "I just can't decide" makes an ineffective ending.

■ **Comments**

This paper has some good points to make: Cats are clean and well groomed; they are well mannered and love people. Dogs can run, jump, and catch things (so they are fun to play with), and they make loyal pets. Each has problems: Cats "cough up fur balls," whereas dogs "eat lots of weird stuff." Two things keep ideas and organization from working well. First, the writer refers to the problems in paragraph 1, raising our expectations, but does not get to them until much later. Second, both good qualities and problems are presented essentially as lists, with minimal development. The sentence "I have a cat, kind of" is bewildering: It isn't really mine? Or it isn't really a cat? Overall, the jump from dogs to cats and back again makes the discussion hard to follow; even the writer is baffled at the end. Questions could help: *What kind of person gets along best with cats (or dogs)? If you could only have one pet, what would you pick?* Smaller issues: The conventions are fairly clean (despite "thereselves" and "to" for "too"). The word choice, by contrast, is quite simple, and the sentences are short and sometimes choppy, disrupting the fluency.

The Write Connection

"Cats or Dogs"

Organization is always easier when the writer has a clear idea or direction in mind. Which do YOU like better—cats or dogs? *Make a choice.* Then brainstorm a list of reasons why you feel as you do. Using your list, revise the paper so that it makes strong, definite, clear points about both cats and dogs—then encourages the reader to lean toward one side. No fence sitting! Oh—and once you revise the paper, you will need to change the title.

■ **Suggested Scores for Other Traits**

Voice: 3, **3**

Word choice: 2-3, **3**

Sentence fluency: 2, **3**

Conventions: 4, **4**

See Chapters 8 and 9 for numerous instructional ideas relating to ideas and organization. For more practice with revision, see *Creating Revisers and Editors* by Vicki Spandel, lessons for student writers in grades 2 through 8 (2008, Pearson Education).

Chapter 4   In a Nutshell

- Ideas form the foundation of any piece of writing.

- Strong organization showcases the ideas, so these two traits work in harmony.

- Focusing on one trait at a time is an effective way of introducing traits; gradually, we need to put them back together to create a "total package."

- Each piece of writing has specific lessons to teach about writing; choosing a paper for the lessons it teaches provides us with good models for instruction.

- Practicing revision on the text of others is a good warm-up for revising one's own writing.

Study Group   Interactive Questions and Activities

1. **Activity and Discussion.** Based on your experience scoring papers in this chapter, how would you rate your understanding of the traits of **ideas** and **organization?**

   _____ *Excellent.* I completely understand both traits and feel ready to lead students in any discussion of writing focusing on those traits.

   _____ *About halfway there.* I need to score and discuss a few more papers.

   _____ *Not there yet.* I need more practice.

2. **Discussion.** When choosing a student sample to use as a model, the grade level of the writer is far less important than selecting a paper that makes a point or illustrates a significant lesson. With this in mind, which papers from Chapter 4 might you choose to score, discuss, or revise with your students?

3. **Discussion.** Did any issues of bias discussed in Chapter 3 influence your scoring on any of the papers in Chapter 4? If so, in what way(s)?

4. **Activity and Discussion.** Rescore one of the papers from this chapter with a partner. As you

do so, use a highlighter to mark specific words or phrases in the scoring guide that influence you. Also highlight words or phrases in the *paper* that influence you. Ask your partner to do the same and then compare. Talk about how this strategy could be helpful in setting up a conference with a student writer.

5. **Activity and Discussion.** This chapter includes many lesson ideas (the Write Connection) based on focused revision: revision that targets a specific feature of the writing. Create a similar lesson based on any writing sample—from one of your students or from a publication. Keep your revision focused and manageable. Don't try to improve *everything!*

6. **Discussion.** Did you and your group use a 5- or 6-point scale for your assessment of these pieces? Was it a good choice for you? How so?

Reflections on Writing

Writing to me is like drinking a cup of hot coffee. At the beginning, it's hard to drink because it's so hot. If you drink, you'll burn yourself. That is like writing. You can't rush your ideas.

—**Ellie Oligmueller,** student writer

Sometimes writing can be like a mosquito. Pesky and annoying. Buzzing around you, as if it will never leave. Finally it bites you, and makes you itch.

—**Chelsey Santino,** student writer

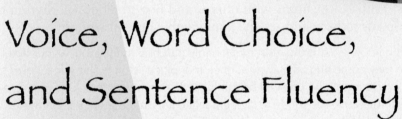

Adding Flavor

Voice, Word Choice, and Sentence Fluency

The writer must learn how to stalk the inner voice.

—**Ralph Fletcher**
What a Writer Needs, 1993, p. 69

Voice allows the reader to hear an individual human being speak from the page.

—**Donald M. Murray**
A Writer Teaches Writing, 2004, p. 21

Voice is the imprint of the writer on the page. It is the heart, soul, and breath of the writing—the spirit and the flavor. Writing without voice is lifeless, dispassionate, remote. More than any other quality, it is voice that speaks to us from the page, that calls us to a favorite chair or hammock and says, "Come with me. Come into the world of the book."

Word choice and fluency are first cousins of voice and indeed enhance voice tremendously. Voice comes, in part, from the words a writer chooses and the way he or she arranges them to create expressive and appealing rhythms. Here are two writers writing about feelings of loneliness—in very different ways. Listen to the voice of author Sandra Cisneros (1991) in this passage about "Four Skinny Trees." Notice the power of her verbs and modifiers and the way her fluency gains momentum until the last four words strike our ears like hammer blows.

> Their strength is secret. They send ferocious roots beneath the ground. They grow up and they grow down and grab the earth between their hairy toes and bite the sky with violent teeth and never quit their anger [p. 74].

Now compare the voice of travel writer Bill Bryson (2001). Notice how his phrasing (. . . *melancholy* . . . *Obviously* . . . *whip away* . . . *facing a pillar* . . .) mixes loneliness with humor and how the bouncy rhythm of his prose helps us to hear and see the annoyingly cheerful waiter.

> Do you know what is the most melancholy part of dining alone in your hotel? It's when they come and take away all the other place settings and wineglasses, as if to say, "Obviously no one will be joining you tonight, so we'll just whip away all these things and seat you here facing a pillar, and in a minute we'll bring you a very large basket with just one roll in it. Enjoy!" [p. 89].

And now, if I shared two more samples, one Bryson and the other Cisneros, you'd have no trouble telling which was which. The language and the way the writer crafted sentences each would reflect the writer's unique voice.

As in Chapter 4, I will break each of these traits out for you first, giving you a chance to read, review, and score two papers just for that trait. Then we will put foundation and flavor together, scoring papers for five traits. And as before, your purpose is twofold: first , to teach *yourself* the traits of *voice, word choice,* and *fluency* first by assessing, discussing, and reflecting on student work; and second, to discover papers you can share with your students as you teach them these same traits.

 # Voice: Fingerprints on the Page

Getting a Mindset

Voice is many things: personality, passion, engagement with the topic, energy and enthusiasm, and audience sensitivity. Because voice builds a bridge from writer to reader, it is much more than a fancy accoutrement; it is a tool for ensuring that the reader pays attention to the message. Voice comes in many guises and shifts with writer, audience, and purpose: "All writing has an intended audience, even the telephone book . . . " (O'Connor, 1999, p. 13). Most of us speak in different voices when we talk with a beloved soulmate on the phone or cheer the local football team on the field. Similarly, our writing voices can (and must) dress to suit the occasion."

> Enthusiasm is the force that keeps you going and keeps the reader in your grip.
>
> —William Zinsser
> *On Writing Well,* 2001, p. 52

FIGURE **5.1** **Trait "Shortie" for Voice**
Use this summary to introduce the trait to students.

Voice
Fingerprints on the Page

- Individual, distinctive

- A "read-aloud" piece

- Passionate, energetic

- Speaks to readers

- Confident, self-assured

- Writer is present on the page

© 2009. Allyn and Bacon, an imprint of Pearson Education, Inc.
Developed by Vicki Spandel for *Creating Writers*, Fifth Edition.

Practice Papers

What To Do

- Be sure that you have a copy of the rubric in front of you.
- Make a copy of the scoring grid (Figure 3.7) if you are working with a group.
- Make copies of papers so that you can write on them.
- Follow the same general procedures as for ideas and organization.

The Inside Track on Voice

Voice is addictive. Once you've read text that is alive with voice, it is much harder to tolerate voiceless writing. One surefire way to measure this trait is

> Voice is the quality, more than any other, that allows us to hear exceptional potential in a beginning writer; voice is the quality, more than any other, that allows us to recognize excellent writing.
>
> —Donald M. Murray
> *A Writer Teaches Writing,*
> 2004, p. 21

FIGURE **5.2** **Books (From Which) You'll Love Reading Aloud**

A Christmas Memory, by Truman Capote (1996)
Amos and Boris, by William Steig (1971)
Angela's Ashes, by Frank McCourt (1996)
Bill Nye the Science Guy's Big Blast of Science,
    by Bill Nye, Terry Marks, and Tom Owen (1993)
Bird by Bird, by Anne Lamott (1995)
Boy: Tales of Childhood, by Roald Dahl (1984)
The Catcher in the Rye, by J. D. Salinger (1951)
Charles Kuralt's America, by Charles Kuralt (1995)
Charlotte's Web, by E. B. White (1974)
Cosmos, by Carl Sagan (1980)
Fables, by Arnold Lobel (1983)
Fried Green Tomatoes at the Whistle Stop Café,
    by Fannie Flagg (new edition, 2005)
George and Martha, by James Marshall (2000)
Guts, by Gary Paulsen (2001)
The House on Mango Street, by Sandra Cisneros (1991)
In a Sunburned Country, by Bill Bryson (2001)
Iron Man, by Chris Crutcher (1995)
The Kite Runner, by Khaled Hosseini (2003)
Leaving Home, by Garrison Keillor (1987)
Lonesome Dove, by Larry McMurtry (1988)

Matilda, by Roald Dahl (1988)
My Thirteenth Winter, by Samantha Abeel (2003)
Name Me Nobody, by Lois-Ann Yamanaka (2000)
No More Dead Dogs, by Gordon Korman (2000)
Out of the Dust, by Karen Hesse (2005)
Pictures of Hollis Woods, by Patricia Reilly Giff (2005)
The Pooh Story Book, by A. A. Milne (1996)
A Prayer for Owen Meany, by John Irving (1989)
Puppies, Dogs and Blue Northers: Reflections on Being
    Raised by a Pack of Sled Dogs, by Gary Paulsen
    (new edition, 2005)
Seabiscuit, by Laura Hillenbrand (2001)
SeinLanguage, by Jerry Seinfeld (1993)
Sleeping Ugly, by Jane Yolen (1997)
Small Wonder (Essays), by Barbara Kingsolver (2002)
Squids Will Be Squids, by Jon Scieszka (2003)
Tar Beach, by Faith Ringgold (1991)
The Teacher's Funeral, by Richard Peck (2004)
This Land Is My Land, by George Littlechild (2003)
To Kill a Mockingbird, by Harper Lee (1960,
    renewed 1988)
Tuesdays with Morrie, by Mitch Albom (2003)
Vintage Cisneros, by Sandra Cisneros (2004)
Wild Thoughts from Wild Places, by David Quammen
    (1998)
A Writer Teaches Writing, by Donald M. Murray (2004)

> Use writing to tell what you saw and experienced and believe. Use writing to tell what you *come* to believe. Don't be circumspect. Don't be mealymouthed. Drive to the heart with detail.
>
> —Tom Romano
> *Crafting Authentic Voice*,
> 2004, p. 49

to ask whether you feel an irresistible urge to share a piece aloud. Think of the books that you like reading to students. I don't mean those you feel you *should* read but those you cannot wait to dive into. See Figure 5.2 for a brief list of books from which I like to take read-aloud moments.

Books that resound with voice are easy to read with expression because the author's sheer joy in the writing comes through in every line. Similarly, if a student's writing has voice, you may feel like tugging someone's sleeve. "Listen to this," you hear yourself saying. You will not feel compelled to share "The Redwoods." This is how you'll know.

Paper 1   **Why You Need a Job** (Persuasive, Grade 9)

Young adults in our country need to learn more responsibility, and having a job while you are going to school is one way to get there.

Many times, young kids take their lives and theyre parents for granit. Parents have been around to care for them as long as they can remember. But it doesnt last forever. Sooner or later you will be out on your own without one clue of your life or responsibility. A job teaches kids to care for themselves without help from their parents. To buy things like clothes and insurance. Jobs are not just about money though. A job shows you how to get a long with people out side your family. A job is good for your future. It introduces you to new skills and new people. This paper gives solid reasons for getting a job while you are in school. Do it. You will not be sorry.

■ Suggested Scores for Focus Trait: Voice

Voice: 3, **3**

■ Lessons Learned from Paper 1

- Generalities weaken voice.
- Persuasive writing requires persuasive examples.

■ Comments

Instead of crafting an argument, the writer simply states an opinion, and generalities squeeze the life right out of it: A job gives you experience, teaches you new skills, and is good for your future. The beginning is fairly forceful, and if the writer had sustained this level of voice, the paper could have become truly persuasive. Notice that voice emerges in spurts—*"you will be out on your own without one clue of your life"*—but quickly retreats. It picks up the tempo in the conclusion: *"Do it."* But by then we're tired. This is functional voice at best and does not seem directed to any specific audience.

■ Suggested Scores for Other Traits

Ideas: 2, 3
Organization: 2, 2
Word choice: 3, 4
Sentence fluency: 3, 4
Conventions: 3, 3

The Write Connection

"Why You Need a Job"

Tom Romano (author of *Crafting Authentic Voice*) tells us that voice is mostly about telling the truth—"Not THE truth," he emphasizes, but "your truth" (2004, p. 49). So do that. Think about how YOU feel about the importance of getting a job. What does it really teach a person? It isn't the perfect experience, is it? What are some of the difficulties or hurdles? Now see if you can make "Why You Need a Job" a little edgier just by saying very honestly how you really feel. Hold nothing back. When you read your revision aloud, do you hear the difference?

Paper 2   Zeena and the Marshmallows (Persuasive/Narrative, Grade 5)

Zeena, I know just how you feel. I love chocolate covered marshmellows too! But let me tell you what happened to me.

My mom came home from the store one day and let me have a chocolate covered marshmellow. It was love at first bite. So lite, fluffy, chewy and slipped down my throat like a small piece of heaven. Just thinking about it makes me want to have another one until I recall what happened when I finished my last bag of those squishy delights.

My mom told me I can help myself to a few and before I knew it the whole bag was gone. My mom called me to dinner, and you know, the last thing I wanted or even cared about was dinner, but you know how mothers are, I had to sit down and take one bite of everything. And after that, I had diaria, diaria, diaria. But I was convinced it wasn't the marshmellows.

Last fall my mom bought me all of these cute clothes for my birthday, shorts, jeans, skirts, so when the weather got warm, and I went to put on my new clothes, they didn't fit to my amazement and not because I had grown too tall, just because I couldn't even zip them up. But it couldn't be the marshmellows, their too lite and fluffy; infact a whole bag of marshmellows doesn't weight as much as one orange.

One day, when I put the tight clothes out of my mind, I grabbed myself some chocolate covered marshmellows, when I was biting down on one, a sharp stabbing pain went up my tooth and the side of my head. And when ever I ate, my teeth hurt. So my mom took me to the dentist, and let me tell you it was not a pretty picture. I had seven expensive, painful cavities.

So Zeena, you can keep popping those marshmellows into your mouth, but before you do, remember not everything about chocolate covered marshmellows is sweet.

■ **Suggested Scores for Focus Trait: Voice**

Voice: 5, 6

The Write Connection

"Zeena & the Marshmallows"

"Zeena and the Marshmallows" is a favorite with readers everywhere—especially when it's read aloud. There are a number of little editorial problems—which usually go overlooked by readers enjoying the humor. See how many you can find. Edit "Zeena" so it's ready to go to press.

■ **Lessons Learned from Paper 2**

• Anecdotes enhance voice and clarity.
• When we identify with the situation, we feel the writer reaching out to us.

■ **Comments**

"Zeena and the Marshmallows" is a knockout in voice. This young writer speaks right to her audience, and the main thing we want to say is, "Thank you for helping us understand why diets do not work." It's that dieter's logic: "A whole bag of marshmallows doesn't weigh as much as one orange." Strong imagery enhances the voice—"*slipped down my throat like a small piece of heaven . . . I had to sit down and take one bite . . . couldn't even zip them up . . . a sharp, stabbing pain went up my tooth.*" Readers love the way this writer pokes fun at herself, along with the dieting world. Although basically persuasive, this paper (contrast Paper 1) uses three humorous anecdotes to make the point. It's a good technique. Many of us can identify with the bingeing, the tight clothes—even the trip to the dentist. A relevant story is nearly always more compelling than a bulleted list.

■ **Suggested Scores for Other Traits**

Ideas: 5, 6
Organization: 5, 5
Word choice: 4-5, 4
Sentence fluency: 4, 5
Conventions: 3-4, 4

Word Choice:
The Bridge from Message to Voice

Getting a Mindset

Choose the just right word, and a simple image creates a world of meaning—and feeling. In Laurie Halse Anderson's classic Speak, the narrator drowns in the despair of her alienation: "I dive into the stream of fourth-period lunch students and swim down the hall to the cafeteria" (1999, p. 7). We not only see the action, but feel it in our joints and muscles with Jane Leavy's reverent description of pitcher Sandy Koufax: "The right knee, as it rose, seemed to touch his elbow. His toe extended like a dancer on point. For an instant he seemed in equipoise, his back leg a pedestal. It was his only point of contact with the earth. Every other part of his body was flying" (2002, p. 12). David Quammen's haunting portrayal of the zoo tiger, its wilder self numbed by dependency on humans, leaves a distinct chill in the air: "When a human looks deep into the eyes of a zoo animal . . . the human is alone" (1998, p. 89).

The Inside Track on Word Choice

Pretend that you're holding a yellow marker in your hand, and imagine that you are going to highlight each

FIGURE **5.3** **Trait "Shortie" for Word Choice**
Use this summary to introduce the trait to students.

Word Choice
Phrasing & Terminology

- Clear, aids readers' understanding

- Original, memorable

- Concise

- Natural

- Filled with strong verbs

- No modifier "overload"

- Paints word pictures

© 2009. Allyn and Bacon, an imprint of Pearson Education, Inc. Developed by Vicki Spandel for *Creating Writers,* Fifth Edition.

word or phrase within a student's paper that strikes you or captures your attention—words and phrases that seem right or noteworthy or commanding in some way. Perhaps you wish you'd written them, or you think, "I never heard it said quite like that." Your word-choice score is a function of how often the words and phrases grab your attention. Every line? That's a 6. Often? That's a 4 or 5. Now and then? Perhaps a 3. Rarely or never? That's a 2 or 1.

> Adjectives and adverbs are rich and good and fattening. The main thing is not to overindulge.
> —Ursula K. LeGuin
> *Steering the Craft,* 1998, p. 61

> I haunt used-book stores, searching for books that contain unusual words. *Elementary Seamanship* has a glossary of sea terms: *scupper, bulwark, winch, windlass, scuttles.* The book is a cup of possibility for those days when I'm thirsty for words.
> —Georgia Heard
> *Writing Toward Home,* 1995, p. 47

Paper 3   Chad (Descriptive, Grade 3)

My friend is great because likes the same things I do. His name is Chad.

If theres nothing to do around the house, we get together and do stuff. I phone him up or he phones me. He's a real neat person. He's fun to do stuff with because we mostly like the same games and TV shows. He comes to my house or I go to his house. He has brown hair and is tall, about five feet! It is cool having a friend who is alot like you and likes the stuff you like. Chad is my friend.

■ Suggested Scores for Focus Trait: Word Choice

Word choice: 2, **3**

■ Lessons Learned from Paper 3

- Words like *stuff* and *things* carry almost no meaning.
- We crave words that help us picture what the writer is talking about.

■ Comments

This paper has the beginnings of a character sketch, but Chad has not become a person yet. We know that he's "neat," "great," and "fun" to be with and that it's "cool" having him for a friend, but we need the clarity of a good close-up to help us see Chad and experience the "stuff" these friends do together. Tired words kill any message. Imagine this paper with just two strong verbs and specific replacements for *stuff, neat, cool,* and *great.* Tiny changes could shoo the fog away.

■ Suggested Scores for Other Traits

Ideas: 2-3, **3**

Organization: 2, **2**

Voice: 3, **3**

Sentence fluency: 3, **3**

Conventions: 4, **4**

The Write Connection

"Chad"

"Chad" is an excellent candidate for revision—and the strategy is simple. Revise by deleting the words *great, things, stuff, neat, fun,* and *cool.* You might find another word or phrase to use instead—or use an example to show what is so *great, fun,* etc. Don't be afraid to invent details. To revise with power, you must write as if you are an authority on the topic, so pretend you know Chad well, and base the character on someone you DO know.

Pets Are Forever: An Investigative Report (Expository, Grade 8)

Many pet owners worry about that difficult day when they must say goodbye for the last time. A new method of preservation could make that day a whole lot easier. It's a sort of mummification of the 90s, minus the fuss of wrapping and the mess of embalming fluid. The new method, believe it or not, involves freeze drying your pet. It's clean, relatively affordable (compared to the cost of a live pet), produces authentic results, and enables you to keep Fluffy beside you on the couch forever, if you wish.

Freeze drying is really a simple procedure. First, highly trained technicians remove all the pet's internal organs. They do leave muscle tissue and bones intact, however, so there will be something to freeze dry. They replace the eyes with lifelike glass marbles in the color of choice. A special procedure temporarily reverses the effects of rigor mortis, allowing the owner to pose the pet as he or she wishes—sitting, lying down, curled by the fire, about to pounce, and so on. It is important to work quickly before the effects of rigor mortis resume. As a finishing touch, the technician uses special blow dryers with a fine nozzle to make the pet look more lifelike. One client posed her cat in the litterbox; apparently, that was her most striking memory of "Tiger."

Freeze drying costs from $500 to $1,000, depending on the size of the pet and the complexity of the final pose. "About to strike" is more expensive than, say, "napping by the woodstove." The entire procedure takes about six months, but satisfied clients claim the wait is worth it. After all, once the pet is returned, you have him or her forever—maintenance-free except for occasional re-fluffing of the fur. Technicians report that freeze-dried pets hold up best in a relatively low-humidity, dust-free environment.

Experts also offer one final piece of advice: It is NOT recommended that pet owners try freeze drying their own pets. Proper equipment and experience are essential if you wish your pet to bear a true resemblance to his or her old self.

■ **Suggested Scores for Focus Trait: Word Choice**

Word choice: 5, 6

■ **Lessons Learned from Paper 4**

• Simple, natural language has power.

• If you enjoy writing it, the reader will enjoy reading it.

■ **Comments**

One secret to putting voice into expository writing is to like the topic. Clearly, this writer does. We get the idea that she is mildly horrified by the idea of freeze-drying and stuffing a pet, yet also intrigued. The humor in this piece is ironic, extremely understated, and highly controlled for a writer this age. Who can help recoiling but snickering at the image of Tiger posed in the litter box? Notice that her language is technically correct yet totally natural: *"mummification of the 90s," "A special procedure temporarily reverses the effects of rigor mortis," "'About to strike' is more expensive than, say, 'Napping by the woodstove.'"* Awareness of audience is very strong, adding

The Write Connection

"Pets Are Forever: An Investigative Report"

Play with the language this writer puts at our fingertips by writing an advertisement for a company that provides freeze-drying services for family pets.

to voice. Each word and phrase seems chosen for impact. The prose is direct, forceful, and crisp, appropriate for expository writing with flair.

- **Suggested Scores for Other Traits**

    Ideas: 5, 6

    Organization: 5, 6

    Voice: 5, 6

    Sentence fluency: 5, 6

    Conventions: 5, 6

Sentence Fluency: Variety and Rhythm

Getting a Mindset

Reading aloud is essential to understanding and scoring sentence fluency. You must hear the writing—put it in motion. Where does the emphasis go? Where do the beats fall? Is repetition purposeful and dramatic, or does it strike the ear like a wrong note? In most instances variety is the soul of fluency. Variety in length. Variety in beginnings. Variety in structure. Sometimes, though, as in the example I have just created, repetition reinforces a key word or idea. Listen. Your ear will tell you the difference: "It was the best of times, it was the worst of times, it was the age of wisdom, it was the age of foolishness, it was the epoch of disbelief, it was the epoch of incredulity, it was the season of light, it was the season of darkness, it was the spring of hope, it was the winter of despair . . ." (Charles Dickens, A Tale of Two Cities, 1859, p. 1).

FIGURE 5.4   Trait "Shortie" for Sentence Fluency
Use this summary to introduce the trait to students.

Sentence Fluency
Rhythm & Flow

- Easy to read

- Enhances voice

- Variety in length, structure

- Easy-on-the-ear rhythm, cadence

- Natural dialogue

- Fragments, if used, add punch, flavor

- Repetition, if used, adds emphasis

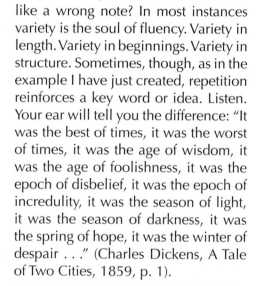

© 2009. Allyn and Bacon, an imprint of Pearson Education, Inc.
Developed by Vicki Spandel for *Creating Writers*, Fifth Edition.

The Inside Track on Sentence Fluency

Read the text aloud. Don't be inhibited, or you'll wind up scoring your own inhibition and not what's in the text. Imagine that you are trying out for a highly competitive part in a stage play; you won't get the part unless you summon every bit of emotional fiber within you and project. *Now* read. Does the text help you to give a good performance? Can you awaken that sleepy guy in the back row? Do you feel as if you're floating from one sentence to the next almost effortlessly? If so, you know the fluency is strong.

■ Caution on Conventions!

What if there's no punctuation? When addressing fluency, read for rhythm and flow, and do some light mental editing with punctuation as needed. If that light editing puts everything in order, the real problem is with *conventions*. Editing may not be sufficient, however. Capitals and periods alone will not solve problems caused by choppy sentences, repetitive structure, or endless connectives. If restructuring is needed, the problem is with fluency—*as well as* conventions.

> Writing is talk on paper. . . . And for centuries before humans wrote, they told stories and passed information along orally. Even when they began to write, the flavor of orality remained.
>
> —Tommy Thomason
> *WriteAerobics: 40 Workshop Exercises to Improve Your Writing Teaching,* 2003, p. 21

Paper 5 **A Rescue** (Narrative, Grade 4)

Once a bunch of my frieneds and I went to this old hounted house and I'm not talking about some amusement park thing or something like that but but this was a for real hounted house, but we couldn't go in because we were too scared and my friend Robert kept making these jokes that made us laugh so hard we couldn't walk so we just kept talking about should we do it or not?.

So the next day we went back and this time we followed Robert into the front door and I was right behind him and I could hear him breathing in this kind of panting way and I told him to keep quiet or he would wake up the gosts. So just then I saw something real creepy move in the corner of the kitchen, and robert said Shhhh its only a stray cat but I said ha I don't think so buddy in a million years so I took off like a rocket from the moon and waited outside in the fog that was nice and creepy and then I saw the thing again and this time I knew it was too big for a cat so I ran back into the house to save my freniends. I grabed Robert by his hair and he let out this inormous shreek but I had to get him out of the monster's claws and I pulled and pulled and finally got him out of the house and he said what in the name of holey moley are you doing?? I had yainked some of his hair clean out of his head and he didn't like it much. I gues he didn't apreschiate beging saved from the gost so I took off for home to have dinner. And then had dinner and went to bed and that is the last time we went to that house, but me and Robert still are best friends as long as I don't pull his hair.

> If you ride, think of a horse's gaits: walk, trot, canter, gallop. If you're musical, use your toe or an imaginary baton to mark the tempo: adagio, andante, allegro, presto. Think of an oncoming train, the waves of the sea, wheels on a cobblestone street.
>
> —Patricia T. O'Connor
> *Words Fail Me,* 1999, p. 79

■ Suggested Scores for Focus Trait: Sentence Fluency

Sentence fluency: 1-2, **2**

The Write Connection

"A Rescue"

Where should the sentences really fall in this piece? Read it aloud, carefully. Then, try revising to "disconnect," eliminating most of the *and's*, *but's*, and *so's*. See how many creative ways you can find to begin sentences, always showing the connections between ideas. Right now this piece is punctuated as if it had only seven sentences. How many do you wind up with after revising for fluency?

■ **Lessons Learned from Paper 5**

• When the reader gets breathless, fluency is usually the problem.

• Endless connectives (*and, and so, so then*) not only impair fluency but also make ideas difficult to follow.

■ **Comments**

While this stream-of-consciousness style may echo the way some people speak, it can cause the reader to lose all sense of the message. Joining clauses like links in a chain creates the illusion that ideas are related, even though the writer has supplied no real transitions or thoughtful connections. It could be argued that this breathless flow reflects how people really feel when exploring a haunted house; I would be more persuaded that the writer were doing this deliberately if he shifted out of it at the end, but he does not. On the bright side, the piece has moments of voice and effective word choice—strengths on which to build. (Note that punctuation alone will not correct the problem.)

■ **Suggested Scores for Other Traits**

Ideas: 2, 3

Organization: 2, 2

Voice: 4, 4

Word choice: 3, 4

Conventions: 2, 3

Paper 6   **The Mysteries of Birds of Prey**
(Informational, Grade 5)

Auburn speckled wings stretch out as the soundless bird swoops down from the horizon. Birds like this one catch prey and are admired by many for their grace and beauty. These birds have many interesting adaptations in their daily life: Strong, sharp talons and a razor sharp beak for tearing prey. But, there is more that you don't know about these brilliant animals.

Birds of prey are probably most well known for their impressive hunting skills. First, they scan the area for any scuttling creature. When they have found their target, they swoop down and capture the petrified animal. Then they swallow it whole—fur and bones. You might be surprised to know that different birds eat many different animals. The owl eats small birds, mice, and insects. The Pygmy Owl, only six inches, eats small birds, lizards, and bugs. Have you ever heard of a bird that eats already dead animals? If not, I have a headline: You're about to find out!

A vulture is a scavenger or animal that finishes scraps. Pretend that a gazelle was killed. A lion ate half and then left. The vulture would come back

(continued)

to the carcass and finish it off. The Cape Griffon feeds its young small bones to make their bones strong. But it's an extraordinary help to people. For example, it removes dead creatures so diseases don't spread. Its sense of smell is so great it can help humans find gas leaks. Another bird of prey is a black kite and let's just say it has an interesting appearance.

Kites are lightweight birds that live in Europe, Africa, Asia, and Australia. Its appearance is a jet black body with a forked tail. It is a scavenger and predator, and eats just about anything. Hundreds of them can be seen flying overhead in tropical places.

So as you know, talons, beaks, and a witty mind are all things birds of prey possess. When you next see a bird of prey, think about their lifestyle and what magnificent creatures they are.

> The act of reading aloud isn't drudgery. It is bliss. I'm doing the important work of crafting a linguistic musical score.
> —Tom Romano
> *Crafting Authentic Voice,* 2004, p. 142

■ Suggested Scores for Focus Trait: Sentence Fluency

Sentence fluency: 5, 6

■ Lessons Learned from Paper 6

- A vivid image makes a good lead for an informational piece.
- Informational writing does not need to be a list of facts; it can include drama—and voice.

■ Comments

This piece shows striking sentence variety. It is easy to read aloud. Word choice is also very strong: *speckled wings, soundless bird swoops down, interesting adaptations, impressive hunting skills, scuttling creature, finishes scraps, lightweight birds, witty mind, scavenger and predator.* Use of strong verbs gives energy to the piece, and in addition, the writer is sufficiently comfortable with pertinent terminology to give the writing an authoritative flavor. Engagement with the topic and confidence (from having good information at her fingertips) makes the voice especially strong. The details are numerous—and satisfying. We are left with *some* questions, though: How does the Cape Griffon help find gas leaks? If the vulture feeds on carcasses, is it still considered a bird of prey? The paper focuses primarily on birds' hunting practices, so the title misleads us just a bit. Just what is *mysterious* about these birds? Or did the writer really mean *fascinating*? The organization is reasonably easy to follow. The lead and conclusion are well done, and transitions are helpful—even if the writer makes sudden leaps at times (from the Cape Griffon and gas leaks to the black kite). Excellent conventions—though paragraphs in the second half do not always seem to begin in the right spots.

The Write Connection

"The Mysteries of Birds of Prey"

Look up Cape Griffon on the Web or from another source. See if you can find information to help this writer answer the question: Exactly how does the Cape Griffon help humans find gas leaks?

Check out *Birds of Prey: A Look at Daytime Raptors* by Sneed B. Collard (Franklin Watts, 2000). This fascinating informational text may give you just the insight you need to create an even stronger conclusion for this piece. Finally, see if you can come up with a title that connects more closely with the body of the text.

■ **Suggested Scores for Other Traits**

Ideas: 4, 5

Organization: 4, 5

Voice: 5, 6

Word choice: 5, 6

Conventions: 5, 6

Looking at Additional Papers

Papers in the remainder of this chapter offer additional scoring practice on five traits: *ideas, organization, voice, word choice,* and *sentence fluency*. (Scores for conventions are also given, but the practice will focus on these five.)

Paper 7   **A Sunflower Seed** (Expository/Reflective, Grade 5)

Now most people I know would think something like a football is most important but this sunflower seed ment a lot to me. It helped me understand the struggles and needs to stay alive in this world. How the seed needed water to live, and that water to me represented the thirst to stay alive. How it needed the sun to grow, and that sun is like our need to be with others.

I thought the sunflower seed died because it had been more than week since I had planted it. The next morning, a clot of dirt was being held midair by the sunflower, so I choped up the dirt to make it softer so the sunflower could grow easyer. In life you have to eas up on other people so they can relax in growing up and don't have to push or force their way up. In life there will be people that will hold you back from what you want (just like the dirt) and you have to break free from them if you want to live your own life.

Just like the seed you must prosper or life will pass you by.

The Write Connection

"A Sunflower Seed"

This writer is responding to a prompt asking him to consider an important object in his life. Hence the reference to the football in the lead. If a reader did not know about the prompt, could the lead be confusing? Revise it so a reader coming to this paper with no knowledge of the prompt would still understand the football reference.

■ **Suggested Scores**

Ideas: 5, 6

Organization: 5, 6

Voice: 5, 6

Word choice: 5, 5

Sentence fluency: 5, 5

Conventions: 4, 4

■ **Lessons Learned from Paper 7**

- Go for the unique topic—the sunflower seed, not the football.
- Strong voice doesn't have to be emotional, just heartfelt.

■ **Comments**

The philosophical message and tone of this piece are very strong. The sunflower seed metaphor works well; it is like the hub of a wheel, to which all other ideas connect. Few papers are so well centered. Organization (along with voice) is a real strength here. Here's a writer speaking from reflective experience. The paper makes us think and makes us want to "[ease] up on other people" and encourage them to do the same for us. Words are simple but carry weight. The writer uses fragments, but they work. Conventions need some attention.

Paper 8   **Reflecting on Saba and History** (Memoir, Grade 7)

Hail to the Queen! My first name Saba comes from the legendary Queen of Sheba from Ethiopia. The sound of my name is like a soothing, calm, relaxing, warm bath. My name has many meanings in different languages. In Swahili, Saba means seven. In Hebrew, it means "wise and knowing grandfather." In Spanish, Saba is a form of the verb "to know." In Persian, it is a poetic term referring to the "Aha moment" when a reader understands the meaning of a poem or achieves enlightenment. In Indian, Saba means community or group.

My name reminds me of the color red, which happens to be one of my favorite colors. It is like biting into a juicy strawberry.

I am the older of two siblings. As the firstborn, I am supposed to be a natural leader and high achiever, as well as punctual and organized. I think being a leader and high achiever describe me best. I am also—as a firstborn—supposed to be moody and lack sensitivity. I highly disagree. These things do not fit my personality.

Under the Chinese calendar, I am a Rooster. My "rooster" personality states that I am an early riser and very industrious, proud, single-purposed, and quick. Also, it states that I tend to express myself in speech, writing, and music. I agree with all these traits.

My zodiac sign is Virgo. It states that I am modest, a worrier, shy, reliable, and intelligent. I believe that I fit the traits of being reliable and intelligent, but disagree that I am shy or a worrier. I am a very outgoing person and do not worry.

Hmm... what am I going to name my kids? I have never given it much thought. But as time goes by, I know I will find the perfect name. As for me, I might be named after a great queen, but I want to be known simply as . . . Saba.

The Write Connection

"Reflecting on Saba and History"

Read the chapter called "My Name" from Sandra Cisneros's book *The House on Mango Street* (Random House, 1991). Use this chapter together with Saba's paper to inspire a piece on your own name. You may wish to check the significance of your birthdate in other cultures (as Saba has done), as well as the history and meaning of your name. You might also consider sharing thoughts on how much you like (or dislike) your name, as well as nicknames you prefer and what they mean to you.

■ **Suggested Scores**

Ideas: 4, 5

Organization: 4, 5

Voice: 4, 5

Word choice: 5, 6

Sentence fluency: 4, 5

Conventions: 5, 6

■ **Lessons Learned from Paper 8**

- Personal connections build voice.
- Examples and images are essential in fully developing ideas.

■ **Comments**

This unusual piece is clear and easy to follow. Ideas are thoughtfully expressed, and the paper is intriguing with an underlying sense of commitment to the topic. The first paragraph is particularly strong. The voice comes through loud and clear when the writer tells how her name reminds her of a warm bath or biting into a strawberry. In the second half of the paper, we get more generalizations: e.g., *I am a very outgoing person and do not worry.* Just the same, we sense the writer's conviction about her identity. The organizational flow is smooth and orderly—here's what my name means, what it reminds me of, connection to Chinese calendar, connection to the zodiac, and thoughts of naming my children. The ending would work even better if the writer had a name or two in mind (or names she plans to avoid). Many sentences begin with "I" or "My," but otherwise, fluency is good. Word choice and conventions are both strong.

Paper 9   Reflections on Writing (Personal Essay, Grade 12)

"Maisha, what do you want to be when you grow up?" everyone used to ask me. I'd look up from my Crayola stick figures and recite, "An author and illustrator of children's books," then go back to my coloring. But as I stumbled through middle school, my concrete dreams broke apart. I considered being a teacher, an advertisement designer, a nurse. The truth was—I didn't know what I wanted to do.

My first two years of high school I struggled through mainstream Lit classes, bored with superficial literary analysis and the formulaic essays it produced. Maybe I wasn't cut out to be a writer after all. Then, in my junior year, I signed up for Advanced Creative Writing. The teacher breezed into the first class of the semester late, clutching a coffee mug and an overflowing purse, and sporting a baseball cap pulled low in an attempt to contain her bad hair

(continued)

day. "Put the desks in a circle, my darlings," she said, accidentally dropping her mug and spilling half the contents of her purse onto a table. One of my friends had warned me about this earlier, in just three words: "Comfort is awesome." She was right.

The class was different from the beginning. The teacher was not some god-like dictator preaching to us from the front of the room. She was just Rosey, real and human, an aspiring writer like the rest of us. Every day was a surprise. The days Rosey showed up with a lesson plan, Nick or Michael or Kaz showed up with performance pieces, music they had mixed, and their own lesson plan. Instead of quashing our enthusiasm, Rosey encouraged us. Discussions were capricious, uncensored. Every clique in the school was represented: jocks, anime geeks, Goths, punks, Lit nerds, rockers, skaters, and preps, brought together by a common interest. Our social differences vanished in that classroom. We learned from each other and about each other—and inevitably, ourselves.

Every single one of us wanted to be there. We were not writing for grades on transcripts. We were writing for ourselves and the world. We put teenage epiphanies to paper and offered up our truths for scrutiny. For the first time in my scholastic experience, I was allowed to be myself. I was not assigned a desk on which to cement myself. I'd been doing that for years—and it hadn't been working. Now I perched on a windowsill, ruled the top of a desk, hid beneath it, lounged in a beanbag chair, spread myself on the floor. I was free.

I was not assigned inane tasks. I took advantage of this expressionistic freedom, allowing my whims to lead me. I was an explorer. I eagerly sampled stream-of-consciousness, dialogues, short stories, slam poetry. This was my niche. English divorced from a rulebook. After a deeply inspiring overnight Creative Writing Retreat, I made a decision: I wanted to use the power of words to open the eyes of the world to the paradox that our differences unite us. I wanted people to understand that even though we all come from different places, we all have voices and we all have a story to tell. I had circled back to my childhood dream.

■ **Suggested Scores**

Ideas: 5, 6

Organization: 5, 6

Voice: 5, 6

Word choice: 5, 6

Sentence fluency: 5, 6

Conventions: 5, 6

The Write Connection

"Reflections on Writing"
Read through the "Reflections" paper and highlight each word or phrase you find striking. Talk with a partner about what makes those moments work. Now, pull out a piece of your own work—anything you are currently revising—and do the same. Then underline any three words or phrases you would like to make stronger. With your partner, brainstorm some possibilities. Remember the power of honesty, showing the true picture—whether it's the bad-hair-camouflaging baseball cap or the student hiding beneath the desk.

■ **Lessons Learned from Paper 9**

- When it comes to voice, nothing beats honesty.
- The teacher having a bad hair day is far more interesting than the perfect teacher.
- When lead and conclusion connect, they hold the piece together.

■ **Comments**

Here's a writer who says just what is on her mind in a no-nonsense, no-holds-barred kind of voice that I find irresistible. She has a knack for finding just the right word for the moment: *clutching a coffee mug and an overflowing purse, quashing our enthusiasm, Discussions were capricious, uncensored, assigned a desk on which to cement myself, ruled the top of a desk.* Other writers may have had thoughts like these—but not many have said it so well. Notice the forceful parallel structure: *perched on a windowsill, ruled the top of a desk, hid beneath it, lounged in a beanbag chair, spread myself on the floor.* This piece is not only powerful, but graceful as well. The picture of the teacher with the baseball cap hiding her bad hair day and the overflowing purse ought to be in a film script. All traits are strong, but it is the voice that drives home the message.

Paper 10   **Fishing** (Narrative/Expository, Grade 11)

"I'm jumping out," I yelled frantically to my father. It was in response to the flopping northern Pike that was near my feet in our boat. I was six and on my first trip to Canada to fish. It was a totally different fishing experience than I was accustomed to in Pennsylvania. It was not like catching Bluegills in Leaser Lake. Surely I had a right to be scared. The Northern Pike is an extremely mean looking fish with sharp teeth which it uses to kill its prey. Being six, I thought I was on its list of prey. My father responded to my plea by saying, "Go ahead and jump, but there are a hundred more in that water."

Most of my knowledge and love of fishing came from that same man who told me to "Go ahead and jump." Since I can remember, I have always fished. My father probably taught me to fish before I could walk. At first he taught me the basics: tying a swivel to a line, threading the line through the pole, removing hooks from any part of the body that they may enter, how to get a lure out of a tree, why to check the inside of hip boots that have been sitting in the garage all year before putting them on, if the sign says "No Fishing—Violators will be prosecuted," it usually means it, and probably most important, if you have to go to the bathroom while on the boat what to do. Occasionally, he also revealed a

(continued)

hot tip while fishing, such as, "See this lure, son? This one is going to catch the big one. It's only legal in two states and this isn't one of them."

The key to fishing, I was taught, is patience. Obviously, my father has a little of that if he could teach me to fish. There were numerous occasions when I crossed my line with his and caused a "rat's nest," or the several times that I used a lure and forgot to close the tackle box, and when he picked it up, all the lures fell out. One time he really showed his patience when I reached back in the boat to cast, but accidentally hooked onto his hat and threw it into the water. My brother and I laughed hysterically while I reeled it in through the water. Eventually, my father joined in.

Since I was young, there was one aspect of fishing my father heavily emphasized. Fishing is not about the amount of fish you catch, but the amount of fun you have. There were times when we wouldn't catch one fish but would still have a great time. I learned fishing is a time to just be with nature and your thoughts, a time to relax and share good times with friends. Anyone who only cares about catching fish all the time is missing the true meaning. Fishing is like an education. It is a lifelong experience. After high school, you could go to college and get a Bachelor's degree. In fishing, if you graduate from regular fishing, you could go on to ice fishing or maybe deep sea fishing. Then, if you move on to get your Master's degree, maybe you could start fly fishing.

One day, I will be teaching my kids to fish and will probably hear them complain about not catching any fish. I will think for a minute what Pop would say: "The worst day of fishing is better than the best day of work."

The Write Connection

"Fishing"

With a paper as strong as this one, tweaking just one moment can make a difference. Notice how the writer begins by painting a clear scene: wanting to jump from the boat to escape the jaws of the Northern Pike. Now look at paragraph 3. Here he states, "One time he [meaning Dad] really showed his patience . . ." Craft a scenario for this scene that is as vivid as the opening lines. Help the reader see the hook fly through the air—and then take Dad's hat with it. Use some dialogue so we hear Dad speak. See what a difference a small "movie moment" can make.

■ **Suggested Scores**

Ideas: 5, 6

Organization: 5, 6

Voice: 5, 6 (7 really)

Word choice: 4, 4

Sentence fluency: 5, 6

Conventions: 5, 6

■ **Lessons Learned from Paper 10**

- Begin right in the middle of things.
- Tell the truth because in the end we want Dad to be human—not perfect.

■ **Comments**

There is so much to love about this paper, from Dad giving the wonderful tip about the illegal lure to the son's recognition of a parent's patience when he spills the contents of the tackle box or uses Dad's hat for casting practice. The voice seems to echo the reverence this writer feels for his father and for the magic of fishing. The beginning and ending are trophy winners. Notice the value of small details, too. Nothing is really wrong with word choice; it just did not shine quite so much as other traits (but then, that's asking a lot). Fly fishing as a master's degree? That's ingenious.

Paper 11 **Review of <u>Exploring the Weather</u>** (Literary Review, Grade 8)

<u>Exploring the Weather</u> by Roy A. Gallant tells how weather is made. The most interesting part of the book is Chapter 4, which gives safety tips for dangerous kinds of storms such as hurricanes and tornadoes. It is hard to believe how many deaths are caused by such storms.

This book covers what to do or not do in a lightning storm—such as staying away from open doors or windows, and avoiding electrical equipment like TV's and radios, or metal objects like golf clubs or fishing rods. Even hilltops can be dangerous, and the best thing to do is hide out in a car, house—or even a cave.

The author goes on and on about the layers of the atmosphere: the troposphere, stratosphere, mesosphere, and thermosphere. Here are a couple interesting facts: The troposphere is the bottom-most layer and has the most gases. It reaches up about eight miles from sea level and the temperature range is vast. On a sweltering summer day, it could be 70 degrees below zero at the top. The stratosphere reaches up about 30 more miles. At the bottom are strong winds that decrease as you go up—and interestingly, the temperature also rises. I found this odd (since the temperature was going down a minute ago), but the book doesn't explain it. Between the stratosphere and mesosphere is the famous Ozone we hear so much of. This layer blocks out most of the sun's radiation—or used to. The mesosphere is the third layer of air, and reaches up another 20 miles or so. It ranges from 30 degrees at the bottom to over 130 at the top.

If you find clouds interesting, this could be your book. Here are some highlights: Cumulus clouds are fluffy with gray, flat bases, and can be found between 2,000 and 4,000 feet up. Cumulonimbus clouds are the ones to watch out for. These are the violent summer thunderheads that often bring hail. Massive clouds, they may extend to heights of 20,000 or more feet. Stratus clouds, by contrast, hang low and solid in the skies, and are usually not more than a few hundred feet thick. Alto-stratus clouds may be so thin you can see the sun or moon right through them. Cirrus clouds race along near the top of the troposphere, where winds carry them along at speeds up to 200 miles per hour.

Chapter 3 encourages trying your own experiments—which might be one way of making this book easier to understand. This chapter has clear pictures with helpful labels. Chapter 4 has quick, exact information. In every other chapter, the important information is spread through paragraphs in bits and pieces. You have to read several times to figure out what is important and <u>then</u> you have to put those details together. It takes 45 minutes to get through 10 pages of this tedious book because it's almost like you are re-writing the book in your head the whole time. Another problem is the very difficult vocabulary. Terms, terms, and more terms! Sometimes the author explained the terms and sometimes he just left you guessing. I also kept wishing this book had more voice. The way the information was presented, like lists of facts, made it very dull. But on the other side of the argument, weather is a difficult topic, so maybe being boring is the only way to pack in enough information.

■ **Suggested Scores**

Ideas: 3, 4

Organization: 3, 4

Voice: 4, 5

Word choice: 5, 6

Sentence fluency: 5, 6

Conventions: 5, 6

■ **Lessons Learned from Paper 11**

• Readers need the "big picture" before you zoom in for the close-up.

• Examples—especially quotations—help support assertions about a writer's skill or strategy.

■ **Comments**

All in all, this is not a bad review, but it needs a stronger sense of purpose. Its most serious problem is a tendency to overload us with small facts—about layers of atmosphere or clouds—rather than sticking with the big picture of how effective (or ineffective) the book might be. What we gain from the piece is a sense that the Gallant text (in this reviewer's mind) is filled with technical detail, but does not necessarily present information in an accessible way. It would be helpful if the writer made this assertion right up front, then went on to show why or how it is true. Quotations from the book would back the claim that the text is low in voice or that the terminology is difficult. Just the same, this reviewer makes some strongly worded and explicit points—especially about "re-writing the book in your head the whole time" you're reading. Paragraphs 3 and 4 tend more toward a summary than a review (This focus shifts sharply in the closing paragraph), but the information is clearly expressed, and this reviewer (unlike some) seems to have read the book attentively. He seems at home with the terminology, even if he did find it difficult. Sentences are well crafted, and the piece is edited. While some encyclopedia writers might agree with that last sentence, I would have preferred a different ending!

The Write Connection

"Review of Exploring the Weather"

Check out any informational book on weather—such as David Suzuki's *Looking at Weather* (1991, Jossey-Bass). Write a review of your own, based on the book's effectiveness. Keep your summary of the book's content to a minimum, focusing on how accessible the writer makes technical information for the reader. Use two, three, or more quotations to show how the writer uses voice, organization, or word choice to make ideas clear. Think about format, too. Do you like the layout on the page or the way chapters or other sections are arranged? What works? What doesn't? What do you learn from this book about writing an informational text of your own?

Paper 12 | **You Whant to be My Friend?**
(Personal Essay, Grade 3)

You whant to be my friend? Well a good friend for me would be a female tomboy. She would like nature, animals and stones. She would like burping and burping the ABCs. If she couldn't & didn't like it she couldn't be my friend. If you don't like Star Wars you are not my friend. I love Star Wars. Oh & viva pinyatas, legos, bionicals. The things I like. You problebly can guse one of my favorite video games. Lego Star wars! Its kind of easy to be my friend just a few minuts or secons & We are friends. But if you don't like drumming thers a big chance you aren't my friend. I am a rocker. I am also very disgusting. Even boys thik so. No matter what age. But be carful. Warning. No vegitarians. I am mostly a carnivore. And last of all exploring & climbin trees are OK. Remember if you do everythin you are my best friend.

The Write Connection

"You Whant to Be My Friend?"

Read this piece aloud to determine where the fluency works and where it breaks down. Try combining some sentences, or turning an awkward fragment into a full sentence. Warning: Keep the voice forceful! This is a writer who means what he says—so don't lose that in the revision! When you finish, read your version aloud to hear the difference.

■ **Suggested Scores**

Ideas: 5, 6

Organization: 3, 4

Voice: 5, 6

Word choice: 4, 4

Sentence fluency: 3, 4

Conventions: 3, 4

■ **Lessons Learned from Paper 12**

- Burping the ABCs makes a great example—chances are, no one else will use that one.

- Reading aloud can help you catch small problems with fluency.

- Writing the way we speak can be effective—but sometimes it gets us into trouble, too!

■ **Comments**

This piece is hilarious. I *do* want to be this writer's friend—and I do like *most* of the same things. Voice is the standout trait here. You have to admire the way this writer just lays the friend qualifications on the line. (Imagine a job announcement a few years down the road.) The ideas are entertaining because they're highly individual. They are shared a bit randomly (hence the lower score in organization), but because the piece is short and focused, it is not as serious a problem as it might be. The lead and conclusion aren't bad either. Moments of word choice jump out: *I am also very disgusting . . . Warning. No vegetarians. I am mostly a carnivore.* Some fragments work, but some do not: *The things I like.* Conventions need work, but do not impair the message. I would read anything this writer wrote, so that says a lot.

Paper 13   **Homeless** (Narrative/Memoir, Grade 6)

Addicted to drugs or mental. I'm homeless, but I'm neither. Not mental or addicted to drugs. My family got robbed. And now I have to try and finish my homework before the sun sets. I sleep over at my friend's house more often to take a nice warm bath and sleep on a comfy bed. My friend understands. But I can never tell one person that I am homeless—the person I love.

He asked me if he could meet my parents. I said that they were busy. He said it would only be for a little while. I couldn't lie—or tell him the truth. So I said . . . Let's just break up. But the truth was I didn't want to break up with him. Being a homeless person is like losing your life.

■ **Suggested Scores**

Ideas: 5, 6

Organization: 5, 6

Voice: 5, 6

Word choice: 4, 4

Sentence fluency: 4, 5

Conventions: 5, 6

■ **Lessons Learned from Paper 13**

- There are many kinds of powerful voice.

- Sometimes, not saying things directly can give a piece even more power.

■ **Comments**

Here's a restrained and very serious voice—quite different from that in Paper 12. It's the quietness and the simplicity that give this voice its power. The meaning is subtle and understated, too: *And now I have to try and finish my homework before the sun sets.* It's harder to work when one has no light. The simple language works well in parts—*I couldn't lie—or tell him the truth.* At other times—*nice warm bath, comfy bed*—it seems more functional than striking. The sentences too are short and simple, but that works fairly well here as it encourages the reader to speak softly. The whole piece builds to the ending, which is a stunner.

The Write Connection

"Homeless"

"Homeless" is a reflective piece, a passionate and understated account of a young woman's personal experience. What about the perspective of her friend, her parents, or the person she loves and felt she had to break up with? Write a short reflection about the same situation from one (or more) of these alternate points of view to explore the many ways that point of view influence voice.

Paper 14   **Movies and Books: A Comparison**
(Expository, Grade 8)

One of the hardest challenges for a movie producer is to make a book as great as <u>To Kill a Mockingbird</u> into a two-hour movie. The director is forced to cut scenes and take out characters so that the movie is not too long. There is also not enough time for description of the town or characters because a movie is based more on action than is a novel.

In the movie version of <u>To Kill a Mockingbird</u>, many of the characters such as Scout's Uncle Jack were taken out. The book contains a long discussion of Maycomb's history and of Atticus, his career, and his family; these were omitted from the movie, along with many scenes showing Jem and Scout at school—scenes that help us understand who these characters are. Some description can be handled in a film (as it was in the film version of "To Kill a

(continued)

The Write Connection

"Movies and Books: A Comparison"

What thoughts do you have about books and the films made from them? Why do directors or screenwriters choose certain books on which to base films—and ignore others? Choose any book from which a film has been made and compare them, as this writer has done. Be sure to cite specific scenes or characters that are included or omitted. Try to capture an important moment of dialogue that is preserved or revised in the film version—and speculate on why. *Note: You will find it helpful to skim through the book one more time—and see the film again before writing.*

Mockingbird") through what directors call "voice-unders," in which a narrator speaks to the audience. "Scout," as an adult, speaks to the movie audience about Maycomb in the very first scene of the film—and off and on, throughout the film. Her speeches make smooth transitions between film segments. In the book, by contrast, she has time to go into great detail about the history of Maycomb, her feelings about Jem and Dill, and her relationship with Atticus—from whom she develops most of her philosophy about life.

The main difference between books and movies is that movies are more visual so they depend more on action. Directors and script writers take the main idea or concept from a book and put it into a movie, but when they do this, they have to sacrifice some dialogue and scenes. A director has to think about what will play well dramatically, such as the trial scene in which Atticus shows that Tom is left-handed (and so is very unlikely to be the person who struck Mayella), or the scene where Scout reaches out to take Boo's hand. Much of the final conversation between Atticus Finch and Sheriff Tate—in which Atticus slowly realizes the roles played by Jem and Boo Radley in Bob Ewell's death—is preserved in the film. That scene is essential to the closure of the story, and so the director gave it quite a lot of screen time.

Sometimes when making a movie, they have to cut so much that the plot thins and the characters are hard to understand. In "To Kill a Mockingbird," however, I think they did an excellent job of trying to preserve as much as they could. Atticus Finch comes across in both the film and the book as a dignified, thoughtful man—strong, courageous, and filled with conviction. Scout is curious, brave, and intelligent. Boo is mysterious and unexpectedly gentle. Bob Ewell is evil and plotting.

It takes a strong book to make a strong movie. To Kill a Mockingbird is an excellent example of a book-to-movie translation. It hit all the major and important points of the book: the encounters with Boo, the relationship between Atticus and Scout, and most of all, Tom's trial. Sometimes you need the movie and the book to get the whole picture.

■ **Suggested Scores**

Ideas: 5, 6

Organization: 5, 6

Voice: 4, 5

Word choice: 5, 6

Sentence fluency: 5, 6

Conventions: 5, 6

■ **Lessons Learned from Paper 14**

• Specific examples help the reader follow the conversation.
• Having a main point to make—*it's a challenge to make a great book into a two-hour movie*—gives writing focus.

■ **Comments**

This is a thoughtful comparison that uses examples very effectively to show how the film reflects the "best" of the book—and suffers minimally from what must be cut. The writer helps us to understand the challenges a director might face—long sections of narrative (that become voice-unders) or numerous characters, not all of whom can make a stage appearance in a film of limited time. It's an intriguing premise, and the writer puts us continually in the position of the director, deciding what stays and what goes. The writer's examples also show a familiarity with both the book and the film (compare Paper 8, "A Great Book," page 73) that give us confidence. The voice is straightforward and restrained—hence the slightly lower scores. We should keep in mind that this voice is quite appropriate for this kind of writing. Still, the writer could kick it up a notch with a quotation or two. After all, both film and book touch us deeply. The review could, too.

| Paper 15 | **Why I Write** (Expository, Grade 7) |

I write for no reason. If I'm forced to write, my pencil is my enemy, but if I'm bored in my room or a teacher won't stop talking and there's a piece of paper in front of me, a pencil is my best friend because in my opinion, writing passes the time better than any conversation.

I write to make people cry and talk to make people laugh because it's easier to make people laugh when you're in the moment than to write it in a story. Sadness is the greatest thing to write about because everybody has a different sense of humor, everybody has their opinion on who's interesting, but everybody knows what's sad: change and death.

I write because everyone thinks writing pieces will never be perfect, so they don't expect my stories to be. If you do sports everybody wants you to be the best, but with writing, they accept the fact that you don't have writing talent. They think that if you're not good at a sport, you can practice and be good. The same is true with writing, except no matter how many workshops you take, you may never have that certain edge it takes.

I write to make people use the dictionary. I think it's one of the greatest books ever written and if I use the dictionary it will create a chain of using it: I look up a few words in the dictionary and use them in my story, the person that reads it looks them up, then they will probably show off their improved

(continued)

vocabulary to their friends, and their friends will want to know what the word is. It's all a process of making the world less idiotic.

I write because writing is like a thousand piece puzzle. There are almost a million ways to arrange the giant thing, but you have to carefully arrange it piece-by-piece, step-by-step. It seems like a never-ending process, some people think it is, but once you have done all of your trial and errors, your mistakes, and slip ups, you find yourself looking at a masterpiece.

I write to teach someone ignorant a lesson. Whether it's something about my life, life in general, or that I'm not a moron, they will learn something. When you read my stories, you might love it, hate it, or just want to shoot me for trying, but when you see the story you will learn a thing or two about a thing or two.

■ Suggested Scores

Ideas: 5, 6

Organization: 4, 5

Voice: 5, 5

Word choice: 3, 4

Sentence fluency: 4, 4

Conventions: 4, 5

■ Lessons Learned from Paper 15

- One key phrase (*"I write . . ."*) can connect otherwise disjointed thoughts in a personal reflection.
- Insight (*"Everybody knows what's sad: change and death"*) is one key to voice.

■ Comments

Disconnected thoughts? Not really. These various reflections together form a cohesive essay. Perhaps the writer thought of several at once or thought of them on different days. They are moments that define who this writer is. The voice in this piece shifts from funny to reflective to philosophical, serious, and even a little superior in the closing paragraph. It's always there, though, a force driving the writing. Word choice is a bit erratic, sometimes strong (*"when you're in the moment," "that certain edge," "thousand-piece puzzle"*), sometimes more routine (*"it's one of the greatest books ever written"*). There are a few small errors in conventions—nothing serious. The trouble is, when you write this well, people start to expect it all the time.

The Write Connection

"Why I Write"

This writer uses one key idea—*Why I Write*—to create a chain of thoughts all centered on this one topic. Try this organizational strategy by creating a chain of your own. Think of *one thing* you do that is important to you. Perhaps it's writing or reading—or something totally different: fishing, playing football or softball, taking pictures, walking with your dog, dancing, listening to music—whatever. Think of all the different reasons you do it, and after listing three or four, begin to write. You may discover that one link in the chain leads to another—until you have a complete essay.

Chapter 5 In a Nutshell

- Voice is the imprint of the writer on the page. It is more than personality. It springs from confidence, enthusiasm, passion for the topic, and sensitivity to the needs and interests of the reader. Voice is also a tool for getting—and holding—a reader's attention.

- Word choice is creation of imagery through colorful language, and precision in selecting the *just right* word or phrase for the moment. Word choice supports voice by relying on strong verbs and original, creative phrasing.

- Sentence fluency is a measure of how writing plays to the ear. Strong fluency is marked by variety in sentence length and structure and is both achieved and measured through continual reading aloud of the text. Sentence fluency also supports voice because expressive sentences echo the writer's thinking.

- Each piece of writing has specific lessons to teach us about writing; careful assessment helps reveal those lessons.

Study Group Interactive Questions and Activities

1. **Activity and Discussion.** Based on your experience scoring papers in this chapter, how would you rate your understanding of the traits of *voice, word choice,* and *sentence fluency?*

   _____ *Excellent.* I can define each trait in my own words and could lead students in a discussion of that trait.

   _____ *About halfway there.* I think I would recognize each trait in student papers or other things I read.

   _____ *Not there yet.* I am not confident I would recognize ___ voice, ___ word choice, or ___ sentence fluency if I read or heard it.

2. **Activity and Discussion.** If you checked "About halfway there" or "Not there yet" for Activity #1, do this: Make yourself a collection of five student samples and five nonacademic samples (from newspapers, books, advertising, etc.), and with a partner, score them all on the five traits we have discussed. When you finish, rate your understanding again. You should see a big change.

3. **Discussion.** Did you find yourself agreeing (within a point) on scores for *most* of the papers in this chapter? If not, what do you think was the cause of the disagreement?

4. **Activity and Discussion.** If you are teaching now, which of the traits discussed so far do you think is strongest in your own students' work? As a group, collectively review five to ten student samples from your own or another group member's class(es). Then answer the question again.

5. **Activity and Discussion.** As a group, identify two short excerpts (50 to 100 words) from literature that you could use to teach *each* of the traits covered so far: *ideas, organization, voice, word choice, sentence fluency.* Discuss the characteristics you looked for in making your selections. Did any of your samples help you expand your definition of a trait?

6. **Activity and Discussion.** Write one to two paragraphs on *any topic* about which you care deeply. Write on every other line, allowing room for revision. Put it away for three days or more. Take it out, read it aloud, and revise by (1) adding a detail you didn't think of originally; (2) rewriting the lead, conclusion, or both; (3) coming closer to the "truth" of things as you see it; (4) eliminating any flat words (*nice, fun, good*) and adding one or two strong verbs; and (5) making every sentence begin in a slightly different way. Read it aloud again. What is the result? What might this same activity show your students about revision?

Reflections on Writing

I write so I can be in my own little world. . . . I love having my own little world because it's all me and most of the time I think the world revolves around me. A lot of people say to me, "Madison, the world doesn't surround you." But I think it does. . . .

—**Madison Sessums**, student writer

In a movie called "Freedom Writers," students had a journal to write in. . . . They wrote to express how they feel, what troubles them in the real world. That's what I think writing should be about, a way to show emotion, to share your personal thoughts on what happens in the real world.

—**Marcus Arellano**, student writer

Framing the Picture
Conventions and Presentation

Conventions belong to all of us. In acquiring them we gain the power to say new things, extend our meaning, and discover new relationships between ideas. For too long, teachers and editors have stood guard over conventions, as if they were esoteric knowledge available only to the few.

—Donald H. Graves
A Fresh Look at Writing, 1994, p. 210

We are dealing with a complicated system, and every element of that system, down to the conventional signs for pauses and nuances, has had a long testing. Its function is to help reproduce in cold print what was a human voice speaking for human ears.

—Wallace Stegner
On Teaching and Writing Fiction, 2002, p. 63

Attention to conventions is, as much as anything, a courtesy to the reader. When we invite guests into our homes, we tidy up, dust, vacuum, dim the lights, turn on the music, light the candles. In so doing, we say, in effect, "I want you to feel at home here." Tidying up text is a way of making readers feel at home within our writing. Editing and formatting also bring closure to writing—in much the same way that framing celebrates and brings closure to an artist's work.

Conventions and Presentation: Editing and Framing

Getting a Mindset

Conventions fall into two categories: textual and visual. Textual conventions cover anything a copy editor would deal with: spelling, punctuation, grammar and usage, capitalization, and paragraphing (which supports organization but is scored here). Such conventions clearly change over time, and so to assess or teach them well, we need to rely on up-to-date handbooks and dictionaries and use them often. Textual conventions not only support meaning but also help readers to understand intended inflection and voice. In Roald Dahl's book *Matilda*, for example, five-year-old Matilda asks her television-addicted father to buy her a book, and conventions (italics, abbreviations) show us precisely how to read his response: "A book?" He said. "What d'you want a flaming book for?" (1988, p. 12).

Visual conventions (also known as presentation) are so called because they visually organize text, guiding the reader's eye and making certain points stand out. They include such things as

FIGURE 6.1 Trait "Shortie" for Conventions and Presentation
Use this summary to introduce the trait to students.

Conventions & Presentation
Editorial Correctness/Eye Appeal

- Edited, polished

- Shows conventional awareness

- Conventions enhance meaning, voice

- No mental editing required

- Virtually ready to publish

- Complexity of text showcases writer's editorial skill

- Presentation eye-catching, helpful

© 2009. Allyn and Bacon, an imprint of Pearson Education, Inc.
Developed by Vicki Spandel for *Creating Writers*, Fifth Edition.

graphics (maps, charts, photographs) that support text or expand meaning, use of bulleted or numbered lists, and use of titles and subheads.

 # Practice Papers

What To Do

- Agree on a handbook that you will use as the *final authority,* if needed.
- Follow the same scoring procedures as for previous traits.

The Inside Track on Conventions and Presentation

This one should be easy, shouldn't it? Isn't it the most clear-cut? Not really. We do not all agree on what is conventionally correct, for one thing. How many commas go in a series? Which words should be capitalized? Which numbers should be spelled out? Is it ever all right to begin a sentence with *And*? Is *data* plural? What about *none*? Do you cringe at *firstly*? *Secondly*? Is second person sometimes *alright*? Do you use it *alot*? Little things get to us all, and we strike back: *Score of 1 for you!* Such things as failing to capitalize the pronoun *i* or writing *alot* as one word might be annoying, but they are not federal offenses and should not cause a drop in a student's score from, say, a 5 to a 1 or 2, but sometimes this is what happens.

Part of the problem lies in our tendency to define conventions strictly in terms of correctness. This is limiting. Conventions exist to serve the message and to make interpretation of the message easier. Thus conventions are clues that guide reading, both reading for meaning and reading for voice. The first time I recall thinking about this was when my sixth grade teacher asked us to consider the difference between these two sentences:

"Let's kick, John!" said the coach.
"Let's kick John!" said the coach.

Here are some keys to assessing conventions well:

1. *Look beyond spelling.* Spelling is important, yes, but it is not the whole of conventions. How is the punctuation? The paragraphing? The grammar?

2. *Score conventions first.* Conventions, for better or worse, often influence how we see a piece as a whole. Therefore, to keep your scoring fair and accurate, it may be helpful to score that trait first and get it out of the way, especially when conventions are noticeably weak or strong.

3. *Look for what is done well,* not just the mistakes. Balance the two.

4. *Do not overreact.* One mistake—or two or three—cannot spoil the whole performance. We go too far when we demand conventional perfection of students, for we cannot teach to such a standard or even meet it ourselves. So ask, "Overall, how well does the student *control* conventions to make meaning clear?"

5. *Do not consider neatness or handwriting in assigning a conventions score.* Such things may be important, but they are separate issues.

6. *Think of yourself as a copy editor.* Ask, "How much work would I need to do to prepare this text for publication?" Heavy editing? That's a 1 or 2. Moderate? That's a 3 or 4. Very light—touch-ups only? That's a 5 or 6.

■ What about Presentation?

If your students are creating newsletter copy, business letters, posters, brochures, or other forms of writing in which layout and graphics play an important role, then by all means take time to consider visual conventions. Look specifically for the following things so far as each is applicable and relevant to the writing:

- Appropriate and pleasing format for a business letter, resumé, citations, etc.
- Use of a title or main heading to capture the essential message
- Use of subheads to mark sections
- Consistency in subheads (e.g., font size and style, placement, spacing)
- Use of graphics that support the text
- Consistent labeling of graphics
- Restraint in the use of fonts (no more than two or three per page)
- Font style and size that enhance readability
- Sufficient margins to make text width comfortable for reading
- Use of bulleted or numbered lists, as needed

These features are easy to recognize and check. I would comment on them and encourage them. I would give them very modest weight in assigning scores, however, and would consider them in assessment *only when the purpose for writing makes presentation critical.* Visual conventions such as graphics and bulleted lists can be very helpful in guiding a reader's eye and certainly can give writing appeal. Most of us look carefully at book covers and front pages of newspapers before purchasing them. In the end, however, serious readers will choose a newspaper for thorough, intelligent journalism, not for layout per se. Writing is not about appearance. It's about *thinking on the page.*

Keep in mind too that in the real world of publishing, layout is usually handled by persons who are gifted specialists in artistic presentation; we must be careful about connecting this skill to writing. What appeals to me may not appeal to you at all (perhaps you like a subdued look, whereas I prefer something more flamboyant and colorful) and coming up with guidelines to govern assessment of layout introduces serious potential for bias and inconsistency.

Let's look at two pieces just for textual conventions: spelling, punctuation, paragraphing, grammar and usage, and capitalization. We'll then briefly consider presentation, and put all six traits together in a number of practice papers.

Paper 1 **Haircut from Hell** (Narrative/Imaginative, Grade 7)

I failed to tell the new worker at "Haircroppers" how I wanted my hair cut. He swung my chair away from the mirror. The noises that fallowed sounded like chainswas, hedge trimmers, and helocopters. Then he swung my chair back to face the mirror. . . .

From the time he swung my chair around, I knew that would be my last visit to "Haircroppers."

My hair, or what was left of it was tinted a brown olive green color. I felt my hair. A slimey sticky residue came off on my hand. I gave a quick smurk and vigorously rubbed the slime onto my pants.

Unbelievably enough, the quick smile I had given the nin-cum-poop barber was taken to be genuine and he quickly responded, "Glad you like it sir That's my best one yet!"

Disgusted, I turned back to my hair. Maybe a wig was the way to go. I felt some of the olive green goop dribbel down my neck.

I felt my hair again and was immediately stopped by a blur of barbers hands. With rage in his voice he yelled "What are you trying to do, ruin my masterpiece?!"

"Your masterpiece??!! More like your mess. What is this junk anyway? Some kind of axel greese?"

His voice was wavery, but refused to crack. "Its my own creation . . . face mud, hair spray, avacado dip . . ."

I let him get as far as turtle wax when I roared "Hold it!!"

My face was beginning to twist, my scalp to burn. "Hose this junk off, you incompitent moron. If my head doesn't just role to the floor, I'll have your hide!" I couldn't wait a moment longer. I grabed the hose and turned it on myself. Whew. The solution came out into a brown puddle on the floor, along with great chunks of my hair.

Fortunatly, I didn't have to pay for what I call today my hair's "mass suicide."

■ **Suggested Scores for Focus Trait: Conventions**

Conventions: 2, 3

■ **Lessons Learned from Paper 1**

- Faulty conventions can distract the reader.
- Good dialogue adds voice.

The Write Connection

"Haircut from Hell"

Make a list of the things this writer does correctly—or even *well*—conventionally. Then edit the piece, correcting all errors you find. Look at the strengths and problems in balance. Do you agree with the score of 3 in conventions? Should it be higher?

■ Comments

Many of the conventional errors in this paper seem to be the result of hasty editing. Apostrophes are overlooked, and commas and capitals missed. There are too many paragraphs. A scrupulous reader will make corrections as he or she goes along, but this should be the *writer's* job. The thing that saves this paper from lower scores in conventions is the writer's skillful use of some conventions, such as ellipses, question marks, and exclamation points to reinforce voice. On the positive side, the imagery is vivid, and voice is *very* strong. Lead and conclusion are excellent, and dialogue is authentic. Notice the strong verbs. Read it aloud to appreciate the fluency. A highly imaginative piece.

■ Suggested Scores for Other Traits

Ideas: **5, 6**

Organization: **5, 6**

Voice: **5, 6**

Word choice: **5, 6**

Sentence fluency: **5, 6**

Paper 2 **The Ritual of Rocks and Sticks**
(Imaginative, Grade 6)

While visiting America I had the opportunity to attend a ritual called the baseball game. In this ritual, an enormous crowd of people gather around, sitting on multi-leveled seats, watching a crowd of people perform.

The performers of the ritual are dressed in striped clothes similar to a zebra. They have pieces of cowhide tied to one hand, and they beat the cowhide with their free hand and make loud grunting noises. Sometimes they spit, and everyone seems to enjoy this part. Their heads are covered in bright colored cloth, which they touch quite often, sometimes running their hands along the front part of the cloth, which hangs over their eyes. When one does this, other performers nod and slap the cowhide hard. Clearly, this is a significant part of the ritual.

The performer in the middle of the flat area is known as the pitcher. He stands on a small hill and throws a hard ball of string at another performer, who holds a long stick. The stick man, also known as a batter, tries to hit the ball of string. If he succeeds, he immediately drops his stick and runs in a huge circle, touching white squares as he passes. The people dressed in stripes run after the ball of string, and then go after the stick man, tossing the ball of string hard as they go. They rarely catch him, but if they do, he yanks the cloth from his head and whacks his leg with it, giving out a mighty yell. The crowd yells with him. This much I have figured out: Once the stick man hits the ball of string, he does not want it back. He is very unhappy if the other performers return it to him.

This hitting and running part of the ritual is performed many times until both the performers and the people in the multi-leveled seats grow tired. As they go, they make more grunting noises and hit one another on the back quite a lot. This means the ritual is over for that day. But they will hold it again. They always take their balls of string and their sticks with them to be ready for the next time.

■ **Suggested Scores for Focus Trait: Conventions**

Conventions: 5, 6

■ **Lessons Learned from Paper 2**

• Understatement can be effective.

• Let the reader figure it out—but be sure you provide good clues.

■ **Comments**

How might the game of baseball look to someone seeing it for the first time? This is the premise of this understated but strong piece. Fans will identify with various parts of the ritual—spitting, slapping the cowhide hard, and the wonderful line about the runner not wanting the hard ball of string back. The pacing is good; the writer provides good imagery but does not take us play by play through a whole game. We go smoothly from players to fans and back again. The language is perfectly functional and includes a few strong verbs—*nod, whack, slap.* The writer's word choice effectively emphasizes the physical side of the game. The rocks mutate into hard balls of string, but this is a minor point—it doesn't confuse us. Sentence fluency is also strong, although more transitions would smooth the flow. Conventions are excellent.

The Write Connection

"The Ritual of Rocks and Sticks"

Despite its clear strength in sentence fluency, this paper includes many sentences that begin with "He," "The," or "They." Try revising it to eliminate all of these common sentence beginnings. Then read it aloud to check the fluency again. Did you take it from a 5 to a 6?

■ **Suggested Scores for Other Traits**

Ideas: 5, 6

Organization: 5, 6

Voice: 5, 6

Word choice: 4, 5

Sentence fluency: 4, 5

 # Examples of Presentation

Let's consider, briefly, three pieces for which presentation is important. I do not wish to put scores on them but only to use them for discussion purposes. The first is a poem (Figure 6.2) that is beautifully formatted to capture the rhythm and guide our reading. Format is important in poetry because it helps determine how we read and how we pick up specific images, e.g., "dark thundering thoughts" or "half-drenched ladybugs." Punctuation in poetry is important, too, but it does not follow the same rules as punctuation in prose. A writer who omits terminal punctuation, for example, creates the sense that thoughts are floating and continuous. In this poem, the short lines are punchlines, and they serve the function of periods.

Figure 6.3 shows page 24 from the Big Book titled *Coco Writes*, part of *Write Traits Kindergarten: Bringing the Traits® to Kinderwriters* (2007, Great Source Education). For this book, my co-author Jeff Hicks and I created

F I G U R E **6.2** **"Rain and Ivy," by Kira (poetry, grade 3)**

Rain and Ivy
By Kira

Green, delicate, smooth, light green
Clumps of ivy
Shadows rain down with
Dark thundering thoughts
Rain
Rustling leaves whisper in your ears
It's silent, then it whispers
Soft, soothing
Mind-reading words
Rain pours down
You reach for your umbrella
Still keeping your eyes on those ivy leaves
You notice that ladybugs shelter under those leaves
Trying to keep dry
Rain thunders down
And your mother is calling you
To come
So you don't get drenched
You go
Leaving the ivy alone in the rain
Sheltering those poor half-drenched ladybugs
The next morning
You go to check on the ivy
After that you always look
At that ivy
With loving eyes.

a series of adventures for Coco the Crab, who lives on the beach, of course, and has numerous adventures—in this case with a person (notice the foot). *Coco Writes* is directed to two audiences: kindergarten students and their teachers. The visual takes up most of the page—because this is where the

FIGURE **6.3** *Coco Writes,* page 24

COCO SAYS:

How fast can you move? Raise one hand if you can move *pretty* fast. Raise two hands if you can move *faster than a crab.* Oh, *really?* So you think you're faster than *I am?* I don't know about that. I am one speedy crab. I whoosh. I tear. I streak. Are you faster on land or in the water? Raise your hand if you can move faster on land. OK, raise your hand if you're faster in the water. Great! I am a water kid, myself. In the water, I glide and slide and float and dive like a champ. This morning I darted through the water with the speed of a jet ski! Guess why? I spotted a shark, lurking around the reef. He was hovering right over my favorite hiding hole, circling and keeping an eye out for something to munch on. Luckily, I was able to *zoom* my way to the beach. There I did my favorite thing—I splashed a human! They always squeal, and I love that. I scuttled off with a chuckle. I want to write about it, but I'm not sure how to spell some of the words. Can you help?

I love to sp_____ hu_____s on the beach!

students' attention is directed. Along the left panel is what "Coco Says," an interactive adventure that the teacher reads aloud. At the bottom in very large print is a sample of Coco's own "writing." Though creative, Coco struggles with conventions, sometimes forgetting punctuation, omitting letters, and so on. Students help her edit, and the large print and extra spacing allow room for that. In her story, Coco tells how much she loves to "splash humans" on the beach because "they always squeal and I love that." When she tries to write about this, though, she cannot spell *splash* or *humans*, and so uses a letter-line strategy for these words. After figuring out what she is trying to say, the kindergartners help Coco to fill in the missing letters. The artist's rendition of each page in *Coco Writes* includes many decisions about design, color, fonts, and spacing. When I submitted the manuscript, it was mostly written in Tahoma 12-point on plain white 8½" × 11" paper. What a difference a few visual conventions have made.

Figure 6.4 shows two covers for Jamal's multipart report on Africa. He is studying the impact of apartheid and the devastating effects of AIDS on African children. The result is a series of reports, grouped in a "journal" Jamal has titled "Thandi" (which, he says, is African for "loved one"). He regretted not having access to a computer, which made design and layout (all done by hand) a bit more challenging.

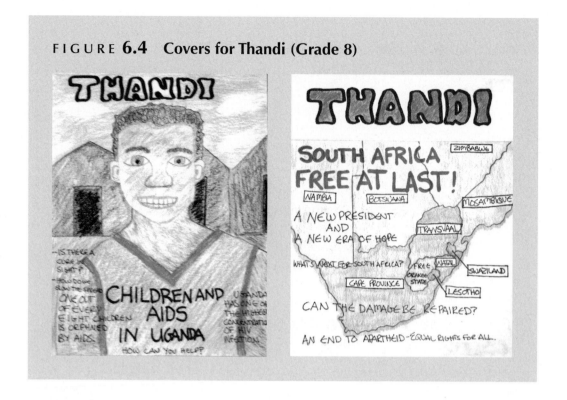

F I G U R E **6.4** **Covers for Thandi (Grade 8)**

Putting All Traits Together

It's time to look at all six traits together, creating a complete performance profile. In assessing the remaining papers, follow the usual procedures, making copies of rubrics and papers, reading pieces aloud, and discussing both scores and lessons learned.

Paper 3 **File Sharing Is Not the Spawn of Satan**
(Persuasive/Expository, Grade 12)

I'm in my car, driving to who knows where, doing who knows what. Sunroof open, windows down, and the radio playing. Life is good. One song ends and another begins. This new song catches my attention. It has a nice beat and rhythm and the lyrics aren't half bad. I think to myself, "Self, who is this song by? I have no idea." I then wait until the song ends for the radio DJ to enlighten me as to who it was. I realize that this is a group that I've never heard of before and I liked the song so much that I may actually consider purchasing their CD. Here presents a problem: What if this band is just a one-hit wonder and the rest of the music on that reflective circle is flat-out horrible? That would be thirteen dollars down the drain. Thirteen dollars for one song is a little pricey for my tastes. So what do I

(continued)

do instead? I start up my friendly file-sharing software and, slowly but surely, get the one song I want to listen to at a savings of roughly thirteen dollars. Who can argue with that? Apparently the Recording Industry Association of America (RIAA) can.

The RIAA claims that users (I am a former user, not because of the impending threats, but because I can only download one song a day in 56k-land and as they say, "Only a song a day keeps the RIAA away.") are illegally downloading copyrighted material and costing themselves and poor, starving artists such as Madonna and Eminem millions of dollars. Because of this, the RIAA is now suing the Al-Gore-invented-pants off of folks who are allowing such a heinous crime, royalty endangerment, to occur on their computer. How much are they saying they have been deprived of and are rightfully due? A mere $100,000 per song.

Songs cost that much these days, right? That's how much an artist receives in royalties for one use of one song, isn't it? Oh, wait, it's not. So how did the amount of this penalty originate? How is it justified as fair retribution? Why am I worried about fairness, you may ask? Oh, I don't know, I just thought that we, as Americans, were protected from unusual punishment or something like that in something I once heard referred to as the Bill of Rights. I could be wrong. Wait a minute, I get it! Madonna lives in England so we're exempt from the United States Constitution! That must be it!

Why is it that in the day of the information superhighway, the RIAA is trying to close it and send us on a detour? Have they just realized that bootlegging is a problem, that we can now, all of a sudden, just make copies of music onto cassettes (gasp!) and CDs? Oh, wait, we've been able to do that for years. Why has it taken them till now to act?

Does the RIAA not realize that trying to fix this problem will make it worse, will make people more determined to try and circumvent the threats of lawsuits? Who in their right mind would voluntarily stop getting something for free and start paying for it? Lawsuits will cause even more people to hate the RIAA and find more ways to get free music. This musical can of worms (which, when opened plays "I Can't Get No Satisfaction" by the Rolling Stones) and can be yours for (insert number of illegally downloaded songs here) easy payments of $100,000) that has been opened will cause many more problems along the way than the RIAA ever dreamed of on its starving-artist-saving stairway to heaven.

■ **Suggested Scores**

Ideas: 4, 5

Organization: 4, 5

Voice: 5, 6 (You may score it lower if you find the sarcasm inappropriate.)

Word choice: 4, 5

Sentence fluency: 5, 6

Conventions: 5, 6

The Write Connection

"File Sharing Is Not the Spawn of Satan"

On the other hand, if you are a writer—of songs or novels—pirating may not amuse you. Whether you agree with the author of this piece or not, imagine that you don't. Try writing a persuasive piece from the other point of view, defending your rights as an artist to be paid for your creation. Imagine that the author of "File Sharing Is Not the Spawn of Satan" is your audience.

■ **Lessons Learned from Paper 3**

- Sarcasm is risky—but it's a voice some readers will love.
- You need to give the other side equal time.

■ **Comments**

This one is good practice because your take on the writer's position—and on his voice—could influence your scores, possibly unfairly. First, let's acknowledge that the writer is highly skilled and (if you respond to the voice) very funny as well. The argument is well crafted in terms of its clarity and the specific examples. Slightly lower scores in ideas reflect the fact that the writer does not seriously consider the infringement of copyright issue—which affects many people less wealthy than Madonna. The point about the severity of the penalty is well taken and well argued. The logic breaks down a bit, though, with the suggestion that downloading music must be okay because we've gotten by with similar stunts for years—and besides, those RIAA people just aren't likable. Sorry, but this doesn't make the pirating of copyrighted materials okay. Nevertheless, despite the flippant tone, this one had me laughing, and I'd like to meet the writer. Notice the masterful use of conventions to reinforce voice. Scathing, risky—well done.

Paper 4　**A Beautiful Dream** (Memoir, Grade 12)

I live in a small town with a low crime rate. The town I come from is so small, I doubt it is even on a map. Everyone knows everything about everybody. In my town, the vast majority of people are white. I, however, come from a mixed background and I am dark-skinned.

I will never forget my third grade year when our class briefly discussed the Civil War, thus leading to a conversation on slavery. Most third graders could care less about skin color, however, I met someone that day whom I bothered a lot because I was not white. After drinking from the water fountain, a boy in my class told me he would never drink from that fountain again because "my black slave lips" were near it. He said that because I looked black, I did not belong in the class. That night, I told my mother what had happened and cried for hours. It was my first taste of the 'real world' and I hated it.

Throughout the rest of the year, I dealt with hurtful remarks made by this boy who did not even know me, just knew I was not white. I dreaded talking about American History and slavery. I would sink down in my seat at the mention of the word "slave." There I was, an innocent eight year old girl who felt ashamed and angry at her parents for not "making her" white.

In my seventh grade year, I found myself sitting across from the very boy that made me resent my color for years. Just seeing him made me want to hide under my desk because I still was not white. That year, we learned about underwater creatures, human life and what made living things 'operate.' Though biology was not my major, I understood the

(continued)

material. He didn't. I could have made fun of him for not understanding the very thing he was—a living creature—but I chose not to. Instead, I offered to help him during class. At first, he was more than just a little skeptical, but I insisted I could help him pass the class. It was the hardest thing I ever had to do that year. I tutored him for a little over a month. Throughout that time, we became friends. When we would pass each other in the halls, we'd smile and say 'hi.' On Mondays, we would talk about our weekends. We were far from *best* friends, but we were friends. That's all that mattered.

We've grown apart since then, and sadly, he converted to his old behaviors. However, he played a crucial influential role in my life. He confirmed my decision to become a teacher. The fact that, despite his intense dislike for me, he was willing to learn and I was willing to teach proved to me that I am capable of being a teacher. I know I can look past students' attitudes and focus on their need to acquire knowledge. I am dependable, caring and unselfish—all traits needed to be an excellent teacher.

Eleanor Roosevelt once said, "The future belongs to those who believe in the beauty of their dreams." I believe my dreams will become a reality with the persistence for a college education. It is my dream to influence and affect students in a positive manner. Now, I think that is a beautiful dream.

■ Suggested Scores

Ideas: 5, 6

Organization: 5, 6

Voice: 5, 6

Word choice: 4, 5

Sentence fluency: 5, 6

Conventions: 5, 6

■ Lessons Learned from Paper 4

- Quiet voices can be powerful.
- Tell the truth and hold readers in your hand.

■ Comments

Voice is the stand-out trait in this heartfelt memoir. Don't overlook the excellent organization, though. The writer sets up the piece and then pulls from memory two distinct but clearly connected events that together lead to the resolution—her decision to teach. Particularly significant is the fact that there is not one formulaic thread in this piece. The closing quotation from Eleanor Roosevelt is a nice touch. There are excellent transitions and smooth sentences. Language is simple, but it works. Clean conventions.

The Write Connection

"A Beautiful Dream"

If you're like many readers, you find the conclusion to this piece more powerful than the lead. Often, good material for a striking lead is found right within the piece, and jumps out once the piece is written. Look through this piece, see if you find such a moment, and rewrite the lead to make it as powerful as the ending.

> **Paper 5** **A Strange Visitor** (Narrative/Imaginative, Grade 5)
>
> The doors flew open, the wind whipped around the room. The startled men looked up. Standing in the door was a man. His royal purple cloak rippled in the draft. The room was silent. There was a sudden noise as the men put down their wine goblets. Tink, tink, tink. The room grew hot and sweaty. Some men tried to speak but nothing came out. The gleam of the strange visiters eyes had frightened the knights who had slain many dragons, and fought bravley for the King. The errieness was unbearable. The visitor's gray beard sparkled in the candlelight giving it an errie glow. The windows let the dark seap in. The large room decorated with banners seemed to get smaller and smaller. The heavy aroma of wine hung in the air like fog on a dull morning. Their dinner bubbled in their stomachs. Their rough fingers grasped their sowrds stowed under their seats. The round table again fell silent. Then slowly the man spoke: "The King has come." The End

■ **Suggested Scores**

Ideas: 5, 6

Organization: 5, 6

Voice: 5, 5

Word choice: 5, 6

Sentence fluency: 3, 4

Conventions: 3, 4

■ **Lessons Learned from Paper 5**

- Disturb the silence with the clink of wine glasses, and the reader will hear it.
- Tension heightens readers' interest.

The Write Connection

"A Strange Visitor"

Try two things. First, highlight each instance of the verb *was*. Change the word (or change the sentence slightly) to eliminate this weak verb. Second, try some sentence combining to create more variety in the sentence lengths. Try not to start more than two sentences with "The." Read the result aloud. You might want to finish by editing this piece for publication.

■ **Comments**

Problems in this piece are minor compared with the strengths. The paper does need some work in conventions, although many things are done correctly (including spelling of difficult words). "The End" can be scrapped—but again, I'm being picky. Sentences tend toward the short side. A little sentence combining and more variety (too many *the*'s and *their*'s) would raise these scores significantly. On the other hand, there is extraordinary attention to detail—mood, tension, colors, sounds. I feel that I'm right there in the castle. Who is the mysterious visitor in royal purple? Why, the very man you've risked your life for—the *king*. Why don't they know? Remember, this takes place in medieval times, when you might not know what the king looked like unless you had met him. This is a great touch. The language has a simple elegance: *"The aroma of wine hung in the air like fog on a dull morning."* The writer uses mostly one-syllable words. This is why it's strong, not overdone.

Paper 6 **The Day My Grandfather Died**
(Personal Narrative, Grade 4)

The day was dark and gloomy. It was the day my grandfather died. I felt like a turtle who couldn't come out of its shell. All I did was cry and mope around the house. I was shocked by the horrifying news. There was so much yet to tell him. I was really hurt but I knew my grandfather wouldn't want me to feel that way. So I didn't let his death hold me back.

I tried to deal with the fact that my grandfather was gone. All I had were memories, but they were good memories. Instead of playing, I wrote in my diary. It became my best friend. That helped me deal with the sorrowful truth. It was a bitter-sweet moment. When my grandfather died, we all knew that his suffering was over. Yet we were sorrowful because my grandfather was gone.

My favorite memory of my grandfather was when we were walking through the park, and he told me of his childhood. It gives me peaceful thoughts just to think of that memory. It seems like just yesterday, but it's a good memory. My grandfather will never leave that special place in my heart.

■ **Suggested Scores**

Ideas: 4, 5

Organization: 4, 5

Voice: 5, 6

Word choice: 4, 5

Sentence fluency: 4, 5

Conventions: 5, 6

■ **Lessons Learned from Paper 6**

- Images make the difference in ideas and voice.
- Some papers touch us in a way that makes scoring very hard.

■ **Comments**

Scoring this paper feels almost disrespectful, so you may find it very difficult to respond in that way. I do. This is a touching and emotional piece. The voice is very strong. Ideas are clear to be sure—the turtle inside its shell, so much left to say (Doesn't that touch a chord?), the best-friend diary, the bittersweet truth. These moments, so strong, so telling, make up for the fact that we do not get to hear the grandfather speak in the last paragraph, the favorite-memory stroll through the park. Sentences are consistently short (with a couple exceptions). This is a minor problem in a paper that is very moving.

The Write Connection

"The Day My Grandfather Died"

This piece currently has twenty sentences, though it is quite short. See if you can combine some sentences to reduce the total number to ten, or even fewer.

Paper 7   A Non-Natural-Born Citizen Should Be Allowed to Be President
(Persuasive, Grade 7)

America is about freedom. Not letting an American citizen be president just because the candidate was not born in the United States of America has nothing to do with freedom. The place one is born does not define how committed or how good a president one will be. The Constitution was written more than two-hundred years ago and some of the requirements for the presidency do not apply to the present day.

When a citizen in the U.S. has experience and knows about politics, funding, welfare, and laws, why shouldn't he/she be president? In America there are many well-educated people and some were not born here. If they know what to do for the needs of this country, we should give them a chance. One example is Arnold Schwarzenegger, an elected governor of the state of California.

In addition, where one is born does not define how good a president you are or how committed one will be. Naturalized citizens do not have an equal opportunity to become president and it is unfair because voters are denied every opportunity to choose a leader for their country. Also, there are some elected representatives who agree with my view, such as Mr. Hatch, a Utah Senator, and Jennifer Granholm, the Canadian-born Democratic governor of Michigan.

The Constitution was written more than 200 years ago; some of the requirements for presidency do not apply to what is in the present day, like the concern that a foreign power might be placed upon the nation, that argument hardly applies. Besides, I still believe that the candidate needs to be at least thirty-five years old and needs to be at least a resident of the U.S. for fourteen years.

Some people believe a president needs to be born in America to *really* understand the problems and needs for America. However, in my opinion we need different views, so more problems will be solved. This country was built from people who came from all around the world, so America is a land with different culture and diverse people and languages, who believe in tolerance and living in peace together; a president from a different place and culture will have the advantage to understand the different views and think of a good compromise. Being a true American does not necessarily mean being born in America. Being a true American means being loyal and obeying laws. If a naturalized citizen meets all of these requirements then the citizen should be qualified to be president.

■ **Suggested Scores**

Ideas: 3, **4**

Organization: 3, **4**

Voice: 4, **5**

Word choice: 3, **4**

Sentence fluency: 4, **5**

Conventions: 4, **5**

■ Lessons Learned from Paper 7

- With persuasive writing, only a strong informational base will help you build a good argument.

- Even when *you* believe passionately in your argument, the reader wants evidence: facts, quotations, examples.

■ Comments

Specifics, specifics, specifics. The irony is, this paper is generally well written, despite a few awkward moments: . . . *like the concern that a foreign power might be placed upon the nation.* . . . As in this example, the writer sometimes comes *close* to saying what he means, but does not quite nail it. Nevertheless, the central argument is strong and expressed with feeling and conviction (hence the relatively high scores in voice). What is needed is more information on which the writer can build an actual case. What have Arnold Schwarzenegger or Jennifer Granholm done that might qualify them to be president? Why is the Constitution outdated—if it is? Why might someone disagree with this premise? The closing paragraph raises an intriguing issue: the idea that someone foreign-born might actually bring refreshing new insight to problem solving in the twenty-first century. But—we want more. Which problems? Terrorism? Border security? International relations? Trade? If the writer shared one solid example including the perspectives of several potential presidential candidates, readers would surely tune in.

The Write Connection

"A Non-Natural-Born Citizen Should Be Allowed to Be President"

Though this piece is fairly well written, some ideas still need clarification. Start with the Constitution. What are the requirements to be president? You may wish to look this up—and include it in a revision of the lead. It can set the stage for the discussion to follow.

Choose paragraph 4 or 5, read it carefully—aloud—and then rewrite it in your own words to make the meaning clear. Consider what specific examples you might offer to strengthen the arguments.

For a thorough (though not lightweight) review of the Constitution, consider (former Reagan attorney general) Edwin Meese's highly acclaimed book *The Heritage Guide to the Constitution* (2005, Regnery Publishing).

Paper 8 **Computer Blues** (Narrative, Grade 12)

So there I was, my face aglow with the reflection of my computer screen, trying to conclude my essay. Writing it was akin to Chinese water torture. It dragged on and on, a never-ending babble about legumes, nutrients and soil degradation. I was tranquilizing myself with my own writing.

Suddenly, unexpectedly—I felt an ending coming on. Four or five punchy sentences would bring this baby to a close, and I'd be free of this dreadful assignment forever! Yes!

I had not saved yet, and decided I would do so now. I scooted the white mouse over the pad toward the "File" menu—and had almost reached home when it happened. By accident, I clicked the mouse button just to the left of paragraph 66. The screen flashed briefly, and the next thing I knew, I was back to square one. Black. I stared at the blank screen for a moment in disbelief. Where was my essay? My ten-billion-page masterpiece? Gone?! No—that couldn't be! Not after all the work I had done! Would a computer be that unforgiving? That *unfeeling*? Didn't it care about me at all?

(continued)

The Write Connection

"Computer Blues"

The "Computer Blues" writer does a fine job of assessing her own work. Try this with a piece of your *own* writing. You do not have to give yourself scores. Just try, like this writer, to identify the strengths. What gives it voice? What makes the ideas strong? What do you think will touch your readers most? If you like, consider what might be improved as well.

I decided not to give up hope just yet. The secret was to remain calm. After all, my file had to be somewhere—right? That's what all the manuals say—"It's in there *somewhere.*" I went back to the "File" menu, much more carefully this time. First, I tried a friendly sounding category called "Find File." No luck there; I hadn't given my file a name.

Ah, then I had a brainstorm. I could simply go up to *Undo.* Yes, *Undo* would be my savior! A simple click of a button and my problem would be solved! *Undo,* however, looked a bit fuzzy. Not a good sign. "Fuzzy" means there is nothing to undo. *Don't panic . . . don't panic . . .*

I decided to try exiting the program, not really knowing what I would accomplish by this, but now feeling more than a little desperate. Next, I clicked on the icon that would allow me back in to word processing. A small sign appeared, telling me that my program was being used by "another user." Another user? What's it talking about? *I'm* the only user, you idiot! Or at least I'm *trying* to be a user! Give my paper back! Right now!

I clicked on the icon again and again—to no avail. Click . . . click . . . clickclickclickclickCLICKCLICKCLICKCLICK!!!!! Without warning, a thin trickle of smoke began emanating from the back of the computer. I didn't know whether to laugh or cry. Sighing, I opened my desk drawer, and pulled out a tablet and pen. This was going to be a long day.

Student's Comments

In this essay, I tried to capture the feelings of frustration that occur when human and machine do not communicate. The voice in this piece comes, I think, from the feeling that "We've all been there." Everyone who works with computers has had this experience—or something close to it. I also try to give the writer—me—some real personality so the sense of building tension comes through. A tiny writer's problem (not being able to find a good ending) turns into a major problem (losing a whole document). This makes the ideas clear, and also gives this little story some structure. I think the reader can picture this poor, frustrated writer at her computer, wanting, trying to communicate in a human way—but finding that in its own mechanical way, the

■ **Suggested Scores**

Ideas: 5, 6

Organization: 5, 6

Voice: 5, 6

Word choice: 5, 6

Sentence fluency: 5, 6

Conventions: 5, 6

■ Lessons Learned from Paper 8

- Good conventions emphasize voice.
- Fragments are working when they sound natural.

■ Comments

This piece flows well and echoes real speech. Anyone who has worked with an uncooperative computer will sympathize with the writer's attitude—and it's that attitude that produces the voice, together with the very effective strategy of having a "conversation" with a machine. Notice the wide range of conventions used effectively to enhance the writing. For an excellent lesson in how conventions work, compare this piece with "The Redwoods" (Figure 3.3, page 39)—also conventionally clean but lacking the nimble conventional manipulations of this writing. The lead and ending are outstanding—very subtle. Does her reflection match your response?

Paper 9 **The Pirate Ship** (Descriptive, Grade 5)

Up above the waters are rippling, but in the watery depths of the ocean floor a sunken pirate ship lies nestled in the golden sand. Its skeleton is battered and broken. Its tall pine mast lay on its side like a soldier fallen in battle. The one deadly ship's cargo of gold is forever lost in its spooky grave.

Hovering above the ship a whale is patrolling the waters of the Caribbean Sea. Like a vacuum, the giant mammal sucks up its scaly meal of krill and small fish until it rises to the surface to take a breath of salty air. The giant sea mammal casts a huge shadow that paints the sea floor a shade of misty gray.

A hammerhead shark lurks in the shadows. It's waiting for any unsuspecting prey to swim by its home in the deep. It blends in with its surroundings, making it nearly invisible in the depths of the ocean.

The jellyfish floats by waiting to catch a fish to feed its simple body. Its elongated tentacles lay limp below its body. Its transparent exterior makes it hard to notice as the jellyfish leaves the scene without a trace of its meaningless presence.

■ Suggested Scores

Ideas: 5, 6

Organization: 5, 6

Voice: 5, 6

Word choice: 5, 6

Sentence fluency: 4, 5

Conventions: 4, 5

The Write Connection

"The Pirate Ship"

When writing a descriptive piece (or *any* piece, really), it can be helpful to brainstorm subject-related words that paint clear pictures. You do not need to *use* them all, naturally (and you will think of others as you write), but having a word bank from which to draw makes writing easier. Try it. Work with a partner—or with your whole class—and put your words into categories so it's easy to pluck out the word you want right when you want it. For example, words for a pirate ship description might fall into these categories: *things you might see in the ocean, colors, motion words, texture words (words of feeling), words that go with sounds.*

■ Lessons Learned from Paper 9

- Verbs really do make a difference.
- Careful word choice not only creates pictures but also creates mood.

■ Comments

This is an exceptionally vivid description, the details painted on the canvas in layers. Clearly word choice is the standout trait: *battered and broken, soldier fallen in battle, patrolling the waters, its scaly meal, unsuspecting prey, elongated tentacles, its meaningless presence.* High scores in voice reflect the fact that this writer thoughtfully chose words that would create an ominous, dark mood, and this is consistent throughout the piece. Many beginning writers choose modifiers for modifiers' sake. Not so this writer. There is drama and suspense in each paragraph. Slightly lower scores in sentence fluency reflect the fact that many sentences begin the same way and tend to follow a subject-verb structure. We'd like to see more of the variety that makes paragraph 2 especially graceful.

Paper 10 ## The Woman a.k.a. the P.B. and J.
(Persuasive/Expository, Grade 12)

In your lifetime, you may meet some interesting people, but none as interesting as me. You may come across persons who astonish you with their intellect, but none will compare with me. You might encounter those with a sense of humor that will have your stomach in knots, and your face muscles cramping from laughing so hard, but no one will make you crack a smile like me. You might think Elle MacPherson is God's gift to men, but once you get one look at me, your mind will instantly change. I am perfect in every way, there's only one problem, I don't exist.

I am the woman every other American female despises. I am the Barbie, the super model, the Julia Roberts, the Meg Ryan, the perfect woman. If you wanted to cook me up and serve me, I'd be the smoked Alaskan salmon dipped in lemon-dill sauce and served on a silver platter at your favorite five-star restaurant.

Yet, for all my beauty, intelligence, and all around excellence, I bring nothing but hurt. In my short lifetime, I've brought about bulimia, anorexia, the sudden popularity in "shrinks" across America, not to mention the dreaded need for tweezers. My presence, while adored by testosterone-driven men, brings nothing but jealousy and "the sore loser" syndrome to ladies. You may ask where plastic surgery came from. Don't worry, you can thank me later.

(continued)

I'm in every make-up set in America. I lurk in the background of every woman's full length mirror. True, I don't exist . . . in physical form. No, for I live only in the back of every woman's mind, thriving on the superficial and self conscious. I am of a greater evil, one which will live forever. As long as womankind allows me to dessimate her self-esteem, I will never die.

The truth of the matter is, with all of women's achievements, political progress and obstacles overcome, it amazes me that I continue to penetrate their vulnerable side. You would think that so much knowledge gained would bless them with the wisdom, that they're more beautiful, and stronger than me in every way. Yet, with every swig of Slim-Fast, every face-lift, every diet pill, they continue to take a step back on a path which they've fought so hard to change.

Perhaps they'll soon come to realize that Alaskan salmon in a five-star restaurant will never compare to that P.B. and J. for a midnight snack.

■ **Suggested Scores**

Ideas: 5, 6

Organization: 5, 6

Voice: 5, 6

Word choice: 4, 5

Sentence fluency: 5, 6

Conventions: 4, 5

■ **Lessons Learned from Paper 10**

• Perspective helps define voice.

• Metaphor enhances meaning if done well.

■ **Comments**

This paper is a strong indictment of the shallowness of American society and our worshipful attitude toward appearance for its own sake. The writer's voice is spunky, self-assured, and insightful. It's edgy but more humorous than bitter. Taking the perspective of the "perfect woman" allows the writer a bit of irony, too—*"it amazes me that I continue to penetrate their vulnerable side."* Here and there, commas link independent clauses: *You may ask where plastic surgery came from. Don't worry, you can thank me later.* Overall, though, conventions are strong. The Alaskan salmon metaphor allows for a nice ending—the reference to the P.B. and J. snack—the woman of real quality, presumably.

The Write Connection

"The Woman a.k.a. the P.B. and J."

Look carefully at the word choice in "The Woman a.k.a. the P.B. and J." Highlight the words or phrases you think are particularly strong: e.g., "astonish you with their intellect." Now, underline any you might consider changing: e.g., " . . . a path which they've fought so hard to *change*." Did they really fight to *change* the path—or to *forge* the path? Make any changes in word choice you wish, working to get at the author's precise meaning. Read the result aloud.

Paper 11   **A Collaboration of Thoughts on Art**
(Essay, Grade 10)

Everyone tries to classify art, but really you can't. The definition of art is different for each person. What I call art could be garbage to others. Art can be anything and everything. Art is created by a person who has a passion for something, or it could be created by accident. Art takes on many forms. It doesn't have to be restrained to paper and pen, canvas and paint, picture and negative. Art flows through our body. It runs in our veins. Art is the way we move, the way we speak, the way we live. Art comes naturally, even if we don't take art classes. It's already inside us. We can say that we aren't artists, but the truth is, everyone is. Art isn't something you learn—you're just born with it. We may take classes to help us express our artistic skill in different forms, but you always have that artist inside you, in your bones.

■ **Suggested Scores**

Ideas: 5, 6
Organization: 4, 5
Voice: 4, 5
Word choice: 4, 5
Sentence fluency: 5, 6
Conventions: 5, 6

■ **Lessons Learned from Paper 11**

- Parallel structure gives rhetoric power: . . . *the way we move, the way we speak, the way we live.*
- Sometimes, short and sweet is a virtue.
- Shifts in person (from *I* and *We* to *You*) can be jarring.

■ **Comments**

Some readers want this piece to be longer. I couldn't disagree more. I love how succinct it is. The writer says what he has to say and then stops. Almost *no one* can do that. I admit, though, I would like one thing clarified: "Art is created by a person who has a passion for something, or it could be created by accident." How so? Accidental art? I love the concept, but I would like a few examples of that one. (Absence of examples brought the ideas score down slightly—it's still strong because focus and clarity are good.) Thoughts are a bit random, but still engaging. The piece overall is elegant in tone; so the word *garbage* feels a little heavy and out of place (Compare *refuse, trash, detritus, castoffs, claptrap, remnants, remains*). Also, the shift from first person (*I* and *We*) to second person (*You*) might feel natural to the writer, but disrupts the flow. Parallel structure just flows from this writer's pen. He's a poet. Strong ending.

The Write Connection

"A Collaboration of Thoughts on Art"

Most of the time, this writer writes in first person, using *I* and *We*. When he shifts to second person—*you*—it is a bit disruptive, even though it is still easy to follow the thought. Go through the piece carefully and highlight each example of second person (*you* or *your*). Revise to eliminate these by either (1) changing them to first person (*I* or *We*), or (2) simply rewording the sentence. See how much the consistency improves the overall flow of the piece.

The Next Step

If you have worked through many of the papers in the preceding three chapters, you should know the traits well—even if you did not agree on all the scores. Use these papers to spark discussions of writing with your students, too. Share hard copies they can mark up, if possible, and encourage them to keep a notebook of lessons learned, adding other pieces of writing you read and discuss together. Read on to consider the many other things you can do to strengthen your students' writing skills.

Chapter 6   In a Nutshell

- Conventions are not just about correctness. They offer a reader interpretive clues about meaning and voice.

- Conventions by nature define what is acceptable at the moment and are continually changing.

- Presentation, or layout on the page, is critical in some forms of writing (e.g., a children's picture book, a poster advertising a play), less so in others.

- For classroom purposes, attention to presentation can focus on such features as sizes and types of fonts, use of headings or subheadings, bulleted or numbered lists, and consistency both in citations within or at the end of text and labeling of graphics.

- Putting all six traits together gives us a thorough and complete profile for a piece of writing.

- Every single piece of writing teaches lessons of the craft and offers opportunities to improve revision skills.

Study Group   Interactive Questions and Activities

1. **Activity and Discussion.** Answer the following question individually; then discuss your responses within your group. How much emphasis do you place on conventions in your own instruction?

    _____ *A great deal*. I consider conventions essential to good writing.

    _____ *Some*. Conventions are important, but should not overshadow other traits.

    _____ *Very little*. I consider conventions less important than other traits.

2. **Activity and Discussion.** Choose a published piece of writing: a brochure, newspaper, menu—whatever. As a group, assess the piece for the trait of conventions and presentation. What issues other than "correct versus incorrect" arise from your assessment? What does this teach you about what you consider "conventionally" important?

3. **Activity and Discussion.** As a group, make a list of ways in which modern conventions are changing in American writing. Which changes do you applaud? Which changes do you find disturbing?

4. **Activity and Discussion.** Choose a book cover that appeals to you. Talk about ways in which presentation might influence you to buy the book. With your group, make a list of the kinds of publications in which presentation plays an important role in appealing to readers.

5. **Activity and Discussion.** By assessing and discussing student work, you have taught yourself what the traits are about and should know them well enough to describe them in your own words. Take the next step by making overhead copies of the trait shorties so you can share these with your students. Then, identify two papers for each trait—one strong, one weaker—that you can share with students, read aloud, assess, and discuss. *You now have one lesson for each trait set to go.*

6. **Activity and Discussion.** As a next step, design one revision lesson for each weaker sample you have chosen. Use the Write Connection sidebars in this and the preceding chapter as models.

Reflections on Writing

I write because it is a way to create a thunderstorm when the weather is too dry. With my imagination, I create rain which turns to thunder, which turns to lightning, which makes the dry land (my paper) wet and beautiful. It is a way to give others a gift without having to take out my wallet.

—Katie Miller, student writer

I wish I could write essays in a way that would let me create my own structure, a structure that would fit my purpose and aid the reader. Not so much writing like I talk, but writing the way I think. The idea sounds a lot more appealing than a five-paragraph structure. Those are easy and thoughtless, and putting any creativity into them is too difficult. If the writer is bored, won't the reader be? Who cares where the thesis is placed? Who decided one quotation per paragraph is the right number? If a quotation fits, it fits. Why fight it? Doesn't that make it worse? Perhaps I care more about the message than the form.

—Meghan Eremeyeff, student writer

Using Traits to Support Writing Process

Assessment is not the private property of teachers. Kids can learn to evaluate their own writing. They must take part in this . . . it is central to the growth of writing. Even before they write, they need to know about what makes writing strong or effective. And they need to know the criteria by which their own writing will be judged.

—**Marjorie Frank**
*If You're Trying to Teach Kids How to Write . . .
You've Gotta Have This Book!, 1995, p. 175*

At the beginning of the composing process there is only blank paper. At the end of the composing process there is a piece of writing which has detached itself from the writer and found its own meaning, a meaning the writer probably did not intend.

—**Donald M. Murray**
Learning by Teaching, 1982, p. 17

Writing process is foundational to writing instruction. A process-based approach, however, is strengthened—*dramatically*—by the inclusion of traits. *Process* provides a *context for the traits*. Process makes the traits *make sense.*

This comes clear at once when we think about what process is at the core: planning, writing, revising—all in a never-ending cycle. For most people, the most difficult part of process to teach (or *do*) is revising. Traits make it easier. With the traits, you can say to your students, "I am going to show you some strategies for making your revision more powerful than you ever thought it could be. I am going to share six writing qualities that will help you make your writing soar."

With the six traits, students learn to do more than fix the spelling. They learn to do the kind of deep-text revision that clarifies meaning and releases voice. Even better, they learn to do it *on their own*, without relying on you to choreograph every step.

 ## Learning Process from the Inside Out

When I first became a teacher, I did not *teach* writing at all. I assigned it. That's because the assigning of writing, followed by the collecting and correcting of writing, is what had been modeled for me. My teachers focused so heavily on the *product* (what kind, how long, how correct) that they scarcely concerned themselves at all with the *how* of writing. I did not see a single one of them write—and so never saw them revise either. My entire instruction in the art of revision went something like this: "Plan to turn in your final draft Monday." I did not know how to think about or choose writing topics, begin or end a draft, or revise for purpose, meaning, or audience.

I did not learn these things by teaching, either. I learned them by *writing*—and then taking my own process apart so I could share it with students, and with teachers.

Research has taught us much about writing process. People like Janet Emig, Donald Murray, Donald Graves, and Lucy Calkins have revolutionized the teaching of writing by documenting things real writers do. They taught us that, as Donald Murray puts it, "meaning is not thought up and put down" (2004, p. 3). They recognized the artificiality of trying to plan every line in advance because we cannot turn our minds off and on like faucets, and writing evolves as we write—and think. Putting words on the page allows us to have a dialogue with ourselves, which is what revision is. A reviser is simply saying, "No—that's not quite it. I can say that more clearly . . . "

It isn't enough to read about writing process, however, or even to attend workshops that show us how it looks. As Mem Fox tells us, we need to *discover* it for ourselves—by being writers, and learning it from the inside out (1993, p. 35).

Getting Started

Here's a logistical tip: Begin your instructional year by *just letting students write for a time*, accumulating rough drafts that they keep in a folder. By the time students have accumulated four or five drafts in their writing folders, they are ready for the traits because they have copy to work with. They have *something to revise*.

Use this generative time to teach writing process, and reinforce what you teach by modeling your own planning, drafting, and revising. Write in front of your students—or at least *talk through* your writing in front of them so they can see and hear how a writer thinks and works. Such modeling is vital, but it is something we must teach ourselves (and sometimes push ourselves) to do.

You'll hear teachers say, "I use process, yet it doesn't seem to make a difference." It can—it *will*—if we let our students see us plan, write, and revise. When teachers say, "I *use* writing process," what they really mean, quite often, is "I *describe* writing process to my students." Describing achieves almost nothing. If we do not *model* the steps, students do not really understand what to do. You are modeling process for students if you are doing those things listed in Figure 7.1, or something like them.

> I started searching for the writing process under the illusion I could find a way to make writing easy—the sword would come right out of the stone. I didn't realize then that the importance of writing lies in the fact that it is not easy, and should not be.
> —Donald M. Murray
> *A Writer Teaches Writing,*
> 2004, p. 9

What about Genres?

You may be wondering where modes or genres of writing fit into this picture. It makes sense to teach forms of writing last, *after process* and *after traits*. This is so because the traits shift slightly from one genre to another. The voice in a mystery story is very different from that in a researched piece. The conventions in a personal narrative or poem will be quite different from those in a business letter, and so on. These differences become much easier to talk about once students know what we mean when we speak of voice, organization, conventions, and so on. What's more, they are precisely the kinds of differences that help students distinguish among genres because every trait is influenced by purpose—and purpose is what genre is all about.

Connecting Traits to Process

Now let's consider how the various steps within the writing process connect to the traits. Figure 7.2 may help you get a "big picture" view of these connections.

FIGURE **7.1** **Important Things to Model for Students**

- Share topics you are thinking of writing about and explain how you discovered them.

- Show students one or more prewriting strategies that work for you: drawing, reading, talking, listing, asking questions.

- Explore possible leads for a piece by writing several possibilities—or by looking for a good quotation with which to begin, or something within the draft that excites your imagination.

- Show students where and how to get information so they can write with confidence.

- Show students how to take notes without writing down *everything*.

- Draft one paragraph—or more—so your students can see ideas flow from your thinking.

- When you finish writing, tell students what you plan to do next—and write yourself a short note as a reminder. This encourages students to do the same.

- Read a draft (or portion of it) aloud so students can respond.

- Work out any small, focused revision problem: *choppy sentences, wrong word, lack of voice, need for detail, need for a conclusion.*

- Brainstorm ideas for a good title—one that really captures the soul of the piece.

- Read aloud *with expression*—and share your thinking about how your own writing sounds to you.

- Use the reviser's friends—double (or triple) spacing, big margins, carets for inserts, deletion marks to take things out, arrows, and (if need be) taped-on inserts.

- Make a mess. Students need to see that thinking on paper is rarely neat.

- Cross out copy you don't need or like.

- Love your work. Just because you're changing it is no sign it isn't any good. That only means it's worth changing.

- If you're nervous, share your feelings. It helps students to know that teachers of writing also need encouragement and support. They will give it to you.

- Ask for specific help. It's important for students to understand that writers need to ask responders for the kind of help they need or want.

 Experience: The Well We Draw From

Writing does not really begin with prewriting, as many diagrams suggest. It begins with life, our personal experience, our sense of what is important, what is worth sharing. In *Winterdance* (1994), Gary Paulsen writes of the Iditarod, the stillness of the Alaskan northlands, the beauty of the aurora borealis, and his near-death experiences from freezing and being attacked by an enraged moose.

In *Travels* (1988), Michael Crichton writes of his personal challenges in completing medical school—how he nearly fainted drawing blood and had to hang his head out the window to keep from passing out in front of his patients, how his hands shook when he dissected his first cadaver.

Occasionally, we take the task of finding writing topics out of students' hands. This is all right sometimes. Part of writing is learning to deal effec-

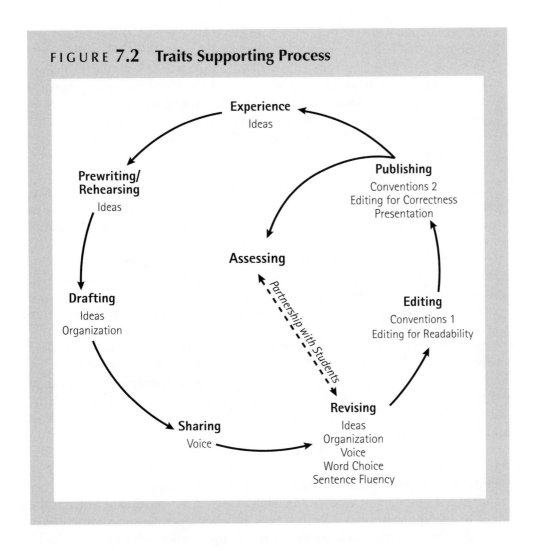

FIGURE **7.2** **Traits Supporting Process**

tively with writing tasks required by someone else, including employers. If we write ourselves, though, we also know how important it is for writers to identify the topics that are important in their own lives. "Children who are fed topics, story starters, lead sentences, even opening paragraphs as a steady diet for three or four years," says Donald Graves (1983), "rightfully panic when topics have to come from them. The anxiety is not unlike that of the child whose mother has just turned off the television set. 'Now what do I do?' bellows the child" (p. 21). Writers must learn to sense the moment when writing begins. Listen to Sue Monk Kidd as she describes the inspiration for her novel *The Secret Life of Bees*:

> The whole idea for the novel began one evening when my husband reminded me that the first time he'd visited my home to meet my parents, he'd awakened in amazement to find bees flying about the room. After he told that story, I began to imagine a girl lying in bed while bees poured through cracks in her bedroom walls and flew around the room. I couldn't get the image out of my head [2002, p. 5].

Sometimes inspiration comes from visiting a place that makes an impression so strong that the characters grow out of the setting:

> I like to tell my as-yet-unrealized philosophers at the start of our journey together that everyone has a philosopher inside and that kids always impress me with their seemingly endless ability to wonder. How high does the sky go? Why are there so many different languages? Does the world look the same to a frog as it does to me? Why do people hurt one another? Does my dog know how much I love him?
>
> —Marietta McCarty
> *Little Big Minds,* 2006, p. 2

When we hear Billie Letts say, "I walked in a Wal-Mart and looked around and I thought, 'You could live here. There's everything you need. You could exist in this place.'" This happening, this walking-into-Wal-Mart, was the beginning that led Letts to write the novel *Where the Heart Is* (1995). So we hear her say this and then we know: writers get ideas for writing when they are away from their desks. Writers can get ideas at Wal-Mart [Katie Wood Ray, *What You Know by Heart: How to Develop Curriculum for Your Writing Workshop*, 2002, p. 4].

Identifying topics requires sifting through the sands of your experience, looking for what is writing worthy, and listening for moments that speak to you. In order to teach this, you must find the treasures buried in the sand of your own life and share what you find with your students.

Donald Murray (2004) tells of pulling topics from his childhood: "I came from a background that was filled with sin, guilt, and threats of Hell and damnation. I was brought up with a grandmother who was paralyzed when I was young, and it was my job when I woke up early in the morning to see if she was still alive" (p. 11).

> It is not the job of the teacher to legislate the student's truth. It is the responsibility of the student to explore his own world with his own language, to discover his own meaning.
>
> —Donald M. Murray
> *Learning by Teaching*, 1982, p. 16

My own writing comes largely from family memories and childhood experiences as well. Among my most vivid recollections is the sight of my mother, an air pistol tucked neatly beneath her apron, preparing to protect my five-year-old friend Gail from an attacking dog. She shot the dog neatly, without a flinch or regret (he was stunned and frightened but not injured), and returned to her baking.

More than thirty years later, I was wheeling my mother—who by then had lost her sense of time and place—through the corridors of a nursing facility, trying to hold back my tears, and she was asking me if I had lost my mind and, if not, why in God's name I had selected this particular hotel as the place to spend our holidays. Both scenes are chapters in an upcoming book.

I also have written extensively of my grandmother, who taught a K-12 class in a single room in North Dakota and who could slice the head off a rattlesnake as cleanly and swiftly as Emeril dices celery. Her kitchen, with its uniquely rustic linoleum-covered table, smelling of vanilla, bread, chocolate, and coffee, was my place of refuge, where I listened to stories of my father, Jack, as a child and of her legendary feral cat, Snooky, who killed everything that dared to invade her territory, including smaller dogs. I remember my grandmother's fierce and sparkling eyes, the reassuring and surprising strength of her arthritic fingers, how her hamburgers (sautéed in butter) tasted a hundred times better than anyone else's, and how she hugged me as if I'd shown up to rescue her. She served me coffee when I was 13 because, she said, "It makes the stories better."

When you model topic selection, help your students to see how writing topics grow out of humble adventures—tasting your first cup of coffee, dealing with your neighbor's biting dog, watching your grandmother bake bread. The best topics, Donald Graves suggests, come from an "everyday reading of the world." If we don't teach children how to seek out what matters, they will think that *only* trips to Disneyland or emergency appendectomies make good copy. They will feel compelled to "draw only on the experiences of others, which they do not necessarily understand" (1994, p. 58).

Prewriting/Rehearsing: Giving Shape to the Ideas We've Chosen

In prewriting or rehearsing, we give shape and focus to the ideas that come from experience. I think of rehearsing as playing with an idea in my head, the sort of thinking a person might do while walking the beach or gardening. Prewriting involves actual planning, putting something on paper or at least talking about it. Rehearsing is more internal, whereas prewriting makes a topic visible, perhaps through webbing, sketching, or listing.

Prewriting techniques are as varied as the writers who use them, so we do well to give our students a wide range of strategies. I like to talk. When my mother was confined to a nursing home, she had a friend named Grace, whom my husband and I visited regularly. Grace was very proud of her hair, which was a beautiful silver color and very curly. As we conversed one day, she confided, "I didn't always wear my hair this way, you know. It was different before the bank robbery." That's an interesting milestone, don't you think? I found myself telling friends about Grace's gravelly voice, her passion for red clothes, her way of punctuating each sentence with a wink—and how dangerous she could be playing wheelchair tag. As I talked about her, I knew I would one day write about her as well.

Many writers like webbing (see Figure 7.3), and although it does not work well for me, I think it's important to teach it and model it because it does work well for many writers. I love lists of potential readers' questions and often will elicit these from a class of students (see Figure 7.4) by presenting them with a one-liner, e.g., *My mother shot a dog.* Then I simply ask, "What would you like to know?" Questions work well for many writers, especially those who struggle with organization, because the draft flows right out of answering the questions.

Prewriting could also include drawing a picture or life map. See Figure 7.5 for an example, courtesy of my teacher friend and colleague Sally Shorr. This

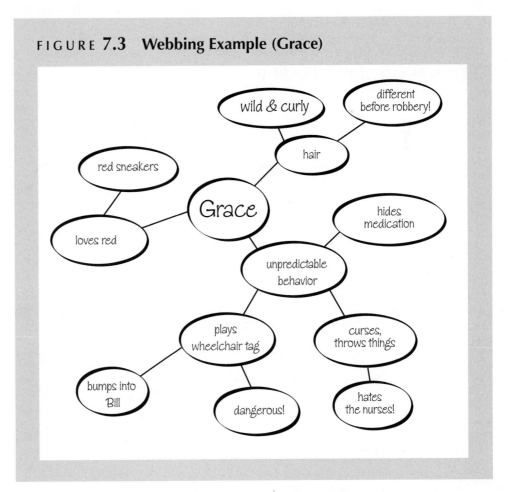

FIGURE 7.3 Webbing Example (Grace)

FIGURE 7.4 Listener's Questions

- ✔ Why did she shoot the dog?
- ✔ Was it your dog?
- ✔ Did it die?
- ✔ How old were you?
- ✔ Was this the first time she did this?
- ✔ What set her off?
- ✔ What happened after she shot it?
- ✔ What sort of gun did she use?
- ✔ How did you feel when it happened?
- ✔ How was she feeling at the time?
- ✔ Were you frightened?
- ✔ Were you angry?
- ✔ Did anyone see her do it?
- ✔ Did you see her do it?
- ✔ Did she ever do it again?
- ✔ What sort of person was she?

sketch captures main events in Sally's life from about 1970 to the present, any of which could provide fuel for a story, poem, or essay. In creating this life map, Sally must reflect very deeply on what memories are most vivid or what events have helped define who she is. Create your own life map and see what adventures emerge.

In Figure 7.5a, you'll see Jamila's charming portrait of Mr. and Mrs. "Woody" (Woodfield) dancing. Like Sally (Figure 7.5), Jamila, a kindergartener, used drawing to jumpstart her writing—and notice her "revision." Originally, she placed the figures farther right, but wanted to have Mr. Woody speak, so needed to move them. This is just the kind of thinking that lets us say, "Good revision, Jamila! You noticed you'd need more space, and you rearranged your drawing. That's just the kind of change good writers make." Mr. Woody seems to be giving Mrs. Woody a rather smart kick, but as we learn from Jamila's text, it's actually a tender moment: "Mrs. Woody and Mr. Woody are having a romantic time dancing at the ball. 'I love you Mrs. Woody,' said Mr. Woody." It doesn't get better than that.

FIGURE 7.5 Sally's Life Map

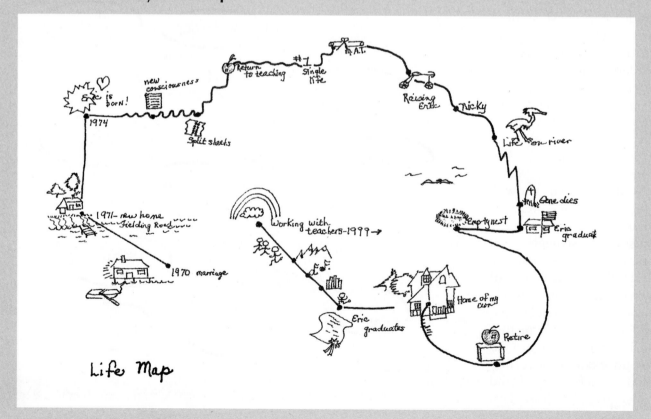

Additional prewriting techniques include include interviewing, reading, viewing a film, browsing through the Internet, or just looking out the window. When I wrote about my grandmother, my prewriting activity was poking through old family albums so I could see the characters of my writing right there on the North Dakota prairie.

Drafting: Going from Beginning to End

You cannot sculpt air; you need clay. Drafting provides writers some substance with which to work. The key to drafting, therefore, is to *keep writing* so that later there will be *something to revise*. Moreover, writing is generative. You discover what you want to say *not* so much during prewriting (as nonwriters often suppose) but during the act of writing itself. One idea leads to another, so writing itself helps you think—more than, say, staring at notes.

As teachers, we often think drafting means stretching and extending ideas. True. But as writers, we soon learn that before we can expand, we must bring our ideas under control. As Barry Lane says, "Write small." Don't write that the "Holocaust was inhuman"; describe a "mountain of children's shoes." Don't write about how messy your brother is; tell the reader how you hate finding hair on the soap (*Reviser's Toolbox,* 1999, pp. 52–53).

Drafting depends on information—a wealth of it—and can go nowhere without the fuel that information provides. When students write in generalities, we often say, "Be specific." This is not helpful advice because we are treating the symptom, not the problem. The student's writing style is not at fault; it's the limited knowledge base—mental "shelves" low on inventory. "Read," we should say. "Investigate. Interview someone. Ask questions. Make notes. Don't write another line until you've collected a wealth of information on this topic."

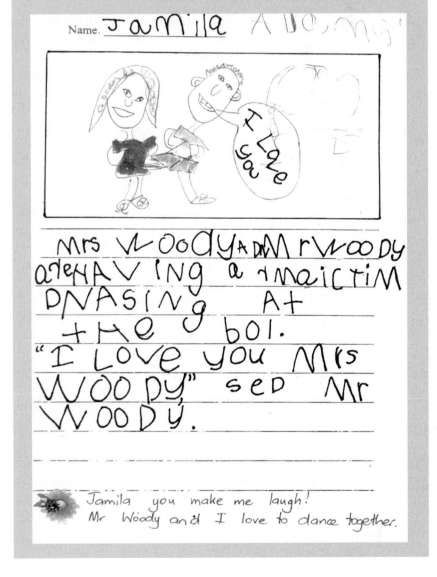

FIGURE 7.5a Jamila's Portrait of Mr. and Mrs. Woody Sharing a Romantic Moment

> Much of the bad writing we read from inexperienced writers is the direct result of writing before they are ready to write.
> —Donald M. Murray
> *A Writer Teaches Writing*, 2004, p. 17

When Sebastian Junger wrote *The Perfect Storm* (1999), he didn't write, "Hurricanes are powerful storms. They do enormous damage and threaten people's lives every year." He waited until he had enough information to write this: "A typical hurricane encompasses a million cubic miles of atmosphere and could provide all the electric power needed by the United States for three or four years. During the Labor Day hurricane of 1935, winds surpassed 200 miles an hour and people caught outside were sandblasted to death. Rescue workers found nothing but their shoes and belt buckles" (p. 129).

In writing about Brian's battle with north woods mosquitoes in *Hatchett* (1999), Gary Paulsen didn't just count on imagination. Instead, he drew on his own experience, which he recounts in *Guts* (2001), a nonfiction book on real-life research:

> I must have attracted every mosquito in the county. The cloud swarmed over me, filled my nostrils and my eyes, flooded my mouth when I breathed. They blinded me, choked me and, worst of all, tore into me like eight or nine thousand starving vampires. I don't know how much blood I lost but I do know that when I regained the house—after a wild, blind run through two hundred yards of dark woods—there wasn't a square inch on my body that hadn't been bitten [p. 60].

> All writing begins life as a first draft, and first drafts are never (well almost never) any good. . . . Write a first draft as though you were thinking aloud, not carving a monument.
> —Patricia T. O'Connor
> *Words Fail Me*, 1999, p. 38

A critical part of drafting is getting everything down on paper so that we have a sense of the "whole." Later we can see where the informational gaps are, and fill in the holes.

Equally critical is reading aloud because only through reading aloud do we discover whether the message makes sense, whether the sentences are fluent as written on the page, and whether the voice is true. Author and teacher Mem Fox talks of reading aloud everything she writes: "As I write this chapter, I hear every cadence, listen to every pause, and check every beat. I'm hoping that if you enjoy the rhythm of my words, you might be inclined to like my content as well" (1993, p. 114).

> There is no substitute for really knowing what you are talking about. The books with staying power are the ones that speak from large knowledge and add something to a reader's comprehension.
> —Wallace Stegner
> *On Teaching and Writing Fiction*, 2002, p. 45

Drafts are not always finished in a single day. This is why it is critical for students to write daily—or at least often. Writing requires continuity. It is easier for me to carry my writing over day to day to day without a break than to leave it for a week. Recapturing my train of thought will be as difficult for me then as finding my car in a huge parking lot after a seven-day absence. As Donald Graves tells us, people who write all he time carry their writing i their heads, testing ideas, rehearsing lines. They enter what Graves calls "a constant state of composition" (1994, p. 104). When children enter this state, they truly become writers, for they are then seeing the world through a writer's eyes.

Sharing Your Voice with an Audience

> The ear hears the voice— and hears when that voice fades or is lost. The ear is aware of the rhythm and melody.
> —Donald M. Murray
> *A Writer Teaches Writing*, 2004, p. 55

For many writers, sharing is the most difficult part of the whole process. Most of us probably felt this way in middle and high school, when we were writing not for an audience but for a grade. We did not always love what we wrote. We mumbled, looked down at our shoes, spoke too softly to be heard, rushed, and never used any inflection because that might have implied that we felt our own writing was worth sharing. The result? No voice.

Sharing becomes meaningful when it's linked to revision. When we begin to write for an audience and not just for a grade, our writing begins to seriously improve—and voice begins to emerge. Your students will learn to share by watching you model it. Read your writing aloud, with confidence, but with an open mind. Read the way you would like your students to read. Don't be afraid to love your writing. That lets students know it's OK for them to love their writing, too.

Focus on two things. First, really listen. Listen for content. Listen for voice. Form a circle, which gives a sense of community to the group and support to the writer. Let your whole demeanor, including your body language, show how tuned in to the writer you are. Truly taking in a writer's message is a profound means of showing respect, and is a way for the very shyest students to participate in the process, even when they do not speak.

Second, ask writers to take control of the discussion, to ask others in the group to listen for something in particular—imagery, mood, language, voice, or whatever. Sharing should not be mechanical, but interactive, with listeners giving the writer *precisely* the kind of help she or he has asked for.

Some teachers will disagree with me, but I recommend not forcing participation. If writers are shown deep respect and given sincere, heartfelt feedback, most students—eventually all—will want to share their writing. Forcing very shy students to participate before they feel ready can cause a retreat from writing process that may effectively stem the tide of creative thinking.

Revising: Letting the Traits Shine

What exactly are we teaching when we teach revision? In a nutshell, we are *teaching the traits*. Scan across levels 5 and 6 from the writing guide (Figure 3.6, page 44) and you will see a whole menu of things writers do when they revise: add detail, take out filler, craft a new lead or conclusion, make transitions stronger, change the order of things, write from the heart to add voice, make the verbs stronger, recraft sentences, and so forth. When students know the traits, the whole world of revision opens up for them.

This is why it is so important for students to have their own student-friendly versions of these writing guides (see Figure 8.1, page 159, for copies). They don't need to *score* their writing, but they need to assess what is working and what needs attention.

It is also important for students to understand the fine line between revision and editing. Professional writers do these things together, usually. But if students do not make the distinction, they may think editing *is* revising, and they may never go beyond tinkering with spelling and punctuation.

You might tell them, "Revision is big and sweeping. If you were revising a house, you'd change the whole look and feel of it by pushing out a wall, adding a room, raising the ceiling, or putting in skylights. Editing is more like moving the furniture around, neatening up, dimming the lights, putting flowers on the table, and turning on the music. Revision changes the structure, while editing makes the room appealing."

> I have an audience for this book—my editor, at least, if no one else. Although I care deeply about it, I wouldn't have dreamed of writing it had I thought that no one would read it and find it interesting, irritating, useful, old hat, provocative, or something.
>
> —Mem Fox
> *Radical Reflections,*
> 1993, p. 38

> I never insist that any child *must* speak, and I make this known at the beginning of the first class. Shy children can be paralyzed by the fear of being called on and forced to answer before they're ready.
>
> —Marietta McCarty
> *Little Big Minds,* 2006, p. 14

> When [my students] saw me, the vulnerable, egotistical writer, offering up my work to their questions, it gave them an incentive to do the same.
>
> —Roy Peter Clark
> *Free to Write,* 1987, p. 41

> I know some very great writers, writers you love who write beautifully and have made a great deal of money, and not one of them sits down routinely feeling wildly enthusiastic and confident. Not one of them writes elegant first drafts. All right, one of them does, but we do not like her very much.
>
> —Anne Lamott
> *Bird by Bird,* 1995, p. 22

Most teachers feel fortunate to get students to revise even once. But so often I am asked how to make trait-based writing work for struggling students and for those who need a challenge. This is the main place it happens: *right here during revision.*

With a struggling writer, instead of asking for a major overhaul of the whole piece (which feels and *is* overwhelming), we should consider asking the student to look at *one small feature* within one trait—and perhaps to apply it just one time. *Features* within the trait of ideas, for example, include a clear main idea, striking details, and focus. This means that when you teach this trait, you are not teaching one big global thing called *ideas,* but rather, each of these individual features. (To get a stronger sense of this, refer back to the trait "shorties" in Chapters 4 through 6, or Figure 8.5, page 171).

So, for example, I might begin by looking at just *one feature* within the trait of ideas—say *details.* What's more, I might ask the writer to consider adding just *one small detail* to *one small piece* of his or her draft—versus weaving details through the whole piece. The tinier I can make the task, the more manageable the revision becomes. I want the writer to experience success, and I will make the task as small as necessary to make that happen. Gradually, the expectations can grow with the writer's confidence, experience, and skill.

For the writer who needs a challenge, I can do just the opposite. I can ask that student to tackle revision more the way a professional writer does it—through multiple drafts across multiple traits.

So often in school we profess to see writing process as a cycle, but we teach it in a linear fashion. A writer prewrites once, writes one draft, then does one revision. This is not a challenge for an exceptional writer—nor is it anything *close* to the way writing works in the world of publishing (or college, for that matter, if you wish to be successful). So instead, we might suggest multiple revisions, with time in between to gather new information or at least gain some mental distance from the draft. With each revision, the writer could ask him- or herself some basic reviser's questions:

- Is my purpose clear?
- Does this writing make sense?
- Do I have enough information—or do I have some work to do?
- Who are my readers? Does this speak to them?
- Did I omit things everyone already knows?
- Does my organizational design make the discussion/story easy to follow?
- Is this my voice? Did I dare to say what I really believe and feel?

Managing multiple revisions is sufficiently challenging even for a professional. But here's one more strategy to kick things up a notch: Ask students *not* to go methodically through a text from beginning to end with every revision. Rather, do as the pros do and enter the text at different points each time, sometimes slipping into the middle or jumping right into the conclusion. That way, every part of the draft gets even attention.

Author Louis Sachar (*Holes,* 2000, reprinted edition) says that he rarely revises any piece fewer than five or six times and that along about draft number 3 he can begin to really sense and feel where he wants to take the writing (Florida Reading Association Conference, Orlando, FL, October 16, 1999). Even as he completes each draft, he is already revising it in his head (maybe on paper, too)—and still prewriting as well, for he is continuing to gather new information. Sharing, for this author, does not occur until after draft number 6; that's the first time, according to Sachar, that his editor, or *anyone* other than himself and his dogs ("who cannot read, anyway"), sees what he has written.

> I learned the need to disrespect the typewritten page, even to take satisfaction in plowing up those neat rows of words with a pencil if they didn't seem to serve my purpose.
>
> —Bruce Ballenger
> In Barry Lane, *After THE END,*
> 1993, p. 119

Editing: Making the Reader Feel "At Home" in Your Text

Every single piece of writing gets edited, one way or another. The question is, *Who will do the work—the writer or the reader?* When *the reader* has to do it, it is difficult for him or her to concentrate on anything else. When *the writer* does it, however, the reader can relax and focus on the message.

Editing involves correcting spelling, punctuation, and grammar; deciding issues of formality (contractions or not?); considering usage and idioms; and ensuring that sentences are complete and grammatical, that parentheses come in pairs, that colons do not follow verbs, and that paragraphs begin where they should. Editing also means ensuring that conventions support meaning. The best editors

- Use excellent handbooks and check what is *currently* correct
- Use every tool available, including personal dictionaries and spell check programs
- Ask for help if another qualified editor is available
- Read text both silently and aloud to check for errors
- Leave text alone for a time prior to editing in order to gain mental distance
- Double space and allow wide margins so that there is room for corrections *or* (if editing on a word processor) so that reading/proofing is easier

Editing can occur at two levels, as I have indicated in Figure 7.2. On one level, we edit text for readability so that we can process it with ease. At this point we want students, as much as possible, to take responsibility for their own editing, doing the best they can. We should ask for attention to detail but not demand perfection. A misspelled word should not keep us from posting a piece on the wall or celebrating other qualities (e.g., ideas, voice) within the writing.

If we publish something formally, whether through a school publishing house or a professional publishing house, editing at another level is required. For that purpose, it is important to make the copy as clean as possible; this means that it needs to be seen by another pair of eyes. This is also the time to attend to layout and appearance in addition to correctness.

Publishing: Honoring and Preserving Writing

Publishing can take many forms. Sometimes it involves making a book or even submitting work to a publishing house. Other times it may be more informal—reading from an author's chair or posting work on a wall. Informal publishing does not, in my view, demand the attention to conventions that more formal publishing requires.

Publication honors the writer's work, but it should not be mandatory. Some classrooms are in a veritable publication frenzy these days. Why? To what end? Stop right now and think. Would you wish to begin today a regimen of having to publish *everything* you write for the next year? How stressful! I sympathize fully when Mem Fox (1993) declares, "It depresses me utterly to see children being forced to finish a piece of writing when they're sick of it, lacking in inspiration, and getting negative feedback in writing conferences. No one forces me to finish my writing, and I'm a published writer, so why should any writer be ruled in such a manner by someone who doesn't own the writing anyway?" (p. 39). Do not ask students to revise everything. Do not publish or assess everything. Toss this burden away like a big rock you just discovered sitting on your left shoulder. You will feel freer, and so will your students.

Formal publication is easier than ever these days. Some agencies will publish student work without the usual hoops of submission and editorial acceptance (or rejection!). Simply search online under "Student Publishing" for numerous resources. If you go this route, use formal publication as an opportunity to ask students to edit with special care, having another pair of eyes review the document, and also ensuring that the layout is both pleasing and helpful to the intended readers. Published documents almost always include work by more than one person. So remember to provide credit to everyone who has worked on a given piece (see Figure 7.6). Not only is this appropriate, but it also helps students understand that most publications are the result of a team effort.

Assessing: For Students, the First Step in Revising

Assessment typically comes at the end of writing process, and is typically teacher-directed and grade-connected. All of this is fine so far as it goes. Teachers, not students, should be responsible for assigning grades (so long as we remain convinced we need grades). However, as Figure 7.2 suggests, what we really need is a partnership, one in which the most important assessor is the student.

Students assess their own work *not* to assign a grade but to see what needs to be revised. Self-assessment is the most important assessment of any piece of writing that can occur—*ever.* That's because this is the *only* assessment to occur during the process of revision, while there is still time for the writing to grow and change. It is also the only assessment (media hoopla notwithstanding) to have major impact upon students' thinking, and hence, upon their writing performance.

Once a grade falls on the paper, the writing process is finished—usually. But when a student assesses to say, "How can I make this stronger?" it is time for the real writing to begin.

FIGURE 7.6 Sample Credit Page

Credits
Written by Jeff Hicks
Illustrated by Fred Wolff & Billie Lamkin
Edited by Sally Shorr
© 2004 Hicks, Wolff, Lamkin & Shorr

Chapter 7 In a Nutshell

- Process-based writing should be the foundation for writing instruction. The six traits do not replace process but support it by giving students a vocabulary for talking and thinking about writing and by strengthening students' understanding of how to revise.

- In planning your instruction, think process first, then traits.

- The reason for teaching genres last is that traits change slightly from one genre to another. Voice in a business letter, for example, is slightly different from the voice in a personal narrative.

- Each step within the writing process connects in an important way to the traits:
  - *Experience:* Living life, finding/discovering ideas.
  - *Prewriting:* Refining thinking about ideas.

- *Drafting:* Getting ideas down on paper; shaping, expanding, and fine-tuning ideas; beginning to organize information—thinking how to begin, where to go next, and how to end.
- *Sharing:* Connecting with an audience through voice.
- *Revising:* Using all traits (except conventions) to reshape text.
- *Editing:* Polishing conventions to ensure readability and to bring out meaning and voice.
- *Publishing:* Sharing writing informally (posting, reading) or formally (book making).
- *Assessing:* As students assess *to revise* and teachers assess *to evaluate*, they become partners in learning about writing.

Study Group Interactive Questions and Activities

1. **Activity and Discussion.** Draw your own diagram of the writing process as *you* see it. Base your sketch on how you teach writing or on how you write, or both. Compare your personal diagram with those of your colleagues and also with the diagram shown in Figure 7.2.

2. **Activity and Discussion.** As a writer, which of the following strategies do *you* use to prewrite? Which might you teach to students? Discuss your responses with colleagues.

_____ Talking
_____ Sketching
_____ Just starting right in with a draft
_____ Webbing
_____ Making a list of questions or key points
_____ Looking up information I don't know
_____ Looking for a literary model
_____ Other _____

3. **Activity and Discussion.** As a writer, which of the following strategies do *you* use to revise? Which might you teach to students? Discuss your responses with colleagues.

____ Writing on every other line to allow room for revision

____ Putting a draft away for two or more days

____ Reading my writing aloud to myself

____ Sharing my writing with a trusted colleague

____ Revising more than once—perhaps looking for slightly different things

____ Starting second or third revisions in the middle—or at the end

____ Using a rubric or checklist as a reminder or guide

____ Other _____

4. **Activity and Discussion.** Consider ways you might ask students who need a challenge to do multiple-draft revisions or to act as reviewers or copy editors for other students wanting to publish their work.

5. **Activity and Discussion.** With your group, brainstorm a list of topics you could write on right now—or would like to write on if you knew more. Star those that would require some research. With your colleagues, talk about where writers get their ideas, and how they know whether they have enough information to begin writing. Plan ways of sharing your list with students to open a discussion of how writers come up with personal topics.

6. **Discussion.** Have you ever found yourself in what Donald Graves calls "a constant state of composition"? Describe and discuss this experience with students or colleagues.

7. **Activity and Discussion.** With your colleagues, look again at Figure 7.1, "Important Things to Model for Students." Which of these things do you model currently as part of your instruction? Which might you consider modeling in the future?

8. **Activity and Discussion.** Make a one- or two-day instructional plan that involves (1) setting up writing folders in which students can collect their work, (2) introducing the fundamental steps within writing process (perhaps through a short writing activity), and (3) introducing students to the six traits. Compare your plan with those of your colleagues.

Reflections on Writing

I write because I know that every bone in my body will appreciate my work, the long hours I put into it, and all the gears in my head working to their full capacity.

—Ryan Sterner, student writer

I've often had these prompts in my Lit classes that ask, "Do you like to write?" It is like asking me if I like to breathe, if I like my heart beating. Writing just is. It is a part of me, and I love every part of it. I enjoy researching, contemplating, screwing up, draft writing, revising, and printing out the crisp, white, finished piece. I love the smell of ink on paper.

—Simona Patange, student writer

Unlocking the Door to Revision

Children are seldom shown how to read their work using actual texts. Rather, they are cajoled into "writing better" without knowing how good writing unfolds or how a writer thinks. Worse, they aren't made aware of strong writing within their own text. Even in my poorest piece, I need to know the best section, the strongest line, or the best use of language.

—Donald H. Graves
A Fresh Look at Writing, 1994, p. 222

We need to think hard about how we talk about writing—to our colleagues, to our students, to ourselves. Language, as the linguists tell us, is also the language of thought. In the end, the words we use to explain such concepts to our students will be the words they use to explain them to themselves.

—Ralph Fletcher
What a Writer Needs, 1993, p. 6

The six traits fit beautifully into virtually any writing workshop format you can design for your classroom. And the best part is, you don't have to change what is already working. The traits do not replace *anything*. They only *enhance* good practice—from personal comments to conferences.

Start with Process . . .

Let's begin by assuming that writing process is the basis for your instruction. In other words, you ask students to think about and plan their writing, often choosing their own topics. They have a folder in which to store their writing, and from that folder they choose pieces to revise and edit. They write in a variety of genres, for a variety of purposes. You do not *assess* everything. They do not *revise* everything. That way, they get to write often without overwhelming themselves or you. This is a very good thing.

. . . then Workshop

Now let's say that you hold writing workshop three to five times a week in your classroom. Also a very good thing.

There is no single right way for this to look. It is very much up to you. Usually, though, writing workshop has three key parts: First, a teacher-led instructional time that might consist of suggestions, reading aloud, direct instruction in the form of short conferences or focused lessons, and so forth. Second, personal writing time, during which students explore ideas for writing and/or go to their folders, choose a piece on which to work, and plan, research, draft, revise, edit, or confer with peers. Everything comes together in the third part of workshop—when students meet to share their writing aloud. Not everyone can share every day, naturally—but students love to hear what other writers are doing and to offer their responses as coaches.

While students are researching or writing, you might be writing too—even if only for a very few minutes. Or, you might be holding conferences. What you do *not* want to do is to make yourself THE person to go to every time a question arises. You want to encourage students to rely on one another as much as possible. This is what keeps the workshop flowing smoothly. It frees you to do some individual conferences, and—equally important—strengthens students' coaching skills and innovation in solving writers' problems when you are not available.

Give It Power

What difference do the traits make in this scenario? You will understand this much better if you think of traits not as a series of mini-lessons, but rather as what they really are: *writer's language.*

This language makes it easier for students to think like writers—and easier for you to talk to them writer to writer. There are countless ways to put language into your classroom: posters and trait-based checklists come to mind immediately. But you'll also find yourself echoing the traits in your written comments. You'll talk writer's language during conferences—and students will use writer's language with one another in response groups and during their sharing time.

Students who know the traits read differently, too. They listen for (and comment on) voice. They notice detail in both text and illustrations. They pay attention to the power and energy created by strong verbs. They'll figure out how many different ways writers begin sentences.

In Judy Mazur's third grade classroom (see Chapter 10 for a description), students use their knowledge of traits to come to a conference with a question or concern in mind: *I need help with my lead, I need a way to show how much I loved my dog without just saying it, I need a last line for my poem on dinosaurs.* This makes conferences purposeful and also makes them go faster. Later, when students share, they also take charge of the sharing and ask for specific help—again using traits to think and talk like writers: *Tell me if this has enough voice, Tell me if this sounds more funny or scary, Let me know if you can picture what I'm describing.*

Do you see how important this difference is? Instead of being personally responsible for every writer's work, Judy has made her students responsible for themselves. *They* control what happens in a conference. *They* control what happens during sharing. Knowing how to talk like writers puts students in charge of their own writing process, and ultimately, their own revision.

Guess What? You're Already Doing It . . .

As you go through this chapter, you'll likely make the happy discovery that you are already teaching the traits, even if you don't refer to them as such. You cannot help it, for it's virtually impossible to discuss or model writing without talking about ideas, details, organizational flow, leads, voice, words, or sentences. When people ask me if the traits really make a difference in writing, it occurs to me that is very much like asking whether numbers make a real difference in math. Numbers and math processes like adding, multiplying, finding the square root, or factoring would be much harder to use or explain, however, if we had no names for them. As one teacher told me, "I never knew what to call that something I responded to in my student's writing. Now I have a name for it—*voice*."

 # Connecting to Research

In 2007, Steve Graham and Dolores Perin prepared a report for the Carnegie Corporation of New York titled *Writing Next* (Alliance for Excellent Education). In that report, they identified eleven instructional strategies (pp. 4-5) that (according to the extensive research cited) appear to have a significant impact on student writing performance. Though the report targets middle and high school students, it is not much of a stretch to infer that many of these strategies—perhaps all—could make a measurable difference even for our youngest writers.

Though it is not my intention to summarize the full report here (to access a copy, type in "Writing Next" online), I wish to point out five *very* strong connections to trait-based instruction as I will outline it in this chapter.

First, the report cites the importance of teaching **specific "writing strategies"** that improve students' skills in planning, drafting, and revising their writing. This chapter—and Chapter 9—are all about such strategies.

Second, the report notes **the value of "collaborative writing,"** which—in direct contrast to what is usually allowed within the scope of writing assessments—actually encourages students to work together in designing and carrying out writing tasks. In a trait-based classroom, students work together continuously. They assess in teams to teach themselves and each other what good writing is. They plan their writing together and share their writing—both during drafting and as part of revision.

Third, the report notes how critical it is to **provide students with "specific, reachable goals"** so that they have no confusion about what success looks like or what they must do to achieve it. Making goals clear is precisely what a good writing guide does. Further, in trait-based writing, students have a voice in setting those goals.

Fourth, the report cites how helpful it can be for students to "read, analyze, and emulate" **carefully selected models of good writing.** This occurs every time students look at and discuss samples of other students' work, or use literary mentors to discover the power of strong details, voice, and more.

Fifth, the report emphasizes the importance of **a process-based approach to writing instruction.** In any successful trait-based writing approach, process is foundational. As Chapter 7 shows, the traits are interwoven throughout the cycle of writing process, but are particularly critical to purposeful revision.

Other critical elements from the research cited in *Writing Next* are also connected to trait-based instruction—notably **summarizing** (a strategy for teaching ideas) and **sentence combining** (perhaps the most effective strategy for teaching fluency). I encourage you to read the report in its entirety. And if you teach the traits now, I am confident that you will feel very validated.

Make a Plan

Teachers who teach the traits all do it differently, and there is no one plan you should feel compelled to follow. As a general guide, I suggest (as noted above) teaching the basics of process first so that students understand the concept of revision. That way, they will see a need for the traits. Give them time to write so that they have drafts on which to practice revision. They don't need to revise all these early drafts. They just need to save them in a special place and in a special notebook or folder—and later choose one, two, or more to revise.

When you first introduce the traits, **introduce them** *all*—by sharing a writing guide. Students need to see the big picture. Then you can take a step back and say, "Now let's look at each of these carefully, one by one, so we can really understand what makes for good writing."

How long you spend on an individual trait is really up to you. Some secondary teachers spend only a few days. Many primary and elementary teachers spend one to two weeks. The time depends on what you do. If you are introducing the trait, scoring and discussing written work, using literary models, revising weak pieces, and writing original pieces, you will surely need a week—perhaps two. So one to two weeks is a good rule of thumb, but you should be flexible about it.

Teach them in the order I present them in this book (with the exception of conventions). Spend a lot of time on ideas, organization, and voice because these are the "deep text" traits—in other words, the traits most affected by true revision. Word choice and sentence fluency are "first cousins" of voice, and really expand and enhance this trait. Once you've taught voice, those generally go quickly. They are easier to grasp conceptually than voice itself—which is a large idea, one most of us define for a lifetime. By the time you get to word choice, your students will be very well grounded in such skills as using a writing guide or checklist, reading critically, talking and thinking like evaluators, and knowing how to apply small lessons learned to their own text.

You may wish to **teach conventions right from the start.** This is my preference. You can start small—with a simple idea such as starting with a capital and ending with a period (or question mark). The span of things to teach under the umbrella of conventions is all but infinite, so don't try to teach (or correct) everything. Identify what is most important, make yourself a list (the top 10 or top 20), and start with the first element right when you begin trait-based instruction. That way, you'll cover a lot of ground.

What happens when you finish all the traits? You simply continue reinforcing them, based on what you see in your students' work. Let the students lead you. If fluency is an issue, spend more time there. If organization is a mystery, work on that. The beauty of the traits is that once you teach the language, it is easy to say, "Remember when we talked about the importance of a good conclusion—one that leaves readers thinking?" You never have to reteach everything.

> Effective writing instruction acknowledges that the smooth deployment of the higher-level writing strategies needed to plan, generate, and revise text depends on the easy use of lower-level skills such as handwriting, keyboarding, spelling, grammar and punctuation, and access to appropriate vocabulary.
> —Steve Graham and Delores Perin
> *Writing Next,* 2007, p. 23

Four Keys to Success

Let me now share with you four keys to making the traits work within your writing workshop:

1. Surround students with writers' language.
2. Teach students to assess writing.
3. Call on literary mentors for examples.
4. Use focused lessons and strategies to build skills.

Key 1: Surround Students with Writers' Language

Students need their own writing guides, written in language that speaks to them. In Figure 8.1 you'll find a student version of the six-point scoring guide. Figure 8.2 provides a student checklist, and Figure 8.3 provides a checklist for younger students. (A five-point student writing guide is included in the Appendix.)

Provide a copy of the student writing guide or checklist to parents too, if possible. When you do this, you ensure that everyone with a stake in creating strong writers is using the same language. Notice that the students' writing guides are formatted in the "leap the river" design, with scores of 1, 2, and 3 on one side to show a pronounced need for revision: In these pieces, problems outweigh strengths. Scores of 4, 5, and 6 have "leaped the river" into the land of proficiency, where strengths outweigh problems. In providing student writing guides and checklists, you've already taken an important step, but there's more you can do to bring writers' language into your classroom.

■ Know the Traits Well Yourself

If *you* know the traits well, writers' language will be a natural part of your instruction and of every writing conference. You can and should use your own version (don't feel compelled to quote a rubric) in the comments you make on students' writing: "Your conclusion surprised me," "The paragraphing in this essay was dead on," "This paper rings with voice—I could hear you in every line."

■ Make Posters

Use posters to highlight the key components of each trait. Make your own, or use the trait "shorties" from Chapters 4, 5, and 6.

Key 2: Teach Students to Assess Writing

Once a week (or more often, if time permits), ask students to assess and discuss writing by anonymous student writers or work by any writer who is not a member of the class. Through your sharing of examples, student writers learn more about what to do—or not do—than they could learn through

FIGURE **8.1** Student Six-Point "Leap the River" Writing Guide

Student Six-Point Writing Guide for IDEAS

6
- [ ] My writing is clear, focused, and well developed. It will hold your attention.
- [ ] You can tell just what my message is about.
- [ ] I know this topic inside and out.
- [ ] I help readers learn, think, and gain insight.
- [ ] The details I chose will intrigue you—and perhaps teach you something new.

5
- [ ] My writing is clear and focused. I expanded on key points.
- [ ] I think the message is clear.
- [ ] I know a lot about this topic.
- [ ] I share important, interesting information.
- [ ] I chose details that make the message interesting.

4
- [ ] This paper is clear and focused most of the time.
- [ ] You can tell what my main message is.
- [ ] I know a few things about this topic.
- [ ] I share *some* new information.
- [ ] I came up with a few details and examples.

3
- [ ] I wrote a list of ideas—I didn't really develop any of them.
- [ ] You might figure out my message or you might not.
- [ ] I wish I knew more about this topic.
- [ ] I ran out of things to say—it was hard to think of new information all the time.
- [ ] I scrambled to come up with details.

2
- [ ] My writing rambles—not all of it makes sense.
- [ ] I'm still figuring out what my message is.
- [ ] I do NOT know enough about this topic to write.
- [ ] I said some things I could not prove or support.
- [ ] I could not come up with many details. Is it OK to repeat things?

1
- [ ] I couldn't figure out what I wanted to say. I don't have a topic or main idea yet.
- [ ] I'm sure I left my reader with a thousand questions.
- [ ] How can I have information? I don't have a topic!
- [ ] These are just random thoughts—whatever came into my head.
- [ ] I just tried to fill up the page.

FIGURE **8.1** Student Six-Point "Leap the River" Writing Guide, *(continued)*

Student Six-Point Writing Guide for ORGANIZATION

6
- ☐ My organization leads you right through the piece like a light in the dark.
- ☐ My lead will hook you—the conclusion will leave you thinking.
- ☐ My transitions show connections you might not think of without my help.
- ☐ I spend time where it counts—on important points.
- ☐ I might have a few surprises, but you'll never feel lost.

5
- ☐ My organization holds the message together.
- ☐ I have a strong lead, and a conclusion that wraps things up.
- ☐ My transitions show how ideas connect.
- ☐ I spend most of my time on key points, not trivia.
- ☐ You can follow my discussion/story without difficulty.

4
- ☐ My organization works with my message.
- ☐ I have a lead and conclusion. They work.
- ☐ My transitions are helpful. They lead you from point to point.
- ☐ I think you can tell what's most important.
- ☐ You can follow it, but you might know what's coming.

3
- ☐ I feel like moving some parts around.
- ☐ My lead and conclusion could use work.
- ☐ I tried to use transitions. I'm not sure they show clear connections.
- ☐ I spend too much time on things the reader knows.
- ☐ Sometimes you have to pay attention to follow this—and sometimes you know *exactly* what's coming next!

2
- ☐ I feel like reorganizing *everything—beginning to end!*
- ☐ My lead and conclusion are ones you've heard a million times—or else they don't go very well with my paper.
- ☐ I wasn't sure how to connect ideas.
- ☐ I spent too much time on some things—not enough on others.
- ☐ This is hard to follow even when you pay attention.

1
- ☐ It's random—here's one thought . . . here's another.
- ☐ It just starts and stops—there's no lead or conclusion.
- ☐ I don't think any of these points are connected—it's just a jumble of ideas.
- ☐ I didn't know how much time to spend on anything.
- ☐ No one can follow this. I can't even follow it myself!

FIGURE **8.1** Student Six-Point "Leap the River" Writing Guide, (*continued*)

Student Six-Point Writing Guide for VOICE

6
- ☐ This writing is as individual as my fingerprints.
- ☐ Trust me—you will want to share this aloud.
- ☐ This is *me*: what I think, how I feel.
- ☐ Hear the passion in my voice? I want you to love this topic.
- ☐ When you start reading this, you won't want to stop.

5
- ☐ This is original and distinctive. It's definitely *me*.
- ☐ I think you'll want to read this aloud.
- ☐ My personal thoughts and feelings come through.
- ☐ My voice is lively. It's enthusiastic.
- ☐ You can tell I am thinking about the reader.

4
- ☐ You might recognize me in this piece.
- ☐ You might share a line or two aloud.
- ☐ I am definitely present on the page.
- ☐ My writing is sincere. I mean what I say.
- ☐ I thought of my reader—most of the time.

3
- ☐ My voice comes and goes. Can you tell it's me?
- ☐ This isn't ready to share—but it's getting there!
- ☐ I need more voice—or a different voice.
- ☐ I was quiet in this paper—I held back.
- ☐ I couldn't think about the reader all the time, could I?

2
- ☐ I'm hiding behind my words—this isn't me yet.
- ☐ This has a hint of voice—but it's not ready to share.
- ☐ I don't think you can tell who I am from this writing.
- ☐ I sound bored—or maybe like an encyclopedia.
- ☐ I'm worried my reader could fall asleep, or go away.

1
- ☐ I'm not "at home" in this paper. I can't hear even an echo of my real voice.
- ☐ I don't think anyone would share this aloud.
- ☐ This is an "anybody" voice. It's not me.
- ☐ I just could not get excited about this topic.
- ☐ Reader? What reader?

FIGURE **8.1** Student Six-Point "Leap the River" Writing Guide, (*continued*)

Student Six-Point Writing Guide for WORD CHOICE

6
- ☐ I found original, creative, clear ways to say things.
- ☐ I stretched for the BEST way to say it—you might even quote me!
- ☐ Every word counts—I didn't use words I didn't need.
- ☐ I used strong verbs—I didn't rely on boatloads of adjectives.
- ☐ My words make pictures in your mind, touch your senses, or help you understand.

5
- ☐ I wrote to make meaning clear—not to impress you.
- ☐ There are moments you'll remember.
- ☐ My writing is concise.
- ☐ I used strong verbs.
- ☐ My words help you understand or picture things.

4
- ☐ My writing makes sense. I used words correctly.
- ☐ You'll spot a few moments to underline or highlight.
- ☐ I might have a wordy moment or two.
- ☐ I need *more* strong verbs, but I used *some*.
- ☐ Strong moments outweigh problems.

3
- ☐ You'll get the main idea.
- ☐ Here and there is a phrase I like.
- ☐ I used more words than I needed—or repeated things.
- ☐ I need more verbs—and I need to stay away from overworked words, like *nice, good, fun, great, cool*.
- ☐ Word problems outweigh my word strengths.

2
- ☐ I wrote the first words that came to me.
- ☐ You'll need to search for a moment to highlight.
- ☐ Wordiness or repetition is a problem for me.
- ☐ Strong verbs rode into the sunset. It's all *is, are, was, were*.
- ☐ I need to stretch for some "just right" words.

1
- ☐ My words might not be "right," but they fill the page.
- ☐ It was HARD writing this.
- ☐ I had to repeat—I couldn't think of new words.
- ☐ I used the same words I always use: *nice, good, great, fun, wonderful, cool, special, really, very . . .*
- ☐ I don't think my message is clear.

FIGURE **8.1** **Student Six-Point "Leap the River" Writing Guide,** *(continued)*

Student Six-Point Writing Guide for SENTENCE FLUENCY

6
☐ This is easy to read with LOTS of voice.
☐ It flows just like a good movie script.
☐ You won't believe how much sentence variety I have.
☐ If I used fragments or repetition, it adds punch.
☐ My dialogue is like listening in on a conversation.

5
☐ You can read this with expression.
☐ I like the sound when I read it aloud.
☐ My sentences don't all begin the same way. Some are long and some short.
☐ If I used fragments or repetition, it sounds right.
☐ My dialogue sounds like real people talking.

4
☐ This would be easy to read aloud.
☐ I can read it aloud without too much trouble.
☐ I have *some* variety in sentence length—sentence beginnings, too.
☐ OK, some fragments, some repetition—but it's not a problem.
☐ My dialogue sounds OK.

3
☐ It's a rocky ride, but you can read this if you try.
☐ Some parts need smoothing out.
☐ I have___ too many short sentences, ___ too many long sentences,___ too many sentences that begin alike.
☐ I have ___ too many fragments, ___ too much repetition.
☐ This dialogue isn't real. People don't talk this way.

2
☐ You can read this *if you practice.*
☐ I have ___ run-ons, ___ choppy sentences.
☐ I have___ too many short sentences, ___ too many long sentences, ___ too many sentences that begin alike.
☐ I have ___ too many fragments, ___ too much repetition.
☐ This dialogue is definitely NOT working.

1
☐ This is hard to read, even for me.
☐ Words are missing—or the sentences just don't flow.
☐ It's hard to tell where my sentences start.
☐ I have___ too many short sentences, ___ too many long sentences,___ too many sentences that begin alike.
☐ I have ___ too many fragments, ___ too much repetition.
☐ Is there dialogue here? I'm not sure.

FIGURE **8.1** **Student Six-Point "Leap the River" Writing Guide,** *(continued)*

Student Six-Point Writing Guide for CONVENTIONS

6
- ☐ I edited this *well*. I read it silently and aloud.
- ☐ My __ spelling, __ punctuation, __ grammar, __ capitals, and __ paragraphing are *all correct*.
- ☐ I worked on the layout. It will catch your eye.
- ☐ This piece is ready to publish.

5
- ☐ I might have a few *small* errors—I'll look again.
- ☐ My __ spelling, __ punctuation, __ grammar, __ capitals, and __ paragraphing are *all correct*.
- ☐ I worked on the layout. It's good.
- ☐ This is *almost* ready to publish.

4
- ☐ I see a few errors I need to fix.
- ☐ I need to check __ spelling, __ punctuation, __ grammar, __ capitals, __ paragraphing.
- ☐ I worked on the layout. It's OK—I could do more.
- ☐ This will be ready to publish once I go through it again.

3
- ☐ I think a reader would notice errors in this piece.
- ☐ I need to check __ spelling, __ punctuation, __ grammar, __ capitals, __ paragraphing.
- ☐ My layout needs work.
- ☐ I need to read this silently and aloud, pen in hand.

2
- ☐ The errors could block my message.
- ☐ I need to check __ spelling, __ punctuation, __ grammar, __ capitals, __ paragraphing.
- ☐ My layout needs work.
- ☐ I need to read this silently and aloud, pen in hand.

1
- ☐ Errors make this hard to read, even for me!
- ☐ I can edit __ the first sentence, __ the first paragraph, __ all of it.
- ☐ I need to check __ spelling, __ punctuation, __ grammar, __ capitals, __ paragraphing.
- ☐ My layout needs work.
- ☐ I need to read this silently and aloud, pen in hand.

FIGURE **8.2** **Student Checklist**

Student Checklist

Ideas

- ❏ My writing is clear and focused.
- ❏ Key points are well developed.
- ❏ You can tell I know this topic very well.
- ❏ I chose my details carefully. They're interesting—and important.
- ❏ I whittled this topic down to manageable size

Organization

- ❏ My lead will pull you into the piece.
- ❏ My conclusion will leave you thinking.
- ❏ Transitions connect ideas clearly.
- ❏ You will never feel lost reading this.

Voice

- ❏ This writing sounds like me—and no one else.
- ❏ It's as if I'm right there having a conversation with you.
- ❏ You might choose my piece to share aloud.
- ❏ I have strong feelings about this topic and it shows.
- ❏ Once you *start* reading this, you'll want to *keep* reading.

Word Choice

- ❏ I found my own way to say things.
- ❏ I stretched for the BEST words—not just the first ones I thought of.
- ❏ I cut words I didn't need.
- ❏ Strong verbs carry the weight.
- ❏ I did *not* overdo the adjectives.
- ❏ My words help you picture things, feel things, or understand my topic.

Sentence Fluency

- ❏ This is easy to read aloud *with voice.*
- ❏ You won't believe how much sentence variety I have.
- ❏ I read this aloud and I like how it sounds.
- ❏ If I repeated phrases or used fragments, it was for emphasis.
- ❏ My dialogue is realistic. It sounds like real people talking.

Conventions

- ❏ I edited this *well.* I read it silently and aloud.
- ❏ I corrected any errors in spelling, punctuation, grammar, capitalization, or paragraphing.
- ❏ This piece is ready to publish.

FIGURE **8.3** **Checklist for Younger Writers**

Simple Checklist

Ideas

- ❏ This makes sense.
- ❏ I used examples.
- ❏ I know this topic.
- ❏ I chose interesting details.
- ❏ I told the *most important* things.

Organization

- ❏ My lead will make you want to read more.
- ❏ My conclusion wraps things up.
- ❏ I showed how ideas connect.
- ❏ This is easy to follow.

Voice

- ❏ This writing sounds like *me*.
- ❏ You will think I'm there talking to you.
- ❏ This would be fun to read aloud.
- ❏ I care about my topic.
- ❏ You'll enjoy reading this.

Word Choice

- ❏ I said things my *own* way.
- ❏ I chose the BEST words I could think of.
- ❏ I didn't use 20 words when 10 would do.
- ❏ Strong verbs make my writing lively.
- ❏ My words make pictures in your mind.

Sentence Fluency

- ❏ This is easy to read aloud.
- ❏ I read it aloud. I like how it sounds.
- ❏ My sentences start in different ways.
- ❏ Some are long and some are short.
- ❏ My dialogue sounds real.

Conventions

- ❏ I edited this *well*. I read it slowly, pen in hand.
- ❏ I corrected mistakes.
- ❏ It's ready to publish.

almost any other means. In fact, research by George Hillocks Jr. explicitly points to use of criteria and student samples—what he calls "environmental" instruction—as being among the most effective of all strategies for teaching writing (1986, p. 247). Here are some tips to keep in mind as you make your choices and share examples with students.

1. *Use samples in pairs to create contrast.* If I were structuring a lesson on ideas, I might begin with one of the weaker papers from Chapter 3, such as "Making Decisions" or "A Great Book." Many students write in this general, floaty way, but they have a much easier time seeing the problem in someone else's work. Then contrast it with a strong piece, such as "Fishing Lessons" (Figure 8.4). As you read this piece, can you picture these two fishermen together, with the sun "just creeping over the horizon"? The detail

---

FIGURE 8.4 **"Fishing Lessons"**
(Narrative, Grade 7)

It was a cool, crisp morning, about the time when the dew begins to form on the grassy banks of the stream. I had been anticipating this moment for some time and now it was here. Grandpa and I were going fishing at an ideal spot swarming with fish. We had left at about 4, but by the time we got there and unpacked, the sun was just creeping over the horizon.

Grandpa pulled the rod back and let it fly, right down stream, farther than I could see. Then, I lowered my toy fishing line down until it was just under the surfcace. Right away, Grandpa got a tug on his line, but it wasn't a fish, it was a baby alligator. The alligator was semi-small, but it still put up a fight. Grandpa would gently reel it in, give it some line, then reel it some more. Just then, I realized he had gotten the scissors and was trying to cut the jumping line. Before I could blink, he cut the line and the alligator swam into a drain pipe. That really surprised me because that was his favorite hook.

I pondered over this while I doodled around with my plastic hook in the water. About when the sun got all the way over the horizon, and it slowly was starting to get hot, we headed home with a puny guppy I caught in my plastic net. On the way to the house, I asked Grandpa why he hadn't just caught the alligator or at least reeled it in. He replied with a question—"Why cause the little fella any more pain than what life dishes out?" I learned that day that all things have a right to life and that life has a reason to be had.

in this story is striking, and you might begin with just asking students to highlight the details they find striking. Talk about the strong sense of friendship in this paper and how the writer develops it. Here's the part that is most important, though: *As soon as you finish your discussion,* ask students to go to their own folders and pull out a piece they are working on now. Ask them, "Is your writing closer to 'Making Decisions' or to 'Fishing Lessons'"? If it's the latter, ask them to highlight those parts of their own work that stand out. If the former, ask them to insert a little caret with a question mark every place within their paper that there's a "hole"—a moment that needs expansion or an example or an image.

2. *Do not worry about the grade level of the writer.* You can use third grade papers with high school students and vice versa. Select papers that clearly make a point; for example, "Detail creates voice" Or "Varied sentence beginnings add interest."

3. *Read the papers aloud.* All writing plays differently to the eye and ear. If conventions are weak or the piece looks a little sloppy on the page, students may have a hard time getting beyond cosmetics to the heart and soul beneath. Ask students to be the readers sometimes.

4. *Encourage students to work in pairs or teams.* It is critical that all students talk, and many will not do so in a large-group setting. They need to share their thinking, the reasons behind the score. Don't let students get by with saying, "It's a five," or, "It sounds like a one or a two." *Anyone* can score writing. It's having to defend your score that teaches you to think like an evaluator, a reader—and a writer.

5. *Do not limit your practice to student papers.* Once you've warmed up a little, apply your skills to scoring other forms of writing: a job application letter, a sample of technical writing, a brochure from the local aquarium, or a test. One of my favorite stories about the student-as-assessor comes from Donald Graves. He tells of a student taking a standardized test ("No talking") who insistently interrupted his teacher, despite her protests, to whisper, "Who wrote this anyway? This stuff doesn't have any voice" (1994, p. 122).

Key 3: Call on Literary Mentors for Examples

When I began teaching the traits to students, I gathered some of my favorite literature and scanned it for samples that would show the traits in action. Passages from *To Kill a Mockingbird* helped to illustrate strong ideas (not to mention one of the all-time great leads), whereas passages from *Lonesome Dove* seemed just the ticket for voice. I chose a passage from Dylan Thomas (1954/1962) to illustrate fluency and creative, unconventional word choice:

> I was born in a large Welsh town at the beginning of the Great War—an ugly, lovely town (or so it was and is to me), crawling, sprawling by a long and splendid curving shore where truant boys and sandfield boys . . . watched the dockbound ships or the ships steaming away into wonder and India, magic and China, countries bright with oranges and loud with lions [p. 5].

Terms like "coherent" and even "specific" are notoriously hard for students to grasp because they do not read stacks of student writing.

—Peter Elbow
Embracing Contraries,
1986, p. 154

The truth is that the reader is always right. Chances are, if something you're reading doesn't make sense, it's not your fault—it's the writer's.

—Patricia T. O'Connor
Woe Is I, 1996, p. 195

You don't need a thesaurus to write "bright with oranges" or "loud with lions." You only have to love language.

Also keep in mind that you *do not need to read a whole book* to illustrate a trait. Short passages work beautifully. Here, for example, are five favorite *moments* you could use for the trait of voice, and notice that because they're so short, you can use them with writers of many ages (even those who are too young to appreciate the text in its entirety):

If students are going to write, they need to regularly experience the best modern voices in the land, the voices of their time.
—Tom Romano
Crafting Authentic Voice,
2004, p. 141

> It's a funny thing about mothers and fathers. Even when their own child is the most disgusting little blister you could ever imagine, they still think that he or she is wonderful [Roald Dahl, *Matilda,* 1988, p. 7].

> Calves come early in the spring.
>   It was how we knew the winter would die, would end.
>   In the dark of the barn night when it was still cold enough outside to make things break, in the warm dark night of the closed barn they came, and when we would open the door in the morning to start chores we could smell them, the new calves [Gary Paulsen, *Clabbered Dirt, Sweet Grass,* 1992, p. 3].

> In English my name means hope. In Spanish it means too many letters. It means sadness, it means waiting. It is like the number nine. A muddy color. It is the Mexican records my father plays on Sunday mornings when he is shaving, songs like sobbing. . . . At school they say my name funny as if the syllables were made out of tin and hurt the roof of your mouth. But in Spanish my name is made out of a softer something, like silver [Sandra Cisneros, *The House on Mango Street,* 1989, p. 11].

> Warts are wonderful structures. They can appear overnight on any part of the skin, like mushrooms on a damp lawn, full grown and splendid in the complexity of their architecture [Lewis Thomas, *The Medusa and the Snail,* 1979, p. 76].

> In Lake Wobegon, we grew up with bad news. Since I was a little kid I heard it wafting up through the heat duct from the kitchen below. Our relatives came to visit on Saturday evenings and after we kids were packed off to bed, the grown-ups sat up late until ten-thirty or eleven and talked about sickness, unhappiness, divorce, violence, and all the sorrows they felt obliged to shelter children from, and I lay on the bedroom floor and listened in, soaking up information. [Garrison Keillor, *We Are Still Married,* 1989, p. xix].

Hearing many voices enriches our understanding of this complex trait, especially when the voices are different. We need the satire of Roald Dahl, the quiet power of Gary Paulsen, the profound humanity of Sandra Cisneros, the enthusiastic eloquence of Lewis Thomas (so unexpected on a humble subject like warts), and the unabashed and insightful honesty of Garrison Keillor. Students need *your* favorites, of course, because you will read them with passion—and passion is voice.

Don't overlook the bad writing. This year, I bought my husband a watch that can be worn (so I'm told) in the water. What they don't tell you when you purchase this item is that you will need to take a course to learn to operate it. Here's a small dose of the 3,000-word (I am not exaggerating) instruction sheet—just the part on alarms (had I seen this first, I would never have made the purchase):

> Press set-recall. Hour flashes. Press + or − to change hour; hold button to scan values.
>
> Press NEXT. Minutes flash. Press + or − to change.
>
> Press NEXT. AM/PM flashes in a 12-hour format.
>
> Press NEXT. Alarm day flashes. Press button to select DAILY, WKDAYS, WKENDS.
>
> Press DONE.
>
> To turn on/off, press START/SPLIT.
>
> Alarm clock icon appears when alarm is on. When alarm sounds, night-light flashes. Press button to silence. If no button is pressed, alarm sounds for 20 seconds every five minutes.
>
> Each of the three alarms has a different alert melody.

Goody. This is *only* the beginning. This watch will also remind the wearer (who has patience to work through the settings) of birthdays, anniversaries, holidays, and *all* daily appointments; it will buzz on the hour or half hour; help the user to time sprints or other physical activities; serve as a stopwatch; work as a nightlight; and keep track of golf scores. It's more than a watch; it's a life companion. But don't forget, someone has to write this copy. One or more of your own students will write this—or something much like it. Teach them (through revision practice) to write it clearly—and to *condense*.

Compare the watch instructions with this introduction from one of my son's college textbooks:

> In most college courses students spend more time with their textbooks than with their professors. Given this reality, it helps if you like your textbook. Making textbooks likable, however, is a tricky proposition. . . . [We] have tried to make [this] book lively, informal, engaging, well organized, easy to read, practical, and occasionally humorous [Weiten and Lloyd, *Psychology Applied to Modern Life,* 2003, p. xxix].

Now I feel pulled into the conversation. And that is precisely the quality I want students to put into their writing—regardless of mode or genre.

Key 4: Use Focused Lessons and Strategies to Build Skills

Focused lessons allow students to tackle writing one small bite at a time. A focused lesson may be as short as three or four minutes (Some people call these *mini-lessons*) or may run 20 minutes or more.

See Figure 8.5 for an example of how to plan individual lessons to fit a specific trait. As noted earlier (see the "shorties" in Chapters 4, 5, and 6), each trait can be broken down into individual features. Organization, for instance, comprises leads, design, transitions, pacing, and conclusions. In Figure 8.5, I took just *three* of those features and imagined several lessons I could use to teach each of them. When you break the traits down this way, you can see precisely what it is you are teaching—not a big something called "organization," but a smaller something called "leads" or "transitions." How will you

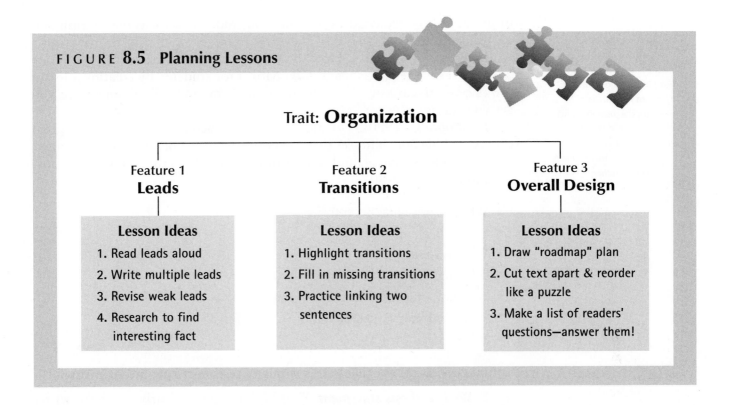

FIGURE **8.5** **Planning Lessons**

Trait: **Organization**

Feature 1 **Leads**	Feature 2 **Transitions**	Feature 3 **Overall Design**
Lesson Ideas	**Lesson Ideas**	**Lesson Ideas**
1. Read leads aloud	1. Highlight transitions	1. Draw "roadmap" plan
2. Write multiple leads	2. Fill in missing transitions	2. Cut text apart & reorder like a puzzle
3. Revise weak leads	3. Practice linking two sentences	3. Make a list of readers' questions—answer them!
4. Research to find interesting fact		

teach these things? As indicated on the chart, *possibilities* for teaching leads include reading sample leads aloud, asking students to write multiple leads for their own drafts, asking them to revise weak leads from writing samples you provide (from this book, perhaps), or asking students to research interesting facts—one of which may turn into a lead. Possibilities for teaching overall design include drawing a roadmap of the text, cutting a draft apart and reordering it, or making a list of readers' questions and then answering them. (A blank master of this planning guide is included in the Appendix.)

Following, trait by trait, are some examples of the *kinds* of focused lessons and strategies that connect to various features of each trait. You do *not* need to use *these very suggestions*; think of them as models. Try to imagine what you are *already doing* that connects to each trait.

Lessons and Strategies for Ideas

- *Main idea*
- *Detail*
- *Clarity*
- *Focus*
- *Interest*

1. Encourage student writers to choose their own topics, at least part of the time. There will be those special times when you're studying the laws

AUTHORS NOTE
For focused lessons that offer students revision and editing practice using a wide range of trait-related skills discussed in this text, please see *Creating Revisers and Editors* by Vicki Spandel (Pearson, 2009). These lessons (30 per set) are available for students in grades 2 through 8. For information, see www.ablongman.com

> Assigned topics aren't necessarily voice blockers. Teachers can make topics more malleable by leaving room for students to make topics personal and relevant within the framework of the assignment.
>
> —Tom Romano
> *Crafting Authentic Voice,*
> 2004, p. 27

of physics or the Holocaust that you wish students to focus their writing on a specified topic, but even then they often can personalize or narrow topics within prescribed bounds. How to find topics? Keep lists, borrow from one another, read extensively—and *talk*. Model for students by creating a list of topics *you* are currently thinking of writing on, and talk about where you get your ideas.

In *Shoptalk* (1990), Donald M. Murray describes himself as a great observer of life but confesses that sometimes even he does not "feel the muse" perched on his shoulder, and so uses questions such as these to uncover possible topics (pp. 79–80):

- What surprised me recently?
- What's bugging me?
- What is changing?
- What did I expect to happen that didn't?
- Why did something make me so mad?
- What do I keep remembering?
- What have I learned?

Your students can ask themselves similar questions to get ideas flowing.

2. *Write a thesis statement.* Writing flows more clearly when the writer has his or her main message clearly in mind. A message, or thesis, is different from a topic. A topic can be expressed as a *single word*; a thesis requires a *statement. Cats* is a topic. *Cats are highly intelligent* is a thesis—a main message, if you will. *Traffic* (one word) is a topic. This is a thesis: *Traffic now moves so slowly that the average commute has lengthened to an hour in our city.* A one-word topic leads to sprawly writing; a thesis gives writing direction and focus.

3. *Write a how-to poem.* Significant details that go beyond common knowledge strengthen writing. Barry Lane (*Reviser's Toolbox,* 1999) calls the good details the "potatoes"—because they're hidden, or at least less than obvious, and you have to dig for them. Try this with your students. Make a list of details on any topic. Look for the "potatoes"—those details that are most striking or that go beyond the obvious. Use them to create a "how-to" poem that might show how to be a shark, an elephant, a teenager, a strong piece of writing—or as in one ninth grader's delightfully diabolical example, a water bug (see Figure 8.6). How-to poems, which are written in a recipe format (*Do this, don't do that*), can be used to explore any concept, term, or person (How to be a democracy, the color blue, a triangle, cubism, a fraction, right field, Ghandi). They are excellent for literary analysis, too (How to be Atticus Finch, Hestor Prynne, Professor Dumbledore, Moby-Dick, Mr. Twit, Stanley Yelnats, Nurse Ratchett).

4. *Put your senses to work.* What sights, sounds, smells, tastes, and feelings (tactile or of the heart) come to mind when you recall a time, place, person, or incident? Begin with a sensory-rich passage from literature. Share it aloud with students, and (if possible) give them a hard copy on which to

FIGURE **8.6** **How to Be a Water Bug**

Boring Facts

- One of the largest insects
- Survives in water—even under ice
- Short breathing tubes stick out as they hunt
- Active in late summer
- Wings overlap abdomen
- Exoskeleton
- Sharp teeth
- Known as boatmen

How to Be a Water Bug

Swim fast below every stream of water.
Breathe out of small tubes.
Don't let your prey suspect you exist.
Row with oar-like hind legs, as a boatman would do.
Attack other insects, small fish, frogs, tadpoles—even birds.
Inject your toxin.
Dine on fresh meat.
When winter comes,
Slip under water.
Hide beneath the ice.
Wait for summer.
Come back to life.

make notes. Ask them, in pairs, to make a sensory chart of the sights, sounds, smells, etc., they notice. One of my favorite passages to use for this purpose is from Kate DiCamillo's classic *The Tale of Despereaux* (2003). This passage comes from Chapter 2, in which Despereaux's sister Merlot tries very hard to teach her odd little brother to eat books, as all normal mice do. The passage begins this way:

> Despereaux's sister Merlot took him into the castle library, where light came streaming in through tall, high windows and landed on the floor in bright yellow patches [p. 21].

They climb together up onto a table, where a book lies open, its pages crunchy and inviting. But something quite unexpected happens to Despereaux as he looks at the "squiggles" on the page—

> [The squiggles] arranged themselves into shapes. The shapes arranged themselves into words, and the words spelled out a delicious and wonderful phrase: *Once upon a time* [p. 22].

Check Figure 8.7 for a sensory chart made by a group of fifth graders with whom I shared this passage. As you can see, they went well beyond the literal, letting themselves surmise how it might feel, smell, look, or sound to actually be in that library. Once you have done this activity, it is a very easy transition to a description or story in which sensory detail plays an important part.

FIGURE **8.7**   **Sensory Details Chart by Grade 5 Students**

Sensory Details Based on

The Tale of Despereaux
by Kate DiCamillo

Sights	*Sounds*	*Tastes & Smells*	*Feelings*
Sunlight	*Mice scurrying*	*Glue*	*Warmth of the sun*
Yellow patches on the floor	*Paper crunching*	*Paper*	*Smooth surface of the table*
Table	*Talking*	*That "library" smell*	*Roughness of paper*
Books	*The words "Once" upon a time"*	*Old furniture*	*Glue on your tongue*
Mice		*Carpeting*	*Paper in your mouth*
Squiggles		*Mouse fur*	*The chills—when Despereaux begins to read*
Words			
Wooden floors			

5. *Revise a weak example.* Start with a writing sample that's problematic—"The Redwoods" (page 39) is an ideal choice for detail because it is written in generalities. Ask students to revise by adding details, giving them editorial freedom to invent. The results will surprise you.

Here's what a high school writer wrote. Notice that even though in her mind she was only revising to add detail, *all* traits came along for the ride.

The Redwoods, Revised (Grade 12)

I'd be the first to admit I've pretty much outgrown the family vacation. So when my father announced that we were going to spend a week down in California seeing a bunch of trees, you can imagine how thrilled I was. Until the day of the trip, I kept hoping for some ailment to rescue me from this world of family fun. No compassionate neighbors volunteered to take me in. No desperate business people called with an urgent job to fill. It looked more and more as if I'd have to go.

The day we set out (or as I like to think of it, "Hell: Day One") arrived. I packed in five minutes, yanking items at random out of my drawer (Who cares what you wear in the woods?), stuffed my bag in the trunk, and plunked onto

(continued)

my side of the back seat—already polluted with my brother's video game magazines and empty Gummy Bear bags.

Dad backed out of the driveway with a cheery "Here we go!" and knowing better than to sigh out loud, I slumped down into my back seat prison. Luckily, I had brought a book.

Finally, we arrived at The Redwoods. I didn't look up from my book at first, even though my parents were pleading me to "Look! Oh, look!" At length, I raised my eyes, and for just a moment, I couldn't breathe. I hadn't thought a sophisticated, worldly high school student like me would be in awe over a few trees. Yet, I was.

I dropped my book, forgetting about the world of courtroom trials, corrupt judges, and the unsolved mysteries of dead wives and lovers. I felt compelled to touch one of the trees, to wrap my arms around it. My reflection was interrupted when Jimmy the Gooey blurted out in his squeaky eighth grade voice, "Stand inside the tree, Dodo-Head, so I can take your picture." I looked deep into his camera and smiled. That photo is still in our album at home. I'll leave it to you to guess what the Video-Maniac wrote as a caption, but I'll give you this hint: He didn't come close to capturing what I felt.

Any paper from this book that has a problem of any sort (however small) is a lesson waiting to happen. This edition includes Lesson Ideas for papers in Chapters 3, 4, 5, and 11 to get you started.

6. *Put it to the test.* Good informational writing teaches. Take this example from one of my favorite nonfiction books, Albert Marrin's *Oh, Rats!* (2006):

> A rat can collapse its skeleton, allowing it to wriggle through a hole as narrow as three-quarters of an inch. An adult rat's jaws are hundreds of times more powerful than a person's. Large muscles allow it to bite down with a force of 7,000 pounds per square inch, about the same force as a crocodile's jaws [p. 10].

You can tell in a heartbeat whether an informational piece actually is teaching you something because you can write a multiple-choice quiz based on it. In the case of Marrin's book, this is extremely easy, for he provides detail-rich information—enough for several questions, in fact—such as this one:

> An adult rat can squeeze through a hole as small as three-quarters of an inch simply by
>
> a. holding its breath.
> b. collapsing its skeleton.*
> c. crashing right through with the power of a crocodile.
> d. eating its way in.

FIGURE **8.8** **Tarantulas**

Tarantulas

The insect world is the tarantula's paradise.

Tarantulas are a type of hunting spider, so they don't build webs. Even some of the largest spiders cannot eat their whole food at once, First, they have to paralyze their prey, its victim, with poison called venom. Now, they drink the prey's blood.

North American tarantulas are easily found in the United States of America, Mexico, and in central South America. Tarantulas live in a burrow, which they call home. Tarantulas are nocturnal hunters like bats.

Can you imagine that some tarantulas eat animals like frogs and snakes? Yikes! But tarantulas aren't that dangerous to humans. Tarantulas attack by biting, but it won't hurt as you think it will.

From the amazing world of spiders, tarantulas are the most interesting creatures.

You're welcome to write about anything, but the places and spaces where you spend time, that's where you'll know the details. That's how you can take readers anywhere, make them see and feel.

—Jeff Anderson
Mechanically Inclined,
2005, p. 28

Writing your own multiple-choice items, by the way, is not only an effective method for checking out detail, but it's also a good strategy for remembering what you have read and guessing (often quite accurately) what likely will be on someone else's test.

7. ***Help students collect information.*** The single biggest reason writers struggle is lack of information. In Judy Mazur's third grade class, students do *a lot* of informational writing. But they do not try to pull the information out of their heads. Judy reads to them, and they read on their own. One whole section of her in-class library is devoted to the current research focus. Students do firsthand research on many topics through observation or field trips. They watch films. They talk and ask questions. *Then*, they write. In Figures 8.8, "Tarantulas," and 8.9, "The Funnel Web Spider," you can see the detail and confidence that comes from having time to explore a topic before trying to write about it yourself.

8. ***Collaborate.*** So often, we do not make the most of student collaboration, waiting until students have drafts before encouraging them to meet with partners or groups to share ideas and offer support. Don't wait. Put students together from the first. They can help one another come up with ideas, figure out how and where to do research, and ask one another prompting questions that make it easier to draft that first line.

9. ***Start with something tangible.*** If you've ever held a photograph, postcard or artifact that takes you to another time or place, you know the power of physical objects to call up emotions and memories. Put this to work in your classroom, asking students to bring in any object they can hold in their hands and that has significance for them—and to use it as a starting point for writing. They do not need to write about the object itself. They can use it as the center of a web or a basis for conversation with a partner. Just let the associations flow, and most students will come up with more than one writing idea. (An excellent text to kick this off is Mem Fox's *Wilfred Gordon McDonald Partridge*, 1989.)

FIGURE 8.9 The Funnel Web Spider

The Funnel Web Spider

Have you ever wondered what crawls underground in Australia? Well, it's called a Funnel Web Spider.

It looks like a tiny ball of hair with legs.

Funnel Webs gorge on tasty insects that get too close. Funnel Webs are the most poisonous spiders in the world. They can kill a human. Luckily, scientists developed a medicine to treat these kinds of bites.

You should be happy that spiders exist because they eat the nasty little creatures we don't like. Enjoy having them in the world.

Lessons and Strategies for Organization

- *Lead*
- *Pattern/structure*
- *Transitions*
- *Pacing*
- *Conclusion*

1. *Nail the lead.* If you are writing a brief essay or story, model three or four leads you *might* use, and ask students to help you choose the most effective one. Here are a few possibilities for my story about a teacher who terrorized our class:

- *She stood six feet tall and ate whole apples, core and stem included.*
- *She used her voice like a weapon.*
- *We could feel her coming before we heard her.*

Which would you choose? Discuss differences, and then ask students to try two, three, or four leads for pieces *they* are working on and to share them in response groups.

You can extend this instruction by sharing leads from a number of sources and asking students to rate them plus (**+**), meaning I would definitely keep reading; check (✓), meaning I *might* keep reading; or minus (−), meaning I would stop right there. How would you rate these?

Lead 1___ (Plus, Check, or Minus?)

People who create computer Web sites to attract attention to catch new customers are borrowing an idea millions of years old. Even before there were dinosaurs, spiders were luring insects to their Web sites [Margery Facklam, *Spiders and Their Websites*, 2001, p. 4].

Lead 2___

Cole Matthews knelt defiantly in the bow of the aluminum skiff as he faced forward into a cold September wind. Worn steel handcuffs bit at his wrists each time the small craft slapped onto another wave. Overhead, a gray-matted sky hung like a bad omen [Ben Mikaelson, *Touching Spirit Bear*, 2002, p. 3].

Lead 3___

My name is India Opal Buloni, and last summer my daddy, the preacher, sent me to the store for a box of macaroni and cheese, some white rice, and two tomatoes and I came back with a dog [Kate DiCamillo, *Because of Winn-Dixie*, 2000, p. 7].

Lead 4___

The title of this book alludes to a scarce resource. Wild places, in the ordinary sense of that phrase, are in precious short supply on planet Earth at the end of the twentieth century [David Quammen, *Wild Thoughts from Wild Places*, 1998, p. 11].

I confess that these are all pluses for me, but you may respond quite differently. That's fine so long as you have a reason. And when you do this with students, you are provoking them to think about why some leads speak to them—and some do not.

2. *Play the scramble game.* Begin with a sample of text that is well organized: good sequencing, clear transitions. It should not be too long—perhaps three lines for younger students, up to nine or ten lines for older students, but not much more. (As an alternative, use whole paragraphs, rather than sentences, as the basic "chunks" of text.) If the piece has a clear beginning and ending, so much the better. Copy it, line by line (or paragraph by paragraph). Cut the copy into strips so that students can play with it like a puzzle. If you're ambitious and can afford it, laminate the strips so that you can use them over and over. Give them to students out of order, and ask them, working in groups of three or four, to order the strips so that they make sense. Try this one (see Figure 8.10) from Sneed Collard's extraordinary book, *The Deep-Sea Floor* (2003). I chose this text because informational writing is slightly more challenging than narrative; yet Collard's writing is always characterized by clear organization and thoughtfully embedded transitions. (*Hint:* There are two paragraphs. The answer is at the end of this chapter.)

Stories work well for beginners because they usually have a clear event-to-event flow. Informational writing (like the Collard example) is a little

FIGURE 8.10 Out-of-Order Lines from Sneed B. Collard's *The Deep-Sea Floor*

The sonar made loud noises that bounced off the sea bottom.

As recently as the mid-nineteenth century, many people believed that the ocean was bottomless or that no life existed in the deep.

During World War I, they began mapping the ocean bottom with a new invention called **sonar**.

In the 1870s, though, scientists began a serious search for deep-sea animals by lowering nets and other collection devices far below the surface.

Photosynthesis, the production of food using light energy from the sun, cannot take place on the deep-sea floor.

The echoes from these noises gave people a detailed outline of what the deep-sea floor looked like.

Others felt sure that the deep sea was filled with terrifying sea serpents or animals that had disappeared from shallower waters millions of years before.

For most of history, the geography and animal life of the deep-sea floor have remained a total mystery.

harder; you have to connect each supporting detail to a main idea. Persuasive writing is harder yet: thesis, support, counterargument(s), closing argument, and conclusion. Consider, though: If you do one of each, you can talk about how organization shifts with mode.

3. *Listen for the ending*. Endings have a sound all their own—a sound readers (and writers) learn to listen for. Often it's the hint of another story or conversation to come. One of the following passages concludes David George Gordon's excellent informational text, *The Compleat Cockroach* (1996). Which one do you think is the actual ending?

- Human beings have the capacity to wipe out cockroaches—along with every other animal and plant on the planet. The only question is, Will we do it?

- The cockroach is a hardy creature, capable of withstanding heat, cold, and even radiation. They are found on all parts of the earth, and come in many sizes from tiny to over three inches in length. They have lived for over 400 million years—and might live for another 400 million. Who knows?

- Who can say if our planet's evolutionary history won't repeat itself—and eventually set the scene from which higher life forms will emerge. It's a good bet that the first land-dwelling animal to appear in this freshly reconstructed world will resemble the cockroach.

If you chose the third, you have a good ear. The first poses a question too sweeping to be truly interesting. The second is a dreary summary—just the ending we want good informational writers to avoid. Only the third offers an enticing prediction based on what we know now—without tediously listing each cockroachy fact. This book offers wonderful in-class research possibilities.

4. *Match design to content*. What things do we organize in our lives? Furniture, closets, curriculum, a trip, a wedding—the list is endless. But we do not organize them all using a *single strategy*. Writing is like that, too—and here's one way to show this to students.

Spend several days researching any topic—say zebras, cell phones, black holes, whatever. Ask *each student* to come up with two fascinating bits of information on that one topic and to write each fact out as a *single sentence*. Make lists of these sentences (one list per group of four students) and, with students' help, cut them into strips. Shuffle them and put them into a bag. If you have thirty students, you will have sixty "factlets."

Group students into teams of four and give each team one set of fact strips. Now—*this is important*—talk about purpose and audience. Are you writing a picture book for young children? A chapter in a textbook? A public relations document, an advertisement, copy for the local science museum? Ask each group to get their purpose and audience firmly in mind. Then ask each group to go through the strips and

- Eliminate what's redundant.

- Isolate what is most important and most interesting, given their purpose and audience.

- "Frame" the writing by choosing a beginning and an ending point (usually, two of the most intriguing bits of information).

- Group what's left into chunks by subtopic.

At any point, they can take information out or put something back in. The organization flows, grows, and shrinks like a riverbed to serve the needs of the content. It's the river that matters. When they finish, ask groups to compare their organizational designs and to talk about why they cut, kept, and ordered things as they did. With luck, you'll have huge variety and renewed appreciation for the ways organization grows out of thinking.

Lessons and Strategies for Voice

- *Individuality*
- *Passion for the topic*
- *Connection to audience*
- *Honesty*
- *Confidence*

Some elements of voice—such as connecting with an audience—can be taught directly. Others, such as honesty, must be invited, applauded, valued, and nurtured. Here are some suggested strategies for drawing out your students' voices.

1. *Provide a safe environment for sharing.* Putting voice into writing is an act of courage. It only occurs in an environment where students feel safe writing the truth and sharing it aloud. When you share your own writing and when you ensure that all writing is received respectfully, you set the stage for this.

2. *Respond to students' work with unabashed enthusiasm.* Of all the gifts we can give our young writers, none is so sweet as full-out appreciation: "Your piece moved me," "Your writing had me laughing aloud," "You seemed so caught up in this story, and you know? So was I." Nothing in all the world of writing is so seductive as the image of an excited reader waiting just to receive your work.

3. *Reward risk.* Nothing happens with voice when writers play it safe. They need opportunities to try something new, to go off-course a bit, to play with fire. If they have to get it right all the time, we get "The Redwoods." And we deserve it.

4. *Remind students to tell the truth.* Take to heart the words of Anne Lamott (1995): "The very first thing I tell my new students on the first day of a workshop is that good writing is about telling the truth" (p. 3).

Truth, of course, is not about literal facts. Truth is the world as you see it—what horrifies or amuses you, what you know to be true, what you know to be right or wrong, what makes you laugh or cry deep inside where no one can see the tears.

In his moving book, *A Dog Year* (2003), Jon Katz opens with the story of his first dog, an animal his parents clearly did not want. When Lucky gets distemper, the parents seize the opportunity to have him "transported to the countryside," where, Jon's dad tells him, Lucky will have to stay for some time. Read between the lines, where the truth lives:

> Then he took me to Rigney's Ice Cream Parlor on Hope Street and bought me a black raspberry cone. Excursions with my father were a rare thing, saved for the most extraordinary occasions. My father never said a word as we slurped our cones, and neither did I. . . . I was young but not stupid. It would be years before I loved a dog that much again [pp. xi–xii].

> Even in a bad piece of writing, the mentor reaches into the chaos, finds a place where the writing works, pulls it from the wreckage, names it, and makes the writer aware of this emerging skill with words.
> —Ralph Fletcher
> *What a Writer Needs,*
> 1993, p. 14

> Composition teachers all know the thrill of hearing—with a student—that student's voice for the first time.
> —Donald M. Murray
> *A Writer Teaches Writing,*
> 2004, p. 2

> We speak differently at home and on the street corner, in class and in the locker room, at the Saturday night party and the Sunday morning church service.
> —Donald M. Murray
> *A Writer Teaches Writing,*
> 2004, p. 22

5. *Read aloud.* Read from the books you love, and as you do, encourage students to listen for the voice within. Ask them to describe the voice they hear. Is it timid, bold, funny, irreverent, brazen, accusatory—what? Each voice is different, and voices have names, character, and personality. Read the three voices in Figure 8.11. One is by Jerry Seinfeld, one is by Dr. Phil McGraw, and one is by Ernest Hemingway. Can you identify each? What word(s) would you use to describe each voice?

You can vary this voices game by identifying the people differently (other than by name, that is); your list might include an irate teacher, an upset parent, or an exasperated fourth grader. How might those voices differ?

6. *Go for contrast.* I often read a passage from Carolyn Lesser's *Great Crystal Bear* (1996) and one from an encyclopedia entry on polar bears—and then ask students which is which and how they know. (They always know.) You could make the same contrast using a sports page account of a basketball game and an encyclopedic summary of basketball. Topic does not matter. You just need one piece that is full of voice and one that is drier.

7. *Ask students to read aloud.* Reading with inflection and writing with inflection are mirror images of the same skill. For this reason, reading aloud

---

FIGURE **8.11** **Three Voices**

Seinfeld, Dr. Phil, Hemingway
Which is Which?

Voice 1

I have no plants in my house. They won't live for me. Some of them don't even wait to die, they commit suicide. I once came home and found one hanging from a macramé noose, the pot kicked out from underneath. The note said, "I hate you and your albums."

Voice 2

Then he began to pity the great fish that he had hooked. He is wonderful and strange and who knows how old he is, he thought. Never have I had such a strong fish or one who acted so strangely. Perhaps he is too wise to jump.

Voice 3

You are sold "self-improvement" the same way you're sold everything else: it's easy; five simple steps; you can't help succeeding, because you're so wonderful; your results will be fast, fast, fast. But we're paying dearly—in more ways than one—for this polluting flood of psychobabble.

Voice 1: Jerry Seinfeld. 1993. *SeinLanguage.* New York: Bantam Books. 143.
Voice 2: Ernest Hemingway. 1980. *The Old Man and the Sea.* New York: Scribner. 48.
Voice 3: Phillip C. McGraw, PhD. 1999. *Strategies.* New York: Hyperion. 23.

is critical in developing voice. Ask students to bring passages from favorite writers to class, to read them aloud with feeling, and to see if other students can identify the voice or at least describe it. Then encourage them to read *their own work* with the same passion and intensity; if they do not bring out the inflection with oral reading, it will be hard for them to "hear" the voice as they write (and also difficult to punctuate properly). Reading one's own text aloud is essential to revision. There is *no* substitute for this.

8. *Do a quick-write on voice.* Build on what you learn from these read-alouds (as well as personal reflective reading) by doing a quick-write in which you and your students create one-liner definitions of voice. Here are a few things students have written:

- Voice is hearing the exclamation point, even when it's not there.
- It's the passion that makes words dance.
- The need to be heard.
- Intense curiosity about life, about the world.
- The writer reaching out to the reader.
- Voice happens when my reader can tell I care about my topic.
- It's writing that really sounds like me and what I think.
- Voice says I want you to read this and feel something.
- Lighting a fire.
- The writer's gift to the reader.

9. *Write letters.* One biology teacher tells his students, "Don't just write about photosynthesis. Explain it the way you would explain it to Miss Piggy." Letters elicit voice because the audience is built in. Students might write to local companies, political figures, sports figures, or favorite authors. Figure 8.12 shows several letters written by elementary students to American armed forces personnel. In 1985, when my mentor Ronda Woodruff first began teaching traits to fourth graders, she used letters to bring out voice. Ronda believed in writing to real people, so she asked her students to write to their favorite authors. One of her student's letters, written to Roald Dahl, appears in Figure 8.13. As Mem Fox reminds us, letter writing is the perfect activity for developing voice because "the audience is so clearly defined" (1993, p. 28). Writing notes to favorite writers is a simple matter these days. Just look up "authors' addresses" on the Web for a long list of sources.

10. *Talk story.* The Hawaiians have a saying—"Let's talk story." This way of communicating heart to heart is an integral part of this rich culture and reflects their understanding that our stories define us; they tell who we are. Stories are important to all forms of writing. They humanize it, make it visual, make it breathe. Even in an informational piece, the occasional image, anecdote, or dramatic moment provides the mental relief we need—a human voice speaking to us through the maelstrom of factual data.

11. *Create a "voice collage" by role playing.* Students who are shy sometimes come out of hiding when they can write in the voice of someone else. Ask students to read a piece of literature, then assume one of the voices from

> You see Pudge Rodriguez step into the batter's box and settle in to prepare for pitch. Even if Pudge was traded and is now wearing a different uniform, you know from watching his unique mannerisms just who's at the plate.... poets and musicians—and even athletes—have an individuality in their approach. They leave their fingerprints on what they do and what they create. In writing, we call it voice.
>
> —Tommy Thomason
> *WriteAerobics: 40 Workshop Exercises to Improve Your Writing Teaching,* 2003, p. 42

> When I write, it feels like I'm carving bone. It feels like I'm creating my own face, my own heart—a Nahuatl concept.
>
> —Gloria Anzaldua,
> Poet and critic,
> In *Deborah Brodie,*
> 1997, p. 139

FIGURE **8.12** **Letters to Soldiers**

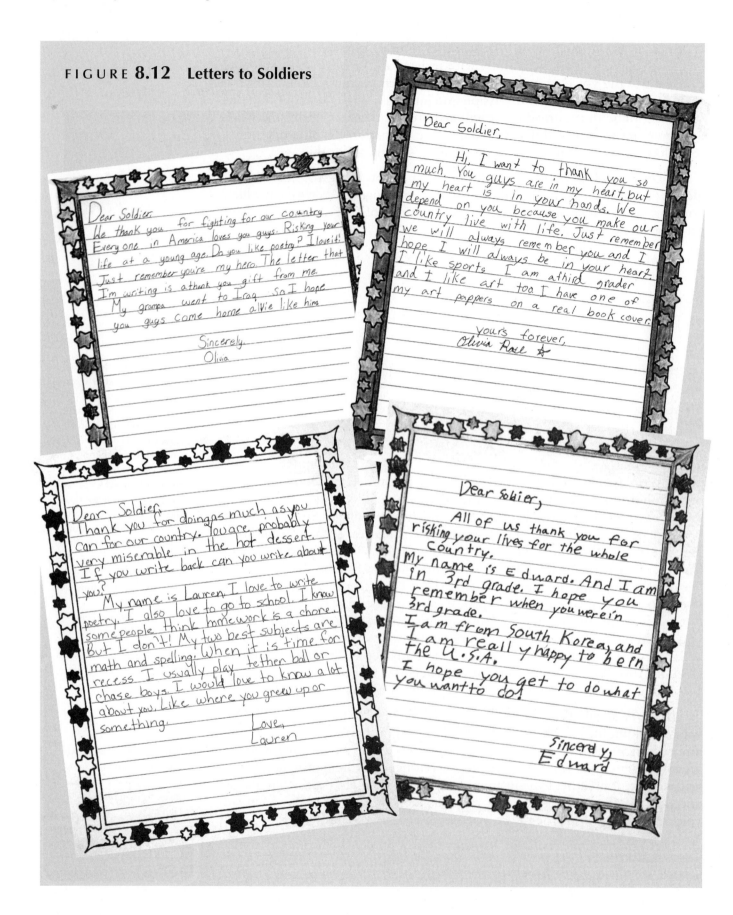

FIGURE **8.13** **Nikki's Letter to Roald Dahl**

Roald Dahl
c/o Bantam Books
666 Fifth Avenue
New York, New York 10013

Dear Roald Dahl:

I'm nine years old. My purpose of writing is to tell you I know all of your books by heart.

I think you should write more books, and make them come out all around the globe. I'm talking about books with voice, like Matilda. Maybe even some sequels. Like Matilda II or Twits II and III.

I've always wondered how you get such creative ideas, and I am hoping if you send back a letter, you will send some tips for putting in just the right amount of information.

When you do send your letter, I would like it hand written and signed in pen. I hope you can come to our school.

I better sign off now. My time is limited.

Your truly grateful, super wonderful fan,
Nikki

the piece. Any sample that has multiple characters and conflict will do—*The Great Gatsby, Harry Potter, Macbeth*, or even *The Three Little Pigs*. The literature can be as simple or advanced as you like; you can also use history or other nonfiction. Choose a dramatic scene no more than 600 words long (shorter for younger students). Divide students into groups of three to five. Within each group, ask each student to assume the role of one character. After they've read the piece, ask them to write a journal entry *in character* as the person they've chosen (6 to 12 minutes). When they finish, ask them to divide their writing into parts and take turns reading aloud, one part at a time, within groups. This way, every voice is heard at least twice—sometimes more. The result is a mini-drama that offers remarkable character analysis and a lesson on perspective. (See Figure 8.14 for a four-part journal by a middle school student assuming the role of a squire in Medieval England.)

12. *Take the voice OUT!* Amazing as it seems, de-voicing a piece of writing is almost as effective in teaching the traits as trying to put more voice in— and is a lot of fun in the bargain. (This strategy works with *any trait*.) Begin with a piece that's strong (e.g., "Mouse Alert" or "Haircut from Hell"), and revise it to minimize the voice. Have students work in teams, and turn it into

FIGURE **8.14** Arthur's Diary

May 3, 1385

My name is Arthur and I have decided to keep a diary. I am 14 and I am a squire, someone who is studying to be a knight. I have seen so many knights killed that I am not sure I really want to be a knight.

May 7, 1385

We just sent over 50 knights off to battle. I have been polishing armor till my shoulders ache. I also have to get the prize hunting dogs ready, and they're as big as I am. I feel sorry for the blacksmith, having to shoe all those horses. Yesterday he got bitten by a horse and they had to stitch it up with cat gut.

May 19, 1385

I really like my room because of its stained glass windows. It used to be the chapel before they built a larger one—and I'm lucky to have it. What I don't like is the person I have to share it with, a stuck up little beast of a squire named Edmond. He has perfect spelling, so the priest thinks he is wonderful. He steals the covers at night, puts boar grease in his hair, shoots birds with his sling shot, and lets them rot on the forest floor. He's going to make a rotten knight.

May 23, 1385

Today I got a haircut in town. The barber is also a dentist and surgeon. I saw him bleeding someone into a bowl. I hope I never get sick. He's a wretched barber. Next time I'll do it myself. We have a visitor from the East who claims to be an astronomer. He has been telling us of temples made from gold. Lord Charles says he wants gold walls in the new chapel. The visitor said people from the East believe the earth is round. Lord Charles says if he keeps on with such nonsense, he'll have him hanged. I think the earth might be round, but I'd better not let Lord Charles know.

a competition. Then talk about what you did. Your strategies in reverse are the secrets to strong voice.

Also remember that voice isn't just about writing. It's about us—who we are. Voice lives in art, dance, sports, and all other expressions of the human spirit. The way we walk, speak, breathe, kiss, dance, bat a ball, or hold a child are all parts of our voice. When we move out of the realm of writing, we make the concept actually easier to teach. Some teachers introduce voice with music, a form of expression as personal as writing. When your students listen to Aretha Franklin, Bob Dylan, and Mozart, they will sense how personal voice is, and how many ways we make our voices heard. Music makes a good introduction to voice because it affects us deeply—and reflects mood. An interesting way to make this clear is to ask students to read their own writing aloud to a musical background they select. Choosing the right music (as if for a film) requires them to think about the mood of their text.

> Give me your best abstract thinking and generalizations, and I do not comprehend them in a meaningful way until I hang a story on them.
> —Tom Romano
> *Crafting Authentic Voice,*
> 2004, p. 29

Lessons and Strategies for Word Choice

- *Accuracy*
- *Strong verbs*
- *Fresh, lively words and phrases*
- *Word pictures*
- *Freedom from redundancy, wordiness, vague phrasing, jargon*

1. *Read, read, read!* The books of William Steig, Gary Paulsen, Roald Dahl, and Mem Fox are all renowned for excellent word choice for younger readers/writers—although I would not overlook them for older writers either. Any high schooler who has not read *Matilda* (which is really more a book for adults than for children) has missed the best of reading times. Don't forget to check out the nonfiction. I wish my history textbooks had contained more passages like Alistair Cooke's description of Eli Whitney's cotton gin:

> Whitney . . . came up with a simple box, the cotton gin. Inside was a suspended wooden cylinder that revolved at the cranking of a handle. The cylinder was encircled with evenly spaced metal spikes that clawed at the deposited raw cotton, shed the seeds behind the cylinder, and let the pure lint come foaming up in front. . . Like so many fundamental discoveries, like the propositions of Euclid, it was so simple that it seemed incredible nobody had thought of it. Once demonstrated, it was indeed so simple that any wheelwright could make it, and it was Whitney's misfortune that most of them did [Cooke, 1976, p. 193].

2. *Harness the power of verbs.* Verbs give writing energy. No passage in recent memory brings this concept home more clearly than Laura Hillenbrand's description of the stirring race between underdog Seabiscuit and legendary thoroughbred War Admiral:

> They ripped out of the backstretch and leaned together into the final turn, their strides still rising and falling together. The crowds by the rails thickened, their faces a pointillism of colors, the dappling sound of distinct voices now blending into a sustained shout. The horses strained onward. Kurtsinger began shouting at his horse, his voice whipped away behind him. He pushed on War Admiral's neck and drove with all his strength, sweeping over his mount's right side. War Admiral was slashing at the air, reaching deeper and deeper into

> **One of the really bad things you can do to your writing is to dress up the vocabulary, looking for long words because you're maybe a little bit ashamed of your short ones. This is like dressing up a household pet in evening clothes.**
>
> —Stephen King
> *On Writing,* 2000, p. 17

himself. . . . Woolf saw Seabiscuit's ears flatten to his head and knew that the moment Fitzsimmons had spoken of was near: One horse was going to crack [Hillenbrand, 2001, pp. 272–273].

To reinforce students' awareness of verb power, try an idea I learned from my colleague, Lynne Shapiro. Read a strong passage such as Hillenbrand's aloud, only deflate the verbs. Imagine, for example, that Hillenbrand had written "War Admiral was *touching* the air, *going* deeper and deeper into himself. . . . Woolf saw Seabiscuit's ears *move closer* to his head and knew that . . . one horse was going to *give up.*" Hear the difference? What happened to War Admiral's desperation and Seabiscuit's cunning? Ask students to help brainstorm alternatives for these weaker verbs—then share the original so you can compare. Don't limit your revision just to verbs, either. In Figure 8.15 you'll see how a third grader revised a short passage from *Creating Revisers and Editors,* a companion book to this one.

3. ***WOW your students.*** If you've ever felt discouraged by the number of students who forget all or most of the weekly vocabulary list within seconds of completing the quiz, this idea is for you. *Word of the Week posters* (WOWs) are an idea borrowed from middle school teacher Susan Doyle. In creating WOWs, students each celebrate one word (chosen by luck of the draw from a basket) by defining it; giving pronunciation, part of speech, and etymology; using it in a sentence; and illustrating it (see Figure 8.16).

4. ***Advertise.*** Sometimes, we get so caught up in building vocabulary that we forget the beauty of simple language used well. Advertisers are experts at this. For some time, the J. Peterman Company has advertised its "reckless, wide-legged" pants ("J. Peterman Dog-Days Manual," August 2003, p. 18) as that dangerous garment that could make you seem "too noticeably lanky,

FIGURE **8.15** **Sample Revision from *Creating Revisers and Editors,* Grade 3, by Vicki Spandel** (Pearson Education, Inc., 2009). Lesson 10: *Word Choice.*

Sample D: Revision With Partners

terrible   worse than terrible.

The weather was ~~bad~~, In fact, it was ~~really~~

pelted the sidewalks.

~~bad~~. Rain ~~fell everywhere~~. The wind was

whipping the branches of the old willow tree I stood next to.

~~blowing~~. If this kept up, we might ~~not be able~~ have to cancel

~~to hold~~ our soccer ~~game~~. match.

FIGURE **8.16** **WOW Poster**

too tallish, too feminine, too elegant." I've always loved the word *lanky* (and wish it really *did* describe me), and I cannot help but think what a masterful choice of words *reckless* is. How many of us, deep down, would like to see ourselves as reckless (lanky, too)—and so wouldn't mind spending $40 or $50 on a pair of pants that might make us so? In the 2001 holiday "Owner's Manual No. 4" (which I saved purely for the pleasure of reading the ads), I find the "Nantucket Sweater" (p. 7): "In winter, you breathe the lost sea smell. Winter is the time to come, I think. Try a small hotel. Bring books, good walking shoes. Give the fire in the fireplace the attention it deserves. Read . . . drink a little wine, eat thick chowder." Book me a room. I'll pack my Nantucket sweater—*and* my reckless wide-legged pants.

Try writing ads of your own; your students can create ads for things they own or things you collect as a class. This activity gives voice and word choice a workout.

5. *Put adjectives to work*. Small changes have power. Begin with a simple sentence:

Tom *walked* down the *dusty* road.

We all know how to make Tom speedy, tired, determined, cautious, frightened, etc., by changing the verb: Tom *raced* . . . Tom *shuffled* . . . Tom *strode* . . . Tom *inched* . . . Tom *fled* . . . and so on.

Now let's try something with that adjective: *dusty*. All roads are dusty, so putting that in doesn't add much. Let's make the dust *do* something by starting the sentence differently. Ask your students what's really happening with Tom and the dust. Make a movie. Then use their ideas to write the script:

Choking on the dust, Tom . . .
With dust reddening his eyes, Tom . . .
Absent-mindedly watching the dust devils, Tom . . .
Brushing dust from his clothes, Tom . . .
With dust coating his face, Tom . . .
Trying to see ahead through the dust, Tom . . .

Lessons and Strategies for Sentence Fluency

- *Smooth flow*
- *Variation in sentence beginnings*
- *Variation in sentence lengths*
- *Transitional words and phrases to build bridges*
- *Fragments for effect*
- *Authentic dialogue*

1. *Hear it*. Developing a sense of fluency is an aural skill. You need to *hear* it. Read aloud yourself, focusing on poetry, where the rhythm's built in. Throw yourself into it, bringing out every drumbeat. Don't be shy, or your students will be shy in their reading, too, and they will never hear the voice that was waiting to be pulled out. For a special lesson that combines sentence fluency and voice, try the "I Am Me" poem (see Figure 8.17) in three parts: *I am . . . I remember . . . I've learned . . .* The result is a poetic essay with rhythm and grace.

2. *Perform it*. Whether it's a bit of drama from Shakespeare, a poem by T. S. Eliot, or any text that allows itself to be divided into sections, your students will benefit by presenting it orally. Seek out samples with dialogue, and you'll find yourself combining voice and fluency. Books for younger students that lend themselves to choral reading include

FIGURE **8.17** "I Am Me" by Katie, Grade 5

I Am Me
By Katie, Grade 5

I am . . .
    The youngest child.
    The Precious Moment who speaks to you.
    The narrator of my own story.
    The stars in Van Gogh's painting.
    A friend a friend would like to have.
    The soaring tire swing on the tree.

I remember . . .
    The gentle sound on my violin.
    The towering oaks in my back yard.
    The pain in my cheek while saying cheese.
    Tears, slowly washing away the pain.
    The glide under my skate.

I've learned . . .
    No one can learn without mistakes.
    Tears are a sign of strength.
    Believing is not always seeing and seeing is not always practical.
    Falling is a sign of courage.
    The expert in anything was once a beginner.

- *Water Dance,* by Thomas Locker (1997)
- *My Man Blue,* by Nikki Grimes (2002)
- *Dogteam,* by Gary Paulsen (1993)
- *Insectlopedia,* by Douglas Florian (1998)
- *Joyful Noise: Poems for Two Voices,* by Paul Fleischman (1992)
- *The Big Box,* by Toni and Slade Morrison

For older students, try

- *Poems from Homeroom: A Writer's Place to Start,* by Kathi Appelt (2002)
- *The House on Mango Street,* by Sandra Cisneros (1989)
- *Seedfolks,* by Paul Fleischman (1997)
- *You Hear Me? Poems and Writing by Teenage Boys,* edited by Betsy Franco (2000)

3. *Cut the clutter.* Create an effective lesson by taking an ordinary business letter and making it grotesquely wordy (see Figure 8.18). See if your

FIGURE **8.18** **Wordy Business Letter**

Acme Enterprises
400 South Main
Anywhere, USA

Dear Mr. Ford:

It is with great pleasure that I accept your very kind invitation to tour the facilities at Acme Enterprises. We are extremely interested in and intrigued by the efficient manner with which you manage your business, and the resulting high profit margin that your company has enjoyed during the past twelve months or so. It is our hope that an on-site visit will reveal some of the corporate strategies that have led you and your company to the exceptional financial results your annual report so proudly displays. Thank you for your cordial invitation to let us observe and learn from the methods you employ.

Sincerely,

Tom Gardner, Manager
Eastwood Company

students can cut it back to sanity. Junk mail is full of inflated letters like this one, awaiting your students' slashing red pens.

4. *Target specific fluency problems.* Problems with fluency often stem from one of several problems (see Figures 8.19 through 8.22). Model solutions asking students to work with you.

5. *"Try dialogue," she said.* In *Bird by Bird* (1995), Anne Lamott notes the heady pleasures of encountering dialogue as we read: "Good dialogue is such a pleasure to come across while reading, a complete change of pace from description and exposition and all that writing. Suddenly people are talking, and we find ourselves clipping along" (p. 64). I agree. Good dialogue does one or more of these things: advances the action, reveals character, or creates mood. Consider this excerpt from *The Secret Life of Bees* (2002) by Sue Monk Kidd:

"You don't scare me," I said, mostly under my breath.

He'd already turned to leave, but now he whirled back. "What did you say?"

"You don't scare me," I repeated, louder this time. A brazen feeling had broken loose in me, a daring something that had been locked up in my chest.

He stepped toward me, raising the back of his hand like he might bring it down across my face. "You better watch your mouth" [p. 38].

FIGURE **8.19**   **Sentences Begin the Same Way**

> In Chicago, there are a million things to do. Chicago is a really interesting city. In Chicago they have museums and a wonderful aquarium, not to mention an art gallery. Chicago is one place you will never get bored.

FIGURE **8.20**   **Sentences Are All the Same Length**

> Calvin was thinking of running away. His life was so very dull. The same things happened every day. He could not take it much longer. Running away could be an answer. He needed a change of scene.

FIGURE **8.21**   **Sentences Are Short and Choppy**

> Samone looked up. The sun beat down. She felt hot. She felt tired. The race was long. It was too long. She would not make it. Her legs were cramping. Her face was flushed. Where was the finish?

FIGURE **8.22**   **Endless Connectives**

> So if I had to find a way to describe Ike, I would say he was this dog you wouldn't notice at first except for his personality which was extremely friendly but he wasn't the sort of dog to catch your eye, not that looks are everything, but he wasn't exactly gorgeous, but then looks are not as important in a dog as a good disposition, if you know what I mean.

This dialogue bristles with tension. The child is courageous—maybe even reckless—and her father is menacing. This is quite different from filler dialogue:

"Let's go outside," said Bob.

"That is an excellent idea," said Wilma.

Nothing is happening here. To dramatize dialogue like this, ask students to work in pairs—each taking one role—and to write out what they would

FIGURE **8.23** **Pop Culture Translation of Shakespeare, Grade 8**

CLAUDIUS: Hamlet! What's up? Where's Polonius?

HAMLET: He's at supper.

CLAUDIUS: At supper? You're kidding! Where?

HAMLET: Well, not any of the usual places, that's for sure. He's the main course! The worms are after him like a bunch of angry politicians. That's how it works—we fatten up the animals so we can eat them to fatten up ourselves. See what I'm saying? But in the end, all we are is food to fatten up the worms.

CLAUDIUS: Sure is depressing talking to you, Hamlet.

HAMLET: No—just think about it! A guy is fishing with a worm and maybe that worm has eaten part of a king. You follow me?

CLAUDIUS: No. What on earth is your point?

HAMLET: No big deal. I'm just trying to say that kings think they're some great shakes, but in the end, they wind up as worm food like everybody else.

really say during a conflict or other discussion. Keep in mind the three purposes: action, character, mood.

Another lesson idea that dramatically improves students' ear for good dialogue involves "pop culture translation," in which students take a dramatic piece from another time and rewrite it in modern vernacular. See Figure 8.23 for an excerpt from an eighth grader's pop translation of Act IV, Scene iii, from *Hamlet*.

6. *Break the rules.* This is what playwright Lynda Barry (in Feiffer and Feiffer, *Home*, 1995) does as she takes on the voice of a teenage boy defending his right to have his own room the way he wants it. Notice her use of conventions to guide the voice in your head as you read:

> Keep Out. Keep OUT. THIS MEANS YOU. Keep! Out! But Mom always comes in with the bogus excuse of "Here are some clean socks and underwear, I'll put them in your drawer." As if I can't get my own socks and underwear from the laundry room, as if I need to get them at all, why can't I just keep them by the dryer but no, she just needs any excuse to come into my room and yell "This room looks like a tornado hit it!" As if she has ever seen anything hit by a tornado, and then she's coming back dragging the vacuum cleaner, as if she has the right to vacuum my room! [p. 153].

Notice how Barry achieves voice by letting the syntax roll on like a river, echoing the speaker's thinking. Students can play with structure, too, as in the excerpt from "The Advice of a Coach" in Figure 8.24 that captures voice and fluency as the players hear it.

FIGURE **8.24** "The Advice of a Coach" (Advice Poem, Grade 10)

Get in the game! Show up for practice. If you don't play, shut up. If you don't play, don't rake the field. Winning is more fun than losing. You guys are KILLIN' ME!! If you ever get the chance to play, then you had better show me something. If you have any questions, always come to me first. Don't try to go over my head. Warm up if you have time. Don't play catch on the apron. Stay warm in case I need to put you in. Always be ready to play. Don't sit on the bench. Don't spit when I'm talking to you. Keep your eye on the ball. Don't forget to warm up the pitcher. Remember to treat the equipment with respect. Try to remember all of the signs. If you are late, don't bother coming. Homework always comes before sports. If you don't show up, you will not play in the next game. You probably wouldn't have played anyway so you could have at least had good grades. Listen when I'm talking to you. You guys think you're good, but you're not. Don't stand directly behind me. Don't ask. Don't tell. At least look ready to play. Don't leave your hat at home. Keep the locker room clean. Don't come to practice without your cleats. And damn it, don't forget your sleeves. Don't talk back to the coach. I have no conscience. I can watch you run all day.

7. *Try sentence aerobics.* This activity builds sentence flexibility. Ask students to work in groups of four to six, and to begin with a half sheet of paper or 3" x 5" card. Every student writes at every step, but as you will see, they are mostly working with someone else's copy. Ask them to follow these steps, writing one complete sentence each time:

1. Write one thing you know to be true (doesn't have to be profound)—your sentence should be no more than 12 words long.

2. Pass your sentence to the left.

3. Read the sentence in front of you and rewrite it—only this time, begin the sentence a different way.

4. Pass to the left.

5. Read and rewrite the second sentence, this time starting with a pronoun: *One, He, She, I, They, We, Everybody.*

6. Pass to the left.

7. Read the third sentence and revise, starting with the word *If.*

8. Pass left.

9. Read the fourth sentence and revise once more, this time turning the sentence into a question.

Return the five sentences to the originator and read some aloud to hear the possibilities. Here's an illustration:

1. Cleaning the garage is not fun.

2. The very last item on my to-do list reads "Clean the garage."

3. No one likes to clean the garage—including me.

4. If you paid me a thousand dollars, I wouldn't clean the garage.

5. Who would clean the garage if there were one other thing on Planet Earth to do?

8. *Use "mentor" sentences.* Borrow an idea from one of the most creative writing teachers around, Jeff Anderson (*Mechanically Inclined*, 2005, pp. 15–29). Jeff collects sentences. He looks for what is striking, beautiful, unusual, or quotable. Then he uses his sentences as models, slipping in a lesson on grammar (how sneaky)—but mostly, showing his students interesting ways they can share information in their own writing. They discuss what makes each sentence special, then use it as a model to create an original sentence of their own. Because the mentor text is so brief, this lesson can work very well for challenged writers or second language learners, especially if you begin with simple sentences. Here are four examples to illustrate the kinds of things you *might* model, but once you begin collecting your own sentences, you'll find, like Jeff, that the number of things you can illustrate is endless:

1. Adverbial phrases and delayed subject-verb (grammar) . . . plus the beauty of repetitive rhythm:

   Away from camp, away from people, away from houses and light and noise and into only the one thing, into only winternight they fly away and away and away. (Paulsen, 1993, pp. 9–10)

2. Compound-complex sentence (grammar) . . . plus the humor created by contrast:

   You can have a wonky nose and a crooked mouth and a double chin and stick-out teeth, but if you have good thoughts they will shine out of your face like sunbeams and you will always look lovely. (Dahl, 1980, p. 9)

3. Prepositional phrases (grammar) . . . a wonderful way of adding detail:

   Over bushes, under trees, between fence posts, through the tangled hedge she swoops untouched. (Davies, 2004, p. 12)

4. Imperative (command) sentence (grammar) . . . a way of getting the reader's attention:

   Imagine, if you will, having spent the whole of your life in a dungeon. (DiCamillo, 2003, p. 103)

Lessons and Strategies for Conventions

- *Editing for correctness*
- *Developing a proofreader's eye*
- *Learning to recognize, read, and use copy editor's symbols*
- *Checking layout and presentation, as needed*

1. *Help students to understand the reasons behind conventions.* Giv thm some unedted copie lik this thet let's their sea what happens? When, convintions is use incorrect. Porlie riten Koppey helpsthem seee the valeu; of Strong convenshons in Klewing. The reader?

2. *Teach copy editors' symbols* (see Figure 8.25). Make a poster. Demonstrate use of the symbols, one at a time, and encourage students to use them. Continue modeling daily to be sure that students understand. Gradually increase the difficulty of your samples, and always ask students to try spotting and correcting errors before you show them how it's done.

3. *Help even very young students to become independent editors* by sharing with them the copy editors' symbols they might be able to make use of (see Figure 8.26) and then gradually adding to the list. (See Spandel, *Creating Young Writers,* 2nd edition (2008), for a more extended discussion of teaching editing skills to beginning writers.)

4. *Strategy: Keep it focused.* *When you design a lesson,* make the print *large,* put *plenty* of room between lines and words for corrections, and make sure you keep the practice *simple* at first. The rule is this: *If you have to do it for your students, it's too hard.* When it counts, you won't be there (unless you plan to follow them on to college and then to the job site). Focus on one kind of problem at first.

For example, in the lesson shown in Figure 8.26a, students are asked only to fill in capitals and end punctuation for six sentences. Keeping the task focused like this dramatically increases a student's chances of success and reinforces a particular editorial skill.

In the actual lesson from which this passage is taken, the teacher models the editorial strategy of capitalizing the first word in a sentence and inserting end punctuation, showing students correct editorial marks for doing these things. Students are encouraged to read the practice sample aloud in order to tell where the sentences begin and end. They edit individually, but check with a partner before coaching the teacher through an editing of the same passage. An edited text (see Figure 8.26b) is also provided as part of this lesson. Other lessons in this set ask students to insert apostrophes, insert quotation marks, insert commas, and so on—*one task* per lesson. Later, tasks are combined in an advanced lesson. In every case, print is big, margins are ample, and text is multiple-spaced to allow editing room. Even the most challenged editor *must* experience success in order to improve. So in this lesson, safety nets are everywhere.

FIGURE **8.25** **Copy Editors' Symbols**

Symbol	Meaning	Example
ℓ	Delete the material.	There are ~~six~~ six traits.
(SP)	Spell it out.	I LOVE the 6 traits. (sp)
⌒	Close the gap.	Organi zation is critical.
ℐ	Delete material and close the gap.	Barry Lane has a w~~r~~y sense of humor.
stet.	Return to the original.	stet Never ~~ever~~ write without voice.
∧	Insert a letter, word, or phrase.	a powerful, original Mem Fox has voice.
∧	Change a letter or letters.	i He's a sl~~a~~ck writer.
#	Make a space.	The lead mustbe a grabber. #
∪	Transpose letters or words.	Gary Paulsen says, "Read a like wolf eats."
∧	Insert a comma.	Write with voice, spirit and detail.
⊙	Add a period.	Say what you think Tell the truth
∧	Insert a semicolon.	Good conventions won't make up for lack of thought they cannot rescue voiceless writing.
∧	Insert a colon.	Use these punctuation marks sparingly colons, parentheses and exclamation points.
∧ —m	Insert an em dash (like two hyphens).	Kate DiCamillo what a fine writer. —m
∧?	Add a question mark.	Who stole my scoring guide ?
∨	Insert an apostrophe.	Garrison Keillors essay on letter writing inspired me.
=	Insert a hyphen.	Novelist poet Maya Angelou rocks the room when she reads.
≡	Change lower case to capital.	Roald dahl never shrinks from reality—even if it's ugly.
/	Change capital to lower case.	The Truth lies in the Details.
¶	Start a new paragraph.	"What can one exclamation point tell us?" queried Watson.¶ "You'd be surprised," retorted Holmes.
No¶	Run lines together. No new paragraph.	*Lonesome Dove* is a long book. No¶ Of course, *Moby-Dick* is long, too, but not everyone finishes *Moby-Dick*.
∨ ∨	Add quotation marks.	I try to leave out the parts people skip, said Elmore Leonard.
ital.	Italicize.	A Prayer for Owen Meany left me breathless—and laughing. ital.
‖	Align.	My favorite books are these: *Lonesome Dove* *Angela's Ashes* *Fried Green Tomatoes*
⌉ ⌊	Center.	⌉ The Origin of Six-Trait Assessment ⌊

FIGURE **8.26** **Copy Editors' Symbols for Young Writers**

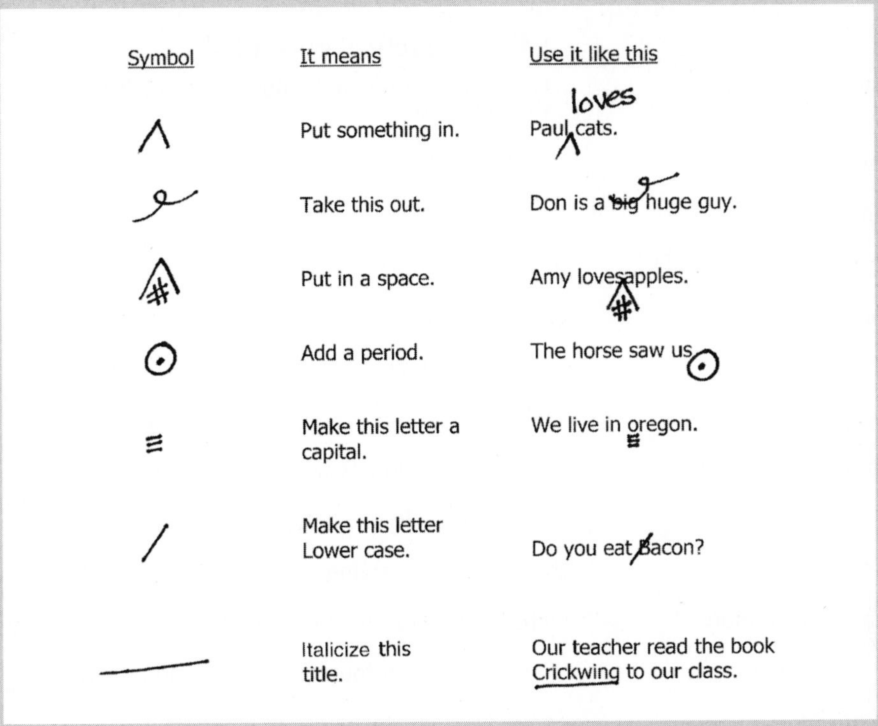

Symbol	It means	Use it like this
∧	Put something in.	Paul∧cats. *(loves inserted above)*
℘	Take this out.	Don is a ~~big~~ huge guy.
⊼#	Put in a space.	Amy loves⊼apples.
⊙	Add a period.	The horse saw us⊙
≡	Make this letter a capital.	We live in o̲regon.
/	Make this letter Lower case.	Do you eat /Bacon?
___	Italicize this title.	Our teacher read the book Crickwing to our class.

5. *Don't correct everything.* We want to fix it *all*; the problem is, the shotgun approach overwhelms many students. The one-thing-at-a-time approach is especially helpful for young writers who make numerous errors. Their own panic over their conventions is infectious. We panic, too, and our remedy is to mark every last problem. Relax. Ask yourself this: Will struggling editors be more successful if we send them into the world armed with corrected copy? We might like to think so, but the truth is that they are unlikely even to look at it, much less learn from it. Better to put one or two editing fundamentals into their arsenal (e.g., capital at the beginning of a sentence, period at the end) with each conference or practice—no more.

6. *Practice on the work of others first.* H. G. Wells once said, "No passion in the world is equal to the passion to alter someone else's draft" (in Donald M. Murray, 1990, p. 187). We can take advantage of this very human tendency by letting students work first on *text that is not their own.* Then they can check their own copy for the *very same kinds of conventional errors.*

Keep in mind that editing our own copy is perhaps the most difficult of all editing tasks. We know what we meant to say, so we do not see what more objective eyes pick up readily. See Figure 8.27 for a summary of how students acquire conventional skills.

FIGURE **8.26a**

Editing Practice

Goal: Fill in end punctuation and capitals for six sentences.

The Mount Rushmore National Monument located near Keystone, South Dakota, covers more than twelve hundred acres and sits on land considered sacred by the Lakota Sioux people the memorial, which is made of granite, has 60-foot sculptures of four presidents, including George Washington, Thomas Jefferson, Abraham Lincoln, and Theodore Roosevelt sculptors spent more than 25 years carving it though a few people were injured during the project, no one died more than two million tourists visit the monument annually it has appeared in many movies

FIGURE **8.26b**

Editing Practice, corrected

Goal: Fill in end punctuation and capitals for six sentences.

The Mount Rushmore National Monument located near Keystone, South Dakota, covers more than twelve hundred acres and sits on land considered sacred by the Lakota Sioux people. The memorial, which is made of granite, has 60-foot sculptures of four presidents, including George Washington, Thomas Jefferson, Abraham Lincoln, and Theodore Roosevelt. Sculptors spent more than 25 years carving it. Though a few people were injured during the project, no one died. More than two million tourists visit the monument annually. It has appeared in many movies.

7. *Avoid over-correction.* Many of us (and many of our students' parents) grew up with worksheets, drills, sentence diagramming, and lots of correction. Research indicates, however, that such an approach is not helpful. In fact, as George Hillocks Jr. points out in *Research on Written Composition: New Directions for Teaching* (1986), an isolated skills emphasis combined with overcorrection actually may *restrict* students' growth as writers:

> The study of traditional school grammar (i.e., the definition of parts of speech, the parsing of sentences, etc.) has no effect on raising the quality of student writing. Every other focus of instruction in this review is stronger. . . . In some studies a heavy emphasis on mechanics and usage (e.g., marking every error) resulted in significant losses in overall quality. . . . [Those] who impose the systematic study of traditional school grammar on students over lengthy periods of time in the name of teaching writing do them a gross disservice which should not be tolerated by anyone concerned with the effectiveness of teaching good writing [p. 248].

8. *Give the red pen to the student.* When you are editing for students, it feels as if you are *doing* something. Actually, it feels as if you are doing a *lot.* You are.

Teachers and administrators feel pressure from a public that worries about handwriting, spelling and grammar. . . . Yet rarely do parents complain about the inability of their children to formulate and express ideas in a clear and logical fashion.

—Donald H. Graves
A Fresh Look at Writing,
1994, p. 32

FIGURE **8.27** **How Students Acquire Conventional Skills**

Step 1:   Recognize a convention on sight.
Step 2:   Name the convention.
Step 3:   Use conventions at random.
Step 4:   Use conventions appropriately.
Step 5:   Explain/teach conventions to others.
Step 6:   Identify errors in others' text.
Step 7:   Edit others' text.
Step 8:   Identify errors in own text.
Step 9:   Edit own text.
Step 10:   Experiment with conventions to add nuances of voice and meaning.
Step 11:   Invent their own conventions.

> Grammar instruction in the studies reviewed involved the explicit and systematic teaching of the parts of speech and structure of sentences. The meta-analysis found an effect for this type of instruction for students across the full range of ability, but surprisingly, this effect was negative . . . indicating that traditional grammar instruction is unlikely to help improve the quality of students' writing.
>
> —Steve Graham and Dolores Perin
> *Writing Next,* 2007, p. 21

You are burning yourself up. Never mind that there is no research to indicate that students learn from these corrections. So when we know better, why do we edit students' writing anyway? Because if we do not correct the copy, who will? *No one.* Some copy is *never going to get corrected,* and effective editing teachers learn early on to live with this. They model appropriate use of conventions. They offer frequent guided practice in editing, with students working *first on the text of others,* then on their own text. They simply do not edit *for* students. To understand why this is so important, imagine yourself teaching multiplication of fractions. If one of your students got 10 of 20 problems wrong, would you provide additional instruction and practice—or would you simply do the problems *for* the student so that he could copy the correct answers?

9. *Remember the 72-hour rule.* Ever tuck a "perfect" piece of writing into the file—only to have it sprout errors before you looked at it again two weeks later? Time is the editor's friend. If you allow students to wait three days—or even more—between writing and editing, they'll edit much more efficiently. That mental break helps you see your writing more the way you'd see someone else's.

10. *Edit daily.* Students need to practice editing *every day,* not just now and then. Practice can be short (5 to 10 minutes), but it must be frequent if you wish to see results. Some students write only once in two or three weeks—or less. Suppose that they are editing only their own work—and only what gets published? How reasonable is it to expect that they will develop any editing proficiency when they are editing about as often as many of us get a haircut?

11. *Use sticky note dictionaries.* Eighth grader Bill made numerous spelling errors in recounting the heart-warming tale of his girl, Tammy, and a number of them involved the word *fiancée,* which Bill spelled "feonsay." A word such as this can go on a sticky note in one corner of Bill's paper. Not

> Traditions in the teaching of English hold that compositions must be marked and commented upon—the more thoroughly, the better. But research reported in this review suggests that such feedback has very little effect on enhancing the quality of student writing—regardless of frequency or thoroughness.
>
> —George Hillocks Jr.
> *Research on Written Composition: New Directions for Teaching,* 1986, p. 239

having to wrestle with an intimidating dictionary makes the correction problem much simpler for a student who finds spelling a challenge.

12. *Encourage students to edit with their ears, not just their eyes.* Good editors read text more than once, and they read *aloud*. Oral reading also helps students punctuate, as well as notice missing or repeated words.

13. *Remind students to read from the bottom up.* Reading from the bottom up is a lifesaver for many students who struggle with spelling. You cannot skim (easily) when you read backwards.

14. *Become sleuths.* Ask students to join you in hunting for samples of conventional problems in textbooks, memos, letters, advertisements, newspaper articles, and elsewhere (A local grocery marquis recently advertised "brocoli," "onoins," and "pottatoes"—all on the same day. Time for "stoo"—or "soop," perhaps.). Give extra-credit points to students who can find a conventions problem in print.

15. *Look for what's done right.* Many teachers find it useful to mark two or three conventions handled *well*, along with, perhaps, *one or two* suggestions for improvement. As writer and teacher Donald Murray (2004) assures us, "We learn to write primarily by building on our strengths, and it is important for the teacher to encourage the student to see what has potential, what has strength, and what can be developed" (p. 157).

16. *Use peer editing with caution.* Teaming for *practice* is an excellent instructional strategy, but when the editing is for real, peer editing should be used with great caution. No one wants to edit herself into a lower grade than she would have received had she left the text alone! Figure 8.28 shows a sample of peer editing gone awry.

What about peer review? Let's be clear. Peer *review* does not call for students to look for errors or to make corrections but rather to respond to voice, clarity, organization, and meaning. It does not entail the same risks.

FIGURE 8.28 Peer Editing Gone Awry

Driving Tests Should Be Harder

If drivers test were more rigorous, every one on the road would be safer.

About 50,000 people die in traffic accidents every year, and thousands more are injured. The most common cause of accidents is drunk drivers but the second most common cause is incompetent driving. Yet we grant driver's lizenses on the basis of a very simple test.

17. *Teach the conventions of your content area.* Do you teach math, music, business, or science? Then you know that there are specific symbols that have meaning in your content area. In math, for example, we use symbols to indicate division, square root, equality, and so forth. Most content areas have their own conventions—and in order to communicate effectively in these contexts, students need to learn the conventions of the territory just as much as they need to learn commas and apostrophes. As Heller and Greenleaf point out (2007, p. 22), "Well-trained biology teachers . . . know technical conventions such as the use of arrows in science illustrations to support their comprehension of visual texts. But they may no longer remember what it was like to learn these things for the first time."

18. *Keep resources handy*—and model ways to use them. Here are some possibilities for any well-stocked serious editor's book shelf:

Ballenger, Bruce. *The Curious Researcher: A Guide to Writing Research Papers*, 4th ed. Boston: Allyn and Bacon, 2004. *Among the most detailed, thorough, and genuinely entertaining books ever written on the how-to's of sound research. Middle school and high school.*

Blake, Gary, and Robert Bly. *The Elements of Technical Writing.* New York: Macmillan, 1993. *A concise, superb guide to the basic elements of technical, informational, and business writing. Excellent examples. Middle school and high school.*

The Chicago Manual of Style, 15th ed. Chicago: University of Chicago Press, 2003. *Complete and authoritative, this is the place to look it up when in doubt. High school through adult.*

O'Conner, Patricia T. *Woe Is I.* New York: Grossett/Putnam, 1996. *Lessons on modern grammar taught with wit and knowledge—plus predictions on where we're headed. Upper elementary through high school.*

Sebranek, Patrick, Dave Kemper, and Verne Meyer. *The Write Source Handbooks for Students*, Second Generation. Burlington, WI: Write Source. *Highly readable, authoritative, and user friendly. Kindergarten through college.*

Strunk, William, Jr., and E. B. White. *The Elements of Style*, 4th ed. Needham Heights, MA: Allyn and Bacon, 2000. *Legendary. The essence of good writing in fewer than 100 pages.*

Truss, Lynne. *Eats, Shoots & Leaves: The Zero Tolerance Approach to Punctuation.* London: Gotham Books, 2004. *A witty enjoyable book filled with tips on putting punctuation to work for you.*

Walsh, Bill. *The Elephants of Style.* New York: McGraw-Hill, 2004. *The best book out there on contemporary usage.*

Zinsser, William. *On Writing Well: The Classic Guide to Writing Nonfiction*, 25th Anniversary Edition. New York: HarperCollins, 2001. *Witty, readable, and straight to the point. Clear-cut, no-nonsense advice on writing about science, art, travel, yourself—or any subject. One of a kind.*

A Message for Parents and Other Caregivers

Even parents who do not spell or punctuate well themselves often have high (sometimes unreasonable) expectations for the speed with which their children will develop conventional proficiency. They look to you to make it happen. You can assure them that it *will* happen, but (1) it will take time and patience because learning to be an editor is harder and takes longer than copying corrections the teacher made for you, and (2) they (parents, that is) can help.

First, let parents know that their children will be taught to think and to work like editors, that they will practice first on text that is not their own, and that as their knowledge and skill improves, they will be responsible for editing their *own* text. It may not come home corrected at first because you will not be editing *for* students, and they may not (unless they're skilled high school editors) be up to editing every line they write—*yet*. They'll get there.

Invite parents in to observe editing lessons (even to participate) and to coach students in small groups or one on one (assuming that they're good editors themselves—*ask*). A note like the one in Figure 8.29 can help.

Chapter 8   In a Nutshell

- Given a process foundation with emphasis on frequent writing, four basic steps will help you teach traits:

  1. Surround students with language (through comments, posters, student-friendly rubrics).
  2. Teach students to assess and discuss writing, both their own and that of others.
  3. Use writing samples of all kinds to illustrate strengths and problems related to each trait.
  4. Use focused lessons to target specific skills related to each trait, e.g., for organization, *how to write a lead*.

- Good literature (along with the not-so-good) provides a basis for numerous focused lessons on traits.

- Each student paper or other piece of writing you share is a "lesson waiting to happen" because students can use it for revision practice.

- Modeling is an integral part of focused lessons as well. Base your modeling on problems students are having, e.g., coming up with a good conclusion, getting rid of choppy sentences.

Study Group   Interactive Questions and Activities

1. **Activity and Discussion.** Think of one thing at which you have been quite successful. Make a list of all the things you did to become successful—the things that *really made a difference*. Which of those strategies could be adapted to fit your writing instruction? Discuss this with your colleagues.

FIGURE **8.29** **What to Tell Parents about Conventions**

Dear Parent,

This year, your child will be learning to both write and edit—and they are not quite the same thing! **As writers**, we will work on ideas, organization, voice, word choice, and fluency—the heart and soul of good writing. You can get a written copy of these traits any time. Please ask. You can also see them posted in our classroom.

As editors, we will work on spelling, punctuation, grammar, capital letters, paragraphs, and making copy look good on the page. As you can see, writing takes many skills!

Students will write and edit often. You can help by asking your child, "Are you working on writing or editing in this lesson? Or both?"

Except when we are publishing your child's work, I will not correct his or her writing. This may seem strange at first since many parents remember that their writing was always corrected by a teacher. The problem is, research shows that when the teacher does the correcting, the teacher also does all the learning. That is not what we want.

I will, however, be showing your child many ways to spot and correct editorial problems, and through the year, you will see your child's editing skills grow. Here are **eight things you can do as a parent to help:**

1. Ask your child to teach you the copy editor's symbols, one by one.
2. Ask your child to also teach you the traits of writing, one by one, as we work on them.
3. Remind your child to skip every other line when writing a rough draft so he or she will have plenty of room to revise and edit.
4. Give your child a pen or pencil he or she likes to work with to make editing more fun.
5. If possible, provide a good dictionary or handbook to use at home. I can give you suggestions if this is something you are able to do.
6. Practice together looking for mistakes in editing lessons I will send home.
7. Look for mistakes in newspapers or other print you and your child read together—and praise your child each time he or she spots an error.
8. When you write, ask for your child's help. Ask him or her to help you spell a word (even if you know it), or to show you where a comma, apostrophe, period, or question mark goes.

Finally, do not expect perfection right away. Editors need time and practice to gain skill. With enough of each, you will see your child's skills grow in ways that will amaze you. Please celebrate with me each step your child takes toward becoming an independent editor!

Sincerely,

2. **Activity and Discussion.** If you are teaching currently, which of the following things do you do? Which might be added to your repertoire?

___ Model writing for students.

___ Ask students to come to a conference with a question or concern in mind.

___ Ask students, during sharing, to tell other students (and me) what they most need help with.

___ Encourage students to work with partners in planning, drafting, or revising their writing.

___ Share writing guides or checklists with students.

___ Ask students to participate in designing or creating their own writing guides or checklists.

___ Encourage students to assess their own work as a prelude to revision.

___ Share written samples—student work, published work—as a way of modeling writing strengths or problems.

___ Invite students to practice revision and/or editing on the work of others.

___ Read aloud to illustrate strategies used by professional writers.

___ Provide a safe environment that encourages risk taking.

___ Present focused lessons that provide a way for even challenged writers to build skills step by step.

3. **Activity.** Using Figure 8.5, "Planning Lessons," as a model, identify three features of each trait (e.g., *details* for ideas, *transitions* for organization) on which you could focus your teaching. Then, identify at least three instructional strategies you could use to teach each feature.

4. **Activity and Discussion.** With a partner, choose a trait on which to focus. Then create a series of lessons on this trait by doing the following:

___ **Select two papers** (one strong, one not) you could use to introduce that trait to students.

___ **Make a list of questions** you will ask about each paper to help students discover the "lessons to be learned" from each one.

___ **Design a revision or editing lesson** based on the weaker sample.

___ **Find one or more samples of literature** you could use to broaden your students' understanding of your chosen trait.

___ **Finally, choose one or more focused lessons** (from this book or your own instructional repertoire) you could use to build skills related to specific features of that trait.

___ **Present your lesson series to the group for critique.** Talk about ways you could expand this series or modify it to meet the needs of students at both ends of the performance spectrum.

5. **Discussion.** Was your own writing (as a student writer) heavily corrected? How did this help or hinder your growth as a writer? Share your thoughts with your colleagues.

6. **Activity and Discussion.** Ask everyone in your group to bring in one favorite picture or chapter book. Within any given book, see if you can find passages you could use to illustrate strengths in *each of the six traits.* If you can find passages to illustrate every trait, all within one book, what does this tell you about finding "books for voice," "books for ideas," etc.?

7. **Activity and Discussion.** Design a editing lesson. Begin with a passage that is edited and error-free—e.g., from the newspaper or other published source. Enter it onto your computer. Then, build in the errors you wish to focus on—but be careful. Include multiple instances of *one kind* of error, but do not include *too many kinds* of errors. Share the lesson with your group for their critique. Is the purpose clear? Is it age-appropriate? Are you asking students to do many things at once? Is it too difficult for struggling writers? If so, how could you simplify it to ensure student success? Where are the safety nets?

8. **Activity and Discussion.** Get a copy of *Writing Next* by Steve Graham and Dolores Perin. Read and discuss it with your group, seeing how many connections you can make to trait-based instruction.

Reflections on Writing

Being a writer has changed my life. It's something I can feel proud about. When I'm trying to think of a story, I will think of different settings and problems and suddenly, one will appeal to me. Or when I'm off doing something else, I'll think of a piece and it will start to grow in my head. At first, all I have is a seed, and while I write, I think, "Well, maybe I should change that dinosaur to a lion," and when I'm finished, my story comes out nicely.

At my old school we had VOCP: vocabulary, openings, connectors, punctuation. That's how we thought about writing. Here at Buena Vista, in third grade writer's workshop, it's very different. Now I'm working on different traits, including word choice, ideas, and organization, as well as different genres, like fiction and poetry. I like workshop because you can write about anything you want any way you want.

I enjoy writing fiction. When I write fiction, I can do the impossible. I can make my enemies lose the state championship.

The bottom line is this: Writing has opened up a whole new door for me . . . a door I once didn't know existed.

—Lily, Grade 3

FIGURE **8.30** **Answers to Sneed Collard Scramble Game Activity, page 179**

Paragraph 1:

- For most of history, the geography and animal life of the deep-sea floor have remained a total mystery.

- As recently as the mid-nineteenth century, many people believed that the ocean was bottomless or that no life existed in the deep.

- Others felt sure that the deep sea was filled with terrifying sea serpents or animals that had disappeared from shallower waters millions of years before.

Paragraph 2:

- In the 1870s, though, scientists began a serious search for deep-sea animals by lowering nets and other collection devices far below the surface.

- During World War I, they began mapping the ocean bottom with a new invention called **sonar**.

- The sonar made loud noises that bounced off the sea bottom.

- The echoes from these noises gave people a detailed outline of what the deep-sea floor looked like.

Note:

The line—

> *Photosynthesis, the production of food using light energy from the sun, cannot take place on the deep-sea floor—*

is not part of the original text! If you deleted it, that was a good instinct. Organization is partly about ensuring strong connections among ideas, and discarding what does not fit.

CHAPTER 9

Troubleshooting
Dealing with Common Writing Problems

Writing is about hypnotizing yourself into believing yourself, getting some work done, then unhypnotizing yourself and going over the work coldly. There will be many mistakes, many things to take out, and others that need to be added.

—Anne Lamott
Bird by Bird, 1995, p. 114

After fifty years of writing, I have pretty much gotten over my fear of writing. Not all, but most of it. I wouldn't want to get over all of it. A little terror is stimulating. Writing is important, and you can say something that is wrong, stupid, silly, clumsy. And you will.

—Donald M. Murray
Shoptalk, 1990, p. 69

While Chapter 8 dealt with strategies for teaching traits in the context of a process-based curriculum, this chapter offers more of a "Dear Trait Person" approach—which is to say, things teachers have found helpful when specific problems arise. At the close of this chapter I also will suggest some strategies that are effective with struggling writers or with students who need more of a challenge.

Problems with Ideas

Problem: The information is too skimpy!

■ Strategies

1. Share students' own voices. Many students who start out believing that they have nothing to say feel differently when they encounter the voices of peers. Suddenly they are inspired to share thoughts about how it feels to be a young person today, the joys (and headaches) of driving, depression, tattoos, "instructions for life," loneliness and alienation, cultural awareness, parents and grandparents, music, work, envy, poverty, love and loss, friendship and betrayal, cosmic truth, violence, self-esteem, and memories. These topics are not mine. They are the selected topics of students assembled in a remarkable little book called, *You Hear Me? Poems and Writing by Teenage Boys* (2000), edited by Betsy Franco. Not many students will tune out when you share Nick's account of growing up with Tourette syndrome, which begins, "It all started in second grade. There was this kid and he would jump on my desk and chair. He also would call me inappropriate things. My teacher would say, Stay away from him. I said, *He* comes to *me*. She didn't care" (p. 20).

As third grader José discovered, poetry sometimes springs from mundane events. He said, "I have nothing to write about," but found that he did (see Figure 9.1).

2. Go beyond stories. Contrary to popular myth, storytelling is extremely difficult. We need to open students' minds to other possibilities. We also need to read good nonfiction aloud, thereby giving them models other than stories. See Figure 9.2 for some favorites to get you started.

3. Make it fun. For dozens of ideas on finding and reporting information with style and energy, I recommend Barry Lane's book, *51 Wacky We-Search Reports* (2003). Barry shows how to put life into the old research report by borrowing sales techniques, creating want ads or posters, writing parody, doing job interviews and talk shows, and otherwise making use of professional writers' proven skills. In "Freddy: A Day in the Life of a Neuron," the student writes, "Freddy was especially fond of Nervana, the neuron nearest to him, whose dendrites were only a synapse away. Many a time he passed messages from his axon to her dendrites but she remained aloof" (p. 89).

FIGURE **9.1** **"Problems," by José Garcia**

Imagine that you know nothing about the subject. Write down every question you'd want answered. Answer them.

—Donald M. Murray
A Writer Teaches Writing, 2/e, 2004, p. 212

4. *Take ten.* An inordinate amount of difficulty with writing comes from sheer procrastination. Here's a way to fight it. Gather around you all the notes (if any) from which you will draw your information. Write the very best lead you can. Then set a timer for 10 minutes, and within that time, write the most complete report your knowledge of the topic allows. Beginning to end: you *must finish.* Here's the trick, though: Write on *every other line*, and once you've finished, go back and use questions to identify gaps where you will need to expand your thinking or add detail.

5. *Ask important questions.* We must ask questions that have limitless and unpredictable answers—answers we *really care about.* Important questions often spring from literature. Who can read William Steig's *Amos and Boris* (1971), for example, without thinking of how much friends have a right to ask of us. Anyone who reads *Beatrice's Goat* (McBrier, 2004) must surely reflect on how much good can come of small gifts, and how important education really is—even to children so poor they must choose between school and clothing. Philosopher and educator Marietta McCarty uses literature, art, and music to challenge her young student philosophers to think, and her questions have a significant philosophical or moral base: e.g., "What

When I wrote reports in school I used a dump truck. I'd take my dump truck to the library, fill it up with facts, and then backload it onto the paper. . . . I didn't know that facts were fun, that facts were funny. Did you know, for example, that a hummingbird's heart is half the size of its body? That the Roman legions used urine as laundry detergent?

—Barry Lane
51 Wacky We-Search Reports, 2003, p. 13

FIGURE **9.2** **Nonfiction Read-Alouds**

For older reader-writers:

- Diane Ackerman, *A Natural History of the Senses* (1995)
- Diane Ackerman, *An Alchemy of Mind* (2004)
- Bill Bryson, *In a Sunburned Country* (2001)
- Bill Bryson, *A Short History of Nearly Everything* (2003)
- Thomas Cahill, *How the Irish Saved Civilization* (1995)
- Malcolm Gladwell, *Blink: The Power of Thinking Without Thinking* (2005)
- Josie Glausiusz and Volker Steger, *Buzz: The Intimate Bond Between Humans and Insects* (2004)
- Temple Grandin, *Animals in Translation* (2005)
- Laura Hillenbrand, *Seabiscuit* (2001)
- Philip Isaacson, *A Short Walk Around the Pyramids and Through the World of Art* (1993)
- Kenneth Kamler, M.D., *Surviving the Extremes* (2004)
- Stephen King, *On Writing* (2000)
- Barbara Kingsolver, *Small Wonder* (2002)
- Barbara Kingsolver, *Animal, Vegetable, Miracle: A Year of Food Life* (2007)
- Julius Lester, *To Be a Slave* (1998)
- Mary Roach, *Stiff: The Curious Lives of Human Cadavers* (2003)
- Carl Sagan, *Cosmos* (1980)
- Charles Seife, *Zero: The Biography of a Dangerous Idea* (2000)
- Robert Sullivan, *Rats: Observations on the History and Habitat of the City's Most Unwanted Inhabitants* (2004)

For younger reader-writers:

- Bruce Brooks, *Predator!* (1994)
- Sneed B. Collard, *The Deep-Sea Floor* (2003)
- Mark Kurlansky, *The Story of Salt* (2006)
- Sneed B. Collard, *Pocket Babies and Other Amazing Marsupials* (2007)
- Nicola Davies, *One Tiny Turtle* (2005)
- Thomas Eisner, *For Love of Insects* (2007)
- Margery Facklam, *Spiders and Their Web Sites* (2001)
- Twig C. George, *Seahorses* (2003)
- Stephen Kramer, *Caves* (1995)
- Kathryn Lasky, *The Man Who Made Time Travel* (2003)
- Alvin Jenkins, *Next Stop Neptune* (2004)
- Morgan Monceaux, *Jazz: My Music, My People* (1994)
- Albert Marrin, *Oh, Rats!* (2006)
- Bill Nye, *The Science Guy's Big Blast of Science* (1963)
- April Pulley Sayre, *Stars Beneath Your Bed: The Surprising Story of Dust* (2005)
- Seymour Simon, *Animals Nobody Loves* (2001)
- Lynne Truss, *Eats, Shoots, and Leaves: Why, commas really DO make a difference!* (2006)
- Jessica Noelani Wright, *Come Look With Me: Exploring Modern Art* (2003)

are some things in your life that you thought you had to have, but when you gave it some thought, they turned out to be unimportant?" (2006, p. 73). As part of a broader discussion on treating people with dignity and respect, McCarty often asks students if they wish to create their own Children's Bill of Rights—and they "jump for the nearest writing utensil" (2006, p. 100). How many prompts can we say that about?

Problem: There's *too much* information.

■ Strategies

1. *Cut the copy in half.* Ask wordy writers to imagine they're writing for a newspaper and can only fill so many inches on the page. Ask them to cut the copy they have by half *without losing content.* That's the trick.

2. *Shrink the topic.* Sprawly topics produce sprawly writing. A student who sets out to write about *Planet Earth* or *Civilization* or *Life* quickly loses all sense of direction. The student who writes about raising silkworms has a much easier time because it's simple to tell what is inside the circle of relevance. A topic like *swimming* might look focused, but to see how big it is, try brainstorming, as a class, all the possible subtopics: learning to swim, getting in shape for a meet, rescuing someone in trouble, keeping fit, and so on—it's endless. We can shrink this topic so that it's manageable. *Swimming* becomes *teaching someone to swim,* which becomes the even more focused *teaching an infant to swim.* Practice this strategy with your students until narrowing the focus becomes a natural way of thinking. Focused writing comes from focused thinking.

3. *Summarize! Summarize!* Summarizing is one of the most powerful strategies for teaching focus—and for teaching writing in general. It requires the writer to zero in on what matters most and to express that message in a condensed, no-words-wasted form. Summarizing is widely used in the corporate world to shrink unwieldy documents down to digestible size, and is a precise, almost infallible test of how well the writer understands the broader message—hence its usefulness in writing across the content areas. Start by asking students to read a piece, then *tell* you what is most important. You may ask them to highlight key points. Start with something small and familiar, then gradually add length and complexity. When students become proficient at identifying what is important, ask them to try writing their summaries, keeping in mind that brevity is the soul of the summary. Summarizing well is an art, and one worth developing. To introduce the topic, read *Once upon a time, the End (asleep in 60 seconds),* Geoffrey Kloske's witty summary of well-known fairy tales and nursery rhymes (2005). Your students will laugh, and by the second or third illustration, they will grasp the idea of the effective summary.

4. *Practice observation.* In *Little Big Minds* (2006), teacher and educational consultant Marietta McCarty recommends asking students to spend up to 10 minutes focused on a single object, such as a blade of grass, a flower, the bark of a tree, or an apple, taking it in through as many senses as possible

> If you give me an eight-page article and I tell you to cut it to four pages, you'll howl and say it can't be done. Then you'll go home and do it, and it will be much better. And after that comes the hard part: cutting it to three.
> —William Zinsser
> *On Writing Well,* 2001, p. 18

> I try to leave out the parts that people skip.
> —Elmore Leonard
> In James Charlton,
> *The Writer's Quotation Book,*
> 1992, p. 27

> Think small. The best things to write about are often the tiniest things—your brother's junk drawer, something weird your dog once did, your grandma's loose, wiggly neck, changing a dirty diaper, the moment you realized you were too old to take a bath with your older brother.
> —Ralph Fletcher
> *What a Writer Needs,*
> 1993, p. 162

(p. 116). You might try this with your students, asking them to take notes. Sometimes, when students feel they have nothing to say, they have simply given up too easily on their sensory powers of observation. In *How the Irish Saved Civilization* (1995), Thomas Cahill writes of the barbarian hordes who plan to attack the apparently invincible Romans: "A crone in a filthy blanket stirs a cauldron, slicing roots and bits of rancid meat into the concoction from time to time. She slices a carrot crosswise up its shaft, so that the circular pieces she cuts off float like foolish yellow eyes on the surface of her brew" (p. 16). In just a few words, Cahill captures the look, feel, and smell of the scene. We are right there. Sensory details make all the difference—and they come from building good observational skills through time, reflection, and patience.

 # Problems with Organization

> One thing that will make it easier to get started is to write three leads to your paper, instead of agonizing over one that must be perfect.
>
> —Bruce Ballenger
> *The Curious Researcher,*
> 1994, p. 168

Problem: My students still have problems with leads.

■ Strategies

1. *Make an off-limits list.* Make a list of leads you're tired of and print them on a poster for all to see. That way, there's no excuse for resorting to such time-worn beginnings as

- *Hi, my name is Sam and I want to tell you . . .*
- *This will be a report about . . .*
- *In this paper . . .*
- *Do you like California? I do. Let me tell you why . . .*
- *This is a paper to explain . . .*
- *Following are the four reasons to . . .*

2. *Offer options.* Some students need a concrete list of "Ways to Begin." Here are a few:

- An anecdote
- A startling fact that wakes readers up
- A scene that sets the stage
- An intriguing quotation
- Action, action, action
- Dialogue
- A promise to readers; e.g., "You'll be a cook within one week!"
- A striking image focused on one unexpected detail
- A summary of a problem—to which the paper offers a solution

You can also have fun by allowing students to create a new lead for an old favorite—as kindergartener Caleb requested permission to do. See Figure 9.3a for Caleb's new take on "Jack and the Beanstalk." It's considerably more suspenseful than the original. Holy Beanstalk, that's refreshing!

FIGURE **9.3a**   **Caleb's New Lead for
"Jack and the Beanstalk" (Kindergarten)**

*Jack and the Beanstalk
HOLY BEANSTALK Jack
wants to clime a big big big
big BIG beanstalk! What
will be up there? and
What will happen? Oh the
Suspense! But what about the
Real Story? how about I Just
tell it to you?*

3. *Go bad on purpose.* Shake out the cobwebs by writing bad leads for one or more of the books you are reading. For example:

- *Hi, I'm E. B. White, and I want to tell you the story of Charlotte the spider and her friend Wilbur. Ready? Here we go!*
- *Do you like chocolate? In this story you'll learn about a determined boy named Charlie and the way chocolate changed his life.*
- *It was a dark and stormy night. Ahab paced the deck, smoking his pipe. Somewhere out there lurked Moby. Moby-Dick. But where?*

Host a "Bad Leads" award ceremony, where you can have some fun reading these aloud and voting for the worst of the lot: "Lead Least Likely to

> Therefore your lead must capture the reader immediately and force him to keep reading. It must cajole him with freshness or novelty, or paradox, or humor, or surprise, or with an unusual idea, or an interesting fact, or a question. Anything will do, as long as it nudges his curiosity and tugs at his sleeve.
>
> —William Zinsser
> *On Writing Well,* 2001, p. 56

Get a Reader's Attention," "Most Action-Free Lead," "Most Obnoxiously Perky Lead," and so on.

4. Go for the kill. Killer leads require killer details. Ask students, in pairs, to *interview* each other for three minutes each. Encourage them to avoid dead-end questions (e.g., *When were you born? What is your middle name?*) and to ask the kinds of questions that will yield intriguing information:

- What bugs you?
- What did you fear most in your life that never actually happened?
- Where would you least (or most) like to be stranded for a week?
- If you could spend a day with one person, living or dead, who would it be?
- What color comes closest to describing you? Why?

Then ask them to pull out the most intriguing detail on which to base a lead. Read results aloud. Use research whenever a good lead or first paragraph just won't come. Lack of information is often the culprit.

Problem: Trying to follow this writing is like running through a giant maze.

■ Strategies

> Write down the five questions the reader must have answered. Put the questions in the order the reader will ask them. Answer them.
>
> —Donald M. Murray
> *A Writer Teaches Writing,*
> 2004, p. 212

1. Tell it orally first. Talking is an excellent organizational strategy because it's quick and because the speaker can see at once if listeners are puzzled or following along with ease. Practice with a story first. You can model this yourself. Think of something unusual, frightening, funny, or otherwise significant that has happened to you in the past year. Tell the story to your students. Then list *everything* that happened on an overhead, including a few details you *don't* need (what time you got up, what TV show you were watching when the phone rang, what you had for lunch). List events in random order, and omit one or two important details. See Figure 9.3b for an example based on my overnight adventure in a strange city. I asked students to eliminate what was not needed, reorder what was left, and ask questions to fill in the blanks, based on their suggestions. This works with any genre.

2. Play with time. Everyone is familiar with the movie moments where time slows to a crawl as we experience the intensity of a lovers' tryst or the heart-stopping tension of a close escape. Or those moments when the screen dissolves into a message—"Five years later . . ." and we know that apparently nothing central to the writer's message has occurred during that time. Ask your students if they recall movie moments like these, and then invite them to play with the pacing of their own writing, slowing things down, or moving right along. In Figure 9.4, third grader Emma writes about her grandfather, introducing him with some essentials in paragraph one, speeding along through the family history in paragraph two, then slowing down to recap Grandpa's memorable coffee break, and coming full circle in paragraph four to echo her lead. This young writer already has a strong sense of how to achieve good pacing.

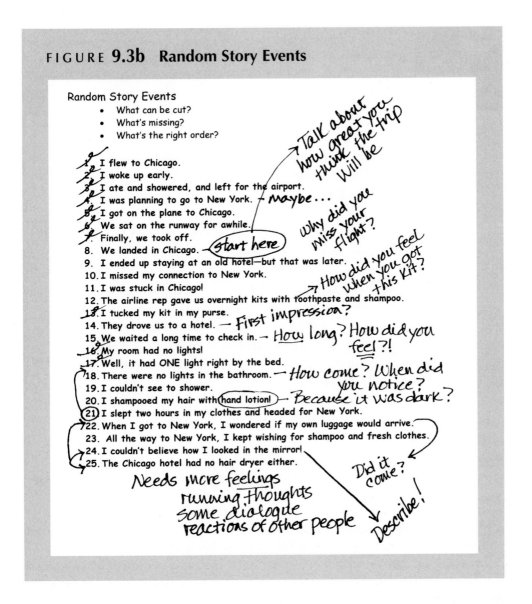

FIGURE **9.3b** **Random Story Events**

3. *Work it like a puzzle.* Skip two to three lines between each paragraph in the rough draft. Then, cut the whole piece apart, paragraph by paragraph. Lay them out on a table and play with them, like a puzzle, *thinking like a reader.* Remember, it helps to pretend you know nothing about the topic. Then you can ask, "What would I need to know first? What would I like to learn next? What surprise do I wish the writer would save for the end? Is there something here I already know that I could skip right over?"

4. *Draw it out visually, like a map.* Show the "stops" (each of which becomes one paragraph or section) the reader will make along the journey, thinking about what he or she will learn at each stop. See Figure 9.5 for a roadmap on nutrition. If you later decide nothing important or interesting is happening at a given stop (paragraph), do what you'd do on a real road trip. Drive on.

5. *Look for clues.* When Louis Sachar introduced the yellow-spotted lizard on page 4 of his novel *Holes* (2000), he knew very well what a crucial

FIGURE **9.4** "My Grandpa," by Emma (Grade 3)

My Grandpa
By Emma, Grade 3

I never met my grandpa. He died before I was born. He fought for my country in World War II. He signed up illegally to be a soldier when he was fifteen. He lived.

Years passed, and he had his first child, my dad. More years passed, and he had my four aunts and two uncles.

My dad tells stories about him. My favorite one is when he and his family were camping when it was raining. My grandpa was drinking coffee on a hill looking one direction while his family floated away in the water, going the other direction. Even though I have heard that story so many times, it makes me laugh so hard. I bet my grandpa would laugh, too.

Even though I have never met my grandpa, I feel like I have known him forever. I know I have.

role this reptilian villain would play. And how disappointed we readers would have been not to have the lizard show his scaly face again.

Before you can learn to leave good clues yourself, you must learn to look for them as you read. So begin there. Ask your students to look for the clues good writers have left along the trail.

In *The Tale of Despereaux* (2003), a charming fairy tale featuring a princess, an arrogant king, a very courageous mouse, and a diabolically evil rat, author Kate DiCamillo deliberately explains how in any fine piece of writing, all things are connected, and no detail stands in isolation:

> The rat's soul was set afire, and because of this, he journeyed upstairs, seeking the light. Upstairs, in the banquet hall, the Princess Pea spotted him and called out the word "rat," and because of this Roscuro [the rat] fell into the queen's soup. And because the rat fell into the queen's soup, the queen died. You can see, can't you, how everything is related to everything else? [pp. 117–118].

6. Give "beginning, middle, and end" a face lift. We know what a *beginning* is: a lead, a hook, a way of getting the reader's attention. Similarly, an *ending* is a resolution of the problem—or sometimes a confession that resolution will be hard to achieve. But what the heck is a *middle?* It's the writer's way of answering questions or expanding ideas raised by the lead, and guid-

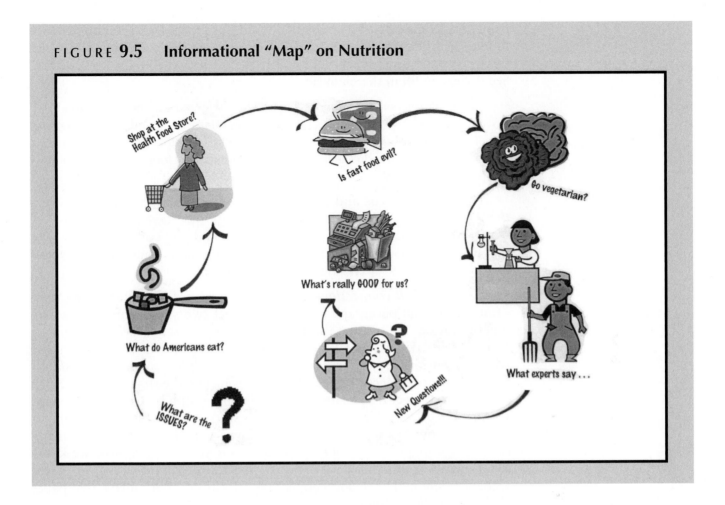

FIGURE **9.5** **Informational "Map" on Nutrition**

ing the reader toward the intended resolution. My suggested face lift, then, is a vision of organizational structure adapted from Barry Lane (1999, p. 37):

Set-Up (*Beginning*), Exploration (*Middle*), Wrap-Up (*End*)

Set up what follows, simultaneously drawing the reader in.

Explore by expanding the main message—and pulling the reader in deeper. Present problems and proposed solutions, details the reader needs. Move forward through action, character development, information, or argument. Then, zap—

Wrap it up. End with a revelation, resolution of the conflict or problem, discovery, moment of truth. Say goodbye.

> Endings grow from beginnings and reveal themselves through clues within the story, characters, or ideas.
>
> —Barry Lane
> *Reviser's Toolbox*, 1999, p. 39

Problem: Transitions are weak or (Help!) missing altogether.

■ Strategies

1. *Invent your own transitions.* Choose a published piece with strong transitions, and rewrite it with all transitional phrases missing. Ask students to fill in transitional words and phrases that make sense. This passage comes from *Jack's Black Book* (Gantos, 1999). In this scene, Jack is taking an aptitude test and has broken his pencil. The rigid Mr. Ploof will not allow him to start over or use a sharpener because the rules say he "must keep going." See if you can fill in the blanks:

> I didn't have a pencil sharpener _____ I began to gnaw at the wood around the lead, spitting out the pulp, _____ I exposed the blunt end. I felt even more like a white laboratory rat, _____ I pulled myself together and raced through the test. _____ it didn't seem too difficult or take very long _____ I got off to a rough start [p. 16].

The missing words and phrases, in order, are *so, until, but, For something so important,* and *even though.* You might not have chosen those very words (your students might not either), but could you come up with words that linked the ideas together logically? If so, you understand the importance of connecting ideas—that's the point of the lesson.

2. Make small connections. Students who have difficulty inserting transitions into a full paragraph can often connect two short sentences—sometimes in various ways—and this helps them begin to see what transitions are about. You may wish to call them "word bridges," a helpful term for some writers. Consider these sentences: *It was cold. Ralph wore his yellow shirt.*

What's the connection here? Well, it depends on the shirt, doesn't it? Ask students to connect these sentences to show that Ralph had a big, fuzzy shirt: *Because it was cold, Ralph wore his yellow shirt.* See how this transition tells us more? Now let's suppose the shirt is sleeveless and made of skimpy material: *Even though it was cold, Ralph wore his yellow shirt.* Now we know two things. The shirt isn't very warm—and Ralph likes it enough to freeze while wearing it. The lesson here is that transitions aren't just verbal paper clips; they *make meaning.*

Problem: Conclusion? What conclusion? It just stops.

■ Strategies

1. Imagine yourself saying goodbye. A good ending feels so right because it gracefully says goodbye to the reader, much the way you might say goodbye at the door after visiting with a friend. You might comment on what you learned about serving a great Caesar salad or suggest something interesting that you might do the next time you get together. Probably you would *not* say, "So, in summary then, we ate, talked, played cards, played with the dog, and spoke of meeting next week."

2. Talk about specific ways to end. Here are some possibilities:

- Something the writer has learned
- Something the writer regrets
- A hint of what's to come
- The writer's emotional response or observation
- A comment on how things have changed
- A stirring image

> The perfect ending should take your readers slightly by surprise and yet seem exactly right.
>
> —William Zinsser
> *On Writing Well,* 2001, p. 65

> Nice story, Aesop. I love the moral too. Very true, but did you ever wonder what happened the next day, the next year, the next decade?
>
> —Barry Lane
> *The Tortoise and the Hare Continued . . . ,*
> 2002, Introduction

- A telling conversation
- An unexpected twist or a secret revealed
- An echo of the lead (coming full circle)
- The answer to a question the reader has likely been pondering

3. *Invent bad endings for books you or your students are reading.* Remember the "Bad Leads Contest"? Host a similar event for conclusions, creating, with your students, some like these:

- Then I woke up and it was all a dream. There was no scarlet letter, after all.
- I hope you liked my book and learned a lot about wizards. . . .
- So Stanley and all the Yelnatses had learned some valuable lessons about life and lizards. . . .

4. *Use the power of the sequel.* In his book *The Tortoise and the Hare Continued . . .* (2002), Barry Lane points out that the ending of one piece is merely the beginning of another. Read this book to your students. Then test the theory: Take the ending from one piece of writing and use it to craft the lead for a sequel.

5. *Picture the reader.* How do you want the reader to feel at the end of the piece? What's the lingering thought you want the reader to have? Structure your conclusion to make it happen.

The Tortoise and the Hare Continued . . .

Problems with Voice

Problem: There is no voice here.

■ Strategies

1. *Encourage students to* **think** *I.* Many teachers object to the use of the personal pronoun *I* in informational or persuasive pieces, and with reason. It's easy for writing to degenerate into a self-serving opportunity to vent: "*I feel that school uniforms are stupid because I hate them.*" The problem is that writing can become *so* impersonal that it is difficult to sense anyone at home within the words: "*One wonders about the motivation underlying school uniforms.*" Somewhere between these extremes lies a balance of supported thinking and personal investment: "*Many people were surprised when a recent survey of local middle schools showed attendance soars when students wear uniforms. But—does that mean the students like them? Apparently not.*"

William Zinsser suggests that even when the pronoun *I* is not permitted, "it's still possible to convey a sense of I-ness." He recommends writing a first draft with *I*, then taking it out, to "warm up your impersonal style" (2001, p. 22)—and *thinking I* even when you cannot use it.

> Writing from the heart is not just about writing from the heart. It's also about writing from and for all the senses. Readers want to feel, they want to taste, they want to smell.
> —Nancy Slonim Aronie
> *Writing from the Heart,*
> 1998, p. 143

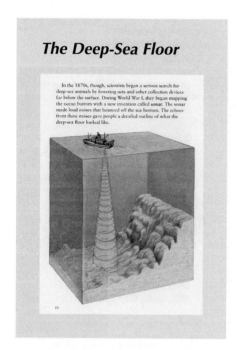

The Deep-Sea Floor

In the 1870s, though, scientists began a serious search for deep-sea animals by lowering nets and other collection devices far below the surface. During World War I, they began mapping the ocean bottom with a new invention called sonar. The sonar made loud noises that bounced off the sea bottom. The echoes from these noises gave people a detailed outline of what the deep-sea floor looked like.

> Go with what comes up. Don't make time for your inner editor to happily announce, "They'll really think you're sick if you write that."
>
> —Nancy Slonim Aronie
> *Writing from the Heart,*
> 1998, p. 77

2. *Make it dramatic.* Sneed Collard, a master of nonfiction writing, maintains that the best nonfiction boasts a sense of drama because readers cannot survive on facts alone. His book, *The Deep-Sea Floor* (2003), for example, opens not with a definition or list of facts but with a scene right from an underwater play (facts come on the following page):

> Far from land, a mile below the sea surface, a tripod *fish* rests on the bottom of the ocean. In total darkness, with water temperatures just above freezing, the fish silently waits for a meal. A shrimplike *copepod* (KO-peh-pod) drifts by. The tripod fish lunges and gulps it down . . . [p. 7].

3. *Get someone talking.* We can plod only so long through text in which no one lives, breathes, or speaks. Yet, it can be challenging to work dialogue into informational text. No problem. Quote someone with something interesting to say on the topic. This can help to satisfy a reader's natural longing for human contact. William Zinsser (2001) does this with stunning timing, inviting such worthy writers as H. L. Mencken, Garrison Keillor, and Loren Eisley into his conversation about good writing. He wraps up his discussion of the invaluable surprise ending by quoting Woody Allen: *"I'm obsessed,"* Woody says, *"by the fact that my mother genuinely resembles Groucho Marx"* (p. 67).

4. *Have a good time.* Voice comes, as much as anything, from loving the writing you are doing and daring to be a little playful about it. One writer who seems to be having a really good time is Anne Lamott. I laugh aloud clear through Lamott's books, but the moment that unhinged me was her description of her mother (it could have been mine) reacting to her book: *". . . whenever I show her a copy of my latest book, she gets sort of quiet and teary, and you can tell that what she's feeling is 'Oh, honey, did you make that yourself?' like it's my handprint in clay—which I suppose in many ways it is"* (1995, p. 150).

5. *Lighten up.* Not everyone can be as funny as Anne Lamott. So it might not be fair to require humor. A respectable first cousin of outright humor is the light touch. Nonfiction writing can become very heavy-handed: *"The Stellar's jay is 11 inches long and makes its home in coniferous forests. Its Latin name is* Cyanocitta stelleri.*"* Such text has a late afternoon in August kind of feel to it. Compare Patricia Lichen's lighter fare: *"I'm not sure who compared Stellar's jays to 'crows in blue suits,' but the description is apt. These birds are in the crow family, and like their basic-black-garbed relatives, they are raucous, bold, and intelligent"* (2001, p. 63). Lichen's voice says, "Pull up a chair—I think you'll find this interesting."

6. *Bring the reader inside.* Find a way to make the reader at home in the text. Bill Nye has a genius for this. I can open *The Science Guy's Big Blast of Science* (1993) to any page and feel as if I have been invited in for tea and physics. Bill helps me relate every topic to my own life: *"As you read these words, you and this book and whatever you're sitting on are being pulled down by gravity. If you're reading in an airplane [I was, actually], the plane* *is being pulled down by gravity. That's why planes need wings and engines"* (p. 35). I looked out, saw the wing, and felt I *was* defying gravity—Bill had said so.

7. **Look to the topic.** Writer Mary Pipher suggests that when writers' work sounds hollow to them, the topic is often to blame. I agree. She suggests (2006, p. 44) finding your voice by posing questions of self-exploration, such as these:

- "What makes you laugh, cry, and open your heart?"
- "What do you know to be true?"
- "What is beautiful to you?"
- "What do you want to accomplish before you die?"

If we focus on the writer, not the writing, if we let students know they are interesting people with an interesting take on the world, and that we cannot wait to read what they have written, we might be surprised at the voice we get.

8. **If it's not your topic, personalize it.** How do you take someone else's topic and make it your own? You stretch it, bend it, and coax it into a slightly different form. Once, in writing about a memorable place, a colleague chose "inside her grandson's eyes." Now that is taking the notion of place to a whole new dimension.

9. **Write to your best listener.** My friend and colleague Sally Shorr, a veteran teacher, offers this excellent piece of advice—which has worked for me and for many students with whom I've shared writing ideas: Think of your *very* best listener, the person in whom you would confide your most important secrets. Write as if you were writing *just to that person.* Who are your own best listeners?

10. **Try role playing.** From Cedar Park Middle School in Beaverton, Oregon, comes a knockout idea that combines writing, drama, historical research, and practice in developing a three-dimensional character. A seventh grader studying the Holocaust assumes the identity of "Isaac Stein," a prisoner who first creates a picture titled "Visions of Hope" (see photograph, Figure 9.6), then writes about it (Figure 9.7)—at apparent risk to his life. This is another case where art inspires writing. Each element of the picture has meaning, and the physical creation of that picture has clearly influenced the writer's essay.

Problem: This voice is wrong for the topic or audience.

■ Strategies

1. **Practice switching audiences.** Students gain a sense of audience only by writing for more than one person or group. Ask students to imagine an uncomfortable situation, e.g., receiving a traffic ticket or getting caught in a lie. Then ask them to write about this incident to several different audiences, e.g., a parent, a good friend, a teacher, and a traffic court official. Does the voice change as the audience shifts? Why?

> The challenge is not to find a unique topic (save that for your doctoral dissertation) but to find an angle on a familiar topic that helps readers see what they probably haven't noticed before.
>
> —Bruce Ballenger
> *The Curious Researcher,*
> 2004, p. 50

> Whenever I write, whether I'm writing a picture book, an entry in my journal, a course handbook for students, or notes for the milkman, there's always someone on the other side, if you like, who sits invisibly watching me write, waiting to read what I've written. The watcher is always important.
>
> —Mem Fox
> *Radical Reflections,*
> 1993, p. 9

FIGURE **9.6** **Visions of Hope**

2. *Get an attitude.* Actors often approach a scene from a particular attitude: *"In this scene my friend is being completely unreasonable—so I need to seem increasingly angry."* It helps to do this in writing, too. What attitude are you projecting? Helpful? Authoritative? Sorrowful? Joyous? Amazed? Get into the mood of your writing. For a masterful example of this, listen to Jim Dale, who plays *all* the parts—with relish and stunning diversity—on the CD version of the Harry Potter series, published by Listening Library (www. listeninglibrary.com). Dale's expressive interpretation of the text can win over even those who don't consider themselves fans, and it's all about *voice.*

3. *Take time to vent.* Almost everyone has an issue with some local business group or other. Express your concerns in letters. The complaint letter is a challenge. You need to hit the right note: serious protest coupled with a professional, courteous undertone. If your students can hit that just-right blend, they have a leg up on achieving good business voice. Save letters (and responses, if you get them) and compile them into a class book entitled, *Effective Business Voices.*

4. *Become the authority.* We want students to write with confidence. Qualifying every statement is a sure way to kill voice. Instead of saying tentatively, "Parasailing can sometimes be rather exciting, given the right circum-

> You are writing for your-self. Don't try to visualize the great mass audience. There is no such audi-ence—every reader is a different person.
>
> —William Zinsser
> *On Writing Well,* 2001, p. 25

FIGURE **9.7** **Visions of Hope by "Isaac Stein"**

I call my picture "Visions of Hope." If I'm caught with this picture, I'll be killed. But it's worth it if people outside see it. I want them to know what life was like in the camp and how we kept our hopes up.

You may be wondering how I got the materials used in this picture. It wasn't easy. I got the material for the prisoner figures from old pieces of uniforms that had been torn off. This was one of the easier things to get. Uniforms get torn all the time from hard work. All the people look alike because to the Nazis it doesn't matter what you look like—only what you can do. To the Nazis we are all just numbers, without faces, without names.

The buildings in the picture are black to represent evil and death. Most of the buildings, aside from the barracks, you would enter but never come out again alive. I got this cloth from an old blanket worn thin from overuse. The Nazis didn't care if we were cold or uncomfortable, so they didn't make any real effort to mend things. Everything in our world needs mending, including our spirits.

Inside the smoke of death from the smokestack you will see the Star of David. This star represents hope. Hope for life and for living. We will never totally die as long as our hope lives on.

My picture has two borders. One is barbed wire. It symbolizes tyranny, oppression, and total loss of freedom. The other border, outside the barbed wire, represents hope and dreams outside the camp. The flowers, sun, moon, and bright colors were all things we took for granted in our old world.

Even though we see sun through the clouds and smoke, we can't enjoy it anymore. The feathers represent the birds we barely see or hear inside the camp. We miss the cheeriness of their voices. The tiny brown twigs are as close as we come to the trees we remember.

I got the bright cloth from a dress. When prisoners come to the camp, they must take off their own clothes and put on the hated prison outfits. All the nice clothes are sent to Germans outside the camps. My job is to sort through the clothes and pick out things that will be sent away. When I saw this beautiful cloth, I tore off a piece and saved it for my picture.

I hope someone finds this and remembers that even when they took away everything else, they could never take our hope.

stances," we want them to write authoritatively, "Parasailing is a thrilling sport, but can be dangerous—even impossible—in truly calm westher."

Of course, you have to know what you're talking about—so doing the homework first is vital. So often teachers complain that research writing has no voice. That is true when students are unsure of their footing, when they write as though they are taking a test and straining to recall the three essential facts they think the teacher will be looking for. Why should teachers—or *anyone*—want to read 30 to 150 papers containing little or no new information? Research papers should be more than essay tests. They should be lively, provocative discussions filled with striking details—at least some of which we did not know. Donald Murray sums it up it best: "Our students should be teaching us the subject while we are teaching them to write" (2004, p. 96).

5. *Relax.* Tension is the mortal enemy of voice. If you can relax as you write, the *self* is more likely to emerge. In the introduction to *Essays That Worked for Business Schools* (1987), Boykin Curry and Brian Kasbar summarize the responses of admissions officers—and their observations are telling:

> The overwhelming complaint from undergraduate admissions officers was that reading 13,000 essays on the same few topics . . . is a mind-numbing experience. Most essays are dry and overwritten. They are often "corrected" by so many friends and relatives that the life gets sucked out. . . . Anxious applicants become so afraid of saying the wrong thing that they end up saying nothing. Such sterilization can mean unbearable monotony . . . so don't treat your essay like a psychological minefield. What seems "safe" to you is probably deadly boring to a weary admissions officer [p. 12].

Curry and Kasbar quote one admissions officer in particular who tries to liven up the essays by reading them on his boat for a change of scenery: *"You know what? Even that doesn't help,"* he claims (p. 12). The moral? Relax. Be yourself. Say what you think.

 Problems with Word Choice

Problem: The vocabulary is too simple, too general, too vague.

■ Strategies

1. *Hunt for striking words.* I like this passage from Margaret Atwood's *Alias Grace* (1996) because it makes a movie in my mind: *"Dora is stout and pudding-faced, with a small downturned mouth like that of a disappointed baby. Her large black eyebrows meet over her nose, giving her a permanent scowl that expresses a sense of disapproving outrage"* (p. 57). Words like *pudding-faced* and *disappointed baby* help me to see Dora and make me less likely to invite her to my birthday party. Reading Atwood reminds me that taking time to find the right word is worth it.

2. *Give "tired" words a rest.* With your students, brainstorm a list of words we could all stand to shelve for a while: *fun* (as an adjective), *awesome, good, great, nice, bad* (meaning *good*), *special, cool* and *way cool, grand, great, super, downer, bummer, pushing the envelope, make it pop,* and so on. Pick six to ten. Write each word or expression in colorful letters at the top of a large sheet of chart paper. Then group students into teams of three to five (depending on how many sheets of chart paper you have), and give one member of each team a colored marker pen. Ask them to do a gallery walk, circling from one tired word poster to the next on cue, and writing as many

One group of researchers tried to sort out the factors that helped third and fourth graders remember what they had been reading. They found that how interested the students were in the passage was thirty times more important than how "readable" the passage was.
—Alfie Kohn
Punished by Rewards, 1993, p. 145

other "ways to say it" as they can think of in one to two minutes (no more). The brainstorming grows more challenging as they go along and the chart paper fills up—but often the options become more creative, too. Once each team has visited each "word stop," ask teams to select their four favorite alternatives and read them aloud.

3. *Read above* (well *above*) *grade level*. This is vital. I would not enjoy being cut off in the bookstore by a clerk who said, "Sorry—you're not ready for that book just yet." *That's* now the one I want. Students learn well before each word or sentence makes sense.

Many young elementary students would be hard-pressed to define these words in isolation: *imprison, individual, invader, renew, elastic, cascade, canvas, harbor*. In context, though, the words reveal their identity in a way that no vocabulary list can duplicate:

> Our skin is what stands between us and the world. If you think about it, no other part of us makes contact with something not us but the skin. It imprisons us, but also gives us individual shape, protects us from invaders, cools us down or heats us up as need be, produces vitamin D, holds in our body fluids. Most amazing, perhaps, is that it can mend itself when necessary, and it is constantly renewing itself. . . . Skin can take a startling variety of shapes: claws, spines, hooves, feathers, scales, hair. It's waterproof, washable, and elastic. Although it may cascade or roam as we grow older, it lasts surprisingly well. For most cultures, it's the ideal canvas to decorate with paints, tattoos, and jewelry. But most of all, it harbors the sense of touch [Ackerman, 1995, p. 68].

This selection is from Diane Ackerman's *A Natural History of the Senses* (1995), a book most would classify as secondary or adult level. I am not suggesting reading this book in its entirety to younger students—or *any* students. I am suggesting harvesting passages with rich language from *many* sources to share with students of *any* age. Will they recall every word? Perhaps not. So what? They'll recall some, and they'll get a *sense* of the deeper meaning. Language in context is infinitely more powerful than language by list.

4. *Predict verbal lifespans*. The Usage Panel for the *American Heritage Dictionary*, which includes teachers, writers, editors, and journalists, meets regularly to discuss what ought or ought not to be considered "acceptable" English: *"Today's spoken garbage may be tomorrow's written gold"* (Zinsser, 2001, p. 42). Words like *nutrient, psychology, presidential, Americanize, checkers, energize, folder, immigrant, penmanship, surf,* and *snowshoe* were all once considered "new" and had to win the approval of time and usage. Which of the words in Figure 9.8—under consideration by *American Heritage* as well as other

---

FIGURE 9.8   New Words

agritourism	hoodie
aquascape	labelmate
bada-bing	mouse potato
belly up	ringtone
big-box	sandwich generation
bling	soul patch
cross train	spyware
drama queen	supersize
the elephant in the room	telemeeting
hardscape	wonky

dictionaries—do you think will make the cut? Do you recognize any of your students' current favorites on this list—or your own? For an even longer list to consider, simply use your search engine to track "new words." This makes an interesting and simple research project for students and can lead to lively discussions of how language does, and should, change.

Not all new words are long-lived: *"The 'happenings' of the late 1960s no longer happen, 'out of sight' is out of sight, and even 'awesome' has begun to chill out. The writer who cares about usage must always know the quick from the dead"* (p. 43).

Problem: This student suffers from thesaurus-chained-to-the-desk syndrome. Everything's overdone.

■ Strategies

1. *Enter the Bulwer-Lytton Fiction Contest at San Jose State University.* You'll need to begin by reading excerpts from *It Was a Dark and Stormy Night*, or *Dark and Stormy Night: The Final Conflict*, or any of the zany, hilarious collections of what is considered to be some of the world's most overwritten writing. Entries are generally only one sentence long and not more than 50 to 60 words. Here's just one example:

> Daphne ran swiftly across the windswept moor scarcely noticing its heather perfume, down to the rocky cliff where she paused momentarily atop the jagged precipice, looked down at the waves crashing far below, and wished that she had been born anything other than a lemming [Little, 1996, p. 83].

Give your thesaurus-happy students a chance to take a crack at this—you try, too. When you've had your fill of laughing at your overbaked results, send the best of them in to the contest:

Bulwer-Lytton Fiction Contest
Department of English
San Jose State University
San Jose, CA 95192-0090

2. *Keep it to one syllable.* This activity is harder than it sounds, but it definitely tames overwritten text. Ask students to write a paragraph on any topic (e.g., weather report, summary of a math lesson, letter to a friend) in one-syllable words only. No cheating. *"The fog crept through the fields. Sun strove to burst through. . . . "*

Problem: Too Many Modifiers!

■ Strategies

1. *Go on a modifier diet.* One of my students once wrote a piece about a sensory-overload deli where the pickles were *tart, juicy,* and *crisp;* the corned beef *succulent* and *delectable;* the mustard *tangy* and *refreshing;* and the bread *fluffy* and *fragrant.* Even the clerk was *gracious* and *accommodating.* I felt stuffed without taking a bite. Put yourself on a low-modifier diet, and the same passage might sound like this:

The pickles snapped when you bit into them, and made your mouth pucker. The bread took you back to grandmother's kitchen. The corned beef required no chewing and the mustard opened even the most resistant sinuses. The clerk always greeted me as if I'd been gone for a month and he'd had nothing of interest to do in my absence.

2. *Spend adverbs frugally*. Adverbs can be useful, but we need to spend them like money. Notice the following examples:

"He shut the door *forcefully*" versus "He *slammed* the door."

"*She talked* loudly and *shrilly*" versus "She *screeched.*"

"Her voice spoke to us *alluringly*" versus "Her voice *seduced* us."

Never let an adverb steal work that should go to a worthy verb.

> I believe the road to hell is paved with adverbs, and I will shout it from the rooftops. To put it another way, they're like dandelions. If you have one on your lawn, it looks pretty and unique. If you fail to root it out, however, you find five the next day . . . fifty the day after that . . . and then . . . your lawn is *totally, completely,* and *profligately* covered with dandelions.
>
> —Stephen King
> *On Writing,* 2000, p. 125

Problems with Sentence Fluency

Problem: Short, choppy sentences break the text up into bite-sized pieces.

■ Strategies

1. *Remember an old friend: sentence combining*. It still works magic. Make your own samples based on creative revisions of famous texts: *Macbeth,* the Constitution, *Winnie the Pooh,* essays by Ralph Waldo Emerson, Edgar Allan Poe's "The Cask of Amantillado," or "Desiderata":

> Go. Go placidly. Go amidst the noise. Go amidst the haste. Remember things. Remember peace. Peace may exist. Look for it in silence. Be on good terms with people. Feel this way toward all people. But only feel this way as much as possible. Do not surrender.

Ask students to reassemble your creations, using as few sentences as possible. Alternatively, chop up some text from a cookbook, lawn mower warranty, legal contract, auto show advertisement, or headline news story. Trade and revise by recombining sentences. Don't forget to compare your students' revisions to the originals.

2. *Read aloud*. Choppiness and awkward moments stand out in an oral presentation; the ear catches them the same way it catches a singer who breathes at the wrong moments or is out of synch with the band. A good tip for the writer is this: *Pretend it's a script—or a song. Write it the way you'd want someone to perform it.*

3. *Count sentences*. Sounds ridiculous—but it works. It's a variation on sentence combining, really. You start with up to a dozen sentences, then see if you can reduce the number to two or three, like this:

- *Jake saw a fish. It was glistening. Its scales were gleaming. The sun shone on them. He raised his spear. He aimed. He let the spear fly. He missed!*

> *He felt disappointed. He was quick, though. He yanked his spear from the water. Right away, he looked for another fish. (12)*
>
> - *When Jake saw the glistening fish, its scales gleaming in the sun, he raised his spear, took aim, and let it fly. Disappointed, he yanked his empty spear from the water and immediately began looking for another fish. (2)*

Can you combine those last two into one? Try it!

Problem: All sentences begin the same way.

■ Strategies

1. *Ask students to list sentence beginnings*—just the first three or four words—on a separate sheet of paper. Do they all look alike? Sometimes awareness is enough to jar a student out of a persistent pattern.

2. *Practice variations.* Start with any sentence: *"You have to be clever to survive school."* Ask students to rewrite the sentence as many ways as they can in three minutes (or slightly longer, if you wish). If you like, give students sample sentence beginnings:

> *Being clever . . .*
> *Surviving school . . .*
> *Survivors . . .*
> *School . . .*
> *Cleverness . . .*

Problem: It has variety—but it still sounds mechanical.

■ Strategies

1. *Hit the end note.* Where is the power of the sentence? At the end. Experienced writers learn to embed the most important word or thought right there—like a punch. After awhile, this becomes automatic, but at first, you have to point it out. Which of these sentences has more power?

- Victor turned, slowly raised the gun, leveled it, and fired.
- Victor raised the gun, leveled it, and fired, even as he turned.

To a writer's ear, the second sentence simply sounds *wrong*, putting the emphasis on *turning*, not *firing*. Read any piece by Diane Ackerman, John F. Kennedy, Winston Churchill, or Carl Sagan (to name a few fluent writers), and you'll hear your voice automatically marking the rhythm of the sentence endings. It isn't just sentences that are guided by this organizational structure; it's writing itself. Sentences, paragraphs, and whole pieces all drive, relentlessly, toward the rhythm, the force, the power of the end note.

2. *Master parallel structure.* Parallel structure, or *patterning*, in sentences adds the same kind of rhythm that percussion adds to music. Read the following passage aloud, and hear the rhythm build to a crescendo in the closing line, a masterpiece of parallel structure:

Lobstermen seek lobsters wherever those creatures may roam, and this means lobstermen chase their prey all over the shallow sea and the cold-water coastline. This means lobstermen are constantly competing with one another for good fishing territory. They get in each other's way, tangle each other's trap lines, spy on each other's boats, and steal each other's information. Lobstermen fight over every cubic yard of the sea. Every lobster one man catches is a lobster another man has lost. It is a mean business, and it makes for mean men. As humans, after all, we become that which we seek. Dairy farming makes men steady and reliable and temperate; deer hunting makes men quiet and fast and sensitive; lobster fishing makes men suspicious and wily and ruthless [Gilbert, 2001, p. 5].

You can teach parallel structure through examples such as this one and through practice. Begin with a piece that is not parallel, and ask students to rework it. Try these yourself:

- She was tenacious. In addition, her manners weren't very good. What's more, she often scared the living daylights out of us.

- Some called the January weather in the mountains dangerous. One thing was certain: You couldn't predict it. Though it wasn't always deadly, it had the potential to be deadly at times.

Problem: Endless connectives turn the whole paper into one monstrous "sentence."

■ Strategies

1. *Encourage the occasional short sentence.* I have often seen assessment rubrics that encourage long, complex sentences. What the writers of these rubrics are thinking I have no clue. Brevity is an invaluable tool. Short sentences are especially important when the content is complex or unfamiliar to the reader; like small steps on a slippery path, they allow the reader to feel in control. Suppose that I am writing about black widow spiders, for example, and I write this:

> Black widows don't really look around for people to bite and in fact they just hang upside down in their webs and so are seldom seen and that is part of their danger because they choose a web site where they will have a good supply of insects, which is where the people usually are, although years ago. . . .

See how tiring this is to read? Fortunately, author Margery Facklam, from whom I borrowed this information, writes much better than this, dividing her text into bite-sized chunks:

> Black widows don't go around looking for someone to bite. They hang upside down in their messy cobwebs, where they are seldom seen, and that is part of their danger. They choose a web site wherever there is a good supply of insects, which is usually where people are, too. Years ago, when most families had outhouses in the backyard instead of indoor bathrooms, black widow bites were more common because the spiders liked living where the fly supply never ran out [2001, p. 15].

2. *Write poetry.* Poems are unique, I believe, in that they are simultaneously challenging enough for our best writers, all the while offering an

> There is no minimum length for a sentence that's acceptable in the eyes of God. Among good writers, it is the short sentence that predominates. And don't tell me about Norman Mailer—he's a genius. If you want to write long sentences, be a genius.
>
> —William Zinsser
> *On Writing Well,* 2001, p. 72

accessible form to beginners. Poetry has potential depth beyond what other forms can usually achieve because so much is expressed in so few words. Further, most poetry is interpretable in many ways, thereby stretching our ability to form connections. In some respects, the poem is the ultimate summary. Notice how many ideas blossom in Elizabeth's poem "Purple" (Figure 9.9). On the other hand, poets can be quite irreverent about sentence structure and punctuation, creating impressions through single words, fragments, or phrases. This makes poetry inviting and manageable for writers who struggle with sentences or conventions. These writers have carte blanch to touch us our hearts without fear of making a mistake.

3. No ands or buts. Ask students to write three paragraphs with no *ands* or *buts* or *becauses* at all. This is challenging, perhaps, but quite possible.

4. *Start with no punctuation.* Build sentence sense by reading punctuation-free writing aloud, pausing clearly and fully for each comma, semicolon, period, or question mark. Ask students to fill in the punctuation they *hear*—then count the sentences:

Outside the rain was falling hard and fast it hit the roof like the thunder of an impassioned drummer we lay in our beds listening wondering when it would

---

FIGURE 9.9   "Purple" by Elizabeth, Grade 3

Purple

By Elizabeth, Grade 3

Purple is the wave, lapping the beach.
Owls hoot at the sight of it.
Purple.
It feels smooth, soft, furry,
Like that blanket your mom gave you
Last winter.
Fresh picked lavender
Is purple.
Calm,
Peaceful,
Happy.
The pillow when you're sleeping.
The blanket when you're cold.
The comfort when you're sad.
Purple.
That relaxed feeling you get when you look up at the sky
Just before dark.
The scent of lavender comes
Through the deep color
The younger sister to blue.

stop like small birds in a nest we looked up at the ceiling as if expecting the rain to come through it never did of course.

This passage has five sentences. Students are sometimes surprised to note that their own writing has relatively few "sentences." With thoughtful punctuation, though, it might have more.

 # Problems with Conventions

Because problems with conventions are so numerous and varied (and because this issue is covered thoroughly in Chapter 8), I will simply add a few tips for making your teaching of conventions and editing easier.

1. *Create a style sheet.* Publishing houses give authors style sheets, which govern many issues of layout: size and format for headings and titles, models for handling citations, margin sizes, use of graphics or photographs, and other design issues. Your classroom is like your own publishing house. Design a style sheet (see Figure 9.10) that reflects your personal preferences—how you'd like graphics titled, where you want titles placed, how you want the writer's name (or yours) to appear, how many fonts you want to see per page, how you'd like references cited, how you'd like captions for graphics handled, and so on. You may wish to enlarge one copy and post it for students.

2. *Model, model, model.* Even though students do their own editing, you must show them what is correct, how to spot an error, and how to correct it using appropriate copy editor's symbols. Model often.

3. *Keep your own conventional skills current.* This is harder than it sounds because conventions are ever-changing. Rely on a good handbook and use it frequently. You can keep a whole shelf full of handbooks, but you should designate one as the class authority and refer to it often. Ask students to help you look up the answers to any questions of usage or correctness about which you feel uncertain.

4. *Encourage students to include samples of their editing practice in a portfolio* or writing folder so that they have a visual representation of how their editing skills are growing. This record also gives parents impressive physical evidence of what their students can do.

5. *Explore the playful side of conventions.* Conventions are not just about correctness. They're about guiding the reader through the text—and sometimes offering intriguing hints about meaning. Writers sometimes create conventional "special effects" by eliminating punctuation on purpose (see poems by e. e. cummings, for example, or *The Sound and the Fury* by William Faulkner). Young writers may enjoy a close-up look at Nina Laden's *The Night I Followed the Dog* (1994), in which Laden shows great originality improvising with fonts, capitals, and other conventions to underscore meaning. Older writers can draw their own inferences about subtle but significant changes in font size in Karen Hesse's *The Music of Dolphins* (1996). Encourage students to help you find other examples of texts in which conventions are about more than simple correctness.

FIGURE **9.9**   **Sample Style Sheet**

1. Use 12-point Times Roman (or similar font).

2. Make major headings 16-point, centered.

3. Make subheads 14-point, flush left.

4. **Boldface** all major headings and subheads.

5. Make all margins 1" wide.

6. Use endnotes, not footnotes.

7. In citing sources, refer to *Write Source 2000*, pages 231–232.

8. Use no more than two different fonts per page.

9. Double space all text (except long quotations—see #20).

10. You may use either bullets or numbers for lists.

11. Label illustrations or other graphics as Figure 1, Figure 2, etc. Refer to each one by number in your text.

12. If you prepare a title page (optional) please include the title of the piece, your name, and the date. Center *everything*.

13. Use *italics*, not underlining, to show emphasis.

14. Avoid **boldface** except for headings.

15. Avoid FULL CAPS except when quoting fully capitalized material.

16. Keep exclamation points to a minimum—no more than two per paper!!

17. Use contractions (*don't, can't, wouldn't, couldn't, we'll*, etc.) if you wish.

18. Number your pages, after the first page, in the upper right corner.

19. If you do not have a title page, include your name, my name, the class period, and the date in the upper right-hand corner of the first page, like this:

Charles Naka
Mr. Price
Period 3
March 1, 2008

20. Set off long (over 25 words) quotations by indenting five spaces on both right and left, and printing the quotation in single-spaced text, like this:

> *Always write with voice. If the voice fades, your reader*
> *will fade with it, and no one wants this to happen. Write like*
> *you mean it, and the reader will not only stay awake, but*
> *may actually purchase your next book.* (Marland, 2008, p. 10)

Helping Challenged/Beginning Writers

Many students dread writing. It may be difficult for them, or they think—rightly or wrongly—that they are not very good at it. A lifetime of negative comments only reinforces this internal assessment. The writing-process approach promises help to challenged writers by offering them more time for writing than many of us used to be given. But time is only useful if you know what to do with it. Traits can help writers understand what it is writers actually *do* when they revise, and even if they do only *one* thing to revise a given paper, that's an important step. Here are some ways to make traits work for writers who find writing difficult or just unappealing:

1. *Focus conferences on the* **writer,** *not the writing.* Ask students to share their interests. What are their favorite activities, hobbies, dreams, hopes, worries? Get to know the person first because out of this well comes the writing.

2. *Keep writing short.* If you're not much of a runner, you probably would rather not sign up for the 26-mile marathon. Fifty yards is plenty. So let students write a little at a time (a paragraph, say) and write *often.*

3. *Do lots of group writing.* Give reluctant or challenged writers partners, and let them co-author a piece or coach each other. They will learn from each other as they talk and work. Brainstorming leads or conclusions or best phrasing lets everyone in on the thinking part of writing.

4. *As a class, critique and analyze* **anonymous** *writing.* Even people who do not like to write themselves or who fear writing enjoy evaluating and discussing the writing of others, and they will learn more from being assessors than you think.

5. *Model writing.* You don't have to razzle-dazzle them. Write simply. Write often. Solicit their help. How should you begin? What should you put in? Take out? Get them to problem solve with you as you go. Then you can tell them—honestly—"Look, you're doing it already as you're guiding me. The only difference is *you* need to be the one moving the pencil sometimes."

6. *Draw.* Many unsure writers discover that they know more than they thought if they are allowed to use two techniques: talking and drawing. Drawing in particular helps many writers to visualize a story or essay or report. Figure 9.11a–d shows four key, randomly selected pages from a longer picture book (titled *A Great Journey*) written by a seventh grader for primary readers. Students were asked to create from seven to ten pictures for a story. Each time something significant happened, it was captured in an illustration. (Look through any picture book to see how carefully choreographed this match is.) Alternating between drawing and writing required the students to think visually, and also to identify those moments that stood out—an important organizational skill. In this story, a small but large-eared mouse named Blake is marooned during a hurricane and uses his ingenuity to fashion a raft. He's about to be reunited with his family in the last illustration

> . . . we need to be gentle. Raymond Carver, writer and teacher, was revered by his students. The harshest criticism he would give to a student was: "I think it's good you got that story behind you."
>
> —Ralph Fletcher
> *What a Writer Needs,*
> 1993, p. 18

> Other instructors are obsessed with motivating writing. When they share their techniques I am reminded of cattle prods that "motivate" the steer up the ramp towards hamburger land. Good writing is rarely "motivated" from the outside but has to be drawn out of the student.
>
> —Donald M. Murray
> *A Writer Teaches Writing,*
> 2004, p. 84

> I'd like to see boys get the clear message that drawing is neither a punishable offense nor merely a way to decorate finished writing but a useful way to think through and flesh out the story, poem, or report they are writing.
>
> —Ralph Fletcher
> *Boy Writers,* 2006, p. 126

FIGURE **9.11** **Four Pages from A Great Journey (Grade 7)**

When hurricane Jerry blew past Hot Sandy Island one July day, it sank the U.S.S. Milford clear to the bottom of the sea. There was only one survivor: Blake, a small gray mouse with unusually large ears.

He was still wearing his orange life vest, but it was hanging from his body like limp rags. He almost tossed it away, but something stopped him. He remembered his mom saying, "Reuse! Recycle!" He decided he could use the vest for something. A pillow maybe. So he kept it.

Just before his trip, Blake had written to his parents telling them he was coming to visit. Now he didn't know what to do. He didn't think that he would ever see his parents again. He thought how worried they must feel wondering what had become of him. He knew then that he must get off the island. He had no idea how he was going to go about it.

FIGURE **9.11** **Four Pages from A Great Journey (Grade 7)**

All this work was making him very tired, and he lay down on top of his raft to rest. He had a wonderful dream that he was in a hammock on his own back porch with his mom on one side and his dad on the other, rocking him back and forth. When he woke up, fear seized him. His first thought was, "Where is my island?!" It took him a minute to figure out that while he had been asleep, the tide had come in and washed his raft out to sea. "What shall I do?" he thought, tugging on his ears the way he often did when he was nervous.

He thought of trying to get back to shore, but he did not know which way to go. The island was nowhere in sight. He had no water, but he did have a few bananas left. "I better ration them," he thought. He hoped he might drift toward the island, but it did not seem to happen. He floated the rest of the day and on into the night.

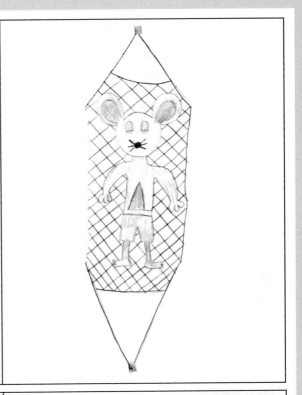

The night was scary to Blake, who had never slept outside his own bed. The waves seemed much bigger. He worried that a shark might eat him or his raft might come apart and strand him. Sudden raft failure. If he fell asleep he might roll off right into the sea, so he tried to stay awake, pinching his nose to keep himself alert.

By morning, he was nearly out of bananas and so tired he had to sit down to keep from falling. Just as he thought there was no hope, he saw a black dot in the distance. He thought he might be seeing things, but the dot kept growing larger and larger until he could make out the shapes of sails. It was a ship!

He flailed his arms frantically and squeaked with all his lung power.

"Help me! Help me!" he cried. Of course, they were too far away to hear anything, but yelling seemed like the right thing to do anyway.

Suddenly, he remembered his vest. He yanked it off and began waving it in the air like a flag.

shown here. This same technique works for informational writing. The illustrations simply capture *main points* the writer wishes to make—versus *events* in an unfolding plot.

7. *Allow more time for prewriting.* Many writers stumble because they are pushed into writing before they are ready. Fear of failure makes them choke, and what we get is limited in length, scope, and feeling. Talking and sketching—or even having quiet time to think (some like writing to music)—allows them to loosen up. Prewriting is also enhanced when we help writers gain access to the information they need to write.

8. *Encourage dictation.* Many students would write more and with greater confidence (and style) if they could dictate all or part of what they say. Talking feels more natural and more comfortable. Let them write on tape—or talk to you. Make notes on what they say so that you can show them that they had more ideas than they thought; they can then use your notes in their writing: "Here you told me your hamster died, but then you went right into your shopping trip at K-Mart. How did you feel when your hamster died? Who buried it? Where did you bury it?" These probing questions from teacher Lois Burdett turned a brief sketch of a hamster's last moments into a touching story of loss, in which we see the second grade writer gently touch the body of her now-dead hamster, hoping for a sign of a heartbeat but finding none, and then trying to hold back the tears. Later we see Dad digging a small grave, watch the writer softly place the body inside and say goodbye and then, after pulling up a soft earth blanket, mark the grave with her beloved Hamster's name—and e-mail address (a reminder of our times).

9. *Keep it manageable.* For challenged students, this is perhaps the most important piece of advice. Writing, revising, editing: All need to be small, confined, manageable. Let your lessons, your conferences, your requests for revision focus on just one small piece, one feature, of writing at a time. A student who quails at the thought of rewriting a whole piece can still add *one* detail, make *one* verb stronger, change *one* sentence beginning. Make the task as small as you need to for the student to experience success. (Refer back to Figure 8.5, Planning Lessons, for a reminder of how to cut a big trait down to size.)

10. *Provide scaffolding models.* Second language students in particular benefit from models: paragraphs, titles, sentences, sentence patterns, or individual words. Gradually, delete more and more of the text, asking them to fill in the blanks. You can do this in one lesson—with students working together to learn new words that make meaning where at first there is none:

The girl raced down the path becomes
The ___ raced down the path, which then becomes
The ___ raced down the ___ , which then becomes
The ___ ___ ___ the ___ , and so on.

Having an opportunity to take small steps gives an unsure writer confidence and the satisfaction of getting it.

> We should see our students as smart and capable. We should assume that they *can* learn what we teach—all of them. We should look *through* their mistakes or ignorance to the intelligence that lies behind [emphasis in original].
>
> —Peter Elbow
> *Embracing Contraries,*
> 1986, p. 149

11. *Put the writer in charge.* Take a lesson from third grade teacher Judy Mazur and insist that students come to a conference or sharing session with a question or concern in mind. Ask them to consider what they need most—no matter how small—and to seek specific help. Writers' questions might range from "What's a good title for this?" to "How do I make a character seem angry?"

12. *Make all students coaches.* When students learn to depend on each other to solve writers' problems, they learn to think like writers. This, and not the creation of perfect pieces of writing, is the true goal of writing workshop.

13. *Build on the positive.* It may be buried or tough to spot. Look harder. Just one moment of voice or convention used correctly is cause for a small celebration. Think *little victories.* And when you comment, don't be gushy, but don't hold back either. No one wants to hear, "Well, your voice is starting to emerge." What is that? A compliment or a complaint? Be enthusiastic: "Your voice grabbed me by the lapels right at this point. I got the chills."

> Your unconscious can't work while you are breathing down its neck. You'll sit there going, "Are you done in there yet, are you done in there yet?" But it is trying to tell you nicely, "Shut up and go away."
>
> —Anne Lamott
> *Bird by Bird,* 1995, p. 182

For Students Who Need a Challenge

Often, I'm asked if there isn't something called *advanced traits,* a term I always find amusing because it sounds as though once we master these basic, simple traits, we can move on to the more sophisticated traits—*wit, innuendo, subtlety, profundity,* and so on.

Actually, working with the traits is like anything else; it can be as simple or as difficult as you make it. If you wanted to get better at bike riding, you'd ride faster or farther or strap weights to your back. You get better at working with the traits pretty much the same way. It is not the *traits* that get more advanced after all, but the *writing, thinking, reading, and discussing.* Still, you don't want to cover old ground. The last thing you need to hear is, "Oh, no, not 'The Redwoods' again!" Here are some suggested strategies for challenging yourself—and your students.

1. *Ask students to reflect on and assess their own work.* They do not need to score their work unless you want them to do so. What is helpful, though, is to reflect on the process (what was challenging or rewarding) and to identify the specific strengths of a piece. In a thoughtful reflection, a twelfth grader (Figure 9.12) discusses the writing process that resulted in her piece on method acting. This is an informational piece with strong voice, and her insight tells her that choosing the right topic was critical.

2. *Create your own writing guides, checklists, or posters.* It's harder than it might seem, and will make you come face to face with what *you* think good writing is, regardless of what the six-trait model says. You can specialize: a rubric for persuasive writing, business or tech writing, drama, or poetry. Start with student samples. Read and rank them: high, developing, beginning. Record what you find, and use the results to create a rubric or checklist written in your own words.

FIGURE **9.12** **Method Acting, Grade 12**

Method Acting

The year is 1880. The theater is dark, except for one figure, illuminated on the stage. The figure, Prince Hamlet, begins his famous soliloquy:

To be, or not to be, that is the question—

The delivery of the lines is perfect, each word enunciated, clear from the rest. However, in the actor's face, there is no indication he feels the pain behind the words. While the character of Hamlet is clearly faced with a difficult decision, the actor is only considering what to have for dinner. The audience does not believe the actor *is* Hamlet. And the reason they do not believe is because the actor does not believe it himself.

The difference between reciting lines from memory and becoming the person characterized by those lines is the difference between acting *before* the Stanislavski Method and *after*. Prior to the twentieth century, when the influence of method acting was first felt in theater, it was up to the audience to figure out what emotions each character might be feeling. Because the lines had to carry all the meaning, one actor's Hamlet might be much like another's.

Enter Constantin Stanislavski, a Russian actor and director, who changed the role of the audience from that of casual observers or critics to that of engaged participants. Stanislavski wanted his audiences to cry and laugh—to feel life. So, in the late 1800s, he introduced the acting technique now widely known as "method acting" (also known as the Stanislavski System). With this method, emphasis on speech and clear delivery decreased, while emphasis on feelings and emotions increased perceptibly. As Foster Hirsch (1984, p. 18) explains, "The spectator ceased to watch the performance, and began to live it."

In method acting, the actor never stops evolving into the character he/she portrays. Actor and critic Sonia Moore points out that an actor must not only learn to "control his voice and body," but also to move across the stage as the character would do it—and to adopt the character's mannerisms and way of speaking, laughing, eating, or talking (1984, p. 13). Say the character is a police officer. The actor might then wear a police officer's uniform routinely—not just on the stage, but all day, even at home. He or she must learn to walk, run, sit, and look totally at home in that uniform so that it becomes an extension of who he or she is.

Method actors improvise. Stanislavski said that "mechanical memorization kills the imagination" (Moore, p. 58). He believed memorized words could never have the power of words that come from the heart—or cause an audience to think deeply about important moral issues. Actor Ellyn Burstyn has said that "to start with the words is to be too literal. Words are the last thing to come to" (Hirsch, p. 210). Many method actors believe they can "personalize" their lines so long as they project the writer's intended emotion and meaning.

Perhaps the most popular way for actors to find the right emotion is through a technique called "affective memory." It works like this: An actor recalls an incident that produced the desired emotion. Suppose she needs to call up anger. She recalls a time a careless driver cut her off in traffic, nearly causing an accident—or a time someone ridiculed the way she spoke or dressed. The recollection triggers the anger, and the audience believes it because what they are seeing *is* real. With affective memory, actors feel emotions intensely, and the audience can sense the difference.

F I G U R E **9.12   Method Acting, Grade 12,** *(continued)*

The influence of Constantin Stanislavski continues to this day. His method is used by many actors, including Al Pacino, Robert DeNiro, Jack Nicholson, Dustin Hoffman, and the late Marlon Brando—to name only a few. Some critics believe they can tell who is using method acting just by the intensity of emotion they project on stage or in films. Many people in today's audiences feel the same way . . .

It is 2006. The theater is dark except for one figure, illuminated on stage. Prince Hamlet breaks into his soliloquy. But this time, it is not the words on which the audience focuses, but the emotion behind them. We see pain on the actor's face, how he is experiencing the very real choice between life and death. Hamlet is no longer a shallow character, but a real human being. He is more. He is *us*. We have felt this pain, too. Art follows reality, and we get a glimpse of ourselves on the stage.

Sources Cited

Hirsch, Foster. 1984. *A Method to Their Madness: The History of the Actors Studio.* New York: Da Capo Press.

Moore, Sonia. 1984. *The Stanislavski System: The Professional Training of an Actor.* New York: Penguin Books.

Additional Sources Consulted

Stanislavski, Constantin. 1961. *Creating a Role.* Trans. Elizabeth Reynolds Hapgood. New York: Hill and Wang.

Stanislavski, Constantin. 1961. *Stanislavski on the Art of the Stage.* Trans. David Magershack.
    New York: Hill and Wang.

Reflection

This paper was easier for me to write than some—perhaps because I did not have trouble coming up with a solid thesis. This gave my writing focus. I think this paper is very easy to follow. It opens with a little drama and offers a bit of history on method acting without growing tedious. I give the reader several examples of how method acting works—enough to invite them to look for it themselves when they see a film or play. Then it comes full circle and ends back on stage. I read it aloud, and I feel it has voice. Al Pacino is my favorite actor, and I enjoyed discovering how he develops a character and makes the person so real. Also, I want to work in theater arts in college, so I had a personal stake in the whole method acting thing. I think that involvement comes through. It's fluent and readable—and it's not dry. The thing I'm working on the hardest right now is making sure an informational piece doesn't sound like a report—just a list of facts. If you don't want to just spit back an encyclopedia entry, you have to come up with a good topic and it has to be something you care about. This means you need time to think and plan. We never have enough time to really figure out what to write about or where to get good information. On the last assignment I wound up writing about Picasso, and it never came to life because I couldn't get into it and I ran out of time to switch topics. What I want to say is that the writing itself is the easy part. Conventions? No problem. It's the ideas and the voice you need to work to achieve. What we need is more time before we do the first draft, to gather information and to think. In spite of the fact I was trying to work on the spring break musical at the same time that I wrote this, it was a good project, and I loved the topic.

3. *Compare traits across modes of writing.* As your students write for various purposes, talk about how voice changes (informational to descriptive to narrative) or how even conventions differ in creative versus business or technical writing. When you bring modes (forms, purposes) of writing into the picture, you open up a whole new world of ways to apply and think about traits.

4. *Invite students to keep portfolios.* Nothing speaks so convincingly of growth and change as the evidence itself: the writing. Edward, a second language student from South Korea, kept a portfolio throughout his third grade year. Notice the many differences—including just an expanding comfort with writing in English—between the fall and spring samples shown in Figures 9.13a and 9.13b, respectively.

5. *Assess and discuss more challenging pieces.* Look at conventions or word choice in a legal document, résumé, or job application letter; voice or organization in a play, recipe, board game, a letter of resignation, or set of directions; word choice in a travel brochure, weather forecast, or college manual; fluency in a film review or set of song lyrics; and ideas in a political speech or doctoral dissertation.

FIGURE 9.13a Edward's Early Poetry

There is a Dragon
By Edward

There is a dragon in a

white small world.

Then it gets filled with wide

dark color.

Nothing else.

Not so bad.

FIGURE 9.13b Edward's Later Poetry

Myself
By Edward

I am a wind blowing under a bright sky.
I am a player who jumps up and shoots
   for the victory.
I am the orange of a burning volcano
   in dinosaur times.
I am a rare mouse who runs for health
   every day.
I am a canyon with large minds.
I am a sunflower shining like sun
   every morning.
I am a statue standing tall and still.
I am moonlight,
   coming out with friendly stars.
I am South Korea,
   south from the battling guns.
I am the sweat of heat after a long game.
I am a son, cousin, and friend.
I am lucky to be me.

6. *Ask students to design their own lessons for teaching traits.* Encourage students to use student writing samples, other writing, literature, or activities to enrich the lesson. Be inventive! Once they've designed lessons for their own classmates (this is just the warm-up), let them create a PowerPoint lesson on trait-based writing for

- Younger children
- Parents
- Members of the business community
- Content area teachers

7. *Conduct your own classroom research.* How do the six traits influence your students' performance—or that of students in another class? Set up an investigation using observation, interviews, and possibly a pre- and postwriting exercise. Document what you learn. Publish the results on the Internet.

8. *Ask for multiple revisions.* As noted earlier, skilled writers revise pieces they are serious about more than once. It is perfectly reasonable to ask that stronger students push themselves in this way. Who knows how far they can take their writing with layers of revision? See Figure 9.14 for a Student Revision Checklist that supports this layered approach.

9. *Ask students to publish their writing.* So much of the way we judge quality writing is influenced by performance on district- or state-level tests. Yet a great deal of writing that is successful in that venue would never be published, and the reason is simple. It doesn't move anyone. It doesn't make a difference. Correctness isn't enough. Formulaic structure might be easy to follow, but without surprise, where is the joy in the reading? If we believe there is a higher and better purpose for writing (and if we don't, why on earth are we teaching it?), let's invite students to put themselves on the line and work on having a piece published. Following are some valuable resources for initiating student publishing (or simply look up "student publishing" online):

- Jim Burke, English Companion, www.englishcompanion.com
- Read Write Think, www.readwritethink.org
- Barry Lane, www.discoverwriting.com
- Linda Hoyt, Excellence in Literacy Instruction, www.lindahoyt.com
- Teachers & Writers Discussion Group, http://groups.yahoo.com/group/teachersandwriters
- International Education and Resource Network (iEARN), www.iearn.org
- Community Works On-Line Resource Center, www.vermontcommunityworks.org
- Schwab Learning, www.SchwabLearning.org
- Teachers & Writers Collaborative, www.twc.org
- www.publishinggame.com

10. *Establish a student drop-in center for writing.* Students with a high level of skill can use that skill as coaches. Consider establishing a drop-in

> You write in order to change the world. . . .
> —James Baldwin
> In Mary Pipher,
> *Writing to Change the World,*
> 2006, Preface

FIGURE **9.14** **Plan for Revision**
Designed to keep revision manageable and support multiple revisions

Plan for Revision

Make a revision plan for your writing. Don't check *everything*. Keep your revision manageable. Check up to four elements across traits or focus on *one trait*. Then, if time permits, put your writing away for three days or more, and when you pull it out, read it aloud and make a new plan. Don't worry about conventions *until the final draft*.

With respect to **Ideas**

I need to—

____ Learn more about this topic

____ Narrow my topic so I'm not trying to cover so much ground

____ Be more clear—perhaps say things another way

____ Expand what I say so it's more than a list

____ Include details that paint a picture in the reader's mind

____ Include other sensory details—sounds, smells, tastes, textures

____ Think of questions the reader might have, and answer them

____ Cut, cut, cut—I have too much information

With respect to **Organization**

I need to—

____ Revise my lead so that the reader wants to know more

____ Focus—stop wandering off-track

____ Show how small ideas and details link to the big picture

____ Have an overall design: *comparison-contrast, visual description, solving a mystery, Q&A, problem-solution, series of events,* and so on

____ Show how one paragraph leads into another

____ Present information in a way that builds interest or understanding

____ Spend more time on what matters—and less on trivia

____ Wrap up the discussion with a conclusion that provides closure

____ Come up with a title that fits the piece—and gets a reader's attention

With respect to **Voice**

I need to—

____ Put more of *myself* into the writing—be expressive

____ Say what I *really think and feel* without holding back

____ Know more about this topic so I can sound confident

____ Be more direct and forceful

____ Consider my audience: *Who are they? What will interest them?*

____ Make the voice match the purpose: *to entertain, to inform, to persuade*

F I G U R E **9.14** **Plan for Revision,** (*continued*)
Designed to keep revision manageable and support multiple revisions

With respect to **Word Choice**
I need to—
___ Stretch for the "just right" word or phrase
___ Drop the clichés and find my own, original way to say things
___ Get rid of generalities (*We had a fun time*) and say what I really mean
___ Use stronger verbs to give my writing life and energy
___ Stop trying to impress the reader with inflated language and just *say it*
___ Cut back on adjectives or adverbs
___ Repeat words or phrases *only* for emphasis
___ Use the "language of the territory"—words that fit my topic

With respect to **Sentence Fluency**
I need to—
___ Read my writing aloud to make sure it flows smoothly
___ Start sentences in different ways
___ Vary length so some sentences are longer, some shorter
___ Use fragments only for effect, not because I forgot to finish a sentence
___ Make dialogue sound natural—like real people speaking
___ Introduce any quotations I use—not just drop them *kerplunk* into the text
___ Use meaningful sentence beginnings—*After a while, For this reason*—to link ideas
___ Avoid weak sentence beginnings: *There is* or *There are*

With respect to **Conventions**
I am now working on my final draft and I need to—
___ Read both silently and aloud to be sure I've caught all errors
___ Hear the punctuation in my head
___ Look up any words I do not know how to spell
___ Use a handbook to check usage or grammar
___ Include enough paragraphs to make the copy visually appealing and signal organizational shifts
___ Double-check homophones: *to, too,* and *two*; *your* and *you're*; *its* and *it's*
___ Make sure the text is readable—good handwriting, clear fonts, wide margins
___ Place any titles or subtitles correctly and set them off from the main text
___ Eliminate "The End"—not necessary
___ Be sure conventions show the reader *how* to read the text

> **Remember . . .**
> Keep your revision *manageable.* You'll have much more success doing multiple drafts and working on a few elements each time.

FIGURE **9.15** **Commitment (Grade 9)**

Commitment

Commitment is the business man who stays late at the office to catch up on work. Commitment is Laziness's alter ego, and loves to get ahead and stay ahead. Commitment goes to poker games on weekends with his best friends/colleagues Determination, Perseverance and Longing. Commitment is married to Devotion and has a very strong and fluent household. Nothing short of puking up a lung will stop Commitment from working hard.

FIGURE **9.16** **Intensity (Grade 9)**

INTENSITY

Intensity is the middle-aged man who yells at the TV during a football game, knowing that the people on the screen won't hear him. Intensity plays on his company softball team with Compassion, and their companionship seems to frustrate everyone else who just wants to have fun. Intensity always plays hard because "It's not just a game!"

center, either within your classroom or as an after-school activity. In this center, students can play the role you usually play, conferring with other students, offering suggestions, giving them a safe place to share their writing.

11. *Personify the traits—and portray them theatrically.* How does Voice dress and speak? Is Conventions really the stuffed shirt everyone thinks he (or she) is? Can Fluency dance? Does Word Choice have a split personality? Does Organization check out everyone's drawers and closets? Create a short play, or just a dialogue. Then extend this playful activity to other abstract qualities, as students have done in Figures 9.15 and 9.16. (For more delightful personifications, see *The Book of Qualities* by J. Ruth Gendler [1988].)

Chapter 9 In a Nutshell

- Even when you work with traits and give students time for writing, they may continue to experience some roadblocks. Be persistent—or just come at a trait from a slightly different perspective.

- To strengthen ideas, voice—and all traits—ensure that students sometimes have the option of writing on personally important topics.

- Encourage students to read everything they write aloud. It will help them to develop an ear for detail, fluency, and voice and to catch small problems with conventions.

- Consider the power of talking and drawing for students who need a comfortable, familiar way to express ideas.

- Model the solution of various writers' problems. Your students will learn from helping you.

- Encourage struggling writers to use strategies such as talking, working with a partner, asking (and answering) questions, and dictation to achieve success.

- Break traits into individual features to make writing and revision manageable.

- Take students who need a challenge to new levels by asking them to assess more difficult pieces, assess and write in various genres, create their own genre-specific rubrics, design their own lessons, keep portfolios, publish, do multiple revisions, or set up their own drop-in writing center.

- Remember that ultimately it is not the traits themselves that are *advanced* but our understanding of how writing and writing process work.

Study Group Interactive Questions and Activities

1. **Activity and Discussion.** Which of the following strategies have you and your colleagues used in working with struggling writers? Which might you use? What other strategies might you add to this list?

   __ Encouraging talking (to prewrite)

   __ Encouraging drawing to plan writing

   __ Encouraging drawing to illustrate text

   __ Providing extra reflection/planning time

   __ Using written models (sentences, words)

   __ Encouraging work with partners

   __ Keeping portfolios

   __ Encouraging work in small groups

   __ Keeping drafts short

   __ Keeping revision small

   __ Limiting emphasis on conventions—at first

   __ Conferring to explore possible topics

   __ Facilitating access to needed information

   __ Using mentor texts written at writer's level

   __ Writing poems

2. **Activity and Discussion.** What strategies have you used (or might you use) in working with students who need a challenge? Do you have additional strategies to add to this list?

   __ Exploring topics that could provide a challenge

   __ Encouraging students to write in other genres

   __ Inviting students to assess and discuss more complex pieces

   __ Encouraging students to reflect on their writing

   __ Keeping portfolios to show growth

   __ Requiring multiple revisions

   __ Encouraging publication

   __ Hosting a "drop-in" center

   __ Inviting students to be mentors/coaches

   __ Asking students to develop/present writing lessons

   __ Encouraging students to do research on writing

   __ Writing poems

3. **Activity and Discussion.** Look through writing samples from your class. Do you identify any writing problems not addressed in either Chapter 8 or 9? With your group, create a strategy you might use for dealing with each one you identify.

4. **Activity and Discussion.** Create a piece of writing on any topic. Wait three days before reviewing it. Then, using Figure 9.14, make a revision plan for that piece. Discuss your plan with colleagues. How ambitious—or realistic—is it? How does this influence the amount of revision you expect from your students? With colleagues, discuss how you might use Figure 9.14 with both challenged students (keeping revision small) and those who need a bigger challenge (and could do multiple revisions).

5. **Activity and Discussion.** Return to Question 6 from the Study Group questions for Chapter 1. How would you answer this same question now?

Reflections on Writing

I write when the day is gloomy and boring. I grab a pencil and a pure white piece of paper. The light bulb is bright and going strong. I look outside and everything is clear. I can write. It's possible.

—Jovana Stewart, student writer

In my portfolio is some of the best work I've done in the past two years. The projects I've chosen to include show I'm a creative person with good ideas. This is my main strength. I have trouble spelling, and I don't have access to a spell checker outside of school. The hardest thing I did all year was write reports. I do not know how to take good notes. I can never figure out what is important enough to write down or how much to write. I hope my portfolio shows I am a strong enough writer to make it in an accelerated class. The thing is, in accelerated classes, the discussions are different. They don't talk down to kids. All classes should be like that. Then students would like school more.

—Nikki Henningsen, student writer

Listening to Teachers' Voices

What happens in your classroom with writing has everything to do with you and the kids. When instruction focuses on the skills . . . the goals . . . the plans . . . the systems—it often becomes mechanical, detached from kids, lifeless. When it focuses on the persons—the writers, it's just the opposite—it has life!

—Marjorie Frank
If You're Trying to Teach Kids How to Write . . .
You've Gotta Have This Book!, 1995, p. 21

Writing begins with listening. Don't we all, as writers, want to be listened to?

—Arlene Moore, K–1 teacher

In this chapter we'll visit the classrooms of several teachers to see how they incorporate the six-trait model into their instruction. As you'll see, they have very different ways of dealing with the traits and teaching them to students. There is no right way, and you should take what is most useful from their examples, finding an approach that suits your own classroom environment, curriculum, students, and teaching style.

In Elaine's Self-Contained Sixth Grade Classroom

Elaine is a veteran classroom teacher of nearly twenty years. She has taught mostly fourth and sixth grades and is an unabashed advocate of trait-based instruction. "It's so much easier for me to think about writing this way, I sometimes wonder why I didn't think of it before. But the funny part is, my *teaching* isn't any different. For instance, we've always done vocab, right? That's word choice. We do a lot of letter writing—now I put that under voice. I've always emphasized good details. That's ideas. So this stuff is not new. My way of *organizing* my teaching is just a little different."

Elaine teaches the traits one at a time, spending one to two weeks on each trait and then reinforcing all traits throughout the remainder of the year with a variety of focused lessons. She teaches conventions as she goes, with *lots* of practice in editing. "My favorite editing lessons are the ones where students watch me write on the board and tell me when they spot a mistake. The first time I did this I was so nervous I dropped the chalk!

"My goal is three hours of writing a week. My kids write in every subject area—social studies, science, math, art, music, and PE. We do reports, posters, letters, invitations to parents to visit our classroom, travel brochures on our community, recipes, directions, maps, and so forth. We write lots of poems—and news stories. We write to people in the community and to favorite authors. Kids love to write letters that get answered. It's like magic. Suddenly, there's a reason for the writing."

Once a week (or so), the class will score and discuss an anonymous student paper. "The kids love being critics," Elaine claims, "and they learn the traits *faster* than we do. They don't come to it with all that baggage we have from years of evaluating student work."

Elaine also uses pre-post tests to gauge her students' progress. "Every class is different, so I use preassessment to tell me where to focus my instruction. One year a class will be strong on conventions; another time it will be ideas or voice." Elaine does her preassessment during late September or early October. "My postassessment usually comes in April. Those results tell me how far my students have come and how well I've taught certain things. This gives me information I can't get from the state assessment. Kids and parents look at those two samples—October and April—and they can see big differences. You'll hear kids go 'Wow! Is that *my writing?*' when they see the October piece, and the parents go 'Wow!' too. Their eyes light up. Nothing speaks as loudly as real samples."

Parents are brought into the process, too. "On back-to-school nights, I ask parents to write—just for three, four minutes, you know. But you should see the fear on their faces. They're terrified! They even ask me if I'm going to collect the writing or if I'm going to read it. I tell them no, it's just for them. But I do ask them to think about how writing was assessed when they were kids. They remember this sea of red marks—so that's what a lot of them expect from me. Then I pass out copies of the *Six-Trait Scoring Guide for Students*—and it's like a whole world opens up. One dad asked me, 'Where was *this* when I was going to school?'"

Parents who are interested can attend a short two-hour training session on the six traits that Elaine does twice a year. Then they're encouraged to volunteer as *writing coaches*. Elaine gives them a writing coach checklist (Figure 10.1)—reminding them to focus on *one trait* at a time—not the whole list!

Key Strategy

Bring parents into the process, as observers and coaches.

"It's like a whole world opens up. One dad asked me, 'Where was this when I was going to school?'"

In Jim's High School Classroom

Jim has been teaching high school for more than fifteen years. Each year, he introduces the traits a little differently, depending on the class and their experience. "This year I will introduce it in the second week as a means of discussing their summer reading essay. They write the essay the first week, and when I return it to them, I will introduce the traits by having them do a somewhat cursory, introductory assessment of their writing. For example, they will have to think about voice and wonder if their writing has any—and this provides an initial frame for us to discuss and work on those things throughout the rest of the year."

Working with the traits, Jim believes, gives his instruction focus and direction. "Students like it because it's very responsive to their needs as writers. It lends a structure, a good one, to the course. We'll work with, say, voice or sentence fluency for a time (keeping in mind other traits we've studied) and link our discussion of other writers to this as well. The traits create and sustain a culture of writing, give us a language for discussing their own writing and that of others. The traits also give their work a purpose. They like me to bring their work before the class on the overhead and work through the assignments we do each week. They read for a purpose, too—to examine and improve upon word choice, for instance. This gives them a compass to steer by and makes them more effective as readers."

Jim is careful to keep his instruction very focused, working on one trait at a time until students have gone through them all. "We are focusing on ideas and development at this point, for example. We'll work through their papers on that one trait using the overhead, handouts, and examples. The feedback they get is very targeted and concrete. They *feel* the difference because their writing visibly improves."

Because Jim's class is integrated with history, students have a wide range of reading samples to draw from in discussing traits, including nonfiction books as well as literature of all kinds.

What is most challenging for Jim's students? "The kids I work with need to work hard in two areas: generation [of ideas] and organization. They

FIGURE **10.1** **Writing Coach Checklist**

(Focus on ONE Trait!)

Ideas and Content

1. Do you have a topic? If not, let's brainstorm possibilities!
2. What is your main message?
3. Is this paper clear? Does it make sense?
4. Can you sum your paper up in one sentence?
5. What do you want your reader to learn?
6. What's the most interesting detail?
7. Will a reader have any questions?

Organization

1. Does your lead hook the reader? Does it set up what comes next?
2. Do the important points stand out?
3. Is your paper easy to follow?
4. Is anything out of order?
5. Are there any interesting surprises for the reader?
6. Does your ending wrap up the discussion—or story?

Voice

1. Does this writing sound like YOU?
2. Did you put your fingerprints on this writing?
3. Does this writing show what you think and feel?
4. Who are your readers?
5. Did you think about your readers when you were writing?
6. What do you want your readers to feel when they read this?

Word Choice

1. Do you know the meanings of all your words?
2. Do you have any favorite words in this writing?
3. Did you use any strong verbs?
4. Do you think you used the BEST words you could?
5. Did you use too many adjectives?
6. Did you use too many "tired" words (*nice, good, fun*)?

Sentence Fluency

1. Did you read your writing out loud? Did you like the sound of it?
2. Was it easy to read aloud?
3. Do your sentences begin in different ways?
4. Are some long—and some short?
5. Did you use dialogue (people talking)? Does it sound like real people talking?

Conventions

1. Did you read your paper over? Silently? Aloud?
2. Did you try holding a ruler under each line so you could catch everything?
3. What do you feel sure about?
   __ Spelling __ Punctuation
   __ Capitals __ Paragraphs
   __ Grammar
4. Do you have any questions?
5. Do you need any help with layout (charts, photos, fonts)?

have ideas, but need to learn how to access them, then organize them. Logic seems increasingly important to me because many students seem to lack a strong sense of reasoning, and this results in muddled writing at best. To me the traits suggest not only a vocabulary of terms, but *habits of mind* when it comes to writing and thinking. I use the traits along with graphic organizers to help struggling students figure out what they have to say—and then make the text say what they want it to. Once they have generated and organized, we can begin to think about voice and fluency to give those ideas some polish, some kick."

The students in Jim's class enjoy comparing their responses to his. One way Jim does this is by marking text together. "They read through their papers and used a highlighter to mark the words or phrases they thought really worked. Then I read with a different color and marked the ones *I* thought worked. It was surprising to see how rarely they matched! This discrepancy initiated a useful series of activities and discussion about what makes language powerful or distinctive. It was remarkably instructive just to ask them why they thought a particular passage worked—and then explain why I responded to something else altogether."

The real strength of a trait-based approach to teaching writing lies, Jim feels, in its flexibility—the fact that you can do with it pretty much what you want. "An approach or strategy sometimes seems a good solution, but after a while you realize it can only take students so far. Because there's no built-in end point, six traits offers the flexibility and room for growth that you seek as a teacher—or as a department that wants to create a long-term program."

Key Strategy

Use traits together with graphic organizers.

"To me the traits suggest not only a vocabulary of terms, but habits of mind when it comes to writing and thinking. I use the traits along with graphic organizers to help struggling students figure out what they have to say—and then . . . we can begin to think about voice and fluency to give those ideas some polish, some kick."

In Billie's Seventh Grade Classroom

Billie teaches middle school in a district where classes tend to be large—usually over forty students. Her seventh graders use rubrics and posters, and are used to assessing writing samples and discussing literature using trait language. For a number of students in Billie's class, English is a second language, and Billie uses many creative strategies to help them gain comfort with the writing process.

"We take brain breaks during class," she explains. "This consists of standing next to our desks and participating in the six traits calisthenics (Lamkin, 2004). It's a total physical response (TPR) activity, which is one way of teaching English language or second language learners, as well as all students who are kinesthetic learners. They work like this. For ideas, we stand with our hands made into fists just above our heads, then reach upward, one hand at a time. As each hand moves up, it opens up just like our ideas spring out of our minds and open themselves up to the world. I ask students to think about a topic they could write about, and I call on a few to share their ideas.

"Then I ask 'What do we need to do with our ideas as we write?' They call out, 'Organize.' Then we move to the motion for organization, which is stacking our hands (with a little space between) right in front of our bodies—put the left hand near your stomach, right hand about six inches above, then continue this pattern till we can't reach anymore—and reverse the process. As we do this, I ask students to call out organizational techniques . . . 'a catchy lead . . . pattern of ideas . . . good transitions . . . smooth ending.'

"Next I ask, 'What do we need to do to make sure the reader believes us?' and they respond, 'Tell the truth.' I add that in telling the truth, we

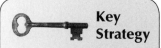

Key Strategy

Teach students the Trait Aerobics—letting them physically act out each trait.

"It's a total physical response (TPR) activity, which is one way of teaching English language or second language learners, as well as all students who are kinesthetic learners."

reveal confidence in our organized ideas, and these must come from our heart—which is where the voice lies. I show the motion for voice by having my hands spring forth from just above my heart. Then I call on a few students to share a comment about something they are confident about in their writing.

"On to word choice. I ask 'If I am going to confidently organize my ideas, what do I need to choose to get my message out?' They respond, 'Words!' I tell them that yes, we need to choose our words wisely. For this trait, we reach and grab at the air in all directions. I bend and stretch as I'm reaching, to show students I want them to reach for the best way to say something. I then ask a few students to share favorite words, maybe one they heard when I read aloud to them today or one they found in their silent reading.

"As they are still reaching, I ask, 'What do we call it when we put a bunch of words together to convey one meaning?' They respond, 'A sentence!' I explain that to get our organized ideas out to the reader we need to choose words wisely and create rhythm with our sentences. Waves of the ocean are different lengths and crash against the shore with different force. We imitate this wave motion by intertwining the fingers of both hands and making a wave with our arms, right to left, then left to right, swaying as we move. As we're imitating fluency, I ask how we create fluency with writing. 'Begin with different words . . . have different sentence lengths,' they say.

"Finally we come to the last trait. I ask, 'What do we do to hold our organized ideas together so our chosen words create sentences that flow in a confident, truthful manner?' And they respond, 'We use periods, commas, and other punctuation!' I say yes, as I untangle my fingers, wrap both arms around my body, and give myself a big squeeze. I explain that conventions hold our thoughts together just the way a good hug holds us together.

"We then have silent peer conferences where the students read each other's writing pieces and are *only* allowed to use hand signals to point out positive trait usage. They will give a 'thumbs up' and then act out the trait that was very strong in the paper."

Billie uses color coding to help students focus in on various traits within a piece of writing: "I color code the traits; then when we review student writing, I have the students color over the parts that help to convey the main idea in blue, organization in orange, voice in red, etc."

Billie has devised her own approach for introducing the traits: "I put a very basic guideline for each of the traits on the overhead and talk with the students about each one. Then I share another outline of what I call RTC—reading, traits, and connections (see Figure 10.2 for a student example). I read Dr. Suess's *Hooray for Diffendoofer Day* aloud to the students [and] then we discuss each of the strategies and how the traits were represented for each. We then complete an RTC with the story. The students use the RTC method as a daily reflection of what they read in class. So we get a daily dose of six traits in a variety of literature as well as an understanding of how the students connect with reading."

The discussions that evolve from this just tumble out of the student's memories.

Billie views modeling as the most important of her instructional strategies. "Modeling my own writing with students is very effective. They look at, critique, and score my writing—then use the same strategies in their writing.

"My students are asked to have three writing pieces of their choice completed per quarter. When a writing piece is assigned, they are also given a blank calendar that shows only a three-week time period. They are also given a list of possible writing stages they may choose to use (brainstorming, drafting, self conference, revision, peer conference, editing, proofreading, publishing, reflection, scoring, etc.). They decide what date they are going to complete the writing piece first and then work *backwards* through the writing stages, allowing a few days for revision or just letting the paper sit and marinate for a few days to give it a fresh perspective until they reach the day that it was assigned. Backwards planning is used widely in the business world and works well in my classroom. The student chooses all of his or her dates and can make appointments for a conference with me based on those choices. It not only teaches students goal setting but also the responsibility of following a plan."

What if another teacher feels reluctant about using the traits in his or her classroom? "I tell that person, 'You are *already* using the traits—you just don't realize it.' I ask them to find their favorite lesson, show me a teacher model of the lesson and a student example; then I sit and point out how the traits are used in that lesson. Once they understand that connection, they are willing to adopt trait-based instruction in their classroom without feeling anxious about it."

What's the secret to good writing instruction? "Modeling, modeling, modeling and humor, humor, humor. Every assignment I ask students to do is presented to them with *my* writing example for that assignment.

"It's important to use a variety of literature, too. I can't think of a better way to start my day than to share a children's picture book or a chapter from Anne Lamott's *Bird by Bird* (1995). I love the chapter 'Lunchroom.' The discussions that pop up from our reading aloud sessions are the best part of my days.

"And laughter . . . laugh a lot, at yourself and with your students. I tell my students that I have the best job in the world because I get paid to act like a 13-year-old all over again. There isn't a job out there that is as rewarding as hanging around middle school students for six hours a day."

FIGURE 10.2   Reading, Traits and Connections

Reading, Traits & Connections
By Hannah

Title of Book: The Sign of the Twisted Candles
Author: Carolyn Keene

The strongest trait in this passage was ideas, I think. I could really picture the whole room in the barn. This part helped me picture it: "The second floor was merely an unplastered attic. A rusted iron bed stood under the eaves, and an antique wardrobe, its doors awry and its once fine mahogany surface green with mildew, leaned against the chimney." The author did a really good job with word choice. I felt like I was there with words like awry, examined, gasped, moldering, betrayed, trembling. Also, there is a cool, mysterious tone (voice) to the writing.

Key Strategy

Backwards Planning

"Backwards planning is used widely in the business world. . . . It not only teaches students goal setting but also the responsibility of following a plan."

In Ellen's AP English Classroom

> Becoming a writer is about becoming conscious. When you're conscious and writing from a place of insight and simplicity and real caring about the truth, you have the ability to throw the lights on for your reader.
>
> —Anne Lamott
> *Bird by Bird*, 1995, p. 225

> But feeling isn't a luxury; it's a necessity. It's your survival. It's your soul life. It's your truth. And without it, your art, your life, your writing will be generic—anybody's voice. With it, work will be authentic, powerful—your voice.
>
> —Nancy Slonim Aronie
> *Writing from the Heart*, 1998, p. 79

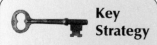
Key Strategy

Reading Aloud

"Listen to television for even a short time and see how we are becoming conditioned to sound bites of language. It isn't just the meaning that's lost. So much of our modern language has no real rhythm. . . . I want them to slow down long enough to read good poetry . . . to hear the rhythm of the lines rising and falling like the tides."

Though the traits are an important focus for Ellen's curriculum, she is also a firm believer in teaching to the *writer*.

"My first step is to help my students envision the world they want to live in, and to imagine how their personal, individual voices will contribute to that world. So I begin with the writers, not the writing; then I shape the writing tasks to what they say and what they see. I like to think I allow my writers to find meaning in contemporary culture—to recognize what's shallow, and even perhaps shoot a few holes in the hypocrisy they see in our society.

"When I teach ideas, I emphasize the importance of a writer opening up people's minds. Your ideas are what you teach your readers, I tell my students. I don't always expect closure, but I do expect them to think: to raise the right questions. 'Who are you? I ask them. Where do you stand on this issue or that? What is your philosophical approach to the world?' I use the traits to build thinking skills."

Ellen shares numerous samples of writing from many sources. "I always read everything aloud. It makes such a difference when the ear is trained. I'm afraid of how little they get to hear. Listen to television for even a short time and see how we are becoming conditioned to sound bites of language. It isn't just the meaning that's lost. So much of our modern language has no real rhythm. I want them to hear language at its best. I want them to slow down long enough to read good poetry, not just process it, to hear the rhythm of the lines rising and falling like the tides.

"To me all the traits are important, but in the end, the final question is, 'How does each trait bring out the writer's *voice?*' It's voice, to my mind, that most influences meaning. We start with an idea, but if our writing is good, we end up speaking person to person. 'When you sign a paper,' I tell my students, 'and you expect me to read it, you've made a commitment to me. I want to hear *your* ideas, *your* voice.' So much of this is missing from today's research writing. There's no passion for the topic, no concern for the audience. That's why it winds up piled in a corner somewhere. Many of our students do not have the patience it takes to sift through volumes of information—our world is so information-laden; we need to show them how. Otherwise, we get informational writing that's just plagiarism, a shortcut. Their eyes glaze over at the thought of doing research, and I think a lot of this is because they wind up writing in someone else's voice, a phony voice, an encyclopedia voice.

"I think it's a breakthrough moment when students are relieved of the burden of having to be someone else. I expect honesty and straightforwardness. I tell them, 'I don't want writing to impress. Write from deep inside you.'"

Ellen also sees writing as potentially therapeutic and empowering for many students. "When I first began teaching twenty-some years ago, students did every assignment. They didn't question anything. For kids today, it's different. So many are emotionally unsure. So many come from broken families and are struggling just to find themselves; school is an additional burden. But it *can* be a place of safety and emotional support, too, if we let it.

I don't want this to sound presumptuous; I know my class is one small part of their lives. But I feel strongly that my job as a teacher is to tell students when they write, 'Your writing moved me. You have the power to change the world with these ideas.' Without that, we—and they—have no real reason to write."

You don't teach writing. You teach WRITERS. And believe me, there IS a world of difference between the two.

—Marjorie Frank
If You're Trying to Teach Kids How to Write . . . You've Gotta Have This Book!,
1995, p. 18

In Judy's Third Grade Classroom

Judy has been working for some time to make her writer's workshop approach as effective and comfortable as her considerable expertise can make it. Her year opens with an opportunity for students to look at and listen to writing and to say what they notice—what makes writing work. This results in their own version of the traits, which they can then compare with those in a student rubric.

One step into Judy's classroom and it's apparent that *everything* is set up to support trait-based instruction. On the walls are trait posters—not purchased, but written and designed by Judy's students. Sentence strips throughout the room capture students' spontaneous comments on what it means to have strong ideas or personal voice, or to use words that move readers (Judy says, "Wait—let me get that," and writes it down on the spot.).

Books are everywhere. Many are organized by category: the solar system, insects, mammals, volcanoes, dinosaurs, U.S. history, biographies, etc. This, together with designated bare table space for taking notes, makes research easy. Students sit and work in small groups of four, so continual conferring throughout workshop time is natural. They have two shelves on which to store three-ring binders containing all their writing from the year. Personal student rubrics are tucked into the front inside pocket. All work is dated so that students can track their growth—which they are often asked to do. Judy rarely sits down—but when she does, it is usually for one of three purposes: (1) to read aloud to students (who move front and form a circle), (2) to participate in sharing (also done in a circle), or (3) to work at her computer, helping students with last-minute editing or using a dictated rough draft from a second language learner to create a printable document he or she can read and save.

Judy's workshop runs for one hour four times a week. She opens each hour with a minilesson, drawing on both writing process and the six traits for her organizational structure. Content might be as simple as one convention or something more complex—explaining what a paragraph is, modeling how to write a strong lead, or sharing a picture book with focus on a particular trait. Students then write for 30 to 35 minutes on personally selected topics while Judy holds individual conferences of about 5 minutes each. "I listen carefully to what the child is saying," Judy says, "and consider his work with respect. I usually ask the student, 'How can I help you today?' They know they need to come to the conference ready to answer that question. I always end the conference by asking, 'What are you going to do now?'" This gives the child a chance to reflect on what he or she has learned and provides a transition into the act of writing.

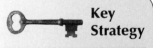

Key Strategy

Expecting the Student to Direct the Conference

"I usually ask the student, 'How can I help you today?' They know they need to come to the conference ready to answer that question."

Judy saves 15 minutes of the writer's workshop for sharing, a process that, she says, "never ceases to amaze me." Writers do not just read their work aloud but also explain why they are sharing, e.g., to get help finding a title or adding details. "You will be amazed by the quality of student comments and suggestions and how quickly the kids pick up writerly talk," Judy comments.

Writing is noisy business, Judy has discovered: "My workshop is not a silent place. . . . I want us to be a community of learners who are (as James Britton described it) 'floating on a sea of talk.'" The talk pays off. Judy was delighted one day when one of her third graders echoed a lesson from earlier in the year during a sharing session: "Remember when we said we don't want to get to the end of the piece and then say, 'Huh?'" These third graders are thinking and working like writers.

Following are two short conferences between Judy and her students K. J. and Margaret—along with the samples of writing to which they refer in their comments.

FIGURE 10.3 The Middle Ages

The Middle Ages
By K. J. Davis

A boy runs off the drawbridge
And spies the blacksmith.
He sees four woodcutters' huts,
One is his father's.
Lord Hickins walks by,
He drops to his knees.
The moat's water sparkles
In the very bright light.
He hears laughter from an inn.
He hears knights swords clack as they practice.
Suddenly, he hears the horn,
It blows a faint sound.
He runs to his house.
He thinks,
Why does it have to be this way?
The enemy catapult flings the heavy stones.
They hit the stone wall
Causing massive damage.
But the enemy falls back.
Later,
That calm smooth swift night,
They have dinner.
They have what they want,
They have meat, cheese, and apples.
The dad says,
"I got five pieces of gold."
The dad says,
"Taxes, taxes, taxes."
The mother is proud,
But the boy is scared
That his dad might lose his job.
For this is the Middle Ages.

Conference 1, with K. J.

Judy: What is your author's purpose in this poem (see Figure 10.3)?

K. J.: Well, I really like the Middle Ages. It was a peaceful time and a hard time. Not a lot of people had money. So it seemed fun to write a poem about something I like.

Judy: Tell me about some of the beautiful word choice in your poem, like "swords clack" and "that calm smooth swift night."

K. J.: Well, since I knew this was going to be shared on Poetry Night, I knew I needed good word choice. I just think of them in my head, and I think, "Well, that's just a really great word," and I put it on the paper.

Judy: Do you think about the way the words sound?

K. J.: Yeah, the word has to sound really perfect for a poem like this.

Judy: How do you decide?

K. J.: I've been reading for a long time. I get these words out of books.

Judy: How do you know what the right word is?

K. J.: The topic—it has to go with the Middle Ages.

Conference 2, with Margaret

Judy: Tell me about your poem "Sunset" (see Figure 10.4).

Margaret: I know what I was thinking. I was thinking about when I went to Pismo Beach and we saw the sunset.

Judy: How did you get some of these beautiful images from that day onto your paper?

Margaret: I just thought about what I saw and I described it.

Judy: Did you think about word choice?

Margaret: Yeah, I thought about *evening* instead of *night*. *Evening* sounds better.

Judy: What about when you talk about the colors "comforting" us?

Margaret: I said that because if it was black or blue, that wouldn't really relax you. The colors I saw were calm colors.

FIGURE **10.4**   Sunset

Sunset

By Margaret Irias

Ssssh
The beautiful sunset goes.
The silent swift Queen of evening.
The red, orange, yellow light
Satisfies your eyes.
Ssssh
Mixed, peaceful,
Bright and dark colors
Fill the sky.
Where does the red come from?
I wonder that too often.
It comforts your eyes.
Ssssh
As colorful as a dragonfly.

In Barbara's Middle School Classroom

At the beginning of the school year, Barbara asks her sixth, seventh, and eighth grade students to purchase a spiral (about 120 pages) for all writing notes, brainstorms, prewrites, etc. Students create a section for each trait. Here she explains some strategies she uses to teach just one trait: *ideas.*

"My sixth grade class includes about twenty challenged writers. I begin by generating a list of things on the white board that *I* want to write about and I talk through this process out loud for all students to hear my thinking. Next, students go to their spirals and they generate their own lists of what Nancie Atwell calls 'writing territories.' From that list, the students pick what they want to write about and then they're ready to begin some planning.

"To give them a context for what works and what doesn't, I write a very weak paragraph and have students break into groups of four and rewrite a much stronger paragraph, using my weak one as a springboard. This gives them a chance to get more 'touchy-feely' with ideas. They also feel more comfortable because they are not working alone, and they're not pressured to write for a grade. I want students to *love* to write and nothing is more fun than doing a lesson with your friends and having the teacher tell you what a great job you have done.

"Here's a process I use all of the time with *all students*—ELL, challenged, gifted, you name it. After we have written a piece (typically done in class with a partner), I put one sample of writing on the overhead and students take out a student rubric for ideas that has been glued into the 'ideas section' of the spiral notebook. We read a paragraph out loud, and using the language of the rubric, each group rates the paragraph. As we discuss the paragraph,

Key Strategy

Revising Weak Example

"I write a very weak paragraph and have students break into groups of four and rewrite a much stronger paragraph . . . They . . . feel more comfortable because they are not working alone, and they're not pressured to write for a grade."

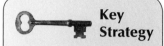

Key Strategy

Voting by Moving to Corners

"Students have to go to the appropriate corner to indicate their scores. They love actually getting up and moving to record their votes."

groups defend their position and we get into some spirited debates about how to score the piece and why. This is how they learn to really get inside the writing and think like writers.

"I also use this process with pre-scored pieces. I use papers from *Creating Writers* and from the *Write Traits Classroom Kits*. I usually do one trait at a time, and typically no more than two traits per lesson for sixth grade. For more experienced traits users, like my eighth graders, I always score for ideas and organization plus a third trait that varies—typically voice or sentence fluency.

"Here is the part that all students, no matter what grade or ability level, really like. I mark corners of the room: All the 1's go here [indicating the corner], the 2's over there, and so on—and then students have to go to the appropriate corner to indicate their scores. They love actually getting up and *moving* to record their votes. In September my sixth graders are all over the place, but as the year moves on, students begin to move to no more than two areas; they're all 5's and 4's, or 4's and 3's or whatever. Once students have moved to an area, they *must* use the language of the rubric to defend their position. This is all done orally so that everyone can hear and participate in the discussion. If some students are more shy (because of language issues, etc.) I call on them *after* they have heard discussion from others. While they may repeat what has been said, they are participating and are feeling more comfortable. The next time we do this, those students are more likely to speak up early on.

"Once we have discussed a paper, students are given another chance to re-vote and they can move if they like. Of course we always end with the big finish, 'And the *raters* say. . . .' Then I read out of *Creating Writers* or one of the kits. My students really get into the game show atmosphere! But the good part is, they're learning to think."

In Andrea's Multiage Second-Language Classroom

Andrea is a specialist in working with second-language students, and her secret is a magical combination of deep respect for students' skills and creative adaptation of the six traits to fit the learning style of someone who is just learning to speak English. Keep it simple is rule one. "My way of adapting the rubrics for non-English or beginning English speakers is to identify the 'key words.' For example, I identify *details* and *main idea* for ideas and development. Students look at those two concepts *only*. We read sample papers and look at the quality of detail and assess if the story/essay sticks to the main point. As the language becomes more familiar, other components of the rubric or trait come in to play."

Andrea is also sensitive to the kinesthetic learning style of many students. "I use many, *many* physical activities. We go on 'digs' around campus, meaning we walk around, collecting words, phrases, and mental pictures of what we see. We put them on index cards, and these cards are later incorporated into dialogue or descriptions or made into found poetry. We listen to music

Key Strategy

Kinesthetic Activities

"We go on 'digs' around campus. . . . We listen to music. . . . We take pictures with disposable cameras. . . . We cook a lot to learn new words. . . . "

and discuss fluency. We take pictures with disposable cameras and talk about details and 'focus.' We cook a lot to learn new words and to discuss following directions as a kind of organization. Just about any snack that can be made in the microwave or on a burner has been made in my classroom."

In addition, Andrea is a whole-hearted believer in the maxim that to become a proficient writer, you must write. "My ESL students write. And write. And write. They write from the first day they arrive. If they have no English skills, they copy a paragraph I have typed out that introduces me and my classroom. If they have some English skills, they practice the act of writing during our writing time. They practice writing their vocabulary words, they practice writing their names in English, if they are not familiar with the alphabet. They never have an excuse not to write. I don't grade it the same, of course, but it is written and turned in and commented on. My philosophy is: If they can write letters, they can learn how to write words. If they can write words, they can learn how to write sentences, and if they can write sentences, they can write *anything*. ESL students can produce written work. They just need some support to get there. Not speaking English is a reason they struggle, but it isn't an excuse not to provide opportunities to stretch them as learners and writers. I provide opportunities to write every day."

To introduce the traits, Andrea doesn't rely on words so much as the concept of categories. "My very first thing is to have students rank pieces of candy into six categories, six being their most favorite. This introduces the concept of a rubric and the fact that a six isn't an 'A.'"

Once they have the vocabulary, Andrea comments, second-language students feel that the traits are "easy" to work with. "They don't have to learn a new set of vocabulary for each class. For EL kids, that is a great thing." She also likes the fact that the traits break instruction into manageable bites: "I like the pacing of the six traits; I know that eventually we will focus on transitions, for example, so I don't need to race to get there. Without the traits, I think that I would feel pressure to teach everything about writing every time we wrote, because I would be afraid I'd forget something later. Students are often overwhelmed when they are writing for school . . . and a lot of that comes from the pressure to learn too many complex things at once."

Like many teachers who work with the six traits, Andrea relies heavily on literature to reinforce learning. "I have so many favorites. I use *Esperanza Rising* by Pam Muñoz Ryan to teach symbolism and sentence fluency. It's a great book for every trait.

"I also used the book to help students understand character. I make a journal for each student. On each page was an outline of a girl. I drew lines in her head, next to her feet, and in her body by her heart. For each chapter, the students found quotations that explain the character. In her head, the students wrote the something that she said or thought and the page number. In her heart, students wrote a quotation that showed something she felt, and next to her feet, students wrote something that showed an action, both again with page numbers. At the bottom of the page, the students wrote an assertion about the character, e.g., "Esperanza is very lonely." At the end of the book, students had collected enough quotations to write a response-to-literature essay, and we didn't have to flip through the book looking for quotations to support their thesis." (See Figure 10.5 for a reproduction of Andrea's outline for this literature response lesson.)

Key Strategy

Using Models for English Language Learners

"They write from the first day. . . . If they have no English skills, they copy a paragraph I have typed out that introduces me and my classroom. . . . They practice writing their vocabulary words, they practice writing their names in English, if they are not familiar with the alphabet. They never have an excuse not to write."

FIGURE **10.5**   **Thoughts, Feelings, Actions**

One of the things Andrea likes best about using the traits in her instruction is the feeling that she is not really adding anything new but only organizing what she would be teaching anyway. "One of the most valuable parts of the six traits is the fact it's broken into parts. I don't have to teach everything I know every time I teach writing. I'm able to relax and really focus on each component until I'm sure my students understand it. Once they understand ideas, they are really on the road to understanding all six traits. Students don't feel overwhelmed and neither do I."

 # In Sue's Elementary Art-Based Classroom

Sue teaches fifth grade to a wide range of young writers, and has found creative ways to teach the traits through art—ways that seem to work well for both challenged *and* gifted writers. Following is her description of a unique vision that has become, for many students, an irresistible learning experience. Notice how she pairs each trait with a particular artist.

Ideas: Norman Rockwell

"Norman Rockwell is an American artist. The subjects of his prints include everyday events people everywhere can relate to. His characters are drawn with sympathy, humor, and understanding. He was the type of artist who could create a sense of American identity and common values.

"When students begin writing, they do best writing about things familiar to them . . . their everyday life. They seem to relate to Rockwell's art. As we discuss his art, we talk about what kind of writing piece might go with each painting. Students begin by writing captions to go with Rockwell magazine covers or illustrations from a Norman Rockwell calendar.

"Rockwell staged all of his paintings, often using his family as his models, and sketching with pencil first. He was adept at painting realistic facial expressions, and using painstaking details in his work. We relate this to a writer—choosing familiar topics, working on a rough copy, and making revisions. We discuss choosing details that make a piece of writing come alive as Rockwell makes his characters come alive with their facial expressions."

Organization: M. C. Escher and Faith Ringgold

"M. C. Escher was a genius at creating tessellations, a special kind of design made from shapes that fit together perfectly. He designed amazing patterns with lizards, birds, and fish. Students make tessellations (in our geometry class) of their own, and see how the shapes need to be organized—that there is a beginning, middle, and a clear end, when their shapes take on characteristics of their own. We share our tessellations in writer's workshop and discuss the beginning, middle, and end of a writing piece and spend time creating strong leads. We compare a strong lead to being intrigued with Escher's tessellation and trying to figure out how he made it—wanting more—just as a strong lead leaves the reader wanting more.

"Faith Ringgold needs organization to complete her writing on quilts. The layout of her quilt is important, and placing details or paragraphs in the right place is important also. We read *Tar Beach*, paying attention to Ringgold's organization of the quilt around the pages. We use wallpaper books to cut quilt-like squares. Students create a story and design the words on their quilt, paying attention to the organization of their story as well as their art."

Fluency: Henri Matisse

"Henri Matisse wanted his artwork to give people pleasure, and be soothing, like a comfortable armchair after a hard day's work. Matisse tried to balance shapes and colors to make the viewer feel good. He often traveled to find new and interesting things to paint, seeking places that were bright and sunny. Many of his paintings are looking out of windows. Students draw a picture looking out of a window to a place of their choosing and write a story about the view.

"We compare fluency to making the reader feel comfortable. We discuss sentence length and sentence beginnings, and how that creates a certain comfort for the reader. Matisse experimented with style, color, and the thickness of his brushstrokes. When Matisse tried a new style called 'fauve' painting (*fauve* means *wild beast* in French), people were shocked. These paintings were done in unusual colors. This period didn't last long, and he moved away from the bright bold colors to more subtle colors. We use that experience to talk about the various stages a writer can also go through.

"At one point, Matisse cut shapes from brightly colored paper to make some of his most exciting art. Students cut shapes to create art like his 'drawing with scissors' and write a story focusing on ideas and fluency."

Word Choice and Voice: Andy Warhol and Pablo Picasso

"Picasso's art is a reflection of his moods. He had a Blue Period when he painted sad pictures, often making his characters with longer than normal hands, or necks, or fingers. He then went through his Rose Period, a happier time during which he painted circus people, acrobats, and harlequins. At one point, he began painting pictures that looked more like puzzles with pieces all out of order. This was his cubist style. Picasso's goal was to get people to see things in a new way. He wanted to show all sides of an object or person at once. Picasso's voice shows in all of his work. My students wrote character sketches and made a cubist style picture of their person to go with their writing. [See Figure 10.6 for one example—and the cover of this book for another.] We also wrote poetry using figurative language focusing on word choice to go with the cubist portraits.

"Warhol fits into pop culture and pop art. We look at a series of his pictures and develop vivid descriptions for them. We try to use figurative language and strong verbs. We have fun using thesauruses at this time. Warhol started all of his pictures in pencil and then went over them all in ink—a form of revision, don't you think? Before the ink dried, he pressed his picture onto a clean piece of paper for a neat blotted-line look. Some of Warhol's first pieces of work were illustrations for stories and for ads."

FIGURE 10.6 **Student Sample of Cubist Portrait**

Conventions and Revision: All Artists

"There is a great painting by Matisse in which you can see how he changed the placement of the person's arms. This is a great piece to use as talking about revision. Rockwell started all of his paintings as pencil sketches. Van Gogh argued with fellow artist Gauguin and they often critiqued each other's paintings; we discuss them as we peer edit. Picasso and Matisse were often critical of each other's work but also admired it and owned pieces of each other's art. Most of these artists tried many different styles before they found the one they were most comfortable with. We compare this to writing in different genres. We need to try many different styles to find where our 'passion' is.

"I am always investigating new artists to use. I am fascinated with the work of German artist Kathe Kollwitz, who created expressive prints focusing on the effects of war upon ordinary people. She lived in Hitler's Germany. Kollwitz used contrast between light and dark areas to suggest feelings. Her prints would be great to use when writing comparison and contrast stories.

"Piet Mondrian was influenced by the cubist work of Picasso. His paintings became increasingly simple and geometric, featuring straight lines, right angles, black, white, and three colors. His work would fit well with organization.

"I also think it would be fun to study an illustrator of children's books, like Maurice Sendak. We often write for our grade level partners (ours are second graders). We could work on ABC books or fables or tall tales using all six traits at the end of the year and capture them in the likeness of a children's illustrator.

"Grandma Moses would also be a fun artist to study. There is a never-ending list! The students love it, and powerful student writing is a direct result!"

Key Strategy

Drawing Parallels between Writing and Art

"Warhol started all of his pictures in pencil and then went over them all in ink—a form of revision, don't you think?"

In Sammie's "Tiger Learning Center"

Sammie works in an *enrichment room*—a special learning center for challenged writers that is devoted half to technology (with a computer lab) and half to personalized instruction in reading and writing. The center is well named. Sammie's students *are* tigers—ready to leap on new ideas and devour everything she has to give. Her main problem is time. She has but half an hour with each group (they spend the other half hour in the computer lab), and with a K–5 rotation, she sees each child only once every six days. Therefore, extended lessons do not work. Everything has to be tied up, package and bow, within 30 minutes.

Sammie has found ways to make the six traits flourish. Her children do numerous poems and books, often class books, to which each child can contribute a page. They write paragraphs (they're short), and they tend to focus on known topics (no research required): themselves, their families, their experiences. Sammie regularly uses brief books or portions of books as models.

Pattern books (e.g., Margery Cuyler's *That's Good, That's Bad* and John Burningham's *Mr. Gumpy's Outing*) have been her mainstay. "When it's a

We need to water the desert so that writing will bloom. By *watering the desert* I mean providing children with the most wonderful literature available: the classics, the new, the beautiful, the revolting, the hysterical, the puzzling, the amazing, the riveting.

—Mem Fox
Radical Reflections,
1993, p. 67

> Worksheets do not develop writers who can think for themselves, who can create extended texts, who can be logical, who can use voice or tone, or who can write with power. It is perfectly possible to be able to fill in endless worksheets correctly yet not be able to write a single coherent paragraph, let alone a longer piece of connected prose.
>
> —Mem Fox
> *Radical Reflections,*
> 1993, p. 69

Key Strategy

Reading Picture Books

"I have many fifth graders—kids practically shaving—who have not heard nursery rhymes before, and love them.... If we don't attach grade levels to things, we give students the freedom to make choices."

pattern the children can see, they can mimic it, and it helps them feel they're doing it. They're writing. Many times they feel they do a better job than the original author, and sometimes, I agree! We do a lot of sharing. The atmosphere is very celebrational. When an author has finished a piece, that's reason to celebrate, to gather around and hear another person's work. We all take pride in what any one of us does.

"I also do a lot of reading. For many of my students it's a totally new experience—being read to. No one has done this with them before. We have a high mobility rate in our area. Many of our students do not regularly converse with their parents—or with *anyone* outside of school. Just talking is hard at first. They haven't had much practice at it. I have many fifth graders—kids practically shaving—who have not heard nursery rhymes before, and *love* them. They love the rhythm and the humor. If we don't attach grade levels to things, we give students the freedom to make choices, and why not? Wouldn't it annoy you if someone pulled a book out of your hands and said to you, 'Oh, you won't like *that*—it's only for 35 and under'?

"I talk traits all the time, right from day one. Fluency is a big trait for us because we use lots of pattern books and lots of poetry—'There Was An Old Woman Who Swallowed a Fly'—that's a favorite with students of all ages. We talk about word choice, too, and keep personal dictionaries. I put lots of words on the walls. And we talk about ideas—what do you picture in your mind? And voice—how does this piece make you feel? I comment on the voice, word choice, and so on in *their* work, too. At first it's just me. But by about the end of the second quarter or the start of the third, they're talking traits, too. This is very exciting because at this point they have some built-in, personal way to measure how their writing is changing.

"We do no skill and drill, no worksheets. We write and we read. I want them to love it, and they do. They *want* to come here, that's my goal, and it shows in the work we do together. We're moving all the time. We're moving to the rhythm of what we write. We yell, we beat on the tables. One of the teachers said to me, 'Sammie, I would swear I saw that portable move right up off its block.' Well, that's what teachers are *for*, isn't it? To rock the walls? The most important thing to me is how the kids feel when they leave here. In this room, I want every child to experience success."

Chapter 10   In a Nutshell

- Every writing teacher who uses the six traits in his or her instruction finds a personal way to make it work.

- Despite differences, commonalities exist among teachers' instructional approaches, e.g., sharing literature, modeling writing or revision, using trait language, expanding students' skills as evaluators, and encouraging students to self-assess.

- Teachers who incorporate the six traits into their instruction need not give up any of the personal instructional strategies they value—such as conferences, writing workshops, or sharing.

- As several teachers show, the traits can be adapted for ELL or struggling writers through art, picture books and other literature, vocabulary support, modeling, kinesthetics, and other activities.

Study Group   Interactive Questions and Activities

1. **Activity and Discussion.** Following are just a few of the many instructional strategies mentioned in this chapter. Which of these might you use in adapting the traits to your writing curriculum? Which might be especially helpful in working with challenged writers? Check each one you might use; then compare your list to those of your colleagues:

   __ Creating student rubrics/writing guides/checklists

   __ Designing trait posters

   __ Conducting pre- and postassessments

   __ Giving writing coach checklists to parents

   __ Pairing traits with graphic organizers

   __ Leading students in the trait aerobics

   __ Color coding to identify strong moments by trait

   __ Using RTC: Reading/Traits/Connections

   __ Using backwards planning for managing writing assignments

   __ Reading aloud

   __ Creating weak samples for students to revise

   __ Asking students to bring questions to conferences

   __ Designing participatory activities (e.g., cooking, collecting) to appeal to kinesthetic learners and build vocabulary

   __ Providing model sentences and paragraphs for ELL students

   __ Grouping books to facilitate research

   __ Using "Thoughts, Feelings, Actions"

   __ Connecting traits to art

2. **Activity and Discussion.** Imagine you are doing a teacher evaluation for any one of the teachers whose classroom is showcased in this chapter. Without the advantage of seeing that teacher in action, write a three- to five-sentence paragraph describing one thing that teacher does well. Share your thoughts with your colleagues.

3. **Discussion.** Some of the teachers in this chapter have adapted traits for kinesthetic learners or second-language learners. If you work with such students, what have you learned from these teachers that might be helpful to you in your classroom?

4. **Activity and Discussion.** One of the teachers in this chapter, Sue, uses art to create a parallel with the six traits. With your group, create similar parallels, using art, music, dance, or any other artistic form. Talk about how you might use the results in your instruction.

Reflections on Writing

Writing is like painting a picture for me. Every color is a different letter. In your mind you have to picture what your masterpiece is going to look like. Then you put all those colors together. . . . Most of the time your inspirations come when you least expect it, like in a dream or when you are actually listening in math class. When you get your story in your mind and onto your paper, it can be a work of art, worth sharing with the whole world—or at least your parents.

—**Stephanie Harris**, student writer

Each year I am amazed at how empowered my students become in working with the traits. They not only have a clear understanding of what makes effective writing, they become much more able to self-evaluate and be reflective of their own work. Through use of the traits, my students have been able to make meaningful revisions that greatly enhance the quality of their own work—and all this without ME as their primary guide! There is no question in my mind that the six traits of writing help to create independent, self-directed writers.

—**Jennifer Wallace**
Grade 4 Teacher, Bellevue, Washington

The writing traits are just the right tools. They just make sense—to teachers and to students. They provide that common language that moves the writer through brainstorming to assessment with such continuity. I think the reason the traits are so successful in my classroom is that they're concrete and practical—and they can easily be found beyond the classroom. If I am talking about voice, my students don't just write with voice . . . they wear clothes that have voice, they demonstrate voice with their hair. They even find voice in the cafeteria lunch!

—**Peggy Fox**
High School Teacher, Lee, New Hampshire

Going Informational

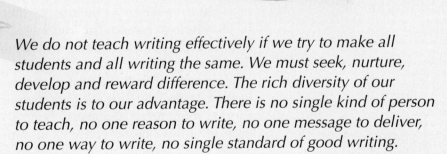

We do not teach writing effectively if we try to make all students and all writing the same. We must seek, nurture, develop and reward difference. The rich diversity of our students is to our advantage. There is no single kind of person to teach, no one reason to write, no one message to deliver, no one way to write, no single standard of good writing.

—Donald M. Murray
A Writer Teaches Writing, 2004, p. 5

The purpose of research writing is not simply to show readers what you know. It is an effort to extend a conversation about a topic that is ongoing, a conversation that includes voices of people who have already spoken, often in different contexts and perhaps never together.

—Bruce Ballenger
The Curious Researcher, 2004, p. 15

Informational writing is different from creative writing—in a number of ways. To honor these differences, the writing guides in this chapter have been adapted from the originals for use with text that a writer could not pull out of his or her own head—in other words, writing that requires research. Every trait in such writing looks a little different.

Take **ideas**. In research writing, the purpose is more to teach than to entertain (though entertainment is *allowed,* of course). Accuracy is also important. So is the writer's ability to synthesize information from multiple sources.

The **organization** in an informational piece is critical. A good informational writer always asks, "What does my reader need to know first—and next—and after that? And what's the thought I want to leave him or her with?" The writer-as-teacher anticipates questions and charts an informational path along which a reader moves toward ever-greater understanding.

So often I am asked if it is possible to have **voice** in informational writing. Not only is it possible, it's vital—*if* you want readers. Consider the work of Barbara Kingsolver, Diane Ackerman, Carl Sagan, David Quammen, Lewis Thomas, Rachel Carson, or any writer who uses voice to make readers care about a topic. Their voices are invariably confident, inspiring, and knowledge-driven. Such voice says to a reader, "I know this topic very well. You can trust me to tell you the truth." If Carl Sagan had written, "The Cosmos sure is a big place," no one would have paid attention. Instead, he wrote this:

> If we were randomly inserted into the Cosmos, the chance that we would find ourselves on or near a planet would be less than one in a billion trillion trillion (10^{33}, a one followed by 33 zeroes). In everyday life such odds are called compelling. Worlds are precious [1980, p. 5].

In creative writing, when we think **word choice**, we often think of imagery or sensory appeal. Informational writers also paint pictures for readers—but to make those pictures technically correct, they need a good grasp of terminology essential to the message, along with ability to make terms and concepts so clear a reader feels as much at home with them as the writer does.

Variety is always the soul of **sentence fluency**, but in most informational writing (especially if it's highly technical) the tendency should be toward shorter, more direct sentences. Longer sentences often require the reader to keep several (or more) concepts in mind at one time. Short sentences let the reader work through the topic bite by informational bite.

Informational **conventions** shift toward the formal (fewer contractions, for example, or less tolerance for slang), and also include correct citation of sources (accurate information, proper formatting). Since there is not a universally accepted format for citations, it is helpful to have a handbook that will be your class authority.

See Figures 11.1 and 11.2 for six-point Informational Writing Guides, one for teachers and one for students. (Note: If you prefer the five-point Writing Guide, see the Appendix for a three-level guide that is adaptable for use as a five- or six-point scale.)

Figure 11.1 **271**

FIGURE **11.1** **Teacher Six-Point Informational Writing Guide**

Ideas

6
- ☐ Clear, focused, explicit thesis—writer has a vision
- ☐ Expansively, accurately answers well-defined question(s)
- ☐ Synthesizes information from multiple sources
- ☐ Offers support and examples that enhance reader's understanding

5
- ☐ Clear, focused thesis
- ☐ Answers important question(s)
- ☐ Pulls information from more than one source
- ☐ Offers credible, helpful support and examples

4
- ☐ Thesis easy to identify
- ☐ Addresses at least one question/issue with broad overview
- ☐ Relies on outside source combined with personal knowledge
- ☐ Offers some support for or expansion of main topic

3
- ☐ Thesis can be inferred
- ☐ Gives broad brushstroke view of topic
- ☐ Limited research, much reliance on common knowledge
- ☐ Evidence and support sketchy, limited

2
- ☐ Thesis still emerging
- ☐ Insufficient knowledge leaves many questions unanswered
- ☐ Broad generalizations, lists of undeveloped ideas
- ☐ Unsupported assertions, observations

1
- ☐ No thesis—topic/key question undefined
- ☐ No informational base, reader left with many questions
- ☐ Best guesses, random thoughts
- ☐ Writing mainly to fill page

Organization

6
- ☐ Thoughtful structure guides reader purposefully from point to point
- ☐ Lead sets up discussion, ending helps reader draw conclusions
- ☐ Transitions suggest connections reader might not think of
- ☐ Design supports reader's understanding of the topic

5
- ☐ Design supports development of thesis
- ☐ Lead introduces topic, ending brings discussion to closure
- ☐ Transitions make important connections clear
- ☐ Design makes discussion easy to follow

4
- ☐ Design lets reader follow discussion without difficulty
- ☐ Functional lead kicks things off, conclusion signals end of discussion
- ☐ Helpful transitions often suggest connections
- ☐ Structure helpful, though sometimes predictable

3
- ☐ Reader must work to stay on track—OR he or she always knows what's coming
- ☐ Lead creates unfulfilled expectations, ending seems abrupt
- ☐ Transitions sometimes missing or unclear
- ☐ Reader must pause or reread—OR *everything* is predictable

2
- ☐ Reader asks, "Where is this going?"
- ☐ Lead does not set up discussion, ending provides no resolution
- ☐ Transitions unclear, missing, or not helpful in linking ideas
- ☐ Information comes at the wrong time—or is continually repeated

1
- ☐ Reader feels lost
- ☐ Starts right in (no lead)—just stops (no conclusion)
- ☐ Transitions missing—perhaps points *aren't* connected
- ☐ Nothing seems related to anything else—a random list

FIGURE **11.1** **Teacher Six-Point Informational Writing Guide**

Voice	Word Choice
6	**6**
☐ Professional, enthusiastic voice welcomes readers into discussion	☐ Explicit, precise words make message consistently clear for reader
☐ Confidence reflects knowledge, inspires readers' trust	☐ Writer uses language of content area with ease and skill
☐ Writer's clear enthusiasm for topic is compelling, contagious	☐ Writer helps reader feel at home with important terms, concepts
☐ Reader feels eager to share the piece aloud	☐ Language builds a bridge to understanding
5	**5**
☐ Professional, sincere voice connects with readers	☐ Carefully chosen words add to clarity
☐ Confidence makes readers open to message	☐ Writer clearly knows language of content area
☐ Writer's enthusiasm for topic is evident	☐ Writer clarifies most new words or concepts for reader
☐ A likely read-aloud candidate	☐ Language supports reader's understanding of the message
4	**4**
☐ Sincere, appropriate voice signals writer's presence	☐ Functional language makes message clear on general level
☐ Confident moments reflect writer's variable knowledge of topic	☐ Writer seems familiar with basic terminology of content area
☐ Enthusiastic moments encourage readers to hang in	☐ New terms are often defined, explained
☐ Some passages could be shared aloud	☐ Reader can readily make sense of the message
3	**3**
☐ Writer hides behind facts, generalities	☐ Some parts are unclear or ambiguous
☐ Confidence and comfort with topic seem limited	☐ Writer not fully comfortable with language of the content area
☐ Quiet voice dampens reader's enthusiasm for topic	☐ New terms not always clearly defined, explained
☐ Not quite ready to share aloud—though moments are close	☐ Reader can figure out meaning with some effort, thought
2	**2**
☐ Voice distant, encyclopedic—or just wrong for audience, topic	☐ Imprecise or vague language creates confusion or incomplete picture
☐ Limited knowledge of topic keeps voice in check	☐ Terms sometimes used incorrectly—or omitted, even if needed
☐ Reader must work to pay attention	☐ Language is general, unclear, wordy, or jargonistic
☐ Not a read-aloud candidate yet	☐ Reader must work hard to "get it"
1	**1**
☐ Voice inappropriate—or just a faint whisper	☐ What is the writer trying to say?
☐ Writer doesn't seem to know or like this topic	☐ Writer lacks terminology to make message clear
☐ Reader feels shut out of discussion	☐ Language does not speak to reader
☐ Feels stiff, mechanical if read aloud	☐ Reader left to guess at writer's meaning

Figure 11.1 **273**

FIGURE **11.1** Teacher Six-Point Informational Writing Guide

Sentence Fluency

6
- [ ] Sentences consistently clear, direct, to the point
- [ ] Text both graceful and designed to promote rapid, easy reading
- [ ] Purposeful beginnings (*For example . . .*) help reader follow text
- [ ] Sentences are varied and balanced—no extremes of long or short

5
- [ ] Sentence structure clear and direct
- [ ] Smooth phrasing enhances readability
- [ ] Purposeful beginnings connect ideas, set up examples
- [ ] Sentences are balanced without extremes of long or short

4
- [ ] Sentences clear and readable
- [ ] No noticeable awkward moments to slow reader
- [ ] Possible repetition—more transitions would help
- [ ] Sentences could use some variety—nothing overly long or short

3
- [ ] Careful reading required
- [ ] Awkward moments make rapid reading difficult
- [ ] Repetitive beginnings noticeable, more transitions needed
- [ ] Sentences tend to be repetitive and choppy—or never-ending

2
- [ ] Processing meaning takes time, effort, attention
- [ ] Confusing structure makes reader pause, go back
- [ ] Beginnings repetitious—or just hard to spot
- [ ] Tangled, awkward, choppy sentences—repeated patterns

1
- [ ] Confusing structure requires constant mental editing
- [ ] Missing words, awkward moments, irregular structure slow the reader significantly
- [ ] Hard to tell where sentences begin and end
- [ ] Non-sentences or endlessly connected clauses, word strings

Conventions

6
- [ ] Thoroughly edited—only the pickiest editors will spot errors
- [ ] Conventions *enhance* meaning, voice
- [ ] Sources correctly cited using appropriate format
- [ ] *Optional:* Enticing layout creates strong, effective overall impression
- [ ] Virtually ready to publish

5
- [ ] Edited well—minor errors that are easily overlooked
- [ ] Conventions support meaning, voice
- [ ] Sources correctly cited
- [ ] *Optional:* Striking layout guides reader to key points
- [ ] Ready to publish with light touch-ups

4
- [ ] Noticeable errors—reader breezes right through, however
- [ ] Errors do not interfere with meaning
- [ ] Sources cited—light corrections needed
- [ ] *Optional:* Layout adequate, pleasing
- [ ] Good once-over needed prior to publication

3
- [ ] Noticeable, distracting errors—editing erratic, things missed
- [ ] Errors may slow reader or affect message in spots
- [ ] Citations need checking—some may be omitted
- [ ] *Optional:* Problems with layout (e.g., small print, no subheads)
- [ ] Thorough, careful editing needed prior to publication

2
- [ ] Frequent distracting errors reflect minimal editing
- [ ] Errors slow reader, affect clarity
- [ ] Citations missing, faulty
- [ ] *Optional:* Layout problematic (e.g., no margins, hard-to-read fonts)
- [ ] Line-by-line editing needed prior to publication

1
- [ ] Serious, frequent errors—not yet edited or proofed
- [ ] Reader must slow down, fill in, decode
- [ ] Sources not cited
- [ ] *Optional:* No apparent attention to layout
- [ ] Word-by-word editing needed prior to publication

FIGURE **11.2** Student Six-Point Informational Writing Guide

Ideas

6
- ☐ I have a clear vision of what I want to say to the reader.
- ☐ I know this topic like an insider and it shows.
- ☐ I give my reader clear, accurate, insightful information.
- ☐ I pulled information from several sources and wove it all together to make my own meaning.
- ☐ Strong support makes everything I say convincing.

5
- ☐ My thesis or key question is clear.
- ☐ I answer some important questions.
- ☐ I give the reader useful information.
- ☐ I pulled information from more than one source.
- ☐ Good evidence makes my main points believable.

4
- ☐ You can tell what my thesis is, even if I don't state it.
- ☐ I answer one or two key questions.
- ☐ I give my reader a good overview of this topic.
- ☐ I did some research, but also relied on what I knew.
- ☐ I have some support—I'm not sure if it's enough.

3
- ☐ I think you can figure out my thesis or main point.
- ☐ I don't know enough to feel comfortable with this topic.
- ☐ Most of what I say is common knowledge.
- ☐ I didn't do a lot of research—I relied on things I had heard.
- ☐ My support is sketchy—it could leave you skeptical!

2
- ☐ My thesis is still coming together.
- ☐ There are BIG gaps in what I know about this topic.
- ☐ Some things I made up—or I took my best guess!
- ☐ I did little or no research. I just wrote.
- ☐ My evidence will convince you only if you already agree with me.

1
- ☐ I don't have a thesis or main point.
- ☐ I don't really know anything about this topic—yet.
- ☐ Without information, it was hard to write!
- ☐ I wasn't sure how to do research.
- ☐ My writing is detail-free.

Organization

6
- ☐ My organization will guide you like a light in the dark.
- ☐ My lead sets up the discussion—and invites you to be part of it.
- ☐ My ending helps you draw important conclusions.
- ☐ This piece is organized to make learning about this topic easy.
- ☐ I show connections you might not even think of if I did not bring them up.

5
- ☐ My organization will help you make sense of this topic.
- ☐ My lead invites you into the discussion.
- ☐ My ending brings the discussion to a close.
- ☐ The organization makes my thoughts easy to follow.
- ☐ I connect ideas to each other—or to a big picture.

4
- ☐ This design works fine for this kind of writing.
- ☐ My lead gets the discussion started.
- ☐ The conclusion lets you know the conversation is over.
- ☐ I don't think you'll ever feel lost.
- ☐ The most important connections are clear.

3
- ☐ You might need to work to stay on track.
- ☐ I think my lead goes one way, my paper another.
- ☐ Maybe I stopped too quickly, or repeated things I had already said.
- ☐ You might need to reread to figure out what is most important.
- ☐ I just followed a formula for transitions: *First, Second,* etc.

2
- ☐ You might find yourself asking, "Where is this going?"
- ☐ My lead is one everyone uses—I'm not sure it fits.
- ☐ My ending doesn't really wrap things up.
- ☐ It's hard to follow this—things come at the wrong time.
- ☐ I didn't know how to connect ideas.

1
- ☐ My writing is random. There is no real design to it.
- ☐ I don't have a lead. I just started writing.
- ☐ I have no conclusion. I just stopped when I ran out of things to say.
- ☐ My writing jumps from point to point.
- ☐ Nothing goes with anything else.

Figure 11.2   **275**

FIGURE **11.2** Student Six-Point Informational Writing Guide

Voice	Word Choice
6	**6**
☐ My voice is professional and enthusiastic—just right.	☐ Every word or phrase is chosen to make the message clear for the reader.
☐ I use my voice to welcome readers into the discussion.	☐ I felt comfortable with terms I needed and used them well.
☐ I feel confident that my message is important and interesting.	☐ I defined or explained things so the reader could follow the discussion easily.
☐ I like this topic, and want you to like it too.	☐ You won't find any wordiness or jargon in my writing.
☐ I feel certain you will want to share this aloud.	☐ I write to inform my readers, not overwhelm them.
5	**5**
☐ My voice is professional and sincere. It suits my topic and audience.	☐ My word choice makes the message clear.
☐ The voice in this piece reaches out to readers.	☐ I know the language that goes with this topic, and used it correctly.
☐ Knowing my topic helps me sound confident.	☐ I defined any terms a reader might not know.
☐ I like this topic. You can hear that in my voice.	☐ You won't find much wordiness or jargon.
☐ You will most likely want to share this aloud.	☐ My word choice should help a reader understand this topic.
4	**4**
☐ My voice is sincere and appropriate.	☐ My words make sense. They get the job done.
☐ You can hear me—especially in some parts.	☐ If I used technical terms, I'm pretty sure they're correct.
☐ I sound confident in those parts I'm sure about.	☐ I think I defined anything I needed to.
☐ I like this topic all right—most of the time.	☐ Wordiness and jargon are not a real problem.
☐ There are definitely some read-aloud moments.	☐ I think a reader can make sense of this.
3	**3**
☐ I think I need more voice—or a different voice.	☐ You'll get the general idea!
☐ My voice either fades away or takes over.	☐ I tried to use terms correctly—I didn't always know the right words for the moment.
☐ If I knew this topic better, you'd hear more confidence.	☐ New terms might not always be explained.
☐ I have to work at sounding enthusiastic.	☐ Wordiness? Jargon? Could be a problem here and there.
☐ It's not *quite* ready to share.	☐ I think you can figure out what I mean if you try.
2	**2**
☐ I think I sound more like an encyclopedia than a person with a message.	☐ Some of this is unclear now that I take another look.
☐ I couldn't get into it. My readers will hear that.	☐ I couldn't seem to come up with the right words.
☐ It's hard to be confident when you don't know the topic.	☐ I was too vague and general—OR
☐ I think you'll need to work at paying attention. I did!	☐ I just kept repeating myself . . .
☐ This is *not* ready to share aloud.	☐ You'll have some work to do to make sense of this.
1	**1**
☐ It's the wrong voice—or it's just a whisper.	☐ This doesn't make sense, even to me.
☐ I don't really care if anyone reads this.	☐ I think I used the wrong words—it's confusing.
☐ I don't know anything about this topic.	☐ The language is pretty vague, OR—
☐ I just wrote to get done.	☐ It's just nonsense. I don't know what I wanted to say.
☐ Maybe if I read this aloud, I'll get some ideas for a new topic.	☐ It's anyone's guess what this means.

FIGURE **11.2** Student Six-Point Informational Writing Guide

Sentence Fluency	Conventions
6	**6**
☐ My sentences are clear, direct, and to the point.	☐ Even a picky editor will have trouble finding an error.
☐ You could read this very quickly and easily—and not miss one important point.	☐ I read this silently *and* aloud—the conventions bring out meaning and voice.
☐ My sentence beginnings make it easy to follow the flow of ideas.	☐ I cited all sources correctly and used the right format.
☐ My sentences show variety, but I avoided extremes of long or short.	☐ *Optional:* My layout will catch your eye.
	☐ This is ready to publish.
5	**5**
☐ My sentences are clear and direct.	☐ I have some tiny errors—you might not even notice!
☐ The whole piece is very readable.	☐ I read this carefully. My conventions help show a reader how to read my text.
☐ Sentence beginnings show how ideas connect.	☐ All sources are cited correctly.
☐ I avoided sentences that were overly long or uncomfortably short.	☐ *Optional:* The layout guides your eye to main points.
	☐ This is ready to publish with only light touchups.
4	**4**
☐ Most sentences are clear and fairly easy to read.	☐ You might spot some errors, but the meaning is clear.
☐ There might be one or two spots I could smooth out.	☐ I proofed this text, but I need to look again.
☐ I need better transitions, and less repetition.	☐ My citations need a few small corrections.
☐ I could use more variety, but there's nothing too long or too short.	☐ *Optional:* The layout is fine for this piece.
	☐ Some light editing should do the trick.
3	**3**
☐ Most sentences come clear if you read carefully.	☐ You will notice errors—and they might slow you down.
☐ Some bumpy moments make it hard to read quickly.	☐ I did not proof carefully—I missed too many things.
☐ My beginnings are repetitious. They don't really show connections either.	☐ I need to recheck my citations carefully.
☐ I have some long, gangly sentences. I have short sentences, too.	☐ *Optional:* I have some problems with layout (such as tiny print).
	☐ This needs thorough, careful editing.
2	**2**
☐ When I read this aloud, it's a bumpy ride.	☐ Errors jump out at you. They get in the way.
☐ You'll need to slow down and pay attention.	☐ This does not look edited. I left all the work to the reader.
☐ Most of my sentences start the same way.	☐ Some citations are missing, or they're not done right.
☐ Most of my sentences are too long or too short.	☐ *Optional:* I have serious problems with layout (such as no margins or unreadable fonts).
	☐ I need to edit this line by line.
1	**1**
☐ This is very tough to get through, even for me.	☐ Errors make my copy hard to read.
☐ You'll have to fix things as you go.	☐ Even patient readers might give up.
☐ It's hard to tell where sentences begin and end.	☐ I forgot about citing sources.
☐ Are these even sentences?	☐ *Optional:* Layout? I didn't worry about it.
	☐ I need to read this aloud word by word, pen in hand.

Sample Papers

I invite you to put the informational scoring guide in this chapter to the test with the following student samples. These papers were selected to represent a variety of topics, grade levels, writing approaches, and skills. For reasons of length, I have not included major research pieces such as might be typical in an AP high school or college freshman English class. Such writing can easily be assessed using the writing guides from this chapter, but it is not handy to use in workshop or study group sessions because of the time required to read and discuss it. If you are using this text as part of a class or study group, however, I encourage you to attempt a longer piece.

Suggested scores and rationales follow each paper, along with lesson ideas and lessons learned. To make your task easier, make a copy of the six-point informational writing guide so that you can have it right in your hand as you look at each paper. As always, feel free to disagree with these scores *if you have a good reason*. Informational papers are scored exclusively on a six-point scale. However, a three-level informational scale, adaptable to a five- or six-point, is included in the Appendix if you wish to use it in your classroom.

Paper 1   Black Widows (Informational, Grade 3)

A small black spot moves slowly and silently across the ground. Her red patch glints in the sun. She climbs up her web.

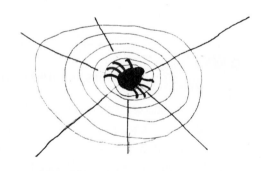

She's a black widow.

A small fly collides with her well-made net. The spider approaches the thrashing insect. Soon, the fly is tightly wrapped up in strong, fine silk.

The spider has a nice, long meal. Its red hourglass stomach sparkles in the sun because no hairs get in the way.

This spider happens to live here in America. It could just as easily live in New Zealand, Australia, or countries surrounding the Mediterranean Sea, though.

She glides down from her web. Suddenly, the shadow of an unlucky person falls over the spider. A bare foot covers her. The black widow sinks her fangs into the skin. It is difficult for the person to breathe or move. Cramps find their way into the person's muscles. Thirty minutes later, the human is in great pain.

If you like breathing, don't step on a black widow spider!

The Write Connection

"Black Widows"

Of the nineteen sentences in this piece, twelve begin with one of these words: *A, She, The, It, This.* See if you can cut this number in half by combining sentences or rewording them slightly to begin in different ways. Can you tinker with the fluency without losing this writer's striking sense of drama? When you finish, see if you can come up with an alternate title that doesn't give away the main character's identity too quickly.

■ **Suggested Scores**

Ideas: 5

Organization: 5

Voice: 6

Word choice: 6

Sentence fluency: 5

Conventions: 6

■ **Lessons Learned from Paper 1**

- A little drama brings an informational piece to life.
- Suspense makes a lead more interesting—but be careful not to give the game away in your title!

■ **Comments**

You can hear this writer's enthusiasm for her topic. She has singled out intriguing details—the strong silk, hourglass stomach, deadliness of the spider's bite—and focuses just on these without giving us a whole truckload of information. We *are* left with some questions, notably: *Is the black widow's bite fatal?* Every image is crystal clear and meaningful. The beginning and ending are excellent—even if the ending is just a little sudden. The word choice and voice seem just right for informational writing with a dark shadow. Sentences are strong, though many begin with *A, She, It,* or *Its.* Just a bit more variety would bump the score to a 6.

| Paper 2 | **Bears in the Wild** (Informational, Grade 4) |

Have you ever watched a black bear before? Once when we were driving I saw a black bear across the river. she was ambling along the river bank, with her two cubs.

Black bears are usually black but they can be brown or white. A black bear has four legs and five claws on each paw. The weight of a grown black bear is about 300 pounds or about 136 kilograms. Black bears are less than five feet long. the black bear has lots of thick fur and it has big teeth, long, sharp claws, and a huge head.

Some bears live in a hole under a tree or in a dug out cave. Bears eat different kinds of berries and some kinds of inseckts they dig out of rotton logs. They normally live in the woods where they are safe from people there main enemy. Bears also eat honey from bee hives. there thick black fur protects them from the bees they also eat many kinds of fish espeshially salmon. when

(continued)

you think about it, they like alot of the same foods we humans like eccept for the inseckts.

Most bears hibernate in the winter, but before they do they need to collect lots of food and stuff themselves to get fat and store food for the winter.

Lots of people think bears will attack you. But the truth is they wont. Bears are mostly gentle. They usually mind there own busness unless you pester them. In the woods in Canada once we got to track a bear but he never would let us get too close because he was just too shy. Its easy to find where bears have been from their tracks and droppings. They rub themselves on tree trunks and leave big tufts of there fur behind.

People are bears only enemies but we could be there freinds if we understood them. we should not kill bears just for bear rugs. there are not enough bears left and if we just keep building houses and shopping malls we will distroy their homes.

■ Suggested Scores

Ideas: 5

Organization: 4

Voice: 5

Word choice: 4

Fluency: 4

Conventions: 3

■ Comments

Though this paper needs a main message, it has good details: Bears are shy, they are threatened by people encroaching on their territory, they eat a variety of food (including insects), and they won't hurt you unless provoked. Although it gets off to a shaky start (the lead does not seem to make a point), the general organizational flow is easy enough to follow. The ending is strong, although a little abrupt. Two personal stories—seeing the mother bear and cubs by the river and tracking the bear through the woods—are begun, but the writer (frustratingly) never follows through. On the positive side, this writer seems to like the topic, and his enthusiasm results in quite a lot of voice. Fluency is by turns mechanical and *very* strong, making some parts highly readable. Conventions need work, and a bibliography would be helpful.

■ Lessons Learned from Paper 2

- Even fairly good organization seems weaker if the lead is not powerful.
- Conventional errors are distracting, even if not serious.

The Write Connection

"Bears"

What is the most interesting message this writer has to deliver? Write it as a sentence—and call this the "theme" of the paper. Revise the piece so that this message or theme stands out. Start with the lead. Then make every paragraph echo or support the overriding theme in one way or another. When you finish revising, edit the paper for publication.

Paper 3	**Thomas Alva Edison: Wizard of Menlo Park**

(Informational, Grade 3)

Boyhood. Thomas Alva Edison was born on February 11, 1847, at Milan, Ohio. He was the seventh and youngest child of his parents, Samuel and Nancy Edison. Samuel was a shingle manufacturer. Thomas' family called him Alva or Al. Alva was a curious youngster and asked many questions. For example, he saw a goose sitting on its eggs in its nest. He then decided to try it. He sat on the nest and crushed all the eggs. Another one of his silly notions was that he noticed balloons could float. So he got one, breathed in the helium air, and fell to the ground ill.

At 12 years of age, he became deaf. Some guy pulled him by the ear. It wasn't bad at first, but as he grew older, he could hardly hear a shout.

Alva only went through three weeks of school and then quit because of his teacher. His teacher got mad because Alva asked too many questions. So his mother taught him at home.

Adulthood. Thomas Alva Edison married Mary Stilwell in 1871. They had three children. Their names were Marion Estell, Thomas Alva, Jr., and William. Mary Edison died in 1884. He then married again in 1886 to Mina Miller. Thomas and Mina had three children also. Their names were Charles, Madeleine, and Theodore. Charles Edison became Secretary of the Navy in 1939. He was then elected governor of New Jersey. Thomas Edison didn't spend much time with his family. He spent most of his time in his laboratory.

His inventions. Thomas made eight major inventions. They were the electric light, telephone, typewriter, motion pictures, electric generator, and the electric-powered train. The other two inventions were the mimeograph machine and the phonograph. The most important invention of his was the electric light. Thomas was called "The Wizard of Menlo Park."

Sources

Frith, Margaret. *Who Was Thomas Alva Edison?* 2005. New York: Grosset and Dunlap.
"Thomas Edison." *World Book Encyclopedia.* 1997. Volume 4.

The Write Connection

"Thomas Alva Edison"

If possible, check out the Margaret Frith text this writer cites in his source list. Use the information you find to answer two questions: Why was Edison called "The Wizard of Menlo Park"? and "Why did he spend so much time in his laboratory—and so little with his family?" Then, do any of the following: (1) revise the lead to make it more enticing; (2) add an interesting detail to the "Adulthood" section; (3) add another interesting detail to the "Inventions" section and get rid of the list; (4) write a new conclusion.

■ **Suggested Scores**

Ideas: **4**

Organization: **4**

Voice: **3**

Word choice: **4**

Sentence fluency: **4**

Conventions: **6**

■ Lessons Learned from Paper 3

- No fair running out of steam in the second half.
- Don't rely too heavily on lists—or your report will sound like an encyclopedia entry, and voice will suffer along with ideas.

■ Comments

What an interesting shift occurs in this paper. It is almost as if the first part—"Boyhood"—was written by a different author. Here we have the rather entertaining exploits of Alva (Al), who actually tried hatching eggs himself, tried to make himself float with helium, and had to be schooled at home because he asked too many questions. Just when we're getting into it, we bump into Part 2, "Adulthood," when Thomas grows inexplicably dull. All we get is the family tree. Part 3, "Inventions," offers a similar list, with none of the charm and drama of Part 1. If the whole paper followed the example of those first two paragraphs, scores would be significantly higher. Conventions are the strength of the piece. Sentences are a little choppy. The lead is standard for a biography, and though the conclusion is on the right track, it needs expansion to work.

> If you're bored by your research topic, your paper will almost certainly be boring as well, and you'll end up hating writing research papers as much as ever.
>
> —Bruce Ballenger
> *The Curious Researcher,*
> 2004, p. 25

Paper 4 **Driving Tests Should Be Harder**
(Persuasive, Grade 7)

If driver's tests were more rigorous, everyone on the road would be safer. About 50,000 people die in traffic accidents each year, and thousands more are injured. Most of these fatal accidents involve 16-year-old drivers. Although one of the problems is driving under the influence of liquor, an even bigger problem is incompetent driving. We could do something about this, but we grant driver's licenses on the basis of a very simple test.

Did you know that the part of the test in which you actually get out in a car and drive is only about 20 minutes long? What's more, the test givers are not demanding at all. They only ask drivers to perform a few tasks, such as turning left, turning right, parking and stopping. It has only been in the last few years that they have added entering a freeway to the test requirements. How often does anyone have to parallel park compared to entering a freeway? Yet it took all this time to update this test.

Tests are not conducted on the busiest streets or during heavy traffic hours. Anyone can pass this simple test in light traffic on a quiet street. It does not mean that driver is competent.

The true test is real-life driving. I mean things like driving in bad weather, such as on icy streets or in fog. Or coping with bad drivers, such as people who tailgate or honk for no good reason. Or learning to handle mechanical

(continued)

problems such as getting a flat tire. The current driver's test does not measure whether a person can handle any of these difficult but common situations.

Of course, a driver's test that had to cover all of these situations would be difficult to set up. It isn't easy to arrange for people to drive on icy roads, for instance. Plus it could be dangerous. Imagine if people got killed while taking their driver's test! Besides, a complicated test might cost more and there could be a long waiting line. Imagine if you were 16 and needed to drive to work and you could not get a license because the wait was so long. There is one solution. They could do part of the test as a computer simulation. That way, you would still need the skills, but you would not need to risk your life to show you were a competent driver.

There are several ways to make the current test better. First, make it longer, so people need to drive more. Second, use computer simulation to test skills under dangerous conditions. Third, make sure people really have to do the things they will do in everyday driving, like changing lanes on the freeway. Then, require a score of 90 to pass, not 70, which is too low. Right now, you can do a lot of things wrong and still pass.

Sure, it will cost a little to make the tests more rigorous. But lives are more important than keeping tests cheap. When was the last time you felt in danger because of an incompetent driver? Remember, almost every person in this country will have a driver's license at some time in his or her life. If even half of these people are not qualified, we are risking our lives every time we go out on the road. We need better driver's tests now!

Source: Oregon Department of Motor Vehicles.

■ Suggested Scores

Ideas: 5

Organization: 5

Voice: 5

Word choice: 5

Fluency: 5

Conventions: 6

■ Comments

The pluses in this paper are many: The voice is strong and sustained, the writer is very aware of his audience, the language is clear and appropriate for the topic, sentences are varied and readable, and the writer makes many good points. Had the writer further explored that intriguing idea of

The Write Connection

"Driving Tests"

This is a well-written paper, but it's long. What if you were going to publish it and you had room for something only half this length? See how much you can cut without losing what's essential.

computerized driving tests, the ideas score would have gone up; the problem of how to make the test more rigorous without increasing costs remains only partially resolved. Still, this writer accomplishes a lot in a short space and expresses himself clearly.

■ Lessons Learned from Paper 4

- When you raise an interesting concept (computerized driving tests), explore it fully.
- Simple, straightforward sentence structure makes an informational or persuasive piece easy to understand.

Paper 5   **Humboldt Penguins** (Informational, Grade 9)

Probably the most startling fact about the gentle Humboldt Penguin is that it is the most endangered penguin in the world. They have been hunted for years. Moreover, their main staple food, krill, are dwindling in numbers with the warming of the oceans, and the range of the Humboldt Penguin is not very big—and is not getting any bigger. Their habitat is unique, and they do not seem able to adapt. The only place it can be duplicated is in the zoo. Odds are, we have only a few decades left—maybe less—to enjoy these remarkable and friendly animals.

Environment

Humboldt Penguins live along the rocky coastline of South America, from Peru to Northern Chile. The warm currents of El Niño bring in plenty of fish and krill—for now—so the penguins do not migrate. They nest right in the rocks, making themselves comfortable along hard, unforgiving rock walls that most creatures would find less than inviting. The rocks and ocean are all they know their whole lives. Because they do not migrate, they know nothing of forests or sandy beaches or even pebbled coves.

Physical Description

Male and female Humboldts are similar in appearance. Both are about 26 inches tall and weigh about ten pounds. They have a black mask with touches of pink around a sharp, heavy beak, well suited to fishing. A black stripe runs like an inverted "U" up and around their sides and down their back. Their belly is mostly white, with scattered black speckles. Penguins have very short legs, perhaps only two inches long, but can nevertheless jump amazingly high, for the leg muscles are very powerful. Their webbed feet are black with pink spots, and they have three toes, with sharp, scaly claws at the end. A penguin's feet work like paddles, propelling the penguin through the water, and are very powerful.

Penguins are normally fairly clumsy on land, and waddle along at a slow pace—though they have been known to "launch" themselves at an enemy if attacked or provoked. They are built for underwater speed, however, and move like tiny torpedoes in the water. Their smooth, oval shape is reminiscent of a dolphin or trout, and they swim with the same ease.

Everyone knows that penguins do not fly. However, scientists believe that once they did. They are almost certainly descended from a flying bird, but so far, nobody has located the "missing link" that would prove this theory.

(continued)

Food

The diet of the penguin is healthy, if a little monotonous. They dine primarily on fish and crustaceans, plus an occasional squid. They are especially fond of fish like anchovies which swim in large schools. Penguins have a lot of body fat to maintain in order to insulate themselves from the cold water, so they must eat a great deal and eat often to maintain their oval shapes.

The bill of the penguin is equipped with small spines which help hook and hold a fish. Once a penguin gets a grip on its meal, the fish rarely escapes.

Predators

Penguins are hunted by seals, killer whales and sharks. For this reason, they like to hunt close to shore and near the surface. If a penguin ventures too far out to sea, it may not have the endurance to outrun a hungry seal.

Land predators include gulls, jaegers, skuas and other large birds. These birds will not take on an adult penguin, which is a fierce fighter, but will prey on young chicks and eggs.

Behavior

A surprising fact about penguins is that they are quite territorial. They will attack others that come too close to their nesting site. Like humans, they sometimes resent neighbors who invade their privacy or become too nosy. If a penguin must walk through a crowded area, he will keep his head high and feathers sleeked down, as if trying to look invisible. Generally, though, penguins are very social. They swim together and hunt in groups for protection. They watch out for one another and are very affectionate with their young. Humboldts have not learned to fear humans, and will often allow people to come quite close.

Conclusion

The Humboldt Penguin is among the most intriguing of all penguin species. It is more social than most penguins, and remarkably like ourselves. With luck, it may survive long enough for us to study its curious ways further.

Sources: Johnson, Russell. "Humboldt Penguins: An Endangered Species." In *Penguin World.* Vol. 4. No. 6. Spring 1992. Seattle Public Zoo. Site visit. May 20, 1994.

■ **Suggested Scores**

Ideas: 6

Organization: 5

Voice: 6

Word choice: 6

Fluency: 6

Conventions: 6

■ **Comments**

This paper is a fine sample of informational writing at its best: informative, readable, well paced, and organized to help a reader understand and appreciate the subject. It does not attempt to tell all there is to know about penguins but selects some significant and intriguing details. It's interesting to learn, for instance, that penguins do not mind nesting in rocks, that they are affectionate with their young, that they bristle (like humans) when nosy neighbors come too close, that they can launch themselves ferociously at a rude intruder, and that they turn into feathered torpedoes in the water. At the end we want to say, "Thanks for sharing so many intriguing tidbits—I learned a lot." Our only complaint (and it's minor) is that sections seem a little out of balance, with a lot of time spent on appearance. The paper has fine conventions and a bibliography, too.

■ Lessons Learned from Paper 5

- Dig for the unusual details. They will make your paper stand out.
- Subheads are extremely useful, for both the writer and reader.

The Write Connection

"Humboldt Penguins"

Skim through this piece, noticing the effect of the subheads. Do they direct your eye to the information you want? Revise a research piece *you* are working on by using subheads as this writer does.

This piece has exceptional voice for research writing—except for the title. Brainstorm other titles that might work better.

Look again at the writer's cited sources. Does the format follow what is expected in your classroom? If not, edit them.

Paper 6   **The Middle Ages** (Informational, Grade 7)

In the time of the Middle Ages many children drempt of being a knight. First they had to become a page. The next step to becoming a squire. Hard training and patience were required. A brave young squire could hardly wait to receive the accolade. During the period of being a squire you had to learn chivalry. Chivalry consisted of loyalty and devotion to the king or lord. Politeness and courtesy towards women was a very big part of being a knight. One also had to be brave and protect the defenseless.

A knight had to be wealthy in order to pay for the equipment. The equipment consists of a suit of armor, a shield, a sword, and of course a horse. The armor consists of many parts we won't name them all because it would take forever. However, we will name the helmet because it is the most important part of armor a knight could have because it protects the head from injury which could be fatal.

Tournaments took up what little free time a knight had. If a knight wasn't out on the battlefield he would be out jousting or sword fighting against another knight. The purpose of a tournament is to test one's strength. The object was not to kill a knight but to capture him.

Manors were the main ways of life during the middle age. They had farms, hunting grounds, people and castles. Castles were the main points of life in the middle ages. Castles were not built for comfort but for defense.

Well, after all that, there isn't much more to discuss, so for now, orevwa.

Source: Caselli, Giovanni. *The middle Ages.* New york, 1988, Peter Bedrick Books, pages 12–17.

The Write Connection

"The Middle Ages"

The writer leaves countless questions unanswered. Make a list—individually or with your class.

Use this same strategy with your own writing, asking, "What reader's questions have I left unanswered?"

As a next step, check out *How Would You Survive in the Middle Ages?* by Fiona MacDonald and David Salariva (1997). How many of your questions does this book answer? What *additional* questions does it answer that you did not even think of? Is it a good example of informational writing? Score it, using the writing guide from this chapter.

■ Suggested Scores

Ideas: **3**

Organization: **2**

Voice: **3**

Word choice: **3**

Fluency: **3**

Conventions: **3**

■ Comments

If you already know a lot about the Middle Ages, you might sail right on through this essay. Otherwise, you are likely to find the information skimpy at best. There are many unanswered questions: Why did children dream of becoming knights? Could anyone become a knight? Were the knights always at war? The writer seems to assume that the audience is right there in the social studies class and therefore can fill in the blanks. We need a better balance of details to give us a sense of history and some little-known information to spark the imagination. The bibliography is short, but at least there is one.

■ Lessons Learned from Paper 6

- Write your title last.
- A good ending should say goodbye metaphorically but not literally.

Paper 7   **Life in the Middle Ages** (Informational, Grade 7)

Imagine yourself living in a time when the average man grew to a height of about 5'2", the average woman to about 4'10". And almost no one lived to be more than 45 years old. At 20 you would be middle aged, and probably would have lost many, if not most, of your teeth. Your skin would be pock marked from chicken pox or acne. At 13, you would either be married or (if you were a male), thinking about becoming a priest or knight. They were about the only people who were educated enough to read, write, or do simple math. This is just a small glimpse of what life was like in the Middle Ages in the part of the world we now call Great Britain. As we will see, life was very different then—in almost every possible way.

Society during the Middle Ages was organized in a somewhat military fashion. At the head of everything was the King, who had life and death control over all his subjects. He could conscript people for service in his "army," or confiscate their goods for use by the state. Not that there was much to confiscate. People during those times owned very little–a few clothes and

(continued)

dishes, some crude tools, some pigs or chickens, and perhaps a small shelter that passed for a house. Only the wealthy had dogs or horses, elaborate clothing, good leather shoes, weapons, jewelry or, in the cases of kings and lords, castles in which to live.

Of course, wealth is a relative thing. Today, we think little of owning things like automobiles, microwave ovens, computers, cameras and televisions, all of which would have seemed like magic to people of the 1300s. On the other hand, they dreamed of living in stone castles, for that was the height of elegance at the time. If we could go back in time and recapture the sights, sounds and smells of the Middle Ages, though, most of us would be horrified. Imagine no indoor sanitation, only crude buckets to dump human waste down the rock walls. Picture hogs, dogs, sheep, chickens and rats all sharing the larger space surrounding the inner castle where the King lived; the noise was deafening, the smell overpowering. Yet people looked on these surroundings as luxurious, for they knew nothing else.

Probably the worst thing to happen to anyone was to become ill or to be wounded. You might be bled into a bowl, or be given an herbal potion to drink, or a so-called doctor might stitch up your wounds with a filthy needle and some cat gut. Strangely enough, people then believed that washing actually pushed germs into your body, so no one washed if they could help it, not even the "doctors." Not only did they smell, but it was dangerous to be treated by one. Few people survived "surgery," which was more of a mutilation.

Entertainment in the Middle Ages was lively, to say the least. Knights practiced their jousting, trying to knock each other from horseback with a lance, in open tournaments. Some engaged in sword fights. They were not usually to the death, but sometimes accidents did occur. Executions were almost always public and were treated as a kind of entertainment. Many people would come to see someone hanged or beheaded. And of course there was almost always a wedding or funeral to attend if nothing else interesting was going on.

All in all, life was hard for people born in 1300. Maybe it's lucky they did only live to 45. Probably for them, that seemed like a long time!

The Write Connection

"Life in the Middle Ages"
Because this piece is so well written, it's easy to gloss over the many instances of strong word choice. Slow your reading down by reading aloud, highlighter pen in hand. Mark any word or phrase that strikes you as strong or "just right for the moment."

Take the next step by doing this with a sample of your own writing. If you do not have enough highlighted moments, underline those passages where you'd like to say something a different way, and revise accordingly.

■ **Suggested Scores**

Ideas: 6

Organization: 5

Voice: 6

Word choice: 6

Sentence fluency: 6

Conventions: 5

■ **Comments**

Compare this piece with Paper 6, "The Middle Ages." This writer has definitely done some research, and the result is an interesting, eye-opening walk through life in the 1300s. We learn how tall people were, how early they married, what they ate, where they lived, what medical treatment was like, what they did for entertainment, and much more. The details are specific, filled with imagery. In addition, this writer sounds truly intrigued by the subject, so the voice is strong. Did you think that the language was pretty simple? Look again. Imagine that you have that highlighter pen in your hand, and ask yourself how many words and phrases you might mark (remember, this is a middle school student). Despite the length, this is an easy one to read aloud. Excellent conventions, but no sources cited.

■ **Lessons Learned from Paper 7**

- Tell what *you* find interesting—and you'll interest your reader, too.
- Know the topic well. That way, you can be choosey about details.

| Paper 8 | **Solar Energy** (Informational, Grade 9) |

In September of 1912, the Italian chemistry professor Giacomo Ciamician proposed an alternative to dependence on coal. He pictured industrial colonies "without smokestacks" where "forests of glass tubes will extend over the plains." Inside these translucent reactors, sunlight would power processes once thought to be the "guarded secrets of the plants." In other words, man would use solar energy to imitate photosynthesis. Ciamician's vision has not quite come to pass—but solar power *is* gaining popularity.

Where Solar Power Comes From
Solar power is derived from the sun's radiation. The amount of energy falling on just .3861 square miles of land (or water) is enough to heat and light a small town. Each second, the sun gives off 13 million times more energy than all the electricity used in the U.S. in one full year.

Unfortunately, despite these striking statistics, it is still remarkably hard to generate a high-energy output from an isolated solar source. One factory built in France in 1970 used giant mirrors to intensify solar radiation, but it was so expensive no other companies would attempt it. So far, the most common and practical use has been in housing. People can collect sufficient solar energy to heat their homes, heat water, and run appliances.

Solar energy is collected by large panels made of black, heat-absorbing material. Inside the panels are pipes through which air or water, heated by the sun, is circulated. *Active solar* uses external mechanical power to move heat from where it is collected

(continued)

to another location where it is stored. An example would be using solar panels to collect energy used to heat a house. Active solar also involves the cost of motors, fans, or other devices needed to move the heat from one spot to another. *Passive solar* uses or stores heat right where it's collected. An example would be a greenhouse or sun room. With passive solar, the only cost is setting up the system, and though this can initially be expensive, the energy itself is free!

Advantages and Disadvantages

The chief advantage of solar power is ready availability. Even in cloudy areas, solar energy can be used, though it does not produce as much energy as in sunnier climates (and it is not practical at all in extreme northern or southern locations). It is also fairly cheap compared to other energy sources, once installed. In addition, it is non-polluting.

On the down side, solar power affects building design. A house, for example, needs a southern exposure, large eaves to support the panels and a strong roof to hold them in place. These things increase building cost. Further, not everyone finds solar panels beautiful.

Even more important, increased use of solar energy could cost jobs. If we drastically cut our use of oil or coal, many people could find themselves out of work. Of course, supporters question how much a thriving economy matters once people can no longer breathe or drink the water.

A New Use—and New Attitudes

A few years ago, gas was cheap, and there was minimal incentive to produce solar or electric cars. Now, things are different. Already the State of California has tightened emission control laws and mandated that a certain percentage of cars be powered by alternative fuels. The receptivity of the country to "going green" suggests that other states may soon follow suit. While slow-moving solar cars have a long way to go to be seen as truly practical, the rising cost of fuel could spur new developments. And sunlight, unlike oil, is not a diminishing resource. Though scientists do predict the sun will one day cease to shine, it's safe to say that is unlikely to happen for a long time.

True enough, solar power is not taking over as scientist Giacomo Ciamician predicted in 1912, but it is gaining fans. People throughout the world see it as a means of becoming independent from foreign, politically volatile energy sources. With increasing reliance on solar, imagine how much energy we could save, and how much pollution we might prevent. "Going green" might mean actually being able to see the green hills now camouflaged by smog.

Sources

Benyus, Janine M. 2002. *Biomimicry: Innovation Inspired by Nature.* New York: HarperCollins.

Bradford, Travis. 2006. *Solar Revolution: The Economic Transformation of the Global Energy Industry.* Cambridge: MIT Press.

The Write Connection

"Solar Energy"

Check out one of this writer's sources—or look up any current newspaper or journal or Internet article on global warming, fossil fuel consumption, solar energy, or the "green" movement. See if you can find two (or more) striking quotations to weave into this piece—without disrupting the writer's organizational flow, of course!

The title is very direct and literal. Should it have more punch? What alternatives might you suggest?

■ **Suggested Scores**

Ideas: 5

Organization: 6

Voice: 6

Word choice: 6

Sentence fluency: 6

Conventions: 6

■ **Lessons Learned from Paper 8**

• Don't be afraid to let authors of your sources in on the discussion.

• When you write as if you want to teach the reader something, you'll probably be successful.

■ **Comments**

When we talk about the "right voice" for an informational piece, this is a good example of what we mean. It's an engaged voice, a confident voice. It reflects both understanding of and curiosity about the topic. The writing is easy to follow and understand, written with a clear intention of making the reader thoroughly familiar and comfortable with the topic. Terms are used with ease and fully explained (*active solar, passive solar*). Skim down the page and notice the numerous ways this writer finds to begin sentences, with openings like *In other words, Each second, Unfortunately, So far, An example* and many others making connections crystal clear. Conventions are particularly strong. The one thing this writer does not do—after the first paragraph, where no page numbers are cited—is to make use of her sources. A strong quotation or two would give the voice (already strong) even more of a boost and further strengthen ideas. Right now, one voice dominates this discussion—the writer's.

Paper 9 **Kill Measure 34—Now!** (Persuasive, Grade 8)

I strongly oppose Ballot Measure 34. No good can come from passing a cruel, unfair law that allows hunters to hunt cougars with dogs or set out bait to attract bears. Hunters can simply sit in a truck enjoying a burger and wait for a bear to sniff out the bait. This is not hunting. There is no sportsmanship in shooting an unsuspecting bear with its head stuck in a barrel.

Similarly, hound hunting is unsporting. Hunters send out dogs with radio collars, then follow them to the place where a cougar is treed and kill it. Before the hunters can catch up, the cougar usually defends itself against the dogs, resulting in death or injury to many hunting dogs—as well as inhumane wounds to the cougar.

Proponents of the measure argue that the bear and cougar populations are threatening to campers and ranchers. Records of attacks do not support the former. Both bears and cougars tend to avoid people unless threatened. Cougar attacks on humans are rare, and

(continued)

sport hunting does not reduce the risk because most of it occurs far from populated areas. Furthermore, trophy hunters only want large, adult lions—the ones least likely to cause trouble. Such lions easily bring down deer or other small game, and are not tempted to seek food from backpackers or by raiding campsites.

Cougars occasionally kill livestock—but it is very rare. There are documented cases of cougars killing llamas, but it is so infrequent most llama ranchers have never experienced it. Such killings are usually made by juvenile cougars seeking territory, and as noted already, these cougars are not the target of trophy hungers. Furthermore, ranchers lose far more money from prey species, such as rabbits, elk, and deer than from cougars. Ironically, cougars help control these crop-devouring species, thereby doing ranchers more good than harm.

There is more at stake than preventing cruelty, though. If Measure 34 passes, it will hand all wildlife management authority over to the State Fish and Wildlife Commission. This group will then have all the power to say when, where, and how everyone can hunt, fish, and trap. It is never wise to put ALL power in the hands of one group, no matter who they are. This measure was already voted down once—and should not even be up for reconsideration. It is opposed by the Humane Society, local Audubon chapters, and responsible ranchers—even sportsmen. The current law allows the hunting of bear and cougars using fair methods—and the taking of any rogue individuals that pose a specific threat. We do not need to "fix" a law that is serving us well. The only thing that should be killed—and now—is Measure 34.

■ Suggested Scores

Ideas: **4/5**

Organization: **6**

Voice: **6**

Word choice: **6**

Sentence fluency: **6**

Conventions: **6**

■ Lessons Learned from Paper 9

- No matter how strong your argument, you need data and opinions of experts to back it up.
- Addressing the perspective of the other side makes any argument stronger.

■ Comments

This writer does *almost* everything right. The argument is clear—and stated right up front. She returns to it in the end and restates it with even more force. Her reasons are convincing, and she addresses counterarguments head-on and well. Word choice is clear and nonrepetitive—even striking at moments:

The Write Connection

"Kill Measure 34— Now!"

Without worrying about Measure 34 specifically, do a bit of research on the issue of hunting predatory animals such as bear and cougars. Then, within your classroom, do a little role playing in presenting your arguments. Perhaps one student could take the position of a trophy hunter, one a local rancher, one a representative of the State Fish and Wildlife Commission, and one a person who likes to camp. Does exploring an issue from several perspectives help you arrive at the "best" policy?

sniff out the bait, head stuck in a barrel, not tempted to seek food from backpackers, help control these crop-devouring species. Fluency and conventions are very strong. What the writer does not do is to cite statistics from the Fish and Wildlife Commission or Humane Society, nor does she interview experts about this issue. Some opposing quotations—with data to help us sort out the truth—would be helpful and make her case stronger. Because the writer says things so well, it is easy to agree with her. But in the end, strong rhetoric is not enough without backup.

Paper 10   **The Violin** (Informational, Grade 9)

vi · o · lin [vahy-*uh*-lin] noun

If you're reading this, you probably want to: a) know how to play the violin, b) learn more about the violin, c) grade this paper (most likely a C). First the bare basic question, "What is a violin?" Excellent question. A violin is a stringed instrument developed more than 600 years ago. The design has barely changed within that time period. The instrument has a body which vibrates when you play the strings, four strings, a bow to play the instrument, and a fingerboard to put your fingers down to play the notes.

Unlike many instruments, such as a kazoo, the violin requires great skill to play well. Many people have to practice for years before they sound like they're actually playing an instrument instead of a dying elephant. If you put your finger on the string a half a millimeter off, the note you play will sound different, thus making the violin a very difficult instrument. Many of the professionals you see on TV and hear on the radio probably had to have played the instrument for years. Many people started playing the violin at age 3 or 4 and have taken lessons for 10+ years.

"But wait!" you must be thinking, "I'm not 3 or 4; I'm practically having a mid-life crisis!" That's OK. You won't be one of the greats, but with enough determination and practice, you can learn to play this majestic instrument.

Now comes the question you've been wanting to ask: "Enough talk. How do I play this thing?" OK, hold on. First, you need the correct size. There are many sizes in the violin family, starting with the largest, the bass (pronounced *base*) violin. This thing is huge, usually taller than the person playing it. Next, a notch smaller, comes the cello (pronounced *chello*). It's just a small base. The next rung down on the ladder is the viola (*vee ola*). The best description for it is a violin on steroids. Last but not least (well, actually, the violin is the smallest so it *is* the least), the violin!

Now I'll tell you how to play it: First, hold the neck of the violin, with your palm up, facing you. Rest the bottom of the violin on your left clavicle (above your shoulder). It should have a shoulder rest on the bottom; if not, you risk damage to your shoulder. Next, hold the bow with your right hand. Make sure your hand is relaxed, but don't relax so much you drop the bow. Finally, rest the bowstring on the strings of the violin. Now you're ready to play.

■ **Suggested Scores**

Ideas: 4

Organization: 4

Voice: 5

Word choice: 5

Sentence fluency: 5

Conventions: 6

■ **Lessons Learned from Paper 10**

• Humor perks up an informational piece.

• Don't just abandon your reader, bow in hand.

■ **Comments**

I confess I like this paper—a lot. Though the first paragraph gets us off to a fairly slow start (I keep getting the feeling that the writer is writing this while lying on the couch), the understated humor is delightful—and spot on. People who do not play the violin well *do* make it sound like a dying elephant (an original and memorable analogy). In addition, I believe this writer actually plays the violin, and so he seems to be an expert on the topic. The problem is one of balance. So much time is spent on the sizes, types, and appearances of various members of the violin family that we barely get round to the playing (reason "a" for reading the paper). Further, I'm finally standing here, bow resting on the strings, when the paper ends abruptly—what *now?* Lesson 2? At all events, we need some sort of wrap-up or promise that the conversation will be resumed next time. Sentences are readable, but could use a bit more variety.

The Write Connection

"The Violin"

In informational writing, an informational base is everything. So if you're not an expert on the violin, revising this piece could prove difficult. You can still help *design* a good revision, though, by indicating places where the current piece could be condensed—and raising questions you wish the writer would answer. Do that. Put brackets around any section where you feel the writer is spending too much time on things you know or do not need to know. Then, put sticky notes along the right-hand side, writing a question you still have on each one. Next time you write an informational piece on your own topic, use this same strategy.

Paper 11   **Libraries** (Informational, Grade 9)

Libraries are nothing new. They have been around almost since there was writing. Libraries did not start out like what we think of libraries now. The earliest libraries did not have codex's (books), but they started with clay tablets in the regions where clay was abundant, then to scrolls, and finally to the books we think of today. Libraries were repositories of information and they are now, too.

In early times, a majority of libraries were connected to temples or monasteries, or were a "royal" library mostly for the use of the king or government officials. Most libraries were run by slaves with a librarian in charge of everything. Being able to check out anything from libraries was mostly nonexistent and a lot were not open to the public. Some that were open to the public, reading books that were looked at had to have a government official supervise from the opening to the closing of the book.

(continued)

One of the earliest known libraries was the library in Sumeria. This library had clay tablets instead of books. A good thing about using clay was that even though fires were a big problem then, the heat would only make the tablets stronger. The library was the king's royal library and mostly kept inventories, temple records, and ownership records, and poems.

One of the most famous library in antiquity is the Library of Alexandria. It was started by Ptolemy Soter when he came to power. He wanted to create the greatest of all libraries with every book in the world. Some of the collecting techniques to achieve that goal was slightly unethical. The king ordered that any ship that docked in Alexandria was to be searched and any scrolls found were to be confiscated. Then the scrolls were copied and since they were copied by hand, the originals were kept and the copies given to the owner. They asked Athens for their original copies of poems by Sophocles and other poets. Alexandria paid 15 talents as a security for their return. They copied them and kept the originals and returned the copies, forfeiting the money.

It has been estimated that the library eventually had a collection of over 500,000 scrolls. The library was eventually destroyed but scholars are unsure why.

Libraries are huge repositories of information and should be treasured forever. They keep history and help make sure we don't lose it.

■ Suggested Scores

Ideas: **4**

Organization: **4**

Voice: **4**

Word choice: **5**

Sentence fluency: **4**

Conventions: **6**

■ Lessons Learned from Paper 11

- Don't end on a generality.
- Keep the emphasis on contrast strong—especially when that is the backbone of your organizational structure.

■ Comments

Here's an intriguing topic—and the writer makes some interesting points: Early libraries were run by slaves and existed mostly for the convenience of royalty, early books were printed on clay, and so were impervious to fire, and

The Write Connection

"Libraries"

See if your school or public library has a copy of a book many librarians love: *The Most Beautiful Libraries in the World* by Guillaume deLaubier and Jacques Bosser (2003). Spend an hour with this book, making a few notes. Then, write a review of the paper "Libraries," noting the important points the author makes—and citing some important information he might have included, but didn't.

many early manuscripts were stolen (a practice that continues to this day). Contrast provides the underlying organizational structure for this piece, but the writer does not take advantage of it as much as he might—by emphasizing the differences. For example, clearly clay provided the benefit of fire protection, yet it must have slowed the copying of manuscripts almost insufferably and made storage quite a problem. A very interesting question, about destruction of the library at Alexandria, is raised but dropped. There must be at least speculation about the cause and reason for the destruction—angry manuscript authors, perhaps! A few sentences need work; though nothing slows the reader significantly, there are some bumps to smooth out: e.g., *Some that were open to the public, reading books that were looked at had to have a government official supervise from the opening to the closing of the book.* With so much intriguing information at his fingertips, it is disappointing when this writer takes the easy way out and ends with a generality: Let's treasure our libraries. Sure. But it might be interesting to know how many volumes are housed in today's libraries, and how many are stored physically versus electronically. After all, libraries are still in flux!

Paper 12	**Expanded Definition: Resonance**
	(Technical/Informational, College Freshman)

Resonance is the vibration of an object caused by a relatively small periodic **stimulus** of the same or nearly the same period as the **natural vibration** of that object. To understand the idea of resonance better, let's first look at some of the terms used in the definition above and then explore some examples to make the idea concrete in your mind.

The first term that needs defining is **stimulus.** A stimulus is something that acts on an object to create a response. For example, a stimulus may be wind, sound, friction, or many other things.

When speaking of **natural vibration,** we must explore an object at its molecular level. All substances are made up of millions of atoms, all either moving around freely, as in a liquid or gas, or attempting to move around, as in a solid. In a solid object, the atoms are packed tightly together, causing the object to hold its particular shape. Because the atoms are packed together, they cannot move freely. This causes the atoms to vibrate against one another, creating that object's natural vibration.

To better understand the definition of **resonance,** the first example we will be exploring is that of an old party favorite, the whining wineglass. When a person has a wineglass and rubs the rim with his/her wine-dipped fingers, a sound can be produced. Finding the glass's natural vibration creates that sound. When you first start rubbing your fingers against the glass rim, no sound is created. Why? Well, the natural vibration wasn't found. Continue to

(continued)

The Write Connection

"Defining Resonance"

Try three things. First, look up the term *resonance* on the Internet or in any physics book or encyclopedia. See if you can add anything to clarify the definition. Second, come up with an additional example (other than the bridge or wineglass) to help make the definition clear. Third, try revising the piece by beginning with the last paragraph. Of course—you will then need to write a new conclusion!

rub the rim and eventually the natural vibration can be found. Once the natural vibration is found and matched, the glass experiences **resonance,** producing the whining sound.

Another example is the Tacoma Narrows Bridge, also referred to as "Galloping Gertie." A suspension bridge has a natural vibration to it, the same as any other solid object. For this reason, it will resonate, given the right conditions. The Tacoma Narrows Bridge was faced with large amounts of wind from the Puget Sound area. This wind blew at the bridge and created a resonance. Much like the wineglass in the example above, the bridge vibrated and twisted because of its flexible structure and lightweight design.

Using what we know about resonance, many new developments have been made to prevent it. Though it is an interesting topic, it can be devastating for the structures that engineers create.

Works Cited

Hill, John W. and Ralph H. Petrucci. *General Chemistry.* Upper Saddle River, NJ: Prentice Hall, 1996.

"Resonance." *Encyclopedia Americana.* 1996 ed.

"Resonance." *Webster's Dictionary.* 1992 ed.

■ **Suggested Scores**

Ideas: 4

Organization: 5

Voice: 6

Word choice: 6

Sentence fluency: 6

Conventions: 6

As you search for the right voice in doing your revision, look for a balance between flat, wooden prose, which sounds as if it were manufactured by a machine, and forced, flowery prose, which distracts the reader from what's most important: what you're trying to say.

—Bruce Ballenger

The Curious Researcher, Fourth Edition, 2004, p. 233

■ **Comments**

This piece is useful in illustrating what technical writing should be: a way of making concepts clear. Perhaps the act of writing this definition helped clarify the concepts of natural vibration and resonance in the writer's mind, too. The text is reader-friendly, with crisp, short sentences, and useful examples a reader can picture and understand. We do wish the writer had defined the term *period* ("nearly the same period as the *natural vibration*"). Also, it is not totally clear how resonance (which seems related to sound, but clearly means more) damaged the Tacoma Narrows Bridge; we need a fuller picture. The voice is professional, appropriately engaging, and controlled—just right for a technical piece, and hence the high scores, even though the writer does not crack jokes or appeal to our feelings. This is a good example of "thinking

'I,'" as William Zinsser (2001) reminds us to do. What's missing is a reason to *care* about resonance. We get to it in the final paragraph, with the comment that it is "devastating" for some structures. Perhaps this would be a place to begin.

■ Lessons Learned from Paper 12

- A dignified, professional tone can still be reader-friendly.
- Sometimes the concluding paragraph provides a good place to begin.

Paper 13   **Pablo Picasso** (Informational, Grade 7)

He was a short man of five foot two inches with dark, piercing eyes, and a bald head. Picasso is his name. Being born in 1881 in Spain, he loved to watch bull fights once he dubbed himself, "The Eye of the Bull."

Struggling with dyslexia he was a poor student that hated authority, he was a leader and hated to be pushed around. When he was 18 he moved to Paris because he thought he could create better art there.

Early in his life he went through two different periods where he produced different kinds of art, the Blue Period was 1901–1904. During that time he created sad pictures using cool colors. One of the pictures created in this period is *The Old Guitarist.* The other period of time was called the Rose Period. That was from 1904–1906, during that short period of time he produced warmer pictures with pinks, reds, and yellows. Those influenced his art work in many ways.

Inspired by many thing like lovely women and naked people. What inspired his famous cubism was sculptures done by Iberian and African people. Cubism is where he uses squares and geometric figures to create a familiar object in his art work.

Women were attracted to him including a ballerina, and other artists. Having four children and being married twice. Entertaining his children was a priority he would, do magic tricks, throw parties were everything is chocolate. As time went on he focused more on his art then his children.

Mr. Picasso taught himself, and wasn't really involved with major art movements. When his flat was robbed the thieves took every thing but his paintings, I bet they sure wish they did though. Pablo Picasso died in 1973 he had created hundreds of pieces of art, he had become quite famous. His estate was valued at $100,000,000 when he passed away. I don't know about you but I think that's a lot of painting to do.

Now he has died, but his soul remains; in his artwork.

The Write Connection

"Picasso"

Unexpected shifts in tense, interruptive comments from the writer, and unintentional fragments make this a choppy ride. Revise the piece just for sentence fluency. Begin by reading it aloud, underlining any sentence, fragment, or phrase that sounds awkward. Revise for fluency, reading aloud as you go, and eliminating the interruptions. How musical can you make it?

■ **Suggested Scores**

Ideas: **4**

Organization: **4**

Voice: **4**

Word choice: **4**

Sentence fluency: **2**

Conventions: **4**

■ **Comments**

This piece has great potential. We learn that Picasso was dyslexic, influenced by African geometric sculpture, had four children and two wives, knew magic, loved chocolate, and was robbed—though not of his paintings. How ironic! In short, there is enough information here to create a very full, satisfying piece. There are two problems. First, the voice is erratic. At times, it is forceful: *"He was a leader and hated to be pushed around."* Then it retreats to encyclopedic mode: *"Those influenced his art work in many ways."* Some sentences are run-ons; some are incomplete: *"Inspired by many thing like lovely women and naked people."* We can put most of the pieces into the puzzle, but *we* shouldn't have to. Be careful not to score down for this skeletal sentence problem in *both* fluency and conventions. I put this one under fluency. The ending would work better if we had more sense of Picasso's soul throughout the piece. The next-to-last line feels interruptive. Still—it's just a draft away: Build on the voice, smooth out the sentences, cite your sources.

■ **Lessons Learned from Paper 13**

- Incomplete sentences and run-ons make your reader work too hard.
- Strong details provide the framework for a potentially strong paper.
- Interrupting your piece with a personal comment may diminish voice.

Paper 14 **Desert Tortoise** (Informational, Grade 7)

Guess what? I am doing a report on the Desert Tortoise and the Desert Tortoise also known as *Gopherus agassizii*. The tortoise is classified into the kingdom animalia, and its phylum is chordata, because it has a backbone. Its class is reptilia because, of course, it's a reptile. The desert tortoise is placed in the order testudines, and its family is testudinidae. A Desert Tortoises genus is gopherus, because it is a burrowing organism. Last, but not least, a Desert Tortoises species is agassizii.

The Desert Tortoises scientific name is *Gopherus agassizii*. Pretty strange, huh? Well this very weird scientific name does have a meaning. The meaning for this scientific name is burrowing, terrestrial tortoise. This means a turtle the burrows and does not swim, and basically stays on land. In this case, the desert.

All of the Desert Tortoises relatives are turtles and tortoises. Some examples of those would be the Berlandier Tortoise, the Gopher Tortoise, and the Gopherus flavomarginatus.

(continued)

Some people in the world probably don't even know what a Desert Tortoise looks like, well I am about to tell you. The upper shell, also know as the carapace, ranges in length from 15 to 36 centimeters, and its color varies from dull brown to a dull yellow. Males are mainly bigger than females. An adult male averages around 20 kilograms in weight, and an adult female averages 13 kilograms. The desert tortoise has two shells, an upper shell, and a lower shell. The upper shell is called the carapace, as I have already noted, and the lower shell is called the plastron. They also have retractable legs and a retractable head. These are retractable because if an enemy or predator came near, the tortoise would pull in its arms and legs, so the predator wouldn't get them, since the tortoise isn't fast enough to run away. The head of a Desert Tortoise is scaly, and the body has thick skin. Desert tortoises also have extremely long nails, which are used in digging through the desert and to find a shelter.

The tortoise ranges from the Mojave and Sonoran deserts of southeastern California, southern Nevada, south through Arizona into Mexico. Desert tortoises inhabit semi-grasslands, desert washes with gravel, canyon bottoms and rocky hillsides, all below 3,530 ft. The tortoises north and west of the Colorado River live in valleys and on alluvial fans. In the Sonoran Desert of Arizona, however, the tortoises happen to live on steep, rocky type hillside slopes in the Palo Verde and Saguaro Cactus communities. As you can tell, the tortoise has only one biome and that is the Desert biome.

One really special adaptation that the Desert Tortoise has is the fact that they can live without water for many years. They do that by ingesting most of their water from plants and then storing it in their bladders. Pretty cool, huh?

The Desert Tortoise is primarily herbivorous, surviving on low-growing plants, such as grasses, herbs, and a wide variety of desert plants. But their primary nutritional source is fresh green grass and spring wildflowers.

Where does the tortoise fit in the food chain, you may ask? Well the Desert Tortoise is the primary consumer because they eat grass, wildflowers, and cacti. All those things are producers, so the tortoise would be the primary consumer. The ravens are the secondary consumer because they are the tortoises' main predator.

The female Desert Tortoises lay their eggs around May, June, and July. A mature female lays 4 to 8 white, hard-shelled eggs in a clutch and produces 2, sometimes 3 clutches in a season. Only a few hatchlings out of 100 actually make it to adulthood. One really interesting fact is that all males are born at temperatures, 79–87 degrees F; females are born at warmer temperatures such as 88–91 degrees F. Pretty interesting, huh? The nests are often dug near the tortoises burrow, but sometimes the nests are dug farther away from the burrow, usually under a shrub. After laying, the female leaves the nest and the soil temperatures support growth of the embryos.

Did you know that the Desert Tortoise is able to live where ground temperatures may exceed 140 degrees F. Also, 95% of the tortoises' life is spent in under ground burrows. How boring is that? Desert tortoise populations have declined 90% since the 1980s, all because people have kept them as pets, or used them for target practice. But the ravens haven't helped because they have caused more than 50% of juvenile desert tortoise deaths, because they have eaten a ton of Desert Tortoises, in some areas of the Mojave Desert. Because of all that the Desert Tortoise is now endangered and it is unlawful to touch, harm, harass, or collect a wild Desert Tortoise.

The Write Connection

"Desert Tortoise"

With so many interesting points to make, why open with the classification data? Decide where else in the essay this information could go, and write a new lead to hook the reader.

Do some ruthless revision. Go through the essay, reading aloud, and cutting anything that is not needed (such as the interruptive questions). See how many sentences you can combine to shorten the document. Try to cut it by one-third or more.

If possible, visit an exhibit where you can see a desert tortoise for yourself. Weave one important thing you learn into this essay.

■ **Suggested Scores**

Ideas: 4

Organization: 4

Voice: 5

Word choice: 5

Fluency: 4

Conventions: 4

■ **Comments**

This writer seems to have done good research. She presents numerous intriguing details but also leaves questions unanswered. For example, if a mature desert tortoise produces, at most, 24 eggs in a season and only a few out of 100 make it to maturity, why is this poor creature not extinct? Why are they such favorites as pets? What's the penalty if you are caught taking one for your garden? The information is well organized, although a little predictable: how they look, where they live, what they eat, etc. What's missing organizationally are a strong lead and conclusion and a way of linking sections together. The writer projects a genuine sense of engagement and curiosity; this is a plus. She does not need the "Can you believe it?" questions that intrude periodically and clash with her more authoritative voice. The whole could be condensed significantly; *many* sentences could be combined. Conventions need another look (inconsistency in capitals; Fahrenheit needs to be spelled out), although nothing blocks readability. A source list would help.

■ **Lessons Learned from Paper 14**

- Open with an image or startling discovery; save the technical information for after the reader is hooked.

- *Think* "Pretty strange, huh?" to give the piece voice; then you do not need to actually ask the question.

Paper 15   **The Chameleon** (Informational, Grade 4)

Creeping through the soggy jungles of Madagascar, there's a colorful sight. He's curling his tail into a spiral, lying relaxed on his branch and bathing in the sliver of sunlight seeping through a crack in the thick mass of vines forming the canopy overhead. It's the most amazing creature, a chameleon. It would be a sad day for everyone if this unique lizard went away.

These fascinating reptiles are all different, just like snowflakes! You know how no snowflake is exactly the same as another. Well, chameleon's scale patterns are the same way. There can be many different facial features too. Some chameleons have horns on their face, bumps, or big noses. All chameleons have a casque, which

(continued)

is a large, backwards-facing arch on the back of their neck. Like us, chameleons have five fingers on each hand, however, they are arranged in a very different way. Chameleon's fingers are in two clumps, one clump with two fingers and one with three, this makes it easier for the creature to grasp branches. Surprisingly, chameleons are the only lizard with this feature. A chameleon's size can range anywhere from two centimeters to three feet long! This gives them a large range of weight, too. No matter how large or small, there are about 134 subspecies of chameleons, and all of them are extremely one-of-a-kind.

As the sunlight falls on a branch, a predator approaches. If the chameleon's changing color fails to save it, there is not much more the creature can do. A Green Winged Macaw comes closer, but swoops right past. The lizard was not blending in, but its casque scared the Macaw away. Once the chameleon is calm again, it sticks it's tongue out so fast it's hard to see! The tongue zaps a fly buzzing by, extending to two body lengths in one-sixteenth of a second. That's faster than any frog!

Extremely sadly, the chameleon's hearing is incredibly poor. But their vision is the best of all living things, they're the only animal in the world that can see in color, 3-D, and in any direction. Another reason their eyesight is superior is they have three eyes. Only two are visible because of a thin layer of skin protecting the third eye, but it is located in the center of the forehead, and though it is covered up, it can still sense heat and light like a regular eye. Chameleons can sometimes give birth to living babies (and sometimes they lay eggs), so it is hard to list them as reptiles. Other incredible facts are that they store fat in their heads for times when they are lean and save the morning dew in their casque for when they are thirsty.

These creatures are extremely inimitable, but they are most famous for their ability to change color. Surprisingly, they do not do this to blend in. Usually, they change color to communicate with each other or show their mood, like a mood ring. The change takes less than a minute and is caused by melanin rising through layers of skin cells.

To wrap it up, chameleons are amazing for countless reasons. Chameleons are all different in some way, they're a living rainbow, and they are exceedingly exclusive.

■ **Suggested Scores**

Ideas: **6**

Organization: **5**

Voice: **6**

Word choice: **5**

Sentence fluency: **4**

Conventions: **5**

The Write Connection

"The Chameleon"

To really appreciate how much information this writer shares, highlight each new or interesting detail. Count your total.

Second, see if you can write a definition of the word *casque* in your own words without looking back at the paper. If you can, the writer has done her job.

Need for revision is very small. Read sentence two in the first paragraph aloud. See if you can condense this sentence slightly (or make two sentences) so that the reader does not have so many images coming at him or her at one time!

Now read sentences seven and eight in paragraph two. Each offers an opportunity to use a semicolon. Can you see where?

Lessons Learned from Paper 15

- Dramatic scenarios provide mental relief from pure statistics.
- Save a surprise bit of information for the end, so you won't have to rely on the trusty old "To wrap it up."
- Even when the instructor provides the information, it's good to cite a source (or sources). Teachers can help with this!

■ Comments

What a refreshing piece of writing this is. We learn so many delightful facts: Chameleons have different (not always attractive) facial features, have fingers much like our own, can extend their tongues for an incredible two body lengths, and have a third eye (!). They can give birth to live babies and change color not to hide from predators—as most of us probably thought—but to reflect their changing mood (much as humans do, to a lesser degree). The writer skillfully alternates drama and fact, allowing us to shift gears and also to picture quite clearly what life is like in the rainforests of Madagascar. The problems are small and easily remedied. The phrases "extremely one-of-a-kind," "extremely inimitable," and "exceedingly exclusive" do not quite work. There can be degrees of exclusivity, but the writer seems to mean "unique" here, and there are no degrees of uniqueness. Similarly, the creature is either one-of-a-kind and inimitable—or not. Excellent conventions, but no sources cited. Appealing voice. A stellar effort from a fourth grade writer.

Paper 16   **The Giant Panda**
(Informational, Grade 4)

A giant panda bends and crushes bamboo with powerful jaws and massive paws, high in the mountains of southern China. A sight rarely seen. There are less than one thousand of these fascinating creatures left in the wild. It is up to us to save them.

Pandas are black, white, and loved all over. Their unique black and white coat helps them blend in with their rocky and snowy background. Newborns are pink and hairless. Pandas live in cold climates so their fur can be two or more inches long in places. The panda's diet consists of vines, tufted grasses, honey, bamboo, green corn, flowers, fish, and small mammals when they can get them. Pandas live from twenty to thirty years in captivity, but are so rarely seen in the wild that scientists are not sure how long they live in the wild. Pandas have the unique features of broad, flat molars and an enlarged wrist bone, both used for crushing bamboo. Females weigh under

(continued)

200 pounds, males about 250. Newborns weigh only 200 grams (one nine-hundredth the weight of the mother) and do not open their eyes until 40 to 60 days after birth. They walk at three or four months, and begin to eat bamboo at about six months. Cubs stay with their mothers for up to three years, but do not mature until they are six to eight years old. Pandas are walking balls of love.

The grown panda doesn't have many enemies. But the cubs do! Chinese leopards and wild dogs may try to eat the cubs. But the mother is always close by! When she or her cubs are threatened, she becomes very aggressive. Pandas use their strong jaws when fighting. Scientists think a panda could snap bones as easily as bamboo, though no one has seen this happen. Pandas have little fear of humans, and one scientist claims he got within one hundred feet of a panda. When a grown panda is threatened, it may swim or climb trees to escape predators. The growing human population is the panda's biggest enemy. As the Chinese population grows, they cut down forests to make way for cities.

If you had to use just one word to describe a panda's homeland, it would be *rugged*. They live in the mountains of southern China about 3,000 meters from sea level. It is freezing in the mountain forests. Snow is on the ground from October to May. When pandas are cubs, they live in snug, protective dens. They share the land with lynxes, tiger cats, Asian wild dogs, deer, and many types of birds. Pandas once lived in the lowlands, but growing human population drove them up the mountainside.

Because their back paws are much weaker than their front paws, pandas are slow moving. It is said they play in the snow like children. A scientist said he once found a place where a panda had sledded downhill in its belly, then climbed back up to do it again! Pandas do not hibernate. They cannot store enough energy from bamboo, so they must go to lower elevations in winter for food. Pandas have twins or triplets occasionally, but usually only one survives. Though the panda has a carnivorous digestive system, it cannot catch much meat. So, to stay healthy, it eats 20 to 40 pounds of bamboo a day! Did you know a newborn panda can fit in a human hand? When scientists catch a panda, they determine its age by checking the wear on its teeth. Bamboo is tough and wears down a panda's teeth over the years. Scientists think pandas were once carnivores but changed almost completely to herbivores for an unknown reason.

Pandas are at the top of most people's favorite animals list. But this species is dying out quickly. We caused it. We must fix it.

The Write Connection

"The Giant Panda"

See if you can identify four or five major subtopics within this piece—list and number them. Then, go through the piece and put a number by each sentence to indicate the subtopic with which it fits. Do you find many sentences or details that should be moved?

You may wish to try this same strategy with a sample of your own writing.

■ Suggested Scores

Ideas: 6

Organization: 4

Voice: 6

Word choice: 6

Sentence fluency: 6

Conventions: 5

■ Lessons Learned from Paper 16

- Keep related ideas together.
- Think of the final impression you wish to leave your reader with—end there.
- Cite your sources—even if you need to check with the teacher for help on this.

■ Comments

Like the "Chameleons" writer, this writer shares an abundance of helpful, interesting information: Pandas have large wrist bones and flat molars from crushing and eating bamboo, their jaws are powerful—yet they're only aggressive in protecting their young, they are tiny enough to fit in a human hand at birth, and so on. The image of the panda sliding in snow for fun is delightful—and indeed makes us want to preserve these special creatures. There are really only two problems. One is with organization. Details on a single topic—such as the panda's diet or newborn cubs—need to be in one place. Otherwise, the reader has a continual déjà vu feeling. Second, this writer knows so much about pandas, we have to assume she consulted sources. These need to be cited. Otherwise, though, conventions are strong. Word choice is excellent. "Black, white, and loved all over"—that's terrific.

Chapter 11   In a Nutshell

- The six-trait model exists to serve you as a teacher—and to serve your students. You should feel free to modify or adapt it as necessary.

- The traits look a little different in research-based writing. Hence the need for an informational scoring guide.

- The informational scoring guide presented in this chapter may be used to assess a wide variety of writing, including informational, persuasive, business writing, and technical writing—in short, any writing involving research or intended for a business or professional audience.

Study Group | Interactive Questions and Activities

1. **Activity and Discussion.** Carefully review the informational writing guides included in Chapter 11. Are there any features of informational or research-based writing that are part of your instruction that we did not include on these writing guides? If so, consider revising our version, making each guide just what you need it to be.

2. **Activity and Discussion.** If you teach research-based writing and your students routinely produce writing of five pages or more in length, copy one paper for your group to review and assess. If you wish, modify the assessment by focusing on those traits you feel are most important to the assignment at hand, keeping in mind that it is not necessary to assess every trait every time.

3. **Activity and Discussion.** What handbooks do you use as a reference in deciding how sources will be cited or about other issues relating to conventions? Bring in a copy to share with your group and discuss why you believe this handbook is a particularly good resource.

4. **Activity and Discussion.** Consider adapting or extending one of the recommended Write Connections lessons from this chapter (presented in sidebars for each paper). Share your version with your study group.

5. **Activity and Discussion.** With your group, develop a checklist for business or technical writing. See the Appendix for models. That appendix includes checklists for narrative, informational, and persuasive writing as well as literary analysis.

Reflections on Writing

I write because I love to write. The words flow from my hand as if I am in the story, as if I am the writing.... I write because I am addicted to writing. I get one idea flowing out of my head and my imagination goes crazy like a maniac in a lab.... I write because I feel free, like an eagle stretching its wings across the canyon.

—**Becca Zoller**, student writer

I don't stress about essays for school anymore. I use the same rhythm, the same words, the same wit as my stories. It's no fun quoting Sparknotes.

—**Simona Patange**, student writer

CHAPTER 12

Exploring the World of Beginning Writers

Children can write sooner than we ever dreamed possible. Most children come to school knowing a handful of letters, and with these they can write labels and calendars, letters and stories, poems and songs. They will learn to write by writing and by living with a sense of "I am one who writes."

—Lucy McCormick Calkins
The Art of Teaching Writing, 1994, p. 83

You do not need to be writing fluent sentences yourself to know what fluency is. Your ears will tell you. You do not need to write stories filled with voice to know voice when you hear it. The smile on your face, the tears in your eyes, or the chill up your back will tell you.

—Vicki Spandel
Creating Young Writers, 2004, p. 7

At the primary level, writing is wondrous and magical. It comes in many forms: sketches, scribbles, dictated stories, recordings, word play, "tadpole people" (mostly head, tiny arms and legs), pictographs—and conventional text as well. Sometimes text goes left to right on the page as we have been conditioned to expect, but primary writers, not yet bound by convention, find their own inventive ways to fill the page: right to left, bottom to top, around in a spiral—or clean off the page and on to adventure.

The writing of the very young reflects both their creative individuality and an uncanny ability to observe, recall, and use the conventions from the print that fills their world. At this age, there are no "errors" in the true sense, any more than beginning walkers make errors in foot placement. Rather, there are hundreds, thousands, of experiments by beginning writers finding their own paths to learning.

If you work with challenged writers . . .

. . . then *everything* in this chapter is for you, too. Many of the strategies that are helpful to primary writers also give struggling writers a safe path in. Students who find writing difficult, who write just a few lines, or who lack confidence in their skills can benefit greatly from an approach that emphasizes the positive and breaks writing into small bites.

Take time to look over the primary continuums, shown in Figure 12.9. You will see that they are not only positive, but designed to include many of the skills beginning writers routinely demonstrate that do not appear on rubrics written for a higher level of skill. What this means—for a beginning writer of *any age*—is a chance to experience success. And that, in and of itself, is the single most important step anyone can take toward becoming a writer.

If you would like more ideas for teaching beginning writers at primary or any level, please have a look at *Creating Young Writers* (Spandel, 2008). It is filled with lesson ideas, student samples K–3, book recommendations, checklists, and much more that will help you guide your writers to success.

Many times children don't realize they can write. An effective writing teacher leads kids to an understanding of the four structures needed for early-childhood writing. . . . Are dictation, scribbling, drawing, and temporary spelling necessary to early writing development? Yes.

—Bea Johnson
Never Too Early to Write,
1999, p. 42

Teaching Ourselves What to Look For

We know that primary writing looks very different from that of older writers. But like impatient parents imagining our children at that first book signing, we watch for paragraphs to emerge, for the first use of quotation marks, for complete sentences and correct spelling. These things excite us and make us feel successful as teachers. We forget sometimes that there is much to get excited over long before these milestones of sophisticated writing ever appear.

Consider the very early piece of writing shown in Paper 1 in picture form by four-year-old Nikki. What we see here may not be conventional writing, but it is remarkably expressive. Notice the look on the face of the bat: humorous, mischievous—that's *voice*. How many writer-artists of this age have noticed that spiders have eight legs and multiple eyes? Notice the toes of the bat, too, and the hollow ears. This is a young writer-artist who takes more than a passing glance at the world around her. As a result, her work is brimming with detail—that's *ideas*.

Another sample of writing—by a slightly older writer, Mike—is shown in Paper 2. This piece is significant because it shows that wonderful moment of stand-alone writer-to-reader communication. We can say, "Mike—I read this without help, and it made perfect sense to me. You are an independent writer." Notice that Mike has created a complete sentence: "Mom, remind me to read my book." He signs his important message "Dear Mike" because when Mom writes to him, that's how she begins, so he now thinks of "Dear Mike" as his complete name.

Consider conventions in this piece, too. Remember for a moment that all conventions, even the simplest and most taken-for-granted things, must be learned. What do you see? Left-to-right orientation on the page and the beginning of spaces between words. Even a period at the end that seems to say, "Stop. This sentence is finished." These things seem so basic, but they are not automatic, nor are they necessarily simple to learn. This writer is also beginning to distinguish between capital and lowercase letters, although he does not yet use them correctly. Remember, though, discovery is worthy of celebration in its own right. Correct placement is a more sophisticated skill.

Paper 1 | **Bat and Spider, by Nikki, Age 4**

Paper 2 | **Mike's Note**

MOM REMiDMe+iReD MiBUk.

DiR Mike

Helping Writers See Their Strengths

By using the language of the traits, we help our young writers see what is strong within their work so that they can build on those strengths. First, we must teach *ourselves* to see what each writer is doing correctly across all dimensions of writing—not the gaps, not what's missing, but what is *there*.

Gentle, gradual encouragement is among the most effective of all teaching strategies. We have more or less abandoned this approach in much of our formal instruction, but most of us, if we think about it, instinctively know the

> Stressing neatness instead of content is an ever-present danger. Many of us were carefully taught the opposite during our school days. But especially in early childhood, all attempts at writing should be celebrated rather than corrected!
>
> —Bea Johnson
> *Never Too Early to Write,*
> 1999, p. 33

It's been a good thing that babies don't understand the concept of "clumsiness" or else they'd never learn to walk.

—Alan Ziegler
The Writing Workshop,
1981, p. 37

power of a teacher who believes absolutely in our capability. Picture a father cheering on his 11-month-old daughter as she learns to walk. "That's it! Come on! One more step. You can do it! Yes! Good! Move your feet—that's it. Come on—I'll catch you. You're doing it! You're *walking!*" We need this image in our heads as we teach writing. We need to notice the little things (not just the big milestones) and then we will see that our young writers are often doing much more than they get credit for.

The father in our scenario knows that correctness is a goal for later; exploration is the right goal for now. How surprised we would be to hear him say, "*No*, Martha, not *toe* first—*heel* first, remember? Do it the way I showed you. No, I really can't call that walking, not *real* walking. It's just kind of stumbling along. I'm afraid I can't give you credit for that. Oops, you fell—well, five points off." Sound ridiculous? How much more ridiculous is it than setting our expectations for young writers too high too soon?

 ## How the Traits Look Early On

Such things as voice, vocabulary growth, fluency, and expression of ideas show up in oral storytelling and in picture writing long before students begin to produce conventional text. So we must learn to *listen* for ideas, voice, and other important qualities even before we see them printed on a page. Next, we must learn to look for hints of these traits in even the earliest text, including pictures—then in letter play, letter strings, word strings, and finally—oh, joy—that first full sentence. Here are just a few things you might look and listen for in young writers' work—and in their responses to literature, too:

■ Ideas

- Little close-up details: veins in leaves, wings and legs on insects, expressive faces
- Signs of movement (e.g., a person or animal running)
- Details of color, shape, size, sound, smell, taste, or texture
- Any message—no matter how delivered—that makes sense to you, the reader (i.e., if you can make meaning from it, the ideas are clear)
- Ability to retell a story (here, the child is making the meaning)
- Ability to recognize another writer's point or message

When children can sit down and put their thoughts on paper quickly and easily, they are fluent writers *even if they make errors.* If the teacher is always correcting the students' spelling and punctuation errors, the children will stop guessing and trying. This will lead to dull writing with students afraid to use words they can't spell.

—Bea Johnson
Never Too Early to Write,
1999, p. 33

■ Organization

- Balance on the page—good use of white space
- Balance within pictures: proportion, sizing, coordination among parts
- Use of a title (an early beginning)
- Coordination of text with illustrations
- Layout that works and that's pleasing to the eye
- More than one detail or events put in order (e.g., through multiple pictures)
- Ability to predict events in a story (grasping the concept of organization)

- Ability to see how a picture and text go together (e.g., What extra information does the picture give you?)
- Ability to choose one beginning or ending over another
- Ability to group "like" things (by shape, color, size, etc.)
- Use of "The End" (often the earliest form of a conclusion)

■ Voice

- Originality and expressiveness
- Emotion (Look at the characters' faces.)
- Individuality, ownership (You can tell it belongs to *this* child and no other.)
- An image, a moment, an idea that makes you *feel* something
- Love of life, love of writing/drawing
- Enthusiasm, exuberance
- Playfulness
- Pleasure in hearing strong voice in the writing of others

■ Word Choice

- Use of *words!* (They might be single letters, letter combinations, or letter strings at first, but in the young writer's mind, these are words.)
- Words that show action, energy, or movement (expressed orally or in writing)
- Words that describe
- Words that convey feelings
- A passion, a love, for new, unusual, or fun-to-say words
- Words that stretch *beyond* the child's spelling capabilities
- Words that help you see, feel, and understand
- Curiosity about new words

■ Sentence Fluency

- Letter strings that translate into sentences
- Word grouping that imitates sentence patterns
- Sentence sense (an ear for what a sentence is)
- That first whole, complete sentence
- Use of multiple sentences
- Patterns that reinforce meaning: "Cats sleep all day. Dogs sleep at night."
- A willingness to try new sentence forms—breaking out of patterns into variety (Compare *"I like my dog. I like my cat. I like school"* with *"I like cats and dogs. But I love my cat the most. Do you like school? Me too."*)

■ Conventions

- Left-to-right orientation
- Top-to-bottom orientation
- Spaces between words or lines
- Association of letters with sounds

> As a society, we allow children to learn to speak by trial and error. But when it comes to reading and writing, we expect them to be right the first time.
>
> —Donald H. Graves and Virginia Stuart
> *Write from the Start: Tapping Your Child's Natural Writing Ability,* 1987, p. 21

- Letters that face the right direction
- *Readable* spelling
- Use of punctuation (whether placed correctly or not)
- Distinction between capital and lowercase letters (whether used correctly or not)
- Use of end punctuation
- Use of a title
- Awareness of margins
- Use of *I* (capitalized)
- Ability to spell own name
- Interest in environmental print

Ideas for Teaching Traits to Beginners

Here are nine general ideas for teaching traits to beginning writers.

Paper 3   **"Clouds," by Nicole (Grade 2)**

> Clouds
> Clouds are big
> puffy things
> but what a
> cloud rely is a big bunch
> of water. You can find
> difrint shaps in them.
> they are some tims fun
> to look at, Clouds are
> vey very big. In other words
> clouds are eanormos.

Idea 1: Don't Worry About Numbers—Yet

The key to good assessment that communicates *to young students* is observing signs of growth and change—not putting numbers on their performances. Describe what you see, as clearly as you can, using language that makes sense to them, but do not worry about whether it's a 2, 3, or 4—or for that matter an A, B, or C. Numbers are used most effectively with students who can begin to understand the meaning *behind* those numbers. If we say to a primary writer, "Well, Bill, this piece of writing is about a 3 in ideas, but we're going to work on getting you up to a 4 or 5," we can't expect this to be anything but gibberish to Bill. It makes much more sense to say, "a while ago, I had trouble sometimes reading your work without your help, but now I am recognizing some letters and even some words. I can read your writing even when you're not there to read it *to* me. This is *so* exciting."

Consider Nicole's paper (Paper 3) on clouds. It has descriptive detail (*"big puffy things"*) as well as good information: "*What a cloud really is [is] a big bunch of water.*"

There's also a stretch for a new word—"*Clouds are very, very big. In other words, clouds are eanormos.*" We also see the beginnings of variety in sentences, something we do not always see at grade 2.

Kean's piece (Paper 4) is highly audience-oriented. It has a sincere, heartfelt tone ("*I relly like Sam*"). Words like *very* and *really* are early ways of injecting voice. But even better is Kean's willingness to share a secret. Psst—come closer: "*I ustu bit his finggers.*" Direct connection to an audience is the very foundation of voice.

Lincoln, also a first grader, writes very lovingly of his brother Nick (Paper 5). "*He plays a lot if hes not bisey.*" We have to be delighted with this line, imagining Nick making time for Lincoln and noting how much Lincoln appreciates it. He generously refers to him as the "faveist" ("favorist," meaning *favorite*). But the last line is best of all: "*His kindnis gits biger avre day.*" Wouldn't you love to have a friend say that about you? We need to tell Lincoln just that.

Some teachers get itchy when they see a line like that last one. They want to write little red corrections right above Lincoln's writing. I wouldn't do that, personally. Why? Because it puts the focus in the wrong place. Instead, I might say to the whole class, "Writers come across great words when they write. One of the words Lincoln discovered for us today is *kindness*. What a terrific word. If we learn to spell it together, we can all use it in our writing when we want to. This word has eight letters, so let me write eight blanks: _ _ _ _ _ _ _ _. Now, let's see if we can fill them in. Who wants to try the first letter?" I want Lincoln to know that his discovery of this wondrous word is more important to me than whether he spelled it right the first time. I also want him to know that by using a word that was new to him, he created a learning opportunity for everyone. That's a gift. The word *kindness* now goes on the wall for everyone to see and use. By the way, no need to attend to *every* misspelled word on each child's paper. Pick two or three from the class. That's enough. Take it easy.

Nicholas is a confident first grade writer, and his confidence fills his writing (Paper 6) with voice. He uses his experience masterfully to fill his paper about the library with rich and personal details.

Paper 4 "Sam is My Friend," by Kean (Grade 1)

me   sam

Sam is my friend we were friends.
Sins we were babys. I relly like Sam.
And I ustu bit his finggers.

Paper 5 "My Favorite Brother is Nick," by Lincoln (Grade 1)

My faverit brauther is nick   he

hase bene the faveist in the famale.

He plays a lot if hes not bisey. His

kindnis gits biger avre day.

Paper 6 — "I like My Library," by Nicholas (Grade 1)

I like my library because I like to learn about every-thing!

and books can Take me anywhere like to the tomb of King Tut, and to the home of the Arctic Wolf. Books have also taken me to den of lions with Daniel and to the site of the first dinosaur discovery.

When I go to the library it's like talking to the smartest person in the whole world — my Dad! First I'm Greeted by my librarian, who always helps me pick out the right book. Then, it's up to me to explore. Luckily, she is patient. When I forget to return it.

the library is my favorite place to be!

To appreciate the sophisticated sentence fluency of this piece, read it aloud. How many different ways does this writer find to begin? "*When I go . . . , First I'm greeted . . . , Then, it's up to me . . . , Luckily, she is patient.*" This is beautiful writing—and quite remarkable from a first grader. We cannot expect that all first graders will attain this level of skill and grace. Nicholas writes with some ease and has begun experimenting with a wide range of conventions, including paragraphing, hyphens, dashes, commas, apostrophes, and exclamation points. Not all first graders yet have this repertoire of skills from which to draw, but we can enrich their worlds with samples of good writing, and we can read to them often with care and expression. We might surprise ourselves with how far we can take them.

Jocelyn shows wonderful fluency for a young writer in an expanded story about a cat and dog on a shopping trip. Look for the moments of voice in Paper 7. It may remind you of some of your own shopping adventures. In addition, this particular piece shows remarkable control of many conventions and excellent experimenting with inventive (*temporary*) spelling. Notice the ellipses ("*ate them in the store . . . then called a taxi*"), as well as the quotation marks and exclamation points ('*this is disgusting!!!*'). The inventive spelling shows a sharp ear for sound: *seriel, grocry* (this is how most of us actually pronounce it), *cupbord*, and *somthing*. In addition, many words are spelled with conventional accuracy: *taxi, disgusting, opened, melted, jokes, uncles,* and *shopping*—not to mention *ice cream sandwiches* (Did she look at the label?). The ending shows the cat and dog doing what most of us do at the end of a long shopping day—swapping stories until they grow punchy.

> **Paper 7** **"Catdog Shopping," by Jocelyn (Grade 1)**
>
> One day my cat and my dog were hungrey so they went to the cupbord to get somthing to eat but there was no cat or dog food in the cupbord and so they wint to the catdog shopping mall. They went to the grocry store and first they went to ial 8 and they looked at all the catfood and dogfood and they said 'this is disgusting!!!' so they went to ial 4 to get some sereil but all of the boxes of seriel were opened so they could not buy any seriel, and so they went to ial number 1 for ice cream sandwiches. they put the ice cream sandwiches in ther cart but the ice cream sandwiches melted and so they went back to ial 1 and got more ice cream sandwiches and they ate them in the store . . . then they called a taxi and on the way home they told jokes about ther mothrs and uncles and the dog laffed so hard he fell off the seat and then they were home and they went in the house.

Paper 8 shows Mason's first book, produced in kindergarten. Notice his organization. He has a cover page, plus two chapters. In Chapter 1 he's a good boy, but then, as so often happens as the plot unfolds, things go downhill in Chapter 2. I was struck by the fact that that he could spell *naughty* correctly, but as his teacher explained, when Mason is acting up, his mom

> **Paper 8** **"Mason's First Book" (Kindergarten)**
>
>

sometimes says, "Oh, Mason is being *n-a-u-g-h-t-y* again," and of course, Mason picked up that spelling at once. Perhaps we should work to keep the spelling of more words a secret.

What *does* it mean to be old—in the eyes of a young child? Perspective is everything. Megan (Paper 9) is quite mature in her thinking, but notice the power of numbers; as soon as she puts a figure with her definition, she is afraid she's offended someone. As soon as it occurs to her that she *might* be hurting the reader's feelings, her focus shifts from defining what it means to

---

Paper 9 **"Old," by Megan (Grade 3)**

OlD

I think you get old when you are 60. If you are 60 it is ok because it is fine you are just like any body else and you should be happy about it. You will probadly get married and you will have grand Kids. Or maybe even kids your self. Love your family and friends and grand Kids. Don't think you are too old for any thing. Be happy and cheer-ful and go to church every Sun-day. Take vacations and get a job probably. So don't be scared of being old. Well I'am not scared of being old but maybe you are. Like I was saying, old is not bad and it doesn't mean any thing bad either I'am 8 and I'am not scare of being 10 but kind of scared about being 60. I can't stop saying Old is not BAD! Actually you should be proud of being old. Think of your self

as a Kid. Say It Kid, Kid. OK maybe not a Kid but like a teenager. You're a teenager not old.

OlD

By: Megan

Paper 10 "Dear Tooth Fairy," by Leah (Grade 2)

Dear Tooth Fairy,

I don't have a tooth right now because my dog ate my tooth.

So my point is, I lost my tooth, my dog ate it, so do I still get my money?

Your still beliver,

Leah

P.S. I don't know if my dog really ate it but I really lost it.

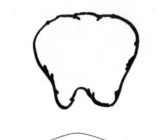

Paper 11 "Jamey The Cat," by Veronica (Grade 2)

" Jamey The Cat "

My name is Jamey. I am a cat. I like this window sill. I can see a lot from here. Sarah is outside. She is having a picnic with a friend. I love Sarah. I love outside. But I can't go outside now. I've been fixed. That means I can't have kittens anymore. I didn't want kittens anyway. They are a lot of hard work. My nails were pulled too. If I go outside I will get clawed till I die. So I don't go outside. I'd like to, but I don't. I love Sarah, but I want to picnic too. When Sarah comes home I'm not letting her pet me!

by Veronica
Grade 2
St. Wilfrid

be old to reassuring the reader that it is okay, it is all right, you're a kid: *"Say it kid, kid. OK maybe not a kid but like a teenager."* Whew. That's a relief.

Letters, as noted earlier, are a powerful means for developing voice—as Leah's note to the tooth fairy (Paper 10) clearly illustrates. Like any good business letter, it comes right to the point. Notice in particular the postscript; Leah seems to reflect when writing to the tooth fairy that it may be best to come clean with the whole story.

Perspective is the foundation for "Jamey The Cat" (Paper 11). Second grader Veronica has had some help with her editing but also has done much of it herself, via computer, and it is work to be proud of. Even more impressive, though, is her take on point of view. Her teacher, an artist, has told the class how different the world can look, depending on who you are and where you are. Veronica's understanding of this concept is quite profound, as is evident in how she adopts the role of a cat who is loving yet a little resentful that her

Paper 12   **Brad's "Pyramid" (Grade 2): (a) Collage Art: The Pyramids; (b) Rough Draft; (c) Final Draft, Revised and Edited in Poetry Format**

(a)

(b) I can pirteot very presish thingslike the mumy and the jewles but soon I will not be abelle to pirtect ang thing for I am crumbling before my eyes. the heat wind and sand are beating awae at me my age is growing today i'm ofi shaly fourt howsin years old But at night when I gaze over all the stars I reamember wen I was being bilt geting a new reasponsebilite to portect a muny. I am a pyramid.

(c)

I can protect very precious things
Like the mummy and the jewels.
But soon I will not be able to protect anything
For I am
Crumbling before my eyes.
The heat, wind, and sand are beating away at me.
My age is growing.
Today I am officially four thousand years old.
But at night
When I gaze over all the stars,
I remember when I was being built
And getting a new responsibility
To protect a mummy.
I am a pyramid.

Paper 13	**"Mr. Bear Is Loving!"** by Andrew (Kindergarten)

Paper 14	**"My Grocery List,"** by Andrew (Kindergarten)

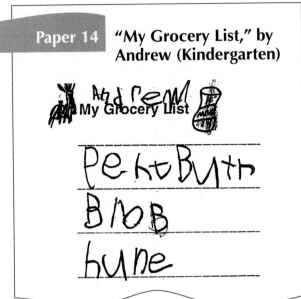

friend Sarah gets all the fun; revenge is afoot—a most sophisticated and subtle ending.

Brad (grade 2) combines art and text to create an impressive reflection on a pyramid, from the pyramid's point of view. Paper 12*a* shows his collage art depiction of pyramids against an Egyptian sky. In his rough draft (12*b*), he does not allow spelling to interfere with his stretch for new, meaningful words (*protect, crumbling, officially, responsibility*). Compare his draft with the final (12*c*) to see how editing and formatting work together to create meaning for the reader. Brad's writing is inspired by the research and teaching of Beth Olshansky (www.picturingwriting.org).

In Paper 13, Andrew (a kindergartner) tries his hand at a full sentence: "Mr. Bear is loving." He gets just the first consonant of the last word and shows us a handy way for beginning writers to indicate a longer word they cannot quite spell yet. He'll be filling in the blanks in no time. He gets in some good practice with detail and spelling, first with his grocery list (Paper 14)—*peanut butter, bread,* and *honey*—and then with his "To Do" list (Paper 15)—*eat, play, [watch] TV, [go to the] park, [ride my] bike, read,* and *draw.* He is bursting with ideas; a list gives him a simple, coordinated format for expressing them.

Notice how much information second grader Connor packs into his piece "My Winter Vacation" (Paper 16). The voice is strong yet very controlled and sophisticated for so young a writer: *"I had to have an IV; it was very annoying."* Annoying! The perfect word. Then there's good old Aunt Helen, who provides Connor with an exceptionally thorough history book. Like many teachers, I was concerned about organization, thinking Aunt Helen had arrived right on the heels of the paramedics. But then, I was thinking

Paper 15	**"My To Do List,"** by Andrew (Kindergarten)

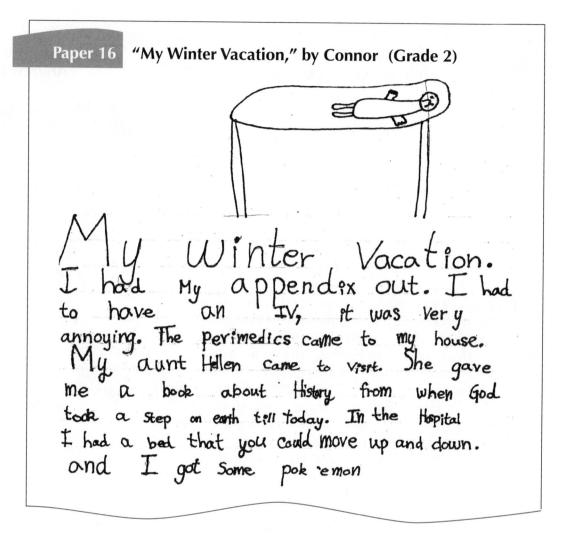

Paper 16   "My Winter Vacation," by Connor (Grade 2)

My Winter Vacation.
I had My appendix out. I had
to have an IV, it was very
annoying. The perimedics came to my house.
My aunt Hellen came to visit. She gave
me a book about History from when God
took a step on earth till today. In the Hospital
I had a bed that you could move up and down.
and I got Some pok'emon

chronological order, you see, and as Connor explained to me, "Uh, no—see, I was trying to explain the parts I *didn't* like so much and then the parts that were pretty good." That makes sense, and I love it that Aunt Helen provides the transition.

Idea 2: Building Awareness with Language

How do we create criteria that primary or beginning writers can use? Simple. No elaborate rubrics—instead, we begin with writers' questions, shown in the primary poster collection called "Thinking Like a Writer" (see Figure 12.1). These questions show young writers, in a simple but clear way, how to begin thinking about their writing without the pressure of formal evaluation.

Introduce *one trait at a time* and *one question at a time*. Don't rush. Use your own writing as a model, and ask yourself these same questions as you go. Then, as you read aloud from favorite literature, ask the same questions about books or other things you read. Let students know from the first that you value their opinions as evaluators. In this way you teach students to ask these questions of themselves as they write. And that is the goal.

Evaluation is embedded in all we do. Every time we make a choice—cereal or toast for breakfast, the black skirt or the black pants . . . each decision involves evaluation. We're all pros at it.

—Jane Fraser and Donna Skolnick

On Their Way: Celebrating Second Graders as They Read and Write, 1994, p. 7

Organization

✐ How does my paper begin?

✐ Did I tell things in order?

✐ How does my paper end?

©2009 Pearson Education. Written by Vicki Spandel.

Ideas

✐ What is my message?

✐ Is my message clear?

✐ Do I know my topic?

✐ Do I have details?

©2009 Pearson Education. Written by Vicki Spandel.

FIGURE **12.1** **Thinking Like a Writer Primary Poster**

Word Choice

✏ Did I use words I LOVE?

✏ Did I use any NEW words?

✏ Do my words make sense?

©2009 Pearson Education. Written by Vicki Spandel.

FIGURE **12.1** **Thinking Like a Writer Primary Poster**

Voice

✏ Do I like this paper?

✏ Does this sound like ME?

✏ How will my reader feel?

©2009 Pearson Education. Written by Vicki Spandel.

FIGURE **12.1** Thinking Like a Writer Primary Poster

Conventions

 Left to right?

Capitals?

Periods and question marks?

Spaces?

My BEST spelling?

Easy to read?

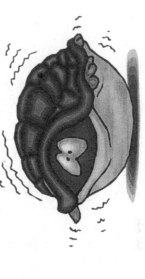

©2009 Pearson Education. Written by Vicki Spandel.

FIGURE **12.1** Thinking Like a Writer Primary Poster

Sentence Fluency

 Did I use sentences?

How *many* sentences?

Are some long?

Are some short?

Do they start different ways?

©2009 Pearson Education. Written by Vicki Spandel.

Idea 3: Help Students Think Like Writers

Use writers' vocabulary routinely to talk about students' writing. *Never miss an opportunity to point out a moment of voice or a small indication of detail, however tiny.* Remember Nikki's picture of the bat and spider in Paper 1? When you get a piece like that, it's a great opportunity to sneak in some trait language (think *writers' language*) that helps shape your student's thinking: "Nikki, you have really taken a close look at spiders! You noticed they have eight legs and multiple eyes. That's detail! And this bat—I love his toes and the hollow ears. Look at this smile on his face. That's what I call voice!" Then perhaps Nikki will think, "I'm a person who takes a close look at things. My writing has *detail*. My writing has *voice*."

With your comments, you plant a seed from which will blossom an amazing flower—*if* you nurture it. Don't paraphrase. Use terms like *details, organization, voice, leads* and *endings, word choice,* and *fluency.* Make these words and phrases part of your students' writing vocabulary. In this way you give them a tool for thinking and talking like writers.

Idea 4: Read and Celebrate Literature

If you love to read aloud (and what teacher of writing doesn't?), you already have at your command the most powerful means available for teaching the traits to beginning writers—or really, *any* writers. Consider a few examples.

Who can surpass William Steig (1971) when it comes to word choice? In *Amos and Boris* we can savor every luscious syllable in his description of friendship between the intrepid, seafaring mouse, Amos, and his benevolent and courageous friend, Boris, a whale:

> Boris admired the delicacy, the quivering daintiness, the light touch, the small voice, the gemlike radiance of the mouse. Amos admired the bulk, the grandeur, the power, the purpose, the rich voice, and the abounding friendliness of the whale.

Listening to someone who relishes language as Steig does, students will find meaning in words they didn't know they knew. That's the power of a master who can make meaning clear from context.

To combine ideas with word choice, try a word picture from Faith Ringgold's (1991) magical tribute to a child's imagination, *Tar Beach:*

> I will always remember when the stars fell down around me and lifted me up above the George Washington Bridge.

We literally see and hear the hushed whisper of falling stars when those words are read aloud. We feel ourselves float.

Do you want to teach the power of a strong lead? Share these opening lines from Petra Mathers's (1991) enchanting tale, *Sophie and Lou:*

> Sophie was shy—so shy she did her shopping during the lull hours, so she wouldn't have to talk to anyone. Every Wednesday the Book-Mobile parked in front of the supermarket, and every Wednesday Sophie almost went in. But the librarian was so tall!

From my own experience I realize that the literature I *heard,* rather than read, as a child resonates again and again in my memory whenever I sit down to write . . . vocabulary and a sense of rhythm are almost impossible to "teach" in the narrow sense of the word. So how are children expected to develop a sense of rhythm or a wide vocabulary? By being read to, alive, a lot!

—Mem Fox
Radical Reflections,
1993, p. 68

What will become of someone so shy that she is afraid of tall people? Make a prediction. Predicting is an important organizational skill, too.

As you read, ask students to listen for the rhythm or hear the beat, the fluency, as in this passage from Deborah Hopkinson's *Under the Quilt of Night* (2001):

> I run so fast, I lead the way; the ones I love race right behind. Pounding dirt and grass, jumping rocks and roots, my feet make drumbeats on the path.

In *Dear Mrs. LaRue: Letters from Obedience School* (2002), author/illustrator Mark Teague shows how perspective (writing from the dog's point of view) can add voice and humor—as in this letter home from Ike, who's been carted off to Brotweiler Canine Academy to learn manners:

> How could you do this to me? This is a PRISON, not a school! You should see the other dogs. They are BAD DOGS, Mrs. LaRue! I do not fit in.

As a follow-up to reading, you might ask students to draw pictures, write letters to the author, pretend to be a character, ask questions, talk in groups about the book, write a similar story using the book as a model—or any of a dozen other things. But it's also important to realize that just reading aloud is often enough. When you share a book, you say, "I love books. I love to read." And when you ask students, "Listen for the voice in this piece," "See if you can pick out one favorite word," or "Tell me what you picture [ideas] as you listen to this story," you are teaching an important writing lesson.

■ Favorite Books for Primary

Following are some of my favorite books to use with primary readers and writers, listed by trait. Many of these—and others—are summarized and linked to lesson ideas in *Creating Young Writers* (Spandel, 2008). Keep in mind that every book listed here can be used for *any* trait—I've simply paired them with the trait I think is a standout.

Books for IDEAS

> **What to look for . . .**
>
> Is it very clear? Does it have a central idea or easy-to-follow story? Interesting details—especially sounds, smells, colors, textures, tastes? Glorious images? Does it make "movies" flow through your mind?

- *Actual Size* by Steve Jenkins
- *Animal Dads* by Sneed B. Collard III
- *Beaks!* by Sneed B. Collard III
- *Courage* by Bernard Waber
- *Everybody Needs a Rock* by Byrd Baylor
- *Fables* by Arnold Lobel
- *Go Away, Big Green Monster!* by Ed Emberley

- *Hottest, Coldest, Highest, Deepest* by Steve Jenkins
- *If . . .* by Sarah Perry
- *I'm in Charge of Celebrations* by Byrd Baylor
- *Shades of Black* by Sandra L. Pinkney
- *Something Beautiful* by Sharon Dennis Wyeth
- *Some Things Are Scary* by Florence Parry Heide
- *Stars Beneath Your Bed* by April Pulley
- *The Three Pigs* by David Wiesner
- *Twilight Comes Twice* by Ralph Fletcher
- *Whoever You Are* by Mem Fox

Books for ORGANIZATION

What to look for . . .

Does it have a powerful beginning? A strong or surprising conclusion? Is everything clearly linked to one idea: bears, insects, oceans, whales, etc.? Does the book follow a pattern young writers could imitate in their own writing? Are there surprises? Puzzles or patterns or storylines to figure out?

- *Dear Mr. Blueberry* by Simon James
- *From Head to Toe* by Eric Carle
- *Growing Frogs* by Vivian French
- *The Important Book* by Margaret Wise Brown
- *My Beak, Your Beak* by Melanie Walsh
- *My Map Book* by Sara Fanelli
- *Rain* by Manya Stojic
- *That's Good, That's Bad* by Margery Cuyler
- *Things That Are Most in the World* by Judi Barrett
- *The Tiny Seed* by Eric Carle
- *The Tortoise and the Hare Continued . . .* by Barry Lane
- *Tuesday* by David Wiesner
- *What Do You Do When Something Wants to Eat You?* by Steve Jenkins
- *When I Was Little* by Jamie Lee Curtis
- *Zoom* by Istvan Banyai

Books for VOICE

What to look for . . .

Will I love reading this book aloud? Will I enjoy it more than once? Will students laugh, cry, get the chills when they hear it? Is the writer totally engaged in the topic? Does the writer sound confident—like an authority? Would students recognize this writer's voice if they heard it again?

- *The Big Box* by Toni Morrison
- *Dear Mrs. LaRue* by Mark Teague
- *Diary of a Worm* by Doreen Cronin
- *Don't Let the Pigeon Drive the Bus* by Mo Willems
- *A Frog Thing* by Eric Drachman
- *I'm Gonna Like Me* by Jamie Lee Curtis
- *I Will Never Not Ever Eat a Tomato* by Lauren Child
- *Julius, the Baby of the World* by Kevin Henkes
- *Koala Lou* by Mem Fox
- *Matilda* by Roald Dahl
- *No, David!* by David Shannon
- *Olivia* by Ian Falconer
- *Once Upon a Cool Motorcycle Dude* by Kevin O'Malley
- *Piggie Pie* by Margie Palatini
- *Scarecrow* by Cynthia Rylant
- *Serious Farm* by Tim Egan
- *A Story for Bear* by Dennis Haseley
- *This Land Is My Land* by George Littlechild
- *The True Story of the 3 Little Pigs* by Jon Scieszka
- *The Twits* by Roald Dahl
- *Where the Wild Things Are* by Maurice Sendak
- *Wilfrid Gordon McDonald Partridge* by Mem Fox

Books for WORD CHOICE

What to look for . . .

Is it filled with words or phrases I'd like primary writers to know and use? Are there words students will want to "adopt" right away? Is language used in creative, appealing, original ways? Does the writer make things "move" with strong verbs? Are adjectives carefully selected—used with a light touch?

- *Amos and Boris* by William Steig
- *The Boy Who Loved Words* by Roni Schotter
- *Click, Clack, Moo: Cows That Type* by Doreen Cronin
- *Crickwing* by Janell Cannon
- *Dr. DeSoto* by William Steig
- *The Great Fuzz Frenzy* by Janet Stevens and Susan Stevens Crummel
- *I, Crocodile* by Fred Marcellino
- *Lord of the Forest* by Caroline Pritcher
- *Max's Words* by Kate Banks
- *Miss Alaineus* by Debra Frasier

- *Roberto, the Insect Architect* by Nina Laden
- *Stellaluna* by Janell Cannon
- *Verdi* by Janell Cannon
- *Walter Was Worried* by Laura Vaccaro Seeger

Books for SENTENCE FLUENCY

What to look for . . .

Does it read like poetry? Does it have sample sentences I could use as models—to show young writers varied sentence beginnings or sentence structure? Does it have interesting dialogue? Are there rhythmic choruses or repeated lines where children could chime in? Are there parts children could memorize or perform?

- *Abel's Island* by William Steig
- *Beast Feast* by Douglas Florian
- *Come On, Rain!* by Karen Hesse
- *Creatures of Earth, Sea, and Sky: Poems* by Georgia Heard
- *Days with Frog and Toad* by Arnold Lobel
- *Dog Team* by Gary Paulsen
- *Extreme Animals: The Toughest Creatures on Earth* by Nicola Davies
- *George and Martha* by James Marshall
- *Great Crystal Bear* by Carolyn Lesser
- *Hey, Little Ant* by Philip and Hannah Hoose
- *Insectlopedia* by Douglas Florian
- *My Man Blue* by Nikki Grimes
- *Oh, the Places You'll Go!* by Dr. Seuss
- *Old Black Fly* by Jim Aylesworth
- *One Tiny Turtle* by Nicola Davies
- *A Pocketful of Poems* by Nikki Grimes

Books for CONVENTIONS

What to look for . . .

Does the book reflect a wide range of conventions I could use as models? Does the writer use conventions creatively to show the reader how to read with expression? Is the layout especially striking or unusual?

- *Hairy, Scary, Ordinary: What Is an Adjective?* by Brian P. Cleary
- *Knuffle Bunny* by Mo Willems
- *Leonard the Terrible Monster* by Mo Willems
- *The Night I Followed the Dog* by Nina Laden
- *Nouns and Verbs Have a Field Day* by Robin Pulver

- *A Poke in the I: A Collection of Concrete Poems* by Paul B. Janeczko
- *Punctuation Takes a Vacation* by Robin Pulver
- *Roomeow and Drooliet* by Nina Laden
- *What! Cried Granny* by Kate Lum
- *When Pigasso Met Mootisse* by Nina Laden

Chances are very good that you have a favorite book that is not on this list. That's OK—just be very sure not to use it. I am kidding. By all means, add it to the list, along with others you love. Read what you like because you'll enjoy it more—and you'll read with passion. Remember that when you read to children, you are modeling not just the love of books, but also how to read with expression and heart. It's very hard to throw yourself into it if you find the book tedious. So don't take anything from my list or anyone else's that you don't love right down to your toes.

Idea 5: View "Mistakes" as Opportunities

As students write, we can stretch our vision to look beyond "mistakes." Is there a new discovery in conventions? Quotation marks? Apostrophes? Terrific. Notice, applaud, celebrate. Fret over meticulous placement later.

Realize too that mistakes—or *any* opportunities for revision—are an instructional gift if we learn to see them as clues, showing us what students might be ready for next. Look again at Paper 7, Jocelyn's story of "Catdog Shopping." Detail, voice, organizational flow—it's all there. Right now, though, Jocelyn is following a sentence pattern many beginning writers use, connecting nearly all of her sentences with *and, so, and so,* or *so then.* These connecting phrases provide an easy way for Jocelyn to make the leap from clause to clause. They also echo the way many people speak. But the result is an endless sentence that doesn't let the reader breathe.

A writer this fluent *may* be ready to move to the next step: disconnecting *some* of the clauses. I might say, "Jocelyn, do you know what is so great about this piece? You have idea after idea after idea. I can picture *everything!* That's what good writers do. They give us details. I think you're ready for a little writer's secret. [*Conspiratorial whisper* . . .] Sometimes, if we hook *all* our little sentences together with words like *and* or *so* and make one BIG sentence, the writer gets out of breath. If you can find some places to put periods, and make *some* small sentences, your reader can pause to take a breath. Want to see how one of your favorite writers does it?"

In his brilliant book *Mechanically Inclined* (2005), teacher-consultant Jeff Anderson talks about the importance of giving students mentor sentences as examples. Jocelyn is a *very* young writer, true, but she is also a sophisticated thinker and an avid reader. She can read some simple sentences with me and help me count periods—*if* I come up with the right mentor text.

One writer who is gifted with the short sentence is E. B. White. He gives short sentences elegance so that they never sound choppy or fragmented. So I choose for my mentor text *Charlotte's Web*—and find just the right passage. In this scene, Mrs. Zuckerman is about to give Wilbur a buttermilk bath: "Wilbur stood and closed his eyes. He could feel the buttermilk trickling

> Children who write before they read become better writers than those who don't.
>
> —Bea Johnson
> *Never Too Early to Write,*
> 1999, p. 1

down his sides. He opened his mouth and some buttermilk ran in. It was delicious. He felt radiant and happy. When Mrs. Zuckerman got through and rubbed him dry, he was the cleanest, prettiest pig you ever saw" (1980, p. 121).

As I share this example with Jocelyn, reading aloud *slowly,* I'll ask her to notice how many sentences White uses, where he chose to write *and,* and how he *sometimes* made the choice to pause and let the reader take a breath—instead of writing *and.* Then I'll ask if she would like to try this writer's strategy with just *one* of her sentences—and I will help. I would *never* ask her to do the whole piece. The point is not to "fix" the *paper*—but to show *Jocelyn* one small technique she can use as a writer.

To begin, I might say, "Let's read your first sentence together and see if there is *any* place we could put a period—so the reader can pause and not lose track of all these good ideas you are sharing. You listen for a spot where you want the reader to take a breath, OK?" I will read aloud very slowly so Jocelyn can listen. I will read more than once so she can think about choices. *Jocelyn* will hold the pencil. *She* will put in the periods. *She* will put in new capitals if needed. I will coach her, taking my cues from her. She will also read her revision aloud so we can see if she likes the choices she made—and if she doesn't, they don't have to stay. And her first sentence may wind up looking something like this:

> One day my cat and my dog were hungrey. ~~so~~ They went to the cupboard to get something to eat, but there was no cat or dog food in the cupboard. ~~and~~ So they wint to the catdog shopping mall.

Jocelyn leaves the conference as a writer who has choices, and if she thinks, even once, "Should I write *and* here—or put in a pause?" then this lesson has been a wild success.

Idea 6: Reward an Adventurous Spirit

Voice is individuality, so every time a writer allows herself to be lost in the crowd, a little bit of individuality is lost. To stand out, to stand alone, takes courage. We must reward students who dare to speak with strong voices. Consider Hollie's tribute to her first grade teacher (Paper 17). She writes

---

Paper 17 | **Guess why I like school? by Hollie (Grade 1)**

Guess why I like school? I like school because I like my teacher. I like her because she is sweet and kind and also butteful. I wish she could be my 2nd grade teacher and all the way to high school. I also like her because she is thoughtful and relly nice. Shes a sweety and a cupcake. Shes a terrific friend In my heart I love her. Shes a loveable teacher. She teaches us good things like how to be friends and she wears nice, pretty, fashionable cloths. That's what I like about school.

directly from her heart about a special teacher who is a "sweety and a cupcake." She also tells us, "In my heart I love her," and "I wish she could be my 2nd grade teacher and all the way to high school." How many teachers would you have hung onto for twelve years? What I want Hollie to know is, "You write with passion. Your paper stood out. I read it several times. I even read it out loud. When you say what you really think and feel, your writing has voice. I can't wait to read your next piece."

Idea 7: Model, Model, Model

Model everything: A list of ideas for writing from which you'll pick one. A first sentence. A list of possible titles. A first draft. A picture to go with a story. Let your students see it happening. Model revision, too—*even if you do not ask it of your young writers.* And probably you will not ask it, for experiencing the joy of writing should be our primary goal for beginners. Many primary teachers feel uncomfortable with the whole notion of revision, and who can blame them? At this level, getting the first draft on the page is often an enormous effort. Now we're supposed to ask students to redo it? Are we insane? Indeed we are if we make revision too big. Copying over or correcting all errors is often a recipe for murdering the child's love of writing—right there on the page. But revision for beginners can be *tiny*—sometimes just adding one small detail (a bird in the tree, a smile on the frog's face) or changing one word (*went* to *skipped*).

Remember: Just because you *model* revision, that's no sign that you expect students to do everything you do. The nice thing about modeling is that you and your students can work together, and they do much of the *thinking* even if you're the one doing the recording. This thinking and planning lay the groundwork for revisions to come. Here's a simple lesson based on an anonymous student paper entitled, "My Dog" (Paper 18).

For this lesson, choose a paper that does not belong to anyone in your class. In that way students will feel free to make suggestions without fear of hurting anyone's feelings. The purpose of the lesson is to show how writers play with writing—and to see, of course, how different it sometimes sounds when they are done. To begin, I share the piece in large print, on a whiteboard, overhead, or chart pack. I leave *lots* of space in between lines for writing, and I draw students' attention to this: "Sometimes after I write, I might want to add a sentence or even just a word, so I need to leave space." Now it's time to get serious about details. So I say, "I want to add some details to my paper. Will you help me?"

> Writing with real honesty takes tremendous courage. Such writing should never be taken for granted. Writers of all ages often find they lack the nerve to write honestly.
>
> —Ralph Fletcher
> *What a Writer Needs,*
> 1993, p. 25

> We want to help children learn how to reread or "resee" their work. Above all, we want them to have a growing sense of options available to them during composing.... What we demonstrate [through our own revision] is not so much how to revise as a certain stance toward the world, a sense of our intentions, and how we listen to ourselves when we write.
>
> —Donald H. Graves
> *A Fresh Look at Writing,*
> 1994, p. 239

Paper 18   **"My Dog"**

My dog is my friend and he plays with me when I come home from school. We do fun stuff. When my mom says to stop we stop. Then we go outside.

From this point on, although I do the actual writing and reading aloud, I engage in a conversation with students the whole time, asking them to do most of the thinking. What I say goes something like this:

This paper is called "My Dog." Do you think we should give this dog a name? <u>Max</u>? *OK, good . . .* <u>Max is my friend</u>—*but how good a friend? . . .Wow—yes, my* <u>very best friend in the whole world</u>. *Terrific. So he plays with me when I come home from school. How soon after I get home do we play? The* <u>very second</u>! *Excellent—I like that. It's specific. So,* <u>The very second I get home, he plays with me</u>. *What does he actually do, though? Can you see him?* He <u>leaps for me</u>? *Great—I can see that in my mind. OK, so—We do fun stuff. What kinds of things do we actually do, do you suppose? Play tag?* <u>Race around the living room</u>? *Can you see this? I can, too—much better than "fun stuff." When my mom says to stop—wait a second. What do you think Mom actually says? Let's hear her voice—right, good—*<u>Mom yells, "It's too noisy in here!"</u> *Then we stop—but what do you think Max and I actually do? Try to picture it—OK, we* <u>fall in a heap on the floor</u>. *And we laugh, right? Should I say that? OK—so* <u>I laugh and Max barks</u>. *All right, and then we go outside—what do you think we do?* <u>Play catch</u>—<u>with my old tennis ball</u>. *For how long?* <u>Till it's dark</u>. *Terrific. Now let's read the whole thing and see how it sounds . . .*

Figure 12.2 shows how it looks when we are finished.

I read the piece aloud with all revisions in place, and ask the students to help me illustrate it. Then I recopy it in its final form, and we give it a title (which we brainstorm together) and post the results. And though I have not requested it, it's likely that I'll see some playfulness with revision in students'

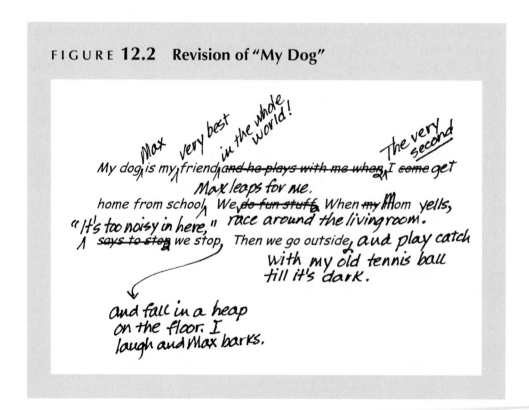

FIGURE **12.2**   **Revision of "My Dog"**

own work. This lesson emphasizes reading aloud, adding little details, asking questions as you write, and using art to expand detail and voice.

Possible illustrations for "Wild and Wonderful Max" (previously "My Dog"):

- Max
- Max leaping for the writer
- Mom yelling, "It's too noisy in here!"
- The writer and Max racing through the living room
- The writer and Max falling in a heap on the floor
- Max and the writer playing catch

Idea 8: Respect the Many Forms That Writing Can Take

Primary students need a variety of ways in which to express themselves, including pictures, dictation, oral storytelling, labeling, and planning. Pictures, as we've seen, reflect the beginnings of ideas (details), voice (emotion, playfulness, individuality, and humor), and organization (format and balance). Further, children who are not quite ready to create extended text (they may not yet have the concentration, ability to form words, or fine motor skills to make writing relatively simple) can dictate stories or simply tell them to others. Through dictation they let loose the creative ideas, knowledge, and voice that they have no means yet to project through standard text. Paper 19 shows second grader Chris's dictated piece on the coyote—clearly one of his favorite animals. The richness of detail and sheer extension of the piece are likely far beyond anything Chris could create if he had to write all this out. The piece was generated through conversation. A few key questions coaxed this young writer to keep going: e.g., *What is special about coyotes? What do they eat? Where do they live?* Now when the teacher (or someone) reads this back to him, Chris can see his thinking on paper—and eventually, he will put it there himself.

Idea 9: Give Primary Writers Editing Tasks They Can Handle

Teaching conventions is not the same thing as *correcting* conventions—or assessing conventions, for that matter. Just because we wait a bit before expecting conventional correctness is no sign that we must wait *even a minute* to begin teaching and talking about conventions. Anyone who works with primary writers for just one day will be struck by how much they notice and how quickly they begin to include in their writing exclamation points, quotation marks, ellipses, semicolons, and parentheses—not always placed correctly, mind you, but present. We can take advantage of this curiosity by filling their environment with plenty of print to borrow from and by continually asking students, "Have you noticed this mark in your reading? Can you find one somewhere in this room? Why do you suppose writers use this? What does it show?"

Start with a treasure hunt. You can use any text at all for this, or you can post bits of text around the room for a true treasure hunt format. Choose pieces that show a variety of conventions; it is *not* essential that students be able to read every word from these passages. Then invite them, with partners

Paper 19 **Dictated Story About the Coyote (Grade 2)**

There is a lot to know about the coyote. It's smart. It lives all over. It can find a home for itself in the country or in the city. It is a little bit afraid of people, but not that much. It will even walk through traffic. It will go right into the back of a restaurant and grab a snack like a doughnut or pizza!

The coyote is brown, mostly, with just a little bit of black. This helps it blend into the grass so the rabbits and other animals don't hear it coming. This is how the coyote catches its food. Coyotes are good at digging. They have strong legs. They dig into the holes where the animals hide. They can also run fast for a long time.

Another way they catch food is to hang out when people are barbecuing and wait for a chance to sneak up and grab hot dogs or other things right off your grill. You could be making dinner and you turn around for a second. Your steak or chicken is gone! It was probably a coyote. Coyotes also eat lizards and snakes. They even eat insects. You might not know this, but they also eat pets like cats and dogs. If you live where there are coyotes, keep your dog inside.

Coyotes have babies in the spring. They have a LOT of babies, but I don't know how many. They live in a cave in the hillside where it is quiet and safe. The cave is dark and is pretty dirty. Coyotes aren't very neat. So in the cave there could be bones or feathers from the last meal. They have big bushy tails and they sleep with their tails curled around them to keep warm. They grow to be about two feet high.

The coyote is one of my favorite animals because it is extremely smart and the babies are very cute. You might want to take one home for a pet, but be careful! Coyotes aren't very good for pets. They bite and will also kill all your other pets. Just enjoy them out in the wilderness. That's what I do.

if you like, to find (and put their finger right on) each convention as you name it. Here are some I've used, but you could make your own list:

- Capital letter
- Period, question mark, comma, semicolon, exclamation point
- Any proper name
- The word *I*
- Any simple word: *and, the, dog, like, see, we*
- Italics
- Ellipses
- Parentheses
- Quotation marks
- Margins (How many fingers fit in the margin?)
- A title (Is the print in the title bigger? How much bigger?)

Because a group of first graders were so exceptionally good at finding everything I could name, I told them I'd give them my conventions "challenge"—*ellipsis*. One girl in the front row put her finger immediately on the ellipsis and raised her hand. When I asked if she could explain how ellipses are used, she said sure. She stood up before the group. "Ellipses," she explained, "are when you . . . [and her voice drifted off for a time, then resumed] pause in your thinking—like that." Not bad.

You can also ask students to do very simple editing tasks, as shown in the "Simple Editing Checklist" shown in Figure 12.3. Even very beginning writers can do these things, and they will feel like independent editors if you call it editing. Later, as skills grow, you can add new skills to create a more advanced editing checklist (see Figure 12.4).

When students begin writing simple sentences, create simple editing practice that invites them to "track down" errors (see Figure 12.5).

FIGURE 12.3 Simple Editing Checklist for Primary Students

Simple Editing Checklist

____ Name
____ Date
____ Capitals to start sentences
____ Capital "I"
____ Periods (.) to end sentences
____ Question marks (?) to end questions
____ Spaces between words

FIGURE 12.4 Advanced Editing Checklist for Primary Students

Editing Checklist

__ My name is on the paper.
__ The date is on the paper.
__ My title goes with the paper.
__ I used capitals to start sentences.
__ I used capital "I."
__ I used periods to end sentences.
__ I used question marks to end questions.
__ I used quotation marks to show talking: "Hello!"
__ I have one-inch margins all around.
__ I used my BEST spelling.
__ You can read everything in my paper!

FIGURE **12.5 Primary Editing Practice**

The cat ate my fish.

The ate my fish.

The cat ate my fish

the cat ate my fish.

The cat aet my fish.

The Cat ate my fish.

The cat ate myfish.

The cat ate my fish?

Notice that in this practice students are given the correct sentence first in big print. In this way you are not modeling errors—but rather helping them to find errors by matching other sentences against the correct one. Each practice sentence (1) is short and complete and (2) contains *only one* error. Put a copy on a board or chart paper, and read sentences aloud, one by one, as you work together. You can do just one sentence or more than one depending on attention spans. Each time, though, you are looking for *one* mistake.

When you do a lesson like this one, make copies for your students. (You can run two to four on a single page and then cut them.) In this way, you can let them correct the text *first,* using the copy editor's symbols for beginning writers (see Figure 12.6).

FIGURE **12.6 Copy Editors' Symbols for Beginning Writers**

Editors' Symbol for Young Writers

Symbol	It means	Use it like this
$\wedge$	Put something in.	Paul $\wedge$ cats. *(chases)*
ℓ	Take this out.	Don is a ~~big~~ huge guy.
⚠	Put in a space.	Amy loves‿apples.
⊙	Add a period.	The horse saw us ⊙
≡	Make this letter a capital.	We live in oregon.
/	Make this letter lower case.	Do you eat Bacon?
———	Underline this title.	Our teacher read the book <u>Crickwing</u> to our class.

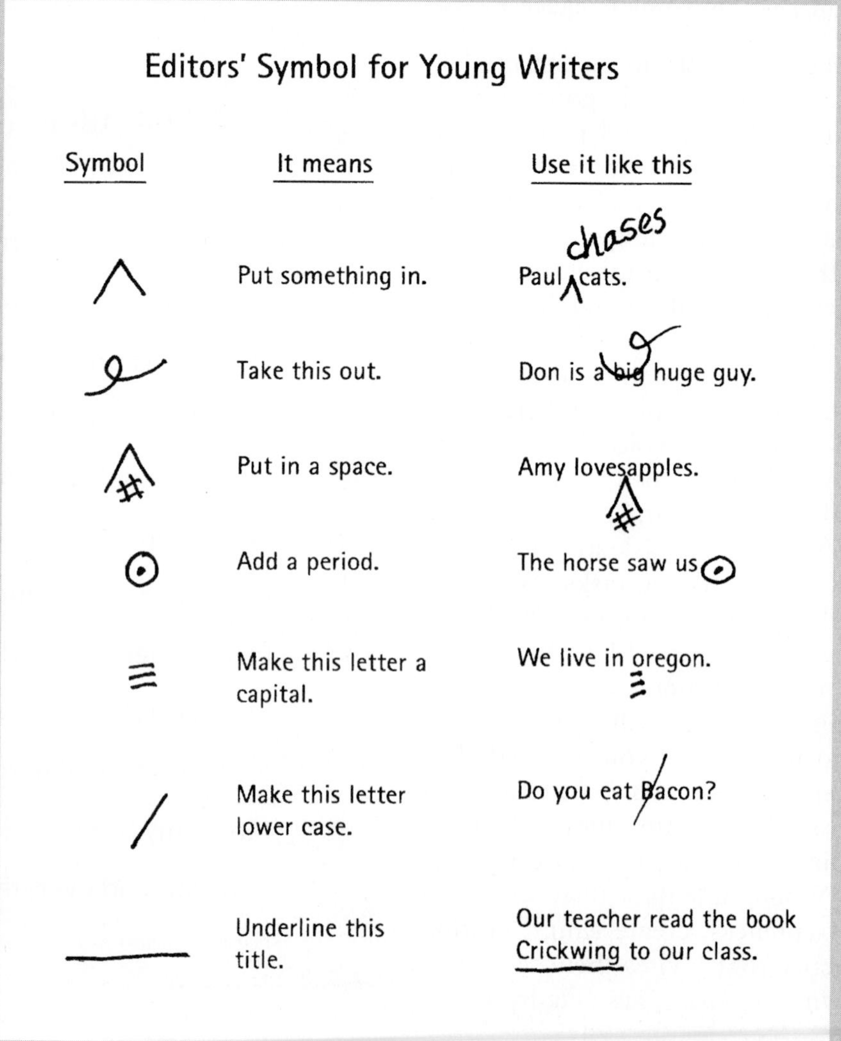

Don't worry if they cannot do all the editing yet; let them try. When they've finished, ask them to check their text with a friend. Then have them tell *you* how to fix the text so that you can do it for everyone to see. The process should be fast, lively, and interactive. No worksheets. Just a group of editors, talking and editing.

Idea 10: Keep It Simple

You do not always need to host a "writing event." For beginners, it's a comfort to know that brief, manageable assignments are sometimes acceptable. Beginners also enjoy interesting shapes on which to write. (See Figure 12.7, "The Shoe.") My friend Arlene Moore, who teaches a K–1 combination, gave her young writers 3" by 5" paper suitcases (see Figure 12.8) on which to write me short messages: "What I should be sure to pack as I travel around

FIGURE **12.7** **"The Shoe"**

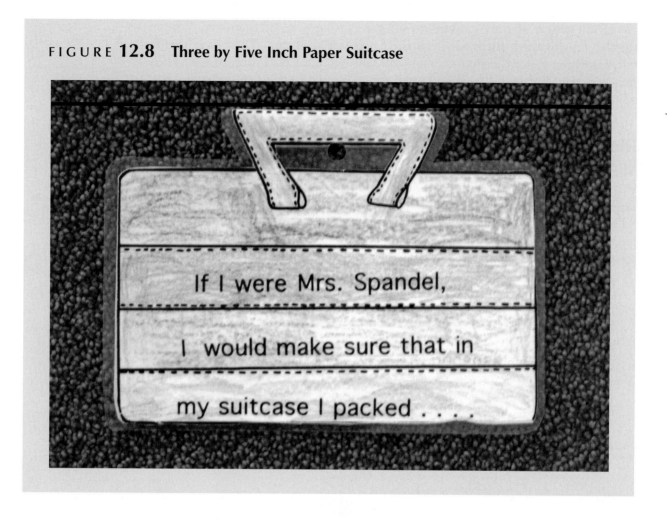

FIGURE **12.8**   **Three by Five Inch Paper Suitcase**

the country talking with teachers and students." Their *very short* recommendations included these—most of which I've followed:

- A snake so no one will steal your stuff
- A book to read
- Earrings to make you beautiful
- Roses for all the teachers you meet
- A charge card
- Plenty of chocolate so you won't get hungry
- Pictures of your children so you won't get lonely
- Clothes so you won't need to run around in your underwear

 # Use Continuums to Chart Growth

This section includes the continuums (see Figure 12.9) that form the basis for the book that complements this one, *Creating Young Writers* (Spandel, 2008). As I discuss at some length in *Creating Young Writers*, the continuums

FIGURE **12.9** Primary Continuum for IDEAS

Beginner	Borrower	Experimenter	Meaning Maker	Experienced Writer
☐ Makes marks on paper.	☐ Uses "words" and pictures to express ideas.	☐ Uses text/art to create interpretable messages.	☐ Creates clear message via text or text plus art.	☐ Creates a clear, detailed message through text/art.
☐ "Reads" own writing, invents meaning.	☐ Uses imitative/borrowed print to create signs, lists, rules, notes, etc. (not always interpretable without help).	☐ Expresses clear main message/idea in one or more sentences.	☐ Expresses complex, extended thoughts.	☐ Uses multiple sentences to enrich ideas or extend story.
☐ Dictates a clear message/story.		☐ Can "reread" text shortly after writing it.	☐ Uses multiple sentences to add detail.	☐ Incorporates significant detail to enhance meaning.
☐ Uses art to convey message/story.	☐ Likes to come up with personal ideas for writing.	☐ Creates decodable lists, labels, notes, statements, short summaries, "all about" or "how-to" pieces and/or poems.	☐ Connects images/text to main idea.	☐ Creates writing that explains, gives directions, tells a story, expresses an opinion, describes.
☐ Recognizes that print has meaning/significance.	☐ Notices detail in read-aloud text and in art from picture books.		☐ Creates images that show detail: eyes, expressive faces, fingers and toes, leaves and grass, etc.	
☐ Hears detail in stories read aloud.		☐ Can talk about main ideas and details based in picture book text/art.	☐ Creates writing that is fully decodable by independent reader.	☐ Creates informational and narrative text; may write persuasive paragraphs or poems.
		☐ Likes to choose own topics sometimes.	☐ Can "reread" text after several days.	☐ Can summarize own text.
			☐ Adds stories to repertoire.	☐ Can recognize and comment on detail or main message in text of others.
			☐ Can interpret or retell message from picture book.	☐ Chooses personally important topics.
			☐ Can think about and choose personal writing topic from several choices.	☐ Can revise own text by adding detail.
				☐ Prefers to choose own topics.

FIGURE 12.9 Primary Continuum for ORGANIZATION

Beginner	Borrower	Experimenter	Meaning Maker	Experienced Writer
❑ Fills space randomly.	❑ Can create art and text that go together.	❑ Consistently creates image and text that complement each other.	❑ Creates balanced, pleasing layout.	❑ Connects all text/art to main message.
❑ Can dictate sequential story or how-to piece.	❑ Creates layout with purpose/balance.	❑ Creates text/art with balanced look.	❑ Writes multiple sentences or images that suggest development/sequencing.	❑ Uses thoughtful titles.
❑ Can point to illustrations that go with text.	❑ May use two or more drawings to express story or message that has extended meaning and continuity.	❑ Can arrange or create sequence of drawings to convey a story or extended message.	❑ Sometimes uses art to express sequence of events.	❑ Writes a true lead (usually, the opening sentence).
❑ Can "hear" beginnings/endings in stories read aloud.	❑ Recognizes titles as beginning points.	❑ Writes more than one sentence on the same topic.	❑ Uses identifiable beginning and ending sentences.	❑ Provides closure (usually with final sentence).
	❑ Recognizes THE END as a signal of closure.	❑ May use title or THE END to signify beginning/ending.	❑ Uses connecting words: *first, next, then, once, after, and, but, or, so, because.*	❑ Follows logical order/sequence.
		❑ Stays focused on message.	❑ Has strong sense of main idea and sticks with it.	❑ Creates easy-to-follow text.
		❑ Often creates labels/lists.	❑ Knows when to use bulleted or numbered lists.	❑ Connects ideas.
		❑ Can organize recipes, all about and how-to pieces, directions, and simple stories.	❑ Creates organized lists, stories, descriptions, or recipes.	❑ Uses elaborate transitions: *After a while, The next day, Because of this, The first thing, Finally.*
		❑ Can predict what will happen next in text of others.	❑ Can make predictions based on text of others.	❑ Creates organized stories, summaries, how-to pieces, short essays, and other forms.
				❑ Can use variety of organizational patterns: e.g., step by step, chronological, comparison, problem-solution, main idea and detail.
				❑ Can revise own text for order, lead, ending.

FIGURE **12.9**   Primary Continuum for VOICE

Beginner	Borrower	Experimenter	Meaning Maker	Experienced Writer
❑ Creates bold lines.	❑ Incorporates voice into art through color, images, facial features, etc.	❑ Uses expressive language.	❑ Creates some text recognizable as "this child's piece."	❑ Creates lively, engaging, personal text/art.
❑ Uses color.		❑ Often incorporates definite tone/flavor.	❑ Writes/draws with personal style.	❑ Creates writing that is FUN to read aloud.
❑ Expresses voice in dictation.	❑ Uses exclamation points/underlining to show emphasis.	❑ Creates expressive art.	❑ Creates individual text, art.	❑ Is able to sustain voice.
❑ Responds to voice in text read aloud.	❑ Uses BIG LETTERS to show importance, strong feelings.	❑ Creates tone that reflects feelings.	❑ Elicits emotional response in reader.	❑ Provokes strong reader response.
	❑ Shows preference for text/art with voice.	❑ Puts moments of voice throughout text.	❑ May use conventional devices (exclamation points, underlining) to enhance voice.	❑ Uses voice to influence meaning.
	❑ Borrows strong "voice" words, e.g., LOVE.	❑ Recognizes voice in text of others, can describe personal response: e.g., "I liked it," "It was funny."	❑ Shows beginning awareness of audience: use of *you*, conversational tone, direct questions: *Do you like cats?*	❑ "Speaks" to audience.
			❑ Shows preference for certain types of voice in read-aloud pieces.	❑ Create voice that is easy to describe: *Joyful, Funny, Moody, Sarcastic, Fearful, Angry, Wistful.*
			❑ Often comments on voice in others' text/art: e.g., "That has voice," or "I want to hear that again."	❑ Shows growing awareness of own voice and is beginning to control quality and strength of voice.
				❑ Can rate extent of voice in other's text/art.
				❑ Can revise own text to strengthen voice.

FIGURE **12.9** Primary Continuum for WORD CHOICE

Beginner	Borrower	Experimenter	Meaning Maker	Experienced Writer
☐ Scribbles.	☐ Borrows recognizable letter shapes from environment.	☐ Writes easy-to-read letters/numbers.	☐ Writes easy-to-read words.	☐ Uses vivid, expressive language.
☐ Creates letter "shapes."	☐ Borrows simple words.	☐ Writes words with consonant sounds and some vowels.	☐ Writes with variety—dares to try new, less familiar words.	☐ Writes with vocabulary that may extend well beyond spelling ability.
☐ Uses favorite words in dictation.	☐ Labels pictures.	☐ Uses titles on text.	☐ Loves descriptive words and phrases.	☐ Sometimes uses striking unexpected phrases: "*I felt like a once contented and proud swan who lost its feathers.*"
☐ Responds positively to text with strong word choice.	☐ Creates letter strings that contain one- or two-letter words: *lk* (like), *dg* (dog), *hs* (house), *m* (my).	☐ Writes decodable words/sentences.	☐ Uses some strong verbs.	☐ Uses many strong verbs.
	☐ Chooses favorite words from read-aloud text.	☐ Uses many simple, familiar words.	☐ Uses words to create images or add clarity, detail.	☐ Keeps extensive personal dictionary.
	☐ Repeats "comfort" (familiar) words in own text.	☐ Uses sight words frequently.	☐ Stretches for the "right word."	☐ Repeats words only for emphasis/effect.
	☐ Guesses at word meanings from read-aloud text.	☐ Has personal bank of favorite words.	☐ Keeps growing personal dictionary of meaningful words.	☐ Can revise own text to add descriptors.
		☐ Attempts new or unfamiliar words in personal text.	☐ Selects some "just right" words to express meaning.	☐ Can revise own text to strengthen verbs.
		☐ Adds new words to personal dictionary.	☐ Usually avoids repetition.	☐ Can revise text to create more vivid images or make use of sensory detail.
		☐ Repeats some words.	☐ Uses language that creates imagery or sensory impressions.	☐ Can recognize and describe strong word choice in text of others.
		☐ Identifies favorite words from read-aloud text.	☐ Favors literature with strong word choice.	

FIGURE **12.9** Primary Continuum for SENTENCE FLUENCY

Beginner	Borrower	Experimenter	Meaning Maker	Experienced Writer
❑ Dictates a sentence.	❑ Creates letter strings that suggest sentences: *nohtipdin.*	❑ Writes letter strings that form readable sentences: *I lik skl.* (I like school.) *I HA DOG.* (I have a dog.)	❑ Creates easy-to-read text.	❑ Can write two short paragraphs or more.
❑ Enjoys poetry, rhythmic language.	❑ Writes text with a "sentence look" that may not be translatable.	❑ Writes more than one sentence.	❑ Consistently writes multiple sentences.	❑ Consistently writes complete sentences.
❑ Enjoys music with a beat.	❑ Dictates multiple sentences.	❑ Usually writes sentences that complete a thought.	❑ Writes complete sentences.	❑ Creates text that sounds fluent read aloud.
❑ Enjoys marching, dancing, clapping to rhythmic beat.	❑ Can hear rhythm, rhyme, and variety in read-aloud text.	❑ Attempts longer sentences.	❑ Writes longer (complex or compound) sentences.	❑ May use fragments for effect: *Wow! Crunch! And how! Really bad.*
	❑ Can hear patterns— and may try imitating them.	❑ Dictates a whole story or essay.	❑ Begins to show variety in sentence lengths, patterns, beginnings.	❑ Creates text that is easy to read with expression.
	❑ Can memorize simple poems for group recitation.	❑ Favors patterns: *I can pla. I can rid my bik. I can red.* (I can play. I can ride my bike. I can read.)	❑ May experiment with dialogue.	❑ Can combine sentences.
		❑ Likes to repeat text read aloud with inflection.	❑ Favors text with complex or varied sentences patterns.	❑ Can revise by changing word order or varying sentence beginnings.
		❑ Likes to memorize and recite simple poetry.	❑ Reads aloud with inflection.	❑ Can read own/others' text aloud with pronounced inflection and voice.
			❑ May experiment with poetry–rhyming or free verse.	❑ Often experiments with poetry/dialogue.
				❑ Can recognize and comment on fluency in others' text.

F I G U R E **12.9** Primary Continuum for CONVENTIONS

Beginner	Borrower	Experimenter	Meaning Maker	Experienced Writer
❏ May create imitative text.	❏ Imitates print: letters, "cursive flow (eee)," punctuation marks.	❏ Uses capitals and lowercase—not ALWAYS correctly.	❏ Uses capitals and lower case with fair consistency.	❏ Uses wide range of conventions skillfully and accurately.
❏ Can point to conventions in print.	❏ Writes own name.	❏ Uses periods, question marks, commas, and exclamation points (often correctly).	❏ Uses periods, commas, exclamation points, question marks correctly.	❏ Creates easy-to-read text with few errors.
❏ Plays with letter or number shapes.	❏ Writes one to several sight words.	❏ Puts spaces between words.	❏ Sometimes uses paragraphs.	❏ Uses paragraphs, often in the right places.
❏ May "write" first letter (or more) of own name.	❏ Loves to copy environmental print.	❏ Spells many sight words.	❏ Correctly spells ever-growing range of sight words and some challenging words.	❏ Spells most sight words and many challenging words correctly.
❏ May spell own name orally.	❏ Creates letters that (usually) face the right way.	❏ Creates readable, phonetic versions of harder words.	❏ Uses some difficult conventions correctly: e.g., quotation marks, ellipses, dashes, parentheses.	❏ Uses conventions to reinforce voice/meaning.
❏ Knows what letters are, what writing is.	❏ Can name/describe many punctuation marks: e.g., period, capital, comma, question mark.	❏ "Plays" with more difficult conventions: dashes, ellipses, quotation marks.	❏ Makes corrections in own text.	❏ Consistently checks/edits own text for many conventions.
❏ Draws to convey meaning.	❏ May use periods or other punctuation marks randomly in own text.	❏ Can name/describe numerous conventions.	❏ Writes left to right, notices margins.	❏ Writes left to right, top to bottom; wraps text and respects margins.
❏ Attempts "words" of personal significance.	❏ Asks about conventions.	❏ Shows concern for correctness in own text.	❏ Writes top to bottom.	❏ Is careful with layout and formatting.
	❏ Often writes left to right.	❏ Writes left to right.	❏ Wraps text easily.	❏ Can edit own text for end punctuation, subject–verb agreement, capitalization, spelling of high-frequency words.
	❏ Often writes top to bottom on page.	❏ Writes top to bottom.	❏ Places title or illustrations thoughtfully on page.	❏ Knows simple copy editors' symbols.
	❏ Can write on a line.	❏ Is beginning to "wrap" text (down and left) to form the next line.		❏ Can edit simple text of others.

reproduced here are not intended for large-scale assessment but for use in the classroom. You might use them as checklists, marking things that your students do well. Or you can highlight skills with a colored marker, attach continuums to four or five writing samples collected throughout the year, and create a portfolio that will show striking growth.

You will notice that the continuums have no numbers. They are intended for use as performance records. To that end, the language is designed to reflect what students *can* do. When a child reaches the "Experienced Writer" stage consistently, across traits and across multiple samples of writing, that child is ready for assessment on the writing guide from Chapter 3 of this book. If you are a primary teacher or if you work with struggling or challenged writers, I invite you to try these continuums with your own students. You will give them a chance to experience success and to celebrate the many things they *can* do.

Create a World of Print

Some children pick up a pencil and begin creating meaning through text at a remarkably early age because for them writing is totally natural. Similarly, some children almost from the first day will write much the way they speak, gracing every line with that truest of voices that flows like water when the writing is an extension of self. As Gloria Wade-Gayles (1994) declares, "In the same way that being alive is about breathing, being alive for me is about writing. . . . Writing simply is. It is an expression of my 'who-ness'" (p. 103).

We must allow primary writers to express their "who-ness" while their belief in the power of writing is strong. It stands to reason they will not all reach milestones of achieving readable spelling, correct spelling, knowledge of terminal punctuation, skill with capital letters, ability to form complete sentences, and so on at the same time. We know this intuitively, yet (as parents and as teachers) we often become anxious when a child seems to fall behind others. "What's wrong?" we ask.

In most cases, not only is nothing wrong, but something is very *right*. That something is that the child is adventuring, playing with language in his or her own way, and finding a personal path to learning. A reading specialist once told me about the importance of filling the classroom with books and other printed materials because young readers were hungry for print. "So this is a way to encourage them?" I asked. She shook her head. "It isn't a matter of encouraging them," she explained patiently. "You can't *stop* them. I'm just providing the tools and getting out of the way."

Chapter 12   In a Nutshell

- At primary level, writing has its own look and may include scribbles, pictures, labeled pictures, letter strings—or sophisticated text of one or more paragraphs.

- Primary writers are not making "errors" in the conventional sense but exploring the world of writing, experimenting, daring, borrowing, and growing.

- Because primary writing looks different from more traditional writing, we must work hard to teach ourselves what to look for.

- We need to help primary writers see their strengths so they will write with confidence and voice.

- New techniques or strategies can be effectively shared as "writers' secrets"—one at a time.

- Young writers "hear" details, voice, fluency, and other significant qualities long before such features show up in their own writing, so reading aloud and otherwise sharing mentor texts is critical.

- We can and should use writers' language (*details, voice, lead, ending*) right from the very first.

Primary writers pick it up faster than almost anyone else.

- At primary level, the four most important things that we can do to teach writing are to provide numerous opportunities for children to write; respond positively to students' work; model writing frequently; and read aloud—with expression—from the very best literature that we can get our hands on.

- Primary writers and challenged writers of any age can handle both revision and editing if we keep the tasks small and manageable, and if we use strategies to help them: providing checklists, working through problem solving as a group, and modeling both revision and editing so that they can see them in action.

- Children learn at very different rates, and we do our primary writers a great service when we believe in them—and do not become overly anxious about correct conventions or other hallmarks of good writing.

Study Group   Interactive Questions and Activities

1. **Activity and Discussion.** Modeling is important with all students—but especially at primary level. Which of the following things do you model with or for your students? Check each one that applies; then, with your group, consider what else you might add to this list:

    ___ Coming up with a topic

    ___ Writing a good beginning—or ending—sentence

    ___ Adding important details to a drawing or text

    ___ Double spacing to leave room for additions later

    ___ Using arrows or carets to add or move a detail

    ___ Coming up with a good title

    ___ Starting a sentence with a capital

    ___ Ending with a period or question mark

    ___ Leaving spaces between words

    ___ Wrapping text that won't fit on one line

    ___ Using sensory details: sounds, smells, textures, tastes

    ___ Sounding out a word you cannot spell

    ___ Breaking up a long sentence

    ___ Combining choppy sentences

2. **Activity and Discussion.** Based on #1, share with your colleagues a modeling lesson involving writing, revising, or editing that you might use with primary students (or challenged writers).

3. **Activity and Discussion.** Without referring to the text, see if you can describe in your own words how each trait looks at primary level. Write out your descriptions; then, compare them with those of your colleagues—and also with the "Thinking Like a Writer" posters (Figure 12.1). If you teach primary writers now, see if you can find one piece of writing that typifies strong performance in each trait.

4. **Activity and Discussion.** Choose one paper from this chapter and highlight those things you notice that the student is doing well, connecting each feature you highlight with one or more traits. Imagine that you are going to have a conference with this student. Rehearse one "writer's secret" you might share to give this student a new strategy he or she can use in the future. If you are currently teaching, follow the same procedure with one of your own student's papers.

5. **Activity and Discussion.** Choose a book you might share with primary writers and build a lesson around it by (1) selecting read-aloud passages (or using the whole book) to reinforce a particular trait; (2) thinking of questions you might ask to help students see how such things as detail, voice, or word choice work in the text; and (3) extending students' learning by asking them to write, using one small lesson they have learned from the book (e.g., *Vivid words help a reader picture what you are describing.*).

6. **Activity and Discussion.** As a group, choose any paper from this chapter—or from your own

students' work—and assess it using the primary continuums (Figure 12.9). You may wish to simply check or highlight each strength. (*Tip: Insert each continuum into a plastic page protector before assessing; that way, you can highlight without affecting the hard copy.*) Discuss your findings. Do you see the student's performance in similar ways? Assess three or four more student papers using this same approach.

7. **Activity and Discussion.** If you work with challenged writers at any grade level, choose two (or more) writing samples and, as a group, assess them using the standard writing guide from Chapter 3 and the continuums from this chapter. What advantages does each approach offer? Which scoring guide offers a more accurate profile of what the student can do? Which offers a better basis for a personal conference?

8. **Activity and Discussion.** Read all or part of *Creating Young Writers* (Spandel, 2008) with your study group, discussing the book's instructional strategies and philosophy about assessment of young writers.

9. **Discussion.** Many educators believe that young students are best assessed at the classroom level rather than on a large-scale basis. Do you agree? Share your thoughts with colleagues. Also, explore your district's policy. If it conducts primary assessment, examine the criteria or rubrics it uses. In your view, are these assessment tools likely to identify a young writer's true strengths?

Reflections on Writing

Who knows? I just might make millions of dollars writing books. I might be the next J. R. R. Tolkien. Would that be sweet or what?

—**Carl Matthes**, student writer

My strange writing took a different form when in second grade my teacher got mad at me because I wrote too much (as if there is such a thing). She did not approve of my twenty-or-so-paged stories with the gorgeous pictures I drew for them. I understand that she expected five pages, but I took the time to write twenty! And no, I couldn't have shortened the story. . . . If you do that, it's not the same story.

—**Meghan Eremeyeff**, student writer

CHAPTER 13

Communicating
with Students . . .

I tell people all the things I like about their piece—how wonderful the atmosphere is, for instance, and the language—and also point out where they got all tangled up in their own process. We—the other students and I—can be like a doctor to whom you take your work for a general checkup.

—Anne Lamott
Bird by Bird, 1995, p. 153

We must speak to our students with an honesty tempered by compassion: Our words will literally define the ways they perceive themselves as writers.

—Ralph Fletcher
What a Writer Needs, 1993, p. 19

A few years ago I was both amused and distressed to hear Grant Wiggins tell a large group of conference attendees about a new teacher who was saying farewell to her students after what had seemed a highly successful term. One of the students, Wiggins explained, paused to whisper a question she'd been too timid to ask earlier: "You've written this on so many of my papers, but I don't understand. What is 'va-goo'?" "Va-goo" (*vague*) all too often describes *us* as we try to clarify our expectations for students.

In this chapter I will talk about four important ways of communicating with student writers: through comments, conferences, peer review, and grades. I'll also talk about bringing parents into the conversation. Let's begin with comments, both spoken and written.

. . . Through Comments

Can you recall the most positive thing anyone ever said to you about your own writing? It might have come from a teacher or perhaps a friend, colleague, parent, child, editor, or anyone—a comment that inspired you and gave you confidence. Now turn the tables. Try to remember the most negative comment you ever received on your work—one that momentarily bumped you off the path or perhaps even stunned you, stopped you short.

Here are two examples from my personal experience. In a class on using writing to think, I had written a poem about moving to Oregon to get married. I'd left my mother distraught and in tears and my father sullen and angry (he thought I was too young to marry or to move so far from home), and we hauled our pathetic cache of belongings, my love and I, in a U-Haul truck that didn't do hills. The Rockies were a challenge. My poem was personal and profoundly emotional, and I felt nervous sharing it aloud. Later, I felt happy that I had shared it when the teacher wrote, "The way words move through you, through your pen. I envy that, *love* that." I saved her words and today have them taped inside a drawer because they gave me both encouragement and courage itself. (Thank you, Elaine!)

In eleventh grade I spent five days writing an essay on *The Great Gatsby*. I didn't know nearly enough about life to appreciate the book at that time, but like many 16-year-olds, I thought classics were supposed to be dull, and anyway, I'd worked hard on my essay, particularly the symbolism involving light. I received only one comment, written at the end: "Your most irritating habit is your relentless, *persistent* misuse of the semicolon. Please revise!" Relentless? Persistent? What an angry man to envision me plotting the strategic placement of semicolons to create maximum annoyance (I wasn't that clever)—not to mention the startling phrase "*most* irritating habit." Apparently, out of my vast array of annoying habits, this was the one—this semicolon thing—that provoked him most. He ended with "Please revise!" but I think what he really meant was "Please revise your*self*. Write differently. Write something else, for some*one* else, or at least, write some*where* else."

I have often asked other teachers to recall positive or negative comments and am startled to learn how long some comments have stayed in their minds.

■ Teachers Recall the Good Times . . .

- You show remarkable insight.
- You have a special way with words!
- You have a creative soul!
- You made me want to keep reading—even at 11 P.M.
- This sounds so much like you that I had to keep looking over my shoulder to see if you were in the room.
- I like your use of the word *flamboyant*.
- I like the way you say what you have to say and then quit.
- I began this paper believing one thing, and though you haven't totally turned me around, you have really made me think.
- Beautiful sentence rhythm. I could use this to *teach* fluency.
- You told me you couldn't write. You can. This proves it.
- Thank you for sharing your poem. It spoke to me.
- You took a technical, hard-to-penetrate idea and made it reader-friendly. I felt like an insider.

■ and the Not So Good Times . . .

- I can't believe what I see here. There is nothing of worth, except that the documentation is perfect. It is only the documentation that boosts this paper to a D–. [*Boosts?*]
- I think you may have it in you to write competently, but not brilliantly.
- In looking at this paper again, I believe it is even worse than I originally thought.
- Reading this has depressed me more than I can say.
- I do not have time to read this much. Please be more concise.
- You simply don't know how to write.
- This is basically verbal vomit.
- No one would read this who was not paid to read it.
- Lay off the exclamation points. This isn't that exciting.
- What in the *world* are you trying to say? Just spit it out.
- You will never, ever be an author.
- You missed the point completely. F.
- Do the world a favor. Don't write.
- I do not believe you wrote this. This is not your work.
- Your writing reminds me of a porcupine—many points leading in meaningless directions.

One teacher's comment came in the form of a gesture: Her teacher shredded her paper and returned it to her in a paper bag. It takes only seconds to create a lifetime memory. We must think before we comment.

> I learned an important idea about teaching writing while preparing for the birth of my son. In our childbirth class, our teacher had this suggestion for husbands (and writing teachers) who are nervous about doing and saying the right thing at the critical moment. Relax, she told us. Try to remember that tenderness is more important than technique.
>
> —Ralph Fletcher
> *What a Writer Needs,*
> 1993, p. 18

Is Anybody Listening, Though? Actually, Yes . . .

While some of the preceding comments seem bitter and rancorous, *most* teacher comments are, from teachers' perspectives at least, well intentioned. Sometimes, though, good intentions are not enough to bridge the communications gap. As the weeks tick by and we note no major changes in writing skill, we may wind up wondering whether anyone is even listening. As the samples that follow show clearly, student writers usually *are* responding to our comments, but often not in the way we had imagined or hoped.

- **When the teacher wrote "Needs work," students responded this way . . .**
  - Kind of rude. Work on what?
  - This is so harsh. It makes me feel hopeless.
  - I have to ignore this or I'll wind up hating the teacher.

- **When the teacher wrote, "Use examples to illustrate your point," students responded this way . . .**
  - If I have to give examples on every little detail, I'll never get the point across.
  - I did use examples. You mean *more* examples?
  - I don't have any other examples.

- **When the teacher wrote, "You need to be more concise," students responded this way . . .**
  - I'm confused. What do you mean by "concise"?
  - I'm not Einstein. I can't do everything right.
  - I thought you wanted details and support. Now you want concise.

- **When the teacher wrote, "Be more specific," students responded this way . . .**
  - *You* be specific. What exactly do you want?
  - It's going to be too long then. What happened to concise?
  - Maybe you need to read more closely. Maybe it's you not paying attention.

- **When the teacher wrote, "You need stronger verbs," students responded this way . . .**
  - I lack verby power.
  - I knew it. I should have used the thesaurus.
  - I don't know any other verbs. Give me some examples.

- **When the teacher wrote, "Weak ending," students responded this way . . .**
  - Weak? No way! That's a great ending. Read it again.
  - I know I need a better conclusion, but I have no idea how to write one.
  - Teach me about endings! *Teach* me!

Research by Maxine Hairston (1986) confirms that these responses are not isolated examples but are, in fact, typical of students who become defensive or overwhelmed by comments they do not understand. It might seem on the face of it that one of the best ways to help a budding writer is to point out what he or she is doing wrong. Yet the truth is that this usually *doesn't* help; it causes the writer to retreat and sometimes to avoid writing altogether.

Positive Comment + Modeling = Path to Success

What *does* help is (1) to point out what is going well and help the writer build on that and then (2) to follow up by modeling ways of dealing with problems. Let's begin with the comments.

This seems like the easy part, doesn't it? It's not. Good comments must be truthful and very specific. It's one thing to say, "Good job, Alex." That's not going to crush anyone's spirit, but you should know that it can, and often does, sound phony. No one appreciates mindless approval. Showing that you actually read the paper calls for comments like these:

- Your examples convinced me that chocolate-covered marshmallows are not a good idea. I'm giving them up!
- I think you were horrified at the idea of freeze-drying a cat, but you were chuckling, too—weren't you? You really know how to connect with an audience.

In Figure 13.1, kindergartener Isabelle writes an end-of-year reflection on what she has enjoyed most: the reward of making friends. It's not a treasure, she tells us, and not just candy either, but the joy of knowing you have—or *think* you have—a friend for life. I love many things about this piece—the fluency, the voice (!), the discovery that a true friend can sometimes be "annoying." Most of all, I appreciate the comment from the sensitive "Mrs. Woody" (affectionate nickname for Mrs. Woodfield) who does not zero in on conventions, but writes as if to a colleague: "I loved the way you talked about 'friends for life.' It made me cry." A comment like that says, "You are a writer. Your words touched me."

What If You Don't Like the Paper?

Sometimes it's tough. Maybe you don't like the paper much, or there isn't that much there. Don't give up. Look within. *Listen.* Find a word or phrase you enjoyed—just one; a detail that enriched the whole; an opening that shows improvement over others or an ending that surprised you; one transition that helped connect ideas; one sentence beginning that made the reading smooth; one line that needs no editing at all. If you look hard, you will find *something.* Make a very big deal of it. Next time there will be another something and then another after that.

Teaching "Small"

We tell our writers to "write small." Sometimes we need to "teach small." Don't model "How to Write." Pick one manageable speed bump you and the

> As writers, what we all need more than anything else in the world is listeners, listeners who will respond with silent empathy, with sighs of recognition, with laughter and tears and questions and stories of their own. Writers need to be heard.
> —Lucy McCormick Calkins
> *The Art of Teaching Writing,* 1994, pp. 14–15

> We have been asked several times by teachers, "What makes for good feedback?"—a question to which, at first, we had no good answer. Over the course of two or three years, we have evolved a simple answer—good feedback causes thinking.
> —Paul Black
> *"A Successful Intervention— Why Did It Work?"* 2003, p. 1

> I genuinely believe it is possible to find something good in each piece of writing, and I think you'll find it becomes an acquired skill that is central to being a constructive critic.
> —Barry Lane
> *After THE END,* 1993, p. 126

F I G U R E **13.1** **"What I Enjoyed," by Isabelle (WithTeacher Comments)**

what I engoyed

I engoyed the rewawd you get when you try hard to make friends, is not treser or candy its a friend for life. I hope I don't get a striked teacher. I'm looking forwod to making new friends in first grarde. I will miss Mrs. Woody, Ms. Suny, Jane, Emily, Sara, Stephanie, Alexa, Ms. Bava, Madeline, Jimmy, and Ryan c the most of all. I leart making friends is not easy eqspeshaly boys! But lukly I have

2 friends that are boys, Liam and Ryan C, But Liam is annoying, but Ryan c is, or I think he is, a friend for life.

Isabelle, I loved the way you talked about "friends for life." It made me cry! You have been an amazing student. Good luck in Grade one.

student can navigate together. You might say, "Notice what happens in your mind when I change 'dog' to 'old black lab with one inside-out ear, nursing a limp in his right front leg.' Do you see the difference in your mind? That's what I mean by specific detail."

Or, "Here you are talking about the different parts of an atom—the *nucleus*, the *protons* and *neutrons*, and the *electrons*. You are probably thinking someone reading this knows all these terms very well. Maybe that's true. But what if it isn't? Write about them the way you would *teach* each term to someone who had never heard it before. Consider using an illustration of an atom, with all these parts labeled. When we did creative writing, we talked about vivid images. Images are important in informational writing, too. Scientists use definitions and illustrations to make pictures in their readers' minds."

My all-time favorite teaching story is told by Don Graves (1983), about a golf professional who was helping him to learn the game. On the first lesson, he simply told Graves to hit the ball. A few minutes later, he told the new golfer to keep hitting—only this time with his head down and his eye on the ball. Gradually, he added one more skill . . . then one more. Patiently—never more than one skill at a time. "Before a few weeks were out," says Graves, "he had quietly attended to my grip, shoulder level, and follow through. A few years later I realized with a start that every single one of my problems was visible on the first lesson. If he had attended to all of them that first day, I would probably have missed the ball entirely and resigned in disgust from ever playing golf again" (pp. 314–315).

 # . . . Through Conferences

The very word *conference* can be horrifying to teachers who are already pressed for time. This is often so because they think that

1. They must control everything that happens during the conference.

2. They must use the conference as an opportunity to "fix" the writing.

3. They must listen as the student reads the entire paper.

Think of a conference as a chat. That's all. I like Tommy Thomason's analogy (in *Writer to Writer: How to Conference Young Authors* [1998, pp. 62–64]) to the two neighbors talking about gardening. One is a veteran gardener, and one is a novice. The veteran might answer a question one day about when to plant lettuce. Another day he offers a suggestion on how to keep the flowers from falling off the tomato plants. But never does he take over the garden himself, examine every plant in the garden—or give a lecture on "All About Gardening." And if he did, then the next time he appeared at the fence, the novice gardener might feel a headache coming on. Like the veteran, we conference best when we stop by to "talk writing" for a moment. Successful conferences are short and focused—and student-oriented.

Our students know a lot about what makes writing work, and if we listen to them, we find out that this is so. Those who know the traits well are often more comfortable in a conference, though, because they also have a language for expressing their concerns or questions in writerly terms:

- I need help with my lead.
- I can't tell if I have one main idea—or two.
- I think this is too wordy, but I don't know how to cut it.

We must also look carefully at how students approach a conference, whether with trepidation or confidence. As Donald M. Murray (2004) reminds us, "the way the student walks into the conference, the way in which the student handles the paper—as if it were a golden gift on a platter or a stinking three-day-old fish—can be revealing" (p. 163). Reading our students is as important as reading their work. Equally important is coming to a conference with our whole selves, ready to listen. Such uncompromising attention is a gift we give to any writer.

Shorter Is Better

In *Free to Write*, Roy Peter Clark (1987) talks about the value of a short conference that focuses simply on where the writer is in the process and the most important problem or obstacle that writer faces—and that's it. This

> Once you learn to listen, teaching a child how to write is easy.
> —Cindy Marten
> *Word Crafting*, 2003, p. xiii

> The important thing to realize is that students can be our teachers.
> —Lucy McCormick Calkins
> *The Art of Teaching Writing,*
> 1994, p. 54

> Students walking away from a writing conference are frequently overwhelmed with information. It's important to teach them to learn how to listen to their own internal critics . . .
> —Barry Lane
> *After THE END,* 1993, p. 109

> If children don't speak about their writing, both teachers and children lose. Until the child speaks, nothing significant has happened in the writing conference.
> —Donald H. Graves
> *Writing: Teachers and Children at Work,* 1983, p. 97

don't-drag-it-out approach comes from his experience as a journalist watching city editors deal with dozens of reporters in 30- to 60-second intervals: "City editors learn these techniques or die" (pp. 36–37).

A student should come away from a conference *not* with a polished, ready-to-go draft but simply with an idea of where to go next.

■ The Amazing Two-Minute Conference

What can you do in two minutes? A lot, actually, if your whole attention is focused on the writer—*and* if you allow the student and his or her needs to direct the conference. Making the paper stronger, after all, is a small victory. What you really want to achieve is improving the writer's skill in solving writing problems—and not just for this paper, either, but for all that future writing he or she will do when you're not around. See Figure 13.2 for a list of things you can do in *under two minutes*.

> Two minutes—amazingly possible. For years I have been running workshops in which I have teachers write and respond to each other's drafts, cutting the conferences at two minutes. After two or three rounds of two-minute conferences, I will hear the teachers' voices fall before the two minutes are up. They have achieved a conversation about a piece of writing.
>
> —Donald M. Murray
> *A Writer Teaches Writing,*
> 2004, p. 173

FIGURE **13.2**   **Two-Minute ConferenceTopics**

- Together, brainstorm two possible leads—or endings
- Brainstorm three possible titles
- Identify the MAIN thing that happens in each paragraph—and see if that's the path the writer really wants the reader to follow
- Identify the MAIN idea of the piece
- Identify each spot where the writer wanders from the main track
- Identify three spots where more detail is needed—information, expansion, an image—and insert a caret with a question mark in those spots
- Ask one question that will help the writer "fill in" informational holes
- Use sounds, smells, textures, or tastes to strengthen one moment or scene
- Identify one place where the writer could "shrink" time and improve the pacing of the piece
- Identify one place where the writer could *slow time down* to help the reader reflect on what is happening—or take in a technical concept
- Identify one moment of strong voice—and one where voice fades
- Replace two flat verbs with something stronger
- Get rid of one "There is," "There are," or "It is" sentence beginning
- Add one line of realistic dialogue to bring a character to life

- Identify one moment where a strong quotation would enliven an informational or persuasive piece
- Connect two choppy sentences to form one smooth sentence
- Disconnect one long, entangled sentence to form two or three easy to read sentences
- Cross out one line or phrase that is not needed
- Rewrite one sentence three different ways—then choose the best
- Show how a semicolon works
- Show how to put periods or commas inside quotation marks
- Brainstorm four alternatives to "said"—then choose the one that fits the mood
- Brainstorm four alternatives to "ran" or "walked" or "went"—then choose the one that creates the right mood and image
- Highlight the first four words of each sentence to check for variety
- Turn the last sentence of one paragraph into a transitional sentence that leads right into the next paragraph
- Highlight every "tired" word (*nice, good, great*) in the piece, and brainstorm alternatives for one or two
- Show how one strong verb (*raced*) can replace a weaker verb and adverb: *ran quickly*

What If the Writer Has Nothing to Say?

Often we *think* this is happening because we're in a hurry, and the student is reflecting. Be patient. Wait. Don't allow yourself to grow uncomfortable. Then, if the student simply can't think of *anything* to ask, here are a few prompting questions that may encourage him or her to think about the writing in a useful way:

- What do you like about your piece?
- What do you think is your *main* message? Can you say it to me in a few words?
- Did you read the piece aloud? What did you learn by doing that?
- What is giving you trouble right now?
- What would you like a reader to see or feel as he or she listens?
- Do you like your topic? Is there any way we could modify it?
- Do you think you have enough information to write? Do you know how/where to get more information?

I want to add one more question to this list: "Have you thought about abandoning this piece and starting another?" I'm not saying that writers should do this as a habit. Writing is always a struggle, and you learn a lot by not giving up. Sometimes, though, the topic just goes dead, and you find yourself trying to make a succulent dish out of four-day-old leftovers. In that case, fixing a lead is like plunking parsley on last week's gefilte fish. Time to start fresh—without guilt.

Writers must write, every day if possible. But there is no law stating that every *piece* of writing that's begun must be finished—tomorrow, next week, or ever. Let go.

> Teach one thing, no more. . . . Overteaching means the child leaves the conference more confused than when he entered.
>
> —Donald H. Graves
> *Writing: Teachers and Children at Work,* 1983, p. 146

> Soup is no good when it's been sitting around coagulating. Potatoes get too mushy when they're old . . . If you tamper too much with your story, you'll lose the immediacy, the edge. Overworking your work is a form of fear.
>
> —Nancy Slonim Aronie
> *Writing from the Heart,* 1998, p. 17

 ## . . . Through Peer Response Groups

One day, watching ABC's *Good Morning America*, I heard Charlie Gibson interview actor John Lithgow and ask him what he considered to be the most satisfying part of his career. Smiling, Lithgow replied that it was his years on Broadway. Why? Charlie wanted to know. Why not television or films? Because, Lithgow explained, on Broadway, you play right to an audience. That's when you find out if you can act. Response groups are like that—a chance to play to an audience. Writers—all writers—need this. Peer review can be a waste of time, though, if it's little more than a social hour, and often it disintegrates into this if students do not know what to do during the time they meet and share their writing. Here are ten things you can do to make response groups more successful (and enjoyable) for everyone:

   1. *Help students develop good listening skills.* Writers learn to be listeners first by having someone listen *to them*. In conferences, we must model what we hope to see. In addition, when students have a directed task—such as paraphrasing, giving their impression of the main point, telling what they see or feel, or noting words or phrases that spoke to them in particular—they learn to listen actively, to truly take in the reader's text, to respond to it, and to think about it. Someone must provide this direction, and it should be the *writer*, not you, who says what kind of response will be most useful.

2. *Show students what* not *to do.* Ask a volunteer to read aloud a short piece of writing: the writer's own or one you provide (e.g., "The Redwoods"). Then illustrate the kinds of responses that do not work: staring at the ceiling, laughing inappropriately, making a negative remark ("How could anyone write with such a flat voice?"), or taking over the revision yourself: "You need to tell what the Redwoods looked like, where you hiked, what you saw, and the things you did." Ask your volunteer to let you know how each kind of response makes him or her feel. Then talk about it as a group.

3. *Distinguish between peer editing and peer review.* In peer *review,* listeners seldom see a writer's text. There is no need. They are not *correcting* the text. They're asking themselves, "What catches my attention here? What confuses me? What does this remind me of?" In peer *editing,* writers work together to proofread a text and correct faulty punctuation, spelling, grammar, paragraphing, capitalization, and so on. This is a completely different experience and should not become the purpose of a response group unless that is your explicit intention. (See Chapter 8 for more ideas on this.)

4. *Define roles clearly.* We often assume, because it may seem obvious to us, that students know precisely what to do in a peer response group. Often this is far from the case. No one is sure who should read first or whether writers must read the whole piece. What kinds of responses should listeners give? Are they responsible for the quality of the writer's revision?

The writer's role. Students frequently believe that the role of the writer is first to subject listeners to a rapid, low-volume, monotone reading of the text and then to sit passively as responders give any sort of feedback that suits them. The writer needs to take control of the group.

First, he or she should give the text the best interpretive reading possible, keeping in mind that it is fine to select just a portion if that's what listeners need to focus on. Second, the writer should tell listeners exactly what to listen for:

- Tell me if this makes sense.
- Tell me what you picture.
- Tell me what you feel as you listen.
- Is my voice too conversational (sarcastic, formal)—or does it work?
- What's a good title for this?
- I can't figure out where to go next. Can you help?

The responder's role. We sometimes think that the writer is the only one in a tough position. After all, it's risky to share your writing aloud. We forget that responders are on the spot, too. They may feel a tremendous sense of responsibility, wondering whether the ultimate fate of the paper rests in their hands.

Help responders understand that they are not in charge of revising the piece; that is the writer's job. As responders, their job involves listening attentively, with every sense in tune—and then to offer supportive but honest feedback. How do they react emotionally? What makes sense, and what questions remain?

> Suggestions for how to fix something may be valuable, but should be offered respectfully. Even if you're sure you see just how it ought to be changed, this story belongs to the author, not you.
>
> —Ursula K. LeGuin
> *Steering the Craft,*
> 1998, p. 154

> Even very young children can listen and look for one colorful word or the most exciting sentence or a line that has interesting sounds or the scariest phrase.
>
> —Marjorie Frank
> *If You're Trying to Teach Kids How to Write . . . You've Gotta Have This Book!* 1995, p. 140

5. *Encourage students to* write *one comment to the reader/author.* This tip comes from a very fine and creative teacher, Rosey Comfort, who taught both my own children. Rosey suggests that writers brave enough to share their writing should receive something for their efforts, so she encourages each listener to write a brief comment on a 3" by 5" note card, all of which then go to the writer. In a group, writers can hold their cards until everyone has shared; then they all read responses together. Writers of all ages treasure written feedback and quickly learn what kinds of notes are most helpful and most appreciated (see Figure 13.3 for samples).

6. *Begin with* I. We can teach students to frame negative responses in positive terms so as to make them less painful for writers. When you start with *I*, you shift the focus from the writing to you and your response, a much less accusatory position:

FIGURE **13.3** **Sample Notes to Writers**

- *Your title doesn't go with your paper* **becomes** *I had a hard time connecting the title to the rest of your paper. I kept listening for something about the Redwoods.*

- *You are writing about two topics* **becomes** *I wasn't sure if you were trying to tell me why writing was important—or how to be a good writer.*

- *You shifted from fairness, justice, and courage to fairness, respect, and courage* **becomes** *I felt confused when the three themes you talked about in the beginning of your paper changed.*

- *You didn't back any of your points with quotations* **becomes** *I was listening for a quotation that would show how Atticus felt about* **justice.**

7. *Participate.* Join one of the class response groups yourself. Not every time—but now and then. Read your own work. Ask for the kinds of responses you'd like; give the kinds you'd like your students to give you.

8. *Remind students not to apologize.* So often we feel compelled to apologize for weaknesses, real or perceived, in our performance. Nowhere do we do this more often or more vocally than in preface to our own writing. "Remember," we say, "this is just a rough draft. I wrote this when I was recovering from knee surgery, and the computer was down. I had a sprained thumb, I had to use a crayon on butcher paper, and the neighbor's dog was howling." See what this does to an audience? It says to them, "Never mind the text; pay attention to *me*. I am very needy here." Most audiences will leap to the rescue, eager to make the writer feel better. Is that the kind of response we want, though?

When you share your own writing aloud, just plunge in. Later (if students do not notice), you can point out your raw courage and tell them, "You do this, too. Be brave. Read your text with confidence so that the feedback you get will be more about your writing and less about you."

9. *Make it real.* Many teachers feel more comfortable with a rule that says, "Each responder will make one positive comment prior to offering other kinds of feedback." This *can* work, provided that the comments are heartfelt and the writer does get his or her most important questions answered. In some ways, however, it seems a little formulaic. First, we'll say something nice to get the writer's guard down; then we'll slam her with the necessary criticism to ensure improvement.

Our responses to writing do not have to be couched in positives and negatives unless we choose to structure them in those terms. And why would we? Our first impression is more likely to occur in terms of asking ourselves, What do I *see* (if anything)? What do I *feel* (if anything)? A student said one day in response to a piece I'd written on a very tense, confrontational family Thanksgiving, "Your family seems very argumentative. *Very.* When you talked about staring into the candlelight reflecting off your mother's blue glass plates, I thought you were trying to escape. I used to do that." I had never before thought of myself as "escaping," but of course that is precisely what I was doing. This response was much more revealing to me than if the student had said, "I enjoyed your description of the candlelight reflecting on the plates." A compliment makes us feel good for a moment; an insight keeps us thinking for hours—sometimes forever.

10. *Don't drag it out.* Peer review is, by nature, a reflective activity, and we must respect that. On the other hand, allowing too much time can make students feel pressured to say more than they have to say, and soon the conversation drifts to unrelated topics. Try this (adjusting if the timing does not work for you): Put students into groups of three. Let students know that they need to stay focused and make comments that are to the point. Ask them to decide who will go first, second, and third. Then give each student 3 to 4 minutes to read his or her work. Allow responders about 2 minutes to give a focused, clear, concise response to the reader's piece, either orally or on note cards. The whole process will take under 20 minutes.

Debriefing

At the end of the peer review session, take 5 minutes to debrief the process. Ask writers, "Who got a response that was really helpful today? What was it? How many of you have a strong sense right now of how you will go about revising your work? Did you get the feedback you need?" When writers take charge and ask for feedback they really need, and when responders listen and offer heartfelt comments, response groups can make a world of difference.

 . . . Through Grades

Even educators who still advocate the use of grades will admit that, for many purposes, there are better, more thorough methods of measuring and recording student achievement. A well-designed portfolio provides a richer and more complete picture of what a student can do than reams of test scores. Similarly, a teacher's narrative record of student performance, if sufficiently detailed, provides a wealth of information no report card can match.

As Barry Lane (1993) tells us, "For a writing teacher who believes in encouraging revision, graded papers are nothing less than a curse. Low grades discourage and high grades imply that a piece is done. Even worse, students begin writing to improve their grade instead of finding out what they have to say" (p. 129). Donald M. Murray (2004) calls grades the "terminal response," meaning that once a grade is assigned to a piece of writing, it virtually dies, for the student will not look at it again.

In his book, *Punished by Rewards*, Alfie Kohn (1993) talks openly about the naïveté of believing that we can motivate students to strive for excellence with a simplistic carrot-and-stick, A-to-F grading system. A student's inner world, he assures us, is far too complex for this. When grades dominate the classroom environment, Kohn argues, students tend to

1. Place minimal value on things learned and to care only about the grade earned.

2. Become dependent on the reward, allowing themselves to be controlled by the threat of the grade.

3. Become unwilling to take any risk, however promising, that might jeopardize their grade point average (GPA).

Kohn suggests that comments are more meaningful and more motivational than grades and are far more likely to inspire excellent performance (p. 203).

What Do Grades Mean to Students?

Ask *students* what grades mean, and you're likely to get some startling answers. Many students will tell you that A's are mostly for parents (or for precollege records)—and sometimes translate into money, the right to drive the car, or other tangible rewards.

Do you think C means average and F means failure? Think again. Many students will tell you that the *worst* grade to receive is a C because while an F means that you didn't try or didn't care (this can even be a badge of honor), a C indicates that you did your best but *still* failed—and that's depressing.

What's more, though many of us hate admitting this, grades have no universal meaning beyond the most general level. To *most* teachers, an A signifies a job well done; an F, significant problems with performance. However, some teachers refuse ever to assign a D or an F because of the potential damage to self-esteem. One teacher I knew assigned grades of A, AA, AAA, and so on, to avoid any confidence-diminishing "lower grades." It didn't work, of course. Within a very short time, his students unraveled the code and were devastated to receive the low grade of "A."

In a workshop one day I asked teachers to define what B− meant to them. Here are just some of their intriguing, diverse answers:

- You tried hard, but it needed work.

- Good job! Just needed that little something more.

> The cost runs high when we coerce students (through grades, praise, favoritism), however subtly, to shoehorn their emerging language into the narrow parameters we set for what constitutes "good writing" in our classrooms.
>
> —Ralph Fletcher
> *What a Writer Needs,*
> 1993, p. 25

> Where do children learn to be grade-grubbers? From this: "You'd better listen up, folks, because this is going to be on the test." And from this: "A B-minus? What happened, Deborah?" And from this: "I take pride in the fact that I'm a hard grader. You're going to have to work in here."
>
> —Alfie Kohn
> *Punished by Rewards,*
> 1993, p. 205

> When I first began to teach, I was a tough grader right from the first day. . . . My students didn't realize I was terrified they might rise up and attack me. I put them in their place with grades.
>
> —Donald M. Murray
> *A Writer Teaches Writing,*
> 2004, p. 142

- Close to what I expected—*almost!*
- Average work. It's what used to be a C.
- Between 80 and 82 percent—it's pure mathematics.
- I tried to like your paper, but I couldn't.

■ Being Consistent

Given these diverse responses, can we ever hope to achieve consistency, a clear definition of performance goals, and all-around fairness? We can. Indeed, we must. By connecting grades to criteria, we say to students, "We will define what we mean by various levels of performance, and we will apply those definitions as consistently as human nature will allow." It isn't a perfect system. How can it be when we are talking levels of quality and not rights or wrongs? But the more we read and write ourselves, and the more we practice assessment with our students, the more consistent our scoring becomes, and the more we draw students into our interpretive community.

How and What to Grade

Certainly student achievement (performance, that is) will be at the heart of most grading systems. But should other factors be considered as well? Let's take a closer look.

■ Achievement

If we grade on achievement, we tell students, in effect, that those who attain a higher level of writing proficiency will receive higher grades. To many people, this seems a fair approach to grading, and I agree. After all, demand for high-level achievement is a reality of life, both in and out of the classroom. Writers whose work no one wants to read do not get published, nor do they get hired as journalists, technical writers, communications specialists, or editors. Performance counts everywhere, not just in school. Having said that, we must determine what kinds of achievement we wish to measure and how we will go about it.

Much of this book is devoted to defining and promoting a performance assessment approach that judges the quality of students' writing based essentially on final products. However, achievement could also include performance on foundational writing tasks, such as spelling tests or editing. In addition, you may wish to look at such things as these:

- The student's ability to self-assess and defend that judgment
- The student's ability to assess the work of others and defend that judgment
- Skill in coaching other writers

Teachers who wish to focus on process as well as product may also ask questions such as these:
- Do students find their own writing topics?
- Do they write for diverse audiences across a range of genres?
- Do they find prewriting strategies that work for them?
- Do they participate actively and purposefully in conferences or peer writing groups?

> We see that our evaluations are usually more trustworthy—and much more likely to enhance learning—when we find ways to describe the performance in question rather than measure or rank it.
>
> —Peter Elbow
> *Embracing Contraries*, 1986, p. 225

> Experienced teachers watch and listen closely for when students get things wrong. . . . Mistakes offer information about how a student thinks.
>
> —Alfie Kohn
> *Punished by Rewards*, 1993, pp. 212–213

> Perfectionism is the voice of the oppressor, the enemy of the people.
>
> —Anne Lamott
> *Bird by Bird*, 1995, p. 28

> If you grade a body of work, you will give students a better picture of their overall strengths and weaknesses.
>
> —Barry Lane
> *After THE END*, 1993, p. 128

- Do they revise their work routinely and thoughtfully, without excessive prompting?
- Do they know how and when to edit?
- Do they have a sense of how they are improving as writers?

■ Effort

One teacher may define *effort* as "completing and turning in all homework on time," whereas to another it may mean "making a positive contribution to the classroom." Such differences lead to inconsistency in grading. Furthermore, haven't we all known people whose specialty was making the next to impossible look easy? And haven't we, honestly, valued and sometimes even envied this capability? Imagine the difference in Fred Astaire's career had he lurched across the stage, huffing and puffing. Would anyone then have said, "Boy, that Fred Astaire is some dancer! What an *effort* the guy makes!" We don't want huffing, really; we want good dancing that looks effortless even when we know that it's not.

Keep in mind, too, that assertiveness can look a lot like effort. The student who is forever asking a clarifying question or seeking additional writing advice is often judged to be highly motivated. This may be a correct perception, but what of the quiet or shy writers who would love to have a fraction more of our attention but are too withdrawn to ask for it? Who knows how much effort it takes for those writers just to share their writing in a group or to compose pieces they know other eyes will see.

Suppose, then, that we do not grade on effort. It's only fair to ask, "What about the student who really *is* making an effort but simply cannot succeed? What, other than effort, will rescue this student from failure?"

Instead of rewarding the effort, which provides a hollow, unsatisfying kind of victory, why not reshape the task to better fit the student's skill? Change the assignment; let the student choose another topic or approach this topic in another way. Allow the student to dictate part of the piece or to flesh out a story with illustrations. If editing is involved, simplify the task by asking the student to search out fewer errors or fewer kinds of errors. Lengthen the time allowed to complete the assignment. In other words, let's find a way to help writers succeed with the business of writing. Then we won't hear ourselves saying to students, via artificially inflated grades (which fool no one), "I see that you cannot make it as a writer, but you seem like such a good person, here are some points for trying." It is condescending and disrespectful to inflate performance scores. Students know when they have done a good job and when they need to work harder. Let's not demean them by pretending we see things differently.

> A low grade for effort is more likely to be read as "You're a failure even at trying." On the other hand, a high grade for effort combined with a low grade for achievement says "You're just too dumb to succeed."
>
> —Alfie Kohn
> *Punished by Rewards,*
> 1993, pp. 208–209

■ Attitude

Do you have a good attitude toward writing? I do—mostly. Perhaps, like me, you actually get a good feeling picturing yourself sitting down at the keyboard with a little music playing and the scent of herbal tea drifting your way. When it's going well, almost nothing feels as good as writing.

I write virtually every day, but I do not feel positive and open about it every day. Once when I was working on a piece on economics (far from my favorite topic), the computer "ate" a large chunk of the chapter I had been struggling with for two weeks. On that day I wanted to be Mad Max—just for an hour—but of course computers are not yet sufficiently advanced to experience pain, so all this energy was wasted. I certainly would not have been happy to be visited just then by someone with a clipboard and checklist, assessing my attitude.

Keeping at it when you don't feel like it is my definition of good attitude. But then another teacher-assessor will look for a cheery disposition, a lengthy journal, or willingness to try a new form of writing. The point is, can we really define or recognize good attitude—any more than we can recognize effort? Bottom line, we should reward effort with an appreciative smile and lavish praise, but we should *not* figure it into our grades.

■ Improvement

Some teachers like to weight later performance because it more closely reflects learning—and also shows how far a writer (or any learner) has come. I agree with this practice. There are several ways to do it. You might, for example, simply toss out an early performance. Or, you might weight the scores of later performances more heavily. Either way, you honor what the student has achieved by putting learning to work.

Translating Analytical Scores into Grades

Begin with the realization that analytical scores do not convert *directly* into grades. This is because a score represents an assessment of one writing trait—not the writing as a whole. Therefore, it does not make sense to say a 6 is an A, a 5 is a B, and so forth. Assessment specialist Richard Stiggins reminds us that the whole point of having a rubric in the first place is to provide the student (or anyone) with much richer, more detailed information than any grade can offer: "If the objective is to communicate thoroughly about student achievement, then don't convert rubric scores to letter grades at all if you can help it. Rather, communicate using the points on the rubric" (2006, p. 316).

Sometimes, of course, you *cannot* help it. Grades—like it or not—are required. In that case, begin by developing for yourself and for your students a "big picture." Spell out, in very specific terms, which tasks, assignments, or tests will affect students' grades and what percentage of the total grade will hinge on each. Be sure that students are familiar with the explicit criteria (e.g., the six-trait model or any other rubrics) that you will use to assess performance. Realize that any grade will be based upon the ratio of scores earned versus scores possible—over time.

Then, consider the following guidelines:

1. *Do not assess everything.* We want to gather just enough information to make confident grading decisions and no more. We know that one or two samples are not enough. When we assess somewhere between four and six samples of writing, though, we see a *body* of work; then we are probably approaching a level at which we can feel confident that our assessment is meaningful.

> The student deserves the teacher's respect, and deserves a grade that indicates how that work measures up. The student is not rewarded for potential, for effort, for commitment; the student is rewarded for accomplishment, for producing writing that stands up to a reader's critical eye.
>
> —Donald M. Murray
> *A Writer Teaches Writing,*
> 2004, p. 170

> When achievement is cumulative over time, base the grade on the most recent work.
>
> —Judith A. Arter
> and Jan Chappuis
> *Creating and Recognizing Quality Rubrics,* 2006, p. 125

With your help, students can be selective about what is assessed. During a given grading period, if you are focusing on specific genres, you might ask students to select samples that they believe are worth taking clear through the writing process; others remain practice drafts—good for developing skills but never assessed. Normally, practice revision, free writing, journals, and beginning drafts would not be assessed (except in the sense that the teacher may check to see that they are done).

2. *For any given assignment, score those traits that are most relevant.* You do not need to assess all six traits each time, although you can if this kind of "full picture" approach makes you more comfortable. Consider, though, that in a piece of technical writing, ideas, conventions, and word choice may be more important than, say, fluency. A student who is explaining how to tie a fishing fly must think about detail, organization, and word choice (terminology), whereas one who is telling the story of a narrow escape from a fire may focus most on details (ideas) and voice.

3. *Do not* grade *individual pieces of writing.* If you are giving students scores, if they know the rubrics, and if you are offering your own personal comments in addition to scores alone, you are providing significant, meaningful feedback. A grade adds no new information. Students who know the traits know that if they're receiving 4s, 5s, or 6s, they're doing moderately to extremely well. Scores of 1, 2, or 3 mean that significant revision is needed. There's never any mystery.

4. *Give students the option to revise.* In many classrooms, students who are unsatisfied with the formal assessment on any piece of writing have the option to revise and thereby raise their scores. This option not only reinforces the value of revision but also says to students, "Assessment is an impression, not an ultimate truth."

5. *Keep written records of all scores earned.* Do not assume that you can recapture scores by looking through a work file or portfolio later. Record scores as soon as they are earned.

6. *Allow students time to self-assess during the revision process.* Early assessment, not for grading but to set up a plan for revision, is essential to making students partners in the overall evaluation process.

7. *Consider basing grades on an average.* This is perhaps the simplest way to compute grades. Simply total the points earned and divide by the number of traits assessed. For example, let's say that I am using a six-point scale and that my students have completed three pieces of writing, each of which is scored on all six traits. One student—Pat—receives (for the sake of simplicity) all 5s (out of a possible 6) on two of the assignments and all 4s on the third. Pat's total points equal $5 \times 6 \times 2$ (or 60) plus 4×6 (or 24), for a total of 84. The average, then, is 84 divided by 18 (the total number of individual *traits* assessed for the three assignments). The resulting score is 4.67. What grade is this? Actually, that's entirely up to you. The way to figure it out is to make yourself a chart, like the one that follows, with grade cutoffs that suit you. Remember, the one in this book is *only a model;* please modify these numbers to suit yourself.

> If you do a complete autopsy on every piece, your writers will perish from too much pruning.
> —Marjorie Frank
> *If You're Trying to Teach Kids How to Write . . . You've Gotta Have This Book!*
> 1995, p. 104

> Grades generate anxiety and hard feelings between students, between students and teachers, between students and their parents, and between parents and teachers. Common sense suggests they ought to be reduced to the smallest possible number necessary to find out how students are getting along toward the four or five main objectives of the program, but teachers keep piling them up like squirrels gathering nuts.
> —Paul Diederich
> *Measuring Growth in English,*
> 1974, p. 2

■ **Possible Grade Equivalents for a Six-Point Scale (The one used for Pat)**

5.2 A	4.2 B	3.2 C	2.2 D
4.8 A–	3.8 B–	2.8 C–	1.8 D–
4.4 B+	3.4 C+	2.4 D+	

8. *Or base the grade on a percentage.* Many teachers like percentages, and this is another (albeit slightly more complicated) way to compute grades. The grade is based on points earned as a percentage of total points possible, a percentage that is adjusted by reason of the fact that it does not represent a true total but an estimated position on a continuum (see Figure 13.4).

Picture that continuum for a moment, and you'll see that a score of, say, 4 is not really a 4.0 at all, but exists somewhere along the path between 4.0 and 5.0. Sometimes it might be a 4.5 and sometimes a 4.9, and so on. To adjust for this, I previously recommended adding a half point to students' scores; however, I was not happy with the resulting percentages, particularly for those students who earned lower scores of 1, 2, or 3. Therefore, I now recommend that you adjust the score by *one full point* (in the grade book, not on the student's paper), making a score of 3 a 4.0, a score of 4 a 5.0, and so on.

An adjustment—not a gift. By the way, in case you are concerned, you are not giving the student extra points by making this adjustment; you are not *giving the student anything.* You are simply making a mathematical adjustment that reflects the fact you are scoring along a continuum. A continuum by nature covers a *range of possible scores*—up to *a full point higher* than the assigned score. This is why scoring on a continuum is very different from, say, earning 76 points on a 100-point geography or math test. So what about the *points possible* then? That number does *not* increase; it remains constant; otherwise, the adjustment would be meaningless.

Scores for Pat. Let's go back to Pat for a moment. First of all, let's acknowledge that a score of 5 on a six-point scale is *very* strong. Logic tells us that a student who is earning *mostly* 5s on this scale should probably receive an A, or something close to it. With our one-point adjustment, Pat's scores of 5 become 6s and the 4s become 5s. Thus, the total points earned become 6 × 12 plus 5 × 6, for a total of 102. We divide this number by points possible on three assignments with all six traits scored: 6 × 6 (points) times

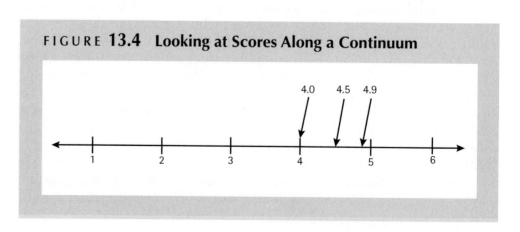

F I G U R E **13.4** **Looking at Scores Along a Continuum**

FIGURE 13.5   Scores for Chris on FiveAssignments

Scores for Chris (based on a six-point scale)

Assignment 1	Assignment 2	Assignment 3	Assignment 4	Assignment 5
2	3	4 = 5	4 = 5	4 = 5
2	2	4 = 5	4 = 5	4 = 5
2	3	4 = 5	4 = 5	4 = 5
2	3	4 = 5	3 = 4	4 = 5
1	2	3 = 4	3 = 4	3 = 4
1	2	3 = 4	3 = 4	4 = 5
	Totals:	28	27	29 = 84

3 (assignments) = 108. Dividing points earned (102) by points possible (108) gives us a percentage of about 94.

Whatever grade you want it to be . . . Again, that percentage can translate into any grade you wish. I would likely look on it as an A minus, but you may see it differently. If we simply computed Pat's percentage as is, with no adjustment, it would come out to 77 percent. This would give Pat a high C in most grading systems. Consider all those 4s and 5s, though, and you'll see at once that this grade is completely inappropriate. This is why adjustment is necessary.

A real-life scenario. Chris is a struggling student. He has started the term with many scores of 2 or even 1—working hard for a 3. On the last three assignments, however (see Figure 13.5), Chris received 4s on ideas, organization, and voice—and sometimes on word choice as well. He hung in with mostly 3s on conventions and fluency. Here's how the grading *could* go.

First, I could decide to weight the *final three assignments* (by discarding assignments 1 and 2) in order to emphasize *growth*—which in Chris's case has been fairly dramatic. So this is a good thing, in my view. Each score of 4 that Chris earned translates into an adjusted score of 5. The six scores of 3 that Chris earned on the traits he struggles with (conventions and fluency) translate into adjusted scores of 4. The earned total is 28 + 27 + 29, or 84. Thus, the final percentage = 84 divided by 108, or about 77 percent. This is a solid C (approaching a B–), and is a more appropriate grade for a student who "leaps the river" much of the time. Just to put this in perspective, Chris's *unadjusted total score* is 22 + 21 + 23 = 66, which, divided by 108, would give him a grade of 61 percent, or barely passing in most systems. As this illustration shows, the adjusted scores *allow the letter grades to make sense.* (Note that Chris's total scores of 66, when divided by the number of traits scored (18), results in an average of 3.6—also a solid C, headed toward B–, according to the grade equivalent chart under Suggestion 7.)

One last comment: The adjusted scores are entered into a grade book for purposes of *computing grades*. Remember, though, that scores are designed to communicate with the student about performance. That, and not the grade, is what is most important. Therefore, *the score that goes on the paper* (the score Chris sees) should be an *unadjusted* score. That way, Chris will know whether the performance "leaps the river" or not.

 . . . Through Communication with Parents and Other Caregivers

Parents are used to letter grades. Now, suddenly, here you are with numerical scores, continuums, scoring guides, strengths and weaknesses, and the rest. How do you explain it all?

Perhaps the best way, if you have the luxury of a little time, is a mini-session in which you summarize the six traits and even have parents attempt to score a paper or two. You might even, if you're very brave, ask them to write a short paragraph and assess their own writing. Nothing brings the traits so vividly into focus as looking at your own work!

■ Writing Goals

Explain that students will be learning the steps within the writing process together with the six traits as writing *goals* and that learning to be strong and independent writers will take time. Also explain that you will be scoring students' work on these six traits, but that you may not score every trait every time. This means that the emphasis will sometimes be on ideas, sometimes on word choice or terminology, and sometimes on conventions—and so on. Make sure parents have copies of the traits in some form, whether as a rubric or checklist or summary. Invite them to sit in on lessons that show how the traits are taught through revision and editing practice—not through teacher correction that has no true impact on students' skills.

■ What Parents and Other Caregivers Can Do

Parents (and others at home) play a critical role in communicating with students, and often want to know what they can do to help their children become stronger writers. Many things, actually. Let them know that they do not need to correct or revise anything. A good first step is to read through one of the student checklists (Figure 8.2 or 8.3), or a rubric that you provide, so that they can use writers' language in responding to their students' work in positive ways. They can also take any of the following eight suggestions to become an integral part of your writing instruction:

■ To Parents and Other Caregivers . . .

1. *Read to your child.* The reading-writing connection is powerful. When you read aloud to your child, you do many things: show that books are exciting and enjoyable to share, expand your child's vocabulary and "sentence

sense," and help him or her to understand why writing matters—as a way of communicating to a reader. When you read, put all the passion you can into your reading. Have fun! Let go of inhibition, and let the text carry you. Don't be concerned if you do not know every word. You and your student writer can work your way through pictures and/or text together. What matters most is that your child sees and hears you enjoying reading.

2. *Encourage your child to read to you.* Students who read aloud learn to read for meaning. They also develop an ear for voice and fluency—two vital qualities of strong writing. When a child learns to read with expression, he or she becomes a confident reader and also learns to put that same kind of expression into his or her own writing. Really listen as your child reads. Sink into the world of the book. Let the text sweep you away.

3. *Be a listener.* Ask your child to share his or her writing—even if it is unfinished. Don't feel that you have to be a grammarian, teacher, or coach. Relax. The most important thing you can do is to listen with full attention and interest. Listen as you would to a cherished letter from a friend you have not seen in a long while. Respond to the content from your heart. Tell the student what you hear; what you love; what you picture in your mind; what you feel, think of, or remember; and what makes an impression on you.

4. *Talk about topics.* Many students have difficulty coming up with topics to write about. You can help. Talk with your child about experiences and interests you have shared. What do you like to do together? Have you overcome a frightening, sad, or challenging experience? Talk it through. Have you laughed together about something? Visited an interesting place? See if you can reconstruct it. Share family stories your child may have forgotten or may not know, including stories of his or her own childhood (and yours). Families make a great resource for writing topics. A family photo album or scrapbook (if you keep one) can be a good place to begin. Perhaps a sibling, aunt or uncle, or grandparent has stories to share or can offer a geographic or historic perspective on life. Other general topic areas: places or people you remember, hobbies, sports, pets, school experiences, work, friends, interesting people, and favorite or least favorite foods.

5. *Write.* Let your child see you write—a note to a friend, a thank-you letter, an invitation, a letter of explanation, a letter of inquiry, a résumé or job application letter, an evaluation or report, a letter to the editor, a recipe, or a list. Each time you write, you show your child that writing is an important life skill and that it has many purposes.

6. *Ask your child to write.* Do you need to request something from an agency or company? Do you want to comment on a product or service? Are you planning a family get-together? Are you putting together an album or scrapbook? Are you sending a greeting card? Writing a review on the Internet? Let your child write captions, letters, notes, explanations, product assessments, or invitations. If he or she is very young, you can help, perhaps even doing some of the writing or keyboarding as your child comes up with ideas. When you do this, the child is still doing the *thinking* part of the writing—the most important part.

"A survey of National Merit Scholars—exceptionally successful eighteen-year-olds crossing all lines of ethnicity, gender, geography, and class—turned up a common thread in their lives: the habit of sitting down to a family dinner table."
—Barbara Kingsolver
Animal, Vegetable, Miracle,
2007, pp. 125–126

7. *Let your child be* your *teacher.* Writers and editors learn by teaching. So let your child be your teacher. Ask him or her to explain the meaning of a passage, interpret a piece of business correspondence, or help you to rewrite a sentence to make it shorter or more clear. Ask for help coming up with the right word, the best way to begin a letter, a correct spelling, or the just-right way to end a piece. You'll find that one of the best things you can do is to seek your child's help.

8. *See your child as a writer.* Virtually *nothing* you can do has more power and impact than believing in your child's ability to write. Take every opportunity you can to encourage him or her and to say to your child, in your own words, "You are a writer."

Chapter 13   In a Nutshell

- The comments we make are a way of sharing our personal responses to students' writing, and the words we choose may have lasting impact.

- The most effective comments are honest and specific. We can (and should) help students to build on their strengths. We can (and should) offer feedback on problems, but in a positive way.

- Often, beginning with *I* is a good way to put a positive spin on a constructive comment.

- Conferences are most effective if they are brief and focus on one or two writing problems, not on the whole piece.

- To the extent possible, the student writer should guide the length and content of the conference.

- Peer response groups serve an important function in the classroom if they are managed carefully.

- Both writers and responders need to understand the roles they are to play.

- Grades are best thought of as one form of communication, not as rewards (or penalties).

- Grades should be based on writing performance and growth, not effort or attitude.

- Several factors can help make grading fair and consistent, including sharing the basis for grades with students; involving students in establishing criteria; not assessing everything; basing grades on a body of work; and remaining flexible about changing grades if change is warranted.

- It is critical to involve parents by letting them know specific ways they can work with their student writers.

Study Group   Interactive Questions and Activities

1. **Activity and Discussion.** What is the most positive or negative comment you have ever received on your own writing? How did it influence you? What are some positive or negative comments you have given to student writers? Do you think you got the response you hoped for?

2. **Activity and Discussion.** With your group, select one student paper from this book.

Independently, write out the comment(s) you would offer this student writer in a conference or on paper—then share them with others in your group. Which of your comments would you expect to be most helpful?

3. **Activity and Discussion.** If you use response groups in your class, which of the following strategies are part of your instructional

approach? Which might you try in the future? Discuss this with your group.

___ Working on listening skills

___ Asking the writer to take charge of the process, identifying the kind of feedback he or she would find helpful

___ Participating myself as a writer and/or responder

___ Modeling helpful (or unhelpful) response behavior

___ Encourage use of the pronoun *I* to make criticism less accusatory and more reflective of listener response

___ Asking responders to go beyond "I liked it" to identify specific strengths or questions

4. **Activity and Discussion.** For fun, act out a "bad response group" scenario, doing some role playing to identify the kinds of behaviors that are least helpful. Imagine ways to use this in your classroom.

5. **Activity and Discussion.** Within your group, take turns sharing samples of your own writing while others act as a response group for you. Ask them to write comments on 3" by 5" cards, which will be handed to you at the end of your presentation. Talk about the most helpful responses you receive.

6. **Activity and Discussion.** Write a one-paragraph rough draft on any topic, and *on purpose* include *at least one* readily identifiable writing problem. Use this piece in a role-playing activity in which you are the student writer. Come to your "conference" (with a colleague from your group) with a question about your piece or your process in mind. See how much you can accomplish in *2 minutes or less.* Take turns so that you also have a chance to rehearse the role of the teacher/coach.

7. **Discussion.** Are grades addictive? Share your experiences and opinions. If you had a choice, would you use grades—or some other way of communicating about performance?

8. **Activity and Discussion.** Individually, complete the following checklist, indicating whether a factor should count at all in determining a student's grade, and if so, what percentage of the grade should be based on that factor. When you finish, share your responses with others in your group.

___ Writing performance ___ %

___ Attitude ___ %

___ Growth ___ %

___ Effort ___ %

___ Participation in writing process ___ %

___ On-demand assessment ___ %

___ Other: _____ ___ %

9. **Activity and Discussion.** *As a group,* choose five comparable (at or close to same grade level) papers from this text—*OR* five papers all written by one of your students. If you pull papers from this book, imagine that all five were written *by the same student.* Score them. Then decide which of them you would include in grading a body of work. All? Three? Four? What grade would the student receive? Compute the grade any way you wish—then adjust the grading procedures, as necessary. What steps do you need to take to arrive at a fair grade? Discuss this.

10. **Activity and Discussion.** Compose an argument for maintaining or doing away with grades. Hold a debate within your study group.

11. **Activity and Discussion.** *From the perspective of a parent or other caregiver,* list specific things your school does (or should do) to create ways of helping make every child successful in writing. *From a teacher's perspective,* list specific things *you do* to give parents or other caregivers a role in the instructional process.

12. **Activity and Discussion.** As an individual or group, compose a letter to parents and other caregivers, offering suggestions for helping their children become stronger writers. Use the list from this chapter as a beginning point.

Reflections on Writing

There were edits on my paper regarding grammar and syntax, which is the most I would have expected of any teacher. But Mrs. Morgan had also typed page-by-page remarks on my dialogue use, plot, and historical facts that I needed to keep in mind. I don't remember what score I got, much less if I even received one. I was young and a good grade was still important to me. But my concern for them decreased significantly after that. There was someone who enjoyed reading what I wrote as much as I enjoyed writing it. That meant the most to me, and no score or grade could ever give me a similar feeling. I was writing for the reader. And I was writing for myself. To me, writing isn't the means to a happy ending of a good grade. Writing is the end in itself.

—Simona Patange, student writer

CHAPTER 14

Expanding the Vision

I believe the ultimate in education is reached when learners—both students and teachers at all levels—take charge of their own learning and use their education to lead rich and satisfying lives.

—Regie Routman
Literacy at the Crossroads, 1996, p. 147

What is needed is a culture of success, backed by a belief that all pupils can achieve.

—Paul Black and Dylan Wiliam
"Inside the Black Box: Raising Standards through Classroom Assessment,"
1998, p. 147

When my students and I discover uncharted territory to explore, when the pathway out of a thicket opens up before us, when our experience is illuminated by the lightning life of the mind—then teaching is the finest work I know.

—Parker J. Palmer
The Courage to Teach: Exploring the Inner Landscape of a Teacher's Life, 1998, p. 1

Let us put our heads together and see what life we will make for our children.

—Tatanka Iotanks (Sitting Bull, Lakota)
New Horizons, 1995

We live in a time of educational skepticism and self-doubt, a time when we often hear only faint echoes of those strong and fearless voices—Donald Graves, Donald Murray, Lucy Calkins, Regie Routman, and others—whose eloquence once charted a path so sure we never questioned the truth at its core. It is growing harder for us to listen these days because, after all, we are very busy—busy launching ourselves full sail from strategy to strategy, never weighing anchor long enough to know for sure whether we have reached safe harbor at last. Our fear makes us frenzied and impatient. Though we fly the flag of "writing process," an agonizing worry gnaws at us: What if teaching writing this way takes too long? The test, after all, is coming. It is *always* coming. So we blaze through articles and Internet sites, looking for a faster approach that will make writers of our students this year, this month, now. And of course, because the test is looming, we simultaneously look back over our shoulders to see if the education critics are closing in. They are, of course. They are forever circling. For some people, criticism is a calling.

In the face of all the doubts, therefore, in that small, quiet place within you where you still recall why you became a teacher, and know that you can and do make a difference, here are seven beliefs I would ask you to cling to:

1. *Believe in the voices that once led us.* Process is the answer—the only answer. People learn to write by writing, by reading, and by living and working within a community of writers who can share their experience and their growing expertise. Writers do not learn to write overnight or through shortcuts. They can learn to fill pages this way, but only writing that touches readers is the real thing.

2. *Believe that the human spirit is too elusive, too vast, and too diverse to be defined by a single assessment.* Assessment gives us useful information (sometimes) and helps us to know where to put our teaching energy (sometimes). A single assessment cannot tell us whether a student can write or whether a teacher can teach. In his last years of public school, a young man received these comments on his writing: "This boy is an indolent and illiterate member of the class." "Ideas limited." "A persistent muddler." "I have never met a boy who so persistently writes the exact opposite of what he means." Some years later, in the early 1940s, this "persistent muddler" wrote an article about his military experiences, an article for which he received a then-amazing sum of $1000 from the *Saturday Evening Post*, and this encouraging comment from the novelist C. S. Forester: "You were meant to give me notes, not a finished story. I'm bowled over. Your piece is marvelous. It is the work of a gifted writer." The young man was Roald Dahl (2000, pp. 187–188, 198–199), and had he allowed those early assessments to define how he saw himself forever, think what we might have missed.

3. *Believe that we can—and must—create assessment to match our vision of good writing instruction.* In the David Mamet film *Heist*, Gene Hackman's character, Joe, explains how he manages to appear more intelligent and clever than he really is: "I try to imagine a fella smarter than myself, and then I try to imagine, 'What would *he* do?'" Let's adopt Joe's strategy. Let's imagine the world's best assessment, 50 years or 100 years from now, run by somebody smarter than we are. What would it look like? Would it be fast and slick, a model of stunning efficiency? Or might today's "rush to judgment" approach be replaced by a more reflective style, tempered by a sense of compassion, which is to say, a genuine desire to help writers?

We are capable of so much more when it comes to writing assessment—but it all comes back to vision. Do we believe—*really believe*—that writing is thinking? Or is that just some idealistic notion to which we automatically pay homage? If we believe it, we must stop assessing as if writing were quick drafting in response to meaningless topics. We must stop it now. This year, this month, today. Instead, let's design—and carry out—the kind of writing assessment built upon a foundational understanding of how good writing comes about.

In such an assessment, students would not only be allowed, but *required*, to choose their own topics. They would spend time exploring, researching, gathering information, talking to others, reflecting, and identifying questions *they* felt were worthy of investigation. In short, they would behave like writers. Armed with real information, a sense of direction, and the confidence that these things provide, they would be given a reasonable period of time in which to compose a first draft—two to three hours at a minimum, more if needed. While drafting, they would have access to dictionaries, handbooks, and technology—the kind of support all professional writers take for granted.

Students would then set their work aside for a time in order to gain the mental distance essential for good revision. During this time, they could, of course, do additional exploration. This is how writers work. Writers do most of their work away from their desks.

At some point, they would have an opportunity to share their writing with fellow writers. Using feedback selectively and thoughtfully is *very hard to do well*. It needs to be built into our assessment because it helps young writers understand that good criticism isn't a blueprint for revision nor is it some sort of final judgment falling upon the writer like a guillotine. It is a wave of human voices, some wiser and more insightful than others. As writers, we must sift and search, determining which voices to pay attention to—and what to do in response. Only nonwriters think that people in a response group can give you the "secret" by telling you what and how to write. If it were that simple, everyone would publish. What writers in a response group *can* do is spark an idea, help the writer to see the writing in a different way, and sustain the energy and courage it takes to write in the first place.

And here's the key—inspired by feedback and by their own reflective thinking, students would *revise* their work. Imagine. Not just touch it up or neaten it up, but *really* revise. They could rethink the whole piece, adding or deleting information, moving things around, changing wording—and in so doing, letting the voice emerge, thereby outrageously increasing the odds that assessors would find what they had written both enlightening and engaging. We could then turn writing assessment on its head, reviewing both rough and revised drafts, so that the assessment would be based in part on the quality and depth of revision—the thinking we claim to value so much, but which now plays virtually no role whatsoever in the way we assess writing.

4. *Believe that students can write.* Although many student writers struggle, I personally encounter students every year whose writing both moves

Given only 25 minutes to write the SAT essay (30 minutes for the ACT essay), students will likely produce a kind of writing that is necessarily formulaic and superficial—writing that is very different from the lengthier, in-depth, and complex writing expected by most college instructors, who tend to discourage rapid, unrevised writing especially because it encourages rote organization and superficial thinking.

—NCTE Task Force
The Impact of the SAT and ACT Timed Writing Tests,
April 2005, p. 3

Research suggests that writing instruction focused on following patterns, writing one draft, and adhering to specific criteria for the text—just the kind of instruction likely to be used to prepare students for the new SAT—prepares students poorly for college-level writing tasks and for workplace writing tasks.

—NCTE Task Force
The Impact of the SAT and ACT Timed Writing Tests,
April 2005, p. 6

FIGURE **14.1** "Family," by Corinne (Grade 4)

> Without family you would be
> a lone wolf
> You'd be a stranger
> to yourself
> You would be the last leaf on the tree
> Without family

and teaches me. Some of their work, such as the poem by Corinne (Figure 14.1) or that by Simona (Figure 14.2) appears in this book. Much of it is stunning. You will not see their talent or success lauded in the newspaper, probably because, as a reporter told me once, "Kids writing well? *That's* not news. People want to hear about the *problems.*" Rubbish. The much-guarded secret that countless American students write somewhere between functionally and brilliantly is definitely newsworthy. Certainly it would be reassuring to parents desperate for their children to succeed in college or at the workplace. It would be emotionally lifesaving to teachers grading papers at 11 P.M. and wondering how else they can help their students "get it."

Admittedly, not *all* our student writers are achieving at a level that we can feel good about. Must we tolerate this? Not for moment. But let's not kid ourselves that intolerance is our most powerful weapon. Intolerance breeds only disdain, not student improvement. Instead of joining the already overflowing ranks of critics or simply wringing our hands, let's do something to help.

If you're an observer of today's educational scene, get involved. Volunteer. Coach. Read to students. Be a writer and share your writing. If you have children in school, read to them and listen to their writing. Talk with your child's teacher about the criteria he or she uses to score or grade work; suggest that those criteria be handed out in written form.

If you're a teacher, don't give up, even if your students seem to dislike writing. Read to them. Write with them and share your writing. Show them how you revise or edit a piece of work. How you come up with an idea. Ask for their opinions. Six-trait criteria can help you. They speak to students in a language that makes sense—and suggest that they are capable and worthy critics, which they are.

Keep up with best practices in writing instruction—and don't assume everything will be captured in state standards. These provide us with a good beginning, but they are not enough. Review the strategies summarized by Steve Graham and Dolores Perin in *Writing Next* (2007) (see Chapter 1 of this book). Ask how many of these you currently incorporate—or could incorporate—into your instruction.

If you are an elementary teacher, provide opportunities for your students to write in connection with social science, physical science, math, art, and other subjects. If you teach at secondary level, work with colleagues in content areas to ensure students write in every area possible—with support from a library of texts that make the gathering of information easy. Such diverse writing teaches flexibility of thinking, moving not only from subject to subject, but audience to audience—and using different "languages" and conventions at the same time. It is as real-world as writing gets. As Heller and Greenleaf (2007) state, "Every academic content area—and every non-academic kind of text, as well—has its own vocabulary, textual formats, stylistic conventions, and ways of understanding, analyzing, interpreting, and responding to words on the page" (p. 8). Historians, they point out,

> Policymakers must recognize that reading and writing are more than just basic skills that permit students to go on and study advanced subject matter; reading and writing are also the very stuff from which academic content areas are made.
>
> —Rafael Heller and Cynthia L. Greenleaf
> "Literacy Instruction in the Content Areas," 2007, p. 6

FIGURE 14.2 "A BadApple," by Simona (Grade 12)

A Bad Apple

will spoil the bunch, the farmers say,
misbehavior spreads easily among fruit; more likely
the apple was just rebellious
and ripened faster, growing up to a different rhythm
from the rest
and incurring the wrath of the farmers.
Misbehavior among apples was a serious problem
in the days of candles and spinning wheels.

These days there are fewer mistakes.
Seeds are taken to labs
of polyethylene and electron microscopes.
Like the elements
people once thought that the seed
was the smallest entity of life.
But science has dissected the psyche of the seed.
Strands of protein are the secret of life,
chemicals that can be created on a Petri dish—
snip snip copy paste into the seed they go
a package of genetic perfection.
This is called scientific breakthrough.

The seeds are injected with codes for sweet red
    immortality.
An evil stepmother couldn't do better.
There is a new alarm clock that prods the seed to
    blossom, grow,
and ripen for maximum profit.
Pluck, pluck zip zip into little bags they go
a package of commercial perfection.
This is called economics.

The trees grow at the same rate creating an orchard
hideout in eleven point seven months.
Apples grow in perfect bunches
saccharine sweet and red
all at the same time
all the same

the same
each
one.

But once in a while there is one who hears the strains
of a cosmic melody
and a deeper life to be lived.
It is the first blossom to be kissed by the bee
before the others are even awake.
It delights in the adventures of the children who come
    to play
and learns of a world beyond the orchard,
of adventure and fairies in disguise and magic mirrors
    and wishes that come true.

The petals fall, the fruit begins to grow,
and the apple forgets about the polyethylene
and being genetically correct.
It hears rainstorms and marvels
at the brilliance of a butterfly
and whispers with fireflies
of midsummer night dreams.

The apple lives as an apple should,
becoming older, wiser, riper than the others—
and yes, a little bruised.
It tells the others that life
is not about lab-injected alarm clocks
mindlessly following the farmer
rushing from one point to the next.
Life is one juicy adventure.
Those who stop to savor it
risk getting bruised and wrinkled
and falling off the tree altogether.
But that doesn't stop them.
And they become more divine as a result.
Perhaps bad apples really are the sweetest.

Distress kills learning.

—Daniel Goleman
Social Intelligence,
2006, p. 274

Writing proficiency develops over time. It begins as a kind of free association of ideas that a reader may find difficult to follow. From this comes a growing knowledge of stylistic conventions and more sophisticated uses of processes for planning, evaluating, and revising.

—Steve Graham and
Dolores Perrin
Writing Next, 2007, p. 23

tend to zero in on "events rich in human significance," and to expand those events through stories, descriptions, and commentary about major events. Chemists, by contrast, favor "precise description and narrative, meant not to elaborate a thesis but to compose an accurate record" (p. 8). Both are important. Students who can cover the range from human perspective to scientific analysis will move easily from one writing context to another.

Above all, work to create an atmosphere in which young writers feel safe, where they will dare to take the risks one must take to become a writer. This is easier said than done in a social context where assessment is so highly valued, and where fear of the test or the test results is a way of life. Fear, though, is not conducive to learning. In his provocative book *Social Intelligence,* Daniel Goleman explores the conditions under which optimal learning can occur, and concludes that one requirement is security: "By offering a secure base, a teacher creates an environment that lets students' brains function at their best" (2006, p. 283).

While we're at it, let's not expect miracles. Be patient. Learning to write takes a lifetime, not a semester. It is *hard.* When our students do not master it quickly, it is usually not for lack of testing, teaching, or effort. It is the complex and difficult nature of the task itself. Once we become writers, we recognize this. We learn not to mistake struggle for failure. All writers struggle; that's how success looks in its early stages. All writers, including professionals, have bad days and write drivel and despair of ever doing better. It is easier to keep heading for the finish line knowing someone believes you will get there.

5. *Believe that writing isn't just a skill for school, but a skill for life.*
A 2004 survey of more than 160 of America's top corporations conducted by the College Board suggests that almost nothing we do better prepares students for work than teaching them to write well. That report states that nearly all corporate executives look on writing as a "marker" of high skill, suggesting that "educational institutions interested in preparing students for rewarding and remunerative work should concentrate on developing graduates' writing skills" (p. 19). One respondent summed it up this way: "You can't move up without writing skills" (p. 3).

Further, corporate leaders offer us important clues about the specific writing skills they seek in new employees—if we will listen. Most value concise, to-the-point writing—with "an appropriate level of detail," and many view academic writing as "wandering" or "verbose" (p. 14). We often hear that businesspeople are sticklers for conventions. Perhaps. But those interviewed by the College Board repeatedly cited accuracy and clarity as top concerns, far ahead of either conventions or visual appeal (Table B, p. 28).

Given their response, is it time to abandon such forms of academic writing as literary analysis? Not at all. Many forms of academic writing give students critical social and historic connections, while sharpening their thinking skills. At the same time, though, we must think innovatively and divergently about how we define writing—and how we challenge student writers to expand their repertoire.

Graham and Perrin (2007) note that in college, most writing tasks are expository in nature—which they define as "reporting, summarizing and analyzing factual information, and expressing an opinion with the support

Extrapolating the findings from Roundtable companies . . . we estimate that annual private-sector costs for providing writing training could be as high as $3.1 billion.

—National Commission
on Writing
*Writing: A Ticket to Work . . .
Or a Ticket Out,* 2004, p. 18

of evidence" (p. 23). Workplace writing also calls for informational writing skills, but the forms such writing takes stretch far beyond what we see in many classrooms, including—among other things—proposals, project evaluations, predictions, reviews, book jacket copy, summaries and integral summaries of multiple documents, keynote speeches, lessons, letters to the editor and rebuttals, news summaries and analyses, interpretive data analyses, economic forecasts, questionnaires, promotional pieces, technical instructions, textbook contributions, social commentary, journalistic reports, video scripts, e-mails and other correspondence, and informational guides for visitors to zoos, art galleries, museums, and other such institutions.

What's more, employees must be prepared to deliver oral presentations, enhanced by video and PowerPoint. As one put it, "We're inundated with e-mail, and people have to learn to think in 'core points.' We need presentation skills on the same basis. Most of us have experienced 'death by Powerpoint'" (National Commission on Writing, 2004, p. 12).

6. *Believe that voice is power.* "Divorcing voice from process," Donald Graves tells us, "is like omitting salt from stew, love from sex, or sun from gardening" (1983, p. 227). Voice is the reason for the writing. Moreover, it is the primary reason—beyond the simple gathering of information—that most of us read. Voice is the human spirit, the essence of all that we feel and believe and know to be true. It is, ultimately, our ethnic, cultural, spiritual, and individual identity. Our verbal fingerprints.

Voice shakes our consciousness, awakens us, and causes us to see and act in new ways. To write with voice is to hold in our hands the power to shape destiny. Our children have this power. We can nurture it—or suppress it. We rob our children of their voice when we—

- Choose their topics for them, requiring them to write about things in which they have no personal interest or about which they know little.
- Force their ideas into universal, uninspired patterns that distort and camouflage rather than reveal thinking.
- Seek convenient, rapid ways to assess instead of taking the time and effort required to "read" their work with understanding and appreciation.
- Fail to identify for and with them the inherent strengths that help them to see how they are growing as writers.
- *Correct* conventions instead of taking time to *teach* them as a way of supporting both meaning and voice.
- Forget to applaud and treasure diversity and individuality.
- Hesitate to lose ourselves in the depths of their writing, and let student writers see, through our laughter, our tears, and our words how much their writing touches us.

7. *Believe that you can teach.* It's what you were born to do, isn't it? Don't allow a test score or a whole battery of test scores to steal your rightful heritage from you. Remember, anyone can be a critic. Not everyone can teach. Only the brave teach.

Treasure that moment when you look out into a sea of faces and eyes look back at you with an unspoken message, "I understand." That moment

Flexibility is now perhaps the most prized goal of writing instruction because the fairly proficient writer can adapt to different contexts, formats, and purposes for writing.
—Steve Graham and Dolores Perrin
Writing Next, 2007, p. 22

The voice is the frame of the window through which the information is seen. Readers can't read voiceless writing . . . any more than they can have dialogue with a mannequin.
—Donald H. Graves
Writing: Teachers and Children at Work, 1983, p. 228

We either teach our children it's okay to write and talk about the things they think to be the truth or else we teach them that it's more acceptable to silence their beliefs. . . .
—Jonathan Kozol
Letters to a Young Teacher, 2007, p. 86

Finally, we teachers know more than we think we know. It's just that our knowing cannot be measured and quantified, and we feel uncomfortable speaking out without hard data. Because we don't value our experiences and intuition enough, the public doesn't value it. We need to rethink how and what we know. . . .
—Regie Routman
Literacy at the Crossroads, 1996, p. 165

is the most powerful assessment of a teacher's skill. So what if no one else sees or records it? Dare to value what cannot be measured.

Know that when you respond to the voice within the writing, you are responding to the writer, for voice is the truest extension of self and is a gift.

Don't give in to the temptation of formulaic writing, which provides the illusion of writing success without any of the satisfaction or flexibility needed for new writing challenges. Almost anyone can be taught to fill in blanks if we make the formula simple enough, just as almost anyone can paint by numbers. Formulaic writing lifts students to mediocrity, but the price is high, for it fosters formulaic thinking. Students who write to fill in blanks rather than to express what they passionately believe will never lead others to new levels of understanding, compel hungry readers to turn pages, knock down barricades of prejudice, or land Oscars for screenwriting. What a hefty toll to pay for a tiny formula that will be of use nowhere save on a test. Formula writers are followers of others' thinking, and we demean our students when we fear that this is all they are capable of. We demean ourselves when we make writing assessment so simple that we can do it at a glance.

Teach students to be strong editors—not by correcting conventions, as was done for us—but by modeling twenty-first century conventions as they are now used by the best editors of our time. Write to publishing houses; get copies of their editorial rules. Check current and reliable handbooks (see Chapter 8 for a list). Read from these sources routinely. Provide students with extensive, frequent practice in editing text of all kinds: poetry, fiction, informational text, technical pieces, journalistic reports—and your own writing. Don't edit for them. No one learns to swim by clinging to the side of the pool. Encourage your students to let go.

Celebrate students' successes, however small, by noticing and sharing what you notice. When a student's writing moves you, don't tell a colleague or friend; tell the writer. Expect of yourself, because you *are* a teacher, that you can look deep within, that you can find even the smallest surprises that others would miss. In a tender and philosophical little book called *The Dot* (Reynolds, 2003), the young and blossoming author/artist Vashti can't bring herself to put more than a single dot on that huge white sheet of paper and is horrified by her own limitations, but she takes sudden pride in her work when her teacher asks if she will please *sign it*—and then posts it on the wall.

Trust your heart. Believe that just round the bend is a new piece of writing to surprise and delight you. Never fear being too readily impressed. Never be ashamed of your unabashed joy at a student's success, however humble; it is the greatest gift you can give a new writer who longs for someone to love the words on the page. Believe that as a teacher you are doing the most important work anyone can do—opening doors to new thinking. As Parker J. Palmer reminds us, no innovation, no reform movement, no amount of restructuring, and no set of standards will "transform education if we fail to cherish—and challenge—the human heart that is the source of good teaching" (1998, p. 3). Believe that every time you listen thoughtfully to your students' work, share your own writing (good or bad), express your sense of joy in discovering a new, fine piece of literature, or help a student writer hear

---

Many students are taught a specific and quite rigid structure for writing an essay, commonly known as the "five-paragraph essay." Skilled writers, however, have more than a single structure to draw on when approaching a writing task.

—Steve Graham and Dolores Perin
Writing Next, 2007, p. 22

Well-intentioned teachers believe they are giving students a helpful boost by handing over a prefabricated structure, but they may in fact be denying students the opportunity to do the very thing that writing is all about— making order, building a structure for the specific ideas at hand.

—Bruce Pirie
Reshaping High School English, 1997, p. 77

"Think about your favorite teachers from your youth: the ones who changed your life. . . . Chances are, these were the teachers with a gift for improvisation . . . Chances are, they didn't teach from a script."

—Linda Perlstein
Tested, 2007, p. 50

a moment of voice in his or her writing that just a second ago that writer did not know was there, you are making a difference—for you are.

How to Be a Flower

I'll start out as a seed and become a colorful flower.
I will grow long roots to drink water.
I will remember to produce oxygen.
The bees will gather my pollen.
I will have a fragrant smell and stand up tall.
I will be a gift to people who like me.
When I die, my soul will become art.

— **Gail Robinson's Fourth Graders,**
Room 106,
Jeffrey Elementary School,
Kenosha, Wisconsin

> Originality, eccentricity, spontaneity, and genius all have a forward, future-seeking momentum. These things cry out for freedom.
> —Marietta McCarty
> *Little Big Minds,* 2006, p. 289

> Even in the most adverse conditions, the work of a good teacher ought to be an act of stalwart celebration.
> —Jonathan Kozol
> *Letters to a Young Teacher,* 2007, pp. 226–227

Thank you, Gail. Thank you, everyone.

Reflections on Writing

I write because the day is over and the night is young and someone had a baby and someone or something just died—and whatever it is, I must write about it.

—Kirsten Ray, student writer

I write because it is a way to give someone the gift of love.

—Katie Miller, student writer

If you open my veins, you will find ink instead of blood.

—Simona Patange, student writer

Appendix 1: Teacher Three-Level Writing Guide

Teacher Three-Level Writing Guide

Ideas and Development

5/6

The writing is clear, focused, and well developed, with many important, intriguing details.

☐ The writer is selective, avoiding trivia, and choosing details that keep readers reading.

☐ The topic or story is narrow, focused, and manageable.

☐ Details work together to clarify and expand the main idea.

☐ The writer's knowledge, experience, insight, and perspective lend the piece authenticity.

☐ The amount of detail is just right—not skimpy, not overwhelming.

3/4

The writer has made a solid beginning. It is easy to see where the piece is headed, though more expansion would be helpful.

☐ Global information provides the big picture, making the reader long for more specifics.

☐ Greater focus might help narrow or shape the topic.

☐ Intriguing details blend with common knowledge or generalities.

☐ Still, the writer draws from knowledge, experience, or research to make some important points.

☐ Sections feel a bit sketchy—or repetitive.

1/2

Sketchy, loosely focused information forces the reader to make inferences. Readers notice one or more of these problems:

☐ The topic or central idea is undefined or unclear.

☐ The topic is so big—*All About Earth*—that it is hard for the writer to focus in and say anything meaningful.

☐ The writer does not know enough about the topic.

☐ The writing fills space, but lacks substance.

☐ Everything seems as important as everything else. No MAIN message pops out at the reader.

Organization

5/6

The order, presentation, and structure of the piece are compelling and guide the reader purposefully through the text.

☐ A strong sense of balance gives main ideas center stage.

☐ The structure showcases ideas without dominating them.

☐ An inviting lead draws writers in; a satisfying conclusion provides closure and prompts thought.

☐ Details fit just where they are placed.

☐ Transitions are smooth, helpful, and natural.

☐ The writer knows just when to linger—and when to move along.

3/4

The order lets readers move through the text without undue confusion.

☐ Key ideas can be identified.

☐ Order may be predictable, but it is not random.

☐ The reader feels an urge to reorder or delete some information.

☐ Transitions are present—they may seem formulaic.

☐ The reader sometimes wants to speed ahead or slow down to reflect.

1/2

Ideas seem loosely or randomly strung together, creating confusion. Readers notice one or more of these problems:

☐ The writing lacks a sense of direction and balance.

☐ Structure is missing—or so formulaic it overpowers ideas.

☐ No true lead sets things up; no conclusion offers closure.

☐ The story or discussion is hard to follow.

☐ Missing or unclear transitions leave the reader to build bridges.

☐ The writer consistently dawdles, or speeds through what needs explaining.

Appendix 1: Teacher Three-Level Writing Guide *(continued)*

Teacher Three-Level Writing Guide

Voice

5/6

The writer's passion for the topic drives the writing, making the text lively, expressive, and engaging.

- ☐ The tone and flavor of the piece are just right for the topic, purpose, and audience.
- ☐ The writing bears the clear imprint of *this* writer.
- ☐ The writer seems to know the audience and to anticipate their interests and informational needs.
- ☐ Narrative text is moving and honest; informational text is lively and engaging.
- ☐ This is a piece readers want to share aloud.

3/4

The writing communicates in a sincere, functional manner. It has lively moments.

- ☐ The tone and flavor are generally acceptable for purpose, topic, and audience.
- ☐ The writer has not fully found his/her voice, but is experimenting.
- ☐ On occasion, the writer reaches out to the audience.
- ☐ Voice comes and goes as the writer's engagement with the topic fluctuates.
- ☐ Readers may wish to share brief passages aloud.

1/2

The writer seems distanced from the audience, topic, or both. Readers notice one or more of these problems:

- ☐ The voice does not suit the topic, purpose, or audience.
- ☐ This writer's individual spirit is hiding behind an "anybody" voice.
- ☐ The reader has difficulty paying attention; the writer is not working to make the topic come alive for an audience.
- ☐ There is no person "at home" in the words.
- ☐ Moments of individuality or liveliness are missing or rare.
- ☐ The writing is not yet "asking" to be shared aloud.

Word Choice

5/6

Precise, vivid, natural language enhances the message and paints a clear picture in the reader's mind.

- ☐ The writer's meaning is clear throughout the piece.
- ☐ Phrasing is original—even memorable—yet the language is never overdone.
- ☐ Lively verbs lend the writing energy and power.
- ☐ Modifiers are effective and not overworked.
- ☐ The writer uses repetition only for effect.
- ☐ Striking words or phrases linger in the reader's memory.

3/4

The language communicates in a functional manner. It gets the job done.

- ☐ Most words are used correctly and convey a general message.
- ☐ Memorable phrases intermingle with overwritten—or underwritten—passages.
- ☐ A strong verb or two—the reader wishes for more!
- ☐ The writer may rely too heavily on modifiers—or clichés, overworked phrases, jargon. (Put the thesaurus away!)
- ☐ Some words or phrases are repeated—it's not a serious problem.
- ☐ Promising words or phrases catch the reader's attention.

1/2

The writer struggles to get the right words on paper. Readers notice one or more of these problems:

- ☐ Words are used incorrectly (*The bus impelled into the motel*).
- ☐ Vague words (*She was nice . . . The decision had impact*) convey only the most general messages.
- ☐ Modifiers weigh the text down—strong verbs are scarce or missing.
- ☐ Inflated language makes the text hard to penetrate.
- ☐ Word choice is repetitive, vague, unclear, or distracting.
- ☐ The words just don't speak to the reader.

Teacher Three-Level Writing Guide

Sentence Fluency

5/6

Easy flow and sentence sense make the text a delight to read aloud.

☐ Sentences are well crafted with a strong, varied structure that invites expressive oral reading.

☐ Striking variety gives language texture and interest.

☐ Purposeful sentence beginnings help connect thoughts.

☐ The writing has cadence, as if the reader hears the beat in his/her head.

☐ Fragments or repetition, if used, add style and punch; dialogue, if used, is natural and effective.

3/4

The text hums along with a steady beat. It is fairly readable.

☐ Most sentences are easy to read aloud with practice.

☐ The text shows some variety in sentence structure and length.

☐ Some sentences have purposeful beginnings: *After a while, As it turned out, On the other hand.*

☐ Graceful, natural phrasing intermingles with mechanical structure.

☐ Fragments or repetition are not always effective; dialogue does not always echo real speech.

1/2

An interpretive reading of this text takes practice. Readers notice one or more of these problems:

☐ Irregular or unusual word patterns hinder readability.

☐ It is hard to tell where sentences begin and end.

☐ Repetitive patterns or choppy sentences are common.

☐ Endless connecting phrases (*and then, so then, because*) create gangly word string "sentences" that leave readers breathless.

☐ The reader must reread or fill in words to create meaning.

☐ Fragments or repetition seem accidental; dialogue sounds forced—or is hard to pick out from other text.

Conventions

5/6

The writer shows excellent control over a wide range of age-appropriate conventions and uses them to enhance voice and meaning.

☐ Errors are so few and minor a reader could skip right over them unless searching for them specifically.

☐ The text appears clean, edited, polished. It's easy to process.

☐ Only light touchups are needed for publication.

☐ Conventions bring out both meaning and voice.

☐ As appropriate, the writer uses layout to showcase the message.

3/4

The writer shows reasonable control over widely used, grade-appropriate conventions.

☐ Errors are noticeable, but the writer also handles some conventions well.

☐ The text is lightly edited; the reader must do a little "mental editing."

☐ Moderate to thorough editing is needed prior to publication.

☐ Conventional problems do not obscure the message.

☐ Layout—if important—is adequate for the purpose of the text.

1/2

The writer demonstrates limited control even over widely used conventions. Readers notice one or more of these problems:

☐ Errors are frequent and/or serious enough to be distracting, even for patient readers.

☐ The text does not appear edited. The reader must frequently pause, reread, decode, or mentally edit (fill in, correct).

☐ Extensive line-by-line or word-by-word editing is needed prior to publication.

☐ Conventional problems slow the reader or obscure the message.

☐ Layout misdirects the reader's attention or is otherwise distracting.

Appendix 2: Student Three-Level Writing Guide

Student Three-Level Writing Guide

Ideas and Development

5/6

My writing is clear, focused, and filled with important, interesting details.

☐ I have a clear main message—or a story to tell.

☐ The topic is small and manageable and I stick to it.

☐ I chose intriguing details that expand my key ideas and answer a reader's questions thoroughly.

☐ I know this topic very well, and it shows.

☐ I cover what matters without burying the reader alive in trivia.

3/4

I have made a good beginning. You can see where I'm headed.

☐ I have a main message or a story. My writing makes sense.

☐ My topic might be a little big. Most of the time, I stay in bounds.

☐ I chose some interesting details—I might have included a few things you've heard before.

☐ I know some things about this topic—I wish I knew more.

☐ Sometimes I didn't tell enough—or I repeated myself.

1/2

I wrote something, but I really don't have a message or story in mind yet. I have one or more of these problems:

☐ I'm not sure what I'm trying to say.

☐ My topic is so big—*All About Earth*—that I can't tell where to begin.

☐ I just wrote to fill space. I didn't know what was important.

☐ I don't know enough about this topic to write.

☐ I repeated things. Or I wrote whatever came into my head.

Organization

5/6

This is so easy to follow it's like I drew you a road map.

☐ I know right where I'm going, beginning to end.

☐ The organization makes ideas easy to follow—but I wouldn't rule out a surprise twist or turn.

☐ My lead draws you right in. My conclusion wraps things up and leaves you thinking.

☐ Every detail comes at *just the right moment.*

☐ I connect ideas so you can tell how one thought leads to another.

☐ I explain what's complicated—but skip over things that aren't important to my topic or story.

3/4

You can follow this if you pay attention.

☐ I go down a few side roads—but you won't get lost.

☐ At times I followed a formula: *My first point, My second point . . .*

☐ I have a lead and conclusion. They could be stronger.

☐ It wouldn't hurt to change the order of some details.

☐ Some ideas are connected. Sometimes you have to make your own connections as you read.

☐ I spend too much time on some things—not enough on others.

1/2

Ideas are just thrown together with no real order or design. I have one or more of these problems:

☐ My writing wanders. I don't really know where I'm headed.

☐ There's no real plan here. It's a list or collection of thoughts.

☐ Lead? Conclusion? I just started—then stopped.

☐ The order is like a messy closet. My ideas are in there—*somewhere.*

☐ These ideas don't seem connected—to each other or any main idea.

☐ I couldn't tell what to spend time on.

Student Three-Level Writing Guide

Voice

5/6

I love this topic—and I want you to care about it, too.

☐ I feel this voice is ideal for my topic and my audience.

☐ This sounds like *me* and no one else. I hear myself in every line.

☐ I thought about my readers all the way through. It's like I'm having a conversation with them.

☐ My writing is honest; it's how I see the world. It's also lively; I worked to make this topic come alive for the reader.

☐ This is a piece a reader will want to share with someone else.

3/4

This is an OK topic. I think I sound interested—most of the time.

☐ The voice seems fine.

☐ At times, it sounds like me. Sometimes, it's an anybody voice (*blah, blah, blah*) or an encyclopedic voice (*fact, fact, fact*).

☐ Sometimes I reached out to the reader. Other times, I was just focusing on getting my ideas on paper.

☐ My voice comes and goes. You'll find moments of honesty or liveliness.

☐ You might want to share a line or two aloud.

1/2

I could not get into this topic, and just wrote to fill the page. I have one or more of these problems:

☐ I can't hear any voice—or else this is the wrong voice for my topic or audience.

☐ I don't think this sounds like me. It's just words on paper.

☐ I wasn't really "talking" to anyone. I wrote what came into my head.

☐ I'm not present in this piece. *Honest? Lively?* I felt bored when I wrote this.

☐ I don't really care if anyone shares this aloud. It's not me anyway.

Word Choice

5/6

I chose every word or phrase to make the message clear—or create a vivid picture (movie) in the reader's mind.

☐ My meaning is crystal clear from beginning to end.

☐ My words and phrases are fresh and accurate. I found *my own way to* say things.

☐ Lively verbs create energy and give my writing power.

☐ I went easy on the adjectives. I left out tired words (*nice, good, really*) that are overworked.

☐ If I repeated words, it was for effect.

☐ A few words or phrases might linger in your memory.

3/4

My words communicate. They get the job done.

☐ Most words are used correctly. You'll get the basic idea.

☐ My words aren't always original or memorable, but they make sense.

☐ I have a strong verb or two—guess I could use more!

☐ Some parts are too flowery—or too flat—maybe I used the thesaurus too much.

☐ I repeated words when I got tired or couldn't think of another way to say it.

☐ There are some good moments if you look.

1/2

I couldn't seem to find the words I needed. I have one or more of these problems:

☐ I don't know the meaning of some words. They might be incorrect.

☐ I used the first words that came into my head: *fun, nice, awesome, bad, cool, real*—you know, the usual words everybody uses all the time.

☐ I needed more verbs—and not so many adjectives.

☐ I overdid it at times: *The baseball game was superlative.*

☐ I repeated words without thinking: *A hard rain was falling hard.*

☐ I don't think these words will speak to my reader.

Appendix 2: Student Three-Level Writing Guide *(continued)*

Student Three-Level Writing Guide

Sentence Fluency

5/6

My writing has rhythm, like music or poetry. It's easy to read aloud.

- You can read this with expression and voice. Try it and see.
- My sentences begin in different ways. Some are long, some short.
- I used sentence beginnings—*After a while, For the first time*—to show how ideas connect.
- You can almost hear the beat. You'll love the sound of it.
- If I used fragments, they work. If I wrote dialogue, it sounds like real people talking.

3/4

This writing hums along. It may not be musical, but you can read it without much trouble.

- It's pretty easy to read aloud—especially if you practice.
- My sentences aren't *all* the same length—and they don't *all* begin the same way.
- Connecting phrases? Like *For example?* I could use more of those.
- It's mechanical in spots—but it has some good moments, too.
- My fragments do not all work. My dialogue needs to sound more like conversation, less like robots talking.

1/2

This is hard to read aloud, even for me. I have one or more of these problems:

- It's hard to tell where my sentences begin and end.
- Too many sentences start exactly the same way.
- I need to combine some sentences and shorten others.
- I used words like *and, and then, so then,* or *because* so much that you can't read this without getting breathless.
- You might need to pause and reread or fill in missing words.
- Did I write sentences or fragments? I'm not sure. I'm not sure if I wrote any dialogue.

Conventions

5/6

I know my conventions and it shows. I used them correctly and creatively to bring out voice and meaning.

- An editor would get bored looking for mistakes in my copy.
- This is edited thoroughly. Spelling, punctuation, grammar, capitals, and paragraphing are all correct.
- It might need light touchups—*if* I missed something.
- Strong conventions guide a reader right through my text.
- I used layout (if needed) to draw your eye to key points.

3/4

I know my conventions pretty well. You might catch a few errors.

- I see mistakes when I read this over, but I did some things well.
- This is edited lightly; you'll need to do a little "mental editing."
- I need to read this aloud, use a ruler to read line by line, and use a dictionary or spell checker to help catch everything.
- The mistakes are noticeable, but they don't get in the way of my message.
- My layout might not be dazzling, but it's OK for my purpose.

1/2

I have trouble with conventions. You'll notice one or more of these problems:

- I have many mistakes. You'll need to read once just to decode.
- This paper isn't really edited yet. I have errors in spelling, punctuation, grammar, or capitals. My paragraphs don't start in the right spots.
- I need to read this aloud, word by word, pen in hand—with a coach to help me.
- This many mistakes will make a reader pause or reread. They could even get in the way of the message.
- Layout? Oops. Never got to that.

Appendix 3: Student "Leap the River" Writing Guide in Spanish

Guía de escritura de 6 puntos del estudiante: IDEAS

6
- ❏ Mi texto es claro, se enfoca en el tema y está bien desarrollado. Seguro llamará la atención.
- ❏ Se puede saber exactamente cuál es mi mensaje.
- ❏ Conozco el tema de arriba a abajo.
- ❏ Ayudo a los lectores a aprender, pensar y comprender.
- ❏ Los detalles que incluyo despertarán tu curiosidad; es posible que te enseñen algo nuevo.

5
- ❏ Mi escrito es claro y se enfoca en el tema. Profundicé en algunos puntos clave.
- ❏ Pienso que el mensaje es claro.
- ❏ Sé mucho sobre este tema.
- ❏ Presento información importante e interesante en el texto.
- ❏ Escogí detalles que hacen que mi mensaje sea interesante.

4
- ❏ El texto es claro y se enfoca en el tema *casi* todo el tiempo.
- ❏ Puedes entender el mensaje.
- ❏ Sé algunas cosas sobre este tema.
- ❏ Presento *cierta* información novedosa.
- ❏ Incluyo algunos detalles y ejemplos.

3
- ❏ Escribí una lista de ideas: no desarrollé ninguna por completo.
- ❏ Puedes entender mi mensaje, o puedes no entenderlo.
- ❏ Me gustaría saber más sobre este tema.
- ❏ No sé qué más decir: fue muy difícil pensar qué información adicional podía incluir.
- ❏ Tuve dificultad para incluir detalles.

2
- ❏ Mi texto es confuso: no todo tiene sentido.
- ❏ Todavía no sé cuál es mi mensaje.
- ❏ NO sé suficiente de este tema como para escribir un texto.
- ❏ Escribí algunas cosas que no puedo probar o respaldar.
- ❏ No se me ocurrieron muchos detalles. ¿Está bien repetir cosas?

1
- ❏ No pude decidir qué quería decir. Aún no tengo un tema o una idea principal.
- ❏ Seguramente mi lector se quedó con miles de dudas.
- ❏ ¿Cómo puedo conseguir información? ¡No tengo un tema!
- ❏ Estas ideas no tienen orden.
- ❏ Sólo traté de llenar la hoja.

Appendix 3: Student "Leap the River" Writing Guide in Spanish (continued)

Guía de escritura de 6 puntos del estudiante: ORGANIZACIÓN

6

- ❑ El texto está tan bien organizado que no tendrás problemas para pasar de una idea a otra.
- ❑ La introducción atrapará tu atención; la conclusión te dejará pensando.
- ❑ Las transiciones presentan conexiones que no se te ocurrirían sin mi ayuda.
- ❑ Me detengo en donde hace falta: en los puntos importantes.
- ❑ Hay algunas sorpresas, pero en ningún momento te sentirás perdido.

5

- ❑ Mi organización del texto le da unidad al mensaje.
- ❑ Mi introducción es llamativa; mis conclusiones no dejan cabos sueltos.
- ❑ Mis transiciones muestran las conexiones entre las ideas.
- ❑ Dedico la mayor parte del tiempo a los puntos clave y no a aspectos incidentales.
- ❑ Puedes seguir mi argumento/relato sin dificultades.

4

- ❑ Mi organización es la adecuada para mi mensaje.
- ❑ Tengo una introducción y una conclusión. Las dos funcionan.
- ❑ Mis transiciones te guían de un punto al otro.
- ❑ A veces es difícil identificar qué es lo más importante.
- ❑ Puedes seguir el texto sin demasiada dificultad.

3

- ❑ Es una buena idea reorganizar algunas partes.
- ❑ Puedo trabajar más en la introducción y conclusión.
- ❑ Intenté usar transiciones. No estoy seguro de que muestren claramente las conexiones.
- ❑ Dediqué demasiado tiempo a cosas que el lector o ya sabe, o no necesita saber.
- ❑ Te puedes sentir perdido en el texto. ¡A veces, también, puedes saber *exactamente* qué es lo que sigue!

2

- ❑ Creo que debo reorganizarlo todo ¡*de principio a fin!*
- ❑ No hay introducción o conclusión, o las que hay son más que conocidas por todos.
- ❑ No hay transiciones, o no tienen sentido.
- ❑ Es difícil identificar los puntos más importantes.
- ❑ Es difícil de seguir, incluso poniendo atención.

1

- ❑ Es como tratar de caminar por un bosque en la oscuridad.
- ❑ Simplemente empieza y acaba: no hay introducción o conclusión.
- ❑ ¿Transiciones? ¿Qué son? ¿Están conectados los diferentes puntos?
- ❑ Todo tiene la misma importancia.
- ❑ Nadie puede seguir el texto. Ni siquiera yo.

Appendix 3: Student "Leap the River" Writing Guide in Spanish (continued)

Guía de escritura de 6 puntos del estudiante: VOZ

6
- ❏ El texto tiene mi sello personal.
- ❏ Con toda seguridad querré leerlo a otras personas.
- ❏ Soy *yo*: lo que pienso, lo que siento.
- ❏ ¿Escuchas la pasión en mi voz? Me interesa que el lector quede prendado del tema.
- ❏ Una vez que comienzas a leerlo, no lo quieres dejar.

5
- ❏ Es un texto original y personal. Definitivamente soy *yo*.
- ❏ Creo que querré leerlo en voz alta.
- ❏ Logro transmitir mis pensamientos y sentimientos personales.
- ❏ La voz está llena de vida; transmite entusiasmo.
- ❏ Es evidente que pienso en mis lectores.

4
- ❏ Puedes reconocerme en el texto.
- ❏ Puedes leer una que otra línea en voz alta.
- ❏ Definitivamente estoy presente en el texto.
- ❏ Mi escritura es sincera. La impresión es que creo en lo que escribo.
- ❏ Pienso en mis lectores casi todo el tiempo.

3
- ❏ Mi voz aparece y desaparece. ¿Se nota que soy yo?
- ❏ Todavía no está listo para leerse en voz alta pero ¡falta poco!
- ❏ Necesito reforzar mi voz o usar una voz *diferente*.
- ❏ No me expresé en el texto: me contuve.
- ❏ No podía pensar todo el tiempo en mis lectores, ¿o sí?

2
- ❏ Me escondo tras las palabras: aún no soy yo.
- ❏ Hay algún indicio de voz en el texto, pero aún no está lista para comunicarse.
- ❏ No creo que el lector sepa quién soy después de leerlo.
- ❏ La voz es aburrida o, a lo mejor, parecida a la de una enciclopedia.
- ❏ Me preocupa que mis lectores se queden dormidos, o me abandonen.

1
- ❏ Me siento "incómodo" con este texto. Ni siquiera escucho un eco de mi voz real.
- ❏ No creo que alguien quiera leerlo en voz alta.
- ❏ Es una voz que puede ser "cualquiera". No soy yo.
- ❏ No logré emocionarme con este tema.
- ❏ ¿Lectores? ¿Qué lectores?

Appendix 3: Student "Leap the River" Writing Guide in Spanish *(continued)*

Guía de escritura de 6 puntos del estudiante: SELECCIÓN DE PALABRAS

6
- ❑ Escribí las cosas de manera original, creativa y clara.
- ❑ Me esforcé por encontrar la MEJOR manera de decir las cosas. ¡Hasta podrías citarme!
- ❑ Cada palabra es importante: no usé palabras innecesarias.
- ❑ Usé verbos expresivos: no dependí del uso excesivo de adjetivos.
- ❑ Mis palabras generan imágenes en tu mente, apelan a tus sentidos o te ayudan a comprender.

5
- ❑ Escribí para que el significado fuera claro, no para impresionar.
- ❑ Hay momentos que vale la pena recordar.
- ❑ Mi escritura es concisa.
- ❑ Usé verbos expresivos.
- ❑ Mis palabras te ayudan a comprender o visualizar las cosas.

4
- ❑ Mi escrito tiene sentido. Usé correctamente las palabras.
- ❑ Habrá algunos momentos que vale la pena subrayar o resaltar.
- ❑ Puede ser que en algún momento me exceda en verbosidad.
- ❑ Necesito *más* verbos expresivos, pero usé *algunos*.
- ❑ Los momentos expresivos superan a los problemáticos.

3
- ❑ Escribí lo primero que se me ocurrió, pero seguramente captarás la idea.
- ❑ En uno que otro lugar hay una frase que me gusta.
- ❑ Use más palabras de las necesarias, o repetí cosas.
- ❑ Necesito más verbos y tengo que alejarme de palabras trilladas como: *bonito, bueno, divertido, grandioso, genial.*
- ❑ Los problemas con las palabras superan los momentos expresivos.

2
- ❑ Cuidado con las palabras trilladas y ambiguas.
- ❑ Es difícil encontrar momentos para resaltar.
- ❑ Tengo problemas de verbosidad o repetición.
- ❑ Los verbos expresivos brillan por su ausencia. Predominan: *es, son, fue, fueron.*
- ❑ Debo esforzarme para encontrar palabras "adecuadas".

1
- ❑ Aunque mis palabras no sean las "correctas", llenan la página.
- ❑ Fue DIFÍCIL escribir este texto.
- ❑ Tuve que repetir; no se me ocurrieron palabras nuevas.
- ❑ Siempre usé las mismas palabras: *bonito, bueno, grandioso, divertido, maravilloso, genial, especial, de verdad, muy. . .*
- ❑ No creo que mi mensaje sea claro.

Appendix 3: Student "Leap the River" Writing Guide in Spanish *(continued)*

Guía de escritura de 6 puntos del estudiante: FLUIDEZ DE LAS ORACIONES

6
- ❏ Es fácil leerlo en voz MUY ALTA.
- ❏ Fluye como un buen guión de cine.
- ❏ No vas a creer la variedad de oraciones que incluí.
- ❏ Si usé fragmentos o repetición, éstos añaden énfasis.
- ❏ Mis diálogos son tan auténticos que son como escuchar una conversación en vivo.

5
- ❏ Se puede leer con expresividad.
- ❏ Me gusta el sonido cuando lo leo en voz alta.
- ❏ Mis oraciones empiezan de diferentes maneras. Algunas son largas y otras cortas.
- ❏ Si usé fragmentos o repetición, suenan bien.
- ❏ Mis diálogos son como si hablaran personas reales.

4
- ❏ Debe ser fácil leerlo en voz alta.
- ❏ Lo puedo leer en voz alta sin *demasiado* esfuerzo.
- ❏ Hay *alguna* variedad en la longitud y en el principio de las oraciones.
- ❏ Es cierto, hay algunos fragmentos y repetición, pero no representan un problema.
- ❏ Mi diálogo suena bien.

3
- ❏ Da trabajo pero, con esfuerzo, se puede leer.
- ❏ Es necesario hacer más fluidas algunas partes.
- ❏ Hay __ demasiadas oraciones cortas, __ demasiadas oraciones largas y __ demasiadas oraciones que empiezan igual.
- ❏ Hay __ demasiados fragmentos y __ demasiada repetición.
- ❏ El diálogo no parece real. Así no hablan las personas.

2
- ❏ Puedes leer esto *si practicas.*
- ❏ Hay __ encabalgamientos y __ oraciones interrumpidas.
- ❏ Hay __ demasiadas oraciones cortas, __ demasiadas oraciones largas y __ demasiadas oraciones que empiezan igual.
- ❏ Hay __ demasiados fragmentos y __ demasiada repetición.
- ❏ Este diálogo definitivamente NO funciona.

1
- ❏ Es difícil de leer, incluso para mí.
- ❏ Faltan palabras; o las oraciones simplemente no fluyen.
- ❏ Es difícil identificar dónde empiezan mis oraciones.
- ❏ Hay__ demasiadas oraciones cortas, __ demasiadas oraciones largas y __ demasiadas oraciones que empiezan igual.
- ❏ Hay __ demasiados fragmentos, __ demasiada repetición.
- ❏ ¿Es esto un diálogo? No estoy seguro.

Appendix 3: Student "Leap the River" Writing Guide in Spanish *(continued)*

Guía de escritura de 6 puntos del estudiante: CONVENCIONES

6

❏ Lo edité *bien*. Lo leí en silencio y en voz alta.

❏ La __ ortografía, la __ puntuación, la __ gramática, el __ uso de mayúsculas y la __ organización de los párrafos son *todos correctos*.

❏ Trabajé en el esquema. Llamará la atención.

❏ El trabajo está listo para ser publicado.

5

❏ Es posible que tenga algunos errores *menores:* voy a revisarlo otra vez.

❏ La __ ortografía, la __ puntuación, la __ gramática, el __ uso de mayúsculas y la __ organización de los párrafos son *todos correctos*.

❏ Trabajé en el esquema. Es bueno.

❏ El texto está *casi* listo para ser publicado.

4

❏ Encontré algunos errores que tengo que corregir.

❏ Debo revisar la __ ortografía, la __ puntuación, la __ gramática, el __ uso de mayúsculas y la __ organización de los párrafos.

❏ Trabajé en el esquema. Está bien, aunque podría hacerlo mejor.

❏ Debo revisar el texto una vez más y estará listo para ser publicado.

3

❏ Creo que el lector notará algunos errores en este texto.

❏ Tengo que revisar la __ ortografía, la __ puntuación, la __ gramática, el __ uso de mayúsculas y la __ organización de los párrafos.

❏ Necesito trabajar más en el esquema.

❏ Debo leerlo en silencio y en voz alta, con un bolígrafo a la mano.

2

❏ Los errores podrían impedir la comprensión de mi mensaje.

❏ Debo revisar la __ ortografía, la __ puntuación, la __ gramática, el __ uso de mayúsculas y la __ organización de los párrafos.

❏ Necesito trabajar más en el esquema.

❏ Tengo que leerlo en silencio y en voz alta, línea por línea.

1

❏ Los errores dificultan la lectura, ¡incluso para mí!

❏ Puedo editar __ la primera oración, __ el primer párrafo, __ TODO.

❏ Tengo que revisar la __ ortografía, __ la puntuación, la __ gramática, el __ uso de mayúsculas y la __ organización de los párrafos.

❏ Voy a trabajar más en el esquema.

❏ Tengo que leerlo en silencio y en voz alta, palabra por palabra.

Appendix 4: Student Checklist in Spanish

Lista de revisión del estudiante

Ideas
❑ Mi escritura es clara y se enfoca en el tema.
❑ Los puntos clave están bien desarrollados.
❑ Es evidente que conozco este tema muy bien.
❑ Escogí los detalles con cuidado. Son interesantes e importantes.
❑ Resumí el tema para presentarlo en un tamaño accesible.

Organización
❑ Mi introducción atraerá al lector.
❑ Mi conclusión dejará pensando al lector.
❑ Las transiciones conectan claramente las ideas.
❑ El lector nunca se sentirá perdido al leerlo.

Voz
❑ En este texto se me puede reconocer; a mí y a nadie más.
❑ Es como si estuviera allí, conversando personalmente contigo.
❑ Es posible que quiera leer mi texto en voz alta a otras personas.
❑ Es un tema que me interesa y el lector lo notará.
❑ Una vez que *empiezas* a leerlo, querrás leer *hasta el final.*

Selección de palabras
❑ Encontré una manera personal de expresarme.
❑ Me esforcé en usar las MEJORES palabras, no las primeras que se me ocurrieron.
❑ Eliminé las palabras que eran innecesarias.
❑ Los verbos expresivos tienen más fuerza.
❑ *No* me excedí en el uso de adjetivos.
❑ Mis palabras ayudan a visualizar y sentir las cosas, o a comprender mi tema.

Fluidez de las oraciones
❑ Es un texto fácil de leer en voz alta *destacando la voz.*
❑ Es sorprendente la variedad de oraciones que usé.
❑ Lo leí en voz alta y me gusta cómo se oye.
❑ Cuando repetí frases o usé fragmentos fue para hacer énfasis.
❑ Mis diálogos son realistas. Son como conversaciones entre personas reales.

Convenciones
❑ Lo edité *bien.* Lo leí en silencio y en voz alta.
❑ Corregí errores de ortografía, puntuación, gramática, uso de mayúsculas y organización del párrafo.
❑ Este texto está listo para ser publicado.

Appendix 5: Trait "Shorties" in Spanish

Ideas y desarrollo
El mensaje

- El mensaje, tema, tesis o argumento principal es claro.

- El tema es preciso y apto para ser desarrollado.

- Detalles complejos y llamativos amplían el mensaje.

- Hay perspicacia.

- Los conocimientos son resultado de la experiencia o la investigación.

- Es interesante; llama la atención del lector.

Organización
Diseño y fluidez de ideas

- Introducción llamativa que captura la atención de los lectores.

- Diseño claro que sirve de guía para los lectores y enriquece la comprensión.

- Transiciones adecuadas conectan las ideas.

- Buen ritmo: se detiene en los puntos importantes.

- El final concluye la discusión.

Voz
Sello distintivo en la página

- Individual, distintivo.

- Texto para "leerse en voz alta".

- Apasionado, entusiasta.

- Llama la atención de los lectores.

- Confiado, seguro de sí mismo.

- El escritor está presente en la página.

Appendix 5: Trait "Shorties" in Spanish *(continued)*

Selección de palabras
Lenguaje y terminología

- Claro, ayuda a la comprensión del lector.
- Original, memorable.
- Conciso.
- Natural.
- Los verbos son expresivos.
- No hay exceso de modificadores.
- Pinta imágenes verbales.

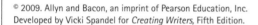

Fluidez de las oraciones
Ritmo y cadencia

- Fácil de leer.
- Enriquece la voz.
- Variedad en longitud y estructura.
- Ritmo fácil de seguir, cadencia.
- Diálogo natural.
- Si hay fragmentos, estos añaden énfasis y color.

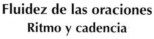

Convenciones y presentación
Corrección editorial/Atractivo a la vista

- Editado, pulido.
- Indica conocimiento de las convenciones.
- Las convenciones enriquecen el significado, la voz.
- No requiere edición mental.
- Casi listo para publicar.
- La complejidad del texto muestra la destreza editorial del escritor.
- Presentación llamativa, útil.

Appendix 6: Student Checklists

Checklist Series for *Creating Writers*

Checklist for Narrative Writing

___ The piece is a story, not a list of events. It has purpose and direction; there is a reason for the telling.

___ At the center of the story is a conflict to resolve, secret to discover, burning question to answer, etc. The story drives toward this.

___ The main character (who could be the narrator) grows, changes, or learns something important as the story unfolds.

___ There is a turning point: a point of change, discovery, or maximum conflict.

___ Every event, image, or speech in the piece has importance—and the writer follows through to show what it is.

___ A strong lead sets up the story and gets the reader engaged.

___ Events unfold in a believable but not always predictable way.

___ Characters are real—not cardboard cutouts. They have feelings, emotions, motivations. They do things for a reason.

___ Dialogue, if used, sounds authentic, like real people talking. It reveals character, advances the action, or sets the mood.

___ The ending ties up the story in a satisfying way. It may also look ahead.

Simple Narrative Checklist

___ It's a story—not just a list of "things that happened."

___ The story solves a problem or answers a question.

___ The main character changes, grows, learns something.

___ There's a turning point: change, discovery, conflict.

___ Everything in the story is there for a reason.

___ It's easy to follow the story—but sometimes, there's a surprise.

___ The characters seem real.

___ If they speak, they sound like real people.

___ The ending seems right, even if it's not happy.

Appendix 6: Student Checklists *(continued)*

Checklist for Informational Writing

___ At the center of the piece is a problem to be solved or a question to be answered.

___ The writer uses examples, anecdotes, substantiated facts, or quotations to validate, support, or expand key points.

___ Information seems thorough, relevant, and authentic/accurate.

___ The text teaches the reader something important.

___ The writer does not try to tell everything, but keeps the writing focused on what is most important.

___ Terminology is used with care and accuracy to aid the reader's understanding of the issue(s).

___ The writer's voice sounds confident and assured.

___ The writing reflects diligent, thoughtful research.

___ Sources are cited as necessary.

Simple Informational Checklist

___ Answers a key question

___ Uses good examples, anecdotes, facts, quotations

___ Gives correct information

___ Teaches the reader something

___ Tells what is most important

___ Explains new or difficult terms

___ Sounds confident

___ Shows that the writer took time to look things up

___ Lists all the sources used

Appendix 6: Student Checklists *(continued)*

Checklist Series for *Creating Writers*

Checklist for Persuasive Writing

___ The writing takes the reader on a journey of understanding, examining an issue or set of issues.

___ The writer makes his/her position clear at the outset and sticks with that position.

___ The writer's main argument is supported by evidence: facts, statistics, studies, quotations from experts, personal observations, etc.

___ The writer does not rely on opinion as evidence *(This is true because most people in this country believe . . .)*.

___ The writer consults and cites multiple sources to build a strong case.

___ The paper clearly summarizes opposing points of view and addresses them in a convincing but fair manner.

___ The writer's voice is strong, confident, and compelling—but not angry, hysterical, or sarcastic.

___ Usually, the writer saves his/her most compelling argument for last, giving it maximum impact.

___ The writer leads the reader to a conclusion that seems all but inevitable, given the evidence—and invites the reader to accept it.

___ The reader understands the issues thoroughly—*even if he or she does not fully agree with the writer.*

Simple Persuasive Checklist

___ Helps reader think through issues

___ Makes writer's position clear

___ More than just the writer's opinion

___ Gives facts, quotations, examples

___ Shows why others might not agree

___ Sounds strong and confident—but not angry

___ Saves the best argument for last

___ Helps reader make up his/her mind

Appendix 6: Student Checklists *(continued)*

Checklist Series for *Creating Writers*

Checklist for Literary Analysis

___ The paper is more than a summary of the plot.

___ The writing makes a point (or points) relating to the work's theme, language, character development, style, or significance in the context of broader social issues.

___ Each major point is supported by direct reference to the work itself and/or quotations from that work.

___ In addition, the writer may quote other sources that offer commentary on the work or its author.

___ The writer may connect this work to his/her own personal experience or research.

___ As appropriate, the writer offers personal responses to the work—but these do not take the place of commentary on theme, social significance, etc.

___ The writer's voice is strong and confident, reflecting familiarity with and understanding of the work at hand.

___ The writer may enrich the analysis by comparing the work to another.

___ The writer may also enrich the analysis by commenting on the author's craft: e.g., providing examples of voice, detail, word choice, fluency, or organizational approach.

Simple Literary Analysis Checklist

___ Explains why someone should read the book

___ Makes important points about the author's meaning or characters

___ Quotes the book to support those points

___ Shows a connection between the book and personal experience

___ Shares how the writer feels about the book

___ Compares this book to others

___ Shows what the author of the book does well *as a writer* (details, lead, voice, words, etc.)

Appendix 7: Teacher Three-Level Informational Writing Guide

Teacher Three-Level Informational Writing Guide

Ideas and Development

5/6

The writing is clear, focused, and purposeful. It answers a well-defined key question in convincing, expansive terms.

- ❑ The main idea or research focus is clearly defined.
- ❑ The writer draws from multiple sources to enrich detail and offer credible, useful, new, or intriguing information.
- ❑ The writer continuously anticipates and responds to readers' informational needs in thorough, insightful ways.
- ❑ Support (facts, anecdotes, quotations, examples, observations) is accurate, relevant, and credible.

3/4

The paper addresses an identifiable key question by offering the reader solid, basic information.

- ❑ The reader can infer the thesis or research question.
- ❑ Some information seems grounded in solid research or experience, some based on common knowledge or best guesses.
- ❑ The writer sometimes responds to readers' informational needs. Some questions, though, are left hanging.
- ❑ Greater knowledge of the topic and more attention to detail—or more credible support—would strengthen a generally good effort.

1/2

No key issue as yet takes center stage. More than one of these problems is evident:

- ❑ The thesis or focus of research is not yet defined.
- ❑ Information is sketchy, limited, vague, redundant, or questionable.
- ❑ The reader is left with numerous questions.
- ❑ The paper would not be helpful to someone who did not already know this topic well.

Organization

5/6

A strong internal structure showcases main ideas, leading readers right to key points or important conclusions.

- ❑ The lead engages readers and sets the stage for the discussion.
- ❑ The order of details promotes readers' understanding and interest.
- ❑ Purposeful transitions help a reader follow the discussion and keep the big picture in focus.
- ❑ The writer slows the pace to explain complex or technical concepts.
- ❑ The closing reinforces earlier concepts, resolves questions, or points the way to evolving, related issues.

3/4

Readers can follow the discussion, but may need to make some leaps or inferences.

- ❑ The introduction may be formulaic—or just prolonged.
- ❑ The order enables the reader to follow the discussion.
- ❑ Ideas are usually connected—but the reader may question the relevance of some points.
- ❑ The writer sometimes lingers too long on obvious or simple concepts while glossing over what is more complex.
- ❑ The conclusion ends the discussion—but may not prompt new thinking.

1/2

Lack of structure leaves readers confused. More than one of these problems is evident:

- ❑ There is no real lead; the paper just begins.
- ❑ The reader struggles to see a pattern that is not there.
- ❑ Pacing seems unrelated to content.
- ❑ The lack of connections makes it hard to track the writer's thinking.
- ❑ There is no real conclusion; the paper just stops.

Teacher Three-Level Informational Writing Guide

Voice

5/6

The writer's passion for the topic drives the writing, making the text lively, expressive, and engaging.

❑ The tone and flavor of the piece are just right for the topic, purpose, and audience.

❑ The writer's knowledge of the topic leads to a confident, authoritative tone that inspires readers' trust.

❑ The writer consistently draws readers into the conversation.

❑ The reader finds him-/herself caught up in the topic, regardless of previous interest or knowledge.

❑ Voice consistently enhances, but never overshadows, the message.

3/4

The writing communicates in a sincere, functional manner. It has lively moments—and some more prosaic, encyclopedic moments.

❑ The tone and flavor are generally appropriate.

❑ The writer seems occasionally hesitant. Greater knowledge might result in more confidence.

❑ The writer seems at least aware of the audience.

❑ As the writer's engagement with the topic fluctuates, readers must work to remain engaged.

❑ Voice sometimes enhances the message—sometimes recedes.

1/2

The voice is faint, stilted, or inappropriate. More than one of these problems is evident:

❑ The voice is inappropriate, overpowering, or distracting.

❑ Lack of knowledge inhibits the writer's confidence.

❑ The reader has difficulty paying attention; the writer is not working to make the topic come alive for an audience.

❑ The writer seems indifferent to the topic, or just writing to be done.

❑ Lack of voice—or the wrong voice—actually works against the power of the message.

Word Choice

5/6

Well-chosen words clarify the message and enhance the reader's understanding.

❑ The writer uses language in a way that helps the reader make sense of and internalize important concepts.

❑ The writer knows the language of the territory and uses it with skill and ease.

❑ The terminology and phrasing suit the topic and audience well.

❑ Technical or little-known terms are consistently clarified or defined.

❑ The writing is concise without compromising meaning.

3/4

Words are sufficiently clear to convey a general message.

❑ Most words are correct and functional—but do not take readers "inside" the topic.

❑ The writer is at home with some content-specific terminology.

❑ The language works—but is not always the best match for the intended audience.

❑ Technical terminology may be used but not defined—or may be missing when it could be helpful.

❑ Some deadwood could be cut.

1/2

The language does not speak to the audience. More than one of the following problems is evident:

❑ The language is too vague to carry the message.

❑ A limited vocabulary makes it hard for the writer to explore the subject in any meaningful way.

❑ Words are not a good match with the subject or audience.

❑ Undefined technical terms leave readers on the outside looking in.

❑ Wordiness slows the reader down or smothers the message.

Teacher Three-Level Informational Writing Guide

Sentence Fluency

5/6

Sentences are strong, clear, and structured to make reading fast and simple.

☐ Meaningful sentence beginnings (*For example, In contrast, To illustrate, As a result*) connect ideas and enhance readability.

☐ While sentences vary in length, most are direct and compact.

☐ Meaning is clear with the first reading.

☐ Quotations (if used) are set up well, and fit right into the flow.

☐ Text is easy to interpret, recall, and summarize.

3/4

Sentences are reasonably clear and complete.

☐ Meaningful sentence beginnings sometimes help readers connect ideas and move from point to point.

☐ Some sentence variety is evident. A few sentences may tend to extremes of long or short.

☐ Meaning is not always clear with the first reading; e.g., *The legislature is voting to re-enact road construction in the spring.*

☐ Quotations (if used) may pop up unexpectedly without introduction.

☐ Text can be interpreted by an attentive reader.

1/2

Reading for meaning takes some effort. More than one of the following problems is evident:

☐ Lack of meaningful sentence beginnings disrupts continuity.

☐ Sentences tend toward extremes of long or short.

☐ The reader must reread or fill in words to create meaning.

☐ Quotations are simply inserted into the text with no apparent connection to the discussion at hand.

☐ Even when paying close attention, the reader cannot always decipher the message.

Conventions

5/6

The writer demonstrates a good grasp of standard writing conventions and uses them to guide readers through the text.

☐ Basic textual conventions are virtually error-free.

☐ Conventions enhance meaning and voice.

☐ Informational sources are correctly, thoroughly cited.

☐ The layout is appealing and enhances readability.

☐ Titles, subheads, bullets, or other visual conventions guide the reader's eye to key points.

☐ Charts, graphs, or illustrations (if used) expand ideas in a way that clearly connects to the text.

3/4

The writer shows reasonable control over widely used, grade-appropriate conventions.

☐ Despite noticeable errors, the writer handles many conventions well.

☐ The reader must do a little "mental editing."

☐ Informational sources are listed—but not always traceable.

☐ The basic layout is acceptable.

☐ Visual conventions (subheads, bullets) are sometimes helpful.

☐ It is not *always* easy to see how illustrations connect to text.

1/2

The writer shows limited control even over widely used conventions. More than one of these problems is evident:

☐ Errors in basic conventions are distracting and impair readability.

☐ The reader must frequently pause, reread, decode, or mentally edit (fill in, correct).

☐ Informational sources are not cited.

☐ Layout misdirects the reader's attention or is otherwise distracting.

☐ Visual conventions could make "print-dense" copy more inviting.

☐ Illustrations (if used) do not appear connected to the text.

Appendix 8: Student Three-Level Informational Writing Guide

Student Three-Level Informational Writing Guide

Ideas and Development

5/6

My paper is clear, focused, and purposeful. It answers a key question in an understandable, convincing way.

- ❑ I make the main idea, thesis, or research question crystal clear.
- ❑ I pulled the best information I could find from various sources: personal experience, research, reading, interviews, site visits.
- ❑ I considered my readers and worked to answer their questions—and teach them something new.
- ❑ You can tell by my examples, quotations, and source list that I have explored this topic carefully and know it well.

3/4

My paper addresses a key question and gives the reader solid, basic information.

- ❑ A reader can easily figure out my thesis or research question.
- ❑ Some of my information comes from research or experience, some from common knowledge or my best guess.
- ❑ I tried to think of questions readers would have and answer at least some of them.
- ❑ If I knew more about this topic or had done more research, my paper would be stronger.

1/2

I don't really have a thesis or research question yet. My paper has more than one of these problems:

- ❑ It's a list of first thoughts—not an answer to a question.
- ❑ My information is sketchy or vague, or not backed by research.
- ❑ A reader would be left with many questions on this topic.
- ❑ This paper would not be helpful to someone new to this topic.

Organization

5/6

My organization is strong and showcases ideas the way a good display showcases merchandise.

- ❑ My lead engages readers and sets up the discussion that follows.
- ❑ I arranged my discussion to make it interesting and easy to follow.
- ❑ Clear connections show how one thing leads to another.
- ❑ I slowed down when I needed to explain something complex—and sped up when covering things most readers know already.
- ❑ My ending answers readers' questions, and points to logical conclusions—or important new questions.

3/4

I think readers can follow what I am saying most of the time.

- ❑ My lead is one we've all heard before—or it takes me a while to get rolling.
- ❑ A reader can follow this—but I do repeat or take some side trails.
- ❑ Ideas are usually connected—but sometimes the reader needs to make the connections.
- ❑ Sometimes I got bogged down in simple concepts—or I didn't take time to explain complex ideas.
- ❑ My conclusion clearly ends the discussion—but it may not make readers reflect or think of new questions.

1/2

My organization is confusing, even to me. My paper has more than one of these problems:

- ❑ There is no real lead; my paper just begins.
- ❑ You can look for a design or structure—but you won't find one.
- ❑ I don't seem to speed up or slow down at the right times.
- ❑ I wasn't sure how to connect ideas. Maybe they're not connected.
- ❑ There is no real conclusion; my paper just stops.

Appendix 8: Student Three-Level Informational Writing Guide *(cont.)*

Student Three-Level Informational Writing Guide

Voice

5/6

The voice strikes just the right chord for my topic and audience.

- ☐ I care a lot about this topic and you hear that in my writing.
- ☐ My enthusiasm and confidence come through in every line.
- ☐ I work at pulling readers right into the discussion.
- ☐ You will find yourself drawn to this topic—even if you didn't think you'd like it that much.
- ☐ My voice makes the message stronger—but it doesn't take over.

3/4

This voice seems fine for my topic and audience.

- ☐ Sometimes my writing is lively and enthusiastic—other times, I sound more like an encyclopedia!
- ☐ Now and then I wasn't sure of myself. It would have helped to know the topic better.
- ☐ I think about my readers—I don't always know how to draw them in.
- ☐ I hope you like this topic—but that's really up to you!
- ☐ Sometimes my voice makes you want to keep reading. Other times, it's too conversational or too quiet.

1/2

This doesn't have much voice—or it's the wrong voice. My paper has more than one of these problems:

- ☐ I didn't care much about this topic, so it was hard to write with voice.
- ☐ I didn't know the topic very well, so it was hard to sound confident.
- ☐ Since I don't care about the topic, I didn't know how to make a reader care either.
- ☐ I just wanted this assignment to be over with!
- ☐ I couldn't seem to hit the right voice for this kind of writing.

Word Choice

5/6

I chose my words carefully to help you understand the message.

- ☐ Every word will help you make sense of concepts and remember them.
- ☐ I know the terms that go with this content area—and teach them to you through my writing.
- ☐ The language goes with my topic—and it's right for the audience, too.
- ☐ If I used any technical terms, I defined them.
- ☐ My writing is clear without being wordy.

3/4

My words are clear enough to get the general message across.

- ☐ I used words correctly. You'll get the big picture.
- ☐ I know a few terms that go with this topic—I'm still working on others.
- ☐ The language works—but it might not *always* speak to my readers.
- ☐ I used a few terms readers might not know—but didn't always take time to define them.
- ☐ My writing is wordy in parts. It could be condensed.

1/2

I don't think my words speak to my readers. My paper has more than one of these problems:

- ☐ The language is vague—or it only speaks to insiders. Either way, you won't get the message.
- ☐ I can't seem to find the right words to really get into this topic.
- ☐ My words don't sound or feel right for my audience.
- ☐ I used jargon or left words undefined. I probably left readers feeling shut out from the discussion.
- ☐ Wordy parts will slow you down—or just bury the message.

Student Three-Level Informational Writing Guide

Sentence Fluency

5/6

My sentences are strong, clear, and easy to read.

☐ I begin my sentences in ways that connect ideas: *For example, In contrast, To illustrate, As a result,* etc.

☐ I have some variety, but most of my sentences are short and direct.

☐ You only need to read these sentences one time to get the meaning.

☐ If I used quotations, I set them up so you could see the point.

☐ My writing is easy to understand even if you speed through it.

3/4

Most of my sentences are fairly clear.

☐ I used some sentence beginnings *(On the other hand, Ironically)* to help readers connect ideas.

☐ Some of my sentences are too long or *really* short.

☐ You might need to read a sentence or two more than one time.

☐ I didn't always set up my quotations—but I think you'll see why I chose them.

☐ You'll get the message if you read carefully.

1/2

Many of these sentences are unclear. My writing has more than one of these problems:

☐ Many sentences begin the same way. Readers need to make their own connections.

☐ Many sentences are so long you run out of breath—or so short the text is choppy. Some aren't complete.

☐ Even when you reread, not all my sentences make sense.

☐ I just popped quotations in wherever—or else I didn't use them.

☐ Even if you read slowly or more than once, you could have trouble figuring out what I'm trying to say.

Conventions

5/6

I know conventions well and used them to guide readers through the text.

☐ I edited my paper thoroughly—I don't think you'll spot errors.

☐ I used conventions to bring out meaning and voice.

☐ Any sources I used are cited correctly—all important info is there.

☐ If layout was important, I spent time on it.

☐ I used titles, subheads, bullets, or other visual aids that make information easy to find.

☐ If I used illustrations, I labeled them and showed how they connect to the main points I was making.

3/4

I know conventions fairly well. My writing is quite readable.

☐ You might spot some errors—but I do a lot of things well, too!

☐ OK—you might need to do a *little* "mental editing."

☐ My informational sources are listed—but I might have left some information out.

☐ I think the layout is OK.

☐ I could have used some bullets, subheads, or labels to help readers find information.

☐ You can figure out the point of most illustrations I used.

1/2

My paper has many errors—and more than one of these problems:

☐ Errors are distracting and/or slow readers down.

☐ You'll need to reread or mentally edit (fill in, correct).

☐ If I used sources, I did not cite them—or even list them.

☐ I did not worry about layout.

☐ I needed subheads or other visuals to break up the text. I filled the whole page with print—or else it's nothing but white space!

☐ I could have used some illustrations—OR, I used them, but they didn't seem related to my message.

Appendix 9: Correlations

Correlating the California Standards Test Scoring Rubric with the 6-Trait Model for Instruction & Assessment

California Standards	6-Traits Connection
The writing— • clearly addresses all parts of the writing task; • includes a clearly presented central idea with relevant facts, details, or explanations.	**IDEAS** • The writing is clear, well-supported or developed, and enhanced by the kind of detail that keeps readers reading. • The writer selectively chooses just the right information to make the paper understandable, enlightening and interesting. • The writer's knowledge, experience, insight or unique perspective lend the writing a satisfying ring of authenticity. **WORD CHOICE** • Precise, vivid, natural language paints a strong, clear, and complete picture in the reader's mind. • The writer's message is remarkably clear and easy to interpret. (Informational Rubric) **IDEAS** • The main idea, thesis, or research question is clearly defined. • The writer seems well-informed and draws from a variety of sources to amplify the main point. • Supporting details are accurate, relevant, and helpful in clarifying main ideas. **WORD CHOICE** • Well chosen words convey the writer's message in a clear, precise, and highly readable way, taking readers to a new level of understanding.
The writing— • maintains a consistent point of view, focus, and organizational structure, including the effective use of transitions.	**IDEAS** • Details work together to expand the main topic or develop a story, giving the whole piece a strong sense of focus. **ORGANIZATION** • The order, presentation or internal structure of the piece is compelling and guides the reader purposefully through the text. • An inviting lead draws the reader in; a satisfying conclusion ties up loose ends. • The entire piece has a strong sense of direction and balance. • Transitions are strong but natural. • Organization flows so smoothly the reader does not need to think about it. (Informational Rubric) **IDEAS** • The paper is clear, focused, and purposeful. **ORGANIZATION** • A strong internal structure highlights main ideas and leads readers right to key points and conclusions. • Purposeful transitions help the reader see how each point connects to a larger concept. • The closing effectively resolves important conclusions or assertions offered earlier. • The reader's understanding of the topic grows throughout the paper.

Created by Vicki Spandel. Great Source Education Group, 2002.

Appendix 9: Correlations *(continued)*

The writing— • demonstrates a clear understanding of purpose and audience.	**IDEAS (Informational Rubric)** • The paper is clear, focused and purposeful. It thoroughly answers a well-defined key question in understandable, convincing, and expansive terms. • The writer continuously anticipates and responds to reader's informational needs. **VOICE (Informational Rubric)** • As appropriate, the writer addresses the audience in a voice that is lively, engaging, and right for the topic and purpose. • The writer seems to know the audience well and to speak right to them. **WORD CHOICE** • The vocabulary suits the subject and audience. • Technical or little-known words are clarified or defined as needed. • Jargon and overly technical language are avoided.
The writing— • includes a variety of sentence types.	**SENTENCE FLUENCY** • Sentences are well-crafted, with a strong and varied structure. • Purposeful sentence beginnings show how each sentence relates to and builds on the one before. • Sentences vary in both structure and length, making the reading pleasant and natural.
The writing— • contains few, if any, errors in conventions of the English language.	**CONVENTIONS** • The writer shows excellent control over a wide range of standard writing conventions and uses them with accuracy and (when appropriate) creativity to enhance meaning. • Errors are so few and minor that a reader can easily overlook them unless searching for them specifically. • Only light touch-ups would be required to polish the text for publication. • Informational sources are correctly cited and would be easy for a reader to check or locate.

Specific Modes	

Fictional or Autobiographical Narrative—
 • provides a thoroughly developed plot line;
 • includes appropriate strategies.
	• See IDEAS
	 • See FLUENCY
	   • original, natural phrasing
	 • See ORGANIZATION
	   • compelling order
	   • natural pacing
	   • smooth flow

Response to Literature— • interpretation shows thoughtful, comprehensive grasp of text; • organizes interpretations around clear ideas or premises; • provides specific textual examples.	• See IDEAS • See ORGANIZATION • See CONVENTIONS
Persuasion— • authoritatively defends position with evidence; • convincingly addresses reader's concerns, biases, and expectations.	• See IDEAS and VOICE • See also WORD CHOICE

Summary—
 • effectively paraphrases the main idea and significant details.
	• See IDEAS
	 • See also
	   • FLUENCY
	   • WORD CHOICE
	   • VOICE

Created by Vicki Spandel. Great Source Education Group, 2002.

LINKING TAKS TO 6-TRAIT WRITING

Focus and coherence...............Ideas, Organization
Organization.........................Organization, Sentence Fluency
Development of ideas.............Ideas, Voice
Voice....................................Voice, Ideas, Word Choice
Conventions.........................Conventions, Word Choice, Sentence Fluency

TAKS Writing Features	6-Traits Connection
Focus and Coherence • Focus of individual paragraphs • Focus of the composition as a whole • Sense of completeness • Lead and conclusion add meaning and depth • Writing contributes to development	**Ideas** • Clear, well-supported information • Details work together to provide focus • Amount of detail is "just right" **Organization** • Compelling order, presentation and internal structure • Natural pacing • Inviting lead and satisfying conclusion
Organization • Progression of thought, sentence to sentence and paragraph to paragraph • Meaningful transitions • Logical movement • Organization enhances clear presentation of ideas	**Organization** • Compelling order, presentation, internal structure • Strong sense of direction • Inviting lead and satisfying conclusion • Strong, natural transitions • Smooth flow from point to point **Sentence Fluency** • Easy flow and sentence sense • Purposeful sentence beginnings that show connections
Development of Ideas • Thorough, specific development of ideas • Thoughtful, insightful development • Unusual or unique perspective • Willingness to take risks	**Ideas** • Text is understandable, enlightening, interesting • Writer draws on knowledge, experience • Unique perspective • Ring of authenticity **Voice** • Evidence of risk • Energy, passion • Lively, provocative, honest text
Voice • Engaging text • Reader–writer connection • Authenticity, originality • Unique perspective	**Voice** • Energy, passion • Lively, expressive, engaging text • The clear imprint of the writer • Knowledge of, concern for audience • Text designed to hold reader's attention **Ideas** • Unique perspective • Authenticity **Word Choice** • Memorable phrasing • Words/phrases that prompt connections in reader's mind
Conventions • Connections contribute to overall effectiveness • Writer shows command of spelling, capitalization, punctuation, grammar and usage, and sentence structure • Minor errors do not impair fluency • Words, phrases, and sentence structure enhance effectiveness	**Conventions** • Writer shows control over wide range of standard conventions (spelling, punctuation, grammar and usage, capitalization, paragraphing) • Conventions used to enhance meaning • Conventions used creatively, as appropriate • Text appears edited • Text easy to mentally process • Minor errors do not impair readability **Word Choice** • Phrasing original, memorable • Precise, vivid language creates pictures in reader's mind • Striking phrases prompt connections, reflections, insights **Sentence Fluency** • Easy flow and sentence sense enhance readability • Variety makes reading pleasant, natural • Sentences well crafted

Created by Vicki Spandel. Great Source Education Group, 2002.

Appendix 10: Blank Version of Figure 8.5 Planning Lessons

Planning Lessons

Trait:_____

Feature 1	Feature 2	Feature 3
_____	_____	_____
Lesson Ideas	**Lesson Ideas**	**Lesson Ideas**
1.	1.	1.
2.	2.	2.
3.	3.	3.

References

Ackerman, Diane. 1995. *A Natural History of the Senses*. New York: Random House.

American Heritage Dictionary. 2003. *100 Words Every High School Graduate Should Know*. Boston: Houghton Mifflin.

Anderson, Jeff. 2005. *Mechanically Inclined*. Portland, ME: Stenhouse.

Anderson, Laurie Halse. 2001. *Speak*. New York: Puffin Books.

Anderson, Richard C., Elfrieda H. Hiebert, Judith A. Scott, and Ian A. G. Wilkinson. 1985. *Becoming a Nation of Readers*. Washington, DC: U.S. Department of Education.

Angier, Natalie. 1995. *The Beauty of the Beastly*. Boston: Houghton Mifflin.

Ansa, Tina McElroy. 1994. In "Tina McElroy Ansa." Rebecca Carroll, *I Know What the Red Clay Looks Like: The Voice and Vision of Black Women Writers*. New York: Crown.

Appelt, Kathi. 2002. *Poems from Homeroom: A Writer's Place to Start*. New York: Holt.

Aronie, Nancy Slonim. 1998. *Writing From the Heart: Tapping the Power of Your Inner Voice*. New York: Hyperion.

Arter, Judith A., and Jan Chappuis. 2006. *Creating and Recognizing Quality Rubrics*. Portland, OR: Educational Testing Service.

Atwell, Nancie. 1987. *In the Middle: Writing, Reading and Learning With Adolescents*. Portsmouth, NH: Boynton/Cook.

Atwood, Margaret. 1996. *Alias Grace*. New York: Bantam Doubleday Dell.

Ballenger, Bruce. 2004. *The Curious Researcher: A Guide to Writing Research Papers*, 4th ed. Boston: Allyn and Bacon.

Black, Paul. April 23, 2003. "A Successful Intervention—Why Did It Work?" Paper presented at the American Educational Research Association annual meeting, Chicago.

Black, Paul, and Dylan Wiliam. 1998. "Inside the Black Box: Raising Standards Through Classroom Assessment." *Phi Delta Kappan* (October), pp. 139–148.

Blake, Gary, and Robert Bly. 1993. *The Elements of Technical Writing*. New York: Macmillan.

Bradbury, Ray. 1992. *Zen in the Art of Writing*. New York: Bantam Books.

Bragg, Rick. 1997. *All Over But the Shoutin'*. New York: Random House.

_____. 2001. *Ava's Man*. New York: Knopf.

Brandt, Ron. 1993. "On Teaching for Understanding: A Conversation With Howard Gardner." *Educational Leadership* 50 (September), pp. 4–7.

Brodie, Deborah. 1997. *Writing Changes Everything*. New York: St. Martin's Press.

Brown, John Seely. 1991. "Research That Reinvents the Corporation." *Harvard Business Review* (January–February), pp. 102–111.

Brown, Ruth. 1996. *Toad*. New York: Dutton Children's Books.

Bryson, Bill. 2001. *In a Sunburned Country*. New York: Random House.

Burke, Jim. 1999. *The English Teacher's Companion*. Portsmouth, NH: Heinemann.

Cahill, Thomas. 1995. *How the Irish Saved Civilization*. New York: Doubleday.

Calkins, Lucy McCormick. 1986. *The Art of Teaching Writing*. Portsmouth, NH: Heinemann.

_____. 1994. *The Art of Teaching Writing*, rev. ed. Portsmouth, NH: Heinemann.

Cannon, Janell. 2000. *Crickwing*. New York: Harcourt Brace.

Capote, Truman. 1996. *A Christmas Memory, One Christmas, & The Thanksgiving Visitor*. New York: Random House.

Charlton, James, ed. 1992. *The Writer's Quotation Book*. New York: Penguin.

Chew, Charles. 1985. "Instruction Can Link Reading and Writing." In *Breaking Ground: Teachers Relate Reading and Writing in the Elementary School*. Edited by Jane Hansen, Thomas Newkirk, and Donald Graves. Portsmouth, NH: Heinemann.

Chicago Manual of Style, The. 14th edition. 1993. Chicago: University of Chicago Press.

Cisneros, Sandra. 1989. *The House on Mango Street*. New York: Random House.

Clark, Roy Peter. 1987. *Free to Write: A Journalist Teaches Young Writers*. Portsmouth, NH: Heinemann.

Collard, Sneed B. III. 2000. *Birds of Prey: A Look at Daytime Raptors*. New York: Franklin Watts.

_____. 2003. *The Deep-Sea Floor*. Watertown, MA: Charlesbridge.

Collins, James L. 1998. *Strategies for Teaching Struggling Writers*. New York: The Guilford Press.

Condry, John. 1977. "Enemies of Exploration: Self-Initiated vs. Other-Initiated Learning." *Journal of Personality and Social Psychology* 35, pp. 459–477.

Conlan, Gertrude, 1986. "Objective Measures of Writing Ability." 1986. In *Writing Assessment: Issues and Strategies*. Edited by Karen L. Greenberg, Harvey S. Wiener, and Richard A. Donovan. White Plains, NY: Longman.

Cooke, Alistair. 1976. *Alistair Cooke's America*. New York: Knopf.

Cramer, Ronald L. 2001. *Creative Power: The Nature and Nurture of Children's Writing*. New York: Addison-Wesley Longman.

Crichton, Michael. 1988. *Travels*. New York: Random House.

Crutcher, Chris. 1995. *Iron Man*. New York: Green Willow Books.

Curry, Boykin, and Brian Kasbar, eds. 1987. *Essays That Worked for Business Schools*. New Haven: Mustang Publishing.

Dahl, Roald. 1980. *The Twits*. New York: Penguin Books.

_____. 1984. *Boy: Tales of Childhood*. New York: Penguin Books.

_____. 1988. *Matilda*. New York: Viking Kestrel.

_____. 2000. *The Wonderful Story of Henry Sugar*. New York: Penguin Books.

Davies, Nicola. 2004. *Bat Loves the Night*. Cambridge, MA: Candlewick Press.

_____. 2005. *One Tiny Turtle*. Cambridge, MA: Candlewick Press.

deLaubier, Guillaume, and Jacques Bosser. 2003. *The Most Beautiful Libraries in the World*. New York: Abrams.

DiCamillo, Kate. 2000. *Because of Winn-Dixie*. Cambridge, MA: Candlewick Press.

_____. 2003. *The Tale of Despereaux*. Cambridge, MA: Candlewick Press.

Diederich, Paul B. 1974. *Measuring Growth in English*. Urbana, IL: National Council of Teachers of English.

Elbow, Peter. 1973. *Writing Without Teachers*. New York: Oxford University Press.

_____. 1986. *Embracing Contraries*. New York: Oxford University Press.

Enholm, Eric. 1963. *Basic Story Structure*. St. Petersburg, FL: Bayside.

Eugenides, Jeffrey. 2003. *Middlesex*. New York: Farrar Straus and Giroux.

Facklam, Margery. 2001. *Spiders and Their Web Sites*. New York: Little, Brown.

Faulkner, William. 1991. *The Sound and the Fury*. New York: Vintage.

Feiffer, Sharon Sloan, and Steve Feiffer, eds. 1995. *Home*. New York: Pantheon Books.

Fletcher, Ralph. 1993. *What a Writer Needs*. Portsmouth, NH: Heinemann.

_____. 2006. *Boy Writers: Reclaiming Their Voices*. Portland, ME: Stenhouse.

Florian, Douglas. 1998. *Insectlopedia*. New York: Harcourt.

Fox, Mem. 1989. *Wilfred Gordon McDonald Partridge*. New York: Kane/Miller.

_____. 1993. *Radical Reflections*. New York: Harcourt Brace.

Frank, Marjorie. 1995. *If You're Trying to Teach Kids How to Write . . . you've gotta have this book!* 2nd ed. Nashville: Incentive Publications.

Fraser, Jane, and Donna Skolnick. 1994. *On Their Way: Celebrating Second Graders As They Read and Write*. Portsmouth, NH: Heinemann.

Frasier, Debra. 2000. *Miss Alaineus: A Vocabulary Disaster*. New York: Harcourt.

Fuller, Alexandria. 2003. *Don't Let's Go to the Dogs Tonight*. New York: Random House.

Gantos, Jack. 1999. *Jack's Black Book*. New York: Farrar Straus and Giroux.

Gardner, Howard. 1993. "Educating for Understanding." *The American School Board Journal* (July), pp. 20–24.

Gendler, J. Ruth. 1988. *The Book of Qualities*. New York: Harper.

George, Twig C. 2003. *Seahorses*. Brookfield, CT: Millbrook Press.

Gerson, Sharon J., and Steven M. Gerson. 1997. *Technical Writing: Process and Product*. Upper Saddle River, NJ: Prentice Hall.

Gilbert, Elizabeth. 2001. *Stern Men*. Boston: Houghton Mifflin.

Gladwell, Malcolm. 2005. *Blink: The Power of Thinking Without Thinking*. New York: Little Brown.

Glenn, David. April 11, 2007. "College Board Researchers Defend New Essay Component of SAT." *The Chronicle of Higher Education*. http://chronicle.com/daily/2007/04/2007041104n.htm.

Goleman, Daniel. 2006. *Social Intelligence: The Revolutionary New Science of Human Relationships*. New York: Random House.

Gordon, David George. 1996. *The Compleat Cockroach*. Berkeley, CA: Ten Speed Press.

Graham, Steve, and Dolores Perin. 2007. *Writing Next: Effective Strategies to Improve Writing of Adolescents in Middle and High School (A report to Carnegie Corporation of New York)*. Washington, DC: Alliance for Excellent Education.

Graves, Donald H. 1983. *Writing: Teachers and Children At Work*. Portsmouth, NH: Heinemann.

_____. 1994. *A Fresh Look At Writing*. Portsmouth, NH: Heinemann.

_____. 1999. *Bring Life Into Learning*. Portsmouth, NH: Heinemann.

_____. 2002. *Testing Is Not Teaching*. Portsmouth, NH: Heinemann.

Graves, Donald H., and Virginia Stuart. 1987. *Write from the Start: Tapping Your Child's Natural Writing Ability*. New York: NAL Penguin.

Grimes, Nikki. 2002. *My Man Blue*. Reprint edition. New York: Puffin.

Hairston, Maxine. 1986. "On Not Being a Composition Slave." In *Training the New Teacher of College Composition*. Edited by Charles W. Bridges. Urbana, IL: National Council of Teachers of English.

Heard, Georgia. 1995. *Writing Toward Home*. Portsmouth, NH: Heinemann.

_____. 2002. *The Revision Toolbox: Teaching Techniques That Work*. Portsmouth, NH: Heinemann.

Heller, Rafael, and Cynthia L. Greenleaf. 2007. "Literacy Instruction in the Content Areas: Getting to the Core of Middle and High School Improvement: An Executive Summary." Washington DC: Alliance for Excellent Education.

Hemingway, Ernest. 1995. The Old Man and the Sea. New York: Scribner.

Hesse, Karen. 1996. *The Music of Dolphins*. New York: Oxford University Press.

Hillenbrand, Laura. 2001. *Seabiscuit*. New York: Ballantine Books.

Hillocks, George, Jr. 1986. *Research on Written Composition: New Directions for Teaching*. Urbana, IL: ERIC Clearinghouse on Reading and Communications Skills.

_____. 2002. *The Testing Trap: How State Writing Assessments Control Learning*. New York: Teachers College Press.

Hopkinson, Deborah. *Under the Quilt of Night*. New York: Aladdin.

Huot, Brian. 1990. "The Literature of Direct Writing Assessment: Major Concerns and Prevailing Trends." *Review of Educational Research* 60 (Summer), pp. 237–263.

Iotanks, Tatanka (Sitting Bull, Lakota). 1995. *New Horizons*. Manhattan, KS: The Master Teacher, Inc.

Isaacson, Walter. 2007. *Einstein: His Life and Universe*. New York: Simon and Schuster.

Johnson, Bea. 1999. *Never Too Early to Write*. Gainesville, FL: Maupin House.

Junger, Sebastian. 2000. *The Perfect Storm*. New York: HarperCollins.

Katz, Jon. 2003. *A Dog Year*. New York: Random House.

Keillor, Garrison. 1987. *Leaving Home*. New York: Viking Penguin.

_____. 1989. *We Are Still Married*. New York: Viking Penguin.

Kidd, Sue Monk. 2002. *The Secret Life of Bees*. New York: Penguin Books.

King, Stephen. 2000. *On Writing*. New York: Scribner.

Kingsolver, Barbara. 2002. *Small Wonder*. New York: HarperCollins.

_____. 2007. *Animal, Vegetable, Miracle*. New York: HarperCollins.

Kloske, Geoffrey. 2005. *Once Upon a Time, the End (Asleep in 60 Seconds)*. New York: Atheneum.

Kohn, Alfie. 1993. *Punished by Rewards*. Boston: Houghton Mifflin.

_____. 2000. *The Case Against Standardized Testing*. Portsmouth, NH: Heinemann.

Korda, Michael. September 1999. "Editing Explained." *Sky Magazine*, pp. 106–112. Reprinted with permission from Michael Korda. 1999. *Another Life*. New York: Random House.

Kozol, Jonathan. 2007. *Letters to a Young Teacher*. New York: Crown (an imprint of Crown Publishers).

Korman, Gordon. 2000. *No More Dead Dogs*. New York: Hyperion Books for Children.

Kuralt, Charles. 1990. *A Life on the Road*. New York: Putnam's.

Laden, Nina. 1994. *The Night I Followed the Dog*. New York: Chronicle Books.

Lamott, Anne. 1995. *Bird By Bird*. New York: Bantam Doubleday Dell.

Lane, Barry. 1993. *After THE END*. Portsmouth, NH: Heinemann.

———. 1996. "Quality in Writing." *Writing Teacher* 9 (3), pp. 3–8.

———. 1997. *Writing As a Road to Self-Discovery*. Shoreham, VT: Discover Writing Press.

———. 1999. *Reviser's Toolbox*. Shoreham, VT: Discover Writing Press.

———. 2002. *The Tortoise and the Hare . . . Continued*. Shoreham, VT: Discover Writing Press.

———. 2003. *51 Wacky We-Search Reports*. Shoreham, VT: Discover Writing Press.

Lane, Barry. 2008. In Vicki Spandel, *Creating Young Writers: Using the Six Traits to Enrich Writing Process in Primary Classrooms*, 2nd ed.. Boston: Allyn and Bacon.

LearningExpress Editors. *411 SAT Writing Questions and Essay Prompts*. 2006. LearningExpress.

Leavy, Jane. 2002. *Sandy Koufax: A Lefty's Legacy*. New York: HarperCollins.

Lederer, Richard. 1994. *More Anguished English*. New York: Dell.

Lederer, Richard, and Richard Dowis. 1995. *The Write Way*. New York: Simon and Schuster.

Lederman, Marie Jean. 1986. "Why Test?" In *Writing Assessment: Issues and Strategies*. Edited by Karen L. Greenberg, Harvey S. Wiener, and Richard A. Donovan. White Plains, NY: Longman.

LeGuin, Ursula K. *Steering the Craft*. 1998. Portland, OR: Eighth Mountain Press.

Lesser, Caroline. 1996. *Great Crystal Bear*. New York: Harcourt.

Lester, Julius. 1992. *The Knee-High Man and Other Tales*. New York: Puffin Books.

Levy, Steven. 1995–1996. "The Year of the Internet." *Newsweek* (December 25, 1995–January 1, 1996), pp. 21–30.

Lichen, Patricia K. 2001. *River-walking: Songbirds and Coyote Singing*. Seattle: Sasquatch Books.

Lunsford, Andrea A. 1986. "The Past—and Future—of Writing Assessment." In *Writing Assessment: Issues and Strategies*. Edited by Karen L. Greenberg, Harvey S. Wiener, and Richard A. Donovan. White Plains, NY: Longman.

MacDonald, Fiona, and David Salariva. 1997. *How Would You Survive in the Middle Ages?* New York: Franklin Watts.

Mamet, David, writer/director. "Heist." A Warner Brothers film.

Marrin, Albert. 2006. *Oh, Rats! The Story of Rats and People*. New York: Penguin.

Marten, Cindy. 2003. *Word Crafting: Teaching Spelling, Grades K–6*. Portsmouth, NH: Heinemann.

Mathers, Petra. 1991. *Sophie and Lou*. New York: Harper.

McBrier, Page. 2004. *Beatrice's Goat*. New York: Aladdin.

McCarty, Marietta. 2006. *Little Big Minds*. New York: Tarcher.

McCourt, Frank. 1998. *Angela's Ashes*. New York: Scribner.

———. 1999. *'Tis*. New York: Scribner.

McGraw, Phillip C. 1999. *Doing What Works, Doing What Matters*. New York: Hyperion.

Meese, Edwin. 2005. *The Heritage Guide to the Constitution*. New York: Regnery Publishing.

Mikaelson, Ben. 2001. *Touching Spirit Bear*. New York: Harper.

Mohr, Marian M. 1984. *Revision: The Rhythm of Meaning*. Upper Montclair, NJ: Boynton/Cook.

Morrison, Toni. In Murray, Donald M. 1990. *Shoptalk*. Portsmouth, NH: Heinemann.

Murray, Donald M. 1982. *Learning By Teaching*. Portsmouth, NH: Boynton/Cook.

———. 1984. *Write to Learn*. New York: Holt, Rinehart and Winston.

———. 1990. *Shoptalk*. Portsmouth, NH: Boynton/Cook.

———. 2004. *A Writer Teaches Writing*. 2d ed. Boston: Houghton Mifflin.

National Commission on Writing. 2003. *The Neglected "R": The Need for a Writing Revolution*. New York: College Entrance Examination Board.

National Commission on Writing. September 2004. *Writing: A Ticket to Work . . . Or a Ticket Out: A Survey of Business Leaders*. New York: College Entrance Examination Board.

National Council of Teachers of English (NCTE) Task Force. April 2005. "The Impact of SAT and ACT Timed Writing Tests." Urbana, IL: NCTE.

Nye, Bill. 1993. *The Science Guy's Big Blast of Science*. Mercer Island, WA: TV Books.

O'Connor, Patricia T. 1996. *Woe Is I*. New York: Putnam.

———. 1999. *Words Fail Me*. New York: Harcourt Brace.

Olshansky, Beth. *Picturing Writing: Fostering Literacy Through Art* and *Image-Making Within the Writing Process*. University of New Hampshire. www.picturingwriting.com.

Palmer, Parker J. 1998. *The Courage to Teach: Exploring the Inner Landscape of a Teacher's Life*. San Francisco: Jossey-Bass.

Paulsen, Gary. 1989. *The Winter Room*. New York: Dell.

———. 1992. *Clabbered Dirt, Sweet Grass*. New York: Harcourt Brace Jovanovich.

———. 1993. *Dogteam*. New York: Delacorte Press.

———. 1994. *Winterdance*. Orlando: Harcourt Brace & Company.

———. 2001. *Guts*. New York: Delacorte Press.

———. 2003. *Shelf Life*. New York: Simon and Schuster.

Perlstein, Linda. 2007. *Tested: One American School Struggles to Make the Grade*. New York: Holt.

Pipher, Mary. 2006. *Writing to Change the World*. New York: Penguin.

Pirie, Bruce. 1997. *Reshaping High School English*. Urbana, IL: National Council of Teachers of English.

Proulx, Annie. 1999. *Close Range*. New York: Scribner.

Purves, Alan C. 1992. "Reflections on Research and Assessment in Written Composition." *Research in the Teaching of English* 26 (February), pp. 108–122.

Quammen, David. 1996. *The Song of the Dodo*. New York: Scribner.

———. 1998. *Wild Thoughts From Wild Places*. New York: Scribner.

Ray, Katie Wood. 2002. *What You Know By Heart: How to Develop Curriculum for Your Writing Workshop*. Portsmouth, NH: Heinemann.

Reynolds, Peter H. 2003. *The Dot*. Cambridge, MA: Candlewick Press.

Rice, Scott, ed. 1992. *It Was a Dark and Stormy Night: The Final Conflict*. New York: Penguin Books.

———. 1996. *Dark and Stormy Rides Again*. New York: Penguin Books.

Ringgold, Faith. 1991. *Tar Beach*. New York: Random House.

Romano, Tom. 1987. *Clearing the Way: Working With Teenage Writers*. Portsmouth, NH: Heinemann.

———. 1995. *Writing With Passion*. Portsmouth, NH: Boynton/Cook.

———. 2004. *Crafting Authentic Voice*. Portsmouth, NH: Heinemann.

Routman, Regie. 1996. *Literacy At the Crossroads*. Portsmouth, NH: Heinemann.

———. 2000. *Conversations: Strategies for Teaching, Learning, and Evaluating*. Portsmouth, NH: Heinemann.

Rowling, J. K. (author), and Jim Dale (narrator). 1999. *Harry Potter and the Sorcerer's Stone*. Audio CD. New York: Listening Library.

r.w.t. Magazine for Writing Teachers K–8. San Antonio: ECS Learning Systems.

Sachar, Louis. October 16, 1999. Keynote address: Author's Luncheon. Florida Reading Association. Orlando.

_____. 2000. *Holes*. New York: Yearling Books.

Sagan, Carl. 1980. *Cosmos*. New York: Random House.

Seife, Charles. 2000. *Zero: The Biography of a Dangerous Idea*. New York: Penguin Books.

Seinfeld, Jerry. 1993. *SeinLanguage*. New York: Bantam Books.

Shaughnessy, Mina P. 1977. *Errors and Expectations*. New York: Oxford University Press.

Smith, Frank. 1984. "Reading Like a Writer." In *Composing and Comprehending*. Edited by Julie M. Jensen. Urbana, IL: ERIC Clearinghouse on Reading and Communication Skills.

Spandel, Vicki. 2005. *The 9 Rights of Every Writer*. Portsmouth, NH: Heinemann.

_____. 2008a. *Creating Revisers and Editors, Grade 3*. Boston: Allyn and Bacon (an imprint of Pearson Education, Inc).

_____. 2008b. *Creating Revisers and Editors, Grade 4*. Boston: Allyn and Bacon (an imprint of Pearson Education, Inc).

_____. 2008c. *Creating Young Writers*, 2nd ed. Boston: Allyn and Bacon.

Spandel, Vicki, and Jeff Hicks. 2008. *Write Traits Kindergarten: Bringing the Traits to Kinderwriters*. Wilmington, MA: Great Source Education Group, a division of Houghton Mifflin Company.

Steele, Bob. 1998. *Draw Me a Story*. Winnipeg, Manitoba, Canada: Peguis Publishers.

Stegner, Wallace. 1992. "Thoughts in a Dry Land." In *Where the Bluebird Sings to the Lemonade Springs: Living and Writing in the West*. New York: Random House.

_____. 2002. *On Teaching and Writing Fiction*. New York: Penguin.

Steig, William. 1971. *Amos and Boris*. New York: Puffin Books.

_____. 1987. *Abel's Island*. Toronto: Collins.

Stiggins, Richard J. 2001. *Student-Involved Classroom Assessment*, 3rd ed. Upper Saddle River, NJ: Prentice-Hall.

Stiggins, Richard J., Judith A. Arter, Jan Chappuis, and Stephen Chappuis. 2006. *Classroom Assessment for Student Learning: Doing It Right—Using It Well*. Portland, OR: Educational Testing Service.

Strickland, Kathleen, and James Strickland. 1998. *Reflections on Assessment*. Portsmouth, NH: Boynton/Cook.

Strong, Richard, Harvey F. Silver, and Amy Robinson. 1995. "What Do Students Want?" *Educational Leadership* 53 (September), pp. 8–12.

Strunk, William, Jr., and E. B. White. 2000. *The Elements of Style*, 4th edition. Boston: Allyn and Bacon.

Suzuki, David. 1991. *Looking at Weather*. New York: Jossey-Bass.

Teague, Mark. 2002. *Dear Mrs. LaRue: Letters From Obedience School*. New York: Scholastic Press.

Thomas, Dylan. [1954] 1962. "Reminiscences of Childhood." In *Thought in Prose*, 2nd ed. Edited by Richard S. Beal and Jacob Korg. Englewood Cliffs, NJ: Prentice-Hall.

Thomas, Lewis. 1979. *The Medusa and the Snail*. New York: Penguin.

Thomason, Tommy. 1993. *More Than a Writing Teacher*. Commerce, TX: Bridge Press.

_____. 1998. *Writer to Writer: How to Conference Young Authors*. Norwood, MA: Christopher-Gordon.

_____. 2003. *WriteAerobics: 40 Workshop Exercises to Improve Your Writing Teaching*. Norwood, MA: Christopher-Gordon.

Thomason, Tommy, and Carol York. 2000. *Write on Target: Preparing Young Writers to Succeed on State Writing Achievement Tests*. Norwood, MA: Christopher-Gordon.

Tredway, Linda. 1995. "Socratic Seminars: Engaging Students in Intellectual Discourse." *Educational Leadership* 53 (September), pp. 26–29.

Trimble, John R. 2000, *Writing With Style*. 2nd ed. Upper Saddle River, NJ: Prentice-Hall.

Van Allsburg, Chris. 1996. *The Mysteries of Harris Burdick*. Boston: Houghton Mifflin.

Wade-Gales, Gloria. 1994. In Rebecca Carroll, *I Know What the Red Clay Looks Like: The Voice and Vision of Black Women Writers*. New York: Crown.

Wasserstein, Paulette. 1995. "What Middle Schoolers Say About Their Schoolwork." *Educational Leadership* (September), pp. 41–43.

Weiten, Wayne, and Margaret A. Lloyd. 2003. *Psychology Applied to Modern Life*. 7th ed. New York: Wadsworth.

Welty, Eudora. 1983. *One Writer's Beginnings*. New York: Warner Books.

White, E. 1985. *Teaching and Assessing Writing*. San Francisco: Jossey-Bass.

White, E. B. 1936. *Farewell to Model T*. New York: G. P. Putnam's Sons.

_____. 1980. *Charlotte's Web*. New York: Harper Trophy.

Wiggins, Grant. 1992. "Creating Tests Worth Taking." *Educational Leadership* (May), pp. 26–33.

Williams, Joseph M. 2002. *Style: Ten Lessons in Clarity and Grace*, 7th ed. New York: Pearson Longman.

Winokur, John. 1990. *W.O.W.: Writers on Writing*. Philadelphia: Running Press.

Wolcott, Willa, with Sue M. Legg. 1998. *An Overview of Writing Assessment: Theory, Research, and Practice*. Urbana, IL: National Council of Teachers of English.

Write Source Handbooks for Students. Wilmington, MA: Great Source Education Group:

Writing Spot. 2006. (Kindergarten). Elsholz, Carol, Patrick Sebranek, and David Kemper.

Write One. 2006. (Grade 1). Kemper, David, Carol Elsholz, and Patrick Sebranek.

Write Away. 2002. (Grade 2). Kemper, David, Ruth Nathan, Patrick Sebranek, and Carol Elsholz.

Write on Track. 2002. (Grade 3). Kemper, David, Ruth Nathan, Patrick Sebranek, and Carol Elsholz.

Writers Express. 2000. (Grades 4–5). Kemper, David, Ruth Nathan, Patrick Sebranek, and Carol Elsholz.

Write Source 2000. 1999. (Grades 6–8). Sebranek, Patrick, David Kemper, and Verne Meyer.

All Write. 2003. (Grades 6–8). Kemper, David, Patrick Sebranek, and Verne Meyer.

Write Ahead. 2004. (Grades 9–10). Kemper, David, Patrick Sebranek, and Verne Meyer.

Writers Inc. 2006. (Grades 9–12). Sebranek, Patrick, David Kemper, and Verne Meyer.

School to Work. 1996. (Grades 9–12). Sebranek, Patrick, David Kemper, and John Van Rys.

Write for College. 2008. (Grades 11–12). Sebranek, Patrick, David Kemper, and Verne Meyer.

Ziegler, Alan. 1981. *The Writing Workshop*. Vol. 1. New York: Teachers and Writers Collaborative.

Zinsser, William. 2001. *On Writing Well*. New York. HarperCollins.

Index

415